C0-ATD-250

Law from the Tigris to the Tiber: The Writings of Raymond Westbrook

Volume 2: Cuneiform and Biblical Sources

Raymond Westbrook
October 1, 1946 – July 23, 2009

Printed in the United States of America.

www.eisenbrauns.com

Library of Congress Cataloging-in-Publication Data

Westbrook, Raymond.
Law from the Tigris to the Tiber : the writings of Raymond Westbrook. / Raymond Westbrook ; edited by Bruce Wells and Rachel Magdalene.
v. cm.
Includes bibliographical references and index.
Contents: v. 1. The Shared tradition — v. 2. Cuneiform and biblical sources.
ISBN 978-1-57506-177-1 (set (2 vols.); hardback : alk. paper) — ISBN 978-1-57506-175-7 (volume 1; hardback : alk. paper) — ISBN 978-1-57506-176-4 (volume 2; hardback : alk. paper)
1. Law—Middle East—History. 2. Law, Ancient. 3. Jewish law. 4. Roman law. 5. Law, Greek. I. Wells, Bruce. II. Magdalene, F. Rachel. III. Title.
KL147.W477 2009
340.5′394—dc22

2009040568

The paper used in this publication meets the minimum requirements of the American National Standard for Information Sciences—Permanence of Paper for Printed Library Materials, ANSI Z39.48–1984. ♾™

Law from the Tigris to the Tiber:
The Writings of Raymond Westbrook

Volume 2

Cuneiform and Biblical Sources

Raymond Westbrook

Edited by
Bruce Wells and Rachel Magdalene

Eisenbrauns
Winona Lake, Indiana
2009

Contents

Preface

On July 23, 2009, as the preparations for this collection were nearing completion, Raymond Westbrook, the W. W. Spence Professor of Semitic Languages in the Department of Near Eastern Studies at Johns Hopkins University, passed away. We had been contemplating the production of these volumes for some time and began work on them in earnest about one year ago, spurred in part by the progression of his illness. Although we had hoped to deliver the completed collection as a surprise, his rapid decline did not permit us to do that. Instead, we made Professor Westbrook aware of the project several weeks before his passing. We are, however, deeply saddened that he was not able to see it in its final form. He was an important role model and mentor for us over the years, and we offer these volumes as a modest tribute to his scholarly achievements, his impact on the field, and his particular contributions to our academic development.

Raymond Westbrook earned his B.A. in Law from Oxford University in 1968, studying with David Daube, H. L. A. Hart, and other prominent legal scholars. He then took his Ll.M. at Hebrew University of Jerusalem, where he worked with Reuven Yaron. Westbrook was called to the Bar of England and Wales in 1976 and practiced law for a brief time. His Ph.D. in Assyriology was completed in 1982 at Yale University under J. J. Finkelstein and C. Wilcke. He arrived at Johns Hopkins in 1987, after he had taught in the Faculty of Law at Hebrew University of Jerusalem.

Westbrook published three books, edited or co-edited five additional volumes, and produced over 90 articles. His books include *Studies in Biblical and Cuneiform Law* (Gabalda, 1988); *Old Babylonian Marriage Law* (Berger, 1988); and *Property and the Family in Biblical Law* (Sheffield Academic Press, 1991). Among his edited volumes are *Amarna Diplomacy: The Beginnings of International Relations* (with R. Cohen; Johns Hopkins University Press, 2000); *Security for Debt in Ancient Near Eastern Law* (with R. Jasnow; Brill, 2001); *A History of Ancient Near Eastern Law* (Brill, 2003); *Women and Property in Ancient Near Eastern and Mediterranean Societies* (with D. Lyons; Center for Hellenic Studies,

2005); and *Isaiah's Vision of Peace in Biblical and Modern International Relations: Swords into Plowshares* (with R. Cohen; Palgrave Macmillan, 2008). A complete list of his publications (at least through 2008) can be found in the bibliography in volume 2.

Deciding the contents of these volumes took some time. In the end, we felt it best to focus on the 25 years of his work that followed directly after the completion of his dissertation in 1982 and to publish what we believe were his most significant works from that period, whether or not previously reprinted. Thus, exceedingly short articles, reviews, dictionary entries, and articles in handbooks and the like are generally excluded. Due to its import, we have included one article published in 1977 and thereby have the exception that proves the rule.

The volumes' structure emerged relatively quickly. Westbrook published across a broad scope. Nonetheless, we felt that these articles could be readily divided into five major areas: 1) his theoretical work on the shared legal tradition of the so-called law codes of the ancient Near East and classical world; 2) his study of particular substantive bodies of law across this large region; 3) the application of his theory and method to Greek and Roman law; 4) his general work on cuneiform legal sources; and 5) his general work on biblical law. These categories were then divided into two volumes named respectively *The Shared Tradition* and *Cuneiform and Biblical Sources*. Such division is not rigid, however, as Westbrook used sources from the ancient Near East, Greece, and Rome as appropriate, whatever topic was before him.

We wish to thank Jim Eisenbraun, publisher of Eisenbrauns, for his ready enthusiasm for the project since its inception. He was always at hand to answer our questions, to guide us, and to lend support. Our colleague, Cornelia Wunsch, willingly assisted with a host of difficult tasks that arose throughout the course of our work; the volumes are greatly improved thanks to her generous labors on our behalf. Finally, because this project was produced for the most part in the Wells' home, we would also both like to thank Marcy Wells, Bruce's wife, for her many gifts of hospitality, which made this project possible.

Bruce Wells
F. Rachel Magdalene
Munich, August 22, 2009

About the Editors

Bruce Wells received his Ph.D. in Near Eastern Studies in 2003 from The John Hopkins University. He is Assistant Professor of Hebrew Bible in the Department of Theology at Saint Joseph's University in Philadelphia. He is currently on a one-year leave at the Ludwig-Maximilians-Universität in Munich as a Research Fellow with the Alexander von Humboldt Foundation. Wells is the author of *The Law of Testimony in the Pentateuchal Codes* (Harrassowitz, 2004) and co-author with Raymond Westbrook of *Everyday Law in Biblical Israel: An Introduction* (Westminster John Knox, 2009).

F. Rachel Magdalene holds a J.D. from the University of Colorado School of Law and a Ph.D. in Biblical Interpretation (Hebrew Bible) from the University of Denver and Iliff School of Theology Joint Ph.D. Program. She also did supplemental doctoral studies in Assyriology, Hebrew Bible, and ancient comparative law at The Johns Hopkins University. She practiced tax and securities law for twelve years before pursuing her Ph.D. She is currently Visiting Research Scholar at the Universität Leipzig and Guest of the Faculty at Humboldt-Universität zu Berlin. She has taught biblical studies, religious studies, and law at both the undergraduate and graduate levels. Magdalene is the author of *On the Scales of Righteousness: Neo-Babylonian Trial Law and the Book of Job* (Brown Judaic Studies, 2007); co-author with James P. Kutner of *Study Guide to Due Diligence: Process, Participants and Liability* (College for Financial Planning Press, 1988); and an editor on G. K. Scott, et al., eds., *Due Diligence: Process, Participants and Liability* (Longman Financial Services, 1988).

Introduction
Law as Method

F. Rachel Magdalene*

In the summer of 1999, Raymond Westbrook left us the key to his office. He was, as usual, going to spend the summer in Europe. His filing cabinet was left open for us. We could look at and use whatever we needed in furtherance of our studies and what later became our dissertations. We worked in his office almost every day and quite a few evenings besides. We were primarily in search of ancient Near Eastern litigation texts, of which we found countless. Along the way, we discovered all sorts of wonderful things tucked away in books and folders: articles and book chapters eventually to be published, innumerable text editions, book and article corrections and comments, bibliographies, class lecture notes, drafts of his notebooks from his student days, and the like. We also found political proposals, poetry, children's stories (with illustrations!), cookbook materials, letters to friends and colleagues, and more. We understood only then the depth and breadth of Westbrook's mind. Yet, working in that environment, surrounded by his large collection of books and papers, we realized that he was fundamentally a legal historian.

As we observed in the first volume of this collection, Westbrook was for many the foremost authority on ancient Near Eastern law. He was, however, not only a specialist in Assyriology but also an important scholar of biblical studies and classics. His work on legal history in each of these areas was prolific.

* With contributions from Bruce Wells.

His scholarship, beginning with his dissertation and monograph (a study of Old Babylonian marriage law) up to the last articles and book chapters, reflects the development of his particular theory of the nature of early law and the hermeneutical method that arises therefrom. This method was an important cornerstone of his careful and detailed analyses of ancient texts from across the Near Eastern and Mediterranean world. As we also stated in the first volume, given Westbrook's varied constituencies, his publications have appeared in a wide variety of venues, including edited volumes and the journals of Assyriology, Bible, classics, history, law, and gender studies. This diversity of venues has allowed many to read his work. It makes it difficult, however, to locate all his pieces and to grasp the full impact of his approach. The varied topics and venues tend to present a scattered picture. Nonetheless, there is a unifying principle to his work, that is, his interest in the origins of law and its earliest expression in the circum-Mediterranean and the outer reaches of western Asia. Westbrook was a legal historian through and through.

We believe that this collection brings that organizing, unifying principle to light. Moreover, this second volume of the collection, which focuses upon the application of his theory of ancient law and the interpretative method that arises from that theory to particular problems and texts of the cuneiform and biblical legal sources, highlights his legal historical thinking particularly well. Consequently, we have entitled this volume simply *Cuneiform and Biblical Sources*. One can observe, of course, in this volume, Westbrook's facility with the many languages written in cuneiform script, as well as Hebrew, Aramaic, Greek, and Latin. We argue, however, that what is most apparent in this volume is his thinking as a legal historian—or, as he liked to call himself, "an intellectual historian whose area is ancient law" or a "scholar of ancient comparative law."

The Ancient Comparative Legal Historian

Each field of study has its own foci, principles, methods, terminology, and so forth. If we were to examine the fields of history, law, biblical studies, Assyriology, and classics, we would quickly discover some of the differences in the loci, assumptions, structures, approaches, terms of art, etc., of each of these areas of intellectual pursuit. Anyone who works in an interdisciplinary field knows how trying it can be to do so, because one has to master the different fundamentals of each field to be able to work within it. Westbrook's work is situated between the five fields just mentioned above, which was quite a scholarly feat, one worthy of admiration. Unfortunately, this breadth often led scholars within each of those separate fields to question his work because they believed his primary allegiance or knowledge belonged to another area. To offer just few examples, we have heard over the years, biblical scholars asserting, in various formulations, that Westbrook was really an Assyriologist, not fully trained in biblical studies. We have heard Assyriologists maintain that Westbrook was not a classic Assyriologist, certainly not a philologist. Others said, "He is just a lawyer." We have also heard legal historians aver that his work was "esoteric" and "irrelevant" because it dealt with law before the Greeks and Romans were dominant. Westbrook did not fit easily into any category because of the nature of his interdisciplinary work, and, consequently, no field ever truly adopted him as entirely their own.

It is accurate to say that his primary intellectual focus was not on the philology of the cuneiform languages, nor on producing text edition volumes, which are critical aspects of Assyriology; yet, his published work, dissertation, papers, and class lectures certainly indicate that he had an easy facility in those areas. Moreover, while Westbrook was a member of the bars of England and Wales and practiced law for some years, he preferred the life of a scholar—an Assyriological scholar to be exact. He did teach law, Assyriology, and classics over the course of his career, but his first love was teaching students to be Assyriologists and Near Eastern historians. In these senses, he was an Assyriologist. Nonetheless, Westbrook's specialty was ancient law, he thought in the categories of law, he used the methods of law, and he embraced the language of law in his writings. It is this organization and expression of his thinking that leads us to maintain that Westbrook was fundamentally a legal historian, using to great success the critical tools of Assyriology, Bible, and classics to probe the substantive and procedural law of the ancient world. Hence, all the fields were important to him. He said repeatedly to us when we were students at Hopkins that one had to know deeply the languages, history, and cultures of the people one studied and one had to be well versed in the principles of law to study ancient comparative law. It would irritate him if he perceived that we were failing to take a particular area seriously enough.

Ancient Comparative Law and Legal Method

All of Westbrook's work reflects, to one degree or another, how he structured this thinking around legal historical concepts, but let us examine first the basic structure of his *A History of Ancient Near Eastern Law*—a work he masterminded, edited, and wrote a great deal of—because it is a later and more encompassing work.[1] Westbrook provided a model form to authors that he wished each chapter to follow. It involved discussing such things as:

1. *the sources for legal historical work*, including the so-called law codes, other scholastic documents, royal edicts or decrees, inscriptions, reliefs, priestly decrees, administrative orders, petitions, trial transcripts and related documents, private legal documents, *kudurrus*, seals, letters, and literary sources;
2. *constitutional and administrative law*, including the organization of power and organs of government, such as the king, basic administrative structures, census-taking, central and provincial or local administration, temple administration, the courts, and compulsory service on the part of freemen;
3. *legal procedure*, including the standing of parties, the rules and organization of trial, evidentiary law, oaths and ordeals, settlements, releases of liability, appeals, and so forth;
4. *personal status law*, including citizenship, class, gender, age, and the institution of slavery;
5. *the major substantive legal areas*, including family law (marriage, children, adoption), property and inheritance law (types of property, land tenure and servitudes, wills and intestate succession, eligible heirs and shares, marital gifts, *inter vivos* gifts, and gifts in anticipation of death), contracts (capacity, sale, loan, pledge and distraint, suretyship, debt and social justice, prebends, the hire of persons, animals, or land, lease/rental, partnership, and apprenticeship), and criminal law (treason, homicide, assault or injury, sexual offenses, theft, damage to property, perjury, witchcraft, runaway slaves, and punishment);

1 Westbrook, ed., 2003.

6. *institutions with particular legal effect that are limited or special* to that particular geographic area and chronological period, such as religious and professional organizations, oracles, and letters to the dead; and
7. *international law*, including special sources (treaties, royal correspondence, letters to gods, historiographic texts, political declarations, oracular queries, etc.), the international system generally, specific imperials powers and other types of states, political relations, treaties generally, and customary international law (such as the law of war and treatment of foreign nationals).

Westbrook's detailed use of legal terms and categories and his particular ordering of the discussions, all reflect his legal historical thinking.

One might argue, of course, that other Assyriological, biblical, and classical scholars use such categories, and, on one level of their discussions, that is often correct. One can certainly find studies from classics, Bible, and Assyriology that use legal terms, such as homicide, marriage, adultery, theft, accusation, complaint, summons, verdict, punishment, and so forth. Yet, if one were to compare the broad works that examine a larger body of law within these fields done by those not also trained in law, one would typically discover the use of profoundly different categories in the content and ordering of these works. They are usually organized by the presence of particular ancient vocabulary or document typologies,[2] rather than by legal concepts, which can mask legal historical concepts.[3]

2 See, e.g., Veenker 1967; and Jas 1996. E. Dombradi's study (1996) of Old Babylonian suits is predominantly philological, but the second half of the study does organize itself around legal administration and procedure. K. Radner's work (1997) on Neo-Assyrian private legal documents is also similarly organized. S. E. Holtz's work (2009) is organized primarily by document typology.

3 Compare San Nicolò (1932) and Wells (2004: 108-26), both of whom have legal historical analyses of Neo-Babylonian conditional verdict documents, with Holtz (2009: 133-65), whose work focuses more on vocabulary and document typologies than on legal categories. Holtz labels these same documents as "summons[es] to establish a case." While the documents certainly are about establishing (Akkadian *kunnu*) a case, we find the term "summons(es)" problematic from a legal point of view.

Westbrook's difficulty with analyses oriented around ancient terminology relates to several key points. First, dissimilar words or expressions can often convey the same legal idea[4] (e.g., in English we can use accurately either "complainant" or "plaintiff" to describe the party who brings a civil lawsuit).[5] Furthermore, instances exist when it is quite difficult to determine whether there are substantive legal differences represented in the use of particular ancient words or whether they function as simple synonyms. In discussing the Old Babylonian courts' use of the words *burrum*, *kunnum*, and *nasāḫum* to describe the actions of both witnesses and judges with regard to facts at issue in a case, Westbrook asks: "In modern systems, ... witnesses *prove* facts but only judges can *establish* facts. Is there a different concept of the court's role at issue here, or merely an ambiguity of language, which did not disturb the pragmatic [Old] Babylonian mind?"[6] Consequently, one has to be quite careful, per Westbrook, to take fundamental legal principles into account and not rely solely on philological study. Using legal historical concepts helps one to see legal connections that might otherwise be overlooked.

Westbrook also viewed legal thinking as critical in the project of philology, at least when it came to legal terminology. We can observe this clearly in his discussion of the Akkadian term *ezēbu* in his article "A Matter of Life and Death," where he asserts that *ezēbu* usually

> means "to leave, abandon"; literally, it refers to physical motion by the subject away from the object, which would normally be stationary. As a technical legal term in the context of marriage, it means "to divorce." The connection between leaving and divorce might seem obvious, except that divorce was achieved in the legal systems that used this term not by physical motion but by the pronouncement of *verba solemnia*. Where a husband divorced his

4 Westbrook 1999e: 123.

5 We can observe this in the definition of complainant in Black et al. (1990: 285): "One who applies to the courts for legal redress by filing a complaint (*i.e.* plaintiff)." We, of course, recognize that English has a significantly larger vocabulary than does Akkadian; nevertheless, we believe that the principle still holds (see Magdalene 2007: 39-40).

6 Westbrook 1999e: 123.

> wife, at least, it was not he but the wife, the object of the verb *ezēbu*, who physically left the matrimonial home. The legal meaning of the term is thus the opposite of its literal meaning, a paradox expressed by MAL A 37: "If a man will divorce (literally: 'leave') his wife,...she shall go out empty.[7]

He concludes this point by stating:

> *A legal context thus provides a new set of clothes, so to speak, for the naked phrase*. Those clothes are invisible, insofar as there is no morphological change in the phrase, but they nonetheless make a very real difference in the way the phrase is read, because they allow it to have a different function, namely to describe not a physical phenomenon but the application of certain legal rules.[8]

Thus, he is able to state his general view of the importance of applying legal principles when attempting to comprehend the meaning of legal language:

> Where a phrase functions as a legal idiom, it takes effect within the confines of a world created by legal rules. Unless the logic of that legal world is taken into consideration, it may be difficult to connect the phrase with its context; indeed, a literal translation may produce bizarre results.[9]

He maintained, in fact, that "the starting point for any [legal] philological investigation should . . . be the presumption raised by legal logic, by their terminological connection, and by strong external parallels."[10]

Westbrook was also concerned with the problem of applying literary methods alone to the exegesis of legal texts. In his article "Law of Biblical Israel," where he again discusses the nature of the biblical "law codes" and difficulties of the evolutionary model of their development, he stresses:

7 Westbrook 1997: 63 (= chap. 17, pp. 254-55 in this volume).

8 Emphasis added. Westbrook 1997: 63 (= chap. 17, p. 255 in this volume).

9 Westbrook 1997: 65 (= chap. 17, p. 257 in this volume).

10 Westbrook 1997: 63 (= chap. 17, p. 254 in this volume).

> The literary model divorces the text from any relationship with the law in force. This is of great advantage to biblical scholars, who are trained in literary criticism and not in jurisprudence. Not all literature is alike, however, and legal literature is simply not the same as scientific literature or myth or historiography.[11]

All legal historical assertions made by those working on the ancient texts of the circum-Mediterranean and larger western Asia must satisfy the logic of law.[12]

Westbrook's view of law was very much based in the analytical school of jurisprudence founded by H. L. A. Hart, with whom Westbrook studied briefly at Oxford.[13] As a mature scholar, he preferred, however, the analytical legal philosophy of H. Kelsen.[14] Law was a coherent whole with a fairly uniform "grammar," as he expressed it to us. One can see that position in his discussion of the failure of diachronic literary methods and the need for all legal historical work to satisfy legal logic:

> We shall seek to show that the law is an organic whole, consistent in its individual parts, that may be explained without recourse to a diachronic deconstruction of its text. In doing so, we shall apply principally the method of legal logic, on the grounds that in a legal text, the sole criterion for resolving ambiguities of language is the most appropriate legal meaning. For that purpose it must be assumed that the law is coherent, and only if all attempts fail should recourse be had to explanations based upon error, inelegant editing, or unresolved difficulties arising from the historical development of legal conceptions.[15]

11 Westbrook 2008a: 108 (= chap. 21, pp. 328-39 in this volume).

12 In many of his articles, Westbrook discussed the importance of legal logic, and the failure "to satisfy legal logic" was often the basis for his critique of a given legal solution. For a good example of this, and even the specific use of that phrase, see Westbrook 1991a: 219 (= chap. 5, p. 80 in this volume).

13 See most importantly Hart 1961; and Hart 1983. See further Gavison 1987.

14 See most importantly Kelsen 1961; Kelsen 1967; and Kelsen 1991. See further Paulson and Paulson 1998; and Paulson and Stolleis 2005.

15 Westbrook 1994a: 391 (= chap. 23, p. 362 in this volume). Westbrook did believe that some editing had occurred within biblical legal material, but diachronic analysis also

Westbrook, therefore, maintained that one simply could not do legal history well if one were not trained in law and history, as well as in the languages, literatures, and cultures of the peoples under study. Legal history was, for him, first about law and society and only secondarily about philology and literature. Thus, Westbrook was a comparative legal historian of the ancient world.

This Volume

There are twenty-eight articles contained in this volume. We believe that these articles demonstrate clearly Westbrook's legal philosophy, the theory of ancient law that arose from it, the hermeneutical principles he used in analyzing ancient legal texts, and how he applied this method to specific legal problems to arrive at interesting, creative, and oft times quite persuasive solutions. The first 19 articles comprise Part I ("Cuneiform Sources") and focus, obviously, on the texts written in the various cuneiform based languages of the ancient Near East. The last nine articles comprise Part II ("Biblical Sources"). Here, Westbrook applies his method to the study of biblical law. Throughout these twenty-eight articles, Westbrook demonstrates how understanding the highly consistent legal logic or legal grammar of the ancient world assists in solving numerous legal puzzles.

As in the first volume, a number of Westbrook's articles were originally accompanied by abstracts, and we have again written abstracts for those that were not. The articles that have original abstracts are: "The Edict of Tudhaliya IV" (chap. 1), "The Phrase 'His Heart Is Satisfied' in Ancient Near Eastern Legal Sources" (chap. 5), "The Case of the Elusive Debtors: CT 4 6a and CT 6 34b" (chap. 6), "Social Justice and Creative Jurisprudence in Late Bronze Age Syria" (chap. 7), "The Quality of Freedom in Neo-Babylonian Manumissions" (chap. 12), "The Enforcement of Morals in Mesopotamian Law" (chap. 16), "Babylonian Diplomacy" (chap. 19), "Lex Talionis and Exodus 21:22-25" (chap. 22), and "The Deposit Law of Exodus 22:6-12" (chap. 23). The remaining articles are accompanied by abstracts written by the editors of this collection.

---

had to be based on sound legal logic. See Westbrook 1999c (= chap. 28 in this volume); cf. Westbrook and Wilcke 1974-77 (= chap. 3 in this volume).

Once again, we have edited according to American spelling, grammar, and punctuation. We have also continued to use the author-date style of citation in all of the footnotes. Finally, this volume, like the first, contains a comprehensive list of all of the scholarly literature cited in these twenty-eight articles. This bibliography, in combination with that of the first volume, should serve as a valuable resource in and of itself for those interested in ancient Near Eastern law.

To be sure, this collection is our way of honoring the memory and work of our teacher, friend, and colleague, Raymond Westbrook. But our hope is that it will be much more than that. We thus conclude with the same statement of purpose with which we ended our introduction in volume 1:

> While the production of this collection and the uniformity of format that it seeks to achieve should help to make Westbrook's writings more accessible and usable, the more important purpose is to give his views a full airing and to reinvigorate the conversations that his scholarship originally stimulated. In sum, we believe and hope that this volume will make a significant and lasting contribution not only to the study of its more immediate topic—the legal systems of the ancient Near East—but also to the study of the larger history of law.[16]

16 See B. Wells, "Introduction: The Idea of a Shared Tradition," p. xx, in volume 1.

Part One

Cuneiform Sources

1

The Edict of Tudhaliya IV

Abstract

A revised translation of this text reveals it to be not a law code that includes reforms but a royal edict that deals with the traditional subjects of such decrees: debt-release and administrative reforms. The content of those sections that can be interpreted is: (I 1ff.) introduction relating the circumstances of the reform; (II 1ff.) debt-release provisions; (III 1-11) provisions concerning access to royal granaries and the local authorities' responsibility for losses therefrom; (IV 4ff.) provisions against oppression of certain classes of royal tenants. Included within the linguistic and philological commentary is an excursus dealing with the problematic verb *šakuwāi-*. It is argued that this form is a reflex of the Proto-Indo-European root *$*sek^w$-* "to follow" and bears remarkable semantic similarity to its Latin cognate *sequi*.

Introduction

The edict of the Hittite king Tudhaliya IV (1265-1240 B.C.E.) was edited by von Schuler in 1959 in an article on legislation in the Hittite and wider cuneiform sphere. The learned editor had recognized the importance of this text to the question of lawmaking in the ancient Near East and attempted to relate it both to other edicts and to the cuneiform law codes. Nonetheless, the obscurity of its language in key passages made the text an unsatisfactory basis for sweeping theoretical conclusions. The purpose of this article is to offer a new translation and legal interpretation,

* Co-authored with Roger D. Woodard. Originally published in the *Journal of the American Oriental Society* 110 (1990): 641-59. Copyright © American Oriental Society. Used by permission.

* We would like to express our thanks to Professor H. Craig Melchert and to Professor James W. Poultney for their valuable comments and suggestions. Responsibility for any errors remains with the authors.

which, although by no means clarifying all parts of the text, does, it is hoped, present a coherent and credible picture of its general character and main provisions.

The two main sources of theoretical law in the sphere of cuneiform civilization are the law code and the royal edict. The former, six principal examples of which are preserved at some length,[1] covers the whole gamut of legal relations, including property, contract, crime and delict (tort), family law, and procedural and administrative law. There has been considerable debate, however, as to whether the codes are true normative legislation or merely academic treatises on the law.[2]

There is no doubt as to the legislative character of the edicts:[3] they are reforms expressly dated to a specific point in time at which their provisions come into effect and there is ample evidence, direct and indirect, of their effect upon legal relations (Westbrook 1989a: 214-17). On the other hand, the subject matter of the edicts is much narrower than that of the codes. They cover three main topics: reform of the royal administration, price-fixing, and retrospective debt release, none of which could be said to represent the central institutions of a legal system.

The edict of Tudhaliya IV begins with a narrative typical of royal edicts, in which former abuses are described and the motivation for reform is given.[4] The text unfortunately breaks off at this point and, when it resumes at the top of column II, appears to be discussing details of homicide and theft, topics outside the normal purview of the royal edict. Hence the importance attributed by von Schuler (1959: 445) to this text, which on

1 Codex Ur-Namma (CU), Codex Lipit-Ishtar (CL), Codex Eshnunna (CE), Codex Hammurabi (CH), Middle Assyrian Laws (MAL), Hittite Laws (HL).

2 For bibliography and a summary of the arguments, see Westbrook 1989a.

3 There are many fragments of edicts preserved and many more references to edicts that are not extant. The Old Babylonian material has been collected by Kraus (1984: 16-110). The most complete examples, apart from the text under discussion, are: Uru-inimgina (Lagash), edition in Cooper 1986; Ammi-ṣaduqa (Babylon), edition in Kraus 1984: 168-83; Horemheb (Egypt), edition in Kruchten 1981; Telipinu (Hatti), edition in Hoffman (1984).

4 Cf. cols. I-VII in Uru-inimgina's edict (Sollberger *Corpus* Ukg. 5.1-7 = La 9.1 cols. I-VII in Cooper 1986: 70-71); and Telipinu paragraphs 7-27. Each narrative provision of Horemheb's edict is preceded by a statement of the former abuse; see Kruchten (1981: 194-98, section C).

this interpretation would seem to be a law code that shows the characteristics of normative legislation.

Von Schuler's interpretation, however, was founded on his translation of the text, which we now wish to call into question. In our view, the text is nothing other than a royal edict, and its content is within the parameters of what is normally found in texts of this genre. It is nonetheless significant in its own right, since it contains two types of edict provisions: reforms of the royal administration and the details of a debt release. This is the first instance of a debt release in the Hittite sphere, since the other Hittite edict, that of Telipinu, is concerned only with administrative reforms. Furthermore, it casts new light on the mechanics of a general debt release, since it covers aspects not dealt with in the debt release decrees from Babylonia.

For the convenience of the reader, a copy of the transliterated text follows. The present text differs from that offered by von Schuler (1959: 446-48) only in minor detail.

KUB XIII 9 + KUB XL 62

Column I

1 *UM-MA Ta-ba-ar-na* ᴵ*Tu-ut-ḫa-li-ya* LUGAL GAL
2 *ma-a-an* ^{URU}*A-aš-šu-wa ḫar-ni-in-k*[*u-u*]*n*
3 ^{uru}*Ha-at-tu-ši* [*ú-wa*?-] *nu-un*
4 *nu-kán* DINGER^{MEŠ} *aš-ša-nu-nu-un* [*nu-*] *mu* LÚ^{MEŠ} ^{URU}*Ḫa-at-ti*
5 *ḫu-u-ma-an-za a-ru-ú-e-eš-ki-u*[*-w*]*a-an da-a-iš mu kiš-an me-mi-ir*

---

6 ^{d}UTU$^{\textit{ŠI}}$*-wa an-ze-el BE-LÍ-NI* ^{LÚ}*la-aḫ-ḫi-ya-la-aš*
7 *zi-ik nu-wa-aš-ša-a*[*n*?] *ḫa-an-né-eš-na-an-ni*
8 [*ḫ*]*a*?*-an-nu-wa-an-zi Ú-UL tar-ra-at-ta*
9 [*ka*?-]*a-aš-ša-wa-kán i-da-la-u-i-eš* UKÙ^{MEŠ}*-ši-iš*
10 [ ] x-*ni ar-ḫa ḫar-ni-in-ki-ir*
11 [$^{\text{Ḫ]I.A}}$ *ú-pa-a-ti*$^{\text{ḪI.A}}$ *Ù* LÚ^{MEŠ} *ša-ri-ku-wa-aš*
12 [*-t*]*i*? *e-eš-ta*

---

13 [ ] x-te-*eš-ša*
14 [ ]
15 [ ] x-*ta*

16 [ ] *mi-iš*

===

Column II

1 *na-aš-ta pa-ra-a Ú-UL tar-na-i nu-uš-ši* EGIR-*pa*
2 *PU-UḪ-ŠU a-pé-e-né-eš-šu-u-wa-da-an* A.ŠÀ *pa-a-i*

---

3 *ma-a-an e-eš-ḫa-na-aš-ša-ku-iš-ki šar-ni-ik-zi-il*
4 *pí-ya-an ḫar-zi nu-za-ta* SAG.DU-*ZU wa-aš-ta*
5 *na-aš-šu* A.ŠÀ^{LAM} *na-aš-ma* LÚ.ULÙ$^{\text{LU!}}$
6 *na-aš-ta pa-ra-a Ú-UL ku-iš-ki tar-na-i*
7 *ma-a-na-aš-za QA-DU* DAM^{MEŠ}-*ŠU* DUMU^{MEŠ}-*ŠU da-a-an ḫar-zi*
8 *na-an-ši-iš-ta pa-ra-a tar-na-i ma-a-an ta-i-iz-zi-la-aš-ša*
9 *ku-iš-ki šar-ni-ik-ze-el pí-ya-an ḫar-zi*
10 *nu ma-a-an* A.ŠÀ *na-aš-ta pa-ra-a Ú-UL tar-na-an-zi*
11 *ma-a-an* ÌR-*ma da-ya-at na-an ta-i-az-zi-la-an-ni ḫar-zi*
12 *na-aš ma-a-an ta-šu-wa-aḫ-ḫa-an-za*
13 *na-an-ši-iš-ta pa-ra-a Ú-UL tar-na-an-zi*
14 *ma-a-na-aš Ú-UL ta-šu-wa-aḫ-ḫa-an-za*
15 *na-an-ši-iš-ta pa-ra-a tar-na-an-zi*

---

16 *ták-ku EL-LAM-ma ku-iš-ki da-i-ya-zi*
17 *nu da-i-ya-zi-la-aš šar-ni-ik-ze-el*
18 n[u] x *n*[*a-a*]*n Ú-UL ta-šu-wa-aḫ-ḫa-an-zi*
19 [ ] *na-an-zi*

===

Column III

1 [ ]x
2 [ ] *e*?-[*š*]*a-ri*

---

3 [ ] x [É].GAL$^{\text{ḪI.A.}TIM}$ *ku-i-e-eš*
4 *m*[*a-n*]*i*-[*y*]*a-aḫ-ḫe-eš-kán-z*[*i ma*]*-a-an*
5 *ki-nu-zu-zi na-aš-ma*[*-ad*?*-du*?*-z*]*a*? ^{LÚ}SIG$_5$
6 *na-an ki-nu-ud-du* ^{L}[^{Ú}AGRI]G?-*ma* $^{\text{LÚ.MEŠ}}$*ḫa-at-tal-wa-la-aš*

7 ^{LÚ}APIN.LAL-*aš* LUGAL-*wa-aš* ARÀḪ[-*an P*]*A-NI* ZI-*ŠU le-e ku-iš-ki ki-nu-uz-zi*
8 *ku-iš ki-nu-uz-zi-ma* [*š*]*u-me-eš-ša-an* LÚ^{MEŠ} URU^{LIM} *e-ep-tin*
9 *na-an* LUGAL-*wa-aš a-aš-ki* [*ú*]-*wa-te-et-tin ma-a-an Ú-UL-ma*
10 *ú-wa-da-te-e-ni nu* ARÀḪ-*an* LÚ^{MEŠ} URU^{LIM} *šar-ni-in-kán-zi*
11 *gi-nu-ut-ma-an ku-*[*i*]*š na-an ša-ku-wa-an-zi*

---

12 *ku-iš-za-an ke-e-da-aš* LUGAL-*wa-aš ud-da-na-aš*
13 *ka-ru-ú-uš-ši-ya-zi na-aš-za na-aš-šu* ^{LÚ}*a-ra-ši-iš*
14 *mu-un-na-a-ši nu*[-*u*]*š-ši ma-aš-ka-an pa-a-i*
15 *nu-za-ta na-aš-šu*[^{L}]^{Ú}*ma-ni-ya-aḫ-ḫa-an-da-aš-ša* LÚ ḪA.LA-*ŠU*
16 *pa-ra-a Ú-UL tar-na-i ne-ez-za-an ud-da-ni-i* EGIR-*an*
17 *ták-ša-an Ú-UL ap-pí-ya-zi ap-pí-iz-zi-ya-an-na*
18 *ut-tar i-ši-ya-aḫ-ta-ri nu-uš 2-i-la-pát ša-ku-wa-an-zi*
19 *an-da-ma ma-a-an ḫa-an-na-an* DI-*šar ku-iš-ki* EGIR-*pa da-a-i*
20 *nu a-pa-a-at ut-tar* SIG$_5$-*in pár-ku-wa-an-zi*

Column IV

2 [*ḫ*]*a*?-*t*[*a-a*]*n-t*[*i*]
3 [-]*mi na-an-ta*
4 [*I*]*Š-TU* ZI-*KU-NU-ma-aš-ma-aš*
5 [*IŠ.T*]*U*? EN ^{GIŠ}TUKUL-*ma PA-NI* ZI-*ŠU da-a-i*
6 [ ] x-*an*? *ta-šu-wa-aḫ-ḫa-an-zi*
7 [ ] x x [*n*]*a-aš-za ku-it ku-it da-a-an ḫar-zi*
8 *ḫu-u-ma-an ta-a-an pé-eš-ki-iz-zi*

---

9 [ ] *QA-TI*
10 ŠU ^{I}*A-li-iḫ-ḫi-ni* DUMU ^{I}AN.ŠUR.LÚ DUMU.DUMU-*ŠÚ ŠA* ^{I}GIŠ.ŠAR.NU
11 KAB.ZU.ZU [*Š*]*A* ^{I}*Zu-wa-a* EN GIŠ.KIN.TI

Translation

Column I

1 Thus speaks the Tabarna Tudhaliya, the great king:
2-3 When I had destroyed Assuwa and returned to Hattusa,

4 I refurbished the gods; the men of Hatti
5 all began to bow down to me, and they spoke as follows:
6 O great king, you are our lord, a leader of campaigns (?).
7-8 Are you not able to judge in matters of justice?
9 Behold, evil people
10 [ ] have utterly destroyed
11 [ ] the feudal holdings (?) and the *šarikuwa* tenants
12 [ ] was.

---

13 [ ]
14 [ ]
15 [ ]
16 [ ]

Column II

1 . . . he shall not release [it/them], but
2 he shall give back to him just such a field [as] its substitute.

---

3 And if someone has given ransom for blood,
4 and he has purchased himself from you;
5 whether [the ransom be] a field or a person,
6 no one shall release [it].
7 If he (i.e., the holder of the ransom) has taken those things along with his (i.e., the offender's) wives [and] sons,
8 he will release him/it to him. And if
9 someone has given ransom for theft:
10 if [it is] a field, they shall not release [it];
11 but if a slave has stolen, and he (i.e., the ransom holder) holds him for the theft—
12 if he has been blinded,
13 they will not release him (i.e., the slave) to him (i.e., the former master),
14-15 if he has not been blinded, then they will release him to him.

---

16 But if some free man steals
17 and a ransom for theft [he has given]
18 [ ] and they will not blind him
19 they shall [ ]

Column III

1 [ ]. . .
2 [ ] he sits

---

3 [ ] who administer the palaces,
4 if such a one opens the granary of the king,
5 or if he sends on his behalf a superior officer [to open it],
6 then allow him to open it. But a steward, doorkeepers,
7 a farmer—let none such open the granary of the king against his (i.e., the king's) will.
8 But who does so open it, you, the men of the city, seize him
9 and bring him to the gate of the king. But if you do not
10 bring [him], the men of the city will make reparation for the granary,
11 and they will track down the one who forced it open.

---

lines 12-20 omitted

Column IV

4 [ ] but by your own will, them
5 [ ] but he takes [from] a ^{GIŠ}TUKUL man against his will
6 [ ] they shall blind him, and him
7 [ ] and whatever he has taken [ ],
8 he will give it all double.

---

9 Completed.
10 Hand of Alihhini, son of AN.ŠUR.LÚ, grandson of GIŠ.ŠAR.NU,
11 student of Zuwa, chief of the artisans.

Linguistic and Philological Commentary

I 6

^{LÚ}*laḫḫiyalaš*. The noun *laḫḫa-* denotes both “military campaign” and “journey.” Likewise, when intransitive, the verb *la(ḫ)ḫiyai-* has the meaning “to travel, go on an expedition,” etc.; in its transitive use, the verb means “to attack, make war on,” etc. (*CHD* 3:4-10). The editors of the *CHD* suggest, however, that *laḫḫiyala-* consistently occurs in the nonmilitary sense of “traveler,” with the possible exception of its occurrence in this text. Either interpretation is consistent with our reading of the text.

I 7-8

nu-wa-šan ḫannešnanni ḫannuwanzi UL tarratta. “Are you not able to judge in matters of justice?” We interpret this phrase as a rhetorical question, which serves as introduction to and justification of the forthcoming royal pronouncements on the matter of debt release.

I 11

upati. See von Schuler 1959: 452. For ^{LÚ}*šarikuwa-*, Friedrich (1952: 185) offers “niedere Bevölkerungsklasse”; see Goetze 1967: 230-32.

II 2

apeneššuwadan. For *apeneššuwandan* “just such,” see von Schuler 1959: 452.

II 4

nu-za-ta SAG.DU-*ZU wašta*. Literally, “he has purchased his own head/person from you”; that is, “he has purchased himself . . . .” Following Goetze (1930: 74), von Schuler (1959: 452) emends the text to read *wa-aš-ta*<*-aš*> “he has transgressed” (pret. 3rd sing. of *wašta-*). There is no epigraphical indication for this emendation, and we interpret *wašta* as simply the pret. 3rd sing. of *waš-* “to purchase” (see Friedrich 1952: 248).[5]

The verb is clearly reflexive in sense as marked by the enclitic particle *-za*. Beyond this, SAG.DU almost certainly functions here as a reflexive pronoun as it does at times in Akkadian. See *CAD* Q 106-7 2b): *kime šamši* SAG.DU-*su māssu inaṣṣaršu* “. . . as the sun watches over himself

5 This analysis of the verb, which we believe to be crucial for a proper understanding of the text, was first brought to our attention by Professor Melchert.

and his land" (KBo I 5 i 50f., 56f.); and cf. 2a): *qaqqassa ana* ŠÁM *iddin* "she sold herself" (literally "her head"; unpublished Old Akkadian text). Typological studies reveal that it is not uncommon for languages to utilize as a reflexive pronoun a word for "head" or "soul." Thus Basque, for example, uses *buru* "head" for a reflexive, and Fula makes use of *hoore* "head"; for a discussion, see Faltz 1985: 33ff.

The inclusion of the second person pronoun *-ta* at first strikes the reader as curious, though, of course, the alternation between second and third person is not uncommon in colloquial speech. Compare the interchange of second and third person verbs in III 8-11.

II 7

mān-aš-za QA-DU DAM^{MEŠ}-*ŠU* DUMU^{MEŠ}-*ŠU dān ḫarzi*. "If he (i.e., the holder of the ransom) has taken those things along with his (i.e., the offender's) wives [and] sons . . ." If *-aš* is construed as a nominative denoting the holder of the ransom, the verb *dā-* is then left without an object, and there is no specification of the entity by which DAM^{MEŠ}-*ŠU* and DUMU^{MEŠ}-*ŠU* are accompanied; consequently, we interpret the enclitic pronoun as an accusative common plural of the later type[6] which has as its antecedent the common nouns of line 5, i.e., A.ŠÀ and LÚ.ULÙ^{LU}. The use of a plural pronoun with what is, strictly speaking, a singular antecedent ("whether [the ransom be] a field *or* a person") could quite naturally be the result of either one of at least two factors: (1) a casual grammatical style, which is exhibited elsewhere in the document (see the discussion of II 4), i.e., the composer may simply be referring collectively to the conjoined referents of line 5; (2) the possibility that the terms A.ŠÀ and LÚ.ULÙ^{LU} merely indicate the nature of the ransom and are not meant to specify the number of items offered (i.e., "whether field or person"). In the latter case, the composer would be betraying his awareness that a multiplicity of items is frequently involved. In the Hittite Laws, one finds that, as a consequence of slaying a man or a woman in a quarrel, an offender is required to present a ransom of four persons (HL 1);[7] if the blood crime is deemed less severe, the penalty levied is either two persons or one (HL 2-4).

6 *CHD* 3:9 identifies this text as Middle Hittite written in New Hittite script.

7 4 SAG.DU *pāi* (Friedrich 1971: 16); literally, "he will give 4 heads."

II 8

n-an-ši-šta parā tarnai. "He will release him/it to him." It seems clearly to be the case that the enclitic pronoun *-an* refers to the debt which is to be released by the ransom holder, though that the common singular of the pronoun should be used is surprising given the plurality of items which are held.[8] Note that lines II 1 and 10 reveal that the object need not be expressed with *parā tarnai*.

II 13/15

n-an-ši-šta. The animate pronoun *-an* most probably refers to ÌR-*aš* "slave."

II 16

takku ELLAM-ma kuiški daiyazi. "If some free man steals . . . ." Along with von Schuler (1959: 453), we interpret Akkadian *ELLAM* as nominative. An identical use of the accusative case for the nominative occurs in KBo VI 4 I 9: [*ták*]-*ku* LÚ-*aš da-me-da-ni* A.ŠÀ A.GÀR *an-da a-ki ták-ku* LÚ *EL.LAM* "If a man dies in a foreign field/meadow, if he [is] a free man" (see Friedrich 1971: 50-51; 1974: 174). This matter will be further addressed below in the Legal Commentary.

II 17

nu daiyazilaš šarnikzel. "And a ransom for theft [he has given]." The phrase *piyan ḫarzi*, "he has given," must here be supplied from context.[9]

8 In a personal communication, Professor Melchert has suggested to us that the antecedent of *-an* is perhaps to be understood as *šarnikzil*. Though the gender of *šarnikzil* is, of course, as with other nouns in *-il*, conventionally identified as neuter, Melchert holds that nouns in *-il* are, in fact, likely to be animate.

9 Unless, of course, this phrase occurred in the lacuna at the beginning of line 18. Within the lacuna, preceding what can reasonably be read as *na-an*, the topmost portion of four (or, perhaps, five) signs is visible. The final character could conceivably be *zi*, though this reading is not straightforward. However, as von Schuler (1959: 446) indicates in his transcription, the initial character of the line looks most like *nu*. If the final sign were *zi*, the amount of space which precedes it—that is the space available for writing *pí-ya-an ḫar-*—would appear to be just slightly less than that utilized for writing these four characters at the beginning of II 4. Could the initial sign of line 18 be a somewhat compressed *pí*? The sign preceding the final visible character could be *an*, but, if the copy is proportionately accurate, there would appear to be insufficient space for *ḫar*. The very small remnant of the second preserved sign does not suggest *ya*.

II 19

[*n-an-ši-šta para* (*UL*) *tar*]*nanzi*. Perhaps line 19 is to be so restored, after II 13 and 15, though it is not possible to determine, of course, whether some entity is to be released or not to be released. Von Schuler (1959: 453) restores the text without the *UL*.[10]

III 3, 4

[. . . É]GAL$^{ḪI.A.TIM}$ *kuieš* (4) *m*[*an*]*i*[*y*]*aḫḫeš-kanz*[*i*] ". . . who administer the palaces," or perhaps " . . . of the palaces—[those] who govern." On the use of *manniyaḫḫ-* "to govern" without an object, see *CHD* 3:165-66.

III 5

n-ašma[. . . *z*]*a* ^{LÚ}SIG$_5$ *peyazi*. Von Schuler (1959: 453) restores as *n-ašma-du-za*, i.e., "If he sends on his behalf a superior officer to you."

III 7

[. . . *P*]*A-NI* ZI-*ŠU*. "Against his (i.e., the king's) will." In other words, without the king's express consent.

III 11

n-an šakuwanzi. "They will track him down." The meaning of the verb *šakuwāi-* has proved quite problematic to identify (see, for example, Friedrich 1952: 177). Goetze (1967: 202-3) examines various occurrences of the form and concludes his examination with the remark, "Mit der allgemeinen Bedeutung 'zur Ruhe bringen' wird man allen Belegen von *šakuwā-* gerecht." However, he returns to a consideration of this verb in his review of Güterbock 1946 (see Goetze 1949: 182), and there states, after summarizing the contexts in which the verb occurs: "It is hard to find the common denominator of all this. For the time being, the best I can find is 'suspend.' If this proves correct, a difference must exist between our verb and *gang-*; the latter may imply balancing."

We believe that *šakuwāi-* is a reflex of the Proto-Indo-European root *sek^w- "to follow" and in the present text has the sense "to track down" or "to pursue." The city officials, having made reparation to the king out of their own pockets, are to pursue the thief in order to recover their own expenditures. As will be discussed further in the Legal Commentary below,

10 Perhaps because line 17 is shorter than line 15? Lines 13 (with *UL*) and 15 (without *UL*) are, however, almost the same length.

there is a close parallel to this injunction in the Code of Hammurabi. In the Excursus we will treat the verb *šakuwāi-* in detail and offer what we believe to be compelling evidence for its identification with Proto-Indo-European *$^*sek^w$-*.

IV 5

EN ^{GIŠ}TUKUL, literally, "owner of the weapon." The term is comparable to LÚ ^{GIŠ}TUKUL and apparently designates a type of fief-holder. For a recent investigation of ^{GIŠ}TUKUL, see Beal 1988.

Excursus
šakuwāi- "to pursue

Among the reflexes of PIE *$^*sek^w$-* are the following: Sanskrit *śacate* "to accompany, follow"; Avestan *hačaite* "to accompany"; and Greek ἕπομαι; Latin *sequor*; Old Irish *sechur*; Lithuanian *sèkti*; Lettish *sekt*—each with the common, basic meaning "to follow." For orthographic reasons, there may be some objection to our inclusion of *šakuwāi-* in this set. It has been held that reflexes of the Indo-European voiceless stops are represented in Hittite orthography as geminate consonants, i.e., **šakkuwāi-* would be expected from the root *$^*sek^w$-*. The evidence clearly suggests, however, that this is not always the case. Note that the Hittite reflex of the homophonous PIE root *$^*sek^w$-* "to see, to show" (Pokorny 1959: 897-98) is likewise spelled with only a single stop: *šakuwāi-* "to see"; *šakuwa* "eyes" (Friedrich 1952: 177-78).[11] This nongeminate spelling of the Hittite reflex of PIE *$^*k^w$* was also noted by Schindler (1967: 290). In his discussion of Hittite *nekuz* "night,"[12] Schindler writes:

> Aus der Einfachschreibung des *-k-* in *nekuz* lassen sich selbstverständlich keine Schlüsse auf ursprüngliche Media (aspirata)

11 Some investigators, including Pokorny (1959: 897), have proposed that the two PIE homophones are ultimately to be traced to a single root (for a recent discussion of this issue, see Baldi 1974). For an opposing opinion, see Chantraine (1968-1980: 2:361).

12 The PIE etymon of which *nekuz* is a reflex has been traditionally reconstructed as *$^*nek^w$-t-* (Pokorny 1959: 762-63). Schindler is responding *inter alios* to Sturtevant (1942: 27), who proposes *$^*g^wh$* for the final consonant of the root.

ziehen. Vgl. *ša-(a-)ku-wa* "Augen" zu **sek^{w}-* "sehen" und *e-ku-zi*, 3. Pl. *a-ku-wa-an-zi* "trinken," das doch wohl zu lat. *aqua* gehört.[13]

While it appears to be generally the case that PIE voiceless stops give rise to orthographic geminates in Hittite, the above observations along with the not uncommon variation between geminate and nongeminate spelling of Hittite consonants call for a careful quantitative study of this aspect of Hittite orthography.

The Hittite reflex of **sek^{w}-* "to follow" is unlike the other IE reflexes cited above in that it consistently shows the *o*-grade of the root. These latter verb forms each exhibit the *e*-grade, though the *o*-grade is found in, for example, Greek ἀοσσέω "to help" and Latin *socius* "companion" (<**sok^{w}-yo-*). Again, the homophonous PIE root **sek^{w}-* "to see" exhibits the same treatment in Hittite as the root meaning "to follow," i.e., it also regularly takes the *o*-grade (*šakuwāi-*); contrast Gothic *saihwan* "to see," Old High German *sehan*, "sight," Greek ἔν(ν)-επε and Latin *inseque*/*insece* "tell"—each with the *e*-grade. The identical evolutionary outcome of the two roots in Hittite may suggest the occurrence of a regular sound change whereby the mid front vowel /e/ was backed and rounded to /o/ when followed by the sequence /labiovelar + back vowel/, i.e., */sek^{w}ai-/ → */sok^{w}ai-/ → /sak^{w}ai-/. Such a scheme is phonologically and phonetically quite plausible, though, for the present this suggestion should, of course, be regarded as tentative.

In the remainder of the excursus, the various occurrences of the problematic *šakuwāi-* will be examined, and evidence will be presented which, we believe, strongly indicates that this verb is a reflex of PIE **sek^{w}-* "to follow."

A. KUB XIII 2 III 16 (von Schuler 1957: 47)

15 . . . *na-aš-ša-an* EGIR-*pa li-e*

16 *ku-iš-ki tar-na-i ku-i-ša-an-ša-an* EGIR-pa *tar-na-i na-an* ***ša-ku-wa-an-za***

13 The inclusion of Hittite *eku-* and Latin *aqua* "water" within the same cognate set is, of course, not universally accepted among Indo-Europeanists; see Puhvel (1984-: 264) for a brief discussion.

15-16 . . . Let no one allow (the exile) to return; that one who does allow him to return, they will **track down/punish**.[14]

In this text from the Instructions for the *Bēl Madgalti* or "Lord of the Border Guards," *šakuwāi-* is used in much the same way as in the Tudhaliya edict. The paragraph in which the text occurs deals with the case of a person who has committed an abomination (*ḫurkel*) and has been banished. The reason for this punishment is that *ḫurkel*-offenses (e.g., incest; see HL 73-82) are regarded as polluting the locale of the offense, with the result that divine anger will inflict punishment on the whole population. For the same reason, the area has to be purified after the culprit's departure. If the culprit subsequently returns, the whole city will again be endangered. The instruction is therefore directed against anyone who might contemplate harboring him or perhaps merely fail to report his presence. Responsibility is laid upon the local authorities, to whom the instructions in this paragraph are addressed, to establish the identity of such persons. Their punishment is not specified, but since they have been instrumental in creating pollution, their fate is not difficult to imagine. Compare Num 35:32-34, where a homicide victim's relatives are forbidden to accept ransom from the killer to allow his return from exile (likewise without specifying any penalty), on the grounds that it will cause pollution.

Both of the nuances "to track down, pursue" and "to punish" are attested among the reflexes of *sek^w- in other IE families. In Lithuanian, *sekti* has the meaning "to pursue" (Pokorny 1959: 897; Senn 1957: 251), and in Lettish, *sekt* means "to pursue," "to track" and even "to smell" in the context of hounds tracking down and sniffing out game (Mayrhofer 1956-80: 417; Pokorny 1959: 897; Ulmann 1872: 255). Greek ἕπομαι also exhibits the meaning "to pursue" as in, for example, *Iliad* 11.153-154:

ἀτὰρ κρείων Ἀγαμέμνων αἰὲν ἀποκτείνων **ἕπετ'** Ἀργείοισι κελεύων.
But, always slaying, lordly Agamemnon **pursued** (the Trojans), exhorting the Argives.

14 On the present indicative third person plural form *šakuwanza* rather than *šakuwanzi*, cf. third plural *ešza* for *ešzi*, and see the discussion in Friedrich (1971: 103).

Also of particular interest is *Iliad* 11.473-75,

> ἀμφὶ δ' ἄρ' αὐτὸν Τρῶες **ἕπονθ'** ὥς εἴ τε δαφοινοὶ θῶες ὄρεσφιν ἀμφ' ἔλαφον κεραὸν βεβλημένον,
> and the Trojans **closed in** about him, as tawny jackals in the mountains (close in about) a horned stag which has been hit (by an arrow),

though there is some disagreement among scholars as to whether the verb in this text is to be identified as ἕπομαι or ἕπω "to busy oneself with" (Chantraine 1970: 363). Also pertinent are occurrences of ἕπομαι in the Xenophon's *Cyn.*, e.g., 6.19; in this passage, Xenophon instructs the reader as to what is to be done if a hare should initially escape a pack of pursuing hounds:

> καὶ ἐὰν πάλιν ἀπαντῶσι διώκουσαι αὐτόν ἀναβοᾶν, εὖ γε εὖ γε ὦ κ΄θνες **ἕπεσθε** ὦ κύνες
> And if again pursuing [<διώκω] (the hare), they should come upon it, let him shout "Well done, well done hounds—**after** (it) hounds!"

By far the most striking parallels, however, are those offered by Latin *sequi*—both the simplex form and its various compositional forms:

> *Eo die quo consuerat intervallo hostes* ***sequitur*** (Caesar, *Bell. gall.* 1.22.5).
> On that day he **pursued** the enemy at the distance to which he was accustomed.

> *Cineres atque ossa peremptae* ***insequitur*** (Virgil *Aen.* 5.788).
> She **pursues/persecutes** (even) the ashes and bones of the slain (of Troy).

> *. . . iuro . . . me L. Tarquinium Superbum cum scelerata coniuge et omni liberorum stirpe ferro, igni, quacumque denique vi possim* ***exsecuturum*** *. . .* (Livy 1.59.1).

I swear . . . that I will **pursue/punish** Lucius Tarquinius Superbus along with (his) wicked wife and all of (his) children with the sword, fire, and whatever additional force I may be able . . . .

Cur, qui vicisti crimine nostro, ***insequeris*** *crimen*? (Ovid *Metam.* 8.130).
Why do you, who have prevailed by my crime, **punish** (my) crime?

sed vindicis ora protervis ***insequitur*** *manibus generosaque pectora pulsat* (Ovid *Metam.* 12.234).
but he **assaulted** and struck with reckless hands the face and noble breast of the avenger.

Reprehende hominem; ***adsequere*** (Plautus *Pseud.* 249).
Catch the man; **get** him!

It is interesting to note that already in early Latin, the term is used in a legal sense:

Quapropter certum est facere contra ac ***persequi*** *et nomen deferre hominis* (Lucilius 920).
Wherefore my mind is made up to do the opposite, and to **pursue** (him) and to report the man's name (to the authorities).

B.-D. In each of these three ritual texts, the neuter participle *šakuwan* is used to modify the term ^{GIŠ}*zup(p)ari*, ^{GIŠ}*zupparu* "torch."

B. KUB XX 10 III 5

3 ^{GIŠ}*zu-up-pa-ru* KASKAL-*ši da-a-i*
4 *ta ta-ma-i* ^{GIŠ}*zu-up-pa-ru*
5 ***ša-a-ku-wa-an*** *lu-uk-ki-iz-zi*
6 *ta-aš* LUGAL-*i pi-ra-an ḫu-u-wa-i*

3 (the chief of the barbers) will place a torch on the road,
4-5 then he will set fire to another **search** torch,
6 and he will run before the king.

In the remaining two texts, *šakuwan* ^{GIŠ}*zup(p)ari* occurs simply within a list of ritual items.

C. KUB XII 55 I 5

4 1 ^{DUG}*ḫu-up-par* KAŠ 1 ME NINDA.KUR$_4$. RA TUR [ ]
5 ***ša-ku-wa-an*** ^{GIŠ}*zu-up-pa-ri* [ ]

4 one bowl of beer, 100 small thick breads, [ ]
5 a **search** torch, [ ]

D. KUB VII 14 I 12 (Starke 1985: 60-61)

11 [*te-pu*] LÀL 2 NINDA.KUR$_4$.RA TUR *ŠA* GA.KIN.AG
12 [ ] x-*ti-ya-ti-iš tar-na-a* ***ša-ku-wa-an*** [(^{GIŠ}*zu-pa-ri*)][15]
13 [2 ^{DUG}*ḫu-*]*pu-wa-i* 2 ^{GIŠ}*in-ta-lu-zi-iš* [(URUDU)] . . .

11 [a little] honey, 2 small thick breads, of cheese
12 [ ]-?, a *tarna* measure, a **search** [(torch)],
13 2 pots, 2 copper shovels, . . .

As indicated by the translations of these three passages, we interpret the participle *šakuwan* as a verbal adjective (see Friedrich 1952: 145) having the meaning "searching." That is, a *šakuwan* ^{GIŠ}*zup(p)ari* is a torch used for tracking or searching at night—a "search torch." That torches were, as one would expect, used in this way among early Indo-European peoples is evidenced, for example, in the Homeric *Hymn to Demeter* (lines 47ff.). Here, as in the various other ancient accounts of the rape of Persephone, the goddess Demeter is presented as carrying torches to light her way as she wanders the earth, desperately searching for her daughter whom Hades has abducted.[16] It is quite interesting that as the above Hittite references to *šakuwan* ^{GIŠ}*zup(p)ari*/^{GIŠ}*zupparu* occur in ritual texts, so the search torches of Demeter also have a ritual connection. Demeter is, of course, the deity of the Elusinian Mysteries. Torches were an important component of the Elusinian purification ritual as well as of the other

15 Restored from the parallel text IBoT III 96 (Starke 1985: 61).

16 Diodorus Siculus *Bib. Hist.* V 4.3; Cicero *Verr.* 2.4.106; Ovid *Metam.* 5.437-443; Ovid *Fast.* 4.491-494; Claud. *Rap. Pros.* 3.330-331; Statius *Theb.* 12.270-273—see Richardson (1974: 168).

various ceremonies and processions of the cult. Consider that the second highest ranking official of the cult was called the Dadouchos ("torch-bearer").[17]

E. KBo VI 2 II 62 (Friedrich 1971: 32-33)

61 *ma-a-an* URU*A-ri-in-na* 11 ITU-*aš ti-iz-zi nu a-pi-e-*[*el* É-*ZU*]
62 *ku-e-la* GIŠ*e-ya-an a-aš-ki-iš-ši* ***ša-ku-wa-a-an*** *a*[*-ra-a-u-wa-an*]

61 If (someone) has been in Arinna for eleven months, then his [house],
62 on the gate of which an *eya-* tree has been **traced**, shall be [exempt from corvée].

HL 50, in which the above passage occurs, specifies certain individuals who are exempt from the state obligation termed *luzzi-* ("corvée"; see *CHD* 3:90-91). Among those who are exempt, as indicated in the above translation, are residents of Arinna of at least eleven months who live in a house which is marked by the sketch or outline of an *eya-* tree on the gate of the house. From descriptions of the *eya-*, it is clear that the tree is some type of evergreen (see KUB XXIX 1 IV 17-20); among those varieties suggested have been the fir, evergreen oak, and yew. The *eya-* tree serves not only as an indicator of exemption or freedom (as also in KUB XIII 8; Otten 1958: 106-7), but, in the Telipinu Myth, as a symbol of the return of prosperity (Friedrich 1971: 100; Puhvel 1984-: 253-57).

Earlier investigators have conjectured that *šakuwān* in this passage has the meaning "erected" (*CHD* 3:90; Goetze 1967: 203; Goetze 1969a: 191), "suspended" (Goetze 1949: 182), or "visible" (from *šakuwāi-* "to see"; Friedrich 1971: 100; Puhvel 1984-: 253). We believe that this occurrence of *šakuwāi-* is again to be understood as a form whose meaning developed historically from a basic sense "to follow"; the specific nuance, as pointed out above, appears to be "to trace" in the sense "to follow the outline" or "to sketch [the shape of something]." It is once again the Latin cognate *sequi* which provides the exact parallel. Thus we find, for example, in Quintilian's discussion on teaching children how to write:

17 For a discussion of the importance of the torch in these celebrations, see Richardson 1974: esp. 165-68; see also Mylonas 1969.

Cum vero iam ductus ***sequi*** *coeperit, non inutile erit eas tabellae quam optime insculpi* (Quintilian *Inst.* 1.1.27).

When (the child) has begun to **trace** the shape (of letters), it will not be without use to inscribe them into a tablet, as carefully as possible.

The tracing of the image of an *eya-* tree on the gate of a house as an indicator of an exempt status is clearly reminiscent of the Passover custom whose institution is reported in Exod 12:21-23 (RSV):

21 Select lambs for yourselves according to your families, and kill the passover lamb.

22 Take a bunch of hyssop and dip it in the blood which is in the basin, and touch the lintel and the two doorposts with the blood which is in the basin; and none of you shall go out of the door of his house until the morning.

23 For the Lord will pass through to slay the Egyptians; and when he sees the blood on the lintel and on the two doorposts, the Lord will pass over the door, and will not allow the destroyer to enter your houses to slay you.[18]

In both instances, a symbol displayed on the entrance to the house is a sign that those within the house are to be held exempt from a particular penalty or obligation.[19] The following instances of *šakuwāi-* occur in texts which exist in varying states of fragmentation; consequently, the sense of the verb is here far less clear.

18 Compare also the statement of the two spies to Rahab in Josh 3:18-19 (Revised Standard Version): Behold, when we come into the land, you shall bind this scarlet cord in the window through which you let us down; and you shall gather into your house your father and mother, your brothers, and all your father's household. If any one goes out of the doors of your house into the street, his blood shall be upon his head, and we shall be guiltless; but if a hand is laid upon any one who is with you in the house, his blood shall be on our head.

19 It is worth noting that the image produced by *touching* a bunch of hyssop dipped in blood to the lintel, etc., would essentially be that of a leafy tree.

F. KBo XX 92 + KBo XI 72 I 3

3] *I-NA* [GIŠ]SAR.SAR[GIŠ-]*ru* ***ša-ku-wa-an-zi*** *n*[*u*
4] GIŠ-*i* *kat-ta-an*[ ]*an*? *ti-an-zi nu A-NA*[
5] 1 UDA.NITÁ 1 UDU.SI[G.SAL ?] *ḫu-u-kan-zi nu-uš*[

3] they will **seek out** a [tre]e in the garden and[
4] they will place [some item(s)] beneath the tree and into[
5] they will slaughter 1 male sheep, 1 fe[male sheep ?] and [

It appears probable that in this ritual text the sense of *šakuwāi-* is "to seek"; thus, the meaning is closely related to that found in other texts considered above, though here the sense is neither hostile nor legal. It is once more the case that the Latin cognate *sequi*, both unprefixed and prefixed, exhibits the identical sense, as, for example, in the following occurrences:

cum flumina et solitudines ***sequeremur***, *quo facilius sustentare nos possemus* . . . (Cicero *Att.* 13.16.1).
though I (pl.) was seeking for streams and places of solitude, by which I would be able to endure (life) more tolerably.

Bonam atque obsequentem deam atque . . . ***exsequontur*** (Plautus *Rud.* 261-262).
They **seek** . . . a good and considerate goddess.

Ego mihi alios deos penatis ***persequar***, *alium Larem, aliam urbem, aliam civitatem* (Plautus *Merc.* 836-837).
I shall **seek** for myself other Penates, another Lar, another city, another state.

G. KUB XXXIII 70 II 5 (Laroche 1965: 161)

4]*da-a-i nu* KAŠ GEŠTIN *ši-pa-an-ti nu te-ez-zi*
5 [([d]UTU-*i* *e-et-za* *m*)]*i-i-ú-un*[20] *a-a-an-ta-an* ***ša-ku-wa-an-ta-an***

20 Restored from the duplicate text Bo 681. See Laroche (1965: 161); and Ehelolf (1933: 3 n. 2).

6 (*nu* Z)]I-*KA mi-i-e-eš-du* . . .

4]he will set . . ., and he will libate beer (and) wine, and he will say,
5 "[(O Sun-god, eat)] the smooth, hot, **scented/fragrant** (?)
6]and may your so[ul] be soft . . . ."

As Güterbock (1968: 68 n. 10) discusses, it is clearly the case that *šakuwant-* is here being used to describe some food—a food which is also said to be "smooth and hot." The name of the food, however, is, most unfortunately, not preserved. Güterbock comments, "Should this *šakuwant-* turn out to be the same as the participle 'seen, visible' one might think of 'conspicuous, beautiful, pleasing' or the like." If, on the other hand, this participle is from the *šakuwāi-* which is a reflex of PIE **sek*^{w}- "to follow," the sense may perhaps be "scented, fragrant," etc. It was pointed out above that in Lettish the cognate form *sekt* means not only "to track" but has also acquired the meaning "to smell." A similar kind of semantic expansion is evidenced in the case of the Greek noun ἴχνος, which normally means "track," but has also acquired the meaning "scent," as is exhibited in Xenophon's *Cyn.*, e.g., in 5.1:

τὰ δὲ **ἴχνη** τοῦ λαγῶ τοῦ μὲν χειμῶνος μακρά ἐστι διὰ τὸ μῆκος τῶν νυκτῶν.
The **scent** (pl.) of the hare in winter remains for a long time because of the length of the nights.

Perhaps it is the case that the Hittite term has been similarly expanded to mean "to smell" and the participle "smelled" has acquired the nuance "scented, fragrant, aromatic," etc.

H. KUB XVII 10 II 16 (Laroche 1965: 92-93)

15 *ka-a-ša* ^{GIŠ}*ša-ma-am-ma ki-it-ta*[
16 ***ša-ku-ú-wa-an*** *e-eš-tu ka-a-ša* ^{GIŠ}MA [*ki-it-ta nu* ^{GIŠ}MA]
17 *ma-a-aḫ-ḫa-an mi-li-id-du Ù ŠA* ^{d}*T*[*e-li-pí-nu* ZI-*KA*]
18 *QA-TAM-MA mi-li-te-e-eš-* *t*[*u*]

15 Behold, *šamama* lies here[
16 let it be **aromatic/fragrant**. Behold, a fig [lies here;

17 Just as [the fig] is sweet, let [your soul, Telipi]nu,
18 so be sweet.

---

19 ^{GIŠ}*ZÉ-ER-TUM-ma-az ma-a-aḫ-ḫa-an* YÀ-*ŠU* ŠÀ-*it* [*ḫar-zi* ^{GIŠ}GEŠTIN-*ma-az ma-a-aḫ-ḫa-an*]
20 GEŠTIN-*an* ŠÀ-*it ḫar-zi zi-ik-ka* ^{d}*Te-li-pí-nu* [
21 *iš-ta-an-za-ni-it* ŠÀ-*it QA-TAM-MA a-aš-šu ḫar-a*[*k*]

19 Just as the olive [holds] oil within it, [and just as the grape/raisin]
20 holds wine within it, so you, O Telipinu, [
21 hold goodness in (your) heart and soul.

As other investigators have pointed out, e.g., Güterbock (1968: 68), it is clear that the structure of lines 17-20, which refer to particular properties of the fig, olive, and grape/raisin,[21] parallels that of lines 15 and 16. This parallelism indicates that the missing portion of line 15 states that " . . . something should be *šakuwan* like *šamama*" (Güterbock 1968: 68). Though some scholars have proposed that Hittite ^{GIŠ}*šam*(*m*)*am*(*m*)*a* is to be identified with Akkadian *šamaššammu* "sesame," Güterbock (1968: 67ff.) has cogently argued that, rather than "sesame" (for which the Hittite term appears to be *šapšama*-), ^{GIŠ}*šam*(*m*)*am*(*m*)*a*- denotes some other food. Noting its characteristics as revealed by an examination of the relevant texts—"*šamama* is the fruit of a tree, it contains oil, and something is thrown away when it is broken"—Güterbock (1968: 70) suggests that ^{GIŠ}*šam*(*m*)*am*(*m*)*a*- may be the name of some type of nut; he indicates that the walnut, hazelnut, pistachio and almond are all possibilities, as they grow in Anatolia.[22] Given the interpretation of *šakuwāi*- which we propose, the identification of ^{GIŠ}*šam*(*m*)*am*(*m*)*a*- as *šakuwan* may further characterize this fruit as "aromatic, fragrant" and is perhaps a reference to the aroma characteristic of roasted nuts—particularly almonds.

21 On the possibility that "raisin" rather than "grape" should be restored here, see Güterbock (1968: 66 n. 1).
22 On this interpretation, see more recently Hoffner (1974: 126-27).

^{GIŠ}*šam(m)am(m)a-* is, in fact, as Güterbock (1968: 70) points out, included in a list of "roasted items" (KBo X 34 I).

I. KUB XXXIII 38 I 6 (Laroche 1965: 144-45)

5 *ki-it-ta nu*[
6 ***ša-ku-wa-an*** *ki-*[
7 *ŠA* ^{d}MAḪ *ud-da-a-a*[*r ša-ku-wa-an*(?)] *QA-TAM*[*-MA*]
8 *e-eš-*[ ]

5 here lies [
6 **fragrant/aromatic** [
7-8 so may the words of the mother goddess be [fragrant/aromatic].

This very fragmentary text appears to be quite similar in form to the previously examined passage from the Telipinu myth, and, accordingly, *šakuwan* is here likely also to modify the name of some food.[23]

J. KUB XVII 7 + XXXIII 93 II 12 (Güterbock1951: 148)

6 [^{d}*Ku-mar-bi-i*]*š* D[INGI]R.MEŠ-*aš ad-da-aš e-eš-zi*
7 [ ] x ^{d}*Ku-mar-bi-in a-uš-ta*
8 [ ] *a-ru-ni i-ya-an-ni-eš*

6 [Kumarb]i, father of the g[od]s, is seated.
7 [ ] he saw Kumarbi
8 [ ] he went to the sea

---

9 [(*nu* ^{d}*Im-pa-lu-ri-iš*)] INIM.MEŠ-*ar a-ru-ni* EGIR-*pa*
10 [(*me-mi-iš-ki-u-w*)*a-an* (*d*)]*a-a-iš* EN- *YA-mu-kán ku-it*
11 [ ]-*at nu-za-kán a-ru-na-an ta-pu-ša*
12 [ ]-*kán x-x* ***ša-ku?-wa-ya-nu-un***
13 [^{d}*K*]*u-mar-bi-iš* DINGIR.MEŠ-*aš ad-da-aš e-eš-zi*

23 Güterbock (1968: 68 n. 13) comes to the same conclusion regarding this similarity.

9 and to the sea [(Imbaluri)] again
10 began [(to speak)] the words: My lord, what to me
11 [ ] and by the sea
12 [ ] I have seen/traced (?)
13 [ ]Kumarbi, father of the gods, is seated.

Güterbock (1946: 14, 57) tentatively translated *ša-ku?-wa-ya-nu-un* as "erblickte," i.e., the form is identified with *šakuwāi-* "to see," while in Güterbock 1951 (p. 194), the word is left untranslated. Goetze (1949: 182), stating that "Güterbock [1946: 57] has correctly pointed out that *šakuwayanun* should be combined with *šakuwayat* KUB XVII 8 IV 32" (see below), argues that this form of the preterite (*šakuwaya-*) is distinct from that for the verb meaning "to see," which occurs in the third singular as *šakuwāit* (KUB VII 57 I 4). Goetze thus interprets *ša-ku?-wa-ya-nu-un* as being a form of that verb which is the subject of this excursus and suggests that its meaning in this text is "to commit to memory." This suggestion is, of course, purely conjectural. Given the fragmentary condition of the text, the precise sense of *šakuwāi-* is not determinable, but a meaning "to trace, seek (out)" or the like is completely possible, if this is, in fact, not a form of the verb "to see" (cf. line 7).

K. KUB XVII 8 IV 32 (Laroche 1965: 168)

30 [ ]x-*an-za la-ap-pí-ya-aš na-aš-ši-iš-ša-*[*an*
31 [ ]*i-ya-u-wa-ni-iš-ki-iz-zi* ZÍZ-*ma pé-e*?[
32 [ ]x-*ti-az* ***ša-ku-wa-ya-at*** *nu-za* ḪUR.SA[G
33 [-]*ša?-na-aš* UZUSA *da-a-aš*

30 [ ] the fever, and for him [
31 [ ]he is healed. Spelt . . . [
32 [ ] . . . he **saw/sought** (?), and the mountain[
33 [ ] . . . he took sinew [

Goetze (1967: 202; 1949: 182) conjectures that *šakuwayat* in line 32 is another instance of the verb with which we are here concerned rather than an occurrence of *šakuwāi-* "to see"; however, the fragmentary context again makes secure identification and interpretation impossible.

L. KUB VII 1 II 39 + KBo III 8 II 5 (Kronasser 1961: 150; 1962a: 111)

38 *ma-a-na-aš* SIG$_5$*-at-da-ma na-at-ši-kán ar-ḫa da-a-i an-da-ma*
39 ***ša-ku-wa-a-ru*** *pa-i nu-uš-ša-an* 2 EME.ḪI.A *nu-kán an-da*
40 UZU*ḫu-i̥t-ya̧ iš-ga-a-ri na-at* TUR*-li ka-li-li*(-?)*ul-li-aš*
41 *kat-t*[*a-an*] *da-a-i nu*, etc. . . .

38 And if he (i.e., the child) becomes healthy, then (s)he will take it (i.e., a cultic object) away from him, and
39 let her/him ***anda šakuwāi-***, (s)he will give (?), and 2 tongues, and
40 (s)he will insert [it?] in the flesh. For the child . . .
41 (s)he will place it under, etc. . . .

Goetze (1967: 203) translates the imperative *anda šakuwaru* in line 39 as "soll aufgehoben werden"; acknowledging Goetze, Kronasser (1961: 151, 154) similarly renders the phrase "soll aufbewahrt werden." These translations are, again, rather conjectural and are, of course, offered on the basis of the particular context in which the form here occurs—a context which would allow many possible interpretations. The problem of interpretation is compounded by the fact that the text of line 39 appears to be corrupt, as is indicated by several factors. (1) The use of an imperative (*šakuwaru*) in the description of the ritual is unexpected. Elsewhere in the ritual, the indicative is used to describe the procedure to be followed and the imperative is limited to occurrences of reported speech. In addition, it should be pointed out that, although Kronasser did not indicate it in his transcription, the final sign of *ša-ku-wa-a-ru* is damaged and only partially legible. The reading *ru* is not a necessary one, given the traces which remain. (2) The occurrence of *pai* after *šakuwaru* is, of course, quite problematic, as is (3) the absence of a verb in *nuššan* 2 EME.ḪI.A.[24]

If, in fact, the verb of line 39, is a form of *anda šakuwāi-*, then perhaps the sense is something like "then this will follow (in the ritual)." The meaning "to follow in order" is attested for Latin *insequor*.[25]

24 Is *pai* to be construed as the verb of this sentence, which the scribe has in some way displaced to the left?

25 Goetze (1967: 203) also identifies an occurrence of *anda šakuwāi-* in KBo IV 2 I 4. The verb describes an action to be carried out on a clay figurine using the wing of an

In his discussion of *šakuwāi-*, Goetze (1967: 203) also cites "*šakuweškizzi* VII 41 Vs 11 bei fehlendem Subjekt and Objekt, sodaß sich nichts Sicheres sagen lässt" and the "verstümmelt XII 56 III 3." Otten (1961: 116-17) interprets the former as an instance of the homophonous verb meaning "to see."

M.-N. KUB VII 41 Vs 11; KUB XII 56 III 3
10b *ki-i* É*-ir ku-wa-at tuḫ-ḫa-it-t*[*a*
11 *ša-ra-a ne-pí-ši ku-wa-at* ***ša-ku-eš-ki-iz-zi***

10b Why does this house gasp?
11 Why does it **look up** to heaven?

Goetze's latter citation, XII 56 III 3, reads simply *ša-a-ku-wa*[. Otten (1961: 114-15) identifies KUB VII 41 and the fragmentary tablet XII 56 as variants of a single text. Another variant, Bo 2072, has *ša-ku-wa-aš* corresponding to the *ša-a-ku-wa*[of XII 56 and, thus, indicates that this is not a verb but is instead a form of the noun meaning "eye."[26]

It has been argued above that the Hittite verb *šakuwāi-* is a reflex of the PIE root **sek*^{w}- "to follow." The meanings here proposed for Hittite *šakuwāi-* are the following: (1) "to pursue, track down"; (2) "to punish, persecute"; (3) "to search, seek out"; (4) "to trace (the outline of)"; and as a participle (5) "scented, aromatic"—the sense of which develops from the meaning "to smell, sniff out" (i.e., "that which is smelled"). Each of these meanings is attested for reflexes of **sek*^{w}- in the various Indo-European languages; moreover, the Latin reflex *sequi* shows remarkable agreement, sharing four of the five meanings exhibited by the proposed Hittite cognate.

It has long been recognized that Hittite *šakuwāi-* is capable of occurring in quite disparate contexts. Our analysis of this verb provides a plausible sense for this problematic form as it is found in each of these

eagle, and Goetze proposes the translation "einwickeln." However, the initial portion of the word is damaged; Kronasser (1962b: 90) reads the form as *x̣-x̣ -ku-i*(-?)*iš-kán-ẓi*, and with appropriate tentativeness identifies the verb as possibly *iškanzi* or, perhaps, *arkuiškanzi*.

26 A third copy of the text, KBo X 45 II 48, reads *ša-ku-wa* (Otten 1961: 125).

varied contexts and clearly links each of these meanings to a common denominator. The naturalness of this solution, which rests upon the above cited agreements between *šakuwāi-* and the various Indo-European reflexes of *sek^w-, argues persuasively, in our opinion, for the correctness of the analysis proposed in this excursus.

Legal Commentary

Column I 1ff. Most of our knowledge of royal edicts comes from the debt release decrees of the Old Babylonian kings. These were typically promulgated on a king's accession to the throne,[27] but also at irregular intervals during the reign.[28] The ostensible motivation was religious: by reestablishing equity and ending abuses the ruler pleases the god of justice[29] and thereby secures the legitimacy of his reign.[30] It is clear, therefore, why a ruler would begin his reign with such a decree, but the sources are silent as to the reason for subsequent decrees. It has been suggested by Bottéro (1961) that fundamental imbalances in the economy led to a build-up of social and economic discontent that had to be relieved by the periodic cancellation of debts. The only express account, however, of the circumstances leading to such a decree is given in the biblical narrative. When the Babylonian army was besieging Jerusalem, king Zedekiah ordered a release of debt-slaves, presumably to obtain divine favor, but possibly also to raise morale in the face of a military emergency (Jer 34:1-10). Obviously, these were not the most typical circumstances for promulgating a decree.

27 Recorded in the first or second year-date of the king, e.g., Hammurabi year 2: "The year that he established equity for the land" (níg-si-sá kalam-ma in-gar).

28 See Kraus (1984: 16-110); Finkelstein (1965: 243-46). They are not, however, periodic, as Finkelstein claims. See Westbrook (1971a: 209-25).

29 Note the reference in BM 80318 (edition in Finkelstein 1965: 233-36): "When my lord raised high the Golden Torch for Sippar, instituting the *misharum* (i.e., debt-release decree) for Shamash who loves him" (lines 1-3).

30 As Hammurabi explains, he was named ruler by the gods "in order to cause equity to prevail in the land, to destroy the wicked and the evil, that the strong might not oppress the weak" (CH prologue I 31-33).

The present text is important, therefore, in that it expressly states the reason for the decree. Abuses had been committed during the king's absence on campaign, and on his return a group of citizens petitioned him—in fairly bold terms—for their removal.

Answering petitions was part of the everyday functions of an ancient Near Eastern king, in his capacity as head of the system of administration of justice. Again most of our information comes from Mesopotamia and the Bible, where such petitions are usually from individuals.[31] Group petitions are rare. An example from the Bible, with a dire warning as to the consequences of disregarding public opinion, is the people's petition (led by Jeroboam) to king Rehoboam to relieve them of public duties (presumably taxation or corvée duties) in 1 Kgs 12:1-20. In practice, group petition could alter royal policy, as two examples from the Hittite sphere show.

In RS 17.130 (Nougayrol 1956: 103-5), the Hittite emperor is petitioned by his vassal, the king of Ugarit, on behalf of the "sons of Ugarit," i.e., the free citizenry, and grants a seasonal restriction on the activities of certain Hittite merchants at Ugarit. A more direct parallel to our text is the account of a successful petition in HL 55:

> When the sons of Hatti, the feudal tenants, came and bowed down[32] to the king's father and said: "No one pays hire; they say to us, 'You are feudal tenants,'" the king's father (decreed) in the assembly and issued a sealed document (saying): "Go! You shall be as your colleagues."

Our text is therefore evidence that pressure of "public opinion," through the customary medium of the group petition, was a factor in the occasional decision to promulgate a reforming edict. Nonetheless, there is also an allusion to religious motives. Tudhaliya mentions that on his return

31 There are many references to petitions in the correspondence of the Old Babylonian kings: e.g., AbB 2 no. 74 where two brothers petition King Abi-eshuh after the local court failed to act in their case. The biblical narratives also mention petitions to the king, e.g., 2 Sam 14:4-11, where the Tekoan woman makes a personal plea to King David.

32 Note that the procedure is described in the same terms as in our text. The petitioners bow (verb *aruwāi-*) to the king and speak.

he "refurbished" (verb *aššanu-*) the gods. It is difficult to see the relevance of this statement to the narrative unless it is to suggest that part of the "refurbishment" was to correct injustices displeasing to the gods.

Column II 3-8. These provisions represent the meeting-point between two areas of law: release of debts and the revenge/ransom system of punishment for criminal offenses.

1. The royal decrees that cancel debts are also concerned to annul transactions based upon the debt, such as pledge and debt-slavery. For example, paragraph 20 of the edict of King Ammi-ṣaduqa of Babylon (Kraus 1984: 20) provides:

> If a son of Numhia, a son of Emut-Balum, a son of Idamaraz, etc., is bound by a debt or sells, gives *ana kiššātim*, or pledges himself, his wife or his [children], because the king has established equity for the land, he is released—his freedom is established.

It is to be noted that the release annuls outright sale as well as less permanent arrangements such as pledge. The kind of sale covered, which arises from a debt, is one that masks the true nature of the transaction, namely distraint for nonpayment of debt. A person who is forced to sell his property to his creditor at the price of the debt loses the inherent benefit of pledge, i.e., its redeemability, while failing to gain the usual benefit of outright sale, i.e., receipt of the property's full value, since the amount of the debt will seldom equal the value of the property pledged or distrained because of it.

The legal systems of the ancient Near East had two measures for dealing with this problem. Firstly, a right of redemption was allowed for family land and certain types of slaves (especially family members). The debtor/seller or his successors could buy back the property at a later date at the same (low) price for which it had been sold (see Westbrook 1985b). But sometimes even this sum was beyond the reach of the debtor, and in that case his only hope was that a debt-release would be decreed, in which case his property (or his own freedom, if he had sold himself) would be eligible for restoration to him by reason of the original debt being canceled. Lev 25:25-28 shows the two measures in effect:

> If your brother grows poor and sells his estate, his redeemer who is most closely related to him may come and redeem his brother's

> property. A man who has no redeemer but who obtains enough to redeem it shall calculate the years of purchase and return the balance to the man to whom he sold and he may return to his estate. If he does not obtain enough to return to him, the property shall remain in the hand of its purchaser until the Jubilee year. It will be released in the Jubilee and he will return to his estate.

The provisions are complicated by the fact that the levitical author had changed the debt-release into a cyclical event, recurring automatically every fifty years, which affects calculation of the price (Westbrook 1971a: 221). The principle, however, remains clear: where family property is sold under financial constraint it may be redeemed, and if this is not possible, the same circumstances make it eligible eventually for automatic release.

2. Homicide gives rise to a dual right in the victim's family: to take revenge on the culprit within the limits recognized by law, which usually means killing him, or to accept ransom for sparing the culprit's life. This principle, effective throughout the ancient Near East, finds its clearest expression in paragraph 49 of the edict of King Telipinu:

> Whoever does blood (i.e., commits homicide), whatever the owner of the blood (i.e., the avenger) says. If he says "Let him die!" then let him die. If he says "Let him pay ransom!" then let him pay ransom.

In cases of aggravated homicide, such as murder, the victim's family has discretion whether to accept ransom and as to the amount of ransom acceptable. For less serious degrees of homicide, such as those involving negligence, the courts will often insist on ransom and set a limit on the amount that may be demanded.[33] In either case, however, the culprit is in a constrained situation where he may be forced to sell his property or his freedom at a discount in order to buy his own life. The whole of his property could be sacrificed in this way, as MAL B 2 demonstrates:

33 For a detailed discussion of the principle, see Westbrook (1988d: 39-71). The payments of slaves for homicide in HL 1-4 represent fixed ransom.

> If one among brothers who have not divided takes a life, he shall be given to the owner of the life (i.e., the avenger). If he chooses, the owner of the life may kill him, or if he chooses, he may come to terms and take his inheritance share.

Where brothers have not yet divided the estate of their father, the avenger is entitled to the equivalent of the guilty brother's inheritance share—in other words, all his property. The ransom agreement is a contract like any other and therefore gives rise to a debt which must be paid or satisfied in some other way,[34] whether by transfer of the debtor's property, his family, or his own person.

3. Because a ransom agreement is a kind of forced sale, the question arises whether the measures for the protection of debtors outlined above would also be available to the payer of ransom. Insofar as a debt release is concerned, it is this question that is addressed by the lines of the edict under discussion.

The edict distinguishes between two cases. In the first, a person has committed homicide and has paid a ransom for his own life: he has "bought himself." Can the property that he handed over as the price of his life be released by the decree? The edict answers in the negative, even if the property be land or persons, which could refer to slaves, or possibly to dependent members of his family.

The second case is harder to determine, because of the ambiguity of the enclitic pronouns in the protasis and apodosis. Our tentative interpretation is that the creditor (i.e., the avenger) has made a general seizure of the homicide's property and family. The change in subject and verb ("has taken" instead of "bought himself") suggests that this was a unilateral act rather than a bargain arrived at between the parties, possibly to force the homicide's hand in negotiations. A comparable situation arises in a Neo-Assyrian document:[35]

34 As the Neo-Assyrian contract ADD 321 provides: "A son of B shall give C daughter of D, the scribe, in lieu of the blood. He shall wash the blood. If he does not give the woman, they will kill him on B's grave. Whichever of them breaks the contract shall pay 10 mina of silver."

35 ADD 164. Edited in Postgate 1976: no. 44; and Kwasman 1988: no. 108.

> A judgment which the *sartennu* imposed upon Hani. 300 sheep with their penalty belonging to the crown prince are to the debit of[36] Hani. The blood of a shepherd, 2 talents of copper per man, is his penalty. Hani, together with his family and his fields is taken in lieu of the 300 sheep with their penalty (and) instead of the blood of the shepherds. Whoever seeks him, whether his captain or officer or anyone belonging to them, shall give 300 sheep with their penalty and the blood of a shepherd, 2 talents of copper per man for the men (and) redeem Hani. He shall see the river ordeal.

The apparent culprit in a case of robbery and murder, Hani, is held together with his family and land pending payment of ransom. The ransom in question has been fixed by a court (or official, at least), which need not have been the case in the Hittite edict. Creditors commonly used self-help, seizing goods or even members of the debtor's family to force payment. For example, an Old Babylonian letter recounts the following:[37]

> To Ahu-kinum, speak. Thus says Awil-Ammur. After you went away on a journey Imgur-Sin came and, with the statement "He owes me one-third of a mina of silver," distrained your wife and daughter. Come and get your wife and daughter released before they die from being kept in detention. Please!

The edict decrees the release of "him/it to him" (line 8: *na-an-ši-iš-ta*). The latter is presumably the homicide himself and the former, on our interpretation, would be the totality of aforementioned property and the homicide's family. It may, however, refer solely to the property, on the assumption that the family is automatically entitled to release.

From the edict of Ammi-ṣaduqa it can be seen that fine distinctions were made between transactions that were eligible for annulment and those

36 Literally, "at the disposal of." The term is taken from Neo-Assyrian debit notes where the debtor has the loan at his disposal and therefore is indebted to the creditor in that sum. Here, the culprit Hani has had the sheep at his disposal only in the sense that he stole them. His debts arise *ex delicto* rather than *ex contractu*.

37 UET 5 9. It is in fact a model letter, i.e., a scribal exercise. See Kraus (1959: 28-29). If distraint turned out to be unjustified, the consequences could be serious for the creditor: see CE 22-24. And see further Jackson and Watkins (1984: 411-19).

that were not. That edict distinguishes basically between arms-length commercial transactions (not eligible) and noncommercial transactions (eligible).[38] The present text reveals another dimension to this jurisprudential activity, extending it to transactions arising from debts *ex delicto*.

Column II 8-10. The revenge/ransom system applies equally to theft (see Westbrook 1988d: 120-26). Except in aggravated cases such as kidnapping,[39] the courts systematically imposed a fixed ransom on the thief, usually in the form of a multiple of the thing stolen.[40] In practical terms this could lead to the thief relinquishing his property or his freedom to pay the ransom. As Prov 6:31 says of the thief: "If he is found he shall pay seven-fold; he shall give all the property of his house."

Similar considerations apply, as in the foregoing case of homicide. Real estate given to satisfy a demand of ransom is not eligible for release. By implication, release would apply to the thief himself and his family.

Column II 11-15. The Hittite Laws recognize the possibility of noxal surrender, i.e., where a slave has committed an offense, his master has the option of handing the slave over to the victim or of redeeming him (Haase 1961). HL 95 reads:

> If a slave burgles a house, he shall give (it back) completely (?).[41] He shall pay 6 shekels of silver for the theft. He may cut off the slave's nose and ears, and they shall give him back to his master. If he steals much, they shall obligate him for a large amount; if he

38 See paragraph 3 for loans that are annulled (at interest or *ana melqētim*), and paragraph 8 for loans that are not (price of goods sold, investment in a trading journey, partnership).

39 The penalty prescribed is death in CH 14 and Exod 21:16. HL 19 requires payment of six slaves. This is extraordinarily high (more than for homicide) and suggests that it was ransom for the kidnapper's life.

40 E.g., CH 8: "If a man steals an ox or a sheep or an ass or a pig or a boat, if it belongs to the temple or palace, he shall restore thirty-fold; if it belongs to a private citizen, he shall restore ten-fold. If the thief cannot make restitution, he shall be killed." Cf. Exod 21:37, which demands four- and five-fold payments according to the type of animal stolen, and HL 57-69 which has a much more elaborate system based on the same principle.

41 J. Friedrich (1971: 47) translates ". . . gibt er (es) ganz richtig (zurück)." Haase (1957: 40-44) argues that *šakuwaššar* should be translated "unverändert"; Goetze (1969a: 193) renders "the respective goods."

steals little, they shall obligate him for a small amount. If his master says, "I will pay ransom for him," he shall pay ransom. But if he refuses, he shall surrender that slave.

The victim of a slave who steals is entitled to mutilate him and keep him as his own slave unless the master is willing to redeem the slave by paying a penalty for the theft: 6 shekels on average, but apparently a greater or lesser sum can be set by the court depending on the scale of the theft.[42]

In the present case, a slave has stolen and noxal surrender has been made, due to the unwillingness or (more likely) inability of the master to redeem his slave. Theoretically, the owner who is unable to redeem may still look to a debt-release to obtain the restoration of his property, as in the case of Lev 25:25-28 discussed above. Here, where the debt is *ex delicto*, a distinction is again made. If while in the victim's power the slave has been blinded as punishment for the theft, he is not eligible for release, but otherwise he is.

The rationale would appear to lie in the seriousness of the offense. HL 95 gives the golden mean, not only in terms of noxal payment but also of the mutilation that may be inflicted. As blinding is the most serious possible mutilation, it may be deduced that the theft was of a correspondingly serious character and therefore the noxal payment set by the court would have been more than a slave-owner could normally afford to pay.[43] Where failure to pay is thus due more to the gravity of the penalty than to the impecuniousness of the owner, the latter is not allowed to take advantage of a general debt-release.

Column II 16-19. This paragraph is close in formation to HL, using *takku*, rather than *man* as in the preceding paragraphs, to designate the

42 Haase (1957: 43) argues that two different penalties are involved: the fixed sum where the stolen goods are returned unaltered, and the sliding scale where the goods have been sold or otherwise altered. But there is no indication of the latter condition in the text.

43 Blinding is known to have been practiced in Sumer on prisoners-of-war who were made slaves, obviously for safety reasons. In the edict here too, then, blinding may have been motivated by fear of the slave's violent character. See Kutscher (1989: 74, 80): "He blinded the young men whom he reached in their cities and gave (?) them as [slaves] in the orchard of Enlil and Ninil and in the orchards of the great gods" (translating text BT 4 [col. IV, lines 15-22], an inscription of the king, Šu-Sin).

conditional clause of the protasis, which may indeed have been extracted from a provision concerning theft in a law code. As pointed out above, we follow von Schuler in taking *ELLAM* (free man) as a nominative, since it is most likely that the free status of the thief is in issue, as opposed to his slave status in the preceding paragraphs. If *ELLAM* were the object of the verb, it would introduce the wholly new offense of kidnapping. It is not possible to interpret the paragraph with confidence, due to the broken condition of the text. Probably it repeats the principle of the preceding paragraph, *mutatis mutandis*, for a free man. Thus ransom was paid rather than noxal surrender being made. But it is not clear then why there should be any question of blinding. It is also curious that the verb "to blind" is in the present-future rather than a past participle as in lines 12 and 14.

Column III 1-11. The subject is no longer release of debts but administrative measures concerning the royal estate, apparently royal storehouses in provincial cities.[44] The edict, directed towards the local authorities, distinguishes between two types of royal officials: high officials, who have authority *ex officio* to open a royal storehouse at their discretion, and lower officials, who may open it only with special permission. If a storehouse is opened without authorization, it is the duty of the local authority to arrest the culprit and bring him before the king. Failure to do so makes the local officials personally responsible for making good the loss. This will apply to any deficit in the inventory, not merely unauthorized withdrawals by officials, and doubtless there was a regular audit for this purpose.

Although the storehouse is called the king's storehouse, its administration was in the hands of the local authorities, who were regarded as depositees of the king's property. Their responsibility is the same as that of the ordinary depositee in CH 125:

> If a man gives his property for safekeeping and his property is lost from the place where he gave it together with the proprietor's property through a breach or climbing in, the negligent proprietor shall make full reparation to the owner of the goods for the property that was given him for safekeeping. The proprietor shall continue to seek out his lost property and take it from the thief.

44 Cf. paragraphs 37-40 of the Telipinu edict.

Where the depositee has been negligent but not dishonest, as witnessed by the loss of his own property as well, he bears primary responsibility for the goods stored with him[45] and must seek to recoup his loss as best he can by locating the thief. In the edict, the same facility is accorded to the negligent local officials against the true culprit.[46]

Column III 12-20. We can make no connected sense of these lines and therefore offer no interpretation.

Column IV 1-8. In these fragmentary lines, the edict appears to return to the theme of the preamble, namely cases of oppression of feudal tenants. If the oppressors are private creditors, then these provisions may be concerned with devices to evade the effects of the edict itself, as in paragraph 7 of Ammi-ṣaduqa's edict (Kraus 1984: 172):

> If a man gives grain or silver as an interest-bearing loan and has a tablet drafted but keeps the tablet himself and says "I did not give it as an interest-bearing or *melqētum* loan; the grain or silver that I gave you I gave as payment of a price or as an investment or for some other purpose," the man who borrowed the grain or silver from the merchant shall bring witnesses to the wording of the tablet that the lender denied and they shall testify before the god. Because he changed his tablet and denied the transaction, he shall pay six-fold. If he cannot meet this obligation, he shall die.

In our text, the punishment of blinding may suggest that whatever oppression was involved was regarded as a form of theft.

If the oppression is by an official, then the edicts of King Uru-inimgina of Lagash and Horemheb of Egypt both provide parallels. Misappropriation by officials is graphically described in Uru-inimgina's edict:

45 Were he dishonest, the depositee would have to repay double: CH 120.

46 It was common for local authorities to be made responsible for loss caused by undetected criminals. According to CH 22-24, the city and its mayor must compensate citizens for loss of property or life caused by brigands who are not caught. HL IV imposes the same duty on the city nearest to the scene of an unsolved murder.

> The . . . administrators felled trees in the orchards of the poor and bundled off the fruit.[47]

No penalty is mentioned for this practice, which Uru-inimgina claimed to have abolished. Horemheb's edict is more explicit. Paragraph III 21-22 recounts that certain officials have been in the habit of requisitioning labor for the saffron-harvest and decrees that this is an abuse which is henceforth prohibited. If an official is found to be still requisitioning labor for this purpose, his nose will be cut off, he will be sent to Tjarou and the fruits of the work performed for him will be confiscated (Kruchten 1981: 194). Likewise, paragraph IV 24-27 forbids officers from appropriating animal skins, on pain of receiving one hundred blows, five open wounds, and having the misappropriated skin confiscated (Kruchten 1981: 196).

47 Sollberger *Corpus* Ukg. 5.5 = La 9.1 col. V in Cooper 1986: 71. Cf. CH 34, which prescribes the death penalty for an officer who takes a soldier's property, oppresses him, hires him out, delivers him up to a powerful person in a lawsuit, or takes a gift given to the soldier by the king.

2

Hard Times: CT 45 37

Abstract

The unusual phrase, *ina maruštim ina mēsirim*, turns up in the Old Babylonian litigation document, CT 45 37. This article analyzes the phrase against the background of Mesopotamian legal traditions dealing with sale under duress and *mīšarum*-decrees. The conclusion is that, in the light of those traditions, the plaintiff's suit should be seen as a claim that the sale at issue has been cancelled by a recent *mīšarum*-decree and that it qualifies for such cancellation because it was made during "hard times."

As a tribute to Professor Veenhof, who has contributed so much to our understanding of early Mesopotamian society, I wish to discuss the implications of an Old Babylonian litigation document, and in particular of one obscure line in it. CT 45 37 reads:

1 *a-na* 1 SAG.GEMÉ *sa-di-ir-du-mu-uq-ša*
2 DUMU.MÍ ^{d}*be-el-ti*-É.*GAL*-*li-um-m*[*i*]
3 *ša ni-ši-ì-*[*lí-ša*(?) LUKUR ^{d}]UTU DUMU.MÍ *nu-ur-*^{d}ZA-BA$_4$-BA$_4$
4 *ša a-na* EREŠ-*ti-*^{d}UTU DUMU.MÍ *sin-ta-ia-ar*
5 *a-na* *KÙ.BABBAR-*im a-*[*n*]*a** *ši-im ga-me-er id-di-nu*
6 *iš-tu* MU.15.KAM *il-li-ku* ^{d}EN.ZU-*iš-me-a-*[*an-ni*]
7 DUMU ^{d}MARDUK-*na-ṣir ša a-bu-šu nu-úr-*^{d}ZA-B[A$_4$-BA$_4$]
8 ^{m}*a-da-an-šu-li-ik-šu-ud ša-pí-ir* *AGA.U[Š.*MEŠ]
9 *im-ḫu-ur um-ma šu-ú-ma* 1 GEMÉ *sa-di-i*[*r-du-mu-uq-ša*]

* Originally published in *Veenhof Anniversary Volume: Studies Presented to Klaas R. Veenhof on the Occasion of his Sixty-fifth Birthday* (W. H. van Soldt and J. G. Dercksen, eds.; PIHANS 89; Leiden: Nederlands Instituut voor het Nabije Oosten, 2001), 547-51. Used by permission.

10 *ša a-ḫa-at a-bi-ia i-na qá-ti* ^{m}EREŠ-*ti*-^{d}UTU D[UMU.MÍ *sin-ta-ia-ar*]
11 *i-ba-aš-ši ša-pir* *AGA.UŠ.*MEŠ *a-na* DI.KU$_5$.MEŠ *iṭ-ru-d*[*a-aš-šu-nu-ti-ma*]
12 DI.KU$_5$.MEŠ *ù li-pí-it-iš*$_8$*-tár* UGULA MAR.TU DUMU *ra-bu-ut-sin*
13 *di-nam i-na* É ^{d}UTU *ki-a-am iq-bu-šu-nu-ši-im*
14 *i-na* É ^{d}UTU *i-na* KÁ PA.PAḪ-*im ṣú-ḫa-ar-t*[*i* . . .]
15 ^{m}EREŠ-*ti*-^{d}UTU DUMU.MÍ *sin-ta-ia-ar*
16 *ki-a-am i-qa-ab-bi ù ši-ma-tu ša* LUKUR.^{d}UTU.MEŠ
17 GEMÉ *an-ni-tam i-na ma-ru-uš-tim i-na me-si-ri-im*
18 KÙ.BABBAR-*am ši-im ga-me-er iš-qu-ul-ma*
19 *lu-ú i-ša-am-ši*
20 ^{m}EREŠ-*ti*-^{d}UTU DUMU.MÍ *sin-ta-ia-ar*
21 *ù sin-iš-me-a-an-ni* DUMU {{SAL}} ^{d}*markuk-na-ṣir*
22 *i-na* É ^{d}UTU *im-ta-ag-ru-ma*
23 1 GÍN KÙ.BABBAR *ta-am-gu-ur-ti* É ^{d}UTU
24 ^{m}EREŠ-*ti*-^{d}UTU *a-na sin-iš-me-a-an-ni*
25 *id-di-in a-na* U$_4$.KÚR.ŠÈ *a-na* 1 SAG.GEMÉ
26 ^{m}*sa-di-ir-du-mu-uq-ša* ^{m}*sin-iš-me-a-an-ni*
27 *a-na* EREŠ-*ti*-^{d}UTU *ú*-[*ul i*-]*ra-ga-am*
28 MU ^{d}UTU ^{d}A-A ^{d}[MARDUK *ù sa-am-su*]-*i-lu-na* LUGAL
29 IN.P[ÀD]
Witnesses (11?), date (Samsu-iluna 27).

Notes

I am grateful to the trustees of the British Museum for allowing me to collate the tablet. The symbols *. . .* mark a reading based on collation.

Line 2. The use of a metronymic with the Assyrian month Belti-ekallim suggests that this was the (house-born?) daughter of a foreign slave-woman, not a debt slave.

Line 3. One would expect the common *nadītum* name Nīši-īnišu, but to my knowledge *ì* is not used in its spelling. The restored name is speculative, based on the analogy of Nīši-DN. Cf. PBS 11/3 55:7.

Line 5. Copy has *a-na ki-di-im*.

Line 14. Cf. an oath to be sworn *i-na pa-ni pa-pa-ḫi-im* in Waterman *Bus. Doc.* 34, lines 9 and 10. I am grateful to Professors Veenhof and Stol for this reading and reference.

Translation

Concerning a female slave, Sadir-dumuqsha, daughter of Belti-ekallim-ummi, belonging to Nishi-ilisha(?), *nadītum* of Shamash (and) daughter of Nur-Zababa, whom she sold for the full price to Ereshti-Shamash, daughter of Sin-tayyar. After 15 years had passed, Sin-ishme'anni son of Marduk-naṣir, whose father was Nur-Zababa, approached Adanshu-likshud, the commander of the soldiers. He said: "A female slave, Sadir-dumuqsha, who belongs to my aunt, is in the possession of Ereshti-Shamash, daughter of Sin-tayyar." The commander of the soldiers sent them to the judges.

The judges and Lipit-Ishtar, the general son of Rabut-Sin, pronounced judgment upon them in the Temple of Shamash as follows: "In the Temple of Shamash, in the Gate of the Shrine, of the 'Girl' . . ., Ereshti-Shamash shall say thus: as for the purchased property of the *nadītum*s, she paid *ina maruštim ina mēsirim* the silver as full price for that female slave and she truly bought her." Ereshti-Shamash, daughter of Sin-tayyar, and Sin-ishme'anni, son of Marduk-naṣir, reached a compromise in the Temple of Shamash, and Ereshti-Shamash paid Sin-ishme'anni one shekel of silver as the compromise payment of the Temple of Shamash. Sin-ishme'anni has sworn the oath of Shamash, Aya, Marduk, and king Samsu-iluna that in the future he will not sue Ereshti-Shamash for the female slave Sadir-dumuqsha." (Witnesses, date.)

Legal Commentary

The facts of the case may be summarized as follows. A *nadītum* sold her female slave to another woman, but fifteen years later, the seller's nephew (and presumably, heir) brought suit against the buyer, claiming that she had not acquired ownership of the slave still in her possession. The court imposed an oath on the buyer and prescribed its terms. She was to swear that in buying the slave she had paid the full price *ina maruštim ina mēsirim*. Taking the oath would have won the case for the buyer; instead she reached a compromise settlement with the plaintiff, whereby she paid him one shekel in satisfaction of his claim.

On what basis did the plaintiff claim that the sale was invalid? The key to this question lies in the phrase containing the buyer's rebuttal, which I have left untranslated for the moment. *CAD* offers two translations in the respective entries under each word: "he paid the full price with bad grace and under duress"; and "with great difficulties, he paid the silver, at full price."[1] Neither would appear to offer a legal rationale for the validity of the purchase. As long as the buyer had paid the price, it is of no legal significance that she had done so unwillingly or had had difficulty in raising the funds. If she had paid under duress, it would be grounds for the buyer to challenge the contract, not the seller.

Before offering my own translation of the phrase, it is necessary to review the principles of Old Babylonian law of sale that would have been applicable to this case. The text emphasizes twice (lines 5 and 18) that the buyer had paid the full price (*šīm gamer*), although the amount is not named. As San Nicolò established, Old Babylonian sale was in principle cash sale: for ownership to pass, it was necessary for the whole of the price to have been paid.[2] Hence the ubiquitous reference to payment of the full price in Old Babylonian sale documents. In the present document, therefore, the issue might be incomplete payment, the compromise payment perhaps representing the unpaid balance. The formulation of the claim, however, does not support this interpretation.

In litigation reports where the claim is based on a balance outstanding, there is usually an explicit reference to that fact. In YOS 12 320, for example, the seller's heir sues the buyer of a slave-girl but formulates his claim as follows:

> When A. bought the female slave from B., my father, A. did not pay him the silver in full (*ú-ul ú-ga-am-me-er-šum*). The balance (*i-zi-ib-ti*) of the silver of the slave remains in A.'s possession.[3]

1 *CAD* M/1 317; and M/2 28.

2 San Nicolò 1921: 7-8, 15-16.

3 Lines 8-13. In this and other Larsa texts, the term *ezibtum* is used. Cf. CT 8 17a from Sippar, where *šapiltum* is used with the same meaning. Cf. YOS 8 150 for another way of expressing a claim of incomplete payment.

It could be that mere mention of payment of the full price is sufficient to indicate a dispute over payment, but in our document the actual amount paid is also absent.[4] Furthermore, the mysterious clause accompanying the assertion remains unexplained. It implies that the issue in dispute was less prosaic than an unpaid bill.

In an earlier study I suggested that the term "full price" could have a second meaning: the full value of the property sold.[5] The background to this meaning lies in social laws such as CH 119:

> If a debt seizes a man and he sells his female slave who has born him children, the owner of the slave may pay the silver that the merchant paid and redeem his slave.

CE 39 similarly allows redemption of a house sold by a man who has "become weak" (i.e., impoverished). Redemption is allowed under certain conditions, the main one being that the seller was acting under pressure of debts. I argued that as a necessary corollary thereto, the sale had to be at under-value, as being essentially a disguised forfeiture of the property for debt. Redemption was therefore the right to buy back the property at the same low price for which it had been bought.

The opposite side of the coin would be that a sale at full value protected the buyer from the possibility of later redemption. In the Old Babylonian period this occasionally finds expression in sale documents, as in the phrase found at Susa "not redemption, not pledge, full price (*ul ipṭiru ul manzazānu šīmu gamru*)"; "as a father buys for his son, X has bought . . . in perpetuity."[6] On this hypothesis, the buyer's oath in the present document would reply to a claim that the purchase price was below the true value of the slave, who could thus be redeemed.

A claim of redemption, however, would accept that the sale was valid and that ownership had passed. It would seek to reverse that condition by repayment of the purchase price. The plaintiff's position in the present

4 Cf. CT 48 19, where the grounds of claim are not specified but the witnesses attest (lines 14-15): *ši-bu ša* 1/3 MA.NA KÙ.BABBAR *ga-am-ra-am ma-ḫi-ru ú-ṣu-nim-ma*.

5 Westbrook 1991b: 90-117.

6 Discussed by Eichler 1973: 78-80, but see Westbrook 1991b: 102-7.

document is that there was no valid sale, and there seems to be no question of his making any payment to the buyer.

The application of a debt-release decree (*mīšarum*), however, could also depend on whether full value was paid or not. Such decrees looked at the substance of a transaction, not its form, and were alert to attempts to evade them by legal fictions.[7] If, on the one hand, the "sale" were really the forfeiture of a pledge securing a debt that had been annulled by the decree, it would be void, and the price would not be repayable at all. Thus in YOS 14 146, land "which A. bought from B. and C. was reclaimed on the basis of the king's order, and he (A.) bought it again."[8] If, on the other hand, the sale were for full value, it would be untouched by the decree. A fragment identified by its editor as a duplicate of paragraph 3′ of the Edict of Samsu-iluna reads:

> "[If a house-born slave of(/or?) a citizen of Numḫia, a citizen of Emutbal, a citizen of Idamaraz,] a citizen of Uruk, etc., or a citizen of the land is sold, given in penal pledge, or left in antichretic pledge for the [full] price (*ana šīm* [*gamer*]), his release shall not be established."[9]

The possibility that a *mīšarum*-decree lay behind our document leads us to consider the circumstances in which the sale of the slave was made. The judges require the buyer to swear that she paid the full price *ina maruštim ina mēsirim*. *CAD* offers for *mēsirum* the translation "hard times," which is equally suitable for *maruštum*. It has a parallel in the phrase "year of hardship" (MU KALAG.GA) found in sale documents at Emar, where persons are forced in a year of famine to sell their property or

7 See, e.g., paragraphs 5 and 7 of the Edict of Ammi-ṣaduqa (edition in Kraus 1984). Special tribunals determined which sales of land were subject to the decree; see Finkelstein 1965.

8 Lines 6-12: *ša it-ti* B. *ù* C. A. *i-ša-a-mu i-na* LUGAL *ib-ba-qí-ir-ma i-tu-ur-ma i-ša-am*. A claim of invalidity on the same basis may have been behind CT 6 42a, where the sellers (for the second time) claimed land from the buyers but were rejected and forced to swear an oath relinquishing all claims "after Sumu-la-el had established justice." See Kraus 1984: 51-52.

9 Edited in Hallo 1995: 79-93.

even their children.[10] On this interpretation, the phrase refers not to the buyer's difficulties but to general conditions affecting the seller. It is significant that, although the purchase in question was from a single individual, who (on the basis of restoration) is specifically designated as a *nadītum*, the terms of the oath refer to the *nadītum*s as a group.[11] It indicates that there was an economic crisis affecting the *nadītum*s that led to a sell-off of their property by the poorer among them.[12] This crisis could have been the occasion for a *mīšarum*-decree, not necessarily for the whole land but perhaps specifically directed to the local area or to the *nadītum*s as a group.[13]

The plaintiff's case would then have been that the buyer took advantage of those adverse circumstances to pay a *nadītum* less than the true value for her slave.[14] In doing so the buyer fell foul of the decree, and the sale was therefore invalid. The court obliges the buyer to take an oath denying that specific allegation. The court expected the buyer to know, at least in her conscience, what would have constituted the full value of the slave, and, if she were uncertain, the gods of the oath would surely know. Rather than tempt divine will on the question, she chose to compromise and pay off the plaintiff with a small sum.

10 See Arnaud *Emar* 6 nos. 20, 138, 158 (land), and 83 (child). Cf. Arnaud *Emar* 6 121, where the debtor himself enters into slavery.

11 From her name and independent status, the buyer also is almost certainly a *nadītum* of Shamash. See Harris 1975: 308.

12 Not all *nadītum*s were rich; Samsu-iluna had to deal with the problem of poverty in their ranks; see Janssen 1991: 3-40. For the exploitation of poorer *nadītum*s by richer ones, see Stol 1998: 100-1; and cf. CT 47 63, lines 1-35.

13 Kraus (1984) does not record evidence of a decree around the time of Samsuiluna 12, when the sale took place. Another possibility is that the courts had a general equitable power to nullify unconscionable bargains. This is a more speculative hypothesis, but one suggested by the social justice provisions of the law codes, unrelated to any specific decree. See Westbrook 1998a: 215-17.

14 Indebtedness may also have been in issue; it is to be noted that *mēsirum* is derived from the noun *esērum*, one meaning of which is "to press for payment." *CAD* creates a separate lemma; see *CAD* E 332 (*esēru* A).

3

The Liability of an Innocent Purchaser of Stolen Goods in Early Mesopotamian Law

Abstract

The laws in Codex Hammurabi that deal with theft reveal several apparent contradictions. It may well be that two different systems of law are the source for these provisions and thus for the tensions among them. When the provisions are separated according to system, however, each set exhibits internal coherence.

The conflicting claims of the owner of stolen goods and a third party who has purchased them not knowing them to be stolen pose a problem for every legal system. In early Mesopotamian sources we find the problem dealt with at greatest length by §§9-13 of Codex Hammurabi:

§9 (col. VI 70-VII 47)

šum-ma a-wi-lum / (VII 1)*ša mi-im-mu-šu ḫal-qú* / *mi-im-ma-šu ḫal-qá-am* / *i-na qá-ti a-wi-lim* / (5)*iṣ-ṣa-ba-at* / *a-wi-lum ša ḫu-ul-qum* / *i-na qá-ti-šu* / *ṣa-ab-tu* / *na-di-na-nu-um-mi id-di-nam* / (10)*ma-ḫar ši-bi-mi* / *a-ša-am* / *iq-ta-bi* / *ù be-el ḫu-ul-qí-im* / *ši-bi mu-de* / (15)*ḫu-ul-qí-ya-mi* / *lu-ub-lam* / *iq-ta-bi* / *ša-a-a-ma-nu-um* / *na-di-in* / (20)*id-di-nu-šum* / *ù ši-bi* / *ša i-na maḫ-ri-šu-nu* / *i-ša-mu it-ba-lam* / *ù be-el ḫu-ul-qí-im* / (25)*ši-bi mu-de ḫu-ul-qí-šu* / *it-ba-lam* / *da-a-a-nu* / *a-wa-a-ti-šu-nu* / *i-im-ma-ru-ma* / (30)*ši-bu ša maḫ-ri-šu-nu* / *ši-mu-um* / *iš-ša-mu* / *ù ši-bu mu-de* / *ḫu-ul-qí-im* / (35)*mu-du-sú-nu* / *ma-ḫar i-lim* / *i-qá-ab-bu-ma* / *na-di-n-nu-um* / *šar-ra-aq id-da-ak* / (40)*be-el ḫu-ul-qí-im* / *ḫu-lu-uq-šu* / *i-le-qé* /

* Co-authored with Claus Wilcke. Originally published in *Archiv für Orientforschung* 25 (1974-1977): 111-21. Used by permission.

ša-a-a-ma-nu-um / *i-na bi-it* / (45)*na-di-na-nim* / KU3.BABBAR *iš-qú-lu* / *i-le-qé*

If a man, whose property is lost, seizes his missing property in the hands of a man, (and) the man in whose hands the lost property is seized says, "A seller sold it to me, (and) I have bought it in front of witnesses," while the owner of the lost property says, "I shall bring witnesses who know my lost property," (and) the buyer brings the seller who sold it to him and the witnesses in whose presence he bought it, while the owner of the lost property brings the witnesses who know his lost property, the judges shall examine their case. The witnesses in whose presence the purchase was made and the witnesses who know the lost property shall declare their knowledge before the god. The seller is a thief. He shall be put to death. The owner of the lost property shall take his lost property. The buyer shall take the money he paid from the estate of the seller.

§10 (col. VII 48-61)

šum-ma ša-a-a-ma-nu-um / *na-di-in* / (50)*id-di-nu-šum* / *ù ši-bi ša i-na maḫ-ri-šu-nu* / *i-ša-mu* / *la it-ba-lam* / *be-el ḫu-ul-qí-im-ma* / (55)*ši-bi mu-de* / *ḫu-ul-qí-šu it-ba-lam* / *ša-a-a-ma-nu-um* / *šar-ra-aq id-da-ak* / *be-el ḫu-ul-qí-im* / (60)*ḫu-lu-uq-šu* / *i-le-qé*

If the buyer does not bring the seller who sold it to him and(/or?) the witnesses in whose presence he bought it (while) the owner of the lost property brings the witnesses who know his lost property, the buyer is a thief. He shall be put to death. The owner of the lost property shall take his lost property.

§11 (col. VII 62-VIII 3)

šum-ma be-el ḫu-ul-qí-im / *ši-bi mu-de* / *ḫu-ul-qí-šu* / *la it-ba-lam* / (VIII 1)*sà-ar* / *tu-uš-ša-am-ma id*-KI / *id-da-ak*

If the owner of the lost property does not bring witnesses who know his lost property, he is a liar and has *made a false accusation*. He shall be put to death.

§12 (col. VIII 4-13)

šum-ma na-di-na-nu-um / (5)*a-na ši-im-tim* / *it-ta-la-ak* / *ša-a-*

a-ma-nu-um / *i-na bi-it* / *na-di-na-nim* / [(10)]*ru-gu-um-me-e* / *di-nim šu-a-ti* / A.RA$_2$ 5-*šu i-le-qé*

If the seller has died, the buyer may take five-fold the claim of that very case from the estate of the seller.

§13 (col. VIII 14-24)

šum-ma a-wi-lum šu-ú / [(15)]*ši-bu-šu la qer-bu* / *da-a-a-nu a-da-nam* / *a-na* ITU.6.KAM / *i-ša-ak-ka-nu-šum-ma* / *šum-ma i-na* ITU.6.KAM / [(20)]*ši-bi-šu la ir-di-am* / *a-wi-lum šu-ú* / *sà-ar* / *a-ra-an di-nim šu-a-ti* / *it-ta-na-aš-ši*

If that man's witnesses are not near at hand, the judges shall set a term of six months for him, and if he did not bring his witnesses hither within six months, that man is a liar. He shall bear the penalty of that very case.

The law presented in these paragraphs of CH gives rise to a number of problems which have been studied at great length by Müller, Koschaker, San Nicolò, Driver and Miles, and Petschow.[1] All these authors agree in stressing two points: (a) the obvious contradiction between the death penalty applied in §§9-11 and the mere ten-fold indemnity to be paid by the thief of private property according to §8; (b) the discrepancy between the liability of the thief in §9 to the buyer for the "money he paid" (*kasap išqulu*) and that of his heirs in §12 for five times "the claim of that very case."

Müller, Koschaker, and San Nicolò sought to explain the contradiction in the first case by the assumption of two different levels in CH, §§9ff. representing the earlier, and §8 a later stage in the development of the law. They were followed with some hesitation by Driver and Miles, whereas Petschow, while not excluding this possibility, suggests "daß grundsätzlich die Todesstrafe für Diebstahl . . . galt wie auch in §7 und §§9ff., daß aber in der Praxis regelmäßig Kompensation in Vermögenswerten erfolgte, deren Festsetzung durch den Bestohlenen mit dem Druckmittel der Kapitalstrafe in beliebiger Höhe erfolgen konnte."[2]

1 Müller 1903: 81-89; Koschaker 1917: 95-100; San Nicolò 1921: 176-204; Driver and Miles 1952: 95-105; and Petschow 1965: 149-51.

2 Petschow 1965: 150.

In the second of the two cases, Koschaker again proposed the existence of two levels, this time with §12 belonging to the later one: "Ich glaube daher die Behauptung wagen zu dürfen, daß §12 in das System des §§9f. beschriebenen Anfangs nicht hineinpaßt und darin scheint mir ein gewichtiges Argument für seine Überarbeitung durch die Redaktoren zu liegen . . . . Wie aber §12 in der Fassung der Vorlage ausgesehen hat, entzieht sich jeder Beurteilung."[3] Again he is followed by San Nicolò and tentatively by Driver and Miles. Petschow does not touch upon this question. None of the authors found a ratio for the five-fold indemnity of §12, although Koschaker came very near to the solution that we shall offer in pointing out the connection between §12 and §8, namely, that both provide fines based on the number five.[4]

In our view the true relationship of §§9-11 to §12(-§13) can only be appreciated when seen in the light of that of §6(-§7) to §8, which deal with theft and receiving stolen goods.

§6 (col. VI 31-40)

šum-ma a-wi-lum / NIG$_2$.GA DINGIR / *ù* E$_2$.GAL / *iš-ri-iq* / (35)*a-wi-lum šu-ú* / *id-da-ak* / *ù ša šu-úr-qá-am* / *i-na qá-ti-šu* / *im-ḫu-ru* / (40)*id-da-ak*

If a man steals property belonging to a god or the state, that man shall be put to death. And he who has received the stolen property from his hands shall be put to death.

§7 (col. VI 41-56)

šum-ma a-wi-lum / *lu* KU$_3$.BABBAR / *lu* GUŠKIN / *lu* IR$_3$ *lu* GEME$_2$ / (45)*lu* GU$_4$ *lu* UDU / *lu* ANŠE / *ù lu mi-im-ma šum-šu* / *i-na qá-at* DUMU *a-wi-lim*[!] (text: LUM) / *ù lu* IR$_3$ *a-wi-lim* / (50)*ba-lum ši-bi ù ri-ik-sa-tim iš-ta-am* / *ù lu a-na ma-ṣa-ru-tim* / *im-ḫu-ur* / (55)*a-wi-lum šu-ú* / *šar-ra-aq id-da-ak*

If a man buys any silver, gold, slave or slave-woman, ox, sheep, or ass, or anything else from the hand of a "son-of-a-man" or a man's slave without witnesses and contract—or if he received it for custody—this man is a thief. He shall be put to death.

3 Koschaker 1917: 81.

4 Koschaker 1917: 98.

§8 (col. VI 57-69)

šum-ma a-wi-lum / *lu* GU$_4$ *lu* UDU / *lu* ANŠE *lu* ŠAḪ / *ù lu* ^{giš}MA$_2$ / $^{(60)}$*iš-ri-iq* / *šum-ma ša i-lim* / *šum-ma ša* E$_2$.GAL / A.RA$_2$ 30-*šu* / *i-na-ad-di-in* / $^{(65)}$*šum-ma ša* MAŠDA$_2$ / A.RA$_2$ 10-*šu i-ri-a-ab* / *šum-ma šar-ra-qá-nu-um* / *ša na-da-nim la i-šu* / *id-da-ak*

If a man steals an ox, sheep, ass, pig, or boat—if it is property of a god (or) if it is property of the state—he shall give (it back) thirty-fold. If it is property of a subject[5] he shall restore (it) ten-fold. If the thief in question has not the means to pay (the indemnity) he shall be put to death.

There is a sharp contrast between §6 and §8, the former providing the death penalty for theft of goods belonging to the temple or the state, while the latter fixes a pecuniary penalty—remarkably high—to be paid by the thief for apparently the same facts. Equally, §8 rules ten-fold damages in the case of theft of private property while the death penalty is decreed by §§9-11 for acts to be regarded as simple theft.[6]

From D. H. Müller[7] onwards, commentators have sought to explain the different provisions of §6 and §8 in terms of the different kinds of temple/state goods involved, since they are described as NIG$_2$.GA (= *makkūrum/namkūrum*) in §6 but by way of an enumeration of movable goods in §8.

Koschaker considered those of §6 as "unter besonderem Verschluß,"[8] and Driver and Miles regarded them as "property . . . sacra . . . stolen from within the precincts of the temple or palace whereas in §8 it is described as various cattle or a ship, i.e. movable property kept without the precincts and so is only *profana*."[9] This division between *res sacrae* and *res profanae* is still maintained by Petschow,[10] but San Nicolò (seemingly

5 We follow the opinion of Yaron 1969: 83-95, and especially of Kraus 1973: 92-117, slightly modifying his view of 1958: chapter 10 (that *muškēnum* in this context means no more than private person, as opposed to state and temple).

6 See Müller 1903: 81ff.; Koschaker 1917: 74; and San Nicolò 1938: 213r.

7 Müller 1903: 79.

8 Koschaker 1917: 74 n. 2.

9 Driver and Miles 1952: 81.

10 Petschow 1965: 149-50; and Petschow's contribution to Klíma et al. 1971: 258.

overlooked by Driver and Miles but quoted by Petschow)[11] had already shown in 1932 that §6 is the "ältere Normierung des gleichen Tatbestandes [sc. like §8] . . ., die den neueren Satzungen vorausgeschickt wurde."[12] His argument was simply that NIG$_2$.GA (*makkūrum/namkūrum*) is in no way restricted to *res sacrae* but is any property. To this we may add: (i) nowhere in §6 is special custody or the temple/palace precincts mentioned, and nothing in §8 points to the goods being stolen outside sacred territory; (ii) *res sacrae* stolen from within the temple precinct may also be movable property; and (iii) there is a stylistic difference between §6 and §8.[13]

Our conclusion is that we are indeed faced with two separate sets of laws dealing with theft and related offenses: on the one hand §6(-§7) and §§9-11, which are based on the death penalty, and on the other §8 and §12(-§13), which are based on a scheme of multiple damages. Whatever their exact historical or geographical relation, the two sets of laws plainly derive from two different systems of law. Accordingly we see little point in attempting to elucidate the meaning of individual paragraphs from one group in terms of paragraphs from the other group. Instead we shall attempt to analyze the working of each system separately and the function of the individual paragraphs within the system.[14]

Beginning with the multiple damages group, we have seen in §8 that simple theft is punished with a ten-fold penalty while theft of temple or palace property is punished with thirty-fold. To these may be added §265, where the shepherd who changes the mark on animals entrusted to him and sells them must pay the owner ten-fold damages. In §12, we are told that the purchaser of stolen goods may take five-fold "the claim of that very case" from the estate of the seller if the latter is deceased. Our explanation of this rule is that the innocent purchaser is being allowed to recoup, at least in part, the payment of multiple damages that he himself has had to

11 Petschow 1965: 149-50 n. 21.

12 San Nicolò 1932: 327-28; see also Jackson 1975: 72-73.

13 §6 is formulated with the utmost economy of words but leaves no doubt as to its meaning. On the other hand, §8 gives a list of individual items, where §6 used only one word (NIG$_2$.GA = *makkūru/namkūru*), and it is not clear from the wording itself if the enumeration in §8 is intended to express the idea of tangible movables in general. This is the intention in §7, but the meaning there is made clear through the addition of *u lū mimma šumšu* "or anything else."

14 See Koschaker's statement above (with n. 3) and below.

make to the owner. "That very case" is the one in which the owner has succeeded in exacting from the purchaser not only restitution of the goods but also multiple damages. Thus the multiple damages system applies in principle to the purchaser, albeit innocent, of stolen goods as much as to the actual thief. But the purchaser can, of course, recover this payment from the seller/thief no less than the price paid for the goods that he has forfeited. §12 presents us with this system at work but deals with a further complication. The seller/thief is dead, and it would be unfair to hold his heirs fully responsible for the personal liability of their late father. The paragraph therefore attempts a compromise by letting the two innocent parties share the burden of the ten-fold damages which the owner is entitled to receive according to §8.

On this basis we can understand the enigmatic provisions of §13. We are not told, whether it concerns the owner or the purchaser, but the latter seems to be the most suitable candidate, both because of the context of the paragraph and because it is more likely that the witnesses of the sale would be itinerant and therefore not at hand. The purchaser, then, must "bear the penalty of that very case." The phrase is unsuitable for the death penalty,[15] which CH does not hesitate elsewhere to impose in explicit terms. But it is to be expected in a case where the penalty that the thief would otherwise bear is variable, e. g., being either ten-fold or thirty-fold. We conclude, therefore, that §13 also fits into the system of multiple damages, inasmuch as it relates to the purchaser of stolen goods.

We must now turn to the contemporary private legal documents to see whether anything like the system posited by us existed in practice.[16] That a system of multiple damages did exist in practice as a penalty for theft is attested by documents coming from the third dynasty of Ur, some three hundred years before the Code of Hammurabi. In *NSG* 186 (edited in Falkenstein 1956-57: vol. 2, no. 186), there is a mention of ten-fold restitution of sheep which appear to have been stolen. In UET 3 25 fish owned by the state and embezzled by an official are to be returned fourteen-fold, and another entry on the same tablet requires the restoration of an unknown amount of money for stolen asses which were temple property.

15 See already Koschaker 1917: 99-100, referring to an even earlier article by Carl Stooß.

16 Leemans (1957) has collected a number of documents relating to our topic; see below on UCP 10/1 107 and n. 36.

It is from the same period that we find the first of our documents relating to the consequences of purchasing stolen goods. MVN 3 219 comes (according to its editor) from Nippur and is available in two slightly differing formulations. We shall follow the tablet, adding the variants on the envelope in brackets.[17]

3 udu nig$_2$-sa$_{10}$-bi(/∅) 1½ (gin$_2$) 15 še ku$_3$.babbar / *Bu-kà-núm* dam.gar$_3$ / DINGER.E$_2$ *ù I-di-lum*-ra / in-ne-ši-sa$_{10}$ / (5)*Na-aḫ-šu-bal* KAB-gi-bi-im /

udu-bi udu-zuḫ-a ba-an-ku$_4$ / *Bu-kà-núm ù Na-aḫ-šu-bal* / IM-zu ba-an-ku$_4$-re-eš / 7 gin$_2$ ku$_3$.babbar aš$_2$-da-udu-še$_3$ (/aš$_2$-da-aš$_2$) ba-la$_2$ / (10)1½ gin$_2$ 15 še ku$_3$.babbar(/∅) / nig$_2$-sa$_{10}$-udu-še$_3$ ba-la$_2$ /

DINGER.E$_2$ *ù I-dì-lum* / su-su-de$_3$ / *Na-aḫ-šu-bal*-ra(/∅) ba-an(-ši)-ku$_4$-re-eš$_2$ / (15)mu-lugal-bi in-pa$_3$-de$_3$-eš$_2$ /

^{m}Šeš-ki-lul-la (šabra) / ^{m}A-ri-a kurušda / ^{md}Utu-an-dul$_3$ (dam-gar$_3$) / ^{m}Lu$_2$-giri$_x$(KA)-zal(ŠIM) / ^{m}Lu$_2$-kalla (ku$_3$-dim) / (20)^{m}DA-an-ZI.BU NIM(/ar$_3$-ar$_3$) / lu$_2$-inim-ma-bi-me / iti še-gur$_{10}$-ku$_5$ mu ^{d}Amar-^{d}su'en lugal

3 sheep, their purchase-price being 1½ shekels 15 grains of silver, Bukanum, the merchant, has bought from DINGIR.E$_2$ and Idi-ilum. Naḫšubal is the guarantor.[18]

17 The symbol (/∅) in the transcription indicates that the sign followed by it was not written on the envelope. The line divisions of the envelope which differ from those on the tablet are not indicated. As tablet and envelope are completely preserved, any sign outside the brackets is found on both tablet and envelope unless it is followed by the symbol (/...) indicating a variant reading of the envelope. Signs inside the brackets are to be found only on the envelope.

18 On the guarantor appearing in contracts of sale and hire, see Falkenstein 1956-57: vol. 1, 125-26; and vol. 3, s.v. lu$_2$-gi-na-ab-tum. See also Szlechter *TJA* 68, line 7. This is the most frequent writing, but as Falkenstein notes, gi- is sometimes replaced by ki-; this is also the case in *CT Nebraska* 63, lines 8-12; DU (= *túm*) is written for *tum* in UET 3 47, line 7, and in NRVN 1 214, line 8.

Clearly used in the same function is the word lu$_2$-KA-gi-na which is nowhere fully preserved (but see MSL XII 137: lú = *ša* IV 272-273, KA-gi-na = *mu-ki/kin-nu*; KA-gi-na = *mu-qi/qip-pu*), but which is attested in UET 3 19, line 2 (reverse), [l]u$_2$-KA-gi-na; in NRVN 1 216, line 10, lu$_2$-KA-[gi-na]; and in NRVN 1 217,

These sheep have been "turned into" stolen sheep.[19] Bukanum and Naḫšubal have been "turned into" thieves.[20] Seven shekels of silver have

---

line 6, lu_2-KA-gi-[na] (this man has sealed the contract). Compare also the expression PN ib_2-gi-ne/ne_2 in UET 3 33, lines 11-12 and in NRVN 1 104, lines 15-16.

The third word for guarantor that is found in Neo-Sumerian documents is the KAB-gi-bi-im of our document, which also appears in NRVN 1 213, line 8, [K]AB-gi-bi-im (contract sealed by him and the seller); cf. MSL XII 58: OB Proto-Lú 697, KAB-gi-en/na, with note by Civil 1969 (= MSL XII): 72-73.

The function of the guarantor is best described by Falkenstein (1956-57: vol. 1, 126): "der für die Erfüllung eines Vertrages einsteht und auch nach dessen Erfüllung im Falle einer Vertragsanfechtung aufzutreten hat. Das gi-na-tum ist dann der Betrag, der im Falle, daß der Vertrag nicht erfüllt wurde, zu leisten war." Recently published documents further inform us that he seems to be a member of the seller's party in contracts of sale who vouches for the correctness of the sales since he is mentioned several times besides the "man who weighed the silver," who vouches for the correct payment by the purchaser; see MAOG 4 191, line 7, PN ku_3-dim_2 ku_3-la-a-bi-im (see Falkenstein 1956-57: vol. 1, 125 n. 3); NRVN 1 213, line 9, PN dam-gar_3 ku_3-la_2-a-bi-im; NRVN 1 216, line 8, PN x-[x x] (?); and CT Nebraska 63, lines 12-13, PN ku_3-dim_2 ku_3-la_2-a-bi-im. UET 3 19, lines 16-17, [dam]-gar_3 simug-bi / [x x]-a-ni (= PN?) could be a similar expression. This man is mentioned also without the appearance of a guarantor to the sale in Ur-III documents and earlier; see *SRU* 57:7 and Krecher *ZA* 63 no. 19:10-11, and the commentaries in both cases.

19 This phrase seems to mean that the sheep had been found (by the court?) to be stolen, though not by the purchasers. See also nn. 20-21.

20 For lu_2-IM-zuḫ/zu "thief," see Falkenstein 1956-57: vol. 2, 74 n. 6, and the references for "to turn into a thief" collected by him (1956-57: vol. 3, s.v. lu_2-im-zuḫ ba-an-ku_4-(re-eš); thus there is no case-morpheme to be expected (at least in script) after IM-zu. The reading of IM in this word may be ni_2, since the very late source TCL 6 35, col. II line 23, of the series Erimhuš glosses it with ni. But we know of no etymological explanation of ni_2 in this place. Therefore Falkenstein's interpretation (1956-57: vol. 2, 74 n. 6) of lu_2-im-zuḫ as "ein substantivierter Satz 'der Mann hat gestohlen'" seems still probable. Without any analogy or phonetic reason we see no need to consider a possible neo-Sumerian *ni_2-zu as developed from the Old Sumerian word for thief, nu-zuḫ. This is attested in the Abu Ṣalabiḫ and Adab versions of the "Instructions of Šuruppak" as compared with the OB version, line 34; see OIP 99 59, col. III line 5 (copy no. 256 III 5 [Abu Ṣalabiḫ]; photo of the Adab tablet on p. 58 fig. 30 II 10b-12 = Luckenbill 1930: no. 56 II 4b-6 [Adab]; Alster 1974: 11, 20, 36/53 line 34 [OB]):

Abu Ṣalabiḫ	nu-zuḫ	ušum?	na-nam
Adab	nu-zuḫ	[pi]rig?	na-nam
Old Babylonian	IM-zu	pirig?	na-n[am]/na-am_3

been paid for the crime committed[21] regarding the sheep. 1½ shekels 15 grains of silver have been paid as the purchase-price for the sheep.

DINGIR.E$_2$ and Idi-ilum have been made obligated[22] to Naḫšubal to restore (the money paid). (To do so) they have sworn by the life of the king.

(Six witnesses); they are the witnesses for it. (Date: –/XII, Amarsuena, Year 1).

Bukanum, the merchant, is very clearly an innocent purchaser of sheep which are later found to be stolen property. He has been found guilty of "theft" in this extenuated sense and has had to restore the sheep to their owner. Most probably he, or rather his guarantor, also had to pay the fine of seven shekels of silver. As the document is not at all interested in this stage of the case, it is simply summarized by the words "turned into a thief." The second stage is that the purchaser recoups from the guarantor the price he had paid and perhaps the seven shekels if the guarantor did not pay it directly. The machinery of payment is not described, since the document is only interested in the fact that the sums have been paid. The third stage, that with which the document is actually concerned, is the obligation of the sellers to restore the money to the guarantor.

The legal principle behind this case, then, is the same as that which we have posited for §§12-13. The innocent purchaser has been obliged not

Abu Ṣalabiḫ	ul-dab$_5$	geme$_2$	na-nam
Adab	u$_3$-dab$_5$	geme$_2$	na-nam$_2$
Old Babylonian	ul-dab$_5$	sag	na-nam

"The thief—he is verily a dragon$^?$/lion$^?$—after being caught is certainly a slave(woman)."

We might note *en passant* that nu-zuḫ "thief" is the second attested nu-compositum with a verbal base (see Edzard 1963: 102ff.). For the rather broad meaning of the word "thief" in ancient Oriental sources, see San Nicolò 1938: 212-13; Falkenstein 1956-57: vol. 2, 74 n. 6; Finkelstein 1969b: 79; and Petschow 1975: 248.

21 We assume the term aš$_2$-da to be related to za-aš$_2$-da in Sollberger *Corpus* Ukg. 6.3.11 and 6.3.24, for which see Falkenstein 1957-58: 91; and Hruška 1973: 121. Its relationship to nir-da = *šērtu* "delict" (see Falkenstein 1956-57: vol. 2, 129-30; vol. 3, 7 and 149; Sjöberg 1973: 34 [line 95] and 45; and MVN 3 342) remains unclear.

22 Note the remarkable use of the verb ku$_4$ in this sentence: that which the people are turned into is construed as a LAL-ed-e form. (On the latter, see Edzard 1967: 41-44.)

only to restore the stolen article but also to pay heavy damages and subsequently seeks to recoup his losses from the seller(s). The fact that the purchaser's liability is not based on any *mens rea,* but is strict, is symbolized by the words "turned into a thief."

The same distinction appears to be behind the phraseology of a northern Babylonian document contemporary with Hammurabi: UCP 10/1 107, from the time of Ibalpi'el II and coming from Nerebtum, which reports a trial for theft.[23] Here the thief—apparently a free man—admits his crime; he loses his freedom, at least in part, since the judges give him to the man from whom he has stolen *a-na ki-it-ti-im.* Finkelstein translates "for penal servitude" (relating this expression to *kinattu* "servants"?), but we suggest that it is an affirmative clause meaning "truly," in actual fact,[24] i.e., the thief is not merely fixed with constructive liability by reason of his possession of the stolen goods. We also suggest the reading ziz$_2$ for aš$_2$, thus yielding ziz$_2$-da rather than aš$_2$-da, and the reading *ki-ša*$^!$*-ti-im* rather than *ki-it-ti-im.*

One further point about MVN 3 219 is that there is no express mention of multiple damages. It should be noted, however, that the denominator for this purpose will not necessarily be the same as the price paid by the purchaser of the stolen goods. It is also possible that the monetary penalty in this case was a fixed sum, as for example, in CU 25, CL 9, and CH 259. At all events, there is no question of the death penalty here; the consequences of theft are dealt with in purely financial terms.

Other documents from the neo-Sumerian period seem to reflect a somewhat different procedural machinery from that which we have seen in MVN 3 219 and posited for CH 12-13. In *NSG* 127 (edited in Falkenstein 1956-57: vol. 2, no. 127), A. in reply to a charge of theft of sheep states that he has bought them from B., i.e., sets up a *defense* of innocent purchaser. B. denies any knowledge of the sale, but A. is able to produce witnesses. A. and one of the witnesses have to take the oath. Subsequent proceedings are not recorded, but the document shows at least the purchaser's ability to join his seller to the action in which he is the defendant, and it suggests that if the purchaser can prove his accusation, the liability

23 Translated in *ANET*^{3} 455.

24 See *CAD* K 472, s.v. *kittu* A 2. Another possibility is that *ana kittim* here means "as rightful property."

for the penal damages will shift from him to the seller, although he still may have to restore the stolen goods. More explicit is the tablet, Kramer *AV* (= AOAT 25) 447 no. 10 (see Sollberger 1976), where a man obviously accused[25] of theft promises under oath to provide "the thief of Lunanna's stolen sheep," or else he himself would be the thief. If the accused's liability arose from his possession of the stolen goods, then the text shows the means by which he could relieve himself of that liability.[25a]

The same pattern is found in two northern Babylonian documents from Old Babylonian times. In a letter to a resident of Šaduppum, modern Tell Ḥarmal, the sender asks the addressee to send him two persons because "cattle belonging to B. were lost, and they have been found in the possession of D. and the merchant Š. They said, 'There are sellers who sold them to us; W. and L., who sold them to us, live in Šaduppum.' Now these two people shall answer their opponents."[26] It seems that the local authorities—not the purchasers, it is to be noted—are trying to get hold of the sellers in order to confront them with the charges made in connection with the property they sold. Nothing is mentioned of documents or witnesses; it is possible that the accused have produced witnesses of the sale. In the light of the facts of the case, D's and Š's statement is tantamount to an accusation that W. and L. had stolen the cattle.

In the second document, *AfO* 25 72-83,[27] the purchaser actually succeeds in producing the seller, who admits the sale and thereby frees the purchaser from the claim brought against him (lines 19-21: *qá-ti* owner *it-ti* purchaser *it-ta-sà-aḫ*). But the seller does not expressly confess the theft, and presumably, the case proceeds as between (purported) owner and seller.

The final document that requires consideration in this context is TIM 4 33 from Malgium(?) from the time of Kuduzuluš of Elam.[28] According to this tablet someone stole some sesame and brought it to a woman. This

25 The verb is ba-da-la$_2$ (cf. Akkadian *ubburum*); the accused is therefore not yet convicted.

25a An Old Sumerian Document (*SRU* 98) mentions an ordeal "because of a stolen slave from Isin" (bar-sag-zuḫ-a-IN^{ki}-ka); for the missing second -ka, see *SRU* 99, line 9, and passim in this document.

26 Goetze, *Sumer* 14 no. 28, lines 4ff (see Goetze 1958).

27 See Kümmel 1974-77.

28 On the approximate date (before Hammurabi 30), see van Dijk 1970: 63ff.

woman in turn passed the sesame to a harlot. The owners were able to trace the sesame to the house of the first woman. She and the thief are brought before the judges. He admits the crime, but she denies any knowledge of the theft. As her daughter assists her with an oath, she is released. The thief is condemned to a payment of (most probably according to the traces) ten shekels of silver, and [if he cannot pay(?)] he shall be put to death.[29]

A number of points should be noted: (1) the thief is available, and proceedings are taken against him; (2) the penalty for theft is pecuniary, although the consequences of insolvency are not; (3) the ultimate receiver of the stolen sesame is not mentioned at all among the persons accused—she does not even face a claim of restitution, but this may be because the goods stolen were fungibles; and (4) in the case of the seller of the stolen goods, a distinction is made between innocent receipt and receipt of goods knowing them to be stolen, and on this basis she is able to avoid liability. Thus the burden of satisfying the owners of the stolen goods falls on the thief alone and, more significantly, the risk of the thief's inability to discharge this burden falls on the owner alone.

We should mention in addition a document from Tell Ḥarmal, *JCS* 14 28 no. 60 (see Simmons 1960) from the time of Ibalpi'el II. A man evidently accused of theft claims that his partner gave the goods to him and subsequently fled to Babylon. The accused is then condemned to pay a certain sum which in part is provided by the mayor of his home town. It is then ruled that if the missing partner turns up, the owner of the lost property may seize him, but the partner who has already paid damages is not allowed to sue his fraudulent partner (perhaps until the owner of the lost property is fully paid—the text is fragmentary). Thus the innocent receiver was held liable only for part of the owner's claim, leaving the owner the responsibility of recouping the rest from the thief. The text does not state what proportion of the claim the payment amounted to, but it seems most likely that the limits of liability in this case were affected by the special rules of the law of partnership. For example, if it were considered that the innocent partner was only a part-owner of the goods (i.e., to the extent of his share in the partnership), it might further be considered right that he

29 See Petschow 1975: 248.

should be liable only in part (to the extent *pro rata* of that share) for liability attaching to partnership assets.

The innocent partner would of course have a claim against the defalcating partner and probably not only on losses arising out of the present case, but the owner is expressly given priority for the satisfaction of his claim to the residue of damages. On this interpretation, the liability of an innocent partner would be more strict but at the same time narrower than that of an innocent purchaser: he is liable for damages arising from stolen goods not acquired by himself and possibly without his knowledge, but only to the extent of his interest in the partnership.

Having surveyed the relevant source material, let us pause to consider some of the policy aspects involved in imposing liability on an innocent purchaser. The typical situation in which a legal system has to render justice is where the stolen property has been bought and resold by a number of persons, is discovered in the hands of the ultimate purchaser by the original owner, but by this time the thief has either disappeared or, if found, has already dissipated the proceeds of his crime and is insolvent. Most legal systems require the innocent party to restore the article to its owner, at least if it is in a recognizable form, but how does a system whose law of theft provides both retribution and compensation by means of multiple restitution deal with such a situation? On the one hand, the interest of the owner of the stolen goods is to seek his remedy against the person most able to pay, which usually means the purchaser, and it is also most convenient for him to be able to claim his penal damages in the same proceedings as his claim for restitution of the stolen article. On the other hand, the interest of the purchaser is that he should be able to buy freely on the open market without lengthy investigations of title. And it is in the interest of the state, both for the suppression of crime and the encouragement of commerce, that the law should distinguish between innocent receipt of stolen goods and theft or complicity therein. On this view the innocent purchaser should not bear the burden of the thief's absence or insolvency.

Any rule of law therefore is likely to reflect a compromise between the various conflicting interests. The documents of legal practice appear indeed to offer several differing compromises of this nature, while our only legislative source on this problem itself represents an even more complex situation, where compromise is required between the owner, the innocent purchaser, and the innocent heirs of the seller/thief.

In our view the differences in the documents show different rules at work only because the law, in its search for a compromise, offers the innocent purchaser a choice of tactics. The law, we suggest, was as follows: the innocent purchaser in whose hands stolen property was found was primarily liable, apart from specific restitution, to pay multiple damages for the theft. He could shift this liability to the actual thief or possibly the handler,[30] who was usually (though not necessarily) the person who sold the goods to him, but the burden of proof would be on the purchaser. The purchaser might well be reluctant to make an accusation of theft against the seller if there were insufficient evidence, in which case he might face a further penalty for false accusation, or if the seller were someone with whom he had long-standing commercial relations. In such circumstances he would prefer to accept liability as a "constructive thief" and seek to recoup his losses in a contractual action against his seller for failing to pass good title, assuming that his contract of purchase allowed for this sort of possibility.

Thus in MVN 3 219, where there is no suggestion that the sellers actually stole the sheep, the action is basically contractual; whereas in the Tell Ḥarmal text (*JCS* 14 28 no. 60), where there is a clear implication of the seller's complicity in the theft, the help of the public authority is enlisted to investigate the matter. In the first case, the purchasers are constructive thieves and bring a separate action against their sellers; in the second the purchasers seek to avoid primary liability by accusing their sellers. And in TIM 4 33, where the real thief is caught by the owner's efforts, the innocent purchaser is not involved at all.

In certain cases the law gave the purchaser a third possibility. According to CH 279, in the case of sales of slaves the seller must satisfy claims made against the purchaser (reverse col. XXIII 70-71 *na-di-na-an-šu ba-aq-ri-šu i-ip-pa-al*). As has been shown,[31] similar phraseology occurs in late Old Babylonian sale contracts in the contractual term that the seller is responsible for claims (to the object of the sale), often with the rider "according to the royal decree." It is reasonable to suppose, then, that CH 279

30 That is, a person who receives stolen goods, knowing them to have been stolen, or who is responsible for disposing of them; cf. English Theft Act, 1968, s. 22. French: *receleur*. German: *Hehler*.

31 Wilcke 1976: 260-62 with n. 17.

originally represented just such a decree. In effect, it inserts into the contract warranty of good title, what in modern law would be called a statutory implied term, but this term imposes upon the seller a more active duty than merely paying compensation for its breach. The way it worked in practice is shown by the tablet published Kümmel (*AfO* 25 72-83), which concerns an action over the title to a slave and undoubtedly turned on such a term in the purchaser's contract. The purchaser can oblige the seller to step into his shoes as defendant against the original owner and thereby free himself from liability altogether (except perhaps for specific restitution if the seller's defense fails). To achieve this, as it appears from the text, the purchaser must actually produce the seller, and the latter must admit the sale or have it proved against him. Thus the primary liability is still on the purchaser, i.e., he bears the risk of the seller being unavailable, but at least he avoids the danger of making a false accusation of theft against the seller. Indeed, as Petschow has pointed out,[32] the procedure in CH 279 applies to claims in general concerning the object of the sale and not necessarily to claims based on an accusation of theft.[33]

In summary, the purchaser's strict liability is tempered by his ability either (i) to avoid the penalty altogether by producing the real thief in his place, or (ii) to sue the seller to recoup the payment of the penalty, or (iii) where specially decreed or even by contractual agreement,[34] to require the seller, thief or not, to replace him as defendant. CH 12, with which we began this discussion, seems to belong to the second case, although the very ambiguity of the situation, where it may be impossible to ascertain the real thief, the late seller, or some unknown seller to him, may be one reason for the compromise ruling. Although we call the claim contractual, it is unwise to press this analogy too far—in particular, we do not know if contractual liabilities inevitably survived their bearer in Mesopotamian law.

32 Petschow *apud* Wilcke 1976: 260-61 and n. 17.

33 Wilcke's remark (1976: 260-61 n. 17), to the effect that §279 does not cover the case of theft because it does not impose the death penalty as in §9, should now be read in the light of our discussion of §§6-13 in terms of separate sources and in particular of the possibility that §§9ff. are intended to demonstrate points of principle and procedure and not to fix a certain punishment for theft; see below, esp. n. 35.

34 As in contracts of sale from Dilbat, Larsa, and Ur; see San Nicolò 1921: 138ff. and 196 ff.; Matouš 1950: 44-47; and Kraus 1955: 121ff. For the late Old Babylonian contracts, see Wilcke 1976: 260ff.

It remains for us to consider the group of laws in CH 6-7 and 9-11, where the death penalty is the punishment both for thief and purchaser of the stolen goods. The paragraphs in question are not internally consistent, for if §§9-11 impose the death penalty for simple theft, there is absolutely no need to have special provision for the theft of temple property as in §6, or for any other form of aggravated theft, for that matter. Furthermore, it would be an extraordinarily harsh legal system that imposed the death penalty in every case of theft. A closer perusal of §§9-11, however, reveals the somewhat theoretical character of its provisions. In §9 there is the simplistic equation of seller with thief, without further consideration of the circumstances. And such a neat case, where the owner receives his property and the buyer his money, will hardly ever occur in practice. The seller may be absent, insolvent, or dead, or some other obstruction will prevent the innocent purchaser from being satisfied in this manner. The owner may require more adequate compensation than simple restitution if his property has deteriorated in the hands of the thief or the buyer, or if he has incurred costs for the rental of a substitute. These are the kinds of practical considerations by contrast that are reflected in the provisions of §12 and §13.

We suspect, therefore, that in spite of its casuistic form we have before us in §9 an intellectual construct, a simple or "standard" case designed to illustrate basic principles. If one is constrained to use casuistic formulation, then the best way to formulate a general principle is surely to state the simplest possible case. Our interpretation applies equally to §§10-11, which are altogether too neatly balanced, considering, as an abstract discussion should, all aspects of the theoretical problem: if the purchaser were in bad faith, if the alleged owner were in bad faith, and if both were in good faith.

Furthermore it may be that the prime interest of whoever compiled CH lay, as far as this legal problem was concerned, not in the substantive law but in the procedural machinery employed in the courts. Thus §§12-13 could be added to the basic discussion in §§9-11 to illustrate the procedure in more complex situations without any concern over their differing penalties for theft.[35]

35 Confirmation that the whole of §§9ff. is somewhat didactic in purpose comes from the explanatory asides (only found elsewhere in CH in §7): §9, col. VII lines 38-39, *nādinānum šarrāq* "the seller is a thief"; §10, col. VII lines 57-58, *šayyāmānum*

Even if §§9-11 is an academic discussion, however, the question remains as to why the death penalty was adopted, and the question applies equally to §6 and §7, which show no outward signs at least of being merely theoretical. In the sources relating to our problem we find no hint of the death penalty; the principle of a pecuniary penalty for theft prevails throughout. There is only one text that is not totally in harmony with the others: TIM 4 33, imposing the death penalty (if correctly interpreted) in the case of the thief's insolvency, as opposed to UCP 10/1 107 and *NSG* 203 (lines 1-6), where the thief is given into the power of the person from whom he stole. But this exception is in accord with §8 of CH, although certainly earlier than the code and from an area not under the jurisdiction of Babylon.

On the other hand, the sources are unevenly distributed: they are found in small groups with large gaps of time and space in between. Those from southern Babylonia come from the Ur-III period, while the sources from northern Babylonia are all Old Babylonian.[36] The latter are in two groups:

šarrāq "the purchaser is a thief"; §11, col. VIII lines 1-2, *sar tuššamma id*-KI "He is a liar and has *made a false accusation*"; §13, col. VIII lines 21-22, *awīlum šū sār* "this man is a liar"; and §7, col. VI 55-56, *awīlum šū šarrāq* "that man is a thief."

This type of phrase should not be equated with the occasional clause in justification of conviction of the *aššum*-type, which always repeats facts mentioned in the conditional clause of the paragraph; see §107, reverse col. II lines 9-10; §136, reverse col. VI lines 68-70; §146, reverse col. VIII line 52; §194, reverse col. XVII lines 35-38; §232, reverse col. XIX lines 87-89; §235, reverse col. XX line 18.

36 If we look at the Old Babylonian documents related to theft collected and studied by Leemans (1957), we find three coming from northern Babylonia which are later than Hammurabi. First, in CT 8 6b a man who had "stolen and eaten" (*ša . . . iš-ri-qú-ma i-ku-lu*), i.e., taken in possession and harvested a field, swears not to claim this field again. There is no penalty mentioned nor any compensation for the crops. Second, TLB 1 144 shows a person standing bail for a robber and thus freeing him from the place where he is confined. Lines 34-36 read: šu-du$_8^!$-a$^!$ PN$_2$ dumu PN$_3$ / PN$_4$ dumu PN$_5$ / *il-qé-ma*$^!$ (text: E) / *a-šar pa-du ú-še-ṣí-šu*; "if PN$_4$, does not bring PN$_2$ (to the court?) within five days he shall answer his (i.e., his own or that of PN$_2$?) liability (*pí-ḫa-as-sú i-ip-pa-al*)"; cf. the neo-Sumerian document ITT 3/2 6225, discussed by Falkenstein (1956-57: vol. 1, 117 n. 2, and 135). Third, TCL 1 164 deals with lost cattle found in the hands of three men (PN$_{1/2/3}$) who are brought before the *abbū ṣābim* in Babylon and report to them (we read line 14 with *AHw* 146-47, under *dabābu*[*m*], [*id*]-*da-ab-ba-a-ma*, but perhaps sing. + ventive). They have to replace (*ri-a-ba-am*) the cattle. Leemans' suggestion that *riābum* here includes also a fine

documents slightly earlier than Hammurabi or contemporaneous with his early years all coming from the left bank of the Tigris, i.e., broadly speaking the Diyala region, and documents later than Hammurabi coming from

---

finds support in the reading and restoration we suggest for lines 17-24: $^{[m]}$*A-wi-il-i*[*št*]*ar* [. . .] / [dumu] *Ib-ni-*^{d}*šamaš* [. . .] / $^{(19)}$*q*[*á-ti* PN$_1$] / dum[u PN$_2$ *issuḫ-ma*] (or: *q*[*ātāt* PN$_1$] / dum[u PN$_2$ *ilqe*]) / $^{(21)}$1 gu$_4$-mu-3 [. . .] / *a-na I-din-*^{d}*marduk* dub-sar-eren$_2$ / *ki-iš-*⸢*ša*!⸣*-at* PN$_1$ dumu PN$_2$ / *id-di-in*; "Awil-I[št]ar [the . . .], [son of] Ibni-Šamaš [the . . .], [pulled off the] h[and of PN$_1$] son [of PN$_2$] (or: [stood] b[ail for PN$_1$ . . .]) [and] gave one three-year-old ox and . . . (silver?) to Iddin-Marduk the army scribe as compensation (for the liability) of PN$_1$ son of PN$_2$." Since the cattle had been found in the hands of PN$_1$, PN$_3$, and PN$_5$ (line 7: *ša* . . . *ik-ka-aš-du-ma*), they could be returned in specie and *kiššātum* must mean an additional payment. Our reading *ki-iš-*⸢*ša*!⸣*-at* (instead of *ki-iš-*⸢*da*⸣*-at*) is based on the same emendation made by *CAD* K 460 to VAS 8 26, line 15, and to TIM 5 62, line 10 (see Hirsch 1970: 114), both with similar context. The fine to be paid is not necessarily a penalty for theft—the word does not occur in TCL 1 164. It could just as well be compensation for loss to the owner arising from the absence of the cattle or payment accruing to the finders from their gratuitous use.

We may now add two more documents from northern Babylonia dealing with theft. First is TLB 1 243, dated Apil-Sin 5, which could even represent the multiple damages system discussed above; the upper part of the tablet is missing. It reads: ⸢x⸣ [. . .] / 3 udu-n[it]a$_2$ [. . .] / *ša šu-ur-qí-im* / ^{m}*Na-ḫi-ilim iṣ-ba-tu-ma* / $^{(5')}$1 sag nita$_2$ *A-na-*^{d}*la-ga-ma-al-tak-la-ku* / *a-na ki-ša-tim* $^{m(!)}$*Ma-ru-ṣum* dumu *An-ne-ilum* / *a-na Na-ḫi-ilim* / *i-di-nu-ú* / $^{(10')}$*a-na ba-aq-ri* sag-nita$_2$ / ^{m}*Ma-ru-ṣum* / *i-za-az* / (9[+ x] witnesses, among them *Be-la-ki* šagina Dil-bat^{ki} and *I-din-*^{d}*uraš* sanga ^{d}Uraš); "[Because . . .] Naḫ-ilim had seized three sheep . . ., which were stolen (property), and Maruṣum, the son of Anni-ilum, then gave the slave Ana-Lagamal-taklaku as compensation to Naḫ-ilim, Maruṣum will stand for vindications of the slave." Unfortunately the reasons for Maruṣum's liability—though somehow related to theft—remain unclear; again we meet the term *kiššātum* (both references should be added to the lexica).

YOS 13 28, dated Ammi-ditana 28, is the second document. It was studied by Finkelstein (1972: 13f.) and mentions a stolen cow and its calf. The person liable for its replacement is not the thief—presumably unknown—but most probably the man from whom the animals have been stolen. He may bring a cow with its calf within ten days; otherwise he will be punished (lines 13-15 should perhaps be restored as: *a-na* U$_4$.10.KAM [*ú-ul ub-ba-lam*] / *a-r*[*a-an* 1 ab$_2$ *q*]*á-du* amar-g[a]-*ša* / [*a-na-a*]*š*!*-ši*; "[If I do not bring (them)] within 10 days [I shall be]ar the pun[ishment for the cow] and its calf"). This punishment is severe: he has to give his wife to the "owner" of the cattle. This may very well be due to the fact that the animals seem to be state property since the "owner," Uṣriya *mār* Warassa, is a state official engaged in agricultural work.

Sippar and Lagaba, i.e., the land between the Euphrates and the Tigris. It is conceivable that the death penalty and with it the laws of §6 and §7, if not §§9-11, did apply in central northern Babylonia before the compilation of CH, but for lack of any documentary evidence it can be neither proved nor disproved. There is, however, another possibility—that these laws were never in force in the Babylonian states and derive from the nomadic background of the Hammurabi dynasty. This might account for their inclusion in the Code alongside flatly contradictory laws well attested in early Mesopotamian practice.

Among the documents from southern Babylonia cited by Leemans (1957), two (Riftin 46 and YOS 8 129) deal with murder and are therefore beyond our scope. In YOS 8 129, lines 8-12 read: *i-na ḫu-ub-tim / ša* sag-ir$_3$ *ša U-bar-*^{d}*šamaš / id-du-ú-ku / it-ti-ia lu il<-li>-ik /* sag-ir$_3$*-ma i-du-uk*; "In the robbery in which the slave of Ubar-Šamaš was killed (?), he indeed went together with me. He did kill that very slave." YOS 8 129 records only the conviction of the thieves and makes no mention of their punishment.

To these could be added CT 48 23, said to be from the south, possibly Isin, which is a personal account of the theft of a pig.

4

The Old Babylonian Term *napṭarum*

Abstract

Various proposals have been made for the meaning of the Akkadian term *napṭaru*(*m*) but with no consensus having been reached. An examination of the term's use in both lexical lists and Codex Eshnunna, however, points to the meaning "visitor." Understanding the term in this way allows a straightforward interpretation of CE 36 to emerge, with the *napṭarum* as a guest lodger with whom goods have been deposited for safekeeping.

In the Old Babylonian sources, the term *napṭarum* is found on a dozen or so occasions in the phrase *bīt napṭarim* but only twice in independent use, in paragraphs 36 and 41 of Codex Eshnunna.[1] In the former, liability is placed upon a *napṭarum* for the loss of goods entrusted to him for safe-keeping, and in the latter, the *napṭarum* is one of three types of persons whose beer a taverness must sell for them at the going rate.

There is no consensus as to the meaning of the word. Goetze in his edition of CE proposed "place of redemption" in paragraph 36[2] and "one awaiting redemption" in paragraph 41.[3] His interpretation was based on

* Originally published in the *Journal of Cuneiform Studies* 46 (1994): 41-46. Used by permission.

1 The term appears once at Ugarit (RS 15.123 + 16.152, line 5) in an exchange of land; see note 18 below. The feminine form *napṭartu* occurs once at Mari (ARM 10 59, reverse line 2) and as an Akkadogram in Hittite texts, where it means a type of wife (see *CAD* N/1 324-25). An abstract form, *napṭarūtu*, also occurs several times in obscure contexts (see *CAD* N/1 326).

2 Goetze 1956: 98. He is followed by *AHw* 742: "Ort des Lösens," as one of three possibilities.

3 Goetze 1956: 107.

the verb *paṭāru* "to redeem"; he did not attempt to justify either translation in its context. Finkelstein saw the *napṭarum* as a person of high status who was immune from search and seizure and whose house, the *bīt napṭarim*, served as a refuge for persons to whom he extended his authority, or alternatively as a place of detention, or as a bonded warehouse for goods, the common element being the responsibility of the *napṭarum* for the safety of things or persons in his care.[4]

His approach was followed by Landsberger[5] and adopted hesitantly by *CAD*, which does not offer a translation, only the description "(person with certain privileges)."[6] Kraus, however, rejected the Finkelstein-Landsberger thesis in strong terms, dismissing the special social class posited by them as a fiction.[7] Taking as his starting point the phrase *bīt napṭarim*, he concluded that the references pointed unambiguously to the simple notion of an inn or lodging for strangers.[8] In no case did it serve as a refuge or sanctuary, nor could the mention of deposit in CE 36 give evidence to conclude that it was anything so elaborate as a bonded warehouse.

Kraus' interpretation on this point is borne out by an examination of the references to *bīt napṭarim*. While several of the Babylonian references are obscure and could be taken, with a little imagination, to refer to some special establishment,[9] the Mari letters offer a number of examples that leave its meaning beyond doubt. Thus, in a series of dispatches, an official

4 Finkelstein 1965: 238; and 1970: 252-53.

5 Landsberger 1968: 98-99. His rendering, "ein Immuner," has been taken up in various German translations, e.g., in *TUAT*.

6 *CAD* N/1 324. But note "sojourner" in the citation of CE 41 under *mudû*, *CAD* M/2 167, which is closer to the sense proposed in this study but in our view would be more suitable, with its biblical connotations, for the term *ubarum* found in the same paragraph of CE. See our discussion of the latter term below.

7 Kraus 1976.

8 Cf. Rowton 1968: 280; Charpin 1988: 142; and Veenhof 1991: 295-95.

9 PBS 7 101 (= AbB 11 101) cited by Finkelstein 1965: 238 n. 17; and CT 4 29c (= AbB 2 97). On the other hand, in TCL 18 91, also cited by Finkelstein, it seems to us that the writer of the letter is concerned about losing his lodgings (which he is not at present using) before the due date for relinquishing them (lines 12-17). In the text edited in Finkelstein 1965 (*Studies Landsberger* 235, BM 80318), a senior official breaks the petitioner's tablets in his *bīt napṭarim*. This could be some special establishment, but it could well be simply his lodgings if, as is likely, the official was a peripatetic official who had come to Sippar specially to enforce the royal *mīšarum*-edict.

reports on his instructions to see to the accommodation of an allied army on its passage through the city: "Let them enter the town and give them *bītāt napṭari*. To Simahlane (their general) give a comfortable *bīt napṭari* in the citadel itself."[10]

In another Mari letter, the writer reports the case of a father who made the journey to town to visit his sick son and stayed until the son recovered. "When his son recovered, he planned to move to Rahatum in the evening. On the day that he planned to move, he took an extended siesta in [his] *bīt nap*[*ṭarim*], and his son cut his throat with a dagger."[11]

Similarly, in a Babylonian letter, the writer, who is due to arrive in ten days' time, sends his servant on ahead and asks the addressee to make the following arrangements pending his arrival: "Show my servant who brings you my tablet a *bīt napṭari* that is nice and roomy and let him look after (it)."[12]

On the other hand, when Kraus goes on to consider the use of *napṭarum* alone, he argues that it must be a *nomen loci* synonymous with *bīt napṭarim*,[13] on the pattern of *aštammu* and *bīt aštammi*. Thus in CE 36, goods are deposited with the "inn," the institution personified, like the *babtum* or the *ekallum*. Unfortunately, in CE 41, *napṭaru* appears in a list of persons, and in the later lexical lists it is universally regarded as a type of person. Kraus can only overcome these difficulties by special pleading—that the list is not to be understood as a list of like concepts, and that the lexical references may be a late error. There is one reference that might seem to support his view: in ARM 2 72:36, a foreign envoy is confined to the "gate of his *napṭarum*" (*bāb naptarīšu*), but in our view the word "gate" can simply be seen here as a metonym for house. The expression is thus no more than a variant of *bīt napṭarim*.

10 *a-na*[!] *a-da-aš-ši-im-ma li-ru-ba-am-ma* $\text{E}_2^{\text{ḫi.a}}$ *na-ap-ṭà-ri i-di-in-šu-nu-ti-im* [*a-na*] *si-ma-aḫ-la-a-ni-e* [*i-na ki-*]*ir-ḫi-im-ma* E_2 *na-ap-ṭà-ri ták-la-am i-di-in-šum* (*RA* 66 116:18-23 [A 2830]). Cf. *RA* 66 116 and 119 (A 826 and A 2801; ed. in Dossin 1972).

11 DUMU-*šu i-nu-uḫ-ma nu-ba-tam a-na ra-ḫa-tim*[ki] *nu-ku-ri-im pa-nam iš-ku-nu i-na* u_4-*mi-im sa a-na nu-ku-ri-*[*im*] *pa-nam iš-ku-nu mu-uṣ-la-lam i-na* E_2 *na-ap-*[*ṭà-ri-šu*] *ú-ša-ar-bi-im-ma il-qe-ma* DUMU-*šu ki-ša-as-su i-na* GIR_2.ZABAR *ik-ki-ìs* (ARM 2 129: 10-18).

12 *ṣú-ḫa-ri ša tup-pí ub-la-kum bi-it na-ap-ṭá-ri ša ki-ma ṭa-bu ù nu-up-pu-šu ku-li-im-šu-ma li-iṣ-ṣú-ur* (VAS 16 21:18-21 [= AbB 6 21]).

13 Kraus 1976: 168-71, following Goetze and *AHw* (see n. 2 above).

It is most probable therefore that the *napṭarum* is the person who either gives or receives the hospitality of the *bīt napṭarim*, i.e., the host or the guest. Kraus insists that if he is wrong in his interpretation as a *nomen loci*, then it can only be the host.[14] Von Soden, who had earlier reached similar conclusions as to the nature of the *bīt napṭarim*, is more ambiguous. He calls the *napṭarum* an "auswärtige Gastfreund,"[15] which suggests a foreign guest,[16] but proceeds to qualify him as one "bei dem man am fremdem Ort absteigt," i.e., a foreigner who acts as host to passing countrymen with whom he has a reciprocal relationship. Such a role hints at the Homeric *xeīnos* and appears to be an attempt to import that social phenomenon into Old Babylonian society.[17]

In our view, there is no need to introduce such complications. *Napṭaru* simply means "visitor" in all the Old Babylonian sources, the *bīt napṭarim* being no more than the house or quarters in which a visitor happens to lodge. It is derived from the verb *paṭāru*, not in the usual sense of "to redeem, loosen," but in the less frequent but sufficiently well attested sense of "to depart."[18] The *napṭaru* is therefore that most favored of guests, one whose stay is only temporary, and whose departure can be relied upon.[19]

To test this hypothesis, we shall examine firstly the evidence of the lexical texts, and then the two relevant paragraphs of CE, to see if our in-

14 Kraus 1976: 171.

15 Von Soden 1949: 371-72. Cf. *AHw* 742, "eine Art von Gastfreund" (second alternative); and Rowton 1968: no. 380, "guest-associate."

16 The term *Gastfreund* is ambiguous as to "guest" or "host." See Grimm and Grimm 1878: col. 1476.

17 Von Soden's definition continues: ". . . dessen Schutz man dort in Anspruch nimmt und dessen Gastlichkeit man selbstverständlich nicht nur im eignen Hause mit Dank vergilt, sondern auch durch tätige Anteilnahme an seinem Schicksal, wenn er einer solchen bedarf." The third definition canvassed in *AHw* 742, "(eine Art von) Vertrautem," seems to be based on the same analogy.

18 See the references under *AHw* 850 meaning 14. At Ugarit, where it appears in a single document to describe persons exchanging land (see n. 1 above), Nougayrol (1955: 223) explains its meaning on the basis of *paṭāru* = "to depart" ("déloger, s'en aller"): "Les *napṭaru* seraient ainsi des 'délogeants,' des hôtes temporaires, (provisoirement) dénués de domicile personnel" (1955: 219).

19 The *napras*/*mapras* form is normally used as *nomen loci, temporis, et instrumenti*, but as Kraus admits (1976: 171), it is occasionally used to designate persons, e.g., *narāmtum*.

terpretation can provide a satisfactory legal meaning in both instances. It would appear that by the first millennium, *napṭarum* was no longer a part of the living language but was confined to lexical lists. In spite of the difficulties that these late lists present, it can be shown that in our case they do preserve genuinely old traditions.

In MSL XIV 211-212 (A = *nâqu* I/2 134), we find the following equivalency: *ni-gìn* LAGAB.LAGAB *nap-ṭá-rum šá* e_2. The association of the Sumerian verb "to wander" with *napṭarum* (when spoken) of the house confirms, we suggest, the proposed derivation from *paṭārum* in the sense of "to leave." A *napṭarum* was associated with someone who did not remain in the house but passed through on his journey.

The association of ideas in a late synonym list is harder to discern. In *LTBA* 2 2:356-357 (var. 1 vi 20-21), our term is given as synonymous with *susapinnu*[20] "paranymph," "best man."

Equally mysterious is the synonym given in an astrological commentary (*AfO* 14 pl. 7 ii 11): *šá* giš.tukul.ur_2 "he who (wears) a weapon at his side." Weidner linked the two by suggesting that the paranymphs carried these special weapons, possibly as a phallic allusion.[21] His hypothesis is confirmed by a bilingual hymn to Ishtar, which states: "I (Ishtar) am the *susapinnu* with the pointed dagger at his side."[22] It assumes, however, but does not demonstrate, that *napṭaru* was such an armed paranymph. As we have seen, there is nothing in the Old Babylonian sources that would remotely connect the term with that function or with marriage at all, for that matter. My tentative suggestion is that the *susapinnu*, as a wedding guest, shares some of the characteristics of a temporary visitor (to the bride's home, when he accompanies the groom, and where they may live for a short period),[23] or that there is possibly a weak play on words between *napṭaru* and *patru*, "dagger," which is how the weapon is described in the Ishtar hymn.

20 And with *anzanīnu*, a term of unknown meaning.

21 Weidner 1954-56a: 78. Cf. Hh. VII 14-15 (MSL VI 85); and Hg. 55 (MSL VI 109): *kakki suni*.

22 *SBH* 56, lines 58-59: *su-s[a-pi-i]n-nu pat-ri zaq-tu ša ina su-nu šak-nu* [*anāku*].

23 Cf. Wilcke 1969: 77-78; and Greengus 1966: 70. Malul (1989), in discussing the *susapinnu*, emphasizes the role of the *napṭaru* as a custodian (of the bride?)—hence the sword (Malul 1989: 258-59, 274-75). On the association of *napṭaru* with guarding, see our discussion of lú = *ša* below.

Our main source, however, is a section of lú = *ša*, which provides us with direct evidence of the term's meaning. Col. III 11′-19′ of ND 4373 (MSL XII 141-142) is a separate section containing the following terms:

gir_5	=	*ú-ba-ru*
$KAŠ_4^?$-e-ne	=	*i-šá-ra-a-nu*
ga-an-uri_3 (ŠEŠ)	=	*nap-ṭa-ru*
ga-an-du_8	=	MIN
šeš-e-ne	=	MIN
ga-ur_5-ra	=	*áš-šá-bu*
ga-an-tuš	=	MIN
lu_2-tug_2-bal	=	*nap-pi-lu*
lu_2-DUN-A	=	*a- ra qa-a-te*
lu_2-šu-DU-a	=	*a-lik i-di*

Napṭaru is given as the equivalent of three Sumerian terms. The first and second belong to a frozen verbal form used as the active participle, which is often found in bilingual lexical texts.[24] The third, on the other hand, is found already in the Sargonic period in an economic document. Westenholz *OSP* 133, from the Philadelphia Onion Archive, records in lines 13-16 the following disbursement of onions:[25]

> 0.1 sum-sikil 0.0.1 sum-gaz / dumu-lugal mar-ḫa-ši / i_3-gen-na-a / šeš-ne šu-ba-ti

We would translate: "60 liters of 'pure' onions, 10 liters of 'crush-onions,' the Prince of Marḫaši, when he came, received as a *visitor*."[26]

24 See izi = *išātu* 97-169 (MSL XIII 163-166); line 102 ga-an-du_8 = *nap-ṭa-ru*.

25 Westenholz 1987. Westenholz notes the connection with *napṭaru* here and also in Westenholz *OSP* 55, line 21 (context unclear), without translating the term.

26 Westenholz (1987: 164) translates: "the Prince received, when he went to Marḫaši" (following Gelb 1965: 60). At first sight this translation seems more in keeping with the rest of the archive, where onions are often disbursed for journeys (kaskal.$še_3$), especially to Agade (e.g., Westenholz *OSP* 129 iii 2-3: $ensi_2$ A-ga-de^{ki} du-ni). According to Westenholz, the same applies to members of the royal family: lugal-igi-nim-ta i_3-im-gen-na-a "when the king went down from the upper country" (Westenholz *OSP* 135:4-5), "when the king's daughter went to the temple of Enlil"

If our interpretation, suggested by the context, is correct, then it is confirmation both of the meaning here proposed for *napṭaru* and of its antiquity. We also assume šeš-(e)-ne (= *napṭaru*) to have been the original lexical entry to which the first two terms were later added.[27] Of these, ga-an-du$_8$ is clearly based on the equivalency du$_8$ = *paṭāru* and confirms at least that *napṭaru* was regarded as a person. The next expression, ga-an-uri$_3$ ("one who guards"), is more difficult to explain. It could simply be a play on the Sumerian sign ŠEŠ, but there is another possibility, that the association derives from the scribe's familiarity with a law similar to that of CE 36, where the *napṭarum* had the function of a depositee of goods for safekeeping. The connection is by no means as strange as it might sound. Codex Eshnunna, like all the cuneiform law codes, was the product of a scribal school, in the same scholarly tradition as the lexical

(Westenholz *OSP* 170:3-6), but in these cases it seems to us more likely that it was the *arrival* of royalty rather than their departure that was the occasion for disbursement, since the king comes *from* an outside location in the one case, and in the other the temple of Enlil was located in Nippur, where the disbursements were made. By the same token, it seems to us more likely that a prince of Marḫaši, a distant land on the southeastern border of the Sargonic empire (Steinkeller 1982: 237-65), would have received supplies at Nippur on his way north on a diplomatic mission to Agade than that a prince of Agade would have received a relatively small supply of onions for a journey to a distant neighbor (Steinkeller 1982: 259).

In Westenholz *OSP* 129, a delegation from Marḫaši in the city of Uru receives onions from the Nippur office. Westenholz connects the prince's journey to Marḫaši with his marriage to a princess there (Westenholz *OSP* 154), but the latter text does not mention Marḫaši at all, and it was standard practice in diplomatic marriages, if such it was, for the bride to travel to the groom's country, where the wedding would take place. (The one exception, in unusual circumstances, was the unfortunate son of Shuppiluliuma.) If anything, Steinkeller's tentative suggestion of "princess" in Westenholz *OSP* 133 (1982: 259) would be more apt.

Against us is the absence of the (ventive?) prefix -m- in the verb gen, which in itself might seem superfluous to describe a visitor, but both of these factors can be explained if it is the case that Nippur was not the foreign prince's final destination but he was just passing through—which exactly fits the sense of *napṭaru* that we have proposed in this study.

27 As Cavigneaux points out, the canonical version of lú = *ša* considerably increases the number of lemmas for certain terms, adding rare and exotic synonyms (1983: 629c). None of the three terms appear in the extant earlier versions of this lexical series, but, it should be added, neither does the grammatical form represented by the first two.

lists.[28] Another of its paragraphs recurs in a first-millennium law code as far distant as Israel;[29] so it is perfectly possible for Neo-Assyrian scribes to have been familiar with the tradition that it represents.

Further information about the meaning of *napṭaru* is provided by the context in which it appears in this lexical section. It is flanked by two terms, *ubaru* and *aššabu* (the meaning of *isaranu* is unknown), both of which refer to types of *temporary* residents.

Aššabu is a tenant, who holds a lease for a limited term. *Ubaru* denotes a resident alien, a foreigner who is accorded the privilege of residing as a free person in the city.[30] In a bilingual hymn he refers to himself thus: "I am a foreigner (*nakrāku*); I am an *ubaru*."[31] Such a person could be of high standing: a document from Nuzi[32] records an official gift by the city of a chariot to an *ubaru* from Hanigalbat on the occasion of a festival. Nonetheless, his status was entirely dependent upon the local sovereign's pleasure. As a bilingual proverb puts it: "an *ubaru* in another city is a slave."[33]

The association of *napṭaru* with *ubaru* is not fortuitous, since it is found already in CE 41, thus providing direct evidence of the connection between the lexical and legal scholarly traditions adumbrated above.

CE 41 reads:

> If an *ubarum*, a *napṭarum*, or a *mudû*[34] will give his beer, the tav-erness shall sell the beer for him at the current rate.

28 Kraus 1960: 288-90, 293-95; Finkelstein 1981: 17-18; Westbrook 1988a: 89-90; Malul 1990b: 129.

29 CE 53 = Exod 21:35, discussed most recently by Malul 1990b: 134-52.

30 Kühne 1973: 29 n. 128. Lewy (1956: 59 n. 250) derives the noun from the root *w-b-r* "to sojourn abroad."

31 *BzA* 10/1 11:10; edition in Meek 1913: 22-24.

32 *AASOR* 16 50 no. 83 (SMN 2058).

33 Lambert 1960a: 259, lines 16-17.

34 The social standing of this class of persons is not known. *CAD* M/2, 167 translates "acquaintance, person known (but in no definite relationship)." Goetze (1956: 111) surmises: "The *mudûm* may be merely a visitor from outside, a citizen's 'acquaintance' who enjoys for a limited time the privileges of hospitality and for whom the host who knows him and his circumstances stands responsible."

Beer is a basic commodity that is supplied to persons by way of rations[35] or payment.[36] If the recipient did not wish to consume the whole quantity himself, then he would of necessity turn to the taverness to dispose of it for him. The rule would then impose upon the taverness the duty to obtain a fair price on her client's behalf. Goetze concluded as much but could not see the rationale for such a rule,[37] and Yaron dismisses it as a peculiar and inherently improbable situation which would not have gained the attention of the legislator.[38] But if the three persons in question were examples of outsiders, such as a resident alien or a visitor, then the rationale becomes clear. Such persons would be open to exploitation by local merchants, with their better contacts and knowledge of market conditions.[39] The authorities were prepared to intervene against the dishonest taverness, as they did in CH 108 and in paragraph 8 of the edict of king Ammi-ṣaduqa.[40]

There remains to be considered CE 36, a paragraph on the basis of which far-reaching conclusions have been made as to the development of responsibility in early Mesopotamian law, but in which the significance of the peculiar use of *napṭarum* has been totally disregarded.[41]

The paragraph reads:

> If a man gave his goods to a *napṭarum* for a deposit, and—the house not having been broken into, the threshold not having been scraped off, the window not having been torn out—he caused the goods of the deposit, which he had given to him, to be lost, his goods he shall replace (variant: to him).

35 Renger 1984: 85-86. Renger points out that since beer was apt to spoil, it was usually distributed in the form of beer bread or of barley, which could be taken to the tavern keeper who would exchange it for beer. Note the receipt of barley by an *ubaru* from Hanigalbat in SMN 3399:15 (see Lacheman 1940: 20).

36 E.g., as rent: VAS 16 62:16 (= AbB 6 62).

37 Goetze 1956: 116-17.

38 Yaron 1988b: 235, also summarizing previous literature on the paragraph.

39 Cf. Cassin 1958: 28, who argues that the palace is seeking to protect the interests of social classes who are financially dependent upon it.

40 Edition in Kraus 1984: 180-81.

41 See Goetze 1956: 101-5; Yaron 1988b: 250-51; and Otto 1988b: 1-31. Yaron and Otto leave the term *napṭarum* untranslated.

At first sight, it might seem logical to understand the *napṭarum* here as the host, thus introducing the interesting legal problem of the liability of innkeepers for the safety of their guests' possessions. But that is exactly what the paragraph does *not* discuss. The question of the innkeeper's liability *in his capacity as innkeeper* only arises if the guest had retained in his possession the goods subsequently lost, while staying on the innkeeper's premises. The moment the guest deposits his goods with the innkeeper, the latter becomes a simple depositee, with the same responsibilities as any other depositee. His status as an innkeeper is irrelevant to the question of liability for loss of the goods deposited with him. It is highly unlikely, therefore, that the special category of innkeeper would have been introduced in this paragraph, when it adds nothing of legal consequence to the position of the depositee.

If the *napṭarum* is understood to be a visitor, on the other hand, then the reason for his liability and the curious sequence of negative circumstances by which it is qualified may be explained as follows. A visitor staying in lodgings receives an item for safekeeping. It is not reasonable that he be held responsible for the security arrangements of the building itself, over which he has no control. Accordingly, if there is physical evidence that the loss was caused by a thief breaking into the building, he will not be liable. In the absence of such evidence, however, it is only right and proper that the visitor should pay compensation for items committed to him which he has lost, presumably through his own carelessness.

5

The Phrase "His Heart Is Satisfied" in Ancient Near Eastern Legal Sources

Abstract

The phrase "his heart is satisfied" is found frequently in Akkadian, Sumerian, Aramaic, and Demotic legal documents. This article deals with its occurrence in the first three sources and seeks to show that it functioned as a conclusive evidence clause as to the receipt by the declarant of a specific quantity, weight, measure, etc. Paragraph 264 of Codex Hammurabi is also explained on this basis.

The term "his heart is satisfied" presents us with a paradox. On the one hand, it is one of the most widespread legal phrases in the ancient Near East, being found in Sumerian (ša$_3$-ga-ni al-du$_{10}$), Akkadian (*libbašu ṭāb*), Aramaic (*ṭyb lbby*), and Demotic versions.[1] On the other, it seems, at first sight, utterly superfluous. It is unnecessary both as a receipt (since it frequently follows an express statement that the receiver has been paid) and as a quitclaim (since it frequently precedes an express statement that no claims may be made). Nor, as Muffs has shown in his classic study of the phrase, can it have anything to do

* Originally published in the *Journal of the American Oriental Society* 111 (1991): 219-24.

* This paper was first presented to the 198th meeting of the American Oriental Society in Chicago in 1988. I am grateful to the participants for their useful comments and criticisms. Responsibility for the views expressed herein rests, as usual, with the author.

1 This paper will not discuss the Demotic sources, which are outside the author's area of competence. It is hoped that an Egyptologist will test the author's thesis on the Demotic material.

with volition (as might be suggested by the similar-sounding expression "in the joy of his heart").[2]

Small wonder, then, that Muffs analyzes it as a "many-faceted term of considerable subtlety,"[3] containing some aspects of practically all the other contractual clauses and forming a kind of bridge between them. The result is, unfortunately, altogether too complex and fails to satisfy legal logic.

Muffs identifies three principal types of transaction in which the phrase has its typical function: sale, settlement of litigation, and receipt of the bride-price.[4] In all three, one party relinquishes rights in return for a *quid pro quo*: The seller relinquishes his rights over his property in return for payment of the price, the litigant foregoes his claims in return for payment or the rendering of an oath, and the father of the bride gives his daughter away in marriage in return for the bride-price.

To take the case of sale, the relevant clauses are, for example:

> We have sold it to you and you have paid us its price . . . and our heart is satisfied with the price you have paid us. We have sold and transferred (description of property) to you and we have removed ourselves from it from this day and forever.[5]

According to Muffs, "the mere objective notation that the full price was paid may still not insure that transaction against future claims by the seller or litigant: he may claim that he was not actually 'satisfied' with the amount received and still demand more payment. In order to prevent that eventuality, the scribes also recorded the personal ac-

2 Muffs 1969: 140-41.

3 Muffs 1969: 45.

4 Muffs 1969: 30-35, 51-56, 63-77, 81-83.

5 TAD B3.4 (= Kraeling 1953: no. 3), lines 5-11, cited in Muffs 1969: 33-35. An example from the cuneiform sphere is the Old Babylonian document CT 8 26b:

> (1-5) [Dimensions and location of field], (6-8) A has bought the field from B, (9-10) he has weighed out its full price, (11-12) his heart is satisfied with the price of his field, the silver, (13-15) his transaction is complete, they shall not raise claims in the future: (16-17) they have sworn the oath, etc.

For an example from the Middle Babylonian period, see Arnaud *Emar* 6 150, line 18.

knowledgement by the former right-holder that he had received the payment in full and that he is satisfied therewith."[6]

This interpretation has the merit of attributing separate functions to the phrase under discussion and to the no-contest clause: the former relinquishes the seller's claims as regards payment; the latter as regards the property. It has the disadvantage of being legally redundant. A completed contract of sale by definition includes an agreed price. Any demand for extra payments after completion of the contract (and *a fortiori* after conveyance of the property sold) would have no basis in law.[7] There is, therefore, no need whatsoever for a clause guarding against this eventuality.

The same applies to the other types of transaction, namely, settlement of litigation and receipt of bride-price. The contractual acceptance of a specific sum in settlement of a claim or in return for giving the bride in marriage fixes the parties' rights and duties in law. Any claim for further payment will be void and unenforceable.

In the cuneiform sources, the phrase is also found in several other types of transaction, such as a simple receipt.[8] For example, Meissner *BAP* 27 reads:

> A has received from his brothers B and C 10 shekels of silver that were assigned to him in his inheritance-share document. His heart is satisfied. He will not contest it again. (Oath, witnesses.)

In such cases the only right relinquished is that which forms the subject of the no-contest clause, i.e., not to challenge receipt of the money due

6 Muffs 1969: 44.

7 It would have no basis in this or any system. No legal system could logically recognize contractual obligations and at the same time enforce claims contrary to the contractual terms on the sole grounds of a unilateral change of heart in one of the parties. The same reasoning does not apply to the no-contest clause, which is designed to counter a later denial that the transaction ever took place or that it was valid. In asking for more, the seller admits the existence and the validity of the transaction.

8 See Muffs 1969: 77-86. The other examples given (all from cuneiform sources) are a division of inheritance and payment for expenses for a common wall.

in the inheritance tablet.[9] Using Muffs' analysis, it is difficult to see what extra element is furnished by the phrase "his heart is satisfied."[10]

A further category of cases does not fit Muffs' analysis at all, and he is forced to classify these texts as "atypical." Thus, in TAD B2.6 (= Cowley 15),[11] a groom lists the items of dowry received by him with their value, and after the grand total declares (lines 14-15):

> And the value of the goods . . . I have received and my heart is satisfied therewith.

Here the phrase cannot refer to the relinquishing of a right, as the groom relinquishes nothing in return for the dowry. Instead, Muffs postulates that the phrase triggers an *obligation* on the part of the groom—to return the dowry in case of divorce. This duty is, in fact, stated expressly in the penalty clauses of the same document; for Muffs, our phrase links it with the acknowledgement of receipt. By declaring himself satisfied with the amount received, the groom relinquishes any future claim against his wife that he did not receive the goods and thus acknowledges his obligation to return the dowry in full.[12]

9 The same is true of division of inheritance; BAP 101 states: "(1-4) [Dimensions and location of property], (5-8) the inheritance share of A that he divided with B and C, (8-12) it is completely divided; his inheritance share is complete; his heart is satisfied; he shall not raise claims." (13-16) [Oath, etc.].

10 Muffs suggests (1969: 79-80) that the phrase (*libbašu ṭab*) originally had an independent existence as a quitclaim and was then incorporated into other instruments. By the end of the Old Babylonian period it had become a "stereotypic fossil." We have our reservations about arguments based on the premise that because the modern historian can find no consistent meaning for a legal phrase, it must have been meaningless to the ancient scribes who used it.

11 Cowley 1923: no. 15; cited by Muffs 1969: 58-59.

12 Muffs 1969: 58-62. The argumentation is hard to follow due to some confusion in the use of legal terminology. Thus, it is stated (Muffs 1969: 61-62): "By declaring, 'My heart is satisfied with the amount received,' he relinquishes any claim, suit, or litigation he might raise against his wife in the future; thus, by relinquishing any claim he might have against his wife, he acknowledges the claim of his wife against him: the obligation to return the dowry in full." The husband's *defense* against the *wife's* claim for return of the dowry seems to have become identified with some unspecified claim by the husband against the wife.

A similar analysis is applied to the second case. In Cowley 2,[13] two agents undertake to deliver their principal's grain to a third party:

> (3) You have consigned to us barley, (4-8) [amounts and consignees] (9) and our heart is satisfied therewith. We shall deliver the (10-11) grain to A and B as written in this document . . . .

By this declaration of satisfaction, it is argued, the agents bar themselves from claiming in later litigation with the owner that delivery to them was short, and in so declaring trigger their obligation to deliver in full, which is detailed in the following clauses.[14]

In both these cases, Muffs' analysis, for all the anomalies it is forced to assume in the meaning of the phrase, still fails to give it a necessary function in the document. There is really no need for a link between the receipt and performance clauses; they appear perfectly sufficient as they stand to create the contractual obligations that they prescribe.

Finally, paragraph 264 of Codex Hammurabi uses the phrase in the context of a herding contract:

> If a shepherd to whom cattle or sheep have been given to herd is in receipt of his full wages (and) his heart is satisfied, (but) he lets (the number of) cattle or sheep fall (and) lessens the offspring, he shall give offspring and produce according to his contract.

13 Muffs 1969: 56.

14 Muffs 1969: 58: " . . . the promises of the agents to perform lack sufficient obligatory basis as long as some possibility of litigation remains. The potential claims of the agents can be obviated in only one way: by a declaration of receipt and quittance. The agents are, therefore, obligated upon receipt of the consignment from the owner to check the goods received in order to determine whether the goods actually received tally with each other; the agents declare that their heart was satisfied with the goods received; they do not want or demand any more from the owner. If they now deliver less than the amount stipulated, they hereby admit that it is not the owner's fault: they have no claims against him; the responsibility to deliver the goods in full, therefore, is all theirs. Thus, in this context at least, the relinquishment of all future claims and litigations against the owner is by implication equivalent to the acceptance of an obligation to be performed." Our remarks in note 12 above as to confusion in the legal terminology apply equally to this passage.

Here, also, Muffs argues that satisfaction of the shepherd's claim to payment is what triggers his obligation in negligence. Thus, if the wage is not fully paid, the shepherd is not fully liable to the owner for his loss.[15]

Such a contractual rule seems to us unlikely. The shepherd, having taken another's animals into his charge, must be liable for negligence in the performance of his contractual duties. At most he could set off any wages owed to him against the debt owed to the owner. (This might often have the same end result as partial liability, but it is a very different concept in law.)

In the light of Muffs' difficulties, Yaron proposes a much simpler, universal meaning for the phrase "his heart is satisfied."[16] In his view it is a mere receipt. It acknowledges annulment of the existing obligation and thus bars the receiver of a benefit under that obligation from raising any future claim.[17] To the obvious objection that this role is already fulfilled by the receipt and no-contest clauses, Yaron's answer would seem to be a denial that the different phrases in these legal documents have distinct, separate functions.[18]

This conclusion is not impossible, but it is an argument of last resort. If distinct phrases are used cumulatively in a legal document, then our starting point at least must be to assume that they each have a distinct purpose,[19] unless the evidence is manifestly to the contrary.[20] In

15 Muffs 1969: 87-90, following Driver and Miles 1952: 456-57.

16 Yaron 1970: 408-16.

17 Yaron 1970: 409.

18 Yaron 1970: 411: "La supposition que toute phrase énoncée dans un document légal privé doit avoir un rôle distinct, spécifique, est l'une de celles que je ne suis pas prêt à appuyer."

19 Compare the approach of Wilcke (1985: 74-77), who takes minor grammatical changes in the formulae and even variations in the order of clauses to reflect developments in law. This seems to us to veer too far in the opposite direction.

20 Yaron has a special explanation for each of these two "atypical" cases in the Elephantine documents. As regards the marriage document, TAD B2.6 (= Cowley 15), Yaron suggests (1970: 412) that in declaring himself satisfied with the dowry, the groom renounces claims to any additional item, in particular, any part of the dowry promised but not yet delivered. This is a possibility, but note that the groom actually declares himself satisfied with the value of the dowry.

our view, the phrase "his heart is satisfied" had a simple, but distinct and very important purpose.

Let us return to the case of sale. The phrase is found after a statement of the weight or quantity of the price and, usually, also the fact that it has been paid or received. In our view it is simply an acknowledgement by the seller that he has checked the weight or quantity of the items received and that they tally exactly with the amount purported to have been paid by the buyer. The phrase is best translated here, "he has no complaint (of short measure)." Its legal function is then that of a *conclusive evidence clause*, which bars the seller from claiming later that he in fact received short measure, even if subsequent verification should prove that this was truly the case.

It is not the same as the payment/receipt clause, as the latter records fulfillment by the buyer of his obligation *in principle*. Nor is it the same as the no-contest clause, since it is not a quitclaim. The no-contest clause bars the seller's right to challenge the existence or validity of the contract; our phrase is not concerned with such legal issues but with the practical performance of one particular part of the contract.

Nor, it should be pointed out, is the idea of satisfaction the same as that posited by Muffs. In the latter's analysis, as we have seen above, the buyer's "satisfaction" is an emotional one, referring to satisfaction with the terms of the bargain. In our analysis, the "satisfaction" is purely empirical, relating to what has been observed, as befits a clause dealing with the performance stage of the contract rather than the stage of conclusion of contract. This analysis applies equally well to the other transactions that we have discussed: settlements, receipts, and supposedly "atypical" cases.

Documents recording the settlement of litigation are of two types. In the first, found in both Aramaic and Akkadian sources, a dispute is resolved by one of the litigants being awarded or accepting a quantity or

---

In the case of the consignment document, Cowley 2, Yaron proposes to restore the missing half line at the end of the consignment clause with a statement of receipt by the agents of their wages—to which the satisfaction clause would then apply. This is again a possibility, but highly speculative in view of the absence of any traces or link with the extant text, and in view of the general tenor of the text.

weight of goods or a measure of land, declaring his heart satisfied therewith, and sometimes undertaking to raise no further claims.[21] Our phrase can be seen to have the same function here as in sale: to acknowledge the accuracy of the quantity, weight, or measure received.

In the second type, represented by the *mrḥq* documents from Elephantine, the litigant declares his heart satisfied, not with the actual items, but with an oath rendered by the other party concerning the disputed items. In Cowley 14 the oath concerns the division of common property.[22] In Cowley 6 it concerns the boundaries of a house alleged by the oath-taker to have been alienated by the addressee of the oath.[23]

This use of the phrase here emphasizes its function as a conclusive evidence clause. The litigant, in declaring his heart satisfied—not with the calculations concerning division of property or measurement of

21 E.g., Cowley 20:

> [A and B sued C and D for goods claimed to have been deposited and not returned. A and B declare:] (8) "Then you were examined and you satisfied our hearts concerning these goods (9-10) and our heart is satisfied therewith from this day forever. I, A, and B, we are removed from you from this day forever. Neither we nor our children can sue you, etc."

VAS 8 101:

> (1-4) A sued B and they judged them and her (A's) claim was accepted. (5-6) Her heart is satisfied. She shall not return and raise claims against B. [Oath, etc.]

TCL 1 112:

> (Before the judges) (16-19) they litigated over the expenses for (cultivating) 1 *ikû* of field and A received (them). His heart is satisfied . . . .

22 See Muffs 1969: 32.

> (4-7) " . . . Then an oath was imposed upon you and you swore to me concerning them (i.e., the property) by the goddess Sati, and my heart was satisfied with that oath that you took for me concerning those goods of yours; and I hereby remove myself from you from this day forever. I will not be able to sue you . . . ."

23 Cowley 6:

> (A declares) . . . (4-7) "You have sworn to me by the god Ya'u ... about my land in regard to which I lodged a complaint against you before X and his fellow-judges, and they imposed upon you an oath to me, to swear by Ya'u in regard to this land, that it was no longer the land of myself, A. (7-11) Now these are the boundaries of this land in regard to which you swore to me (description). (11-13) You have sworn to me by Ya'u and have satisfied my heart concerning this land. I shall not be able to sue, etc. . . . ."

land, but with an oath taken as to those calculations—is barred from subsequently questioning their accuracy, even if the calculations are shown to be incorrect.

The next category of documents is that of simple receipts. In the light of our interpretation, the function of the phrase in such documents is obvious and needs no further comment.

We come now to those instances classified by Muffs as atypical. The first is the receipt of a dowry by the groom in the context of a marriage document (TAD B2.6 [= Cowley 15]). It can now be seen that the groom's declaration of satisfaction with the value (presumably total and individual, since the items are so carefully listed) has nothing to do with any contingent obligation to return the dowry but is simply an acknowledgement that the value stated is accurate. Should he at some time be obliged to return the dowry, this acknowledgement will be of great assistance in ensuring full performance of that obligation.

The receipt of grain by agents in Cowley 2 can also be seen to reflect a perfectly typical use of the phrase. As Muffs correctly noted,[24] the agents are acknowledging that the grain received by them tallies with the quantity stated in their contract. This acknowledgement does not create an obligation to deliver to the third party—that is the essence of the contract—but if they deliver short, it will prevent them from shifting the blame onto the original owner.

Finally, we turn to the use of the phrase in CH 264. Here, its function is not so apparent, because the context is very different from that of private legal documents. It is necessary, therefore, to explain the background.

The usual arrangement under Old Babylonian herding contracts was for the shepherd to be remunerated with a share of the profits, by taking any growth in the flock in excess of an agreed minimum. If the shepherd was unable to produce the agreed minimum, he was obliged to make up the deficit himself.[25] Naturally, this form of remuneration would fall due only at the end of the contractual period, when the sheep were brought in for shearing.[26]

24 Muffs 1969: 58.

25 Postgate 1975: 1-10; and Finkelstein 1968: 30-36. Cf. Kraus 1966: 48-52, 58-63.

26 Postgate 1975: 4.

There are, however, occasional references to fixed wages, either in silver, rations, or in kind.[27] The shepherd would still be expected to furnish a minimum growth in the flock and be liable for losses, which would be deducted from his wages.[28] Again, it is most likely that these wages would be paid, or at least payment completed, at the end of the contractual period;[29] hence the ease of deducting losses from the shepherd's remuneration.

The statement in CH 264 that the shepherd "is in receipt of[30] his full wages (and) his heart is satisfied" (*idīšu gamrātim maḫir libbašu ṭāb*) tells us three things: first, he is paid a fixed wage; second, it is payable *in advance*; and, third, he has not complained of non-payment (or short payment).

This last fact raises an evidentiary presumption that full payment has, in fact, been received by him. If he, then, fails to furnish his contractual minimum, the effect of the presumption is to bar him from claiming that there are unpaid wages against which he can set off the shortfall. The rationale of the presumption is to prevent the shepherd from employing an allegation of non-payment (or short payment) as a tactic in his defense to a claim of contractual negligence where he had not previously raised it as an independent claim.

By way of postscript to this discussion we should note the associated phrase "he shall satisfy his heart," which occurs in a small number of cuneiform legal sources and appears to be an undertaking that actual delivery will tally with legitimate expectations. We would suggest that it imposes the burden of proof as to actual payment upon the *payor*.

27 Postgate 1975: 9-10. E.g., VAS 9 59-60:

> (1-7) A has hired B from himself for one year to herd the sheep of C. (8-11) He will measure out 8 kor of grain as wages for one year and will weigh out 1 shekel of silver for wool-ration. (12-13) He entered (into service) on 24th Nisan.

28 UCP 10/1 58 (cf. Finkelstein 1968: 33; Postgate 1975: 5 n. 2):

> (1-6) A hired B for one year in the month of Ab. (7-9) 5 kor of grain are his wages, 2.2 kor his grain-ration, 1 shekel of silver his wool-ration. (9-12) Of the sheep that are the increase, he shall give 80 out of 100(?) and he shall be responsible for any lost: (13-14) He shall pay it by forfeiting from his wages (*i-na-ad-di-šu i-na i-di-šu i-te-el-li*).

29 Note the *consecutio temporum* in VAS 9 59-60, note 27, above.

30 Note that the verb "receive" is in the (active) stative, not in the preterite tense.

Thus in CH 178 an unmarried priestess is to relinquish her inheritance share to her brothers in return for an equivalent income in the form of rations: "they shall give her grain, oil, and wool like the value of her inheritance share and shall satisfy her heart." If they fail to give her these rations and do not "satisfy her heart," she may give her property to a farmer and take the full income herself.

The point of the phrase here, we suggest, is that it is for the brothers to prove that actual delivery was proportionate to the inheritance share, not for the sister to prove that it was inadequate.

Likewise in CT 8 34b (= Schorr 1913: no. 202) a husband assigns property to a wife who may (during widowhood) give it to such of her sons as will support her and satisfy her heart (*ipallaḫši u libbaša uṭabbu*). Again, it is the son claiming the inheritance who will have to prove actual delivery of rations in satisfaction of the customary norms. Finally, in BE 6/2 14 the joint owner of a wall will have to satisfy the heart of the co-owner with silver representing a proportionate share of the expenses of building the wall, and the burden of proving that his payment represents a full share, therefore, rests upon the payor.[31]

31 In the few business documents in which the phrase occurs, the context is insufficient to show why assignment of the burden of proof to the payor should have been necessary. These documents all concern payments outstanding in grain or silver for items sold (BE 6/2 27) or hired (BIN 7 192) or upon loans to be returned with interest, usually at harvest-time (BE 6/2 16, 20, 25, 27; cf. YOS 8 111).

6

The Case of the Elusive Debtors: CT 4 6a and CT 6 34b

Abstract

A dossier of two Old Babylonian litigation records is explained as a creditor's attempts to claim penal damages arising from breach of a contract to supply goods and his two debtors' maneuvers to avoid immediate payment. The interpretation also reaffirms the interpretation of the disputed term *mitḫārum* as an additional equal amount.

Introduction[1]

Two Old Babylonian legal documents, CT 4 6a and CT 6 34b, form a dossier relating to the same litigation. A creditor (C), the well-known financier Erib-Sin, is suing two debtors, Sin-iddinam (D1) and Etel-pi-Sin (D2), over a debt arising from the non-performance of their contractual obligation to him. The documents are depositions before witnesses by each of the debtors in turn, following a formal confrontation by the creditor.[2] Although only one of the documents is dated, it is clear from their content that CT 4 6a, the confrontation with D1, preceded CT 6 34b, the confrontation with D2.

The dossier, which has attracted the attention of numerous scholars, has most recently been studied by Zaccagnini (1996: 104-107) and by

1 The abbreviations in this article follow those of *CAD*. [Editors' note: see p. 451 for the complete list of abbreviations used in this volume.]

2 For a discussion of the legal act of *ṣabātum*, see Dombradi 1996: vol. 1, 295-302.

Dombradi (2000: 40-64). Their efforts have considerably advanced our understanding of the texts but have resulted in radically different interpretations of their content, centering around the enigmatic term *mitḫārum*, which is used several times in CT 6 34 b. The purpose of this article is to build upon their insights in order to reconstruct more clearly the original transaction and the course of the dispute.

For the full text of the two documents, we refer the reader to the meticulous edition of Dombradi (2000: 41-46, 59-61). We will reproduce here only excerpts that are germane to our discussion.

Contract and Breach

In CT 6 34b, lines 7-11, C makes the following claim against D2:

> . . . 2 GIN$_2$ KU$_3$.BABBAR
> *a-na* UDU.NITA$_2$ *nu-da-ma-qá-am*
> *a-na ka-ši-im ù* D1
> *ad-di-in-ma*
> UDU.NITA$_2$ *ú-ul tu-ša-bi-la-nim*

> I gave you and D1 two shekels of silver for a ram *nudammaqam*, and you (pl.) did not deliver the ram to me.

Dombradi (2000: 46-55), after a thorough review of possible contract types, argues that the transaction here described was a partnership between all three parties, creditor and debtors. The purpose of the loan was to purchase a ram for their mutual benefit, on the analogy of an *ana šīmim* contract (*Lieferungskauf*), although not using that technical terminology. From her description, it seems to have been not so much a credit transaction as a mandate by one partner to the two others.[3]

3 She compares it to the medieval *commenda* partnership, although she admits that it lacks the element of sharing profit or loss on a joint venture. Rather, the two agents' profit would have been in the margin between the capital supplied and the purchase price of the ram.

Dombradi relies on two pieces of evidence in the text. Firstly, in line 12, the term "partner" is used of one of the parties, and secondly, the curious term *nudammaqam*, which she has confirmed by collation as the correct reading of the signs at the end of line 8. She translates "wir werden für mich etwas Gutes tun," thereby implying a mutuality of purpose.[4]

Neither argument is sustainable. The term "partner" is used by C, who in addressing D2 actually refers to D1 as "your partner" (*tappaka*), thereby excluding himself from the partnership (otherwise he would have said "our partner"). The partnership is thus between D1 and D2, with C standing outside as the creditor. Likewise, the translation of *nudammaqam* would create not a partnership for mutual benefit but a *societas leonina* ("for me"), where one partner has all the profit and the others only the risk. The translation is in any case at best awkward, verging on the syntactically implausible in any language.

Dombradi is forced into an artificial translation of *nudammaqam* by the fact that it appears to be a non-motion verb with a ventive ending.[5] There is, however, another solution to this problem, which is suggested by Dombradi's own insight that the word is inserted here in parenthesis to allude to the type of the transaction agreed. It is a peculiarity of the use of the ventive that where two verbs are joined by the copula, only the second being a verb of motion, the first may nonetheless take the ventive as well. For example: *ašammam-ma . . . attallakam* "I will buy and come hither."[6] The parenthetical quality of *nudammaqam* suggests that it is being used here elliptically—that it is only the first of two verbs joined by a copula, the second part of the clause remaining unstated. The second verb is revealed three lines later: *šūbulum*. The full phrase would have read *nudammaqam-ma nušabbalam**—"we will make it (i.e., the ram) good and deliver it."[7]

4 Dombradi analyzes the verb as an intransitive D-stem with a personal ventive ending (2000: 43-44).

5 See the detailed discussion in Dombradi 2000: 43-45.

6 *GAG* §82c; see now Kouwenberg 2002: 218-222, who calls it the anticipatory ventive.

7 Although Kraus (1987: 35) took this as a case of *dummuqum* without a second verb joined by the copula, his translation assumes an elliptical use of *nudammaqam* here: "Wir werden einen guten Hammel (liefern)." Ellipsis is found in Old Babylonian contractual clauses, as in the phrase "if X hates," which is sometimes used instead of the

Thus interpreted, the term has a parallel in the Old Babylonian matrimonial adoption contract recorded in CT 47 40. A woman adopts a girl as daughter and daughter-in-law from her parents, pays them in advance her betrothal payment (*terḫatum*) and undertakes that *udammaqši-ma ana mūtim inaddišši*, "she will make her good and give her to a husband." Landsberger (1968: 94) translated the verb *dummuqum* "ausstaffieren," a surmise justified by the context, but perhaps a trifle too specific.[8] The point of the arrangement is that the adoptress will raise the adoptee, making the necessary investment, whether material, social, or moral, to turn her into a suitably marriageable woman. In the same way, in our case the partners D1 and D2 agreed to deliver a ram with value added, possibly by purchase but more probably by breeding and fattening a lamb.[9] For this purpose they received two shekels from the creditor.[10]

The arrangement is closely analogous to the receipt of advance payment for the supply of goods to be manufactured, as in VAS 8 86:

> A and B have received (šu ba-an-ti-meš) one shekel of silver from C. From the financially sound and reliable one . . . . In the month of Elul they shall give sixteen *sar* of bricks. If they do not give, they shall pay two shekels of silver.

The contract is dated to the month of Adar; so they have six months in which to make the delivery. The silver advanced is regarded as a debt, as shown by the use of technical terminology, with payment in the manner of *datio in solutum* (see Skaist 1994: 22-25). Note that the contract contains two clauses relating to performance—a two-fold penalty for failure to de-

---

full formula "if X hates and says [*verba solemnia* of divorce]." See Westbrook 1986b: 399-401.

8 Not relevant to our discussion is the well-attested use in letters of *dummuqum* in hendiadys with another verb with the meaning "do a favor and (action of second verb)"; see *CAD* D 63; and Kraus 1987: 26, 34. Contracts are about obligations, not favors.

9 In our view, Kraus' translation—"Wir werden einen guten Hammel (liefern)"—while interpreting the phrase as elliptical (see n. 7 above), misses the point of the speaker using a verb rather than an adjective (quote in Kraus 1987: 35).

10 As suggested by Leemans' translation (1991: 318): "pour rendre bon un bélier." Whether this was a *tadmiqtum* transaction is of little consequence, since we know so little about that type of contract.

liver and a joint liability clause. The effect of the latter is to enable the creditor to collect the whole of the debt or penalty from any single debtor, without regard to the existence of co-debtors (Landsberger 1937: 120-123; Skaist 1994: 231-237).

The litigation in our dossier concerned breach of a similar contract to supply, and in the same way, the injured party sought payment of silver, not performance of the contract. Whether the contract also contained the two extra clauses, of double repayment and joint liability, depends upon our analysis of the parties' statements. As we shall see, the presence or absence of these clauses is crucial to our understanding of the course of the litigation.

The First Claim

D1 and D2 have borrowed two shekels from C in return for a promise to supply a ram, which they have failed to honor. C brings suit with regard to the debt but meets with complications. His first step is against D1, as recorded in CT 4 6a. D1 replies to C's (unstated) claim with three offers to pay:

a) one shekel on deposit with a third party, which C may take from the latter;
b) two shekels if D2 fails to acknowledge[11] and pay one shekel "of receipt" (*ša* ŠU-TI-A);[12]
c) one shekel received from C, on a contingency involving an order by two other persons.[13]

11 Following Dombradi's interpretation (2000: 45-46) of the verb *burrum* here and in CT 6 34b as *bestätigen*.

12 The logogram may represent either *namḫartu*, "goods/sum received," in which case it tells us nothing of the transaction behind it, or *melqētum*, a type of loan. According to the Edict of Ammi-ṣaduqa §7, it is a type of loan which, like *ḫubullum*, is subject to annulment by a royal debt-release decree. Otherwise, it is seldom attested, and its nature is not clear. It could relate to the type of transaction recorded in VAS 8 86, but cf. our remarks on *tadmiqtum* in n. 10 above.

13 Lines 20-25: "As for the one shekel of sealed silver that you gave me, if A and B declare/order (reading *i-qá-bu-ma*), I will pay one shekel of silver." Notwithstanding

According to Zaccagnini's analysis (1996: 106-7), payment a) does not belong to the transaction that is the subject of CT 6 34b, while according to Dombradi (2000: 61), it is payment c) that does not belong. We see no good reason to exclude either. It is true that we cannot identify the parties in payments a) and c), nor are we told their connection with the litigants, nor the nature of the contingency in c). None of this means that they were not interrelated. It should be enough that they are part of D1's statement before witnesses in a record of litigation. Methodologically, we must assume that all the matters in this document relate to the same claim, unless we have evidence to the contrary. The fact that one payment would not fit a presupposed calculation is no such evidence.

On the face of it, then, the document tells us that:

a) D1 and D2 have received one shekel each from C;
b) if D2 fails to acknowledge and pay his shekel *ša* ŠU-TI-A, then D1 must pay two shekels;
c) D1 agrees to pay C in total a maximum of four shekels (two that he admits to owing directly and two on the contingency of D2's default).

The payments in this document thus fit the pattern of a loan with a two-fold penalty. The only objection might be that D2 appears to owe only one shekel, but we do not know what payment terms lie behind the enigmatic qualifying phrase *ša* ŠU-TI-A (literally, "of receipt").

The Second Claim

The problem with D1's convoluted offer is that it does not include any immediate payment. C is referred in all cases to third parties. He indeed appears to have obtained nothing, for his next move is to turn to D2, confronting him with D1's statement, albeit formulated in somewhat different terms. According to CT 6 34b (lines 12-24), C declares:

Dombradi's collation, her reading is admittedly speculative. Our own collation did not resolve the problem: the final sign is over-written by the date formula. We agree with Dombradi, contra Zaccagnini, that B (Sin-iddinam) is not identical with D1.

> "I seized your partner D1, and he said: 'If D2 acknowledges it, he will give you one shekel of silver *mitḫāršu*, and I will give you one shekel of silver *mitḫāršu*. If he does not acknowledge it to you, I will give you two shekels of silver *mitḫāršu*.

Earlier commentators (e.g., Landsberger 1924: 24-25) interpreted the offer in a straightforward way: each debtor is to pay one shekel of the debt of two shekels; but if the one defaults, then the other is responsible for the whole debt. Obvious as this solution may seem, on our reconstruction of the contract, it does not make commercial sense, since the creditor only gets back his capital, with no provision for interest or other compensation for being kept out of his money—not to mention any penalty for a blatant failure to perform. In principle, the purpose of a contractual remedy is to fulfill the injured party's legitimate expectations, not to return him to the *status quo ante*. In this case, expectations are particularly important, since the debtors had a duty to create value added.

Aside from the rationale of the claim, the premise of repayment *in simplum* ignores two factors of a formal nature. They are D1's statement in CT 4 6a, discussed above, and the repeated use of the term *mitḫāršu*, which would seem to be superfluous.

The basic meaning of *mitḫārum* is "of equal amount" (*CAD* M/2 137, meaning 1c). Landsberger (1924: 24) understood it in this text as indicating the proportionate share of each partner—". . . den (auf ihn/mich entfallenden) Teil(?) davon."[14] As Dombradi (2000: 55) points out, however, since the term also refers to the two shekels, it cannot mean an equal share. Furthermore, as Zaccagnini (1996: 106 n. 53) notes, Landsberger's interpretation forces him into the inaccuracy of translating the second *mitḫāršu* as "my share."

Dombradi (2000: 55-59) argues instead that *mitḫāršu*, "its equivalent" ("sein Gegenwert"), in all instances refers to the value of the ram that the partners failed to supply.[15] The difficulty with this interpretation is that the same ram would then be worth one shekel in two instances and two shekels in the third. (In fact, if the creditor is to realize any profit, the ram

14 Likewise, Leemans (1991: 318) explained *mitḫāršu* here as "sa quote-part," and cf. Schorr (1913: 316): "seinem Teile entsprechend."

15 Following an informal suggestion of C. Wilcke.

would have to be worth more). The two instances where the ram appears to be only one shekel are explained as follows: "Das geforderte Silber ist sein (anteiliges, weil es 2 Schuldner sind) 'Entsprechendes,' i.e. sein Gegenwert."[16] The qualifying word "anteiliges," however, reintroduces the concept of proportional share which Dombradi rightly rejects. It does not become more acceptable by being implied in one case and not in another. Either the term refers to the value of the ram (2 shekels), or it refers to the value of a partner's obligation (1 shekel).

Zaccagnini (1996: 105) translates the three contingencies in the passage: "he will give you the *mitḫārum* of 1 shekel; . . . I myself will give you the *mitḫārum* of 1 shekel; . . . I myself will give you the *mitḫārum* of 2 shekels." In all instances, therefore, he interprets the term as the equivalent of the sum mentioned immediately beforehand, that is, a doubling of the sum to represent the penalty.[17] It seems to us that this is the preferable interpretation, because, on the one hand, it can properly apply to both sums and, on the other, the total payable will be four shekels, as in CT 4 6a.

The Final Offer

D2's reply to C's claim is as follows (CT 6 34b, lines 25-29): "D1 will pay you your two shekels. I will bring you D1. He owes me ten shekels; if I do not bring him, I will pay the *mitḫārum*."

16 Citing Wilcke's communication (Dombradi 2000: 57 n. 67). This interpretation makes not only the possessive suffix *-šu* with *mitḫārum* refer to the ram but also the accusative suffix in line 15: "if he acknowledges it (i.e., the ram)." The materiality of this translation, however, is more apparent than real. One can do many material things with a ram, but acknowledging it is not one of them. What is being acknowledged is of course an abstract element—the contractual obligation that relates to the ram. Wilcke admits as much when he translates, "Den Schafbock, d. h. die Verpflichtung ihn zu liefern, wird Etel-pi-Sin bestätigen." Even more so, Dombradi's rendering (2000: 42) ". . . ihn (= den Schaf[bock], sc. die Verbindlichkeit betreffs eines Schafbocks)." Since the real subject of *-šu* is the contractual obligation, mention of the ram is in fact otiose.

17 Dombradi's objection (2000: 56 n. 63) to this construction is an exercise in grammatical determinism. We would take the phrase "x, its *mitḫārum* . . ." as a straightforward *casus pendens*: "as regards one shekel of silver, I will pay its *m*." Note that the word order in two of the three instances (lines 18 and 21) is: x – pronoun – its *m*. The resulting meaning is the same as in Zaccagnini's translation.

D2 could not reasonably argue that D1 owed the whole of the debt. Rather, he is tacitly accepting his share of the debt, that is, one shekel plus one shekel penalty, while trying to avoid paying the whole four shekels. He therefore offers to stand surety for D1's appearance, a tactic that will at least buy time. Should he produce D1, C will still have the task to extract the money from him—that which he signally failed to do at their previous encounter, in spite of D1's effusive declarations of willingness to pay all.

Only if he fails to produce D1 will D2 agree to pay the *mitḫārum*, meaning the equivalent of the two shekels already paid by him (or at least acknowledged by him as his responsibility). Even then, there is a hint that payment will not proceed smoothly: D2 talks of taking the funds from D1's assets, on the basis of what D1 owes on their partnership account. Execution upon D1's assets might be a long drawn-out procedure, delaying final settlement for C even further.

Conclusions

The contract between the creditor, Erib-Sin, and the two partners, Etel-pi-Sin and Sin-iddinam, is of a type only rarely attested in writing. It may have belonged to the large class of contracts made informally, possibly between persons with a long-standing business relationship, that relied on part performance (here the advancing of a loan) to found liability. The fact that in litigation the question arose whether the debtors would acknowledge the debt points to the lack of a formal procedure. The other main issue would then be what terms, express or implied, were included in the contract.

The sum of four shekels payable in CT 4 6a and the use of the term *mitḫārum* in CT 6 34b attest to the presence of a double-payment penalty clause, while the peregrinations of the frustrated creditor testify unequivocally to the absence of a joint liability clause. Otherwise, he could have claimed the full four shekels from either of his debtors without reference to the other debtor's share of liability. Instead, the law appears to have regarded the loan as given severally to each of the debtors.[18] The creditor

18 This is certainly the thrust of D1's argument in CT 4 6a, lines 20-25, when he talks about "one shekel . . . that you gave me."

was thus forced to approach each debtor separately for his share and to rely on their partnership contract to make each liable for the other's debt. Partnership made each a surety for the other, but suretyship was still a residual obligation, which could be invoked only upon default by the principle debtor.

The creditor's first claim, against D1, proved to be a failure. D1 declared himself willing to pay his share, but his assets just happened to be "tied up" with third parties, and C apparently was unable to extract them. D1 also declared himself willing to pay D2's share, but only on default by D2.

The creditor then sued D2, perhaps with more success, since D2 appears at least not to have contested his share of the obligation. He temporized, however, on D1's share, offering himself only as surety for D1's appearance in court.

Whether the creditor ultimately recovered the whole sum owed him is not known, since the two tablets record only interlocutory proceedings. The fact that those tablets remained in the archive, however, intimates that he was no more successful than in his previous efforts.

7

Social Justice and Creative Jurisprudence in Late Bronze Age Syria

Abstract

The private legal documents from Emar and its vicinity (late 14th to early 12th centuries B.C.E.) show evidence of creative jurisprudence in their attempts to reconcile the wishes of the parties with the norms of general law imposed by the courts, in particular the principles of social justice. Two areas are examined: i) contracts of sale and their relationship with the right of redemption by an impoverished seller; ii) testaments and their relationship with the customary status of women within the family.

The legal texts from Emar and its vicinity (late 14th to early 12th centuries B.C.E.) provide us with great insight not only into the law of Late Bronze Age Syria but also into deeper aspects of the cuneiform legal tradition. The scribes of Emar, writing in Akkadian, drew upon the inheritance of Mesopotamian law, but at the same time their documents contain much phraseology that is unique or that is shared only by their close contemporaries. Through the interaction of these two influences, the local and the external, in the legal documents, we can perceive something of their jurisprudence, of the means by which they sought to reconcile through law conflicting socioeconomic interests within their society and the competing demands of ethics and pragmatism.

It was W. Leemans who made the first steps towards a juridical analysis of the Emar material, in an article published in this journal (Leemans 1988). This study acknowledges its indebtedness to his pioneering work.

* Originally published in *Journal of the Economic and Social History of the Orient* 44 (2001): 22-43.

We will consider two aspects of Emar jurisprudence: the influence of principles of social justice on the formulation of certain contracts of sale, and the effect of testamentary dispositions on the role of women in the family.

Contractual Freedom and Social Justice

Sale of Land

Two land sale documents, Arnaud *Textes syriens* 53 and 65, are remarkable for their similarity to each other and for their atypical character in the Emar corpus.[1]

Arnaud *Textes syriens* 53

1. ^{m}*ia-'-za-nu* DUMU *šu-ši-a*-E$_2$-^{d}*iš*$_8$*-tár*
2. E$_2$ *a-bi-šu a-na* ^{m}*ki-it-ta*
3. DUMU *la-al-i a-na* 20 GIN$_2$ KU$_3$.BABBAR.MEŠ
4. *a-na* ŠAM$_3$ *id-din šum-ma*
5. *ur-ra-am še-ra-am* ^{m}*ki-it-ta*
6. *i-qáb-bi ma-a* E$_2$*-ka ul*
7. *a-la-qì-mi a-na* KU$_3$.BABBAR.MEŠ*-šu*
8. ŠU*-šú li-i-li ù šum-ma*
9. ^{m}*ia-'-za-nu i-qàb-bi ma-a*
10. E$_2$*-ia te-er-ra-am-mi*
11. KU$_3$.BABBAR.MEŠ TEŠ$_2$.BI *a-na*
12. ^{m}*ki-it-ta i-na-din*
13. E$_2$*-šu lil-qì*

14-22. Seals (2) and witnesses (7)
lower edge
23. *ù qa-ta-ti-ša* E$_2$ *an-ni-i*

1 Both are Syro-Hittite style texts, but they do not share the samre parties or witnesses. Arnaud *Textes syriens* 53 was written by the scribe Belu-malik, but unfortunately the name of the scribe is not given in Arnaud *Textes syriens* 65. On the two different scribal schools at Emar, Syro-Hittite and Syrian, see Wilcke 1992a. Despite considerable differences in formulation, we have been unable to detect any differences of substantive law in the documents drafted by the two schools.

24. A.ŠA$_3$.MEŠ-*šu i-na* EDIN.NA
25. ^{m}*ki-it-ta i-ṣa-bat*

1-4 Ia'zanu, son of Šuršia-bit-Aštarti has sold the house of his father to Kitta, son of Lalu, for 20 shekels of silver.
4-8 If in the future, Kitta syas: "I do not take your house," he shall forfeit his silver.
8-13 And if Ia'zanu says: "Return my house to me," he shall pay Kitta the silver, the equivalent, and he may take his house.
14-22 (Seals and witnesses.)
23-25 And Kitta will seize his fields in the country as a pledge for that land.

Arnaud *Textes syriens* 65

1. ^{f}*a-da-ma*-DINGIR-*lì* DAM ^{m}*a-bi-ka-pí* DUMU *ga-a-ki*
2. *it-ti* ^{fd}KUR-*ni-wa-ri ù it-ti* ^{f}*im-mi*
3. ^{f}*ḫa-ab-ú ù it-ti* ^{f}*a-bi-ú* 4 DUMU.MEŠ *a-bi-ka-pí*
4. E$_2$-*tu*$_4$ *ša* ^{m}*a-bi-šu-nu a-na* ^{m}EN.GAL
5. *ù* ^{m}*tu-ú-tu* 2 DUMU.MEŠ ^{m}IR$_3$-DINGIR.MEŠ
6. *a-na* 45 GIN$_2$ KU$_3$.BABBAR.MEŠ *a-na* MU.MEŠ^{ti} *dan-na-ti*
7. *a-na* ŠAM$_3$.<TIL>.LA^{àm} *it-ta-an-nu-ú*
8. *ur-ra-am še-ra-am šum-ma* DUMU.MEŠ ^{m}*a-bi-ka-pí*
9. ^{ki}*er-ṣe-tu*$_4$ *iš-tu* ŠU ^{m}EN.GAL
10. *ù* ^{m}*tu-ú-tù i-le-eq-qu-ú*
11. 90 GIN$_2$ KU$_3$.BABBAR.MEŠ TEŠ$_2$.BI *a-na* ^{m}EN.GAL
12. *ù* ^{m}*tu-ú-tù li-id-<<id>>din-ma*
13. ^{ki}*er-ṣe-tu*$_4$ *šu-nu lil-qu-ú*

---

14. *ú šum-ma* EN.GAL *ù* ^{m}*tu-ú-tù a-na* 4 DUMU.MEŠ *a-bi-ka-pí*
15. *a-kán-na i-qáb-bi ma-a* E$_2$-*ku-nu la-a a-la-qì-mi*
16. *a-na* KU$_3$.BABBAR.MEŠ NU.TUKU

---

17. *a-nu-ma* KU$_3$.BABBAR.MEŠ ŠAM$_3$ E$_2$^{tu4} *a-na tu-ra*-^{d}KUR
18. DUMU *at-tu-wu e-te-ru-ub*

Seals (3) and witnesses (7)

1-7 Adama-ili, wife of Abi-kapi, son of Gaku, with Dagan-niwari and with Immi, Ḫabu, and with Abi'u, the four children of Abi-kapi, have sold the house of their father for the (full) price to Ba'al-kabar and Tutu, the two sons of Abdi-ili, for 45 shekels of silver in a year of famine.

8-13 In the future, if the children of Abi-kapi will take the land from Ba'al-kabar and Tutu, they may pay Ba'al-kabar and Tutu 90 shekels of silver, the equivalent, and take their land.

14-16 And if Ba'al-kabar and Tutu say to the four children of Abi-kapi as follows: "I do not take your house," they have no claim to the silver.

17-18 Furthermore, the silver, the price of the house, has gone in to Tura-Dagan, son of Attuwu.

The documents share four features:

1. They are formulated *ex latere venditoris*.
2. Neither the dimensions nor the location of the property are given; it is described merely as the house of the seller's father.
3. They contain a redemption clause.
4. They contain a clause penalizing the buyer for revoking the sale.

The first three features make it abundantly clear that the background to these sales is indebtedness. Sales of land at Emar are typically formulated from the buyer's point of view; formulation from the seller's point of view is relatively rare. Most such documents contain a redemption clause and reflect a sale under special conditions—either within the nuclear family (Arnaud *Emar* 6 156; Beckman *Emar* 7; Arnaud *Textes syriens* 81) or due to economic difficulties, such as famine (Arnaud *Emar* 6 82) or insolvency (Arnaud *Emar* 6 123). Sale into slavery was always formulated *ex latere venditoris* and inevitably resulted from debt and impoverishment (see the next section). Description of the land as the "house of the father" emphasizes the fact that the heirs are selling the family estate, which implies the death of the head of household—a common cause of economic distress.[2] In Arnaud *Textes syriens* 65 the sellers are a widow together with her four children, although only the children are mentioned as potential redeemers. They may still have been too young at the time of sale to negotiate for themselves.

Further clauses in the two documents confirm this impression. In Arnaud *Textes syriens* 53:23-25 other lands of the seller are pledged as security. This clause is characteristic of a loan transaction; it is unexpected in a sale document.[3] Arnaud *Textes syriens* 65:17-18 reveals that the purchase price was paid not to the sellers but directly to the sellers' creditor. This arrangement is found in two other sale documents (Arnaud *Emar* 6 15 and Arnaud *Textes syriens* 33), but is more frequent in other types of transactions involving insolvent debtors, where a financier takes over the debtor's property or person in return for paying off his debts (Arnaud *Textes syriens* 78; Arnaud *Emar* 6 121; Beckman *Emar* 10). The financier is either adopted as the debtor's heir or else acquires the debtor as a slave or as an antichretic pledge.

Finally, Arnaud *Textes syriens* 65:6 adds that the sale was made in a year of famine, a notice frequently found in standard sale documents, although this is the only Syro-Hittite style example. Fuller versions refer to a year of war and famine, when the city was besieged and the price of grain was inflated.[4] Although not mentioned in Arnaud *Textes syriens* 53, it may have been the background to that sale also, given the close correlation between the two documents.

Thus it seems clear that the sellers in both cases were parting with family property under pressure of debt and economic hardship caused by the death of the father and a general calamity, possibly the siege of the city

2 Cf. *ASJ* 13 no. 21; Arnaud *Textes syriens* 56, 80.

3 It may be tied to the possibility that the buyer has not yet taken possession of the land sold, but there would seem little rationale in seizing fields outside of town when he could simply seize the property being sold itself. We consider it more likely that the clause served in lieu of a warranty of title, to ensure that the buyer could obtain compensation from the sellers if a third party (namely, another creditor) was able to make good claims against the property sold. Cf. Arnaud *Emar* 6 209.

4 See Zaccagnini 1995: 96-100. The notices may have referred to more than one such emergency.

by "Hurrian" troops.[5] It is against this background that we must interpret the fourth, and most curious, feature of these two contracts—the clause penalizing the buyer for revoking the sale.

To our knowledge this clause is absolutely unique in the cuneiform record. It provides that the buyer will forfeit his payment if in the future he declares "I do not take (your) house."[6] This is not the same as a penalty for repudiating the contract, as is frequently found in cuneiform documents of sale. The clause assumes that the buyer could assert a right to relinquish the property bought and receive back his purchase price. No such right, however, is recognized anywhere else in the ancient Near East. On the contrary, it would contradict the purpose of a contract of sale. A contract is by its nature designed to freeze the process of bargaining at a given point, so that the parties can no longer change their minds. The purpose of a contract of sale is to effect the permanent transfer of ownership in certain property in return for the permanent transfer of the purchase price. Once these two actions have been completed, the results should be irreversible. In this case, the verb "I do not take" might suggest that the buyer may not yet have taken possession of the property. Although it explains why he might be tempted to withdraw, it would make no difference in law. The price has definitely been paid, since the penalty is that it be irrecoverable. In all ancient Near Eastern legal systems, full payment of the price was the point at which ownership of land passes.[7] The fact that the buyer had not yet taken possession of the property would give him no right in law to withdraw from the contract.

There was, however, one legal exception to this principle of finality, and that was the right of redemption. The concept of redemption derives

5 Arnaud *Emar* 6 42 and *ASJ* 12 no. 7 (cf. Arnaud *Textes syriens* 25). See Astour 1996; Skaist 1998.

6 The nearest equivalent is CT 45 60, an Old Babylonian litigation record in which one party to an exchange of land later says (lines 21-22): "(the land) which I took in exchange I do not take; it is returned to you" (*ša ana puḫḫim elqû ul eleqqe turrakkum*). The case is not comparable, however, as the statement is not a contractual clause.

7 That is why payment of the price is always present in the operative section of sale documents, from the Fara period on (see Steinkeller 1989: 22-29). It is also why at Ugarit, the local verb *ṣamata* meaning "to pass (of ownership)" glosses the logogram ŠAM$_3$.TIL.LA "full price." On this point, see Westbrook 1991b: 90-117, esp. 114-15; and cf. Huehnergard 1989: 68. For Emar, cf. *ASJ* 12 no. 11.

from the law of pledge, which is its natural setting. In a contract of loan secured by a pledge, the creditor and debtor each transfer property to the other, but the contract foresees that the transfer will be reversed: the debtor will repay the loan (plus interest, if applicable) and the creditor will return the pledge. The principle of reversibility is the very essence of the contract.

In many ancient Near Eastern systems, however, the right to redeem appears also in the law of sale. In that context, it is an unnatural extension of the principle, for it allows the seller to do what it was earlier suggested the buyer could not, namely, to overturn the principle of irrevocable property transfer that is the whole purpose of the contract.

The rationale of this extraordinary right lies in the realm of social justice. It was designed to correct the injustice that could be caused when family property—ancestral land or members of the family—was sold under pressure of economic hardship, in particular, debt. Where the sale amounted in practice to the forfeiture of a pledge securing a loan, the right of redemption restored the real underlying nature of the transaction, treating the price as a loan and the property sold as a pledge, which might thus be recovered upon repayment of the original purchase price (Westbrook 1991b; Veenhof 1999). The right of redemption was just one of the measures of social justice that ancient Near Eastern kings were obliged to impose as part of their religious duties. According to an Old Assyrian decree granting a special right of redemption for family homes, it was given by the "grace of (the god) Assur to his city" (*ennan ālišu*: Veenhof 1999: 600, 603). Lev 25:1-2, 24 attributes it to the command of the god of Israel. It is not surprising then, that the right should appear in ancient Near Eastern law codes. Nonetheless, the provisions of the codes are careful to surround the right with restrictions—such is the potential for economic disruption in this unnatural encroachment upon contractual freedom. All the codes that provide for redemption confine it to circumstances of impoverishment and insolvency, and individual codes add different restrictions to its applicability: certain classes of property (land and family members sold as slaves), certain beneficiaries (the seller himself), and certain conditions, e.g., when the buyer decides to resell or within one year of sale for urban land.[8] The background to all these different rules was, we

8 See CE 39, CH 119, and Lev 25:25-26, 29-30.

suggest, the local application of a generally acknowledged principle, through ad hoc decrees, precedent, and a residual discretion in the ruler and his courts to intervene against inequitable bargains.[9] Naturally, the parameters of that discretion would differ between individual jurisdictions.

Its appearance as a contractual clause is more surprising. This is the case with a few slave and land sales from Emar, among them the two documents under discussion.[10]

Were buyers, under orders from their rulers, dutifully inserting the rules of social justice lock, stock, and barrel into their contracts? It would not appear so. In Arnaud *Textes syriens* 65:8-11, the redemption payment is set at 90 shekels, double the purchase price, and in Arnaud *Textes syriens* 53:8-13 as the "equivalent" (TEŠ$_2$.BI = *mitḫaris*) which, as Zaccagnini has shown, means the same, i.e., the price plus its equivalent.[11] Double payment is in fact standard in Emar land sale redemption clauses.[12] At that level, it is more akin to a penalty clause in the buyer's favor.

9 Decrees were sometimes promulgated allowing limited redemption of property sold previously: see the discussion in Veenhof 1999 of the decrees from Assur and Sippar. Judicial decisions would be needed in individual cases on what was a fair price and whether special local criteria for the applicability of the right had been met.

10 There are also scattered examples from other periods. Note especially an Old Babylonian land sale from Khafaji (*JCS* 9 96 no. 82), stipulating that the seller must redeem with his own funds, which has possible parallels at Emar in Arnaud *Emar* 6 121:13-14 and Arnaud *Textes syriens* 25:10-17. For the Old Assyrian period, see Hengstl 1987; for the Neo-Babylonian period, see Oppenheim 1955.

11 Zaccagnini (1996) rejects the earlier accepted interpretation of this phrase as meaning simple payment (also assumed by us in Westbrook 1991b: 14-16). A recent study by E. Dombradi (2000) questions Zaccagnini's conclusions for the Old Babylonian period, interpreting the phrase as simple payment in the one significant source: CT 6 34b. We do not find Dombradi's interpretation of that document compelling, but a detailed discussion would be outside the bounds of the present article. However, in the same article Dombradi announces a forthcoming study with the same results for the Emar texts. As that study is regrettably not available to us at this time, our own conclusions in what follows, insofar as they are based on our present understanding of the phrase, must be regarded as provisional. Nonetheless, we would note that the striking parallelism of TEŠ$_2$.BI and a numerical double in these two documents, and the logic of the reciprocal penalty clauses within each document, seems to us very strong evidence of the correctness of Zaccagnini's interpretation of the use of the phrase at Emar.

12 The term redeem (*ša ipaṭṭar*: *AuOr* 5 9) is used interchangeably in these clauses with other terms for claim: *ša ibaqqar*(*u*): Arnaud *Emar* 6 90, 122, 123; *mannummê* . . .

Leemans takes the opposite view, that redemption at Emar was purely a creature of contract, brought into existence only when bargained for. This contractual stipulation was entirely different in character from the right of redemption found in the law codes (Leemans 1988: 229-32). Leemans cites Hengstl's analysis of comparable clauses that appear in a small number of Old Assyrian slave sales. According to Hengstl, the purpose of those transactions was (in the light of later Greek and Roman models) to provide a pledge by way of interim security for a creditor (Hengstl 1987: 110-11). That hypothesis seems to us unlikely. From the buyer's point of view, outright purchase encumbered by a right of redemption would suggest not that he anticipated repayment, but rather that he had despaired of it. Indeed, for an interim measure designed to ensure repayment, it is remarkable (as Hengstl himself notes) that repayment lies at the discretion of the seller/debtor.

A different approach would be to argue that the transaction was an outright sale, but that the double payment was truly a penalty, in the buyer's interest, to deter any future claims on the property. In this role, however, the clause is a little half-hearted. Unlike a real penalty clause, it does not block redemption altogether or interpose an impossible payment. On the contrary, it admits that if the sum is paid, the redeemer will in fact acquire ownership.[13] It is not that harsher terms are unknown to the Emar sale documents. Many Syro-Hittite style documents totally exclude the possibility of reopening the sale, stating that "this tablet will defeat" any claimant, even one who would redeem (*ša ipaṭṭar*: Beckman *Emar* 80). Only one Syrian style tablet, Arnaud *Textes syriens* 82, mentions redemption at all; otherwise they impose huge fines on anyone raising a claim.

Could the (relative) weakness of the clause indicate that it was inserted for the benefit of the seller? In a context of free bargaining this seems equally unlikely. The documents frequently stress the economic difficulties of the sellers, most of whom were insolvent, some on the brink of

---

ibaqqaru: Beckman *Emar* 12, Arnaud *Textes syriens* 33; *ša iraggum*: Arnaud *Textes syriens* 66; *mannummê bēl dinīšu . . . illa*: Arnaud *Textes syriens* 68; seller . . . *iraggum*: Arnaud *Textes syriens* 64.

13 In the case of the slave sales, discussed in the next section, a few are redeemable at par, e.g., *ASJ* 13 no. 18.

starvation. There would seem to be no motivation for a buyer to accord any right of redemption whatsoever.

In summary, the redemption clause in the Emar land sale documents defies easy characterization. It can be classified neither as a simple reflex of the social justice measure found in the law codes nor as the untrammeled initiative of a party to a free market transaction, whether the buyer or the seller. Its relationship to both is more subtle, as a broader investigation of its use at Emar shows.

The double-price redemption clause at Emar is not only found in contracts of sale. It appears in other transactions involving debt, and where it does so, it emerges that the redeemer did have a right to redeem at par which he had forfeited, and for good reason. The contract of personal antichretic pledge at Emar has in its basic form no minimum period of service before redemption, as for example is found in *tidennūtu* contracts at Nuzi.[14] There is, however, a variant form: in return for a minimum period of service, namely, the lifetime of the creditor and his spouse, the creditor forgives part or all of the debt (Arnaud *Emar* 6 16, 117). The penalty for premature redemption by the debtor is repayment of the principal, with a doubling only of the forgiven portion of the debt. It is a fair bargain, particularly since it is balanced by forfeiture of the debt by the creditor if he demands repayment prematurely. The same principle is applied to straightforward debt slavery in Arnaud *Emar* 6 205: on the death of the debtor, the creditor took his two children as slaves, but before a public tribunal offered their uncles the opportunity to redeem them for the value of the debt. The uncles refused, whereupon the creditor confirmed the children as his slaves, with the proviso that anyone in the future who claimed to redeem them would have to pay two slaves for one.

Analogous considerations seem to underlie the opposite case, namely, the few land sale contracts where redemption is allowed at the original selling price. In Arnaud *Textes syriens* 82, where the owner's brother in his absence bought his land in return for paying his debts, the owner will be allowed on his return to redeem at par. Their other brothers are excluded altogether by a prohibitive penalty. In Arnaud *Emar* 6 123, an insolvent debtor who sold his land directly to his creditors for the exact sum owing

14 *ASJ* 10 no. A; Arnaud *Emar* 6 77; *ASJ* 13 no. 35. For Nuzi, see, e.g., Eichler 1973: 134, no. 43. On antichretic personal pledge see the next section.

(instead of to a financier who would then pay off his creditors, as is usual), may redeem at par, albeit within a limited time, while any other claimant must pay double.[15]

It is worth comparing two other cases. In Arnaud *Textes syriens* 81, where a brother sells to his sister, he can reclaim only upon payment of four-fold the original amount. It is clearly she who is regarded as the weaker party, in need of protection. In Arnaud *Emar* 6 115, two brothers sell off family land in order to pay the family debts. Should the third brother turn up and claim the property, he must pay double. It would appear that he is being penalized for his absence during a family crisis, but the assumption seems to be that he would otherwise be entitled to redeem at par.

Accordingly, it is reasonable to suppose that the rules of social justice at Emar were a hidden hand, setting the parameters within which a fair bargain could be struck, so as to avoid interference by the courts. In the case of those land sales that contained a redemption clause, double the purchase price was considered fair, due to circumstances that the parties were well aware of but that are not usually stated in the text.

The same hidden hand may account for the curious phenomenon of statements against interest in the sale documents. Documents recording the sale of property were drafted for the buyer's benefit, to provide him with proof of title. Matters against his interest would be recorded only if the seller were strong enough to insist on them or if they were necessary to ensure the legal validity of the transaction. One such element is the frequent statement that the sale took place in a year of famine. In spite of their pathetic appeal, such references were, in our opinion, intended to

15 Lines 10-16: *šúm-ma ur-ra-am še-ra-am* ^{m}ZU-*ba-la a-du* U$_4$.1.MU.KÁM KU$_3$.BABBAR.MEŠ 30 GIN$_2$ KU$_3$.BABBAR *ša-a-šu a-na* EN.MEŠ-*šu i-na-din* é-*šu lil-qí ia-nu-ma-a* U$_4$.2.MU.KÁM *e-ti-qa ša i-na* EGIR U$_4$-*mi* E$_2^{tam}$ *ša-a-šu i-pa-qa-ru* KU$_3$.BABBAR.MEŠ TE$_2$Š.BI *li-din-ma* E$_2$-*šu lil-qí*. The difficult phrase *a-du* U$_4$.1.MU.KÁM . . . U$_4$.2.MU.KÁM *e-ti-qa* is translated by Arnaud in his edition (1986: 131) "en un seul jour . . . deux jours ayant passé" and by Zaccagnini (1996: 93) "within the term of one year . . . (the term that marks the beginning of) the second year." Neither can be conclusively deduced from the word order. On the first interpretation, the seller has a day's grace to exercise his option to the exclusion of another claimant's offer; on the second (which seems to us more likely), the seller has an exclusive option for one year, after which other claimants may buy.

justify harsher terms in the contract than the seller would have been permitted in normal times. As a matter of public policy, it might be deemed advisable to relax the rules of social justice during a siege or similar national catastrophe, in order to encourage those with sufficient financial means to use their resources to keep their fellow citizens alive. The phrase was thus an argument to a potential interfering court that the contract was still valid.

It is against this background that we may interpret the unique clause in the two contracts under discussion barring reversibility by the buyer. It reveals that the sellers in these cases had an interest in the irreversibility of the whole transaction.

Buying houses in a year of famine, especially a famine occasioned by war, is a speculative operation. The land is not naturally productive, and if the war continues, the seller may be unable to realize his investment by leasing or reselling the house.[16] The danger for the Emar sellers was that the buyers might be tempted to turn the weapon of social justice against them, claiming that the house was in reality a pledge and the sale price a loan. Under those circumstances the buyers could return their unprofitable investment and still have a claim for their money, with the possibility of seizing other assets of the sellers or their persons.[17]

The clauses of the two contracts were thus designed to achieve a balance: the sellers are penalized with a double redemption payment but a further provision protects them from any attempt by the buyers to foist redemption upon them. The message to the courts was that although the parties were well aware that the land was eminently redeemable, it was in the interests of social justice that the underlying transaction not be treated as a redeemable pledge.

16 A graphic parallel is found in Jer 32:6-15, when in the midst of the Babylonian siege of Jerusalem, his cousin Hannama'el asks him to purchase a plot of land from him, in Jeremiah's capacity as heir and potential redeemer. Jeremiah agrees to do so, confidently predicting that he will be able to recoup his investment: "For thus says the LORD of Hosts, God of Israel, 'Houses and fields and vineyards will again be bought in this land.'" Of course, Jeremiah was acting altruistically on behalf of a relative, whereas the buyers at Emar were concerned only with the profit motive.

17 As we have seen, the seller in Arnaud *Textes syriens* 53 in fact had other land, which he offered as security to the seller (lines 23-25).

Sale into Slavery

When free persons entered into slavery, it was by reason of debt or famine or both (Zaccagnini 1995: 92-105). Some documents refer to a general calamity, e.g., "in the year of famine when three seah of barley cost one shekel of silver" (*ASJ* 13 no. 37), "in the year when enemy troops besieged the city and one seah of barley cost one shekel of silver" (Arnaud *Textes syriens* 25). Others refer to personal disaster, e.g., that "her creditors seized her and she could not pay them" (*ASJ* 13 no. 36). A common practice was for a financier to pay off the various creditors in return for the debtor becoming his slave (Arnaud *Emar* 6 121, 215).

Where a person gave a relative into slavery, the transaction was formulated as a straightforward sale *ex latere venditoris* "for x shekels of silver, the full price, of their own free will, into the slavery of X" (*AuOr* 5 11: *a-na* 70 GIN$_2$ KU$_3$.BABBAR.MEŠ ŠAM$_3$.TIL.LA *iš-tu* SAG.DU-*šú-nu-ma a-na* IR$_3$.MEŠ *ša* X).[18] Where self-enslavement was involved, the debtor was said to have "entered into his (= creditor's) slavery" (Arnaud *Emar* 6 121: *a-na* IR$_3$-*ut-ti-šú e-te-ru-ub*). Legally, the effect was the same, as demonstrated by Arnaud *Textes syriens* 44, where the debtor "entered as a slave for X for 20 shekels of silver, the full price."[19]

About half the relevant documents contain a special phrase which is the particular object of our discussion: "dead or alive (BA.UG$_6$ TIL.LA), X (= slave) is his (= purchaser's) slave."[20] For example, Arnaud *Emar* 6 83 reads:[21]

> A gave B, his unweaned daughter, for 9 (shekels of) silver, [the full price, in a] year of famine [in slavery] of her own free will to X.

18 Debtors sold their wives (*ASJ* 13 no. 18), grandchildren (Arnaud *Emar* 6 7), brother (with his wife and child; *AuOr* 5 11), sister-in-law (Arnaud *Emar* 6 118), daughter-in-law (*AuOr* 5 12), nephews (Arnaud *Emar* 6 205) and niece (Arnaud *Textes syriens* 52).

19 All the enslavement documents but one are Syro-Hittite. The one Syrian style document, *ASJ* 13 no. 18, a slave sale, does not differ in formulation or substance.

20 Arnaud *Emar* 6 7, 83, 121, 205; *AuOr* 5 11; *ASJ* 13 nos. 18, 36; Sigrist *Kutscher Mem. Vol.* no. 1; Arnaud *Textes syriens* 26, 44.

21 Restoration of the broken parts of the tablet is assured on the basis of standard clauses in parallel texts.

[Dead or ali]ve, she is the slave of X [and] X is clear.

If in the future A says to X, "Return my daughter to me and take [your silver]," he shall give 2 persons [. . .] and take the slave.

(Seals and witnesses.)

The legal purpose of this clause is not immediately apparent. A literal reading would suggest that the corpse of the slave is to remain the property of the purchaser. What benefit the purchaser would derive from such a gruesome arrangement is unclear. To our knowledge, there is nothing in the relatively well-documented cultic practices of Emar that would point to some religious or symbolic significance.

Another possibility is that it refers to a problem discussed by various law codes: the potential penal liability of a slave owner should his debt-slave die due to maltreatment (CE 23-24; CH 115-116; Exod 21:20-21). The purpose of the clause would then be to establish that the purchaser is free of liability in any circumstances. If the formulation seems unsuitable, it may be recalled that Exod 21:21 excuses liability on grounds that can be translated "for he is his silver" (*ky kspw hw'*). In Arnaud *Emar* 6 83, it is to be noted, the phrase is followed by the statement "[and] X is clear" (*za-a-ku*).

Nevertheless, we would reject this interpretation as too far-fetched. There would seem to be no rationale for this particular contingency to be included: the Emar contracts are otherwise exclusively concerned with economic interests. It is inherently unlikely that a slave owner could exclude liability for homicide by a contractual clause or would seek to do so. From a formal point of view, where the scribe has drawn a separating line across the tablet in relation to this clause, it invariably appears after the clause (as in the example of Arnaud *Emar* 6 83 above). By that means, this clause is associated with the operational clauses of the contract, which it concludes, and is separated from the final clauses, such as redemption, which deal with contingencies.[22] The significance of the *zakû* clause in

22 In some cases there is no line between the terms, only a line separating the terms from the witness list (Arnaud *Emar* 6 205; *AuOr* 5 11). True (but not invalidating) exceptions are Arnaud *Emar* 6 121, where a line is drawn only after the redemption clause,

Arnaud *Emar* 6 83 does remain to be explained, and we will return to it below.

In our view, this phrase performs a similar function to the clause in the land sale documents discussed above, which barred the seller from reversing the sale. It operates in that same sphere of ambiguity between pledge and sale that we have seen arise from the existence of the right of redemption. Some, but not all, of these slave sale contracts contain a redemption clause, the terms of which vary from simple to multiple payments. As we have seen, however, redemption was an underlying right that was only regulated in part by contractual terms. The existence of principles of social justice in the background must be presumed all the more so in the case of debt slavery, which involved family members or the debtor himself.

The most common form of pledge of persons, found throughout the cuneiform record, was antichretic pledge. The debtor gave the creditor a member of his household or himself in pledge, and the work of the pledge for the creditor was deemed to be in lieu of interest on the loan. On repayment of the principal, the pledge was allowed to leave the creditor's employ.

Antichretic pledge at Emar was known as *amēlūtu*. There are few contracts of *amēlūtu* as such, and they are very tersely worded (Arnaud *Emar* 6 77; *ASJ* 13 no. 35), but it is also mentioned in a number of legal documents dealing with its transformation into a different legal relationship (Arnaud *Emar* 6 16 and 117, discussed above, and Arnaud *Textes syriens* 39 and 40) or with termination of the contract. The one example of the latter, *ASJ* 10 no. A, gives a very clear picture of the working of the institution:

> A together with his sons B and C was staying as an antichretic pledge of X for 105 shekels 40 grains of silver. Now A has repaid 40 shekels of silver to X from that sum and has released himself. B and C, and their mother D and their sisters, stay in X's house for 65 shekels and 40 grains of silver. When A pays their silver he will break their tablet. Further, when A was staying in X's house he was freed and went about for 9 months. Accordingly, when A

and Arnaud *Textes syriens* 44, where a line is drawn only before the last clause, detailing payments to the creditors.

> pays his silver, he shall give one son of his to X, and he shall do work for 9 months.

A standard clause not attested at Emar deals with permanent loss of the pledge due to flight, disappearance, or death.[23] These contingencies are met by various provisions, such as calling in the loan, charging interest, or the obligation to provide a replacement pledge. Where the debtor is also the pledge, a clause at Nuzi shifts the burden of the debt onto his heirs, who will be held as pledges in his stead. JEN 302 reads:[24]

> Tablet of antichresis (*tidennūtu*) of A. He has received 20 shekels of gold from the house of B and for the 20 shekels of gold A will stay in the house of B. When he returns the 20 shekels of gold, he may leave.
>
> If A dies, his sons shall pay the 20 shekels of gold, and they may go (where they please).

The point is that the risk of loss of the security lies with the debtor even where it was due to no fault of the pledge or the debtor, as is the case with death of the pledge. In this respect it is distinct from sale, where the death from natural causes of a slave, once purchased, is the loss of the purchaser alone (with some reservations for latent diseases and a few other conditions). It could not found a claim for reimbursement of the purchase price. The distinction is illustrated by another contract of antichresis from Nuzi, JEN 192:[25]

> Thus says A: I owe B two men, and now I have given B one man of the Lullu land as her sl[ave]. If that man acquires a claim, A will clear it and give (him back) to B.
>
> A has given B a second man in antichresis (*tidennūtu*) in lieu of the second man.

23 For the Old Babylonian sources, see Kienast 1978: 92-94, 116-18. For Nuzi, see Eichler 1973: 25-26. Temporary absence from work was penalized by a *per diem* payment.

24 Edition in Eichler 1973: no. 46. Also discussed in Eichler 1973: 28-29.

25 Edition in Eichler 1973: no 21.

> A shall give B a good quality man and he may take (back) his man. If that antichretic pledge dies, disappears, or flees, it is to (the loss of) A that he dies, disappears, or flees

The contract distinguishes between two types of transfer. The first, into outright slavery, transfers full ownership and thereby extinguishes that part of the debt. The transferor must guarantee good title, as is usually the case in sale, but has no obligations beyond that. The second, by way of pledge, leaves the remainder of the debt still owing and therefore leaves open the possibility of redemption. At the same time, an express clause places the burden of loss of the pledge on the transferor. It does not say what his specific obligations are in that eventuality; it is considered sufficient to express it in terms of risk.[26]

In the light of this discussion, the phrase "dead or alive" in the Emar contracts is in our view designed to emphasize that the nature of the transaction is final sale, not pledge. It is placed at the end of the operational clauses to show that, notwithstanding the possibility of redemption, ownership has passed irrevocably as far as the buyer is concerned. As we have seen in the case of family land, it prevents redemption of slaves, which is a measure of social justice, from working in favor of the buyer rather than the seller.

Although expressed in terms of property, its effect is contingent. If the slave should subsequently die, the purchaser cannot claim that he must be replaced because the debt is still outstanding or (in the case of self-sale) that the heirs inherit liability.[27] Sale of the slave amortized the debt altogether: his death was now the erstwhile creditor's risk, in his status as purchaser.

A final matter that remains to be clarified is the term *zakû* in association with the phrase under discussion. Although *zakû* normally means "free of obligations," it can in an appropriate context have a different nuance, as sale contracts from the Late Bronze Age on illustrate.

26 Cf. the expression in Neo-Assyrian antichretic pledge documents: "if he (the pledge) dies or flees, it is upon (UGU) his owner (i.e., the pledger)" (*ARU* 126, 127).

27 At Emar, a person could be a debt-slave while his children and other members of his family remained free: Arnaud *Emar* 6 18. In *AuOr* 5 11, an express clause was considered necessary to secure the slave status of the debt-slave's future children.

Among the standard terms we find a multiple clause used to describe receipt of payment by the seller: *maḫir apil zakû* "he has received, he is paid, he is clear" (or variations on this pattern). The third leg of the claus cannot refer to the end of an obligation of the seller, since he has none in relation to the purchase price. Accordingly, Cardascia translates for the Middle Assyrian documents: "a reçu; il est payé, désintéressé."[28] The term must, like its synonyms, express the notion that the seller is not entitled to anything more, because the transaction is complete. The same nuance, we would suggest, applies very aptly to the word *zakû* in respect of the purchaser in Arnaud *Emar* 6 83.

Female Inheritance

Daughters as Sons

At Emar, as elsewhere, the normal lot of a daughter was to be married off and to receive a dowry, which presumably passed into the control of her husband. Occasionally, however, she could be given an inheritance share exactly like a son. No change in status was necessary, since a daughter was already within the circle of potential, but not necessary, heirs. Thus in *ASJ* 13 no. 23, a daughter is allotted an inheritance share along with her three brothers. After their father's death, the four are to enter upon the estate and divide it among themselves. Arnaud *Textes syriens* 80 records just such a division of the paternal estate, between two daughters.

Nonetheless, the testator might also adopt his daughter into the status of a son when bequeathing her an inheritance share. In Arnaud *Emar* 6 31, the testator had three daughters. He allots the first, a *ḫarimtu*, furniture and female slaves, i.e., typical dowry items. He adopts the second and third as sons (*a-na* DUMU-*ut-ti-ia e-pu-uš-šu-nu*), and gives the second in marriage. Notwithstanding her marriage, she and the third daughter are ultimately to enter and divide the paternal estate. In Arnaud *Emar* 6 181 the daughter is called the "second

28 Cardascia 1980: 517a. Cf. Gurney's translation of the MB phrase *aplū zakû rugummâ ul īšû*: "They are paid, they are quit, they have no claim" (1983: nos. 21, 22).

son," mainly to emphasize the fact that she does not take a firstborn's share, even though it is clear that she is older than the two brothers with whom she is to inherit (it is her duty to marry off her brothers).

Thus far, the pattern is the same as established by Paradise for the Nuzi texts (Paradise 1980: 193-98). He suggests that the testator's motivation for changing his daughter's status to that of son is to protect her from the predations of potential heirs, such as her uncles or stepmother, especially when she is the sole heir (1980: 197). On the other hand, lack of male heirs was not the sole motivation at Emar for instituting a daughter as heir, as *ASJ* 13 no. 23 and Arnaud *Emar* 6 181 show.

A feature that is peculiar to the testaments from Emar and the vicinity is the occasional statement that the testator has made his daughter "male and female" (NITA$_2$ *ù* MUNUS).[29] Some commentators have assumed that this step was necessary to enable a daughter to inherit, but from our discussion above it is clear that this is not so.[30]

In most of the texts, however, the designation is immediately followed by a clause imposing upon the daughter responsibility for the family cult.[31] Most frequently she is called upon to "invoke my gods and my dead" (DINGIR.MEŠ-*ia ù me-te-ia lu-ú-na-ab-bi*).[32] In all cases but one, she is also bequeathed the entire estate.[33] The one exception, Arnaud *Textes syriens* 72, reveals the link between the two. It states that as regards her, the gods belong to the main house. This phrase, as van der Toorn points out, means that it is the main heir who will get

29 *ASJ* 13 nos. 25, 26; *AuOr* 5 13; Fales 1989: no. 66; Beckman *Emar* 15, 85; *Semitica* 46 12-14. In Arnaud *Textes syriens* 72 she is made DUMU.NITA$_2$. Sometimes the status is accorded to another female relative, a sister (*UF* 26 197 no. 9) or a wife (Beckman *Emar* 23).

30 Huehnergard 1985: 429: "The purpose of the legal fiction is to enable a daughter to inherit, something which—apparently—she would not otherwise be able to do." Likewise Ben-Barak 1988: 97.

31 In Arnaud *Textes syriens* 72, a complicated adoption and inheritance document, there are some intervening clauses. It is absent from Fales 1989: no. 66 and Beckman *Emar* 15.

32 *ASJ* 13 nos. 25, 26; *Semitica* 46 12-14; Beckman *Emar* 85: "honor"; *UF* 26 197 no. 9: "inherit." Beckman *Emar* 15 refers indirectly to the duty (see below).

33 In *ASJ* 13 no. 25 there is no direct mention of an inheritance, but the penalty on her younger brothers/sons if they claim their inheritance share during her lifetime shows that she holds the undivided household.

the main house, and with the main house also the gods. Concomitant with his position was the main heir's duty to take care of the household gods. Possession of the main house and responsibility for the domestic cult were thus two sides of the same coin (van der Toorn 1995: 36).

Accordingly, if a testator wished to assign the continuation of the domestic cult to a female member of the household, he needed to fulfil two conditions. First, he needed to make her a male in the eyes of the law, since it would appear that in theory the cult was practiced only by males. Second, he needed to make her the principal heir, or at least heir to the main dwelling, since only the owner of that land could perform the cult. The purpose of the appellation "male and female" was not therefore to provide the daughter with an inheritance but to provide for the continuation of the family cult, the inheritance being only a means to this end.[34] In Arnaud *Emar* 6 181, where the daughter was made "second son," her performance of the cult was thereby excluded. The cult was an obligation; inheritance was a right that gave rise to it.[35]

This device was used by the testator when he had no suitable male heir but also as an insurance policy if he feared that the male line would fail.[36] Thus in Beckman *Emar* 23 the testator grants the status, together with his estate, to his wife in the event that his son dies, and in *Semitica* 46 12-14 to a daughter if her brother should die. If the brother does not die, he is to marry her off, i.e., she is to resume the normal female role. In *UF* 26 197 no. 9, the testator makes his sister male and female prophylactically: if she bears children, she will inherit his gods and dead, which means that she will have to perform the cult. She is already heir to his estate, following a life estate in favor of the testator's wife.

34 At Nuzi, the same concept is expressed in Lacheman and Owen 1981: 386-87, no. 6:27-31, by the testator adopting his three daughters as sons (*ana marūti*) and providing "whoever among my daughters holds my fields and houses and dwells in my house shall serve my gods and my ghosts."

35 Ben-Barak (1998: 94) misleadingly assumes that the cult was a right. Gross (1987: 84) recognizes that the cult was a duty but sees it merely as one of the incidental consequences of giving a daughter "the full status of son," the main purpose being to attach the daughter's children to her father's lineage.

36 In *AuOr* 5 13 the testator states: "I have no male son; I have made ^{f}X my daughter male and female."

Wives as Fathers

In a large number of testaments, the testator makes his widow "father and mother of my house," sometimes adding that she is "head" (*qaqqadu*) of the house.[37] In *ASJ* 13 no. 23 this status is given to her jointly with a daughter, in two documents to a daughter alone (Arnaud *Emar* 6 31; Beckman *Emar* 57), and in Arnaud *Textes syriens* 28 to the testator's mother.[38]

As Kämmerer points out, this status has nothing to do with inheritance. In a few cases, a separate provision gives the "father and mother" the whole estate (Beckman *Emar* 15, 71; Arnaud *Textes syriens* 47; *UF* 26 197 no. 9), and in others a mere share of the inheritance (Beckman *Emar* 57; Arnaud *Textes syriens* 50; *UF* 26 194 no. 8). Nor can it be for the material benefit of support, which is invariably the subject of a separate provision (Kämmerer 1994: 187, 201).

In Kämmerer's view the woman's new status is of a social nature, although it is not altogether clear what he means by this term. Earlier (1994: 190), in discussing Arnaud *Emar* 6 31, where a daughter is given this status, he suggests that it is to give her the high social position of "mother."[39] In *UF* 26 197 no. 9, however, the testator makes his own mother "mother and father." It is hard to see what gain in social standing could have been achieved for the woman. It is in any case unlikely that a legal document would concern itself with according a purely social status. In his main discussion (1994: 201-2), Kämmerer defines the new status in terms of legal capacity (she is *rechtsfähig*), which is further defined as not being legally subordinate to another but having full capacity to conduct transactions (*Geschäftsfähigkeit*). There is, however, no basis for assuming that a widow at Emar, or even a wife, was legally incompetent if her husband had not happened to accord to her this special status. To whom would a widow, for instance, with young children be subordinate?

37 Arnaud *Emar* 6 15, 91, 181, 185; *SMEA* 30 no. 7; *Semitica* 46 12-14; *ASJ* 13 nos. 24, 26, 30; Dalley and Tessier *Iraq* 54 no. 6; Beckman *Emar* 15, 28, 37; Arnaud *Textes syriens* 45, 50, 71; *UF* 26 194 no. 8; *UF* 26 197 no. 9.

38 In Arnaud *Textes syriens* 47 it is given to two women of indeterminate status.

39 Beckman (1996b: 72) also sees the purpose as an "expanded social role" as head of household.

On the other hand, it is equally unlikely that her new status would have given the woman a free hand over the testator's estate.[40] Since in most cases the inheritance shares of the heirs are assigned to them by the same document, to be taken on the widow's death, the widow would have only a life interest in the estate. She could not therefore alienate the property on her own. Nor was management of the estate necessarily the aim. In *ASJ* 13 no. 23 where the testator makes his widow and his daughter (a *qadištu* priestess) joint "mother and father," he also expressly assigns them possession (*ana qāti . . . addin*), which presumably meant management of the property.[41] In no other case is an express power given, and in many of them it would be unrealistic to infer that the testator's intention was to grant management for life to his aging widow, as opposed to his heirs. Such an inference would seem to be excluded in Arnaud *Emar* 6 15 where the widow, notwithstanding her new status, is also granted a right to dwell in the matrimonial home.

In our view, the testator's purpose in assigning the status of "mother and father" is revealed by the penalty clauses used in a few cases. In Arnaud *Textes syriens* 71, any heir who states "my share!" during the widow's lifetime forfeits his share. In *UF* 26 194 no. 8 the heirs are enjoined not to "make a share" (*zitta epēšu*) until the "mother and father's" death, on pain of forfeiture.[42] Normally speaking, on the death of the *de cuius*, his heirs entered the estate and divided it at their own initiative either in accordance with the *de cuius*' testamentary allocations or "according to the custom of the city" (*kīma āli*: *ASJ* 13

40 Instances of a widow as testatrix, cited by Kämmerer 1994: n. 41 (Arnaud *Emar* 6 30, 59 and 128), give no indication that the woman had been made "mother and father" by her late husband; on the contrary, they could equally be cited as evidence that such a disposition was unnecessary.

41 One could argue that this was the purpose also of the express grant of the entire estate to the wife, which is found in a few testaments (*ASJ* 13 no. 22; Beckman *Emar* 15; Arnaud *Textes syriens* 47). We consider that the right being granted was more abstract (see below).

42 Cf. *UF* 26 197 no. 9, where the testator's sister, the sole heir, forfeits the estate if she denies her sister-in-law's status as mother and father and refuses to support her. Also of interest is *ASJ* 13 no. 25, where a testator makes his daughter the mother of his three sons. They are not to claim their inheritance share during their "mother's" lifetime (*zitta ul qabî*). The household is to remain undivided under their sister's nominal ownership.

nos. 23, 25; Arnaud *Emar* 6 201; Beckman *Emar* 8). It could happen, however, that the heirs postponed division, sometimes for years, in which case the paternal household continued to exist in theory, as if the *de cuius* were still alive (Westbrook 1991b: 118-41). By making his wife "mother and father," the testator indicates his desire to keep his household undivided after his death, at least for the lifetime of his widow. Since he can only ensure this result if there is a head of household, he attributes that status to his widow (or another female relative in special circumstances). She is theoretically owner of all the assets, but it is likely to have been a purely nominal ownership, except where greater control had been expressly given. The heirs will have to farm the estate and hold the houses in common, but without the usual option to divide it into new households.[43] That decision, which will trigger the residual provisions of the will, lies solely with the widow as nominal head of household and need never be exercised by her. The testator's motive in making this arrangement is not evident. Since it is invariably coupled with the duty of the heirs to support the new head of household, it may have been considered an extra safeguard for securing that support. As long as the heirs could not claim a specific share of the estate, they were tied to it and more likely to fulfil the condition of support.

Summary

A testator at Emar could bestow two different conditions of status upon the women of his household: "male and female" and "father and mother." They had separate functions: the former relating to continuation of the family cult, and generally given to a daughter; the latter relating to the continuation of the undivided household, and generally given to a wife. The two can sometimes be found together in the same

43 Arnaud *Textes syriens* 47 does not appear to fit into this pattern. Two women are made "mother and father" and given free disposition over the estate, for which there appear to be no heirs. There is also no mention of support. It is not, however, a testamentary document but the report by a witness testifying after the testator's death as to his oral testament. Doubtless important details have been omitted from the record, which was concerned with some particular question, probably connected with litigation.

testament, but they are not occupied by the same person.[44] It is possible that the office of "father and mother" included the cultic duty, which did not have to be spelled out, since the widow merely continued her husband's household. In that case, the daughter who was appointed "male and female" would only take up her duties with her inheritance, on the mother's death, when the last vestige of the father's undivided house ceased to exist.[45]

Conclusions

The Emar archives contain no law codes, edicts or orders, which would give us direct access to their juridical thinking. Their legal sources consist of transactional records, drafted according to a body of rules whose existence is assumed but never expressed. Nonetheless, from the interstices of their technical clauses we can extract some of the features of their jurisprudence and appreciate its subtleties. The two topics discussed in this study illustrate the importance of legal fiction as a juridical tool and at the same time an awareness of the dangers inherent in a reality that is an intellectual construct.

On the one hand, where the general law had assigned to women a more restricted legal capacity than men, ingenious testators were able to overcome those limitations through formal devices, in reliance on

44 In *ASJ* 13 no. 25 a daughter is called "mother" of her three younger brothers but is not made "mother and father," although the undivided household is preserved by penalty clauses against the brothers claiming their shares in her lifetime. On the other hand, she is made "male and female" in her capacity as daughter and given the cultic duty to perform. Why the testator chose this mode is not clear. In two other cases the testator makes his daughter "mother and father," but in both she is already a woman of unusual status: in Arnaud *Emar* 6 31 a *ḫarimtu*, and in Beckman *Emar* 57 a *qadištu*.

45 Of the cases where both offices are found, Beckman *Emar* 15 and *UF* 26 197 no. 9 expressly grant the estate to the "mother and father," so that the "male and female" will only inherit after the former's death. In *ASJ* 13 no. 26, which is missing the usual details of support, the "male and female" (daughter) and not the "mother and father" (widow) is made sole heir. In the light of the above texts, we would interpret it as applying only after the widow's death. In the meantime, the widow, daughter, and the latter's husband would continue to live in the undivided household. The interpretation of Arnaud *Emar* 6 185 is too doubtful, since it is broken at the relevant place.

the idea that the law can create its own reality, even to the point of turning a woman into a man. On the other hand, where the law set up equitable mechanisms that saw beyond the fiction of outright sale into the reality of a debt-driven transaction, it was sometimes necessary to re-establish the opacity of the contract, for fear that equity might be abused to create a new legal fiction. In both cases the draftsman's creativity was not arbitrary but the result of manipulating established legal concepts such as undivided ownership or burden of risk within limits set by the unseen hand of traditional law and the potential for intervention of the ruler and the courts.

8

A Death in the Family: Codex Eshnunna 17-18 Revisited

Abstract

This article attempts to explain the peculiarities of paragraphs 17-18 of the Code of Eshnunna and to show how these provisions fit within the literary context of where they now stand. Rather than being fundamentally about marriage, the two laws are of a commercial nature, focusing on property exchanged as part of a marriage agreement, and its possible restitution.

It gives me great pleasure to dedicate this contribution to a teacher and scholar whose now classic study has done so much to enhance our understanding of the Old Babylonian law code from Eshnunna.

Paragraphs 17-18 of Codex Eshnunna read as follows:[1]

Col. I, lines 13-18

DUMU.LU$_2$ *a-na* E$_2$ *e-mi-im tir-ḫa-tam li-bi-il-ma*
šum-ma i-na ki-la-al-li-in iš-te-en a-na ši-im-tim
it-ta-la-ak KU$_3$.BABBAR *a-na be-lí-šu-ma i-ta-a-ar*
šum-ma i-ḫu-ús-si-ma a-na E$_2$-*šu i-ru-ub*
lu-ú a-ḫi-za-n[u-u]m [l]u kal-la-tum a-na ši-im-tim it-ta-la-ak
ma-la ub-lu ú-ul ú-še-ṣi wa-tar-šu-ma i-le-eq-qé

* Originally published in *Studies in Honour of Reuven Yaron* (ed. M. Rabello); *Israel Law Review* 29 (1995): 32-42. Used by permission.

1 The transliteration is of Tablet IM 52614 = Text B in Goetze's edition (Goetze 1956). Text A presents only a garbled version of these two paragraphs, due to an error of homoioteleuton by the scribe.

17 Should the son of a man bring the betrothal payment to the house of the father-in-law, if one of the two dies, the silver shall return to its owner.

18 If he marries her and she enters his house (and) either the marrier or the daughter-in-law dies, as much as he brought he shall not hand over; he shall take its surplus.

As Yaron has pointed out, the two paragraphs should be seen as a *single* unit.[2] In this paper, I intend to address three problems that arise from the text: the identity of the parties, the justice of the ruling, and the position of these paragraphs in the code.

Identity of the Parties

The interpretation of these obscure provisions has generally relied on the context supplied by a parallel in Codex Hammurabi (§§163-164):

163 If a man marries a wife and she does not bear him sons and that woman dies: if his father-in-law has returned the betrothal payment (*terḫatum*) that the man brought to his father-in-law's house, then the husband has no claim to that woman's dowry; her dowry belongs to her father's family.

164 If his father-in-law has not returned the betrothal payment, he shall deduct it from the amount of her dowry and shall return her dowry to her father's house.

CE 18 presents a direct parallel to CH 164, whose more explicit provisions establish a set-off arrangement for return of the dowry and betrothal payment when the marriage is ended by death (and there are no children to inherit).[3] In contrast to the clear language of the Hammurabi law, its for-

2 Yaron 1988b: 35.

3 CH 163 contains a complication which does not concern CE, namely, the need for the set-off arrangements to take into consideration a custom whereby the betrothal payment had already been returned to the groom upon marriage as a supplement to the dowry. See Van Praag 1945: 135-36; and Yaron 1988b: 176-79.

mulation is so terse that scholars have been unable to reach a consensus on the exact meaning of its provisions, especially as regards the identity of the parties in the apodosis.[4] If we are to assume, however, that the meaning was clear to contemporary readers, then there must have been some factor in the text itself which limited the number of possibilities and thereby avoided ambiguity at first reading. That factor is, I suggest, that the same two parties are the sole protagonists throughout paragraphs 17 and 18.

Paragraph 17 has not been regarded as causing any problems. It has been taken by all commentators (including myself) to refer to the same events at an earlier stage, when death of the bride or groom annuls the betrothal.[5] The only parties mentioned expressly, however, are the groom and the bride's father. I would therefore suggest that it is the death of either of these two which triggers the restitution provisions.[6] It is true that in the following sentence we are told that the groom proceeds to marry *her*, but I take the pronoun as looking forward to the next clause where the bride is referred to directly, rather than backward.

The idea that the death of the bride's father should vitiate the betrothal contract, or at least give grounds for rescission, may seem strange at first, but it is not so surprising when seen in its cultural context. Marriage in the ancient world, it has often been stressed, was an alliance between two families.[7] The groom might be reluctant to marry into a family whose configuration had now been changed by the loss of its head. Another possibility is that the contract between the two men was regarded as a personal one, which was frustrated when either of the two was unavailable to fulfill his promises.

On the other hand, death of the bride before the wedding might not necessarily vitiate the contract, as paragraph A 31 of the Middle Assyrian Laws reveals:

> If a man brings the betrothal payment to the house of his father-in-law and his (inchoate) wife dies, (but) his father-in-law has

4 The scholarship is reviewed by Yaron 1988b: 183-87.

5 E.g., Goetze 1956: 62-63; Szlechter 1954: 47- 48; Yaron 1988b: 179-80; Westbrook, 1988b: 47.

6 Goetze 1956: 63, raises this possibility but dismisses it as not probable without further discussion.

7 See e.g., Cardascia 1969: 66-67.

> daughters, if the father-in-law wishes, he may marry a daughter of his father-in-law instead of his dead wife, or if he wishes, he may take the silver that he gave.

While the Middle Assyrian Laws are some centuries later than Codex Eshnunna, the cultural attitudes that they reveal are still considerably closer to those of the Eshnunnans of the Old Babylonian period than our own. The same attitudes, it may be added, appear to be behind Laban's ability to substitute his daughter Leah for Rachel as Jacob's bride in Gen 29:15-26.

Evidence that death of the bride's father could give grounds for rescission of the marriage contract is provided by an Old Babylonian document, Riftin 48, the opening lines of which read:

> [Because of the ma]rriage-gift which Sin-ashared, the district commissioner, and his brothers brought to the house of Belaniya as a marriage-gift, though the daughter of Belaniya was not given [to him], Lamassum wife of Belaniya was seized for the marriage-gift. (Officials) examined his case, and they paid his marriage-gift to them. They shall not sue Lamassum wife of Belaniya again.

My earlier analysis of this document has been criticized by Van der Mieroop for not recognizing the contradiction between this document and CH 160 which requires repayment *in duplum* by the bride's father for breach of the contract of betrothal.[8] In that study, however, I had tentatively suggested that the reason for payment *in simplum* here was that the betrothal had been ended by frustration as in CE 17, not breach as in CH 160.[9] The frustrating event, moreover, was the death of the bride's father, which might be inferred from his curious absence from the proceedings and the seizure of his wife alone for not repaying the money received. If the death in CE 17 is also that of the bride's father, then the connection between the two sources is considerably stronger.

If my interpretation of §17 is correct, then in §18 there is a shift in the identity of the persons who die. This accounts for the express statement in the protasis "either the marrier or the bride dies," which would otherwise

8 Westbrook 1988b: 47. Van de Mieroop 1991.

9 Westbrook 1988b: 47.

be otiose.[10] The bride replaces her father, and the groom is identified in relation to her by the use of a new title, *āḫizānum*. When appended to the participial form, the *-ānum* ending denotes the subject of the verb in the particular case, "the one who married in this instance," and not a separate status. In the apodosis of §18, on the other hand, the subjects of its three verbs are not identified and should therefore remain the two protagonists, the groom and the bride's father.

As between these two, the subject of *mala ublu* is more likely to be the groom, since the phrase refers to a past event expressly mentioned earlier, namely, bringing the betrothal payment, for which the same verb is used.[11] On the other hand, neither of the other two verbs in the apodosis can refer to the groom, since on one contingency assumed by the protasis he is already dead. Accordingly, they must refer to the father of the bride, who on the analogy of CH 164 need not hand over[12] the betrothal payment made to him by the groom, but is entitled to receive only the excess over that sum of what he had paid, namely, the dowry. Our finding thus confirms Yaron's interpretation of the apodosis, if arrived at by a different route.[13]

10 Goetze 1956: 59-60, originally restored line 17 as *ù*(?) *a-aḫ-ḫa-ru-um*(?), an otherwise unattested term, which he took to mean "afterwards," translating "but soon afterward the young woman deceases." On this interpretation, the paragraph dealt only with the death of the wife, as in CH 163-164. The present reading of line 17 was proposed by Landsberger (1968: 73) and confirmed by collation by R. Ellis (see Finkelstein 1970: 249 n. 39). The legal difficulties that arise due to the new reading have been detailed by Yaron 1988b: 181-83.

11 It might be argued that on the same grounds the phrase could refer to the bride, since the verb *wabālum* can be used of her transfer of the dowry, as in CH 156. There is indeed an allusion in the protasis to the dowry having been transferred, but it indicates a different verb. The statement "she entered his house" suggests the phrase commonly used in contemporary marriage documents: "this (dowry) is what A. (bride's father) gave to her and caused to enter the house of B. (groom's father/groom)." See, e.g., BE 6/1 84 (Westbrook 1988b: 113) and CT 8 2a (Westbrook 1988b: 118-19).

12 Cf. Yaron 1988b: 183-84, who translates "relinquish" on the same understanding, namely, that the subject causes an object to go forth from his possession. Although the verb *šuṣûm* has many different connotations, this meaning is clearly established in Old Babylonian contexts involving silver or commodities, e.g., AbB 3 88 (lines 15-17): *še-a-am ma-ḫi-ra-at i-la-ku*$_{13}$ KU$_3$.BABBAR *i-na bi-ti-i-ka la ú-še*$_{20}$*-ṣú-ú* "give her barley at the going rate, but let them not hand over silver from your house."

13 Yaron 1988b: 186-87

Justice of the Ruling

The difficulty with a solution following the pattern of CH 164 is that the wording of the Eshnunna text makes it apply not only where the bride has died but also where she is left a widow by the untimely death of the groom. Under these circumstances a widow would normally be entitled to her dowry. As Yaron points out, failure to restore it to her here leaves her in an invidious position. "She is no longer a virgin (and that in a society which sets much store by virginity). As a widow, her prospects in the marriage market are greatly impaired. In circumstances so unequal, a ruling based on 'equality' becomes a travesty of justice; what was seen as *summum ius* turns into *summa iniuria*."[14]

In an earlier study, I could only suggest that the widow followed her dowry back to her father's house, to be dowered again on a subsequent marriage, although the Old Babylonian sources provided no evidence of such an arrangement.[15] On the contrary, such contemporary evidence as there is suggests that the wife on termination of the marriage was a free agent. In Codex Hammurabi, the most common phrase is "the husband of her choice may marry her" (§137, §156, and §172), which clearly indicates that she did not return home. In the case of a sick wife, it is provided that "she shall go" without stating the destination (§149). CH 142 might seem to furnish an example: the slandered bride "shall go to her father's house." In my interpretation, however, the marriage in question had not yet been completed, so that the bride had not in fact left her paternal domicile.[16] The point of the phrase in that context was to state that the bride went to her father's house rather than her husband's. It therefore provides no evidence of a return to the paternal home after termination of a marriage. Finally, in private marriage documents, the phrase "she shall take the hand of her daughter/sister and leave" is applied to a divorcee, which likewise suggests that she was a free agent.[17]

14 Yaron 1988b: 189.

15 Westbrook 1988b: 91-92.

16 Westbrook 1988b: 14-16, 45-47.

17 E.g., BIN 7 173, lines 16-22 (Westbrook 1988b: 116); VAS 18 114, lines 15-20 (Westbrook 1988b: 136).

There is, however, a later source which addresses directly the question of the wife's destination after termination of the marriage. TAD B3.8 (= Kraeling 7) is a marriage document from Elephantine, dated to the fifth century B.C.E.[18] Although drafted in Aramaic, it is closely connected with cuneiform legal traditions.[19] Its divorce clauses foresee two possibilities. If the husband divorces his wife, he must return her dowry to her and pay her divorce money and "she shall go away from him whither she pleases" (lines 21-24). If the wife divorces her husband, she is to take her dowry minus betrothal payment (*mōhar*) and divorce money, and "she shall go to her father's house" (lines 24-28).[20] The reason for the distinction is not explained, but it is clearly deliberate. It would not appear to lie solely in the fact that the wife is to blame for the divorce, since in a second marriage document from the Elephantine archives the phrase "go whither she pleases" is applied in the penalty clauses for divorce by both husband and wife.[21] The only unique feature of TAD B3.8 (= Kraeling 7) that we can discern is the aforementioned loss of the betrothal payment.[22] Thus the wife who returns to her father's house has received back less than the full value of her dowry, having had the betrothal payment (*inter alia*) deducted from it. It should be noted for good measure that in all the instances in Codex Hammurabi above where the wife left to remarry, she took with her the full value of her dowry and sometimes a good deal besides.

The possibility existed, therefore, in ancient Near Eastern legal practice of the bride returning to her father's house after the termination of her marriage, in circumstances where her financial situation had deteriorated. Apparently, there was some consciousness of the concerns expressed by Yaron about the widow's situation. More definite conclusions about the

18 Edition in Porten and Yardeni 1989: 78-83.

19 See, generally, Yaron 1961: 101-7, 114-20; and Muffs 1969: 173-94. Cf. Westbrook 1986b: 399-403; and Geller 1978: 228-37.

20 The betrothal payment had been included in the dowry, in accordance with the custom already attested in CH 163. See n. 3 above and Geller 1978: 227-28.

21 TAD B2.6 (= Cowley 15; edition in Cowley 1953: 30-33), lines 22-29. A third marriage document, TAD B3.3 (= Kraeling 2; edition in Kraeling 1953: 60-63), does not specify the wife's subsequent fate in its divorce clauses. In the remaining marriage documents from Elephantine the divorce clauses are not preserved.

22 In TAD B2.6 (= Cowley 15) and TAD B3.3 (= Kraeling 2) there is only payment of divorce money, not loss of the betrothal payment.

background to CE 18 cannot be drawn from this one enigmatic parallel but must await further evidence.

Textual Context

Paragraphs 1-14 of the Code form a patently distinct thematic unit, concerning the fixing of prices for various goods and services, and problems arising from the latter. Likewise in §§25-35, a common theme of family is immediately apparent in rules on betrothal, marriage, and children. The intervening unit of §§15-24 could be characterized as loans and related transactions were it not for the existence of §§17-18 in the middle:

15 A merchant or a taverness shall not receive silver, barley, wool, or oil from a slave or slave-woman *adi ma-di/ṭi-im.*[23]
16 The undivided son of a man, or a slave, shall not be entrusted with a deposit of fungibles.[24]
17 (see above)
18 (see above)
18A 1 shekel will add 36 grains as interest. 1 kor will add 10 seah as interest.[25]

23 The reading of this term is disputed and the meaning of the phrase unclear. For a review of the proposals, see Yaron 1988b: 52-53.
24 *qīptum*. For a discussion of this term, see Westbrook 1991b: 120-22.
25 The verb *waṣābu* "to add" is normally personal with the borrower as subject. Accordingly, some commentators have regarded §18A as part of §18, in accordance with Goetze's original division (see esp. Landsberger 1968: 73-74). Attempts to see this as the imposition of interest on a payment by one of the parties in §18, however, confuses restitution with loan and produces legally absurd results (see Yaron 1969: 11 n. 36). Recently, Otto has suggested that the percentages in §18A represent the proportion that the bride's father may deduct for each year of the completed marriage from his repayment of the *terḫatum* (Otto 1992: 75-81). The rationale for this extraordinary arrangement is said to be the financial benefit to the bride, but on one contingency given in the law the bride is dead. In any event, an impersonal meaning of the verb with the capital sum as its subject, although uncommon, is by no means impossible. It is well attested in Old Babylonian Alalakh in the phrase *kaspu šū ul uṣṣab u ul iddarrar* "this silver will not increase and will not be cancelled" (e.g., AT 31 = Wiseman 1953: no. 31, lines 8-9; and *JCS* 8 5 = Wiseman 1954: no. 30, lines 7-9). The same conclusion

19 A man who wishes to lend against an equivalent shall collect it at the threshing floor.

20 If a man lends barley at interest and changes the barley to silver as regards him (the debtor), at the harvest he shall take barley and 10 seah per kor as its interest.

21 If a man lends silver originally, he shall take 36 grains per shekel as its interest.[26]

22 If a man is owed nothing by a man but distrains the man's slave-woman, the owner of the slave-woman shall swear the divine oath—"You are owed nothing by me"—and he (the distrainor) shall pay silver to the value of the slave-woman.

23 If a man is owed nothing by a man but distrains the man's slave-woman, detains the distrainee in his house, and causes her death, he shall restore two slave-women to the owner of the slave-woman.

24 If he is owed nothing by him and distrains the wife of a *muškēnum* (or) the son of a *muškēnum*, detains the distrainee in his house, and causes their death, it is a case of life. The distrainor who distrained shall die.

Consequently, commentators have regarded §§17-18 either as a stray provision from the unit on family law (§§25-35) or as the beginning of that unit that has somehow been separated from it by intrusive provisions on loans.[27]

Petschow at first offers a purely mechanical explanation: §17 was attracted to §16 because they begin with the same words (*mār awīlim*), and §18 proceeds to complete the subject thus broached.[28] With §18A, the draughtsman returns to the main topic. Petschow, however, then tries to salve the honor of Codex Eshnunna by identifying a system of sorts based on parallel leapfrogging: just as paragraph 18A picks up the theme of loans

has been reached, with further Old Babylonian examples, by Yaron in a new study that reached me after this article was in press (Yaron 1993a: 206-18).

26 For the translation of *ana pānišu* as "originally," see Rosen 1977: 35-38.

27 See Korošec 1964: 86.

28 Petschow 1968: 135-39.

from paragraph 16, so §25 picks up the theme of marriage from §18, after interruption.[29]

Otto proposes an even more elaborate scheme.[30] The marriage laws were originally a single unit, into which at some point §§18A-21 (the loan provisions) were inserted. The reason for the interest rate in §18A being added was to give it a specific role in calculations regarding the "surplus" in §18. Paragraphs 19-21 then had to be added to deal with problems in the sphere of interest law that arose from this rule, so as to prevent false analogies being made from marriage law to the law of loans. Furthermore, the placing of §§17-18 after §§15-16 changed the legal purpose of §§15-16, which henceforth concerned not loans in general but acquisition of money for the betrothal payment.

The reason why such complicated theories of composition are necessary is the assumption by all commentators that paragraphs §§17-18 are marriage laws. I would question that assumption. Old Babylonian marriage had two components: the status of marriage itself and the marriage contract, an ancillary agreement which preceded the marriage and regulated various aspects of it, in particular property matters. The betrothal payment (*terḫatum*) reflects this dual character: it had an important effect on status in that it created inchoate marriage, but it was also a property arrangement that functioned on the margins of the marriage relationship like dowry and marital gifts. The *terḫatum* was not a part of the status of marriage; it derived from and was a term of the marriage contract. Where the focus of the law was on this latter component, there is no reason why it should not have been included in a series of provisions on contractual and property matters.

Our understanding of paragraphs 17-18 has, paradoxically, been distorted by the parallel of CH 163-164, those same paragraphs that we rely on to understand the substance of the Eshnunna law, where return of the *terḫatum* is discussed in the context of marriage laws. Notwithstanding the existence of many close parallels in substance, the two law codes are capable of wide divergencies in both formulation and structure. An example

29 Petschow does initially suggest a wider classification in qualifying the group of paragraphs from §15 apparently to §35 as contract law. It would seem that he regards marriage as a contract, although he avoids using the term in discussing §§17-18, preferring to refer to them as "Rechtsgeschäfte."

30 Otto 1989: 61-66.

is the case of the goring ox. Codex Hammurabi situates its provisions on the goring ox in the context of laws about oxen (§§241-252): their distraint, their hire, harm caused to them, and lastly harm caused by them. CE 53-58 places them in the context of an owner's liability for harm caused by his dangerous property: an ox, a dog, or a wall. The arrangement is more than a matter of chance or convenience; it is a different jurisprudential analysis, albeit within a modest compass, achieved through structure.

If the perspective is commercial rather than marital, then §§17-18 fit without difficulty into their overall context. Paragraphs 15-24 form the second part of a chapter on commercial relations which precedes that on family relations (§§25-35). Whereas the first part (§§1-14) concerned permanent transfer of assets, through sale of goods or services, these paragraphs deal with my property in your hands, when the question of its restitution arises. Three possibilities are envisaged, which are treated in three separate groupings of provisions:

1. Cases where the transfer is void, either because the transaction is forbidden, as in §§15-16, or because its purpose is frustrated by subsequent events, as in §§17-18. In the first two cases no sanction is mentioned, but as Petschow has pointed out, it is reasonable to suppose that invalidity was the sanction.[31] The consequence was that in §15 the merchant or taverness was obliged to return commodities received from a slave, while in §16 the value of goods transferred as a deposit of fungibles could not be reclaimed. By the same token, in §17 restitution of the betrothal payment is required but in §18 does not occur because it is set off against the value of the dowry that the bride's father receives back.
2. Cases where the transfer is valid and is expected to return to its owner. These are all commercial loans, in §§18A-21, and the concern of the law is only to regulate the terms upon which the profitability of the loans is calculated.
3. Cases where the transfer is wrongful and not only invalid but gives rise to a penalty. These are the provisions on the wrongful distraint of persons in §§22-24.

31 Petschow 1968: 135-46. See also Petschow 1961: 197-200.

9

The Adoption Laws of Codex Hammurabi

Abstract

A careful reading of paragraphs 185-193 of the Code of Hammurabi shows that all of these laws have to do, not merely with adoption, but with primary adoption as opposed to secondary adoption. Primary adoption entailed a unilateral act on the part of the adopter. It could be dissolved equally by a unilateral act, in this case of either the adopter or the adoptee, so long as the correct *verba solemnia* were utilized. Finally, certain classes of palace and temple personnel were given absolute protection when they adopted via the primary mode, probably because they were forbidden or unable to have natural offspring.

Paragraphs 185-193 of Codex Hammurabi (CH) deal with a single topic: adoption.[1] In this study, dedicated to a dear friend and colleague, a new translation of these paragraphs will be offered, together with a legal interpretation that, it is hoped, will shed light on the general principles of Old Babylonian adoption law.

Adoption may be achieved by two modes: primary or secondary. By the primary mode, a person adopts an orphan child and in a unilateral act creates *ex nihilo* the legal relation of parent and child between himself and the adoptee. This is expressed in Babylonian by the phrase "to take for

* Originally published in Kinattūtu ša dārâti: *Raphael Kutscher Memorial Volume* (ed. A. Rainey and M. Anbar; Tel Aviv: Institute of Archaeology of Tel Aviv University, 1993), 195-204. Used by permission.

1 David (1927: esp. 18-19, 25-28, 33-36; followed by Donner 1969: 90-96) distinguished between full adoption and other lesser conditions such as wardship. It is not possible to enter into a full discussion within the scope of this article, but we would note: (1) David's interpretation was based in part on a mistranslation of §185 (see n. 4); and (2) the term "son" or "sonship" occurs in every provision of this section of CH.

sonship (/daughtership)": *ana mārūtim* (/*mārtūtim*) *leqûm*. By the secondary mode, a person adopts a child from its natural parents. Two legal acts are therefore necessary: a contract between the parents and the adopter whereby the parents relinquish their rights over the child and an act by the adopter whereby he creates the same relationship (in law) between himself and the child, as in the primary mode. This is expressed in Babylonian by the phrase "to take for sonship from PN_1 and PN_2, his father and mother" (*itti* PN_1 *abīšu u* PN_2 *ummīšu ana marūtim leqûm*).[2] It is important to note that whatever mode of adoption is used, the resulting legal relationship is one of *status*. It is not to be confused with the contract in the secondary mode, which is a condition precedent to, but legally separate from, the status of "sonship."

In our view, all the paragraphs of CH under discussion concern adoption by the primary mode. We shall examine them in turn in order to test this hypothesis. Paragraph 185 reads:

> If a man adopted a child in its water and has brought him up, that one who has been raised shall not be reclaimed.

Borger (1967-75: vol. 1, 30) and Yaron (1965: 171-73)[3] have shown that "its water" refers to the amniotic fluid, being an abbreviated version of the phrase "in its water and blood." The situation is therefore that a new-born infant has been adopted, before even the normal post-natal ablutions have been performed. Such an action is a clear sign that the parent is abandoning the child, as is explicitly stated in a document from Susa:

> Manniyatu the *istarītu* abandoned Mar-ešre in his water and blood in order to acquire her property.[4]

The phrase occurs elsewhere in contracts of adoption, where its purpose was presumably to emphasize the natural parents' relinquishment of

2 Adoption of an adult uses the secondary mode; the adopter adopts the adoptee "from himself" (e.g., YOS 8 120).

3 The many theories based upon David's earlier translation "unter seinem Namen" (1927: 24) must therefore be abandoned.

4 MDP 23 288. See Wilcke 1981: 88 n. 3, for a discussion of the translation of these lines.

all rights as against the adopter.[5] Nonetheless, we would suggest that its original context was not contractual; rather, it describes the typical situation of a foundling. Malul (1990a) has pointed to the same phraseology in Ezek 16:4-6, in a graphic description of the abandonment of a new-born infant:[6]

> At your birth, on the day you were born, your cord was not cut, nor were you washed in water nor rubbed with salt nor wrapped in napkins. No eye pitied you to do any of these for you, but you were cast into an open field in contempt for your life on the day you were born.

Driver and Miles nonetheless argue against the adoptee being a foundling in CH 185, on the grounds that if the parents had exposed the child, they would be unlikely to wish to reclaim him (1952: 391). But exposure is not the only possibility; the child may have been lost by his parents, rather than abandoned. Such a possibility is described in a vignette given in the lexical text *ana ittišu.*[7] An adoptee was one who "has no father and mother" or who "does not know his father and mother." The adopter rescues him from a series of alternate perils—a well, the street, the mouth of a dog, or of a raven—and pays for his upbringing, but should the adoptee's[8] natural family ever turn up, they will be able to claim him back, upon payment of compensation for expenses.

Where therefore, a foundling's natural family (but not necessarily his parents) claim him back from his adopter some time after the event of the adoption, the case may turn on whether the natural parents had abandoned their child or not. The court will be faced with the rather difficult task of determining the parents' intentions at the time of the original

5 AbB 7 103 (letter), YOS 12 331. The special circumstances that necessitated the phrase in these contracts are not clear. See Wilcke 1981: 89-94.

6 We disagree, however, with Malul's conclusion that the Ezekiel passage involves adoption, *inter alia* because in the same narrative the "adopter" goes on to marry his "adoptive daughter."

7 MSL I 3 III 28-57 (Landsberger 1937: 44-46). Although the text is from a later period, it is recognized as containing traditional material that dates back to the Old Babylonian period.

8 Line 53 *leqâšu* "his adoptee." Cf. *CAD* L 130-31.

adoption.[9] As is usual in Old Babylonian law, recourse is had to evidentiary presumptions. Evidence that the child was a newborn infant who had not received the normal post-natal ablutions raises a presumption of abandonment. What evidence, then, would raise the alternative presumption? Paragraph 186, in our view, gives an example:

> If a man adopted a child *inūma ilqûšu abašu u ummašu iḫiāṭ*, that one who has been raised shall return to his father's house.

The paragraph presents the opposite ruling, where the natural family's claim is successful, but the circumstances upon which it is grounded have given rise to many conflicting translations. David (1927: 25) makes the clause in question part of the protasis: "und sobald er es genommen hat, nach seinem Vater oder seiner Mutter forscht." But as Driver and Miles rightly ask (1952: 389-90), why should a man actually adopt the child if he only meant to keep him until he found the child's parents? The same consideration applies *a fortiori* to the *Chicago Assyrian Dictionary*'s version (*CAD* Ḫ 161): "if a man adopts a small child (as a foundling), he (may) trace its parents after he has adopted it." There is no conceivable reason why the adopter should need legal permission to trace the natural parents.

Driver and Miles' own suggestion makes the child the subject of the verb *iḫīaṭ*: "when he (the adopter) has taken it, it persists in searching for its father and mother" (1955: 75; cf. Finet 1973: 107e). The case contemplated is one in which a man has adopted a child in infancy which, as soon as he is taken away, pines for his father and mother and is therefore returned to them (1952: 390). On their interpretation, therefore, the case does not involve a foundling but is adoption by secondary mode, a contractual arrangement which the law allows to be frustrated for the benefit of the child. As we shall see, however, the adoptee could theoretically dissolve the adoption at any time, and one of the purposes of the contract was to prevent such a possibility. Even assuming, therefore, that Old Babylonian society showed such concern for the wishes of children, it is difficult to contemplate a law that would indirectly render useless the express terms of standard contracts of the period. Nevertheless, we consider that Driver and Miles' translation points in the right direction: the subject of *iḫīaṭ* is the

9 Unless a ruling was given by the court at the time the child was found: UET 5 260.

child, its meaning in this context is "to search," and its being in the durative tense cannot be ignored. There is no need, however, for the durative to relate solely to present or future action (*GAG* §78a.). We would therefore translate the paragraph as follows:

> If a man adopted a child, and at the time when he adopted it, it was searching for its father and mother, that one who has been raised shall return to his father's family.

The circumstances once again refer back to the moment of adoption, but this time the evidentiary presumption that they raise is that the child was lost rather than abandoned.

CH 188-189 likewise form a couplet, with the same contrasted results as in the previous example, but with circumstances that are the direct opposite of each other:

> If a craftsman adopted a son in order to raise him and has taught him his craft, that one who has been raised shall not be reclaimed.
>
> If he has not taught him his craft, that one who has been raised shall return to his father's house.

It is tempting to regard this case as a straightforward breach of contract leading to dissolution of the adoption. Nevertheless, the result would be too banal: the condition discussed goes to the root of the contract and must exist as an express or implied term, breach of which would lead to dissolution by the very nature of a contractual obligation. There is even less need to state the opposite—that fulfillment of a contract precludes a claim for breach. In the light of our discussion of the previous paragraphs, we consider it more likely, therefore, that the fate of a foundling is once more at issue. This time the focus has shifted to the period of upbringing. If adoption gives the adoptee the status in law of a son, then all the incidents of that status should apply, including inheritance. The inheritance of a craftsman, however, is not his property but his craft. By failing to teach the adoptee his craft, the adopter in this instance has adopted him in form but not substance, thus giving the court good grounds for allowing the natural family's claim against him.

Similar considerations apply to §190:

> If a man has not counted among his sons a child whom he adopted and raised, that one who has been raised shall return to his father's house.

Szlechter (1967: 87) considers the phrase "has not counted among his sons" to refer to a particular act of disowning by the adopter, but the use of a negative is inappropriate for that purpose. In §191, where an act of disowning is at issue, it is described in different terms (cf. Driver and Miles 1952: 395-96). It is difficult to discern the exact connotation of such a vague phrase, but elsewhere in CH, in §170, being counted with the sons refers specifically to the equal inheritance rights of adoptees, and thus it would seem here to refer to a course of conduct, objectively verifiable, from which it may be presumed that the adoptee will not inherit along with the natural sons. As we shall see, it was an easy matter for the adopter to disinherit the adoptee at any time. As in the previous case then, the adoption has been one of form and not of substance, and may be challenged by the natural parents. And again we conclude that the context is adoption of a foundling, not a contract. The adoption contracts contained clauses amply protecting adoptees from any infringement of their inheritance rights (see below, nn. 11 and 14).

If the previous paragraphs gave room for dispute, §191 leaves no doubt that its subject is primary adoption. The remedy provided is for the adoptee alone, without any indication that the rights of the natural parents are at issue:

> If a man *ṣeḫram ša ana mārūtīšu ilqûšūma urabbûšu bīssu īpuš*, and afterwards acquired sons and decided to expel the one who has been raised, that son shall not leave empty-handed. The father who raised him shall give him one third of his inheritance from his moveable property; he shall not give him from his field, orchard, and house.

Apart from one clause in the protasis which we shall consider below, the basic meaning of the rule is clear. It awards a third of his erstwhile inheritance to the adoptee on being expelled by his adopted father. The phrasing of the award incidentally confirms that the original adoption necessarily included the status of heir for the adoptee. As Szlechter points out (1967: 90), "one third of his inheritance" is used in the apodosis although no mention of an inheritance was made in the protasis, and inheritance must thus have been understood as an ordinary incident of adoption. We might well conclude, then, that adoption placed the adoptee in all respects in the position of a natural son and heir, were it not for Szlechter (1967: 92) further drawing our attention to CH 168-169 and the apparent conflict of our paragraph with the latter. In §§168-169 elaborate obstacles are placed in the path of a father who wishes to disinherit his son: he may only do so with the permission of the magistrates after proving to their satisfaction that the son has twice committed an offense of sufficient gravity. How then is the father able in §191 to disinherit his adopted son without any procedural hindrance, apparently at his own whim, the only sanction being the requirement to provide a partial indemnity? Szlechter takes the law of disinheritance to be the same for natural and adopted sons, and the rule in §191, although subject to the procedural restraints laid down in §§168-169, to be in its generosity an exception to the general rule of total disinheritance stated therein, the reasons for this exception lying in the special circumstances related in the protasis (1967: 91-92).

Szlechter's attempt at reconciling the two rules requires a series of assumptions and would leave a father without the possibility of totally disinheriting a certain category of adoptee, however gravely the latter may have sinned against him. Moreover, the paragraph indicates that the acquisition of natural sons is the occasion for disinheritance, without regard to any question of fault.

In our opinion, the apparent conflict between the two rules reflects a fundamental difference between the position of natural and adopted sons with regard to disinheritance. Theoretically, adoption created in law an exact replica of the status of natural son. But in one aspect it remained different.

As the existence of the primary mode shows, adoption was created by the unilateral act of the adopter, most probably by pronouncing a solemn formula of words.[10] In this respect it is analogous to marriage, and like marriage it could equally be dissolved by a unilateral act, in this case of

10 "(You are) my sons!" CH 170-171.

either the adopter or the adoptee (Westbrook 1988b: 69-70, 80-83). The only restriction was one of form: that a solemn formula of words be used, the contrary act to that of its creation. As Greengus has shown (1969: 517-20), the words "You are not my son" pronounced by the adopter or "You are not my father" by the adoptee were employed to dissolve the relationship and status created by adoption.

Adoption contracts sought to block this facility of unilateral dissolution by imposing sanctions on the adopter or adoptee who dared to pronounce the fatal formula. For example, "if A (the adoptee) says to his father B (the adopter), 'You are not my father,' he shall be sold into slavery, and if B says to his son A, 'You are not my son,' he shall forfeit house and chattels."[11] The foundling, however, has no such protection. His is an adoption by primary mode, without the benefit of a contract. Should the adopter choose to exercise his right to dissolve unilaterally, the adoptee will lose his status as a son and thereby automatically any right to inheritance. The provisions of CH 168-169, therefore, which apply to natural sons, will not avail him. It is at this point that CH 191 intervenes. While not challenging the fundamental dissolubility of adoption, any more than do the contractual clauses, it tempers the consequences in certain special circumstances where equity demands some measure of compensation for the adoptee.

Those circumstances are the subject of the untranslated clause in the protasis to which we now turn. Driver and Miles translate: "If the man, who has taken the infant in adoption to himself and has brought him up, has built him a house . . ." (1955: 75). They presume that the adopter has provided the adopted son with his own house, probably on the occasion of the latter's wedding, this being the reason why the adoptee then receives no more than a third of what he would have inherited and no land (1952:

11 E.g., Meissner *BAP* 95 and 96. Note that where the adoptee receives a *vested* future interest in the adopter's estate, in the form of a specific share of the inheritance or of specific property, it will survive dissolution of the adoption. Accordingly, in such cases, forfeiture of that interest is sometimes deemed a sufficient penalty upon the adoptee, e.g., CT 45 101, UET 5 94 and 96. David (1927: 19-20) concluded from such contracts that there could be two types of adoption, with or without inheritance. But the difference lies in whether the inheritance, which applies in all cases, is already vested in the adoptee (whether given present possession or not) or is merely a contingency that will vest on the adopter's death.

396-98).[12] The paragraph assumes, however, that the adoptee would otherwise be entitled to nothing: "that son shall not leave empty-handed."

Most commentators follow the interpretation of David (1927: 36-37), who takes "his house" (*bīssu*) to refer to the adopter's family. The resulting translation, however, is an awkward *casus pendens*, with the addition of words not in the text: "Wenn ein Mann ein kleines Kind, welches er zu seiner Kindschaft angenommen und grossgezogen hat, (wenn er) sich einen Hausstand gründet . . . ." Szlechter's translation (1969: 88) is less awkward: "Si un citoyen, qui avait adopté et élevé un jeune enfant, a créé (fondé) sa (propre) famille . . . ," but it is syntactically incorrect, since it assumes the word order *awīlum ša ṣeḫram*, while the actual order is *awīlum ṣeḫram ša*. Finet admits as much in referring to the syntax as "deceptive,"[13] but there is no need to distort the syntax in order to arrive at a satisfactory interpretation. On the contrary, strict attention to the rules of syntax reveals a legal rule with a clear and logical rationale.

The term *ṣeḫram* is the object not of the verbs *leqûm* and *rubbûm* in the subordinate clause as the above translation suggests, but of the main verb *epēšum*. The main verb thus governs two accusatives, *ṣeḫram* and *bīssu*, a phenomenon which in Akkadian most often means that one of the accusatives is instrumental (*GAG* §145a-c.). Normally it is a thing that is the instrument, but here we suggest that the context makes it singularly appropriate for the person to be the instrument, and we translate the protasis as follows:

> If a man made his house with a child whom he adopted and brought up, but later acquired sons and decided to remove the one who has been raised . . . .

Making a house, as the earlier commentators saw, indeed refers to founding a family. The point of the law is that a childless man has founded his family, i.e., has ensured the continuation of his line, by adopting a child. For this reason the law inclines to help the adoptee when the adopter

12 Following a suggestion by Koschaker (1924) in the *Reallexikon der Vorgeschichte* (not available to us).

13 "Littéralement, la syntaxe est trompeuse: si un homme, le petit qu'il avait pris pour la filiation et qu'il a élevé, il a fondé son foyer" (Finet 1973: 109a).

subsequently begets natural sons and decides to discard the person on whom he had earlier based his ambitions. A similar danger is seen and guarded against in contracts involving a childless adopter by sanctions against not only disinheritance but even loss of the firstborn's preferential share: even if A and C (the adopting couple) have ten sons, B (adoptee) is their principle heir.[14] The adoptee by primary mode had no such protection, of course.

The last group of provisions requires little comment:

> 187 The son of a *girseqûm*, a *muzzaz ekallim*, and a *sekrum* shall not be reclaimed.
>
> 192 If the son of a *girseqûm* or a *sekrum* said to his father and mother who have raised him: "You are not my father, you are not my mother," they shall cut off his tongue.
>
> 193 If the son of a *girseqûm* or a *sekrum* identified[15] his father's house and hated[16] his father and mother who have raised him and went to his father's house, they shall tear out his eye.

Certain classes of palace and temple personnel are given absolute protection when they adopt by primary mode, probably because they were forbidden (or unable) to have natural offspring (Driver and Miles 1952: 392; 1955: 245). The natural parents cannot reclaim the child in any circumstances. Dissolution by the adoptee using the appropriate formula of words is visited by a sanction in the same manner as with contractual sanctions, but with a far harsher content. Conduct by the adoptee that amounts to repudiation in fact but not yet in form receives a similar, "sympathetic" sanction. Thus in terms of content these last two provisions reflect (chiastically) the provisions of §§189-191.

14 E.g., Meissner *BAP* 95, ARM 8 1; cf. *ana ittišu* in MSL I 3 IV 3-6.

15 Cf. the contractual provision in UET 5 92, lines 14-22.

16 For the technical meaning of this term, see Westbrook 1988b: 22-23.

10

The Female Slave

Abstract

Although female slaves were treated in many respects in like fashion to their male counterparts, their reproductive capabilities raised special legal problems. In particular, rules governing family law often came into conflict with those governing property. This article examines evidence from across the ancient Near East in order to clarify these issues. It looks especially at situations where a female slave had a split legal status. For example, she could be owned by a free individual, on the one hand, but simultaneously married to another free person, on the other hand. The article argues, however, that a woman could not be the wife and the slave of the same man simultaneously.

In the legal systems of the ancient Near East, male and female slaves were for the most part subject to the same rules.[1] Of necessity, however, there were special rules for female slaves in respect of their sexuality and reproductive capacity. Regrettably, sources that deal with female slaves as a separate category are scattered and few. My interest in gathering them together is twofold. First, concentrating attention on material concerning females alone may throw new light on familiar sources that are usually considered only in their immediate textual context or from the viewpoint of slavery in general. Secondly, the rules that governed the condition of

* Originally published in *Gender and Law in the Hebrew Bible and the Ancient Near East* (ed. V. H. Matthews, B. M. Levinson, and T. Frymer-Kensky; JSOTSup 262; Sheffield: Sheffield Academic Press, 1998: 214-38. Copyright © Sheffield Phoenix Press. Used by permission.

1 Sigla such as *Nbn.* 682 refer to publications of copies of cuneiform texts. The full titles are given in the "Provisional List of Bibliographical Abbreviations" of *The Assyrian Dictionary of the Oriental Institute of Chicago* (see Oppenheim 1956-). All translations in this article are the author's.

female slaves are of particular jurisprudential interest because they arose from a conflict between family law, which applied to slaves as persons, and property law, which applied to slaves as chattels. Sometimes the one institution prevailed, sometimes the other, and sometimes the rules represented a compromise between the two.

The legal framework for sexual relations between free persons was either concubinage or marriage.[2] Both applied to female slaves, but in differing measure.

Concubinage

Status of the Woman

Since a female slave was property, her owner could exploit or dispose of her sexuality like any other beneficial aspect of property. She could thus be made her owner's concubine or could be given in concubinage to another at her owner's behest. Where concubinage resulted in motherhood, however, the slave might be accorded some qualified protection from the consequences of her status as property. According to CH 171, a slave concubine who had borne her master children had to be freed by operation of law after his death. The provision in CH 146-147 discusses the case of a wife who gives her female slave to her husband as a concubine:

> If a man marries a *nadītu* and she gives a slave-woman to her husband, and after she has borne children that slave-woman makes herself equal to her mistress, because she has borne children, her mistress shall not sell her; she may place the slave-mark upon her and count her among the female slaves. If she does not bear children, her mistress may sell her.

The slave's legal personality is split: she remains the slave of her mistress while becoming the concubine of the latter's husband. The mistress may

2 A third possible framework was prostitution, but being a transitory arrangement it was obviously not relevant to relations between master and slave. Female slaves were used for prostitution with third parties, e.g., *Nbn*. 682.

therefore discipline her or sell her, at will. If the slave's concubinage results in offspring, however, the mistress's ownership rights are restrained; she may only discipline her slave by reducing her social status within the household.

A word of warning must be given about the effect of law code provisions such as the above. The ancient Near Eastern law codes were not legislation in the modern sense, and their provisions should not always be attributed with the absolute, peremptory character of modern laws. In my view, the paragraphs in the codes often represented an ideal of justice: principles that should apply in the formulation of contracts or that only applied in absence of express contractual clauses to the contrary. At most, they might represent the equitable discretion of the court (especially the royal prerogative) to strike down or modify bargains that offended the principles of social justice.[3] Particularly indicative of the royal prerogative are CH 117, which declares an automatic release of debt slaves after three years' service, and CH 171, mentioned above, which does the same for a slave concubine (and her children) on the master's death. They usurp the language and overlap the functions of debt release decrees, which were declared intermittently by the king at his discretion.[4]

Consequently, it is not surprising to find contracts with express provisions that contradict the law codes. Paradoxically, they may be evidence of the validity of the principles expressed by the law codes, if not of the formalistic application of their provisions in the manner of a modern statute, since a contracting party would not normally bother to insert special clauses into the contract merely in order to establish rights that he had

3 This is not the much-debated issue of whether the cuneiform law codes were prescriptive or descriptive. Even if the law codes were not a source of law, the law that they described, whether from custom, decree, or judgment, was still valid, and the relationship between the principles that it embodied and the provisions of contracts needs to be established. A systematic study of that relationship has yet to be undertaken (cf. Westbrook 1995e: 1631-76, esp. 1657). The range of possibilities may be illustrated by an example from modern legal systems. The general law often implies certain clauses in a contract of sale. Those clauses may sometimes be excluded by an express clause inserted by the parties, but sometimes (e.g., in the realm of consumer protection) they may not.

4 See Westbrook 1995e: 1656-58. As regards CH 171, the parallel provision in CL 25, discussed below, assumes that release of the slave concubine is purely a matter of her master's choice.

anyway, in the absence of contract. How far a contract might modify the principles of social justice without running foul of the equitable discretion of the courts is impossible to tell.

In the light of these considerations, the following express provisions in an Old Assyrian marriage contract should perhaps be read as designed to overcome a restraint similar to the one in CH 146-147.[5]

> If within two years she (the wife) has not provided him (the husband) with offspring, she will purchase a slave-woman, and after she (the slave) shall have provided him with a child by him, he/she may sell her wherever he/she pleases.

Contractual terms depend on the bargaining power of the parties, which could vary, even when the contract concerned slavery. Accordingly, special terms did not always restrict a slave's rights; they could equally be used to extend those rights beyond the customary limits of protection. Another Old Assyrian contract expressly protects a concubine who did not yet have the advantage of motherhood.[6]

> Shalim-beli, who has taken Kitidi (as a concubine), shall not cause her to enter the house of Amur-Ashur (his patron?). He may lead her where he wishes. Neither Amur-Ashur nor his sons nor Shalim-beli shall sell her or cause her to enter. If anyone sells her, Shalim- beli shall pay one mina of silver to Shat-ili.

We do not know the background to this enigmatic document, but it would appear that Kitidi has been given into slave concubinage by Shat-ili (her mother?) to Shalim-beli, who is in some condition of dependence upon Amur-Ashur. The contract protects the concubine from exploitation by the patron or from sale by the patron, his heirs, or his client, the immediate owner.

Motherhood could lead to another form of protection for the slave concubine, as CH 119 provides:

5 ICK 1 3:7-16 (see Hrozný 1939: 108-11).

6 KTS 1 47a (edition in Eisser and Lewy 1930-35: 2-3).

> If a debt has seized a man, and he sells his slave-woman who has borne him children, the owner of the slave-woman may pay the silver that the merchant paid and redeem his slave woman.

The right of redemption was widespread in the ancient Near East. It was a measure of social justice, for the benefit of native citizens, whereby a sale under pressure of debt was treated as if it were a pledge. The right appears to have been limited principally to two cases: family land and members of the family sold into slavery.[7] The slave concubine fell into neither category, but where she had borne children, a special rule was formulated in her regard, which neatly illustrates the type of compromise that resulted from the conflict between the rules of family law and property law. She was sufficiently regarded as a member of the family to benefit from the privilege of redemption, but whereas a free wife or a son sold into slavery would on redemption by the husband or father regain their former free status, the slave concubine merely returned to her former master as a slave, in the manner of family land that had been redeemed.

In other circumstances, concubinage could vitiate the right of redemption. Exod 21:7-11 reads:

> If a man sells his daughter as a slave-woman, she shall not go free as the male slaves go free. If she displeases her master who assigned her to himself (/who has not assigned her), he shall let her be redeemed; he shall not have authority to sell her to a foreign people, in breach of faith with her. If he assigns her to his son, he shall treat her according to the status of daughters. If he takes another for himself, he shall not reduce her food, clothing and oil.[8] If he does not provide her with these three, she shall go free without payment of silver.

7 On the question of social justice and redemption of land, see Westbrook 1991b: 15-16, 90-117. On redemption of family members, see Yaron 1959: 155-76; and Westbrook 1995e: 1651-56.

8 The meaning "oil" for the *hapax 'nh* was established by S. Paul (1969: 48-53). It is astonishing that this simple identification, supported by copious evidence of a banal formula found throughout the ancient Near East, has still not been universally accepted by scholars.

A preliminary question is whether this text concerns concubinage at all. Most commentators assume that a form of marriage is being regulated by the law, but there is nothing in the terminology to suggest that marriage is meant.[9] As we shall see, when ancient Near Eastern sources wished to indicate that a female slave was a wife, they did so explicitly, both in the language of formation and dissolution. Here, the slave is assigned and taken, but never specifically as a wife, and the relationship is ended by sale or manumission, not by divorce.

Confusion as to the slave's status has been caused in part by Mendelsohn, who compared this law with the institution of "daughtership and daughter-in-lawship (*mārtūtu u kallatūtu*)" at Nuzi.[10] The latter was a commercial transaction in which the adopter (usually a woman) acquired a girl from her parents as a daughter, with the explicit right to give the girl in marriage and receive her betrothal payment. According to Mendelsohn, it was a "scheme whereby certain sales into slavery of young free-born girls assumed a semblance of legitimate marriage, i.e., conditional sales whereby the giving into marriage of the slave girl was made obligatory upon her purchaser."[11] This is incorrect. It may well be that in social terms the girls' condition was little more than slavery, but in law the distinction was maintained. The terminology of neither slavery nor sale is employed in the texts; there is nothing to suggest that they were anything but a transaction involving the adoption and marriage of a free woman. Mendelsohn systematically mistranslated the operative verb "gave" (into daughtership, etc.) as "sold," without a shred of justification.[12] The Nuzi texts do not furnish a legal model for the law in Exodus. Confusion has also been caused because the difference between concubinage and marriage has not been directly discussed in the context of this law. We shall see, however, that the distinction is of vital importance, with implications both for the consequences of the law's provisions and for the jurisprudential coherence of the legal status of female slaves as a whole.

For the moment I am concerned with the first part of the law, which deals with the question of redemption. The woman's situation differs from

9 The scholarship on this law is reviewed by Chirichigno 1993: 24-55.

10 Mendelsohn 1935: 190-95.

11 Mendelsohn 1935: 191.

12 The Akkadian for "to sell" is "to give for silver" (*ana kaspim nadānum*).

that of the female slave in CH 119 in that she is a free woman who has been sold by her father into debt-slavery, as the reference to redemption reveals. The father would normally have the right to redeem his daughter, but that right is lost because her enslavement is for the purpose of concubinage. The right of redemption revives only if the purchaser fails to abide by the special purpose of the contract—if he fails either to consummate the assignment himself (*qere*) or to assign her for concubinage altogether (*ketib*).[13] In either case, the purchaser has treated the contract as one of ordinary servitude, not concubinage, and has denied the slave-woman the possibility of gaining the protection available to a concubine through motherhood. In those circumstances, it is logical that the ordinary right of redemption should apply notwithstanding the fact that the slave is female.[14]

Verse 8 provides a second measure of protection. Her master "shall not have authority to sell her to a foreign people (*'am nokrî*)." To understand the purpose of this prohibition, it should first be pointed out that alienability is not the opposite of redeemability. The two concepts should not be confused.[15] A right of redemption does not make a slave inalienable, because it can always be exercised against a subsequent purchaser—the seller cannot transfer a more absolute ownership than he has.[16] In the present law, therefore, there was no danger that the mere act of selling the woman to a third party would make her irredeemable. On the contrary, because such an act treated the contract as one of ordinary servitude, in breach of the concubinage clause, it would automatically turn her into a slave who was redeemable from her new owner. In one circumstance only would the woman's redeemability be irretrievably lost: if she were sold abroad. She would then be a foreign slave for her purchaser, who would

13 In order to have legal consequences, his displeasure must have some external manifestation and a concrete act (or omission). Accordingly, the provision is unlikely to refer to a change of attitude after consummation. This eventuality is covered by v. 10, where he takes another concubine in preference to her. It is possible, however, that his displeasure could be manifested through an attempt to sell her to a third party, which again would contravene the purpose of a concubinage contract.

14 Deut 15:12 makes it clear that a female debt-slave in a non-concubinage arrangement has exactly the same status as a male.

15 As does, for example, A. Schenker 1988: 547-56, esp. 547.

16 Yaron 1959: 158-59.

not see himself obliged to respect her rights under Israelite law. For this reason, I prefer to translate the term *'am nokrî* as "foreign people" rather than "outsiders," "other clan," or the like, which would imply a total prohibition on alienation.[17]

Status of the Offspring

Because she could bear children, the female slave was a special economic asset. A child born to an unmarried slave-woman was a house-born slave.[18] The child was reckoned to be the offspring of its mother; it had no father. Like its mother, the child would be the property of her owner, no different from the offspring of the owner's herds. If her master himself took his slave-woman as a concubine, his rights over the issue of the union would be those of an owner, not of a father.

The difference can be seen clearly in an Old Assyrian document. In TuM 1 22a, four brothers divide the estate of their father.[19] The agreement stipulates:

> 18-22 As for the residue (of the estate), whether wheat or slave-woman or slave or (other) share, they shall take according to their father's testament.
>
> 25-32 Agi'a either here or in the city of Assur may take a slave-woman for his(!) concubinage[20] and is free of claims; Asu, Puzur-sadu, and Alahum may take one each from the slave women whom they have known sexually (*lamdū*), but she shall be deducted from their share. They (the brothers) will make their (the slave-women's) offspring equal (*lillissina šunu umta*[*ḫḫ*]*urū*]).

17 See Chirichigno for the contrary view (1993: 249). Support for my interpretation is provided by MAL C+G 2-3, which punish the sale abroad of an Assyrian taken in pledge, who might otherwise be redeemed (Westbrook 1995e: 1660-62).

18 Akkadian: *wilid bītim* (Old Babylonian period), *dušmu* (later periods); Hebrew: *yĕlîd bayit* (Gen 17:13, 23).

19 Edition in Eisser and Lewy 1930: 330-34; cf. Kienast *Altass. Kaufvertragsrecht* 3e and 20 (see Kienast 1984: 92-93 and 98).

20 *ana ištariūtīšūnu ilaqqe*. See *CAD* I-J 271.

The *CAD* translates the last phrase: "they will assign equal rank to their [the women's] offspring."[21] These are fine sentiments but misconstrue the situation. It is a matter of indifference in a division of inheritance what status the individual brothers will assign to the children of their slaves once they have received their inheritance. The problem was a mathematical one: for example, if the three brothers had slept with three slaves who had borne one, two, and three children respectively, should each brother receive the children born to the slave-woman whom he took as his inheritance, or should all receive an equal number, that is, two each? The agreement prefers the second solution, irrespective of who was the father.

The same considerations lead to exclusion of relations with a slave-woman from the ambit of certain sexual taboos. According to HL:

> 191 If a free man has intercourse with free maternal sisters and their mother—one in one country and one in another—it is not an offense. If it is in one place and he knows, it is an abomination.
>
> 194 If a free man has intercourse with slave maternal sisters and their mother, it is not an offense. If brothers sleep with a free woman, it is not an offense. If a father and his son sleep with a slave-woman or a prostitute, it is not an offense.

These provisions do not mean that in Hittite law sexual taboos never applied to relations with a female slave; HL 196 foresees the possibility of a male and female slave committing a sexual act together that amounts to an abomination. The Hittite prohibitions as regards family members cover a wider range of relationships than pure incest (that is, relatives having sexual relations with each other) because their rationale is also to prevent confusion in relations of parentage. In the examples given in the paragraphs above, would the sons of a mother and daughter by the same man be brothers or uncle and nephew? Would the daughters of a woman by a father and son be sisters or aunt and niece? The problems for the family tree, family worship, and inheritance are evident. It is not a problem, however, in certain special cases:

21 *CAD* L 55-56.

1. Where family ties are no more than theoretical, due to geographical (and perhaps jurisdictional) separation.
2. Where two brothers have offspring by the same woman, because the vertical family lineages are not affected. The offspring will be half-brothers or half-sisters, and it is of no great consequence that they are also cousins.
3. Where a father and son sleep with a prostitute, because the offspring of a prostitute have no paternity. The same applies to a slave concubine: in law, her offspring have no father; they only have an owner. Thus uncertainty as to whether her offspring are by the father or his son could at most lead to a property dispute. For the same reason, the offspring of a slave mother and daughter are not related in law, even if they have the same father in fact.

The law codes emphasize that slave concubinage cannot confer legitimacy on the offspring of the relationship, even if both mother and child are freed. CL 25 reads:

> If a man married a wife and she bore him a child and that child is living, and a slave also bore a child for her master but the father granted freedom to the slave and her children, the child of the slave shall not divide the estate with the child of the master.

Likewise CH 170-171, which order that the children of a slave concubine be freed on the father's death, nonetheless bar them from sharing the inheritance with the legitimate children, unless the father had adopted them in his lifetime.

There is nothing surprising in these provisions; indeed, it is strange that they should have been deemed necessary. It is in the nature of concubinage that it cannot have the prime consequence of a legitimate marriage, namely, the creation of legitimate heirs to the father's estate. Hence the offspring of a free concubine had no better right to inherit than the offspring of a slave concubine. On the other hand, if a man died without legitimate heirs, natural or adopted, the law codes do make provision for his illegitimate children to be recognized as his heirs. The examples that they give, however, all concern the offspring of a union with a free woman: his child by a prostitute in CL 27 or by a free concubine in MAL

A 41. Whether the freed children of a slave concubine were equally entitled in those circumstances, or whether a distinction was being drawn between slave and free concubines, cannot be determined.

Position of Third Parties

Ownership implied the exclusive right to exploit the sexuality of a female slave. Accordingly, the law protected her owner against unauthorized use of her by a third party. The penalty was a relatively small payment, which appears to represent compensation for economic loss. The penalty for the wrongful defloration of another's female slave is set at 5 shekels of silver in CU 8, 20 shekels in CE 31, and 30 shekels in an Old Babylonian report of a trial from Nippur.[22] CE 31 adds: "and the female slave remains her owner's." The purpose of this clause was to distinguish the case from that of the defloration of a free maiden, where the penalty imposed represented a betrothal payment and might lead to marriage (e.g., MAL A 55; Exod 22:15-16; Deut 22:28-29). It was an emphatic statement that the principles of property law, not family law, applied in this instance.

Marriage

It is a salient feature of ancient Near Eastern law that, unlike Roman law, it recognized as legitimate the marriage of slaves, whether with other slaves or with free persons. With one exception, which I shall discuss below, marriage and slavery were not legally incompatible, although their different rules led to conflicts.

The marriage of slaves can be divided into three categories: marriage between slaves, marriage with a third party who was free, and marriage with one's own master.

Between Slaves

The slave law of Exod 21:2-6 is emblematic of the conflict between the principles of family law and property law that resulted from recognition of

22 Finkelstein 1966: 355-72, esp. 359-60.

slave marriage. The law distinguishes between marriage prior to enslavement and marriage during slavery. If a married couple enter into debt-slavery, then release of the husband after six years' service automatically includes release of his wife. There is no theoretical difficulty in this case, since the debt for which they both were enslaved is deemed extinguished. If, on the other hand, the master gave a female slave of his own in marriage to the debt-slave, the latter's release has no effect on his wife's status. The master's property rights take precedence over the husband's marital rights.

The ambiguous language of CU 4 is best interpreted as reflecting the same rule. Following Yaron, the subject of the apodosis should be understood as the wife, not the husband.[23]

> If a slave marries a slave-woman whom he loves and that slave is freed, she shall not go out from the house.

Free Person and Slave

Marriage between free persons and slaves could arise from the enslavement of one of the partners to an existing marriage or by the voluntary marriage of a free person with a slave. In the first instance, enslavement did not affect the validity of the marriage or the husband's exclusive sexual rights over his wife, although it might limit his remedies.[24] In the second instance, two situations are covered by the sources: the general case where there is no material family relationship between slave owner

23 Yaron 1985: 131-42, esp. 138-39. Contra the original editor, Yildiz 1981: 96. A Nuzi contract is cited by Yaron in support of his interpretation (JEN 610; see Greenberg 1955: no. 64, cited by Yaron as no. 65), but the situation there is somewhat more complicated. B enters into slavery with A for A's lifetime and is given a wife by A. The contract further obliges B to serve A's son, C, and imposes a penalty upon him for breach of this provision, which includes forfeiture of his wife and children. It is not clear that the relationship between B and C is one of slavery or is contractual in nature, and in any case forfeiture of the wife is an express penalty for breach, not the natural consequence of the end of B's slavery.

24 A reading of Lev 19:20-22 in this sense has already been proposed and argued at length by me (Westbrook 1988d: 101-9).

and free spouse, and a special case where a family relationship between the two is the essence of the arrangement.

1. The General Case. In the general case, most of the evidence relates to the marriage of a free woman with a male slave. The provision in CH 175-176 lays down the principle that both the woman and her offspring remain free; the slave owner has no claim to either. CU 5 assumes the same principle as regards the woman but requires one male child of the marriage to be placed at the owner's disposal.[25]

The Hittite Laws, on the other hand, appear to call into question the freedom of a woman who marries a slave, but the terms of the relevant provisions are very obscure. HL 34-35 read:

> If a slave brings a betrothal payment for a woman and takes her as his wife, no one shall release her.[26]
>
> If a steward or a herdsman causes a free woman to run [elopes with/abducts?] and does not bring a betrothal payment for her, she shall become a slave in [/for?] three years.

25 In my interpretation, that child is not a slave, I translate as follows: "If a slave marries a free woman, he/she shall place one son at the disposal of his master. The son who was placed at the disposal of his master will [divide] half the property of his father's house, the wall, the house [...] The free woman's son is not [...] with the master; he shall not cause him to enter into slavery."

Other translations assume that this final provision relates to the other children of the marriage, although not explicitly indicated, either by the wording or the grammar (Yildiz 1981: 96; Roth 1997: 17; Borger and Kaiser 1982: 20). The couple have to supply the master with one son, who will work for him. Far from being a slave, however, after his father's death, that son apparently gets the half of his estate that the master must forego, as in CH 175-176. (Any other children will have to content themselves with their mother's dowry, it seems.) The master cannot claim the son as a slave in place of his father.

26 There have been numerous attempts to translate the final verb in a way that spares the unfortunate bride from slavery. The latest is the *Chicago Hittite Dictionary*, which translates, "no one will hand her over [to a slave master]" (P/2 125). Since the normal meaning of *para tarna* is "to let go, release, set free, let out" (see P/2 115), it is proposed as a special use ("legal idiom") on the basis of E. von Schuler's translation of passages in the Edict of Tudhaliya (von Schuler 1959: 446-48). Not cited by the dictionary is an article in which the law of the relevant passage of the edict was completely reinterpreted, so as to validate the normal meaning of the verb (Westbrook and Woodard 1990: 641-59, esp. 643, 653-57).

The juxtaposition of the two paragraphs would suggest that making a betrothal payment changes the woman's status immediately, whereas in its absence, three years must elapse. In the absence of any background to these laws, it is impossible to do more than speculate as to their rationale or the parties or interests involved. The purpose might be to distinguish a betrothal payment from a loan, which would allow the recipient (her father?) a right of redemption. Another possibility is to regard the release as being from the marriage, not from slavery. In Yamada's view, these paragraphs mean that a slave cannot take a free woman to wife without paying the brideprice; if he dares to do so, it changes her status to that of a slave.[27]

As for the offspring of a marriage between a slave and a free woman, the principle of freedom expressed in the Mesopotamian law codes was frequently overridden by express clauses in marriage contracts (to which the owner was a necessary party), which assigned some or all of them to slavery.[28] There is insufficient evidence to determine whether the same principles applied where it was the wife who was a slave. Children of the marriage are mentioned in only one source: a series of legal documents from Elephantine recording the changing relationships over a period of years between an owner, his female slave, and her husband.[29] In the first

27 Yamada 1995: 301-16 (311).

28 CT 48 53 (edition in Westbrook 1988b: 123); and JEN 120 (edition in Saarisalo 1934: no. 25). On the other hand, circumstances, especially love and affection, might make the contractual terms as generous as those of the law codes. Two Middle Assyrian documents record a remarkable arrangement. In the first, a slave redeems a woman from slavery with a third party, presumably with his master's silver, and frees her (KAJ 167). In the second, while remaining a slave, he marries her (KAJ 70:2-10, 20-29): "Ilima-iriba slave of Amurru-natsir redeemed [f]Asuat-Idiglat from the house of Ashur-retsuia son of Ibassi-ilu and, with Asuat-Idiglat's consent, Ilima-iriba cleansed her of her slave status and established her as his wife. Ilima-iriba is her husband and Asuat-Idiglat is his wife . . . . Asuat-Idiglat and her children shall be villagers (*ālaiū*) of Amurru-natsir and his children. They shall do village-service (*ālaiūtu*) for Amurru-natsir and his children. But Amurru-natsir and his children shall not seize Asuat-Idiglat and her children for slavery."

29 See Porten and Yardeni 1989: vol. 2, 60-63, 72-73. In an analysis of Kraeling 2 (= TAD B3.3), Porten and Szubin argue that not only the conditions of the wife's marriage contract, but her very slave status, is subtly altered by successive revisions of the document, and by later documents, so that she gradually moves from a status of slavery to one of emancipation (Porten and Szubin 1995: 43-64). I disagree with their analysis on two grounds. (1) The concept of a gradual emancipation is legally incoher-

document (Kraeling 2 = TAD B3.3) the master gives his slave in marriage to a free man. In a later document (Kraeling 5 = TAD B3.6), the aged master frees the slave and her daughter who has been born in the meantime. The master refers to the daughter as "your daughter whom you bore me" (lines 4-5). It is clear, however, that the daughter is the biological child of the husband. The phrase can only refer to the master's ownership of the daughter, which he is now relinquishing. It is not known, however, whether his ownership was based upon the general law or upon another contractual arrangement which has not been preserved in the archive.[30]

The only provision in the law codes that considers the case of a slave-woman married to a free man is HL 31, which makes equitable arrangements in case of divorce:

> If a free man and a slave-woman are in love(?) and they enter and he takes her as his wife and they make a house and children for themselves but afterwards they either become bad or separate, they shall divide the house equally. The man will take the children for himself; the woman will take one child for herself.

It is important to note that the wife receives only one child because she is a slave, not because she is a woman. In HL 32, where it is the husband who is a slave, and in HL 33, where both are slaves, the husband receives only a single child.[31]

---

ent, leaving the rights and duties of the parties uncertain at any one time. The ambiguities noted by Porten and Szubin may be readily accounted for by the division of the slave's legal personality between her master and her husband (see further below). (2) As Porten and Szubin themselves point out, the marriage contract is ancillary to the status of marriage, not determinative of it (1995: 44-45). Changes in the contract can ameliorate the slave's status, but they cannot alter it.

30 In Kraeling 2 (= TAD B3.3), lines 13-14, it emerges that there was already a son of the couple prior to the marriage. The master reserves the right to reclaim that son for himself in the event of a divorce. If he was the issue of concubinage and not marriage, the son would in principle have had no paternity and hence no right to freedom. Porten and Szubin appear to confuse, or at least to conflate, him with the later daughter, attributing the phrase "whom you bore to me" in Kraeling 5 (= TAD B3.6), line 8, to the son (1995: 59).

31 In HL 32 the key words are restored, but the restoration is compelling in the light of HL 33. See the edition in Friedrich 1971: 26 n. 6, and 27 n. 4.

2. The Special Case. The special case (where a family relationship between slave owner and free spouse is the essence of the arrangement) is best exemplified by the practice of a first wife giving her female slave in marriage to her husband as a second wife. Once again, the legal personality of the slave was split. As the Old Babylonian contracts express it: "To H, W_2 is a wife; to W_1, she is a slave."[32] It is necessary that the slave achieve the status of wife and not merely concubine, because the purpose is to provide legitimate offspring, primarily for the husband and secondarily for the first wife. This is made clear by the examples given in Genesis. Sarah, Rachel, and Leah all give a slave to their husbands *as a wife*, with the express purpose of acquiring offspring for their husbands and themselves. Gen 16:1-3 reads:

> Sarai, Abram's wife, had not borne children to him, but she had an Egyptian slave-woman by the name of Hagar. Sarah said to Abram, "Behold, God has prevented me from giving birth. Come in to my slave—perhaps I shall be established through her." Abram listened to the words of Sarai. Sarai, the wife of Abram took Hagar the Egyptian, her slave . . . and gave her to her husband Abram as a wife to him.

What then were the rights of the first wife over the slave and her offspring? The law is complicated by the fact that the first wife is subordinate to her husband within the household; she cannot assert against her husband the rights of a slave owner as she would against an outsider. Accordingly, her ownership rights become residual, both as regards the slave and her offspring. This is illustrated in Genesis by the actions of Sarah. When she wishes to punish Hagar for impudence, she first has to seek permission from her husband (Gen 16:5-6). And later, when Sarah bears a son herself and wishes to prevent Hagar's son from sharing Abram's inheritance, she cannot act directly by expelling her own slave; she must prevail upon Abraham to divorce Hagar (Gen 21:10).

32 H = Husband; W = Wife. W_2 is the slave. See CT 4 39a; CT 8 22b; CT 48 48; TIM 4 49 (see Westbrook 1988b: 104); CT 45 119 (edition in Wilcke 1984: 170-80).

In the same way, the Old Babylonian contracts, in their use of express terms, demonstrate that the first wife could no longer rely on her bare ownership to assert her rights.[33] According to CT 48 48:

> Ahassunu has adopted Sabitum daughter of Ahushina and Ahatani from her father Ahushina and her mother Ahatani. Sabitum is a slave to Ahassunu, a wife to Warad-Sin: with whom she is hostile, she will be hostile; with whom she is friendly, she will be friendly.[34] The day she distresses Ahassunu, she will shave her and sell her.

However sweeping the first wife's powers appear, they are the result of an express contractual clause, not of her normal rights as an owner.

It will be recalled that in CH 146 the wife was forbidden to sell her slave that she had given to her husband as a concubine when the latter had borne children. In the light of the above examples, that provision may be seen as an attempt to extend to a slave concubine some of the natural protection afforded a slave by marriage.

There remains the question of the relationship between offspring of the marriage and the first wife. If her ownership rights over them are limited, does her status as owner at least make them her legitimate heirs? The latter possibility is suggested by a clause in an Old Babylonian contract that asserts: "If she (W_2) bears ten children, they are the children of W_1."[35] At the same time, its appearance in an express clause suggests that this was not the automatic result of the relative status of the two women, but that some further process was necessary.

The same appears true for the cases in Genesis. Rachel declares to Jacob (Gen 30:3): "Here is my slave Bilhah; come in to her and she shall give birth on my knees, and I too will be established through her." Both Rachel and Leah also name the children that their slaves bear to Jacob

33 There are further complicating factors in these contracts, namely, adoption and sisterhood, which do not concern us here. For full discussion, see Westbrook 1988b: 104-7; and Wilcke 1984: 171-75.

34 Correcting my translation of this phrase in Westbrook 1988b: 109 ("whenever she is angry, she will be angry; whenever she is friendly, she will be friendly") in the light of the parallels with international treaties drawn by Weinfeld 1970: 184-203, esp. 194.

35 CT 48 67, but see the discussion in Westbrook 1988b: 106.

(Gen 30:5-13). It may therefore be that, as has been often suggested, some form of adoption was involved, whereby ownership rights were turned into filiation.[36]

Slave and Master

In my view, marriage of a female slave to her own master is the one situation where marriage and slavery are altogether incompatible: a man cannot be a master and a husband of the same woman at the same time. The reasons derive from the logic of the two institutions. Before expounding them, however, it is necessary to consider a preliminary problem of terminology. In a small number of texts, a married woman is called the slave of her husband. The texts are concentrated in three widely separated clusters of sources, altogether different in genre and in the context in which the term appears.[37]

1. West Semitic. Lipiński has drawn attention to first millennium West Semitic seals and tomb inscriptions where in each case the woman named is referred to as the slave (*'mt/'mh*) of a man who from the context appears to be her husband.[38] As Lipiński points out, however, the context also makes it clear that these are free women, indeed, that they are of high status. One is even a queen![39] The explanation most probably lies in the semantic relativity of slavery terminology. As has often been noted, the term for slave, male or female, was used indiscriminately in ancient Near Eastern languages to refer to any hierarchical inferior, for example, a subject before a sovereign, a king before an emperor, or an emperor before a god, without necessarily implying the strict legal relationship of ownership of the former by the latter.[40] In introducing oneself, the expression "Your slave" was commonly used as a formula of polite self-abasement. In the

36 See e.g., Skinner 1930: 386-87.

37 My statement in an earlier study that wives are never referred to as slaves of the head of household is therefore incorrect, having failed to take into account the following, albeit marginal, instances (Westbrook 1995e: 1635).

38 Lipiński 1994: 12-16.

39 Queen Gahimat, who is qualified as *'amat* of the *mukarrib* of Saba in a South-Arabian inscription (Lipiński 1994: 14).

40 A good discussion of this phenomenon may be found in Yamada 1995: 301-16.

sources under discussion, therefore, it would appear to have served the purposes of euphemistic modesty rather than legal classification.[41]

2. Old Assyrian. Among the Old Assyrian tablets that document the affairs of Assyrian merchants in Anatolia there are several instances collected by Kienast where the standard Akkadian term for female slave, *amtum*, appears to refer to a wife.[42] While some of them might fall under the category of euphemistic modesty, as above,[43] there are two marriage documents which suggest that the term *amtum* refers to a definite legal status.[44] ICK 1 32 states that one Pilah-ishtar divorced "his slave-woman" (*amassu*) and paid her a divorce settlement in the presence of her mother and brothers.[45] The second is a marriage document according to which,[46]

> Puzur-ishtar took (*ēḫuz*) Ishtar-lamassi, daughter of Ashur-nada "for female slavery" (*ana amtūtim*). He will take her with him to Purushhaddum or to Hattum or wherever he journeys, and he will bring her back to Kanish with him. If he divorces her, he will pay 5 mina of silver; if she divorces him, she will pay 5 mina. Besides his wife (*aššitīšu*) in the city of Assur, he shall not take (*eḫḫaz*) another. If Ishtar-lamassi does not see a child within 3 years, he may buy a slave-woman (*amtam*) and take (*eḫḫaz*) her. Ashur-nemedi, Anina, and her mother gave her.

41 This is its purpose in 1 Sam 25:41 and 1 Kgs 1:17, where the phrase is "your slave" in direct speech. Lipiński is therefore wrong in attributing the meaning "wife" to the term in these passages, which no more indicate marriage than they do slavery (1994: 12-15).

42 Kienast 1984: 94-95, 100.

43 Especially a wife's letter to her husband, listed by Kienast (1984) as no. 1f (= Kienast *Altass. Kaufvertragsrecht* 44:25-28a), in which the following statement is found: "Today, have I not done well for you like a slave-woman 'with a beaten head,' so that you should measure out the rations to the slave-woman (i.e., me)?" (Kienast 1984: 95).

44 A third marriage document is cited by Kienast (1984: 94), but the key term is written over an erasure and needs to be restored; hence it cannot serve as evidence (no. 1b = ICK 1 3). Kienast restores it as GEMÉ (the Sumerogram for *amtum*); *CAD* (A/1 175) restores it as DAM (wife).

45 Edited in Lewy 1956: 3-6. Published only in transliteration (Lewy 1956: 6).

46 Published only in transliteration (Lewy 1956: 6).

The verb "to take" (*aḫāzum*) in principle requires further specification in order to refer to marriage: "to take a wife/to take for marriage." It can be abbreviated, but the context would have to be unambiguous. Otherwise, when used alone, it refers to concubinage.[47] Hence the second occurrence here indicates marriage, but the third, concubinage. On the other hand, Ishtar-lamassi herself, although taken "for female slavery," cannot have become thereby a slave. The decisive reason is the penalty clause, which obliges her to pay her husband upon divorce. A slave, being owned, could not own property separately from his or her master.[48] Hence the "female slavery" of Ishtar-lamassi was legitimate marriage as a free woman.

The question remains why this particular terminology was employed. The reason would appear to lie in the unusual bigamous practices of the Assyrian merchants, who maintained one household at home in the city of Assur and another in the trading colony in Anatolia. It is the latter that is documented in these records. Lewy conjectured that the Assyrian merchants "did not and could not accord to their wives the title *aššatum* [wife] whenever they were married to an *aššatum* residing elsewhere—for instance in the city of Assur—or wished to retain the right to marry another woman whom they intended to make their *aššatum*."[49] Lewy does not explain why both wives could not bear the same title, a practice that is well attested elsewhere, but in support of his view, some legal fiction would definitely have been necessary if, for example, the merchant did not want the children of his Anatolian marriage to share his estate in Assur with his Assyrian children, or if his marriage contract with his Assyrian wife prohibited him from taking a second wife. The term *amtum* avoided

47 For a full discussion of *aḫāzum*, on the basis of the Old Babylonian sources, see Westbrook 1988b: 10-16. Old Assyrian examples are: KTS 1 47a (*aḫāzum* alone = concubinage); TCL 4 67 (*aššatam aḫāzum* = marriage; edition in Eisser and Lewy 1930: 1-2; see also *CAD* A/1 175); Matouš 1973: 312 (*aḫāzum* alone = marriage, but in preamble to divorce document).

48 It is true that a slave in the ancient Near East might have a *peculium*, a fund allocated by the master with which the slave could transact independently and even make payments to the master. But ultimately a *peculium* remained the master's property. In a confrontation between master and slave there would be no point in forcing the slave to pay a penalty to the master with funds that belonged to the master anyway. See Dandamaev 1984: 384-97.

49 Lewy 1956: 4.

difficulties that might arise from an overt admission of bigamy, even if it was understood under local law that the Anatolian partner was a free person and a legitimate wife.

3. Biblical. There are two verses in Genesis where the slaves given by Sarah, Leah, and Rachel as wives to their husbands Abraham and Jacob respectively are referred to as the slaves of their husbands. In Gen 21:12 God reassures Abraham, who does not wish to send Hagar away: "Do not be perturbed on account of the boy and of your slave-woman (*'ămātekā*)." In Gen 32:23 Jacob "took his two wives and his two female slaves (*šipḥōtâw*), and his eleven children and crossed the ford of the Jabbok."[50]

This sudden shift to calling Hagar, Bilhah, and Zilpah the slaves of the husband rather than of the wife, although in a narrative, cannot be dismissed simply as euphemistic modesty, especially in the second passage, where it is explicitly contrasted with the term "wives."[51] Nor would any comparison with the very special situation in the Old Assyrian documents be appropriate. I suggest (albeit reluctantly) that the explanation lies in an inconsistent narrative rather than in the nature of the law. Either there was some confusion in the tradition as to whether they had been given as concubines or wives, or the author of these passages was concerned to maximize the status of the primary wives at the expense of the secondary wives. Support for the latter view comes from Gen 35:22, where the same Bilhah is called the "free concubine" (*pîlegeš*) of Jacob, a designation that is totally inappropriate. The narrator's motive is obvious—to spare Reuben, Jacob's son, whose crime in sleeping with Bilhah would have been far more heinous if she were Jacob's wife. On the other hand, as we have seen in the Hittite laws, if Bilhah were merely Jacob's slave concubine, there would have been no breach of a sexual taboo at all. The narrator's main goal was to impose an appropriate level of moral opprobrium, in pursuit of which he was prepared to sacrifice legal or narrative consistency.

50 It is unnecessary for the purposes of this study to distinguish between *'āmâ* and *šipḥâ* in Biblical Hebrew. Whatever else they mean, they certainly both mean female slave.

51 Lipiński argues that *'āmâ* is an honorific title in Gen 21:9-13, where Hagar is presented as an Arabian queen (1994: 14). But at that point she is still far from becoming a queen, and when Sarah uses the same term of Hagar in v. 10, it is anything but an honorific title.

Notwithstanding the above evidence, I consider that in ancient Near Eastern law a man could not be master and husband at the same time, because of the conflicting logic of the two institutions. The purpose of marriage is to produce legitimate offspring who can inherit from their father, if there is anything to inherit. Children begotten upon a slave are the fruits of their father's property. As such, they are not capable of inheriting from him; rather, they are part of his estate, to be inherited by his legitimate heirs.[52] Even if it were conceded that by a special rule the children were free while their mother was not, the logic of the law would still produce absurd consequences: on the father's death, the children would inherit their own mother as a slave.

Further difficulties arising from the logic of the two institutions are illustrated by an Old Babylonian document:[53]

> Mar-ertsetim son of Ayatia has taken Atkal-ana-belti, her [Ayatia's] slave for marriage. If Atkal-ana-belti says to her mistress Ayatia, "You are not my mistress," she will shave her and sell her. Everything that Ayatia has acquired and will acquire belongs to Mar-ertsetim. As long as she [Ayatia] lives, both of them shall support [her].

A woman has given her slave-woman to her son as a wife but has not freed her.[54] If slavery and marriage were compatible in this instance, the husband would, on his mother's death, inherit his wife as a slave. It seems to me more reasonable to suppose that the slave's personality is split. She is a free woman as regards her husband and a slave as regards her mistress.

52 CH 171, in decreeing the release of a slave concubine and her children by her master on the master's death, seeks to avoid the unseemly but logical consequence of the law, namely, that the legitimate heirs will acquire their own siblings as slaves. It specifically (and unnecessarily) adds that the master's legitimate children are not to claim his children by the slave concubine as slaves. Nonetheless, the concern of CH does not appear to be reflected in its parallel provision in CL 25, which assumes that release of his children by a slave concubine is purely a matter of the master's choice.

53 CT 6 37a (see Westbrook 1988b: 117).

54 The background to this arrangement is almost certainly that the "son" is adopted, possibly a slave whom she has manumitted. The tell-tale sign is the duty of support which falls on the son as much as upon his wife. See Obermark 1992: 45-47, 83-94.

The mistress's ownership rights as regards her slave are limited and therefore have to be restored in part by express contractual clauses, as we have seen above—in this case a penalty clause and a support clause. On her mistress's death, any inheritance rights that her husband might have had in her will be stultified by his status as her husband.

Accordingly, marriage to one's own slave will nullify or at least suspend her slave status, as regards her husband. An Old Babylonian polygamy document makes this consequence clear.[55]

> Bunene-abi and Belessunu have purchased Shamash-nuri daughter of Ibbi-Shahan from her father Ibbi-Shahan. To Bunene-abu she is a wife; to Belessunu she is a slave. The day that Shamash-nuri says to her mistress Belessunu, "You are not my mistress," she will shave her and sell her. He/she has paid 5 shekels of silver for her full purchase-price. He has caused her to climb over the pestle; the transaction is complete; his heart is satisfied.

As in the previous document, the slave's legal personality is split between her mistress and her husband. In this case, however, she was originally the property of her husband, who purchased her jointly with his wife. He then married his newly acquired slave, although the document does not inform us of this directly. It is drafted for the benefit of the first wife, to show that she retains some of her rights of ownership, even though the husband has lost his through marriage.

I now propose to analyze two biblical laws in the light of my understanding of the law of slavery and marriage. The first is Deut 21:10-14:

> When you go out to war against your enemies and God has given them into your hand and you have taken captives, and you see among the captives a beautiful woman and you desire to take her for yourself as a wife: you shall bring her into your house, and she shall shave her head and pare her nails and remove her captive's garb and sit in your house and mourn her father and mother for a period of one month. And afterwards you may come in to her and take her, and she shall become your wife. If it comes about that

55 CT 8 22b (see Westbrook 1988b: 119).

> you do not want her, you shall divorce her to herself; you shall not sell her for silver. You shall not trade in her, because you degraded her.

There is no question of slave concubinage here; the text explicitly refers to the formation of marriage and to its termination by divorce. The Hebrew verb *šlḥ* usually translated "release" or the like, is also a technical term for divorcing a wife, as in Deut 24:1, 3. In my analysis, the captive woman is initially a slave, marriage makes her a free person, but subsequent termination of the marriage revives her previous status: her husband becomes her master again, and therefore can in principle sell her as a slave. The law forbids him to do so; instead, he must divorce her "to herself (*lĕnapšâ*).[56] This curious and seemingly redundant expression is another facet of splitting the juridical personality. The woman is reunited with herself, that is, she receives back the ownership of herself that was ceded to her captor when she became a slave, regained during marriage, but lost again to him following her divorce.

The second law is Exod 21:7-11, which I have identified as regulating a situation where a slave-woman is the concubine, not the wife, of her master. The opening provisions have already been discussed. We are now concerned with the second part of the law, which deals with her rights if she remains within the family of the purchaser:

> If he assigns her to his son, he shall treat her according to the status of daughters. If he takes another for himself, he shall not reduce her food, clothing, and oil. If he does not provide her with these three, she shall go free without payment of silver.

Two situations are envisaged:

1. She is assigned to a son of the purchaser. Many commentators (including myself), have assumed that the "status of daughters" is an oblique reference to marriage with the son.[57] In the light of my earlier discussion of this law, I now consider it more

56 See *HAL*^{3} 673a.

57 Westbrook 1988d: 61.

likely that the provision is designed to counter another attempt by the purchaser to subvert the purpose of the contract. Assignment points to future consummation, which gives the purchaser the opportunity to temporize regarding the female slave's position while she waits for his son to come of age. The law insists that her master must in the interim give her the standing of a daughter within the household, not a servant, because the purpose of the contract is that she provide sexual and reproductive services, not labor.

2. The master takes her himself but subsequently takes a second concubine. Since he has fulfilled the purpose of the contract (and presumably taken the woman's virginity), unraveling it by redemption is not an appropriate solution to his failure to provide her with proper sustenance, which in any case was a more serious breach. It was a form of physical abuse, not merely a loss of rights in the abstract, and accordingly it annulled not just the contract of concubinage but the underlying debt.[58]

The mention of rations provides a final indication that this law was regulating concubinage, not marriage. The duty of a husband to provide his wife with sustenance was so self-evident that it went virtually unmentioned in ancient Near Eastern sources. Only where the husband is missing abroad does the issue come to light. The law codes consider the inadequacy of his property for providing sustenance sufficient grounds for his wife to marry another (CH 134; MAL A 36). Rations are the stuff of servants and dependants, not wives. Were the slave-woman married to her master, she could have relied on the protection given by her status as wife to ensure her sustenance and would not have required special measures.

58 The same principle may be reflected in MAL A 39. The protasis describes a complicated and obscure situation in which a girl is pledged for her father's debt and then apparently becomes the object of rival claims between the pledgee, another creditor of her father, and a man to whom she has been given in marriage (apparently by the plegdee). Our concern is with yet another contingency (lines 34-35): "if she is badly provided for, she is free of claims, in favor of the one who sustains her," following the interpretation of Veenhof (1978: 292-95) and not of *CAD* L 249.

Summary and Conclusions

In the legal systems of the ancient Near East, the female slave, no less than her male counterpart, was property. The special features of her gender were property interests of her owner, to be exploited or disposed of as the latter saw fit. Thus the owner's interest in her sexuality was protected against interference by outsiders through the rules of property law, just as the integrity of any asset might be protected. By the same token, offspring of the slave, even when fathered by her owner, were in principle subject to the rules of property law, like the fruits of any asset.

At the same time, however, the female slave's sexuality and reproductive capacity brought into play the rules of family law, either through special applications of the principles of social justice, which tempered the condition of slaves in general, or directly through the status of marriage. In certain circumstances occasioned by the exercise of her sexual and reproductive functions, the principles of social justice could override the owner's property rights to render her inalienable, redeemable, or protected from physical abuse. The status of marriage, if with the owner himself, altogether excluded the application of property law to her person.

The question of which regime—property law or family law—was to prevail varied according to circumstances and sometimes was resolved by compromise. For example, the principles of social justice could be avoided by express contractual provisions. Presumably such provisions could not override the equitable jurisdiction of the courts altogether, but they were employed so widely as to leave little doubt as to their efficacy, the limits of which cannot be ascertained. Similarly, where marriage was to a third party, there was a wide range of possibilities. If the slave was married to another slave of her owner, the owner's property rights prevailed, but if to a free person, the slave and her offspring enjoyed some of the consequences of a free marriage.

Finally, mention should be made of the special legal mechanism employed to regulate the status of a female slave. Where the property and family interests in her person were located in different persons, the law employed a subtle jurisprudential device: her legal personality was split between them, the two parts being governed by property and family law respectively. No better symbol could have been devised for the conflicting attitudes of the law towards the female slave.

11

A Sumerian Freedman

Abstract

Several different definitions have been offered over the years for the Sumerian term dumu-gi$_7$. This article examines several sources in which the term is used and proposes that, in legal and administrative texts, it is best to understand the term as referring to a slave who has been freed.

A free person is most commonly referred to in Sumerian as lu$_2$ ("man, householder"), a term which assumes rather than asserts free status.[1] A more specific term is "son/daughter of a man" (dumu/dumu-munus lu$_2$), asserting that the person was freeborn. As a definition, it seems to beg the question, since the criterion of being freeborn only removes the inquiry to an earlier generation. Like ownership of property, however, it recognizes that an absolute right remains at bottom a relative one: title to land depends on having acquired it from someone with good title, and that owner's in turn from the same process. Since infinite historical inquiry is impossible, at some point relative rights are accepted as absolute.

Two other terms define freedom by reference to geography. "Son of the city (X)" (dumu uru X) is a widely used expression that focuses on the status of citizen (and therefore free person). It is often used in the plural to describe the burghers of a particular state.[2]

* Originally published in *Literatur, Politik und Recht in Mesopotamien. Festschrift für Claus Wilcke* (ed. W. Sallaberger et al.; OBC 14; Wiesbaden: Harrassowitz, 2003), 333-39. Used by permission.

1 I am grateful to my colleague Professor Jerrold Cooper for reading the first draft of this article and for his helpful comments and criticisms.

2 In the di-til-la documents of Ur III: *NSG* 185: 8. Cf. the same usage in the late second millennium at Ugarit: e.g., DUMU.MEŠ KUR *ú-ga-ri-it* (RS 17.42; edited in

The second term is dumu-gi$_7$, which is found mostly in legal and administrative texts of the Ur III period and occasionally in literary texts derived from that period. Unlike the other terms, it has no Akkadian equivalent and is not attested beyond the early Old Babylonian period. Steinkeller translated "native son," on the analogy of ur-gi$_7$ ("domestic dog").[3] Our contribution will explore more closely the meaning of this term and in particular its legal usage as a designation of free status.

Where the term is found in literary sources, freedom is not at issue. When applied to gods, the epithet dumu-gi$_7$ illustrates rather their position as city-dwellers. Thus in the Lamentation over the Destruction of Sumer and Ur, Nanše, although a dumu-gi$_7$, is obliged to dwell outside the city (line 167), and Nanna, a dumu-gi$_7$ who loves his city, is forced to leave it (lines 370-373).[4] In Gilgamesh and Agga, Utu asks Gilgamesh: "Young man, you are a city-dweller; what will become of you in the mountains?"[5] In the Curse of Agade, it is in parallelism with lu$_2$ sag$_5$, illustrating two types of prosperous inhabitants (lines 249-251).[6]

In legal sources, on the other hand, the term is typically found in opposition to slavery. It is attested four times in di-til-la court records and twice in Sumerian law codes.[7]

1. *NSG* 76 (lines 1-8) reads:

> Case closed. A son of X sued B daughter of Y. He said: "I bought her." Because the witnesses denied his word and he was pronounced a wrongdoer (lu$_2$-ni$_2$-zuḫ ba-an-šu-še-ša), B was pronounced a dumu-gi$_7$ (dumu-gi$_7$-ra ba-an-šu-še).

Nougayrol 1956: 171-72). Note that it is used interchangeably with LU$_2$.MEŠ KUR *ú-ga-ri-it* (RS 17.145; edited in Nougayrol 1956: 172-73).

3 Steinkeller 1993: 112-13 n. 9. The term gi$_7$ or gir$_{15}$ (sign ŠE$_3$) is also found in phonetic writing (dumu-gi) in some of the Ur III di-til-la's.

4 Michalowski 1989.

5 Edzard 1991: 174-75, line 20: ĝuruš dumu-gi7 ni2-za-a ḫe2-me-en kur-ra a-na-bi-me-en.

6 Cooper 1983a.

7 The di-til-la documents are edited in Falkenstein 1956-57, vol. 2 (abbreviated as *NSG* followed by the edition number).

The case in part concerns a false claim of ownership of a woman, which results in a finding as to her true status. (There are further proceedings involving a statement by the successful defendant, but the report is too broken to establish their content.) The term that we have translated "pronounced" refers to a judgment of the court creating a legal status or condition (presumably by a speech act).[8] As Falkenstein points out, it is not strictly necessary, since a false claim could not in itself have changed the defendant's status.[9] The extreme terseness of the report does not permit an exact reconstruction of the situation, but the court's action suggests that the situation was more than simply a false claim against a free woman. The most likely scenario is that the woman had been a slave and the dispute was whether she had been freed or sold. Such disputes would typically arise on the death of the master, concerning actions that he had taken during his lifetime;[10] hence the court's decision here to resolve the defendant's ambiguous status.

2. Falkenstein in his edition of the di-til-la documents translated dumu-gi$_7$ throughout as a conditionally free person ("bedingt frei"). His interpretation was based on *NSG* 177, lines 17-20:

> 1 dumu ir$_{11}$ dumu-gi / geme$_2$-uš-ki-ĝar-ra-ke$_4$ / ku$_3$-diĝir-ra ir$_{11}$-a-tu BAPPIR-še$_3$ in-ši-in-tud-a / a-tu-e ama-ar-gi$_8$-bi in-ĝar^{ar}
>
> "Die Sklavenkinder, die 'bedingt Freien,' die Geme'uškigarra dem Kudiĝirra, dem Sklaven des Atu, des Brauers, geboren hat, hat Atu freigelassen."

8 šuš/ku$_4$; see Falkenstein 1956-57: vol. 2, no. 76, note to line 7; and 1956-57: vol. 3, 169, s.v. tu(-r), meaning 3 "zu etwas machen." The shift š > t posited by Falkenstein is not valid with the reading ku$_4$, but the two verbs must still be synonymous. For this legal usage of ku$_4$, see also MVN 3 219, most recently edited in Steinkeller 1989: 330-32; cf. Wilcke 1988: 26-28 n. 97.

9 Falkenstein 1956-57: vol. 2, no. 76, note to line 8.

10 Cf. *NSG* 99, where the heirs promise not to challenge a manumission made by their mother during her lifetime.

Falkenstein's reasoning was impeccable: since free persons cannot be freed a second time, dumu-gi must refer to a condition less than freedom upon which the final release could operate. He surmised that it referred to *paramonē*, which, following Koschaker, he interpreted as a state of half-freedom.[11]

Kraus rejected Falkenstein's interpretation as incoherent, for two reasons. Firstly, the combination dumu x signifies a state into which one was born. It could not apply to a state which was acquired or imposed, like *paramonē*. He did admit to one exception, which we shall consider below. Secondly, in all the legal sources the term was consistently used in contrast to slave; in two thereof manumission was expressly mentioned, and in two there was no mention of anyone to whose benefit *paramonē* could operate. The translation "free/free citizen" therefore fitted exactly in all cases.[12] The logical difficulty in *NSG* 177: 17-20 was only apparent: the appearance of dumu-gi in that position could be explained as an anticipation of the outcome of the case.

Kraus' explanation of *NSG* 177: 17-20 is artificial and unsatisfactory. In a report consisting of one short sentence, an anticipatory statement of the outcome is unnecessary and would only be confusing. There is, however, another way to overcome the logical difficulty. Charpin has shown that the Sumerian term for "to free" (ama-ar-gi$_4$ . . . ĝar) has, like its Akkadian counterpart (*andurāru*), a basic meaning of "to restore to its previous condition." In most cases restoration will be synonymous with freedom, but in special circumstances, for example where a slave was previously not free but owned by another, it will indicate return to the original owner. Thus in CH 280-281, where a foreign merchant returns with the slaves of a Babylonian whom he purchased abroad, the original owner is entitled to redeem his slaves if the latter were foreign-born. If the slaves were native-born, "their release will be established (*andurāršunu iššakkan*) without payment." In the special context, this phrase must refer to the merchant's duty to return them to the owner.[13]

11 Falkenstein 1956-57: vol. 1, 94-95. Cf. already Siegel 1947: 43 n. 47.

12 Kraus 1970: 55-60. Kraus cited only five sources, the tablet containing the text of CU 5 not yet having been discovered. See below.

13 Charpin 1987: 36-44.

In the same way, in our text, Atu did not free the child of a slave who was already half free but caused the child's restoration to a previous condition. At some point the child had indeed been freed, but Atu went before the court in order to obtain the right to re-enslave the child.

3. In the above example, the child's mother appears to have been a free woman married to Atu's slave, which may have had a bearing on the case. The response of early Mesopotamian law to the competing claims of the free mother and the father's owner varied and may not have been consistent even within a single system. CH 175 roundly declares that the owner may not claim the children as slaves, but an Old Babylonian marriage contract from the reign of Samsu-iluna (CT 48 53) declares that all the couple's children belong to the owner.[14] Our third source, paragraph 5 of Codex Ur-Namma (CU), adopts a compromise approach:

> If a (male) slave marries a dumu-gi$_7$, he shall provide the owner with one male child. Together with the son provided to the owner, half the property of his father's house, the wall, the house [. . .]. A child of the dumu-gi$_7$ (dumu dumu-gi$_7$) who is not with the owner shall not enter for slavery.

The assumption is that dumu-gi$_7$ means a free woman, on the analogy of dumu-munus *awīlim* in CH 175, although why this term should have been used (and not, for example, dumu-munus lu$_2$) is not clear, nor the exact status that it embodies. (The question is not mere pedantry, as we shall see below.) The broken clause referring to half the father's property may have provided that the owner was entitled to half the slave's acquired property on his death, as in CH 176. It is unlikely that it was regulating the inheritance of the slave's son who had been given as a slave. At all events, the duty to provide one child as a slave is clear.

4. That dumu-gi$_7$ is not simply a synonym for dumu lu$_2$ is demonstrated by *NSG* 75, which reads:

14 Edited in Westbrook 1988b: 123.

> Case closed. X, Y, and Z swore the oath that A and B, the sons of F, had come forward and declared with regard to C, who was the slave of F: "Oath of the king: let the slave C be freed (ama-gi$_4^{gi_8}$-ni ḫe$_2$-^{ĝa_2}ĝar^{ar}), and let him be made like the son of a man" (dumu lu$_2$-AŠ-gin$_7$-na-am$_3$ ḫe$_2$-dim$_2$). And (they swore) that C had called PN$_{1\text{-}7}$ (to attest that) the slave was freed. C and his children were pronounced dumu-gi$_7$ (dumu-gi$_7$-ra ba-an-ku$_4$).

The court by its judgment gives C a new status, which is described in two ways: he is a dumu-gi$_7$, but he is only "like" a dumu lu$_2$. Had C been born free, the effect of ama-ar-gi$_4$ would have been to restore him to his previous condition. Evidently, he had been born a slave and, notwithstanding the power of the law to change a person's status, it was felt that manumission could not go so far as to make a person freeborn when he had not been free at birth. What the law could do, however, was to deem C's status *analogous* in law to that of a freeborn person and thus endowed with the same privileges.

The same applies to the term dumu-uru. In *NSG* 74 and 178 (lines 12-15), a slave is freed and made *like* a son of the city (ama-ar-gi$_8$ i$_3$-ĝar-ra dumu uru-gin$_7$ in-dim-ma). The term dumu-gi$_7$, by contrast, is used in *NSG* 75 as a direct designation of the manumitted slave's new status.

5. It is in the light of this analysis that we should interpret paragraphs 25-26 of the Codex Lipit-Ishtar:

> If a man marries a wife and she bears him a son and the son is living, and a slave woman bears her owner a son and the father frees the slave woman and her children, the son of the slave woman shall not divide the estate with the son of his (former) owner.
>
> If his first wife dies and, after the death of his wife, he marries his slave woman, the son of his first wife is his heir; the son that the slave woman bore to her owner is like the son of a dumu-gi$_7$ (dumu dumu-gi$_7$-gin$_7$-nam)—he shall enjoy his house (e$_2$-a-ni ib$_2$-du$_{10}$-ge).

The second situation in paragraph 26 is a slight variant on the first: instead of freeing his slave who has borne him a son, he marries her after his first wife's death. The effect of the marriage is to free the slave woman, since the status of wife, although not legally incompatible with the status of slave, is incompatible when the owner and husband are the same person.[15] On the father's death, therefore, the question arises as to the status of her son by him, who was born while she was still a slave-concubine and not expressly manumitted. Although the situation is different from the court cases above, the underlying legal principle is the same. The law cannot change the circumstances of his birth, but it can put him in the same position as if they had been otherwise. The ruling is that he is deemed free *as if* he had been born subsequent to his mother's marriage. Note that the term dumu-gi$_7$, which applies to his mother, refers to her condition as a freed slave, the issue being not whether she was free but when she had been freed.

The consequences of the son's change of status depend upon the meaning of the last phrase ("he shall enjoy his house") which unfortunately is not clear. If the house in question is the father's estate, we still do not know whether the slave's son inherits a share subject to the firstborn privilege of the legitimate son or is merely entitled to some sort of usufruct or right of habitation. In the first alternative, subsequent marriage would not merely free a son born out of wedlock but make him also a legitimate heir. Another possibility (which would account for the unusual expression) is that "his house" is the son's *peculium*, i.e., separate assets that his father gave him or that he otherwise acquired during the father's lifetime but were deemed his father's as long as he was regarded as a slave.

6. The final legal source adds little to the discussion, if only because its interpretation relies on the restoration of a key verb. *NSG* 184 (lines 9-15) informs us that because a certain woman was a dumu-gi, she was [redeemed] (ba-[du$_8$]). The silver for her (ku$_3$-ga-ni) was charged to the palace for the benefit of an official. Siegel, who proposed this restoration, made the plausible suggestion that it was a case of ransom from captivity abroad of a captive by a merchant who was then reimbursed by the palace.

15 Discussed by Westbrook 1998a: 214-38, esp. 229ff.

The palace was responsible because she was a free citizen.[16] If his interpretation is correct, this is the only legal source in which dumu-gi_7 exemplifies the local/foreign dichotomy that is the perspective of the literary sources.

Conclusions

In the four legal sources where some context can be established for the term (nos. 1, 2, 4, and 5 above), dumu-gi_7 arguably refers not to any free person but specifically one freed from slavery. In *NSG* 75 it is explicitly distinguished from a freeborn person. It is impossible to conclude from such a narrow sample that dumu-gi_7 was used exclusively to refer to freed slaves, but its use calls to mind the term *libertus* ("freedman") that designated a manumitted slave at Rome. Without wishing to import any of the special conditions of that status in Roman law, we note that the *libertus* was a fully free citizen of Rome but with a slightly lower legal and social status than an *ingenuus*, a freeborn citizen. A lower status of citizen would account for the specific designation as dumu-gi_7 of numbers of guruš in ration lists, and in particular Jones and Snyder 252 ii 25: dumu-gi_7 lu_2 uru X^{ki}-me.[17] The appellation "citizens (lu_2) of city X" was sufficient to establish that the men in question were free citizens; the designation dumu-gi_7 would be redundant if that were its only purpose.[18]

Our suggested nuance could only apply in a legal or administrative context; elsewhere the broader connotation of locally born would apply. The gods, after all, could never be described as freed slaves. By way of a bridge between the two aspects, we would return to Kraus' assertion that the form dumu x applies exclusively to a state into which one is born—directly contradicted, as Kraus admitted, by *NSG* 75. Kraus' explanation was that it fell within the typical exception to the rule, namely, the use of dumu for an adopted son. Just as the adoption of A by B makes A into

16 Siegel 1947: 42-46.

17 Jones and Snyder 1961.

18 Kraus (1970: 60) wonders why only few out of thousands of names in these lists are called dumu-gi_7. A narrower status than simply "free person" would go some way toward explaining the rarity of the term.

dumu B, so the manumission of a slave in Nippur made him into a dumu nibru.[19] As we have seen, however, that is precisely what manumission does not do: it makes him dumu-gi_7 but only *like* a dumu uru. Accordingly, either dumu-gi_7 does not follow the grammatical rule, or it refers to a birth condition not necessarily connected with freedom. In the latter case, it is possible that dumu-gi_7 referred essentially to a native-born person, and that it was adopted as a euphemism in legal texts for houseborn slaves who were freed, since they could claim local birth, if not freedom at birth. Perhaps as a social class it even colored literary texts. The two characters juxtaposed in The Curse of Agade could be taken as a merism for Agade's prosperous citizenry, being examples from each end of the social scale:

249 May your freedman (dumu-gi_7), who eats fine food,[20] lie hungry in the grass.
250 May your prominent nobleman (lu_2-sag_5)
251 eat the *thatching* on his roof!

19 Kraus 1970: 58.

20 Social status and economic status are not necessarily identical. Freedmen at Rome could be fabulously wealthy, as one might expect with persons who had essentially bought their freedom with their own enterprise. Or the verse could be a comment on how prosperous all classes of Agade's citizens were before the curse.

12

The Quality of Freedom in Neo-Babylonian Manumissions

Abstract

The status of *mār banî*, generally understood to be free citizen, and the status of *širku*, temple slave, would seem to be incompatible, yet they appear in combination in certain Neo-Babylonian and Achaemenid period texts. The reason lies in the Greek institution of *paramonē*, first identified in Mesopotamian sources by P. Koschaker. It is not, as Koschaker thought, a semi-free status, but a contract of service. Applied to manumitted slaves, it gives them free status, although dedication to a temple upon a future contingency may make their freedom temporary.

The document[1] OIP 122 38 (= A 32117), a record of litigation from the reign of Cyrus,[2] contains a paradox that has led to two radically different interpretations of its contents. If either interpretation were accepted, it would have widespread ramifications for our understanding of Neo-Babylonian law and society.

According to the document, a slave named Ištar-ab-uṣur is suing his former mistress. His declaration tells a long and complicated story of his transfer from one owner to another. The essence of his plaint, however, lies in two contradictory steps taken by the defendant, Innina-eṭirat:

1. "Arrabi and Innina-eṭirat his wife sealed a tablet of my *mār banî* status (IM.DUB DUMU-*ba-nu-ti-ia*). They wrote in my

* Originally published in *Revue d'Assyriologie* 98 (2004): 101-8. Used by permission.

1 This article was first presented as a lecture at the Centre National de la Recherche Scientifique, UMR 7041—Archéologie et Sciences de l'Antiquité, at Nanterre on 28 May 2004. I am grateful to the participants for their helpful comments and criticisms. Responsibility for errors rests with the author.

2 Published and edited in Weisberg 2003: 70-74 and pl. 21; also edited in Roth 1989b.

tablet: 'Ištar-ab-uṣur (and his children) . . . are [*mār banî* (?)][3] pure ones of Ištar of Uruk' (^{lú}*za-ku-tu šá* ^{d}INNIN UNUG^{ki}) . . ." (lines 12-17).

2. "Now, 9 years later Innina-eṭirat wife of Arrabi, who had sealed my tablet of *mār banî* status, after the death of her husband Arrabi sold me to Anu-ah-iddin son of Ṣilla, and he has inscribed my hand (with a slave mark). Render a judgment against Innina-eṭirat!" (lines 20-28).

The court, after hearing evidence from the defendant that the purchaser forced her to sell on the grounds that he was still owed money by her late husband, ruled that "they would not change the *ṭuppi zakūti* of Ištar-ab-uṣur; they would not change the curse of the great gods; they confirmed (the status) of Ištar-ab-uṣur and his children in the tablet of their oblate status/redemption" (*ina* IM.DUB *ši-ir-ku-ti-šu-nu*/*pi-ir-qú-ti-šu-nu*; lines 42-45).

Roth, who reads *širkūtu* in line 45, assumes that three conditions of status were at issue in this trial: slavery, *mārbanûtu*, and *širkūtu*. The second, *mārbanûtu*, is generally taken to be the status of a free citizen. The third, *širkūtu*, is that of an oblate—a person dedicated to a god as a temple slave. The phrase "pure ones of Ištar of Uruk" alludes to the well-known process in this period of persons dedicating their slaves or children as oblates: "purify them to DN" (*ana* DN *zukku*).

The result, however, appears to be that the slave in this case gained the status of free citizen and temple slave at the same time. To avoid this contradiction, Roth re-interprets the term *mār banî*, suggesting that it did not mean "free" in the Western or Classical connotations of that term, but could involve some degree of dependence. It is difficult, however, to consider the term as indicating anything but a fully free citizen, as studies by Dandamaev and others have shown.[4] A document of manumission, BM 6650, expresses the idea forcefully (lines 1-10):[5]

3 Restored by Roth 1989b; doubted by Weisberg 2003, but without another suggestion for the traces.

4 Dandamaev 1981; San Nicolò 1930; and *CAD* M 256-57.

5 Edition in MacGinnis 1993. See also OIP 122 37.

> Ištar-eṭirat, the daughter of the king, of her own free will sealed for Nabu-mukki-elip a tablet of *mār banî* status in perpetuity (*ana umi ṣati*). Nabu-mukki-elip is clear (*zakû*); he belongs to himself (*ša ramānišu šū*). No other person may make a claim against him.

Weisberg seeks to avoid the contradiction in status by denying that the text mentions temple slavery at all.[6] The plaintiff had been manumitted but then sold into slavery illegally, and he now obtained through the court a judgment confirming his status as a free man (*mār banî*). In order to achieve this result, Weisberg firstly gives a new reading (collated) to the word in line 45 that Roth read as *širkūtu*, namely *pirkūtu*, which he translates "redemption," on the basis of the Aramaic root *prq* "to release."[7] The word *pirkūtu*, however, is attested neither in Akkadian nor in Aramaic. *AHw* derives a Neo-Babylonian word *pirqu* with the meaning "Auslösung" from the Aramaic root, but Stolper has since shown it to be a phantom lemma.[8] Moreover, notwithstanding Weisberg's collation, the first sign of the word could just as well be read ŠI as PI.[9]

Weisberg secondly seeks, like Roth, to redefine one of the terms used. Ištar-ab-uṣur is called a *zakû ša Ištar* (*ša*) *Uruk*, which Weisberg translates "one whose status has been clarified by the Lady-of-Uruk." It is not clear to us how the basic meaning of *zakû*—"pure; free of obligation,"—can be stretched to cover ascertainment of the facts, which is the meaning that Weisberg gives to "clarified" here. He produces no other example for use of the phrase with this meaning, which would imply a hitherto unknown

6 Weisberg 2001.

7 We assume that by redemption he means simply "release," since there is no evidence that anyone paid money to release Ištar-ab-uṣur from slavery, as redemption would imply.

8 *AHw* 867; Stolper 2000. The word is *pišku*/*pirku*, meaning "harm." Weisberg points out (2001: 1173-74) that *širkūtu* is spelled *šir-ku-tu* in the extant examples, but the spelling *ši-ir-ku* is common. It is less of a stretch to postulate an orthographical variant than an entirely new word. Furthermore, the value *qú* proposed by Weisberg (*pi-ir-qú-ti-šu-nu*) is rare in Neo-Babylonian, being found only in royal inscriptions (oral communication of F. Joannès).

9 Certainly according to the photograph supplied by Weisberg (2003: pl. 21). I am grateful to Profs. Martha Roth and Jonathan Tenney for reexamining the tablet at my request. They agree that no unassailable verdict can be given but incline to the reading ŠI.

jurisdiction of the temple courts in verifying the free or slave status of individuals. On the other hand, *ša Ištar*/DN *zakû* is frequently attested for the designation of persons as temple slaves. *RA* 67 147-56, for example, makes the connection abundantly clear: temple officials claim a slave woman from the private individual whom she is serving. The latter states that he had purchased her, but the officials claim that she is nonetheless *zaqītu ša* ^d^*Nanaya* (lines 9-10) and point to the star inscribed on her wrist, the mark of an oblate. She in turn testifies that her former master "purified me to ^d^Nanaya" (lines 18-19: *a-na* ^d^*na-na-a uz-zak-ka-an-ni*). After a scribe has given expert testimony that the inscriptions on her wrist (to Nanaya and Ištar of Uruk) are genuine, the judges assign her to the Eanna temple, to be counted among the basket-carriers (*zābil tupšikku*) of Eanna.[10]

The paradox of OIP 122 38 cannot, therefore, be resolved by redefining any of the commonly used terms found in it. That two eminent scholars should have been led to strain the semantics of legal terminology, albeit in different directions, is not surprising, for the coexistence of free citizenship and temple slavery seems to be an impossible contradiction. A more fruitful approach may be to reexamine the underlying legal situation. The explanation for the anomalies that the text presents and for the quality of freedom that its protagonist enjoys, lies, we suggest, in another ancient legal condition whose nature has been misunderstood: *paramonē*.

Paramonē is a Greek term found in Hellenistic contracts from the third century B.C.E. onward. It is a condition that one party will "remain with" the other for a fixed period or for the latter's life and perform work for him. There are three main transactions in which the *paramonē*-clause is found: suretyship, in which a surety remains with the creditor; antichresis, in which a pledge works for the creditor in lieu of interest; and manumission, in which a freed slave remains with his former master.[11] Our study is chiefly concerned with *paramonē* following manumission.

It was Koschaker who first connected the Greek institution with the ancient Near East.[12] He identified *paramonē* in two sources: firstly, a

10 See also YOS 6 129, where a *zakīti ša* ^d^*Bēlti ša Uruk* is also marked on her wrist with the oblate's star.

11 See Samuel 1965, discussed below.

12 Koschaker 1931: esp. 70-83.

group of Old Babylonian manumission documents where the slave was freed (and sometimes adopted) by the master and obliged to support (*našû*) the master for the rest of the latter's life; secondly, Neo-Babylonian documents where the master dedicated the slave to the temple, but the slave continued to serve (*palāḫu*) the dedicator during his lifetime.

Koschaker explained *paramonē*, in both the Greek and ancient Near Eastern sources, as a half-free status. In the case of manumission (*Freilassungsparamone*), the slave remained under the authority (*Gewalt*) of his master, who therefore still had some rights of ownership. The slave gained full freedom only after the end of the period of *paramonē*. Where the slave had been dedicated to a temple, he did not gain his freedom at all. Instead, there was a division of ownership: the master retained sufficient rights during his lifetime to be designated owner as well as the temple.

Koschaker's identification of *paramonē* in the cuneiform sources was a great insight, but in the light of subsequent research and with many more examples to draw upon, his conception of its legal nature is no longer sustainable. Three main criticisms may be noted:

1. Koschaker identified the verb *palāḫu* as both a tell-tale sign of *paramonē* and of a relationship of slave and owner between the server and the served. It does not necessarily imply either. It refers to the care and sustenance of a person, usually in their old age when they are unable to look after themselves.[13] It may be used of the service of slaves but may equally apply to that of a son or daughter, and even of an outsider, that is, of free persons, by contractual arrangement.[14] The Old Babylonian examples cited by Koschaker of an owner adopting a slave who was then obliged to serve him demonstrate that the server in question was free. It is impossible to be son or daughter of a person and their slave at the same time.[15]

13 Greenfield 1982.

14 See *Nbn.* 697 discussed below. In Beckman *Emar* 10 from Emar (see Beckman and Hoffner 1996: no. 10), the person providing the service is a financier.

15 Regrettably, there are no Neo-Babylonian examples of manumission and adoption; see MacGinnis 1993: 99-101. On the other hand, a use of *palāḫu* that was confined to free men was the Achaemenid term *palāḫ šarri* ("royal service"). It refers to a tax payable by the holders of bow lands; see Stolper 1985: 61-62.

2. Koschaker laid emphasis on the restrictions placed on the server's freedom of movement and residence, the fact that the server had to work for the served under his instructions, and the possibility that he could be assigned to work for third parties, as evidence of continuing rights of ownership.[16] Restriction of freedom, however, cannot simply be equated with property rights. There is no reason why a person's freedom should not be restricted by contract, as is frequently the case in modern society. The documents from Emar (unavailable to Koschaker) reveal that *paramonē* in the ancient Near East occurred in other situations besides slavery. As in Greece, it could be a term in an antichretic pledge, known at Emar as *amēlūtu*. Pledged persons did not have the status of slave but were bound by contract.[17] For example, in Arnaud *Emar* 6 16, a creditor takes over a debt in return for the debtor serving him (*palāḫu*) for the creditor's lifetime. Thereafter the debtor can choose between paying back half the debt as full payment or continuing to serve the creditor's heirs.[18]

3. Koschaker's understanding of the legal nature of ancient Near Eastern *paramonē* was predicated upon his analysis of the Hellenistic institution. A papyrologist, A. Samuel, has since refuted that analysis.[19] It is not appropriate to review Samuel's reasoning in detail here, but in summary, he brings evidence to show that a freedman subject to *paramonē* had the rights of a free man: property rights, the right to have freeborn children, immunity from arbitrary arrest or slavery while performing his obligations. In particular, a freedman customarily was obliged to make an extra payment to his manumitter's heirs for release

16 Koschaker 1931: 19-20, 27, 74.

17 See Westbrook 1995e: 1636-37. Note that the term *amēlūtu* at Emar is an abstract noun and has no connection with the Neo-Babylonian use of *amēlūtu* meaning a slave. Eichler (1973: 43-44) refutes Koschaker's view that the pledge in *tidennūtu* at Nuzi becomes the slave of the creditor.

18 There are contractual penalties on both parties for prematurely ending the arrangement: the creditor loses his debt; the debtor must repay the whole debt plus 50 percent.

19 Samuel 1965.

from his *paramonē*-obligations upon the death of the manumitter. He paid in his own name, thereby showing that he was already free and could own property. The arrangement bears a striking resemblance to the Emar contract discussed above.

Paramonē was not, therefore, a form of partial ownership, but a contractual term. In manumission, the essence of *paramonē* was that the legal relationship between the freed slave and his former master changed from one based on property to one of contract. The existence of *paramonē* as a contractual arrangement in the Neo-Babylonian period is confirmed by a document (not referred to by Koschaker) recording breach of such a contract. *Nbn*. 697 reads (lines 1-16):

> Iqiša gave his slave Remanni-Bel the name Rimut and sealed a tablet of his free status (^{lú}DUMU-DU$_3$-*ú-tu-šu*), so that he (Rimut) might supply him with his food and clothing. Remanni-Bel . . . after his tablet of free status was sealed ran away and did not give food, oil, and clothing, but Esagil-ramat (the daughter-in-law of) Iqiša served, honored, and looked after him (*ta-ap-laḫ-šu ta-du-ur-šu ù tu-sa-ad-di-*[*is-su*]). She gave him food, oil, and clothing. Iqiša voluntarily annulled Remanni-Bel's tablet of free status and transferred him to Esagil-ramat . . . .

An owner manumitted his slave on condition of continuing care, which, as the document subsequently instructs us, is the content of *palāḫu*. Roth is troubled by the fact that the status of *mārbanûtu* appears to be revocable by the former master, which she claims is not to be expected if it meant a fully free man.[20] The explanation, however, lies not in the nature of a *mār banî*'s status but in the basic principles of contract law.

Manumission with *paramonē* was a contract between owner and slave in which the owner freed the slave in return for future payment, in the form of services. If the owner stipulated in the contract that manumission was to be conditional upon performance of those services, failure by the *paramonar* to fulfill that condition at any time would annul the contract,

20 Roth 1989b: 486-87.

with the result that he would simply revert to being a slave.[21] Accordingly, when Remanni-Bel broke his *paramonē*-contract by running away, his former owner was entitled to annul the manumission.

In the Neo-Babylonian period, Koschaker identified *paramonē* not in simple manumission but only in the special arrangement whereby a slave's owner dedicated the slave as an oblate but the slave remained with the owner for the latter's lifetime. It is not *paramonē* as we now understand it, since in the examples given by Koschaker, the slave is never freed, even in a limited sense, but merely transferred from one owner to another. It is nevertheless necessary to consider the legal nature of the arrangement, as it will have some bearing on the issue that this study seeks to resolve: the contradiction between *mār banî* and *širku* status.

Koschaker postulated shared ownership between donor and temple, in that ownership passed immediately to the temple but the donor retained some residual rights. He could not, however, point to any positive right of ownership that the temple could exercise during the donor's lifetime. The idea of such a shared ownership appears to have been different from joint ownership in that different elements of ownership were divided up between the two owners. An obvious analogy is usufruct, but Koschaker did not employ it, probably because the one "residual" right in the donor that he adduced as evidence was the right to sell the slave, which would hardly be conducive with usufruct. His concept of shared ownership thus remains an artificial construct, without parallel in other legal systems—certainly not in the ancient Near East—and relying solely on analogy with manumission-*paramonē* as he understood it.

Koschaker acknowledged that his was not the only possible analysis; the dedication could be interpreted as a future gift, which would give the temple no immediate rights in the slave. He rejected the idea of a future gift on the grounds that the contracts declared ownership to have passed.[22] Nonetheless, *donatio mortis causa* (gift to take effect on death) is a well known device in cuneiform law, in the realm of adoption and inheritance law. It is often deceptively presented as a gift, in order to establish a vested

21 For a similar analysis of the Greek contracts, see Samuel 1965: 275.

22 Koschaker 1931: 81.

right, but the right is to future property.[23] The same interpretation can apply to dedications of slaves. YOS 7 17, for example, reads:

> Nabu-ahhe-bulliṭ, son of Nabu-šum-ukin and descendant of the priest of Ninurta, and his wife Bulṭa, daughter of Bel-ušallim and descendant of Kuri, have voluntarily given their slave Ah-iddin to Ištar for the preservation of their lives. As long as Nabu-ahhe-bulliṭ and Bulṭa live, Ah-iddin shall serve them. When they die, Ah-iddin is an oblate (*širku*) of Ištar.

The preterite of the verb "give" expresses irrevocability, not immediacy. The gift actually takes effect only after the death of the donors.

The idea of a division of ownership in time is in our view crucial to understanding the legal nature of these dedications to the temple. If accepted, it means that most such dedications did not involve *paramonē* even in Koschaker's sense, that is, of a slave simultaneously owned by the temple and by the dedicator but remaining with the latter to serve him. The slave remained entirely the property of the dedicator until the latter's death or until transfer to the temple.[24] Nonetheless, the association made by Koschaker with *paramonē* is still of value, if it is applied to the concept of

23 As pointed out by Koschaker himself (Koschaker and Ungnad 1923: 131); see also Klíma 1940: 84-85, 97-98.

24 The prohibition on alienation, on which Koschaker placed great emphasis as evidence of some residual ownership, has a perfectly practical rationale if the dedicator is taken to remain the full owner for life. In BRM 2 53, for example, discussed at length by Koschaker, the owner of a five-year old girl dedicates her to the temple for brick-making (1931: 80-81). He does not expressly reserve any right to her services but is forbidden to alienate her. It is apparent therefore that she remains in his possession for the meantime, at least until she is old enough for the work for which she has been designated, but possibly for the owner's lifetime. If he is deemed to own her until his death or until some other relevant date (e.g., her reaching a certain age), then he has the right to alienate her. The new owner would have an ownership limited in time by the alienator's life or the slave's maturity, at which point the slave would automatically vest in the temple. However neat the situation might be in legal theory, the temple would face a practical problem of recovering the slave after she has passed into different hands, perhaps more than once. It is reasonable to expect that the temple would attempt to secure its interests by supplementary contractual provisions, notwithstanding its rights in law.

paramonē as modified by later scholarship. In conjunction with the practice of *donatio mortis causa*, *paramonē* explains the few documents in which manumission and dedication as a temple slave are found together. *Cyr*. 322 reads:

> (lines 1-4) [. . .] of Bel-uballiṭ [. . .] in year x of Nabonidus king of Babylon, [Hašda] and his wife Ayartu [sold] Mušezib-Šamaš for the full price to Nur-Šamaš son of [. . .].
>
> (6-8) Nur-Šamaš wrote the document of Mušezib-Šamaš in his own name, but in year 7 of Nabonidus king of Babylon he transferred him to his wife Burašu in lieu of 30 shekels, Burašu's dowry.
>
> (8-10) Nur-Šamaš died. After the death of Nur-Šamaš, Burašu and her second husband, Tabbanea, pledged him for 30 shekels to Appanu son of Abu-nur.
>
> (11-13) Subsequently, in year 6 of Cyrus king of Babylon, king of the lands, Burašu and her husband Tabbanea sold their slave Mušezib-Šamaš for 110 shekels of silver, full price . . . .
>
> (14-17) . . . Now in year 8 of Cyrus [. . .] Ayartu wife of Hašda [has come forward] to claim Mušezib-Šamaš from me (on the grounds that) he is a temple slave of DN [. . .]. I came before you [. . .]. With Ayartu [. . .].
>
> (17-20) [Bel-uballiṭ] priest of Sippar, [. . .] the preben[dary of Shamash, and the elders of the city . . .], he brought Ayartu and stood her before them. They questioned Ayartu, but she did not demonstrate anything of the temple slave status and free status of Mušezib-Šamaš . . . (*mim-mu šá* [lú]ŠIM-*ki-ú-tu ù* [lú]DUMU-DU$_3$-*ú-tu šá M. la tu-kal-lim-mu*).
>
> (20-24) Bel-uballiṭ priest of Sippar, the prebendary of Shamash, and the elders of the city had read to them the contracts of Mušezib-Šamaš's slavery (*ardūtu*) from year 6 of Nabonidus king of Babylon to year 8 of Cyrus king of Babylon, king of the lands, which Iddin-Nabu brought before them; Ayartu did not demonstrate anything of the temple slave status and free status of Mušezib-Šamaš . . . .
>
> (24-27) The judges conferred and imposed a payment of 110 shekels plus x shekels upon Ayartu and gave it to Iddin-Nabu, be-

cause Ayartu had made a claim against Iddin-Nabu regarding the free status of Mušezib-Šamaš . . . .

Dandamaev and Roth both translate the phrase *širkūtu u mārbanûtu* in lines 19-20 and 23-24 "a temple slave *or* a free man" [author's emphasis], not being able to conceive that the two conditions could be compatible.[25] It is the combination of the two, however, that was the basis of Ayartu's claim. She claimed that, prior to his being sold, her slave had been both made a free citizen and dedicated as a temple slave. This must be understood to be immediate manumission with a *donatio mortis causa* to the temple, but in the meantime, *paramonē* for the lifetime of her late husband Hašda and herself. (Evidently she brought this case as a widow.) Accordingly, any intervening sale would have been invalid, since the couple no longer owned Mušezib-Šamaš, who was a free man. He physically remained with them, but his services were only available to the couple on a contractual basis. The defendant, the current purchaser, would have no title to Mušezib-Šamaš, who would still theoretically be bound to his former mistress by the contract of *paramonē*.

Ayartu was not a mere witness; she was an interested party—the plaintiff, in fact. She would have no interest in a simple claim *either* that Mušezib-Šamaš was a free man *or* that he was a temple slave. In the first case, no advantage would accrue to her, except perhaps from the sentimental desire to aid a loyal formal servant. In the second case, it would be the temple's concern, not hers, and the temple authorities would be bringing the claim against the present owner. It was only the combination of freedom, *paramonē*, and *donatio mortis causa* that gave her an interest in reclaiming her former servant, albeit not as her property. She was trying to exploit the invalidity of the original sale for her own ends. She ultimately failed only because she was unable to provide evidence to support her claim.

The same process lies behind the seeming paradox in OIP 122 38, which was the point of departure for our investigation. A couple made their slave a *mār banî*, that is, they manumitted him, and dedicated him as a temple slave, but with the gift only to take effect on their deaths. In the meantime, he remained with the couple and continued to serve them as

25 Dandamaev 1984: 192-93; Roth 1989b: 487.

before, but as a free man under a contract of *paramonē*. It was because of his physical presence and the absence of any outward manifestation of the change in his status that the mistress had the opportunity to sell her former slave, even if she did not have the legal right to do so. She claims that she was coerced into selling him, in order to pay off a debt owed by her late husband. The former slave was made of sterner stuff. He brought the suit against his former mistress, in order to defend his free status. It is true that his freedom was limited in time and practical effects, but it had at least the great advantage that he could not be forced to serve a different master, and his former mistress might still live for many years. It is no wonder that he objected to being sold.

To summarize, a master who dedicated his slave to a temple performed a pious act through which he hoped to obtain divine favor. If the gift was to take effect only on his death, he had the further advantage of not relinquishing the earthly benefits of slave ownership. Nor was it to the disadvantage of the slave, who was assured of a secure place in which to end his days. This type of *donatio mortis causa* was the most commonly attested form of dedication.

Occasionally a slave owner might go one step further and add immediate manumission on condition of *paramonē* to the *donatio mortis causa*. Although the freedom gained thereby would be temporary, the advantage to the slave was that, at least in law, he could not be sold or transferred into an unknown fate, even on an interim basis. The principal advantage to the owner was that he retained the slave's services while putting him beyond the reach of his creditors, since his relationship with the slave was henceforth one of contract, not property.[26]

26 In this period, debt slavery is not employed against the person of the debtor, and creditors can find themselves helpless before an "insolvent" debtor who has managed to divest himself of all his assets. Cf. the case of the husband in Dalley *Edinburgh* 69, whose assets are declared by the court equal to the amount he owes his wife and stepmother for their dowries, excluding other creditors (editions in Ries 1984 and Joannès 2000).

13

Judges in the Cuneiform Sources

Abstract

Drawing on cuneiform texts from across the ancient Near East, this study examines the function and duties of those who had the authority to adjudicate trials, whether they are referred to as "judges" in the texts or not. While definitive conclusions are somewhat elusive, several points can be inferred from the evidence: the king was the supreme judge; administrative officials often served as judges; judges rarely presided over trials alone; and they typically cited only evidence and not law as the basis for their verdicts.

This survey covers the societies of Mesopotamia, Syria, and Anatolia, which between the third and first millennia B.C.E. shared the use of cuneiform writing. Their legal systems show a close structural similarity, and they all drew upon a common Mesopotamian legal tradition. Local differences notwithstanding, they share a common conception of the status and role of the judge in the administration of justice.

The Machinery of Justice

In considering the court system, it should be borne in mind that there was no distinction between the executive and judicial branches of government. The same officials or bodies made administrative decisions and judgments, and the same legal character was attributed to both.

There appears to have been no special place for the court to sit. The term "courthouse" (*bīt dīni*) does not appear until the Neo-Babylonian

* Originally published in *Maarav* 12 (2005): 27-39. Used by permission.

period (seventh century B.C.E.).[1] Nor was there a special term for a court of law; parties speak of going before a particular official or administrative body, or simply before "the judges."

Three levels of court may be discerned: royal, provincial, and local, corresponding to the three levels of administration. The king was everywhere the supreme judge, although his judicial activity is better attested in some periods than in others. He could try cases both at first instance and on appeal. There was no formal machinery of appeal from a lower court; rather, a subject would petition the king to redress an injustice suffered by a lower court or official. The correspondence of Hammurabi shows that he could act in three ways in response to such a petition: he either tried the case himself and gave final judgment; decided a point of law and remitted the case to a local court for a decision on the facts; or remitted the entire case to a local court.[2] Provincial officials, appointed by the king, acted in much the same way, combining judicial and administrative functions. They could have a fixed seat, as in the case of local governors, or be peripatetic. In the Hittite emperor's Instructions to the Commander of the Border Guard (*bēl madgalti*),[3] an official with wide-ranging military, administrative and cultic duties in border territories, the Commander is enjoined:

> When you come to a city, call out all the citizens. Whoever has a claim, decide and make it in order. If the slave or the slave woman of a man or a single woman has a claim, decide it and make it in order (III 29-32).

Whereas the king and his officials essentially sat alone, the guiding principle at the local level seems to have been collegiality. The city council or town elders, however it is described, had judicial functions as a collective body, as did other bodies such as the council of merchants (*kāru*[*m*]), who presided (not surprisingly) over commercial disputes. Most

1 See the examples in *CAD* D 156. A variant is "house of the judge(s)." Assurbanipal in a letter to the Babylonians cites a proverb: "At the gate of the house of the judge, the word of a sinful (i.e., adulterous) woman prevails over her husband's" (SAA 18 1; edition in Reynolds 2003: no. 1).

2 See Leemans 1968: 107-29.

3 Schuler 1967: 36-65.

frequently, however, reference is simply to "the judges," without stating who those judges might be. A judge by that title sitting alone is a rarity in any period. Most frequently, the bench consisted of two or more judges. In the Neo-Sumerian period (twenty-first century B.C.E.), the norm seems to have been three; in other periods, references to an "assembly" (*puḫru[m]*) suggest a considerably larger body. In the Old Assyrian trading colony of Kanish in Anatolia (eighteenth century B.C.E.), a council of "big men" decided whether a case was to go to the plenary assembly ("big and small"), where the judgment would be by a majority vote.[4]

The Office of Judge

There has been debate among scholars concerning the level of professionalism among the judges: they were certainly not trained jurists in any sense, but were they permanent? Was the position of judge an office or merely a function? On the one hand, the title "judge" (Sumerian: di-ku_5; Akkadian: *dayyānu*) is sometimes appended to the names of persons acting in other capacities, such as a witness.[5] On the other, it may also be combined with another, permanent office or be a function exercised by an official not normally called upon to adjudicate, such as the Old Babylonian head of the irrigation bureau (seventeenth century B.C.E.).[6]

At Kanish in the Old Assyrian period, the parties may voluntarily choose arbitrators to settle their disputes, who are called "judges." The latter, if they fail to resolve the conflict, give evidence on the proceedings in a deposition to the merchants' council (*kārum*).[7] On the other hand, the judges in the Neo-Sumerian trial reports are often the same triad and may sit on a variety of cases recorded in a single tablet, evidently the day's docket.[8] But what is one to make of a document from the same period recording the sale of a slave? Atypically, the sale was not made in the presence of witnesses; instead it is recorded that "the seal of Lu-Enlil, the

4 See Larsen 1976: 165.

5 AT 6:31 and 56:48 (witnesses); *ZA* 53 73 no. 14 (surety); BE 9 75:16 "judges of the Sealand" (notarizing a tax payment).

6 YNER 4 45; edition in Waters 1970: 64-66.

7 See Veenhof 2003: 442.

8 E.g., *NSG* 211 (edition in Falkenstein 1956-57: vol. 2, no. 211).

judge, was rolled." The actual impression of this same Lu-Enlil on the tablet, however, describes him as "the sea-faring merchant"![9]

The term "judge" might therefore cover a variety of situations, from one among many duties of an administrator to the sole occupation of a person dedicated to that vocation. The occasional mention of "royal judges" might indicate that professionalism was a question of rank.[10] In the Neo-Assyrian period (ninth-seventh centuries), it should be noted, the term "judge" is not used at all in the context of mortal justice; the function of judging is reserved exclusively for royal officials.[11]

Certain local courts might acquire a special reputation for the quality of their justice. In an Old Babylonian letter, the writer advises a litigant: "Go to Nippur, to the city of judges, and let them decide the case for you" (AbB 11 7). In another letter, the mayor and elders of the city of Isin write to "our fathers, the judges of Nippur" reporting the claims of the parties in a case and adding: "Because the case is very [difficult (?)], we have not decided it, and we have not assumed binding jurisdiction over them (*ul niprus u dīnam ul nušāḫissunūti*). We have sent them to our fathers; decide their case and assume over them the binding jurisdiction that is within your authority" (AbB 11 159).

The question remains on what basis the judges made their decisions. Where a decree of the king was being enforced (or of the city, in the case of the Old Assyrian merchant colonies), the court certainly had recourse to that source.[12] Citation of legal text or precedent, however, never established itself in the cuneiform sphere, where only a few harbingers of the concept (not in a legal context) can be found in first millennium texts.[13] On the other hand, there existed an immense body of traditional, unwritten law. It might be thought that knowledge of the traditional law would have

9 Steinkeller 1989: 302-3.

10 They are called di-ku$_5$ lugal in the Neo-Sumerian reports (although the term is not used specifically of the named judges) and *dayyānē ša* RN in Neo-Babylonian texts.

11 Radner 2003: 886-90.

12 In Old Babylonian sources it is sometimes mentioned that decisions are to be made "according to the decree of the king" (*kīma ṣimdat šarrim*); see Veenhof 1997-2000: 49-83. In Old Assyrian sources, there are references to "words written on the stela" or "words of the Council" (*kārum*); see Veenhof 1995: 1717-44.

13 For example in omen texts. See Leichty 1970: 7-11; and Parpola 1993: xxvii and no. 33.

been considered a facet of wisdom, but the fact is that the term "wise" (*emqu*) is not attested in association with judges or judging. Traditional law may simply have been regarded as a matter of common knowledge. It is noteworthy that scribes—the one profession that might have been regarded as having a superior knowledge of the law, by reason of their drafting of legal documents and trial records—are seldom found acting as judges (except when they are also administrative officials). The scribe's name and profession is frequently appended to lists of witnesses to litigation, but not as one of the judges.

Moreover, officials acting as judges were expected to inquire about the traditional law from local sources. Hammurabi dispatches some litigants to a high official with the instruction: "When they arrive, examine their evidence, decide their case, and cause them to have judgment in accordance with the law that is currently practiced in Emutbal" (*kīma dīnim ša inanna ina E. iddīnu*; AbB 13 10). The Instructions to the Hittite Commander of the Border Guard are even more explicit:

> Further, the Commander of the Border Guard, the City Prefect, and the Elders should try and decide cases properly. In the lands the binding rule applied is as from olden times: in any town in which they were accustomed to execute, let them continue to execute, but in any town in which they were accustomed to banish, let them continue to banish (III 9-44).

Thus a good judge is not necessarily a font of the law; on the contrary, he may sometimes have to discover what the law is from others.

Jurisdiction

We have seen that higher courts, of the king or his officials, could hear cases at first instance. The principles upon which a case went to a particular court are not clear. According to CE 48, cases in which the penalty was up to sixty shekels were for the "judges," whereas a capital case was for the king. Elsewhere, capital jurisdiction appears to have been a royal prerogative, by no means his exclusive preserve. Certainly, he could delegate capital jurisdiction to royal officials or even to a local court, as in a case of murder remitted to the assembly of Nippur.[14] Adultery and witchcraft were a special concern of the king but could also be tried before the judges.[15] On the other hand, the Hittite Commander of the Border Guard is ordered to refer difficult cases to the king (III 23-24).

Royal officials, especially peripatetic officials, could sit together with local bodies to form a bench. For example, in the Hittite empire in Syria in the thirteenth century B.C.E., an imperial official called "the overseer of the land" (^{lú}UGULA.KALAM.MA) is found sitting on a court together with the local city elders.[16] An Old Babylonian royal decree annulling debts brought together a vast array of officials and judges to judge cases arising from the legislation:

> When my lord raised the golden torch for Sippar and established equity for (the god) Shamash who loves him, and convened in Sippar Taribatum the "overseer of troops," the judges of Babylon, and the judges of Sippar, they examined the cases of the men of Sippar, heard the tablets of field, house, and orchard purchases and had broken those that were to be released by the equity decree (AbB 7 153:1-6).

The text continues with a complaint arising from the decisions of certain of those officials. It reveals yet more layers of bureaucracy and the fact that some of the judges constituting an assembly could be officials in their own right:

> I took my tablets to the assembly. Riš-Šamaš, the "resident" of Sippar, Kudiya, the "chair-bearer," and Sin-nadin-šumi, the cadastral scribe, examined my tablets and sealed them and had them sent to Šalim-teḫušu at his house. Šalim-teḫušu, the "overseer of barbers," without hearing me broke the tablets in his lodgings in Sippar. I was informed, and in consternation I collected the pieces

14 Jacobsen 1970.

15 E.g., MAL A 15, where the husband who catches his wife *in flagranti delicto* can bring the lovers before the king or the judges.

16 E.g., J. Westenholz *Emar* 2.

> of my tablet from his house and showed them to Riš-Šamaš, Kudiya, and Sin-nadin-šumi. But they said, "What can we say to the 'overseer of barbers'?" (AbB 7 153: 30-45).

The victim's only recourse was a petition to the king. The king himself typically sat alone, at the peak of the system, but in one instance, in Assur of the Old Assyrian period, we find the king of a city-state sitting together with the city-council.[17]

One type of court that we have not discussed is the temple court. In the earlier periods, the temple was the place where evidentiary oaths were administered but not the location of the courthouse. Priests do not seem to have played a role in secular jurisdiction, unless the interests of the temple were involved. From the Middle Babylonian period on, however (fifteenth century B.C.E.), we begin to see priests playing a greater role as judges, even in disputes that have no obvious connection to the temple or sacral aspect. In one Middle Babylonian document, a high priestess (*entu*) interrogates a party, although it is not clear from the broken text that she judges the case.[18] Incidentally, this is the only cuneiform record known to us in which a woman appears (potentially) as a judge; otherwise, judging appears to have been a strictly male role, as with other aspects of public life.

In the Neo-Babylonian and Persian periods, the great temples of southern Babylonia, such as the temple at Uruk, seem to have had wide-ranging jurisdiction. It is impossible to know whether it was a sign of growing religious influence on the legal system or merely the distortion of our archival record. At all events, joint benches were assembled of temple officials, royal officials, and members of the city assembly.[19]

Powers

A vexed question is: did the judges have power to compel a litigant to appear in court? Note that the question is not: did the courts have the power?

17 Veenhof 2003: 439-441.

18 UET 7 7; see edition in Gurney 1983.

19 As for example in a prosecution concerning the theft of ducks from the temple in *Iraq* 13 96 (see Figulla 1951).

An official acting as a judge would have coercive powers by virtue of his office, not necessarily deriving from his judicial function. In the Neo-Assyrian sources, where only officials are found acting as judges, the judge is often said "to impose a judgment" (*dēna emādu*) on the litigants.[20] For a bench of local judges, on the other hand, the position is not self-evident, and raises the deeper issue of the basis of their authority.

If authority comes from above, then the coercive powers would come with it. In a trial for homicide, we are told that the case of four persons accused of murder was taken to Isin before the king. "Ur-Ninurta, the king, ordered the assembly of Nippur to take their case" (di-bi dab$_5$-bi-da bi-in-du$_{11}$).[21] It is clear that the accused had been taken into custody at the king's command and were delivered to the local court to stand trial without consideration of their own wishes in the matter.

The same cannot be said of litigation purely at the local level. Whether it is at the initiative of one or both litigants (or indeed ordered by a higher authority), the judges are said to "cause them to hold the case/judgment" (*dinām ušāḫizūšunūti*). There has been much debate as to the meaning of this clause: one possibility is that it involved the litigants submitting to jurisdiction.[22] Whether submission was a direct consequence of the court's action or needed the parties' agreement, at least nominally, is not clear. It cannot be said with certainty that a bench of local judges, even as august a body as the assembly of Nippur, could force a reluctant defendant to come to court. It may well be that self-help by the plaintiff was sometimes necessary, as in the case of the cuckolded husband who strapped his wife and her lover caught *in flagranti delicto* to the bed and brought them, bed and all, before the assembly of Nippur.[23]

Once the litigants were before the court, the judges appear to have had extensive powers in the conduct of the trial itself. A hymn to Gilgamesh sets out the activities of an ideal judge in trying a case: "You question, you investigate, you judge, you establish the truth, and you set straight" (*tašâl taḫâṭi tadâni tabarri u tuštāšer*).[24] We suggest that the list is a chronologi-

20 See SAAS 5 (= Jas 1996) nos. 1-9.

21 See the text in Jacobsen 1970, lines 17-19.

22 As we translated in the text AbB 11 159 above. The different theories are discussed by Dombradi 1996: vol. 1, 312-20.

23 Greengus 1969-70: 33-44.

24 Lambert *BWL* 40 (line 7).

cal one in as much as the first two activities result in judgment and the last two are the result of judgment. Judges were not mere passive witnesses to the parties' presentation of their respective cases but are known to have had active powers to intervene by interrogating witnesses, ordering the parties to summon witnesses, imposing on a party or witnesses oaths that would make their evidence decisive, or ordering the parties to undergo the river ordeal. After weighing the evidence in this way, the judge by his judgment establishes the facts of the case. The verb *barû(m)* is also used for the art of the diviner, who establishes the true meaning of ominous phenomena.[25] In consequence, he does justice, since a judgment has two aspects: the verdict on the facts and the orders that may flow from it for punishment, compensation, restitution, etc. The courts, of whatever level, certainly had powers to make all manner of orders; they were more than mere arbiters of the facts. For example, in the Code of Lipit-Ishtar 30, the judges issue an order restraining a young married man from consorting with a prostitute, while in a Middle Babylonian record of litigation a judge named Sin-shapik-zeri issues a similar order (*rikiltu*) restraining a woman from entertaining a man.[26] Old Babylonian judges frequently imposed a penalty (*arnum*) on vexatious litigants, which in one case took the following form: "they had half his hair shaved off, they pierced his nose, stretched out his arms, and had him led around the town."[27]

The king and officials had power to impose their judgment upon both parties, however unwilling, but there is no decisive evidence as to whether local judges did. HL 173 contains the following harsh provisions:

> If someone rejects the judgment of the king (*DĪN* LUGAL), his house (i.e., whole family) will be destroyed. If someone rejects the judgment of a dignitary (*DĪN* [LÚ]DUGUD), they shall cut off his head.

25 It is in fact used in the latter sense a few lines later in the same text (line 10). The use of *barû(m)* is unusual with respect to a judge and is obviously deliberate in the context. It may be a play on the common term for establishing the facts of a case: *burru(m)* (based on the root *bâru[m]*). See *CAD* B 129-30.

26 UET 7 8 (see Gurney 1983: 41-45).

27 See Dombradi 1996: vol. 1, 100.

The judgment of mere judges is not mentioned, leaving us unclear whether an analogous punishment or none at all would apply. In an Old Babylonian case, the plaintiffs did not accept the local court's decision to impose a particular oath on the defendants. They therefore convened a second court, with mostly the same judges. They did not accept the second judgment either, however, which left them only with recourse to a higher authority, the king.[28] Rejection of the decisions of the two lower courts did not necessarily mean, however, that a litigant could simply disregard the local judges; more probably it was an indication that the plaintiffs had not yet exhausted their remedies within the system. On the other hand, the complaint of a litigant that "the judges told him (the defendant) to release the distrainees, but he did not release (them) . . ." (AbB 11 158) suggests a certain lack of effectiveness in the authority of the local court.

The situation is further complicated by the practice of one or both parties being obliged, after the verdict had been rendered, to take an oath not to litigate on the same matter again. In his classic study of Old Babylonian court procedure, J. Lautner drew the conclusion that the judgment of a local court (as opposed to the royal courts) was no more than a proposal for the settlement of the dispute, which then had to be formally accepted by the parties.[29] E. Dombradi, however, points out that the same undertaking is found in cases decided by the royal courts.[30] The practice is therefore best understood as an additional precaution rather than a necessary condition. Nonetheless, it reveals how deeply ingrained was the idea that a judgment was a settlement that should end any sentiments of dissension.

In considering the attitude of the courts, the nature of the litigation needs to be taken into consideration, although no formal distinctions are made in the sources as between criminal and civil jurisdiction, for example. Adversarial judgments are necessary to suppress anti-social behavior, whereas they need be used only sparingly in private disputes, where the court has more the role of an arbiter. T. Hertel notes that the essential aim of the courts of the Assyrian merchant colonies in Anatolia was to get litigants to settle their disputes by mutual agreement, which he takes to be an

28 CT 29 42-43; see Wilcke 1992b: 65.

29 Lautner 1922: 35-67.

30 Dombradi 1996: vol. 1, 362-365.

exceptional feature of the Old Assyrian system.[31] It is, however, only to be expected in private disputes, especially commercial disputes, where courts throughout history have typically encouraged settlement by the parties. Even the reports of decisions by the judge-officials of the Neo-Assyrian kingdom sometimes indicate the finality of their judgment with the statement "there is peace between them (the parties)" (*šulmu ina birtišunu*)—an expression more resonant of settlement than judgment.[32]

Duties

The sources give little indication of the duties of a judge. He is of course expected to do justice; the question is, what constituted justice? The conduct expected of a righteous judge is portrayed in the Hymn to Shamash, the sun-god, the god of justice, in both negative and positive terms (lines 97-102):[33]

> To the corrupt judge You reveal the sight of prison,
> On the taker of bribes, who does not set straight, You inflict punishment;
> But he who takes no bribe, who intercedes for the weak,
> Is pleasing to Shamash, He lengthens his life.
> The judicious judge, who gives equitable judgments (*dīnāt mēšari*),
> Makes whole the palace, makes the seat of princes his place.

Clearly, bribery and corruption were the antithesis of justice. The Hittite Commander of the Border Guard is not to conduct a case in favor of a lord, a brother, his wife, or his friend, nor must anyone take a bribe. He is not to make a good case lose or a bad case win. By way of summary the order concludes: "Do justice!" (III 25-28).

Only once is punishment of a judge for misconduct mentioned. According to CH 5, if a judge "changes his judgment" after recording it on a sealed tablet, he must pay twelve times the claim in that case and is

31 Hertel 2006: 543.

32 See, e.g., SAAS 5 (= Jas 1996) no. 9.

33 Lambert *BWL* 121-138 (edition of these lines in Lambert 1960a: 132-33).

removed from the seat of his judgeship in the assembly, never to sit in judgment with the judges again. It is not clear exactly what was involved in changing a judgment, but obviously it does not relate to the actual conduct of the judge in the trial itself.

The positive aspect, intercession for the weak, is already stressed in sources from the early third millennium, where kings speak of their divinely mandated duty to uphold the rights of the widow and orphan, of the weak against the strong, of the poor against the rich. In the prologue to his law code, King Hammurabi speaks of his equitable judgments (*dīnāt mīšarim*) and of his application therein of the "beaten path" (*kibsum*), "mores" (*rīdum*), and "established law" (*kittum*). At the same time, he ensures "equity" (*mīšarum*), which implies a breaking of strict legal rules in order to do justice, as in the case of a decree annulling debts. The latter may have been the prerogative of kings; upholding the traditional law was presumably incumbent upon every judge.

Conclusions

From this rapid survey of the cuneiform sources, the judge emerges as a shadowy figure, sometimes an official, sometimes a local dignitary, with no fixed duties or base of operations. It is not possible to draw firm conclusions, only to point to certain impressions given by the sources.

i) Judging was regarded as an inseparable part of an official's duties, even in offices that would seem to us to be purely administrative in character. At the same time, judging was an activity that could be detached from the other functions of government and be practiced as a sole function. In the latter case, the judge seems rather to have been drawn from the society than imposed upon it and may have derived his authority in part from the quality of his judgments.

ii) Although gods and kings may judge alone, there is a marked predilection for collegiality. Even officials who could sit alone are often found forming a bench together with local judges and other officials. In the absence of a formal system of appeal, this may have been seen as a safeguard against abuse of power or miscarriages of justice. Although the presiding judges are often named in records of litigation, the practice of referring simply to "the judges" or "the assembly" lends an aura of anonymity and perhaps impartiality to the activities of the court.

iii) Judgments do not cite law, only evidence as the basis for the decision. This is not surprising, given the absence of jurists as a profession in the ancient Near East. The legalization of the judiciary would have to await the advent of the Rabbis and the Roman jurists, with new techniques of legal science at their command. Those qualities which are emphasized are not knowledge of the law but a sense of right and justice, honesty, and regard for the weak. Possibly they were regarded as more essential qualifications for the office. In a system where judges could have other functions and interests, even interests in the case that they were deciding, probity, like collegiality, was an important safeguard against miscarriages of justice. It and the other desired qualities to some extent fulfilled the role that adherence to the letter of the law nowadays plays in ensuring the impartiality of judges.

iv) The coercive quality of the courts' jurisdiction is evident in the case of the official hierarchy: kings, governors, and various bureaucrats. The power of the local judges is less certain. The impression gained is that at least in criminal matters (i.e., homicide, theft, and acts of violence that were a danger to the community) they functioned as a part of the government apparatus and could rely on the support of the king and his administration. As regards the settlement of private disputes, the sources are much more enigmatic. The system seems to have been more than voluntary arbitration, but what mechanisms of coercion were applied—whether physical force, social pressure, or the charisma of the judges themselves—cannot be determined. It is doubtful that the situation was as extreme as in classical Athens, where judgments of the courts, with no coercive forces at their disposal, were frequently disregarded or incapable of execution, leading to repeated litigation on the same dispute.[34] The king and his officials had a gendarmerie (*rēdû*) at their disposal, which may also have been available, at least on occasion, to the local courts; sometimes, the court itself had bailiffs to carry out its bidding (e.g., the *manzatuḫlu* at Nuzi). On the other hand, judgments are disregarded,[35] and litigants are often required to take an oath by the king or a god that they will not challenge the decision that was supposed to end the dispute.

v) Finally, the role of the divine should not be underestimated. Behind and above the whole system stood the gods, to whom recourse might be had if human justice failed, and whom the judges themselves did not hesitate to call in aid. Through the evidentiary oath and the ordeal, human judges could remove the burden of decision-making to a divine court, while the promissory oath acted as a powerful sanction upon would-be scofflaws. If retribution from human justice was uncertain, there was no doubt in the mind of ancient litigants as to the inevitability of divine retribution. A favorite reason for last-minute settlement between the litigants was the reluctance of one party to take an oath ordered by the court and the reluctance of the other party to see the oath taken. At the same time Shamash, the god of justice, oversaw the work of the judges, ready to punish the venal, corrupt, and partial, and to reward those who pursued only justice.

34 Hunter 1994: 120-50.
35 Veenker 1974: 1-15.

14

Evidentiary Procedure in the Middle Assyrian Laws

Abstract

The verbs *burru* and *kunnu* are used together a number of times in the Middle Assyrian Laws. This article argues that the former stands for rational methods of proof (e.g., witness testimony); the latter, for supra-rational methods (e.g., the oath, the ordeal). The combination of both often indicates that the accuser in a case must pass a threshold of credibility with rational evidence before recourse will be had to supra-rational procedures.

Introduction[1]

The phrase *ubta''erū*(*š*) *ukta''inū*(*š*) appears (with slight variations) some twenty times in the Middle Assyrian Laws (MAL).[2] Both verbs are well known, having the same basic meaning in the D-stem ("make firm"). Nonetheless, the exact meaning of the couplet has proved elusive. In their classic commentary, Driver and Miles called it "a curious phrase" and translated "they have brought charge (and) proof against him."[3] In their interpretation, the subject is always the accusers or witnesses. The verb *ubta''erū* refers to an accusation and *ukta''inū* to adducing sufficient

* Originally published in the *Journal of Cuneiform Studies* 55 (2003): 87-97. Used by permission.

1 This article was first presented as a paper at the annual meeting of the American Oriental Society in San Diego on March 14, 2004, and in longer versions to the Institut für Orientalistik, Universität Wien, on March 19, and the École Pratique des Hautes Etudes, Paris, on May 25, 2004. I am grateful to all the participants for their helpful comments and criticisms. The usual caveats as to responsibility for errors apply.

2 Tablet A §§1 (/*ši*), 9, 15, 16, 20, 21, 40, 47 (/*šunu*), 53; B §§4, 8, 9, 13, 14, 20; C+G §§3 (/*šu*), 8 (/*šu*), 10 (/*šu*), 11 [restored] (/*šu*); E §1; L §3.

3 Driver and Miles 1935: 339.

evidence.[4] They admit, however, that the presence or absence of the procedure in MAL seems arbitrary. More difficulty is caused by the fact that in nine instances the verb *burru* appears alone, as in A §12, where a man is to put to death for rape if witnesses *ubta''erūš*.[5] Following Driver and Miles' interpretation, this would mean that the rapist's punishment is imposed on the basis of a mere accusation, without sufficient evidence.

Cardascia attempts to refine Driver and Miles' approach, suggesting that the two verbs represent a gradation of evidence: *burru* means to gather sufficient evidence for a presumption of guilt; *kunnu* means to provide irrefutable proof.[6] In this way, Cardascia is able to account for five of the cases where *burru* is used alone (A §§3, 14, 18, 19; N §2) as having a weaker meaning, as where a man brings charges that he is unable to sustain.[7] He further manages to eliminate two (A §25 and §36), by asserting that the verb has a special meaning, "to claim" (property).[8]

Nevertheless, there still remain two instances which Cardascia is forced to label true exceptions: A §12, the case of the rapist already mentioned, and A §7, a parallel case in which witnesses testify that a woman laid a hand on a man. Furthermore, if Cardascia's theory of gradation is followed, the dual expression would seem superfluous: what is the point of mentioning a *prima facie* case when irrefutable proof is demanded?

Two more recent translations adopt a different approach. Roth translates "they prove the charges against him and find him guilty,"[9] and Borger similarly "man es ihm beweist und ihn überführt."[10] As Driver and Miles already noted, this translation requires a shift in subject between the two verbs, between the witnesses (who prove) and the court (that convicts). They therefore rejected this solution, on the grounds that it was more likely that both verbs would have the same subject.[11] The shift in

4 Driver and Miles 1935: 341-43.

5 The other cases are: A §§3, 7, 14, 18, 19, 25, 36; N §2.

6 Cardascia 1969: 94-95 note c.

7 Even this interpretation requires adding nuances to the literal meaning. In §18, *anāku uba''er ba'ura la ila'e la uba''er*, literally "(saying) 'I will make firm,' but he cannot make firm, he does not make firm" becomes ". . . je porterai des charges . . ., (s'il) ne peut porter des charges (et s')il n'a pas chargé (suffisamment)."

8 "réclamer." Cardascia's translation of §36 actually reads (inadvertently?) "il prouvera (les faits)" (col. V 1).

9 Roth 1997 153-94 *ad loc* (in the 1995 edition).

10 Borger 1982b: 80-92 *ad loc.*

11 Driver and Miles 1935: 341.

subject has the merit of accounting satisfactorily for the use of *burru* alone but at the same time leaves the dual phrase with more than a whiff of superfluity about it. It stumbles, however, at the hurdle of A §1, where the two verbs are used as alternatives: *lu-ú ub-ta-e-ru-ú-*[*ši*] *lu-ú uk-ta-i-nu-*[*ši*] (col. I 6-7). This cannot logically apply to two successive, complementary stages in the judicial process. The context is that a god is consulted to determine the punishment of a woman who has committed sacrilegious theft. A rule that the procedure applies *either* when the charges have been proved *or* when she has been found guilty is absurd. Borger, translating correctly, walks into the trap: "man es ihr beweist oder sie überführt." Roth, sensing the logical difficulty, translates here: "they prove the charges against her and find her guilty." In the same way, one interpretation in CAD takes the phrase as hendiadys: "they prove it of her by means of witnesses KAV 1 i 8 (Ass. Code §1), and *passim* in this phrase in the Ass. Code," as if it were the same form as elsewhere in the code.[12] The Assyrian form *lū . . . lū*, however, can only mean "either . . . or."[13]

Methods of Proof

If the dual phrase is not to be dismissed as meaningless repetition,[14] a separate role must be found for it that leaves the individual verbs with discrete functions and neither conflicts with those functions nor renders them superfluous. I propose the following hypothesis: the couplet *ubta''erū(š) ukta''inū(š)* refers to the burden of proof on the accuser and more specifically to the different methods of proof required to discharge that burden in court. In its use in MAL, *burru* means proof by rational methods, such as witnesses or documents, whereas *kunnu* means proof by supra-rational methods such as the oath or the ordeal.

It should be noted that these conclusions are unique to MAL. The combination of *burru* and *kunnu* is attested elsewhere only in reverse order, in two literary compositions in the Standard Babylonian dialect. In

12 *CAD* K 168, meaning 4; similarly, *AHw* 109 *bâru*(*m*) III, meaning D 4b: "meist vor *ukta''inūš* als Hendiadyoin: sie ihn (sie) völlig überführen."

13 Cf. A §3 (col. I 23-24): *šum-ma* LU$_2$ *lu-ú ma-ri-iṣ lu-ú me-et*. A man cannot be ill and dead at the same time.

14 This is the role assigned to it by *CAD* B 130: "if they establish and prove that."

Šurpu, it occurs in a list of sins, in a context that reveals nothing of the two verbs' function; they could simply be synonyms (*Šurpu* II 60: *ukannu ubarru ušaṣbaru*). Their context in the Assyrian Dream-Book, on the other hand, implies that the verbs are cumulative, not alternative. The omen in question reads (330, reverse col. ii, lines 40-41):

> If he walks constantly in dark waters, a hea[vy] lawsuit [. . .], they will sum[mon him] *ana kunni u burri*.

Because the lawsuit is a difficult one, the witness will be obliged to furnish more than one mode of proof.

The reverse order of the verbs in these late sources is significant, as it may reflect an earlier difference between the Assyrian and Babylonian dialects. In Old Babylonian sources, the two verbs, appearing individually, have the same functions as proposed here but with exactly the opposite application: *burru* is used of proof by supra-rational means, whereas *kunnu* is mostly used of proof by rational means.[15]

Only two forms of supra-rational evidence are positively attested in Mesopotamia, namely, the evidentiary oath and the river ordeal. The ordeal is far less common than the oath, and its procedure is not well understood.[16] Both are imposed by the court and are decisive.

The evidentiary oath is imposed on one side—on the party or his witnesses or both.[17] If taken, it decides the case in favor of the oath-taker. It is, however, a burden as well as a privilege, for a person may be reluctant to expose himself to the wrath of god or king through a self-curse. Thus there are many attested instances of the imposition of the oath leading to a last-minute compromise settlement.[18] On the other hand, the danger arising

15 See Dombradi 1996: vol. 1, 335, for the evidence from private legal documents. The distinction is clear-cut in Codex Hammurabi: *burru*: §§23, 120, 126, 240; *kunnu*: §§1, 2, 3, 5, 42, 106, 107, 108, 113, 116, 124, 127, 133, 141, 194, 255, 265, 282. In §2, if witchcraft is not proved, then they resort to the river ordeal.

16 Although there are references to the river ordeal from all periods (for a survey of the sources, see *HANEL* 155, 196-97, 375-76, 495-96, 529, 575-76, 891, 925), the only accounts of the procedure come from OB Mari; see Durand 1988. It sometimes involved an agreement between the parties. An oath or oaths may also have been required; see Joannès 1997: 172-73.

17 For a detailed account based on the Old Babylonian sources, see Dombradi 1996: vol. 1, 330-34. See also Démare-Lafont 1997: 185-93.

18 See e.g., CT 4 47a; and CT 48 1 (both Old Babylonian).

from the oath's self-curse is merely potential, which might tempt a hardy or desperate soul to risk its consequences.[19]

The ordeal applies to parties, not to witnesses. It appears to have been imposed on one side, but it could be undertaken by substitutes.[20] As with the oath, there are cases where a party refuses to undergo the ordeal. Unlike the oath, it involves immediate risks and immediate results, which would make the subject of the ordeal even more reluctant to undergo the procedure.

The court has a discretion whether to impose the oath or ordeal and on which side. The most common form of oath is an exculpatory oath on the defendant. Otherwise, the sources, especially the law codes, refer to particular circumstances in which the court imposes an oath or ordeal but never articulate the principles underlying the exercise of its discretion.

The verbs *burru* and *kunnu*

Most of the cases in which the two verbs appear in MAL, whether as a couplet or *burru* alone, do not provide us with sufficient context to determine what sort of evidence they refer to, whether rational or supra-rational. A few cases in which *burru* appears alone, however, indicate that rational evidence is meant.

In A §17 a man makes the assertion that another man's wife is notoriously promiscuous:

> If a man says to a man, "Your wife is always being slept with," and there are no witnesses, they shall make a contract and go to the River.

In the absence of witnesses, that is, of rational evidence, supra-rational evidence is expressly prescribed, in the form of the ordeal. In A §18 a man makes the same allegations, but then rashly declares that he will prove it (*burru*):

19 An Old Babylonian prayer to Nanna documents a case of successful perjury: UET 6 402 (edition in Charpin 1986: 326-29).

20 Durand 1988: 518-21.

> If a man says to his companion, whether in private or in a dispute, "Your wife is always being slept with," and "I will prove it," but he cannot and does not prove it (*a-na-ku ú-ba-ar ba-ú-ra la-a i-la-'-e la-a ú-ba-e-er*), that man shall be beaten with 40 strokes.

The proof must refer back to what was stated to be missing in A §17, namely, the testimony of witnesses.

In A §12 a man is charged with seizing a married woman as she is passing in the street and raping her. He is to suffer the death penalty "whether he is caught upon the married woman or witnesses prove that he had intercourse with the woman" (col. II 20-22: *lu-ú i-na* UGU DAM-LU$_2$ *ik-šu-du-uš ù lu-ú ki-i* MUNUS *i-ni-ku-ú-ni še-bu-tu ub-ta-e-ru-uš*). In my view, the protasis is canvassing the two standard types of rational proof: seizing in the act and testimony *ex post facto*.[21] There would be no need to impose an oath on the witnesses, whose credibility is not in issue. This law is not about setting a minimum level of proof. The point being made by the apodosis is that the death penalty applies whether the culprit is caught in the act or not. The context is the principle commonly found in ancient legal systems that being caught *in flagranti delicto* aggravates the offense.[22] It is a stylistic feature of MAL to give a list of alternatives in order to show that the ruling is indifferent to them.[23] I shall return to this point below.

The provision in A §25 makes a clear distinction between rational and supra-rational modes. The text reads (col. III, lines 82-94):

> 82 *šum-ma* MUNUS *i-na* E$_2$ *a-bi-ša-ma us-bat*
> 83 *ù mu-us-sa me-e-et*

21 A third type, documentary, applies essentially to transactions. A confession might also be regarded as a form of proof. See Démare-Lafont 1999: 165. Seizure in the act does not at first sight look like an independent type of evidence, since there will still be testimony about it at the time of trial. It becomes sufficient proof in itself when it is such as to exclude deniability by the culprit. See below.

22 E.g., a thief caught in the act, as in CH §25, suffers the death penalty. Cf. the case of Laban's stolen idols in Gen 31:30-32, where the death penalty is to be imposed on the thief caught in possession after a hot pursuit. The distinction is expressed in early Roman law as between manifest and non-manifest theft. See Gaius *Inst.* III 184-185 and 189-190 (edited in de Zulueta 1946-53).

23 Compare the list of different circumstances of a rape in A §55: "whether in the town or in the country or at night in the street or in a granary or at a town festival..." As Landsberger put it, they signify "Tatort gleichgültig" (1968: 63 n. 1).

84 ŠEŠ-MEŠ *mu-ti-ša la-a ze-e-zu*
85 *ù* DUMU-*ša la-áš-šu*
86 *mi-im-ma du-ma-a-qé ša mu-us-sa*
87 *i-na* UGU-*ša iš-ku-nu-ú-ni*
88 *la ḫal-qú-ú-ni* ŠEŠ-MEŠ *mu-ti-ša*
89 *la-a ze-zu-ú-tu i-laq-qé-ú*
90 *a-na re-ḫa-a-te* DINGIR-MEŠ-*ni*
91 *ú-še-et-tu-qú ú-ba-ar-ru*
92 *i-laq-qé-ú*
93 *a-na* ^{d}ID$^{i\text{-}id}$ *ù ma-mi-te*
94 *la-a iṣ-ṣa-ab-bu-ú-tu*

If a woman is dwelling in her father's house and her husband dies, her husband's brothers have not divided, and she has no son, her undivided husband's brothers may take any jewelry that her husband placed upon her that is not lost. As regards the remaining (property?), they shall cause the gods to move past (it) and shall prove and take (it). They shall not be seized for the River God or the oath.

The brothers must engage in a procedure involving the gods, the content of which is not clear, but would seem to engage the gods as witnesses. It is not an oracular procedure, for which different terminology is used, as we shall see. Nor is it one of the two known supra-rational means of proving an assertion in court, for they are expressly excluded. The brothers must in any case still prove (*burru*) their claim to the items of property. The conclusion must be that *burru* alone is used when rational means of proof are intended.

Finally, A §1 is the sole source in MAL in which both *burru* and *kunnu* appear together but not as a couplet. The text reads (col. I, 1-13):

1 [*šu*]*m-ma* MUNUS [*lu-ú*] DAM LU$_2$
2 [*lu*]-*ú* [DUMU-MU[NUS LU$_2$]
3 [*i-na*] E$_2$-DINGIR [*t*]*e-ta-ra-ab*
4 [*i-na*] E$_2$-DINGIR [*mi*]-*im-ma*
5 [ ] *tal-ti-i*[-]*ri-iq*
6 [(*lu-ú*) *i-na qa-ti-ša*?] *iṣ-ṣa-bi-*[*it*]
7 *lu-ú ub-ta-e-ru-ú-*[*ši*]

8 *lu-ú uk-ta-i-nu-*[(*ú*)-*ši*]
9 *ba-e-ru-ta* [ ]
10 [D]INGIR *i-*[*š*]*a-'u-*[*ú-lu*]
11 [*k*]*i-i ša-a* [DINGIR *a-na e-pa-še*]
12 *i-*[*q*]*a-ab-*[*bi-ú-n*]*i*
13 *e-ep-pu-šu-ú-ši*

If a woman, whether the wife of a man or the daughter of a man, enters a temple and steals something . . . , (and) it is seized [in her hand], or *ubta''erūši* or (else) *ukta''inūši*, [they shall perform] a divination and shall inquire of the god. They shall treat her as [the god] orders.

Notes

line 5 Collation by Freydank 1994: 204.

line 6 The dubious verbal form led Postgate to suggest (tentatively) *iz-za-qa*[*p*], with an unattested intransitive meaning "come to light, turn up" (1973: 21). Otto proposes the Neo-Assyrian verb *zaqāpu* B, "vor Gericht erscheinen (um Klage zu erheben)" but then translates "völlig überführt" (1993b: 158 n. 49). Claiming, however, is far from proving, and the form would in any case be *izzaqqup*.

line 7 A duplicate fragment (Postgate 1973: 19-21) reads *ù lu-ú ub-ta-e-ru-ši* [. . .]

line 9 On the form, see Deller 1987: 65.

In this paragraph, three different types of proof are presented as alternatives: being caught in possession of the stolen goods or perhaps in the act of stealing, and two others. In the light of the paragraphs previously discussed, it is reasonable to suppose that the remaining two would be the testimony of witnesses, and the results of a supra-rational procedure, possibly an ordeal. Thus MAL presumes three standard modes of proof: seizure *in flagranti delicto*, *ex post facto* testimony, and referral to the divine court. As we have seen in A §12, the ruling itself concerns punishment, not proof. Its point is that whatever means were used to prove the woman's guilt, her punishment is to be determined by consulting the oracle.

The Couplet *ubta''erū(š) ukta''inū(š)*

A preliminary objection to my interpretation of the dual phrase is that the oath, and more particularly the ordeal, would normally be imposed on a single person, whereas the verbs in the dual phrase are in the plural. The answer is that the third person plural of the verbs should be understood as an impersonal form. Consequently, the unspoken subject may and often will be an individual: the plaintiff, a witness, or the victim (as in A §16, where the victim testifying is the plaintiff's wife), whoever they may be. Tablet A §40 reveals the individual behind the impersonal phrase:

> If a man sees a slave woman veiled and lets her go—he does not seize her and bring her to the gate of the palace—*ubta''erūš ukta''inūš*. He shall be struck with 50 strokes of the rod, his ears shall be pierced, threaded with a cord, and tied at his nape. His denouncer (*bātiqānšu*) will take his garment. He shall do the king's corvée for a month.

The denouncer is thus the hidden subject who has to testify as to the accused's dereliction of duty and to confirm his testimony by submitting to the oath or ordeal.

A more serious objection to my interpretation is that it has not solved the problem of redundancy. If the method of proof is to be a supra-rational procedure, why require rational evidence as well? The answer lies in what I will call the condition of threshold credibility.

Supra-rational procedure is the removal of the case from the human tribunal and its referral to a divine tribunal. The human court has first to decide under what circumstances it will refer a case, then which procedure is to be applied and which assertion is to be tested, the plaintiff's or the defendant's (or their witnesses'). The most obvious reason for a referral is the absence of evidence. For example, in an Old Babylonian suit by a seller reclaiming property from a buyer, "The royal judges gave Ḫaliya'um (the buyer) to the oath because they had fixed a day and his witnesses could not be present."[24] Nonetheless, in many cases the court would only

24 OECT 13 91 (lines 12-15): DI-KU$_5$-LUGAL *ḫa-li-ia-ú-um aš-šum u$_4$-mu iš-ku-ú-ma ši-bi-šu ú-la i-ba-aš-šu-ú-ma a-na ni-iš* DINGIR [*i*]*d-di-nu-šu*. The example is Old Babylonian. Unfortunately, there are no litigation documents from the Middle Assyrian

reach its decision after considering the evidence. Thus in another Old Babylonian case, where one heir sued the purchaser of land from another heir, the plaintiff relied on a tablet of division of the estate, but the defendant adduced witnesses to the existence of a later division. "The judges heard their statement (*šaptišunu*) that there was a later division, and the judges ordered them to speak their testimony (*šibussunu*) before the god."[25] In a royal decision from Ugarit, the content of the witnesses' evidence determines who is to take the oath (lines 17-34):

> Takia (the debtor) said as follows: "I paid the son of Zibaia (the creditor) the 800 shekels of silver that I owed him and I have witnesses: Attanu and Aiu." If his witnesses say, "(The debt) is settled: Takia paid the 800 shekels of silver to the son of Zibaia," then let Takia swear together with his witnesses, and let the son of Zibaia relinquish his claim. And if Takia's witnesses say it is not so, let the son of Zibaia swear together with his (Takia's) witnesses and let Takia pay him his silver.[26]

The court might therefore decide that for an assertion to be tested by supra-rational procedure, the person making the assertion must first have attained a certain threshold of credibility, whether through testimony, documents, or material evidence. The condition is more appropriate to the oath than to the ordeal, because the oath was applicable to a wider range of persons and was open to abuse by a party with a weak case or by a dubious witness. The immediate peril of the ordeal would have acted as more of a deterrent against the temptation of perjury. Nonetheless, it was not an absolute deterrent, and threshold credibility could be regarded as necessary for the ordeal, depending on the circumstances of the case.[27]

---

period to illustrate the oath or ordeal in practice, but there is a rich fund of sources from Mesopotamia in other periods (especially the Old Babylonian period), and the basic principles of supra-rational procedure appear to remain constant throughout the cuneiform record.

25 BE 6/2 49 (lines 25-29). The plaintiff thereupon agreed to a compromise settlement rather than allow the witnesses to swear.

26 RS 20.22 = *Ugaritica* V no. 27: 5-34. For a legal analysis of this and the preceding text, see Loewenstamm 1980a: 341-45.

27 Démare-Lafont argues that A §17 shows that rational and irrational modes of proof were in theory mutually exclusive, because the ordeal is prescribed in the absence of

In many instances where the dual phrase is used in MAL, it is reasonable to infer that the court heard evidence before deciding whether to impose the oath or the ordeal and on whom. Thus the landowner who claims that a neighbor has encroached upon his land would need to bring some *prima facie* evidence of title before the court would impose the oath (or ordeal) on him rather than on his neighbor who also claims the land (B §§8, 9, 13, 14, 20).[28] Again, the victims of fraudulent practices in C+G §§8, 10, and 11 would need first to show that the property of which they were defrauded was theirs. C+G 3 imposes a punishment on a creditor who sells abroad a son or daughter held as pledge, unless the debt equals their full market value.[29] The procedure *ubta''erūš ukta''inūš* is invoked against him. Aside from the question of sale abroad, the debtor, who is the father of the pledged child, needs to show that the child was given as a pledge and not sold as a slave, and furthermore that the child was not pledged for its full value. The issue is one of the state of accounts between the creditor and debtor, for which some rational evidence would be required, before allowing the debtor to swear an oath (or submit to an ordeal).

Supra-rational procedure, therefore, does not necessarily eliminate the need for rational evidence as a preliminary step. It follows that the dual requirement in the couplet *ubta''erū* (*š*) *ukta''inū* (*š*) is not redundant. It is a gradation, although not in the sense that Cardascia meant. The law could simply have prescribed an oath or ordeal, deeming that the circumstances warrant it. It does so in A §17 where, as we have already seen, the ordeal is expressly provided where there are no witnesses. The law thus orders (or empowers) the court to apply a supra-rational procedure *instead of* rational evidence. The dual phrase is not used. I would argue *a contrario* that the dual phrase was used only in cases where the law chose not to eliminate the preliminary step but to require (or perhaps to allow) the court to proceed to the ordeal (or the oath) once that threshold requirement had been satisfied.

By far the most common application of the oath or ordeal was exculpatory, to allow a defendant to disprove an accusation. It is not surprising,

witnesses (1999: 259). As I shall hope to show below, the paragraph represents a much narrower principle.

28 Where boundaries are fixed by tradition of usage they are hard to prove; there will be no deeds of sale, and boundary stones are notoriously movable.

29 The object of the latter clause, an Assyrian man or woman, refers to an Assyrian citizen, not an inferior social class. See Démare-Lafont 2003: 530-31.

therefore, that most of the paragraphs of MAL that prescribe the oath or ordeal in explicit terms refer to an exculpatory procedure. In six paragraphs, the law imposes an oath using the verb *tamû*. In two of these (B §10; C+G §1), the tablet is too broken to establish the context, but in A §§22 and 56, an exculpatory oath is imposed upon the accused. In A §5, the oath is imposed upon the accuser, but is analogous to an exculpatory oath, in that the alleged victim of theft must prove that he did not incite the theft. The final instance, A §47 (lines 16-17), also concerns an unconventional oath that is exculpatory in purpose: a hearsay witness exonerates himself (*zakû*) by proving what an eyewitness told him. Likewise, of the three cases of ordeal in MAL, at least two (A §§22 and 24) are undergone by the accused and are clearly exculpatory.

The dual phrase, by contrast, refers exclusively to proof in support of an accusation. Herein, I suggest, lies both the rationale for its existence—to indicate an application of supra-rational procedures that was less common—and the rationale for its duality. It is precisely because the oath or ordeal was being imposed upon an accuser, not a defendant, that threshold evidence was regarded as necessary.[30] It is significant that A §17, which as we have seen imposes the ordeal not by the dual phrase and explicitly excludes threshold evidence, also appears to impose the procedure on the accuser.[31]

The Dual Phrase in Action

The rationale for prescribing the procedures indicated by the dual phrase may be illustrated by contrasting two fairly straightforward cases from MAL, one that uses the dual phrase and one that uses *burru* alone. The provision in A §20 reads:

30 A similar distinction exists in CH: *tamû* is used where the oath is exculpatory (§§206-207, 227); but *ina maḫar ilim burru* for accusations or claims of lost property.

31 Driver and Miles argue that the ordeal was undergone by the wife, in order to clear herself of suspicion, which would make it exculpatory (1935: 68-69). In order to maintain that interpretation, they are obliged to regard the statement about the wife not as slander but as a friendly word to the husband. As Cardascia points out, the maker of the statement must be the same as in the following paragraph, where his allegation is definitely an unfriendly act (1969: 127-29).

> If a man has intercourse with his companion and *ubta''erūš ukta''inūš*, they shall have intercourse with him and turn him into a eunuch.

A man claims that he was sodomized by an associate. Two factors affect the evidentiary procedure to be applied. First, there would be no outside witnesses to such an intimate sexual act. Second, the evidence of the accuser himself is a statement against interest. As Daube has pointed out, the offense is not homosexuality at large but imposing upon a free man the despicable passive role in intercourse, treating the victim sexually like a woman; hence the punishment of the offender—to be treated like a woman and turned into a woman.[32] For the victim to admit publicly that he had played the passive role, whether willingly or unwillingly, would be deeply shaming. Accordingly, the personal, uncorroborated evidence of the victim will cross a threshold of credibility—not enough to prove his accusation outright, but enough to persuade the court to refer it to a divine tribunal, for example by imposing the oath upon him.[33]

The provision in A §36 considers the case of a man who has gone abroad, or perhaps just to the provinces (*a-na* A-ŠA$_3$ *i-it-ta-la-ak*), apparently on business, and fails to leave his wife with provisions or to send her provisions from abroad.[34] After five years she is free to remarry, and if the husband subsequently returns, he has no right to reclaim his wife. There is one exception, however (col. IV 103-V 3):

> If he is delayed beyond 5 years but was being held against his will or a . . . seized him and he fled or he was seized as a criminal and delayed, on his return he shall prove it (*ú-ba-a-ar*) and give a woman like his wife, and he may take his wife.

The absentee claims that he is entitled to take his wife back because his absence beyond the statutory limit was due to *force majeure*, in particular judicial measures taken against him. Again, two factors influence the evidentiary procedure prescribed. First, other evidence would be available,

32 Daube 1986: 447-48.

33 In this and the following example, I will assume for the sake of argument that the more common supra-rational procedure, the oath, was intended.

34 Literally: "to the field." See Cardascia's discussion of the context (1969: 187-89).

even though the events in question took place elsewhere, since they would have been witnessed by fellow merchants or be demonstrable from court records.[35] Second, he has a strong incentive to lie in his own self-interest. Accordingly, the claimant's personal testimony suffices neither to prove his claim outright nor to cross the threshold necessary for referral to a divine tribunal. He must prove his case by rational means alone; he is not to be granted the benefit of an oath.

Two more complex cases, both revolving around the definition of seizure in the act, illustrate further details of the dual procedure in practice. I distinguished above between three standard types of evidence: seizure *in flagranti delicto*, testimony, and oath or ordeal. Seizure *in flagranti* does not at first sight look like an independent type of evidence, since there will still be testimony at the time of trial. It becomes sufficient proof in itself when it is such as to exclude deniability by the culprit.

Lack of deniability arises from the circumstances of the seizure, which may cover a broad spectrum of time, place, or actions: in a public place, in a private place where there can be no innocent explanation for the culprit's presence, in possession of incriminating material in the immediate aftermath of the crime. Thus the rapist caught in the act in public by a crowd of bystanders has no deniability (MAL A § 12), nor does the burglar caught trespassing, especially at night (CE §§12–13), nor the thief in whose possession stolen goods are found after a hue and cry and formal search (Gen 31:22–35).

Seizure in the act may fail to exclude deniability, on the other hand, where it is done by an interested party alone, or where an innocent explanation is available for the presence of the accused, or where too much time has elapsed between the crime and the seizure. The court will then need to revert to other modes of proof in order to establish the link between seizure of the accused and the alleged crime.

The law on witchcraft in A §47 rules that seizure of incriminating materials does not exclude deniability. In laying down further evidentiary requirements, it reveals the key elements inferred by the dual phrase: duplication of testimony and oath by an individual witness in support of an accusation. The opening lines read (col. VII 1-6):

35 Sources from the Old Assyrian period show that the Assyrian courts had great experience in dealing with the problems of witnesses or parties absent abroad and the time needed to gather evidence. See Veenhof 2003: 443-45.

> If a man or a woman practices witchcraft and they (the items) are seized in their hands;[36] *ubta''erūšunu ukta''inūšunu*; the makers of witchcraft shall be killed.

Witchcraft was regarded as a danger to public safety. In the war against witchcraft, the palace needed to be informed and could take extreme steps to identify and apprehend sorcerers. At the same time, false accusation was all too easy, since the link between cause and effect was intangible. Seizure of "incriminating" items was not enough; the accuser had to testify as to the practice of witchcraft and also take an oath or submit to an ordeal. The final section of the law confirms that he had in fact to take an oath. The eyewitness has informed another who in turn informs the palace, but the eyewitness then denies his statement. Evidently fear of the sorcerer deters the eyewitness from testifying. The palace, however, has a remedy (lines 20-23):

> The king shall interrogate him as he is able and shall see his back (LUGAL *ki-i i-la-'-ú-ni il-ta-na-'-al-šu ù ku-tal-lu-šu e-em-mar*), and the exorcist shall cause the man to speak when he is purified.

The meaning of this enigmatic phrase is in my opinion that the king will interrogate the reluctant witness under torture, so as to counteract fear of the sorcerer with an equal terror.[37] If the purpose were merely to gain information, there would be no problem, but it emerges from the continuation of the law that as a result of his "interrogation" the eyewitness has sworn an oath by the king and the prince (lines 24-31):

> He (the exorcist) shall say: "He will not release you (pl.)[38] from the oath that you swore to the king and his son. You swear in accordance with the tablet that you are swearing to the king and his son."

36 *i-na qa-ti-šu-nu iṣ-ṣa-ab-tu*. The reference is to magical preparations or products; see Cardascia 1969: 230-31.

37 The use of torture in judicial interrogation is attested in Neo-Babylonian times, when a "ladder of interrogation" was used to extract confessions; see Jursa 1996: 199, 210. The phrase "see his back" could refer to a reversal of his denial. I am grateful to Professor Jursa for this suggestion.

38 Possibly a reference to the oath-taker's family, who would be included in the curse.

The exorcist is on hand to reassure the witness that the sorcerer will not be able to release him from the curses attendant upon his oath, which the sorcerer might perhaps justify on the grounds that the oath was not given voluntarily. From our point of view, the significance of the law is that it reveals that not only must seizure of incriminating evidence be corroborated by testimony, but that the testimony itself must be confirmed by oath.

Confirmation by testimony and oath of what at first sight seems to be covered by seizure *in flagranti delicto* may also be behind a use of the dual phrase in A §15 that has puzzled commentators. In this case, it is a cogent parallel that supplies the context. The paragraph reads (col. II: 41-57):

> 41 *šum-ma* LU$_2$ *iš-tu* DAM-*ti-šu* LU$_2$ *iṣ-ṣa-bat*
> 42 *ub-ta-e-ru-ú-uš*
> 43 *uk-ta-i-nu-ú-uš*
> 44 *ki-la-al-le-šu-nu-ma*
> 45 *i-du-uk-ku-šu-nu*
> 46 *a-ra-an-šu la-áš-šu*
> 47 . . .

> 41-46: If a man seizes a man with his wife, *ubta''erūš ukta''inūš*, it is both of them that shall be killed; he has no liability.
> 47-57: If he seizes them and brings them to the king or the judges, *ubta''erūš ukta''inūš*; if the woman's husband will kill his wife, then he shall kill the man. If he will cut off his wife's nose, then he shall turn the man into a eunuch, and his whole face shall be mutilated; if he will let his wife off, he shall let off the man.

A husband catches his wife "with" another man, that is, strictly speaking not *in flagranti delicto* but in circumstances that could be construed as indicating an adulterous relationship. The distinction may seem overly subtle but is confirmed by the brutally graphic language of A §12, where the rapist is caught "upon" (*ina muḫḫi*) the woman.[39] The second part of the law

39 Driver and Miles noted the difference in terminology, but dismissed it as unimportant (1935: 48); Cardascia took the same view but was troubled by the fact that proof by witnesses should also have been required in a case of seizure *in flagranti delicto* (1969: 120 note a). Native sources were conscious of the distinction, however. The report of a trial from Old Babylonian Nippur relates that the husband actually tied his wife and her lover caught in the act to the bed and brought them, bed and all, to the

not unreasonably requires the husband to prove the case against the man before a local or royal court (*ubta''erūš ukta''inūš*) and also to refute any suspicion of entrapment by punishing his wife and her lover in equal measure (lines 47-57). The first part of the law creates a difficulty in that it seems to allow the husband to exercise summary justice (lines 41-46), but with the same requirements, including *ubta''erūš ukta''inūš*. Driver and Miles postulated an informal trial with the neighbors as witnesses, citing Greek parallels.[40]

In an earlier study on the law of adultery, I conjectured that the proving might refer to a procedure *ex post facto* of the husband killing the lovers on the spot, in a trial in which he was the defendant.[41] The result would be that any oath sworn by the husband would be exculpatory. The conclusions of the present study, that *ubta''erūš ukta''inūš* refers only to an accusatory procedure, render my earlier conjecture, which was difficult to reconcile with the syntax, untenable.[42] At the same time, they reveal a closer parallel in the Gortyn Code, one of the Greek sources mentioned by Driver and Miles, which gives added credibility to the scenario that the latter postulated.[43]

The Gortyn Code discusses the case of a man seized while committing adultery (*moikiōn*) with a free woman in the house of her father, brother, or husband (II 20-28).[44] The text continues (28-45):

> Let him (the captor) before three witnesses declare to the relatives of the one seized that he is to be ransomed within five days . . . . If he is not ransomed, it is for the captors to do (with him) as they wish. If he (the captive) claims to be the victim of fraud, the captor is to swear . . . with five others, each cursing himself solemnly, that he was taken committing adultery and was not the victim of fraud.

---

court. See Greengus 1969-70: 33-44. Cf. also Démare-Lafont 1999: 68, arguing in favor of the distinction.

40 Driver and Miles 1935: 45-46, 50.

41 Westbrook 1990b: 552-53.

42 See also the criticisms of Démare-Lafont 1999: 69-70.

43 Edition in Willetts 1967.

44 The Greek term *moicheia* covers a broader scope than adultery in the ancient Near Eastern sense, being illicit intercourse with a woman under the authority of any close relative.

It emerges from this account that the adulterer is held by the accuser, who makes a formal declaration before witnesses but does not bring him before a court. If the accused claims, presumably before those witnesses, that it was a fraudulent trick, then the captor must swear a declaratory oath. Apparently, this procedure also takes place in the captor's home, where the accused is being held, not before a court. It thus conforms with Driver and Miles' reconstruction of the circumstances in the first part of MAL A §15. From our point of view, what is important is that this extra-judicial procedure is twofold: a declaration before witnesses of the circumstances of the seizure and a supra-rational stage.[45]

There is, however, an important difference between the Greek and the Assyrian law. The Greek oath is in fact two-fold: an accusatory positive oath that the oath-taker seized the accused in adultery and an exculpatory negative oath that it was not a fraudulent scheme to entrap the accused. Adultery was an offense against the husband; if he agreed to another sleeping with his wife, he would have no claim against him.[46] The second oath is not present in the Assyrian version because a different safeguard is employed against entrapment, namely, the requirement (emphasized by the enclitic *-ma* in line 44) that both the wife and the lover be killed. The result is the same: the husband will be immune from future suit by the relatives of the man he killed, a suit in which he would be the defendant. Nonetheless, in the present extra-judicial procedure the oath is accusatory, not exculpatory.[47]

45 The Gortyn law requires oaths not only by the captors but also by four others, whom I take to be members of the captor's family who would be suspect of conspiring with him to entrap an enemy (and who probably stood to profit with him from the ransom). The older view that they were oath-helpers, whose sole task was to establish the principal witness's credibility, has been disproved. See Gagarin 1990: 29-54, esp. 51-52. A further illuminating feature of the Gortyn law is its shift between single (captor) and plural (oath-takers) subject, and impersonal verbs. A similar background would account for the switch between singular and plural verb forms in MAL A §15 that has disturbed commentators. See Driver and Miles 1935: 48-50; and Démare-Lafont, who argues on the basis of the 3rd person plural verb forms in lines 42-45 (*ubta''erūš ukta''inūš . . . iddukūšunu*) that the first part of A §15 is a formal procedure before the court just like the second part (1999: 71-72, 90). As I have argued above, these forms can not only be impersonal but can hide an individual subject.

46 See Westbrook 1990b: 564-68.

47 Note that the husband's immunity is described as *aranšu laššu* (cf. A §59), whereas in A §47, line 17, the exculpatory oath makes the oath-taker *zakû*.

The Assyrian procedure is a hybrid born of the special circumstances of the case. The husband is allowed to execute summary justice on the lovers without recourse to a court. As a safeguard against abuse, he must first demonstrate their guilt in two stages. Firstly, by rational means, namely, presentation of the lovers to witnesses in the compromising circumstances in which they have been found. This is insufficient to prove the case definitively (should the alleged paramour deny wrongdoing) but is sufficient to cross the threshold of credibility, thus opening the way to proof by supra-rational means, presumably an oath. In that respect there is a trial, before a divine tribunal. The procedure may therefore justifiably be called *ubta''erūš ukta''inūš*, in spite of its informal setting.

Conclusions

The provisions of MAL express the requirement of a supra-rational evidentiary procedure in two ways. They either set out the procedure explicitly, whether by oath or ordeal, or they employ the enigmatic phrase *ubta''erū(š) ukta''inū(š)*. The latter is used in order to substantiate an accusation, when both rational and supra-rational means of proof are required.

Accordingly, I would propose as a (non-literal) translation of the phrase *ubta''erū(š) ukta''inū(š)* wherever it occurs in MAL: "(if) the burden of proof against him(/her/them) has been discharged by all means, human and divine."

15

ziz_2.da / *kiššātum*

Abstract

This article argues that the terms ziz_2.da and *kiššātum* were listed as equivalents in lexical lists because they both refer to punishment for certain offenses. That punishment, however, had two aspects, ransom and revenge. The Sumerian term mostly reflects the idea of a ransom payment, while the Akkadian term largely points to the idea of revenge in that the wrongdoer is forced into servitude in the household of the victim.

In the lexical lists of the first millennium, the Sumerian term ziz_2.da has as its equivalent the Akkadian term *kiššātum*.[1] The Sumerian term is found in a small number of documents from the third millennium, from which its meaning can be established without difficulty.

MVN 3 219 records the case of a merchant who had purchased sheep which were found to be stolen.[2] He was declared a thief but was able to invoke his contract to join the guarantor of title to the action, and it would appear that the latter had had to indemnify the merchant for the value of the sheep that he had forfeited and was also obliged to pay a ziz_2.da amounting to four-fold the value of the sheep, presumably to the real

* Originally published in *Wiener Zeitschrift für die Kunde des Morgenlandes* 86 (1996): 449-59. Used by permission.

1 Hh. I 34, XIII 87; Erimhuš V 78; Ea I 329, wrongly attributed to **kiššatu*, "emmer" in *CAD* K 459 by Borger 1973: 175. The reading ziz_2.da for $AŠ_2$.da has now been confirmed by a recently published Neo-Sumerian text from Umma (*SNATBM* 373; see below); see Wilcke 1991. It is to be identified with za.$aš_2$.da in Sollberger *Corpus* Ukg. 6 iii 11′, 24′. For the earlier discussion, see Wilcke 1979: 95-96; and Steinkeller 1980: 178-79.

2 Edition in Steinkeller 1989: 330-32, cf. 85-86.

owner.[3] In the present document, the guarantor is claiming the refund of his outlays from the sellers.

In *SNATBM* 373, stolen meat(?) was found in the possession of A.'s slave.[4] B. seized two mountain sheep (udu.kur) per fattened sheep (udu.niga.e) from A.'s herd and "made them into the ziz₂.da for the stolen sheep" (line 8: zi.iš.da udu.zuḫ.a.še₃ in.na).

In a third document, Sigrist *Messenger Texts* 190, A. purchased grain from B. that came from the granary of the millhouse, a state institution.[5] A. is required to replace it (su.su.dam), but the tablet notes that B has already "replaced its ziz₂.da" (ziz₂.da.bi i₃.su). Thus the buyer found with goods that were stolen or at least to which the seller did not have good title must replace them (as these are fungibles he cannot simply restore them), but liability (to the owner) for a further payment has been discharged directly by the seller. Finally, in OIP 14 76 II 4, a payment of 15 shekels of silver is qualified as a ziz₂.da, but without indication of the purpose.

The Edict of Uru-inimgina confirms the connection of ziz₂.da with theft (Sollberger *Corpus* Ukg. 6 iii 10′-13′): "theft, its ziz₂.da is dropped; missing property is hung up at the city gate."[6] The expression ziz₂.da therefore designated a penalty for a crime, typically theft, and took the form (where specified) of a payment in silver or kind.[7]

3 Following our interpretation in Westbrook and Wilcke 1974-77: esp. 114-16. There we raised the possibility that the purchaser first paid the penalty and then recouped it from the guarantor, but since the guarantor is also declared a thief, it would appear more likely that the purchaser was successful in his bid to transfer liability for the penalty to the guarantor.

4 For a transliteration, see Ozaki (Gomi) and Sato 1990; amended readings by Wilcke 1991.

5 This was the e₂.kikken; see Milano 1994: 30; and Uchitel 1984.

6 Written za-aš-da-bi. Edition in Steible 1982: 318. A further enigmatic passage states (iii 20′-24′): "the women of former times had two men; the women of today, its ziz₂.da is dropped." The significance of this passage will be discussed below.

7 Although the verb su in Sigrist *Messenger Texts* 190:8 leads Wilcke (1991: 14) to explain ziz₂.da in terms of "Ersatzleistung," there is a clear distinction in that document between the latter payment and restitution of the stolen property. The four-fold payment in MVN 3 219 definitely points to punitive rather than compensatory damages. Steinkeller's rendering "penalty" (1989: 85) is therefore to be preferred to "indemnity" (1989: 331).

The term *kiššātum* is attested in a growing number of sources from the Old Babylonian period—law codes, letters, and legal records—but a reference in a Sargonic source indicates respectable antiquity for the Akkadian term.[8] Several meanings have been attributed to it by various scholars over the years. The closest to ziz$_2$.da is *CAD*'s "indemnity (for a lost object), replacement (for a distrained person),"[9] albeit as a secondary meaning, following Harris' proposal of "substitute" for persons or "replacement" for things.[10] The latter proposal is based on the appearance in several texts of the construction PN$_1$ *kiššāt* PN$_2$ and of x shekels *ana kiššāt* (object lost) in YOS 8 53. In the three cases where the identity of PN$_2$ is clear, however, it is respectively an offender (TCL 1 164: 23), a debtor/victim of abduction (VAS 8 26: 15), and a creditor (AbB 8 100: 11-12). It is best to regard the construction as being a loose genitive of respect: "the *kiššātum* in respect of PN/Object," which gives no direct indication of its exact meaning. On the other hand, the mention of payments in juxtaposition to *kiššātum* in several documents shows that the term could have a pecuniary value, like ziz$_2$.da.[11]

The primary meaning attributed to the term, however, suggests a condition rather than a payment. CH 117 presents the case of a man who is unable to pay a debt and has therefore sold his family or given them *ana kiššātim*. After serving in the house of their purchaser or *kāšišum* for three years, they are to be released. In the same way, the correspondent in AbB 8 100 reports that a woman has been released from *bit kiššātīša*, while another letter concerns a slave-girl taken *ina hiššātim*. Her owner gives five shekels to a merchant who promises to secure her redemption, but in the meantime she dies *ašar illeqûma ina ṣibittīša*.[12]

8 MVN 3 102; edition in Steinkeller 1980: 179.

9 *CAD* K 459-60. The association with ziz$_2$.da had led us to translate "compensation" in TCL 1 164 (Westbrook and Wilcke 1974-77: 120 n. 36).

10 Harris 1955: 98.

11 See, for example, TCL 1 64 (lines 21-24): 1 gu$_4$ mu$_3$ / *a-na* PN dub.sar erin$_2$ / *ki-iš-ša-at* PN$_2$ *id-di-in*. See also TIM 5 62 (lines 10-11): 10 gin$_2$ ku$_3$.babbar *ki-iš-ša-ti-šu* / PN i$_3$.la$_2$.e; and VAS 8 26 (lines 14-15): *ki-iš-ša-at* PN / *a-na* 1/3 ma.na 3 gin$_2$ ku$_3$.babbar.

12 Boyer *Contribution* 122 (= *RA* 15 140). For the variation *h*/*k*, see Speiser 1956: 4-6; and 1964: 44-45. Speiser's claim of a Hurrian origin for the term *kiššātum* seems improbable in the light of a Sargonic attestation.

Accordingly, most commentators consider the legal term to refer to a type of servitude. Kraus translates simply: "Dienstbarkeit."[13] Others emphasize the origin of the servitude in question in debt: "debt-servitude,"[14] "'Gewalt,' die, auf Personen bezogen, die 'Schuldhaft' bezeichnet,"[15] "Schuld(sklaven)dienst,"[16] "status of a person given as a distrainee for a debt."[17] The idea of a penalty is completely absent and that of payment virtually so.

The term, however, must have a different, or at least narrower, application than debt-slavery, since CH 117 lists *kiššātum* as a separate arrangement alongside sale into slavery for debt. Fleishman surmises that in that paragraph the one who has been handed over *ana kiššātim* works for the creditor and thus pays the debt, but there is no evidence that *kiššātum* functioned in this manner.[18] If it differed from sale in the possibility of redemption by payment of the debt, by whatever means, then it would in turn be indistinguishable from certain types of pledge. Kienast tries to distinguish it from the latter on the grounds that pledge is normally taken at the beginning of the debt whereas *kiššātum* in CH 117 occurs only after the debt falls due.[19] Kienast does not specify, but if it is a voluntary arrangement made after the due date, then it is based on novation of the debt; hence the new pledge will still be prior to the new debt. If it is involuntary, then it is indistinguishable from *nipûtum*, which involves seizure for debt. Kienast's argument can thus only apply to a contract of loan which provides for the taking of a pledge on default. As we shall see below, the documents of practice show *kiššātum* to be anything but a contractual arrangement.[20]

13 Kraus 1984: 181, cf. 267.

14 Steinkeller 1980: 179.

15 Kienast 1978: 67.

16 *AHw* 492.

17 *CAD* K 459, meaning 1.

18 Fleishman 1990: 250 n. 4.

19 Kienast 1978: 67.

20 Two texts where *kiššātum* is not based on a contract of loan, VAS 7 149 and YOS 8 53, are dismissed by Kienast (1978: 67 n. 281): "es scheint zweifelhaft, ob überhaupt das Rechtsinstitut der *kiššātum* vorliegt." Since both texts use the relevant term, it must be concluded that they do represent the relevant legal institution, albeit not in the form postulated by Kienast's theory.

In UCP 10/1 91 the verb *kašāšu* is used to describe the act of the judges in handing over a slave guilty of burglary to his victim: *ana* PN *bēl šurqīšu ikšušūma*. On the basis of this text, Landsberger understood *kašāšu* *N as "eine Schuld (nicht Geldschuld, sondern Verbrechen) durch Dienst im Hause des Geschädigten abbüßen" and *kašāšu* G as "dieser Diensthaft unterwerfen."[21] Thus crime could be a condition for the application of *kiššātum*. Indeed, in those documents of practice where the cause of *kiššātum* is stated, it is always a crime. In YOS 8 53 a boat was sunk;[22] the five other texts are all records of trials concerning theft or missing property, which result in an order for or act of *kiššātum*.[23] Accordingly, in UCP 10/1 107, where a burglar is handed over to the householder *ana kiššātim*, Finkelstein translated "for penal servitude." What distinguishes *kiššātum* from other forms of debt-slavery, then, is that the debt from which it arises is *ex delicto*, not *ex contractu*, and its legal conditions will therefore be shaped by the special features of such debts.

The difficulty remains, however, that in some sources *kiššātum* is equated not with servitude but with payment, and its lexical equivalent, ziz_2.da, is always in the form of a payment. In our view this discrepancy may be resolved by reference to a special characteristic of ancient Near Eastern "criminal" law that we have expounded in earlier studies.[24]

Serious offenses such as murder, rape, wounding, etc., gave rise in the legal systems of the ancient Near East to a dual right that the victim (or his family) could exercise through the courts: to revenge upon the culprit or his family, or to the payment of ransom in lieu of revenge. That right was regulated by the courts by setting an appropriate limit on revenge in accordance with the gravity of the offense—"an eye for an eye," for example, or vicarious revenge upon a member of the culprit's family rather than on the culprit himself. Alternatively, the victim could accept ransom from the culprit to buy off his right of revenge. Theoretically, the level of ransom was a matter for free bargaining between the parties, but here also the

21 Landsberger 1968: 75 n. 4.

22 Kienast (1978: 67 n. 281) refers to the document as "Darlehen betreffend ein Schiff." This would appear to be on the basis of an erroneous interpretation by Kraus in his first edition of the Edict of Ammi-ṣaduqa (1958: 178). Kraus corrected his error in 1984: 273 n. 430.

23 TCL 1 164; TLB 1 243; UCP 10/1 91, 107; VAS 7 149.

24 Westbrook 1988d: 39-128; and 1990b: 564-66.

courts sometimes intervened, to fix the appropriate ransom, especially in less serious cases. Revenge would then be exercisable only if the culprit would not or could not pay the fixed ransom. The law codes provide examples sometimes of appropriate revenge and sometimes of appropriate ransom, but the one does not exclude the other; they are two sides of the same coin.

Theft in modern law covers a very broad range of sins, from armed robbery to shoplifting, and in ancient Near Eastern systems it was even wider, covering kidnapping, fraud, receiving stolen goods, and even the innocent possession of stolen goods. For the most serious forms such as kidnapping (for sale into slavery) of a free person (CH 14) or theft of temple property (CH 6), the appropriate revenge was death, and ransom would have been a matter of free bargaining. For theft of movables that turned out to be temple property, a limit of thirty-fold payment by way of ransom is imposed, but the small likelihood of the thief being able to pay leads CH 8 to mention expressly that the alternative is death. CH 9-12 also suggests that simple theft of movables was liable to a ten-fold payment or death,[25] and the Edict of Ammi-ṣaduqa 7 lays down death as the alternative to a six-fold payment for fraud connected with the cancellation of debts, but in practice most cases of theft may have been punished by lower payments, multiples of five or less or fixed sums, and, we have suggested, by revenge in the form of enslavement to the victim of the culprit or his family.[26] The latter is thus very close to debt-slavery, albeit not identical.

In the same way, we suggest that ziz_2.da and *kiššātum* both refer to a type of penalty, but one which possessed this dual aspect: revenge or fixed ransom. It was imposed by the courts on a particular range of offenses, mainly in the realm of theft, where revenge was limited to enslavement.

The process is illustrated by a reexamination of CH 117, where a man "seized by a debt" gives his family *ana kaspim* or *ana kiššātim* to the purchaser or *kāšišu*. The phrase *ana kiššātim* does not mean that they are given "into servitude" any more than he gives them "into silver"; reference is to the grounds of the enslavement, namely a type of penalty. The victim of a petty offense is entitled to a fixed ransom under the penalty of *kiššātum*. The culprit, however, is unable to pay the ransom. Unpaid ran-

25 Westbrook 1988d: 114-15, 123.

26 Westbrook 1988d: 113-28, esp. 121-26. Cf. Petschow 1986: 41-66.

som is no less a debt than one based on a loan; it arises *ex delicto* rather than *ex contractu*. The judgment-creditor is therefore entitled to his alternative under the penalty of *kiššātum*, namely revenge in the form of enslavement.

It is in the light of this system of alternatives that we would interpret the famous "polyandry" clause of the Edict of Uru-inimgina (Sollberger *Corpus* Ukg. 6 iii 20′-24′): "the women of former times had two men; the women of today, its ziz$_2$.da is dropped." The first man was her father or husband; the second, a judgment-creditor to whom the first had been obliged to hand her over in lieu of payment of ransom for a crime.[27]

In the documents of practice involving ziz$_2$.da, the amounts payable are relatively small. In MVN 3 219, it is four-fold the stolen property, amounting to a mere seven shekels. Moreover, the offense itself carries no serious moral culpability, being the innocent receipt of stolen goods. In *SNATBM* 373 the payment levied on the owner of the dishonest slave appears to be only two-fold, and although the document is not clear, it is possible that there is a call by the steward of the slave's owner for a more serious punishment (on the slave?) involving adjudication by the ensi, which is referred to as a šer$_7$.da (*šērtu*). In OIP 14 76 the offense is not stated, but the payment is fifteen shekels, while in Sigrist *Messenger Texts* 190, the amount of the payment is omitted, but the offense amounted to the misappropriation of one kor (300 liters) of grain.

The pattern revealed by this admittedly small sample is thus one of petty theft or related offenses and of relatively low payments by way of sanction. It is appropriate to ransom in lieu of a low level of revenge, namely enslavement, as found in the context of *kiššātum*. By the same token, the highest sum mentioned in connection with *kiššātum* is twenty shekels.

Enslavement by way of revenge could be the primary penalty imposed by the court, in which case the ransom would be a matter of free bargaining between the parties, or it could be the alternative to a fixed ransom. Within this schema there are further alternatives. The enslavement could be of the culprit or vicariously of members of his family. The fixed ransom could be a multiple of the thing stolen, a slave, their equivalent in silver or

27 I am obliged to my colleague Professor Jerrold Cooper for pointing out to me this interpretation as the logical consequence of my own thesis.

a fixed sum in silver. In free bargaining, further possibilities are open to the parties, such as sale of a slave or member of the family or item of property. It is not surprising then that the documents of practice show a wide variety of arrangements in respect of *kiššātum*, and that it sometimes is equated with payment rather than servitude. The documents are difficult and obscure, but those that bear interpretation yield five categories.

1. The court hands the culprit over to the victim *ana kiššātim* (UCP 10/1 107; cf. UCP 10/1 91: 9-10, K, verb *kašāšu*). This would appear to be direct revenge in the form of enslavement. There is no mention of payment—ransom may possibly have been available only by free bargaining.

2. In two cases (TIM 5 62; VAS 8 26), a surety guarantees the appearance of a debtor by a certain date. If the debtor fails to appear, the surety must pay a fixed sum referred to as the *kiššātum* of the debtor. As the document is concerned with a later stage, no details are furnished of the circumstances causing the debt, but we surmise that it was a fixed ransom which if unpaid would entitle the judgment-creditor to enslave the culprit by way of revenge. In VAS 8 26 the creditor is cheated of this opportunity by a third party who abducts the debtor. The surety in fact guarantees the abductor's production of the abducted debtor.

3. A sum in silver paid by the culprit is referred to with the term *kiššātum* (YOS 8 53). In our view, this is because it is ransom, representing the value to the culprit of not being enslaved. In a lawsuit concerning possession of missing oxen, a payment of one ox is made, referred to as the *kiššātum* of one of the culprits (TCL 1 164).

4. A slave is given by the culprit to the victim *ana kiššātim* (TLB 1 243). If the slave was regarded as a means of payment, then this is ransom to avoid enslavement of the culprit or his family; if as a family member, then it is revenge, and payment of the appropriate ransom could theoretically redeem the slave at a later date. In Boyer *Contribution* 122, a slave-girl taken *ina*

hiššātim is to be redeemed for five shekels, while in AbB 8 100 a girl serving in the house of a merchant for ten shekels writes to her "brother and master" that "the *kiššātum* of the merchant has power over me"[28] and claims that two shekels will be enough to release her.

5. A slave or family member is sold. In the Sargonic text MVN 3 102 the sale of a daughter for ten and one-third shekels is noted at the end of the document as a *kiššātum.* This is paralleled in the Old Babylonian period by CT 45 14, where five and a half shekels are the price paid for the sale of a child, and by *JCS* 9 114 no. 84, where a priest buys a slave-girl for a sum unspecified but noted as the full price, in both cases *ana kiššāt* PN, whose identity is unclear. Possibly these are bargains designed to avoid enslavement of the head of household. The obvious question is why these slaves were not given directly into servitude as in TLB 1 243. Before answering that question, it is necessary to examine the relationship between debt, sale, and *kiššātum.*

Sale is not always final. If the sale was in fact no more than the foreclosing of a debt, i.e., when the "price" of family property such as land or family members was the debt owed, then it could be tempered by the right to redeem by paying that debt.[29] Enslavement for *kiššātum*, as we have seen, is inherently subject to redemption. If the debtor lacks the means to pay, however, redemption remains a hollow right. Consequently, the court sometimes intervened to prevent the loss of family members by setting a limit on the time that they need serve the creditor/purchaser. In CH 117,

28 Lines 11-13. Cagni's transliteration reads: ki-iš-ša-[a]t/dam.gar$_3$-ri x x ma-aḫ-ri-šu / i-be$_2$-la-an-ni, evidently seeing more in line 12 than is shown on the copy in TIM 2 100. His translation—"Es ist schuldhaft, mein Gläubiger hält mich"—relies on an otherwise unattested stative use of *kašāšu.* We take *kiššat* to be a normal *status constructus* and restore dam.gar$_3$-*ri*-[*im*/*ia*].

29 See Westbrook 1985b. For persons, CH 119 provides a clear example of the right to buy back a member of the family (in that case a slave who is deemed a family member) for the same price as that at which she was sold under the constraint of debt, i.e., in fact the amount of the debt.

where a man "seized by a debt" is forced to give his family *ana kaspim* (i.e., by way of sale) or *ana kiššātim*, they are to be released after three years. It is thus a case where redemption was in principle available after sale as after enslavement for *kiššātum* but has failed as a remedy.

In paragraph 20 of the Edict of Ammi-ṣaduqa a different solution is provided for the same situation: immediate release and by implication cancellation of the underlying debt, whether *ex contractu* or *ex delicto*. The cancellation of debts *ex delicto* in a debt-release decree, earlier identified by us in a Hittite edict, thus has two counterparts in Mesopotamia: this paragraph and the Edict of Uru-inimgina (Ukg. 6 iii 20′-24′, which effects the release of a woman from her second man (in our interpretation, the judgment-creditor) by a cancellation of the ziz_2.da.[30]

Ammi-ṣaduqa 20 extends the range of possibilities in CH 117 to include the debtor himself and a further transaction, *mazzazānūtu*, antichretic pledge.[31] In *mazzazānūtu*, the persons handed over served the creditor by way of interest until the debtor repaid the loan. As with *kiššātum*, therefore, it was inherently subject to redemption, but that right was illusory when it had been transacted because the debtor could not repay an existing loan that had fallen due.

Under certain circumstances, slaves may be regarded as family members for the purposes of release or redemption, but Ammi-ṣaduqa 21 expressly excludes slaves given *ana kiššātim*. CH 118 contains an enigmatic clause allowing the creditor to sell a slave given *ana kiššātim* after an unspecified time has passed.

The status of slavery has two aspects: the loss of personal freedom, as a result of which the slave must serve his master, and the quality of a chattel, as a result of which ownership in the slave may be freely transferred. We tentatively suggest (in the absence of direct evidence) that servile conditions arising from *kiššātim*, *mazzazānūtum*, and *nepûtum* were less than full slavery because only the first aspect applied; they had to serve the creditor but were inalienable.[32] This would explain, for example,

30 Westbrook and Woodard 1990: 642-43 (col. II), 654-56.

31 On the nature of the *mazzazānūtu* contract, see Eichler 1973: 47-88.

32 A Mari letter, ARM 14 47, combines *nipûtum* with *kiššātum*, using the otherwise unattested D-stem of *kašāšu*: *nipûssu ana ekallim likaššiš*. It is a threat made with respect to any carpenter sent to the palace who deserts on the way. The expression, although curious, is not altogether illogical: this is a crime where by definition the criminal is

why conditions of *nepûtum* were so harsh:[33] the creditor could not realize his capital by selling the distrainee; he could only extract labor from him or put pressure on the debtor by harsh conditions. A slave given *ana kiššātim*, however, is already a marketable commodity. CH 118 may therefore refer to a rule whereby slaves given for that purpose benefited only temporarily from the rights of family members; if not redeemed after an interval (of three years?), the restrictions of *kiššātum* ceased, and they were treated as ordinary slaves, at least as far as alienation was concerned.[34]

In the light of this tentative theory, we could offer an equally tentative explanation of the contracts of sale of persons in the context of *kiššātum* discussed above. The reason may have been the creditor's desire to overcome the limitations of *kiššātum* and to have immediately full, alienable slaves in satisfaction of the debt. But the underlying basis of the sale, a debt *ex delicto*, was noted, so as to preserve (at least temporarily) the right of redemption in the seller.

To summarize: the legal terms ziz_2.da and *kiššātum* were listed as lexical equivalents because they both signified punishment for a category of petty offenses. That punishment, however, had two aspects, ransom and revenge. In the extant sources, the Sumerian term mostly reflects the ransom aspect, in the form of payment, while the Akkadian term for the most part reflects the revenge aspect, in the form of servitude.

---

unavailable for punishment. Enslavement of his family therefore serves both as vicarious punishment (*kiššātum*) and as a means of pressure upon him to secure his appearance (*nipûtum*). For a discussion of the text, see Finet 1978: 12-18.

33 In both CE 23-24 and CH 116, *nipûtum* serves as the model for discussing the death of a servant through brutal treatment by the master.

34 Alienation still need not have affected the right of redemption, since they could always be purchased subject to existing rights.

16

The Enforcement of Morals in Mesopotamian Law

Abstract

The article examines three cuneiform sources from different periods and reinterprets two of them in the light of the third by showing the underlying legal principle common to them. The principle involved is the intervention of public authorities to restrain certain extra-marital liaisons by husbands when considered *contras bonos mores*.

Adultery is an offense severely punished in the Mesopotamian law codes,[1] but it is one defined soley in terms of the extra-marital relations of the wife. The male partner commits adultery only inasmuch as he is the paramour of a married woman: his marital status is not considered of any significance. The contingency of a married man having relations with an unattached woman is not dealt with in the codes in the context of adultery, and would not seem to constitute a marital offense or even grounds for divorce. The few private legal documents relating to adultery follow the same pattern: they concern the relationship of a married woman with a paramour of undefined marital status.[2]

This is not to say that a married man in Mesopotamia could with impunity engage in extra-marital relationships. Intercourse with an unmarried

* Originally published in the *Journal of the American Oriental Society* 104 (1984): 753-56.

* For comments and criticisms, I am grateful to Professors C. Wilcke, O. Gurney, and R. Kutscher, and especially to Mr. C. Locher of the Phil.-Theol. Hochschule St. Georgen, Frankfurt, who first brought the text BM 13912 to my attention. Responsibility for the opinions expressed is, of course, entirely my own.

1 CU 4, CE 28, CH 129, MAL A 12-16, 23.

2 UET 5 203; editions in Van Dijk 1959: 12-14; 1963: 70-77; Greengus 1969-70: 33-44.

woman could lead to claims against the seducer by her father, but this again was irrespective of the seducer's marital status.[3] There is, on the other hand, some evidence that certain casual sexual relationships which were otherwise perfectly permissible, were considered not proper for a married man, and steps were taken to prevent him from continuing in them. This is the import of paragraph 30 of Codex Lipit-lshtar (CL):

> If a prostitute from the street holds a young married man[4] and the judges forbid him to return to that prostitute, (if) after that he divorces his wife, (even) if he has paid divorce money, he shall not marry that prostitute.

The authorities intervene twice to bar what are in themselves perfectly legitimate actions. A married man apparently commits no offense by consorting with a prostitute,[5] but the authorities make a specific order forbidding its repetition with that particular woman, and the man will presumably be punished if he disobeys that order. The second act, marriage following divorce, is also legitimate in normal circumstances but is here prevented and possibly even rendered void by a specific order. The married status of the man is therefore the crucial factor in the attitude of the law towards his actions.

3 YBC 2177 paras. 7-8, MAL A 55-56 (although it affects the type of punishment inflicted); cf. CE 31, CU 5.

4 Col. xvii 50-53: tukum-bi guruš-dam-tuku karkid-dè tilla_2-a in tuku-àm. Edition by Civil (1968: 2) who translates: "If a married man joined a prostitute from the street . . ." (see also Wilcke 1973: 161). Strict grammar, however, requires the prostitute to be considered as the subject of this clause, even though it makes the content of her action yet more obscure. The verb tuku is used again twice in this same law with the man as the subject, but if we accept the meaning "marry" in those two cases, the same translation cannot apply when the prostitute is the subject. Wilcke's translation, with the man as the subject, suggests a sexual relationship (as one would expect), but it seems unlikely that a woman, even a prostitute, could "take" a man sexually. The other known lexical equivalent, *rašû* "to possess," does not seem any more appropriate. We tentatively suggest, therefore, that in this context the verb has the same meaning as *kalûm* "to hold" in BM 13912, to be discussed next. See notes 10 and 21 below.

5 In CL 27 it is considered perfectly legitimate for a married man to have a child by a prostitute.

A word of explanation needs to be added about the phrase "young married man" (guruš-dam-tuku). This is not a special law protecting newlyweds. Rather, it refers to a man who has not yet had children of his marriage and in our view is not mentioned in order to limit the law to that class of person, but because the practicalities of divorce make him the most likely candidate for application of the apodosis of this casuistic law to the concrete situation described. There is a general rule, as evidenced by CE 59 and CH 137, that once children have been born of a marriage, the husband cannot divorce his wife (without grounds) except upon forfeit of all his property and even, in certain circumstances, expulsion from the matrimonial home.[6] Prior to the birth of offspring, however, the penalty for divorce without grounds by the husband is merely a limited sum by way of compensation to the wife.[7] In the law under discussion, therefore, only a married man without children could seriously contemplate the tactic described to avoid the effects of the prohibition on him—i.e., to divorce his wife and marry the prostitute. The point of the law is that this *prima facie* legal procedure will not be allowed, even though the wife has been fully indemnified. The purpose of the law is therefore not to protect the rights of individuals (except indirectly), but to uphold certain standards of morality.[8]

A practical example of the judicial prohibition mentioned in the protasis to the law is found in the OB text BM 13912, published and edited by Anbar.[9]

> 1-5 In the matter of Aḫuni son of Ilšu-ibbi, Šat-Marduk swore the oath of King Samsu-iluna thus, saying:
>
> 5-6 "As for Aḫuni son of Ilšu-ibbi, I do not hold[10] him, I am not sworn to him.

6 This question is discussed in detail in chapter four of the author's doctoral dissertation (Westbrook 1982a; since published as Westbrook 1988b).

7 CH 138-140.

8 "die gute Sitte" as Wilcke puts it (1973: 162).

9 *RA* 69 120-125; edition in Anbar 1975.

10 Verb *kalûm*. We would suggest that this represents the counterpart to the second phrase of this couplet ("I am not sworn to him") and therefore means that the woman does not hold the man to performance of his oath. The use of *kalûm* in this sense is not

7-9 He shall not again propose sexual relations to me; he shall not kiss my lips; I will not accord him sexual relations.
10-12 If he calls me for lying in the lap, I will verily inform the city elders and the mayor,
13-15 If I am seen[11] in (his) company, let them treat me as if I had disregarded the oath of the king."
16-18 And Aḫuni son of Ilšu-ibbi swore the oath of King Samsu-iluna thus, saying:
19-21 "I shall indeed not go to Šat-Marduk and propose sexual relations to her."
22-29 Witnesses.
30-33 Date.

Anbar considers the text to record a public agreement between husband and wife to a legal separation.[12] There are, however, a number of objections to this interpretation.

Firstly, it is nowhere stated that the man and woman involved are husband and wife. The relations from which they are to abstain, translated by Anbar as both "relations conjugales"[13] and "relations intimes,"[14] are simply "those of a man and woman," (*ša* nita *ù* munus). In the lexical lists, where this phrase is also found,[15] its purpose is to explain that the verb *lamādu* is being used in the sense of "to have sexual intercourse," (as opposed to acquiring knowledge). The verb *lamādu*, in turn, is by no means confined to sexual intercourse in the context of marriage.[16]

Secondly, the agreement is exclusively concerned with the sexual aspect of the couple's relationship, to the neglect of aspects that are vital from the point of view of marriage, such as matrimonial property, subsistence of the wife and the matrimonial home. If Anbar's assumption is

attested by the dictionaries but would not conflict with the basic meaning of the verb. On the content of these mutual oaths, see note 21.

11 Literally: "they see me." Impersonal form of 3rd plural.

12 Anbar 1975: 125.

13 Anbar 1975: translation to lines 7, 9, and 21.

14 Anbar 1975: 125.

15 CT 12 29 iv 5, Nabnitu A 274-275. See *CAD* L 53a.

16 See, e.g., CH 154-156.

accepted that this separation involved the husband leaving the wife,[17] then such matters would have to be regulated no less than they are in the extant divorce settlements.[18] Instead, intimate details of sexual conduct are given, such as are never found in any cuneiform legal source on marriage, whether laws, contracts, or litigation.

Finally, the idea of a legal separation falling short of divorce is otherwise unattested in cuneiform sources, and its purpose is difficult to see in a system which admits of divorce by the unilateral act of one of the parties. Anbar suggests economic advantages in remaining married but does not state what they might be or to whom they would redound.[19] In short, a judicial separation is an alien concept, express reference to which would need to be found in the cuneiform sources before it could be applied to this context.

On the other hand, the roles of the man, the woman, and the authorities fit neatly into the situation described in CL 30. The mutual oaths have clearly been imposed upon the man and woman by the mayor and elders of the city, or some other authority (such as the ward or the judges) in the same line of hierarchy. They amount to a prohibition on the man against continuing to consort with the woman. Although she renders a more detailed oath, this is because she is being called upon to police the enforcement of the prohibition.[20] She is obviously someone with whom the authorities have sufficient leverage to be able to force her to act as informer on matters of the utmost intimacy—a position that one can readily ascribe to a public prostitute. It is reasonable to suppose therefore that the background to the prohibition was the unseemly association of a married man with a prostitute.[21]

17 Anbar 1975: 123, note to line 7.

18 Meissner *BAP* 91, NCBT 1900, VAS 8 9-11, VAS 18 1. See Westbrook 1982a: chapter 4, I pt. 3.

19 Anbar 1975: 125.

20 This answers Edzard's comment (1976): "Bemerkenswert ist, dass der Eid auch den Nichtvollzug einer Handlung durch die Gegenseite (Z. 7 *lā iqabbi'amma*) beschwört" (*apud* Anbar 1978: 137 *ad* 120-123, no. 8).

21 The possibility of the man marrying the prostitute as in CL 30 is hinted at in lines 5-6. The prostitute opens her statement with a denial of the existence (or perhaps rather a repudiation) of mutual oaths between herself and the man (see note 10 above). We would tentatively suggest that these were promissory oaths to marry, i.e., a betrothal

The missing element in the above source is the cuckolded wife, which leaves some doubt as to whether the man was in fact married (although it is less evident why he should be prohibited from consorting with a prostitute if he were not). This missing element is, however, supplied by a third text—a text that also provides evidence of the survival of this system in a later period.

UET 7 8, a document from the Kassite period, has recently been edited by both Gurney[22] and Wilcke.[23] They offer radically different interpretations. According to Gurney, a married man (H) frequents the house of a certain woman (X) and in consequence his wife (W) leaves him. H, hoping for a reconciliation, blames X on the ground that she has locked him in. His brother brings X before the judge. On being asked why she acted in this way, X promises never to see H again.[24] Wilcke, on the other hand, explains the case as follows: X has distrained W for a debt of H and forced H to divorce her in lieu of payment. Then H enters into sexual relations with X (without actually marrying her), but his brother obtains a court order to terminate the relationship. Wilcke in fact mentions in this context the prohibition in CL 30.[25]

We disagree with both these interpretations, while accepting that there are valid elements in each of them, and translate as follows:

1-3 Sin-erimanni, son of Sin-rimanni, married the daughter of Gula-ereš, the herdsman of the governor, and
4-5 Ilatu daughter of Arkaya held her (?)[26] for *napṭarūtu*,[27] and

contract. This would be a stage prior to inchoate marriage (see Westbrook 1982a: chapter 1), and where the bride was *sui iuris*, the parties would be herself and the groom. Had the prostitute in CL 30 obtained such an oath? See the discussion of tuku in note 4 above.

22 Gurney 1982: 91-94.

23 Wilcke 1980: 138-40.

24 Gurney 1982: 93-94.

25 Wilcke 1980: 138.

26 *ik-la-ši*[!]*-ma*. In spite of his copy, Gurney read *ik-la-šu-ma* "held him," making the husband the object of the prostitute's action. In a private communication, he has informed me that he now considers the original reading *ši* to be the correct one.

27 The meaning of *napṭarūtu* is unknown. Wilcke translates "distrained her for redemption" (*zwecks Auslösung*), presumably on the basis of the verb *paṭāru* "to redeem." But it is unlikely in terms of legal logic that redemption would be given as the purpose of

6 caused him to divorce his wife, and

7-9 his brother, Sin-bel-tabini, brought Ilatu before Sin-šapik-zeri, the judge, and

9-11 said: "She caused Sin-erimanni, my brother, to get divorced."

11-14 The judge questioned Ilatu, and said: "Why did you cause Sin-erimanni the herdsman to divorce?"

14-15 Ilatu heard the word of the judge, and

16-20 said: "Sin-erimanni, the servant of my lord, has been having intercourse with me[28] until now; now that my lord has questioned me, he shall not cross my bed-post."[29]

20-26 If Sin-erimanni again enters the house of Ilatu, whether passing the day for rest or passing the night, he will be arrested, examined, and questioned, in accordance with the order to Sin-šapik-zeri.

27-30 Witnesses.

31-33 Date.

34 Finger-nail of Bana-ša-Šeriš instead of his seal.

---

distraint by the creditor. Redemption may be the essential motive of the person repaying the debt, but for the creditor it is a mere side-effect of repayment and not the only possible outcome of distraint. The purpose of the creditor in distraining is rather to ensure satisfaction of his debt, either by forcing repayment or by selling or using the security to obtain the equivalent value.

Gurney tentatively suggests "for cohabitation," citing the term *napṭartu* which in Hittite texts refers to a special kind of royal concubine. (This will not apply if the object of the verb is a woman.)

We would note that the verb used in the present context, "to hold" (*kalû*) is found also to describe the prostitute's actions in our second text, BM 13912 (line 6), where we have interpreted it as meaning to hold someone to performance of a promissory oath. But we would expect the husband to be the object of the verb as in BM 13912, CL 30, and in fact the following clause of the present text.

28 Literally: "has been taking me . . . ." Our study of the verb *ahāzum* (Westbrook 1982a: chapter one) shows the verb not to have had a purely sexual meaning in OB sources, but that strict OB use of marriage terminology broke down in subsequent periods. It is thus perfectly possible in an MB document, as the context shows, for the verb to mean "to marry" in line 3, and in the *t*-form in line 17: "to have (regularly) sexual intercourse."

29 Literally: "the edges of my bed."

In our view, although certain circumstances recorded in the opening lines are obscure, this case is on a similar pattern to CL 30 and reflects the same thinking. A married man is seduced by another woman and in consequence divorces his wife. There appears not to have been a judicial prohibition on his conduct prior to the divorce: indeed, it is probably because of that omission that he is able to continue cohabiting with the woman. The facts, however, are then brought to the attention of the court and a judicial prohibition is imposed, not only on marriage but even on cohabitation. As in our second document, BM 13912, the woman is obliged to ensure enforcement of the prohibition. It is not stated that the woman is a prostitute, but the fact that H continued to cohabit with her without marrying her is suggestive of that status, as is perhaps the explicit nature of the woman's statement to the court on her relations with him.

A final point of interest is that it is not the injured wife but the brother who brings the philandering husband to court, possibly to forestall marriage with the other woman. Perhaps, Wilcke surmises, the brother's interest is to preserve the good name of the family.[30]

30 Wilcke 1980: 138.

17

A Matter of Life and Death

Abstract

Taking the expression—"he shall die; he shall not live"—in Codex Eshnunna as its starting point, this article examines various uses of similar expressions in ancient Near Eastern texts. The conclusion is that such wording can carry one of three connotations: a king's right to pardon or not to pardon someone; the state's right to enact summary justice; or the right of a private citizen to enact summary justice. The provisions in question from CE fit within the third category.

This study is in direct response to a recent article by Reuven Yaron.[1] It gives me particular pleasure to disagree with Professor Yaron in this instance, because, if I succeed in refuting his argument, I only succeed in proving him correct.

The phrase "shall die; shall not live" (*imât ul iballuṭ*) occurs three times in Codex Eshnunna as the punishment for a crime.

12 A man who is seized in the field of an ordinary citizen in the sheaves at midday shall pay 10 shekels of silver. He who is seized in the sheaves at night: he shall die; he shall not live.

13 A man who is seized in the house of an ordinary citizen in the house at midday shall pay 10 shekels of silver. He who is seized in the house at night: he shall die; he shall not live.

28 . . . If he makes the contract and libation with her father and mother and marries her, she is a wife. The day she is seized in the lap of a man she shall die; she shall not live.

* Originally published in the *Journal of the Ancient Near Eastern Society* 25 (1997): 61-70. Used by permission.

1 Yaron 1993b.

Szlechter suggested a dual meaning: that the death penalty was mandatory and that the victim was entitled to kill the offender on the spot.[2] Ambiguity being incompatible with law, however, only one of the two is possible. Yaron originally opted for immediate retribution, on the grounds that it was legally the most appropriate solution,[3] but subsequently revised his view because he could see no connection between the language of the phrase and the idea of immediate retribution by the aggrieved party.[4] He concluded that the phrase was without special legal significance. The dual formulation was legally redundant, a rhetorical device serving merely as emphasis. His most recent article attempts to support that conclusion by examining use of the same phrase in non-legal contexts and demonstrating that it has the same function, or rather lack of one, as in the law code.

It is my opinion that Yaron's original proposal is the correct one. His misgivings, however, were fully justified in that other commentators, including this author, had failed to pay sufficient attention to the connection between idiom and legal meaning. A legal idiom can only be understood if we can visualize the image of the law that it is intended to represent. The purpose of the present study is to address those misgivings by reviewing the relationship between legal and non-legal meaning and reexamining the legal function of this particular phrase both in its individual parts and in its duality. Our findings will then be applied to Codex Eshnunna, to demonstrate the connection between the phrase and our legal interpretation of the paragraphs in which it occurs.

Legal Evidence

Before entering into a discussion of the idiom, it is worth reviewing the evidence in favor of interpreting CE 12, 13, and 28 as allowing the aggrieved party the right to kill the culprit on the spot. All three paragraphs concern cases of seizure *in flagranti delicto*, using the same terminology (*iṣṣabtu*). Furthermore, the two situations described therein are familiar from the many parallels in laws not only from the ancient Near East but

2 Szlechter 1954: 110-11.

3 Yaron 1969: 173.

4 Yaron 1988b: 259-62.

also from Greece and Rome. The first is the burglar caught at night, and the second is the wife caught in adultery. All the sources have the same common feature—the culprit is caught *in flagranti delicto*—and offer the same legal solution: the victim is entitled to kill the culprit on the spot without trial and is not liable for murder.

The case of the burglar is found in three sources. Exod 22:1 reads: "If the thief is caught breaking in and is struck dead, he has no blood. If the sun has risen on him, he has blood. He shall surely pay. If he cannot, he shall be sold for his theft." The laws of Solon are recorded as having had the following provision: "For a theft in daytime of more than 50 drachmas, a man might be arrested summarily and put into custody of the Eleven. If he stole anything, however small, by night, the person aggrieved might lawfully pursue and kill or wound him, or else put him into the hands of the Eleven, at his own option."[5] Finally the Roman Twelve Tables include the provision (VIII 12-13 [= I, 17-18 in Crawford 1996]): "If he commits theft by night, if he kills him, he is lawfully slain. By daylight . . . if he defends himself with a weapon . . . having called for help."

In all three the distinction is made between seizure by day, when the victim is not entitled to kill the burglar but only to claim the normal penalties for theft, and seizure by night, when he can kill with impunity.

The case of adultery is found in the Hittite Laws 197: ". . . if the husband finds them (the adulterers) and kills them, there is no liability upon him." The same principle is possibly to be found in the Middle Assyrian Laws A 15, a difficult text that I would translate as follows: "If a man seizes a man with his wife (and if) it has been established and proved with respect to him: (on condition that) both are killed, there is no liability upon him."[6] The same right of the husband in early Roman law is described by Aulus Gellius, quoting M. Cato, as follows: "If you should take your wife in adultery, you may with impunity kill her without trial."[7]

In my view, these parallels are no accident. The two cases are scholastic legal problems from Mesopotamian scribal schools, part of a body of learning that spread across the ancient Near East and even found its way

5 Demosthenes, *In Timocratem* 113.

6 See further Westbrook 1990b: 551-54.

7 . . . sine iudicio inpune necares (Gell. *NA* 10.23.5).

into the Mediterranean countries.[8] In a sense, it is the Eshnunna provisions that provide the connection between all the parallels. An outside observer may note that the parallels all happen to have the same special legal solution to two different cases; the Eshnunna laws self-consciously link those two different cases through use of the same special terminology for their legal solution.

On the other hand, as Yaron has shown, the alternative proposal of a mandatory death penalty makes little sense in terms of the severity of the offense, especially since adultery is assumed by other cuneiform codes to be pardonable.[9]

The starting point for any philological investigation should therefore be the presumption raised by legal logic, by their terminological connection, and by strong external parallels that these three laws in their apodosis condone immediate, private retribution. Yaron's present solution, that they impose the death penalty, pure and simple, is legally unobjectionable but raises the far less attractive presumption that they are an anomaly among parallel provisions.

Legal Phrases

Technical legal phrases originate either within a legal system or as lay terms which acquire a special nuance in a legal context. The latter are especially common in ancient Near Eastern languages, and the relationship between lay and legal meaning can be complex. Although the search for the meaning of a legal term will always begin with its literal meaning, it will often end in a totally different semantic sphere. For a legal meaning may not only restrict or nuance the literal meaning of a term, as might be expected of any specialized use; it may subvert that meaning altogether. For example, the Akkadian term *ezēbu* means "to leave, abandon"; literally, it refers to physical motion by the subject away from the object, which would normally be stationary. As a technical legal term in the context of marriage, it means "to divorce." The connection between leaving and divorce might seem obvious, except that divorce was achieved in the

8 See Westbrook 1988a.

9 Yaron 1969: 173.

legal systems that used this term not by physical motion but by the pronouncement of *verba solemnia*. Where a husband divorced his wife, at least, it was not he but the wife, the object of the verb *ezēbu*, who physically left the matrimonial home.[10] The legal meaning of the term is thus the opposite of its literal meaning, a paradox expressed by MAL A 37: "If a man will divorce (literally: 'leave') his wife, . . . she shall go out empty."

A legal context thus provides a new set of clothes, so to speak, for the naked phrase. Those clothes are invisible, insofar as there is no morphological change in the phrase, but they nonetheless make a very real difference in the way the phrase is read, because they allow it to have a different function, namely, to describe not a physical phenomenon but the application of certain legal rules.

The Parts of the Dual Formula

Yaron avers that the sum of "shall die; shall not live" expresses no more than its parts because the latter are synonymous.[11] In terms of the lay meaning of the phrase, this is perfectly correct. "Shall die" is a prediction of a future change of physical state. "Shall not live" predicts exactly the same change. It adds no new information; it is superfluous.

The same is not true of the legal meaning. That meaning becomes evident once it is realized that the phrase under discussion is merely a variant of a much more common phrase using the same verbs. It was Yaron himself who established the connection over thirty years ago in a seminal article that curiously has not been cited in discussions of the Eshnunna provisions.[12]

Yaron pointed out that in the Latin phrase *vitae necisque potestas*, "power of life and putting to death," the second part referred to a judicial death sentence and the first to a judge's power of pardon. By way of evidence for this proposition, Yaron adduced sources from the ancient Near

10 In *CAD* E 416-17, under meaning 1. a) 1′ ("to abandon, to desert . . . persons"), in fact there are many passages where the term should be translated "divorce." Cf. the Hebrew term *šlḥ*, "send away," which is more faithful to reality.

11 Yaron 1993b: 144ff.

12 Yaron 1962b: 243-51.

East. Thus in HL 187 a man found guilty of bestiality is brought to the gate of the palace and "the king may kill him; the king may cause him to live." In Dan 5:19 Nebuchadnezzar's power is described as follows: "Whom he wished, he would kill; whom he wished, he would make live; whom he wished, he would raise up; and whom he wished, he would bring down." Finally, a letter to king Assurbanipal makes explicit the judicial nature of the king's actions: "He for whose crime death had been ordered, my lord the king has made live; they who have been prisoner for many years, you have redeemed."[13]

The dual formulation in these sources was explained by Yaron as follows:

> The first part of the formula "power to put to death" implies a tendency to concentrate jurisdiction in the hands of the king, at least as far as capital cases are concerned. In this connection it ought to be noted that in texts like the Hittite laws, the vassal treaties of Esarhaddon, and also in Daniel . . . the "power to put to death" is not arbitrary. The king decrees the death of him who has committed a capital crime; he is not given power to decree the death of a law-abiding subject. . . .The second part of the notion, "the power to keep alive," means that the king, in his discretion, is entitled to prefer mercy to strict justice, to grant pardon if he so pleases.[14]

In the light of Yaron's exposition, we may conclude that "to kill" ceases to be a physical act where the subject of the verb is a court or a sovereign acting in his judicial capacity. It refers rather to its imposition of the death sentence. In the same circumstances, the intransitive form "shall die" also refers to the death sentence, but from the condemned man's point of view; it is a normative statement, asserting that a person ought to be put to death. It informs us that he is guilty of a crime and of the sentence applicable to that crime.

The formula "shall not live," however, does not contain the same information. It refers to a separate judicial process, that of pardon, which, although it may on occasion be coterminous with condemnation or sen-

13 ABL 2, lines 21-24; edition in Waterman 1930: no. 2.

14 Yaron 1962b: 248.

tencing, is in principle independent thereof. The formula negates the possibility of pardon where a sentence of death is applicable or has been imposed.

This interpretation was espoused by Yaron in his article on *vitae necisque potestas* with regard to a passage in a letter to king Esarhaddon: "the writer, who committed a grave offense and had been pardoned, profusely thanks the king: 'Great sins against the house of my lords I have committed; . . . I (deserved) to be killed, not to be kept alive.'"[15] In his most recent article, however, Yaron cites the same passage as attesting to the meaninglessness of the dual formulation: "The double phrase implies no addition to the substantive import, only a desire to impress, a wish to be taken seriously."[16] This may well have been the desire of the writer in question, but there remains a substantive difference between deserving justice and not deserving mercy.

Legal Death

Where a phrase functions as a legal idiom, it takes effect within the confines of a world created by legal rules. Unless the logic of that legal world is taken into consideration, it may be difficult to connect the phrase with its context; indeed, a literal translation may produce bizarre results. The dual formula that we are considering can only work outside the legal sphere in the hands of a divine ruler. According to 1 Sam 2:6: "The LORD puts to death and makes live; he brings down to the Netherworld and he brings up."

Mere mortals can achieve the same, but only within the world of their own creation: the artificial world of legal rules. Consider the following law in Deut 17:6: "The dead man shall be put to death on the word of two or three witnesses; he shall not be put to death on the word of one witness." The apparent absurdity of my literal translation disappears once we realize that it is legal death that is in issue.[17] A man who has been found guilty of

15 Yaron 1962b: 246; ABL 620 (edition in Waterman 1930: no. 620).

16 Yaron 1993b: 145.

17 Standard translations typically ignore the word "dead man" (*mēt*) in the Hebrew text, even though the Septuagint tries to take account of it (*apothnēskōn*: "dying man").

a capital offense is deemed dead in the eyes of the law; his physical death must await his execution, which is not a foregone conclusion. For, as the prophet Ezekiel puts it (Ezek 18:32): "'I do not desire the death of the dead,' says the Lord GOD, 'so repent and live.'"

A letter to king Assurbanipal from one of his officers begins by reporting success in a minor skirmish, but it then emerges that the officer is in disgrace due to an earlier military disaster:[18]

> Since Birat was sacked and its gods carried off, I am dead (*mītu anāku*). Had I but seen the golden ring of my lord the king, I would live (*abtaluṭ*). But behold, when I sent my messenger to my lord the king, I did not see the ring of my lord the king and I did not live (*ul abluṭ*). I am dead (*mītu anāku*); let my lord the king not forsake me!

Clearly, the death in question is figurative, referring to the officer's disgrace. The king has punished him in some way, and the officer seeks a reversal of that order. There is hyperbole in the officer's statement in that he compares his punishment to a death sentence, but the principle is not affected. The sequence of events narrated is: 1) punishment, 2) petition for remission of punishment (messenger, see the king's ring), and 3) rejection of petition (not see the king's ring). "Dead" refers to the original punishment, whereas "live" and "not live" refer to the petition and its failure. Of course, as a result of that failure, the officer remains in his previous status; hence repetition of the term "dead."

In Isa 38:1 (= 2 Kgs 20:1) King Hezekiah falls seriously ill. God informs him through the prophet Isaiah: "Put your house in order, for you are dead, and you shall not live." As in the letter of the Assyrian officer, "dead" refers to Hezekiah's status as a condemned man. Sickness was regarded in the ancient Near East as, *inter alia*, divine punishment for sin,

---

See, for example, "the death sentence shall be executed" (Oxford Bible); "a person shall be put to death" (JPS); "on ne pourra être condamné à mort" (Bible de Jérusalem). It should be noted that the Hebrew root *mt** meaning "man" is not attested in the singular.

18 ABL 259; edition in Pfeiffer 1935: 22 (reverse lines 1-10).

and a mortal illness was therefore a death sentence.[19] "You are dead" thus means that Hezekiah has been found guilty of a capital sin by the divine judge; "You shall not live" means that he can expect no mercy. Hezekiah, however, refuses to take God at his word and begs for mercy (vv. 2-3), with the result that God eventually relents somewhat and grants Hezekiah another fifteen years of life (vv. 4-5). The message is that prayer and repentance may soften even the harshest decision, at least where the divine king is concerned.

In the light of these examples, we see that within a legal framework the notion "make live" is a perfectly logical counterpart to "kill." The condemned man is legally speaking dead, and the effect of pardon is to bring him back to life again.[20]

Ellipsis

So far we have been examining the dual phrase, but there is no reason why "live" or "make live" should not be used alone to indicate pardon or even to indicate by ellipsis the whole process of condemnation and pardon, if the context is sufficiently suggestive. In the "Nippur Homicide Trial," an account from the early second millennium B.C.E. of a trial for murder before the assembly of the city of Nippur, three men conspired to kill a fourth and, when they had done the deed, informed the victim's wife.[21] She kept her silence. All four were brought to trial. One group in the assembly argued as follows:

> As men who have killed a man they are not live men (lu$_2$-lu$_2$-u$_3$ in-gaz-eš-am$_3$ / lu$_2$-ti-la nu-me-eš). Those three males and that female shall be killed before the chair (of the victim).

19 See, e.g., *Šurpu* (edition in Reiner 1958), a series of incantations designed to remove sin from a sick man by means of confession and ritual purification. Cf. Num 27:3 and 2 Kgs 5:20-27.

20 This approach was already adumbrated by Yaron in his earlier article: "by his god-like intervention [the sovereign] 'keeps alive,' perhaps even 'restores to life,' the offender who has been condemned to death" (1962b: 248).

21 Edition in Jacobsen 1970: 193-214.

Another group, however, argued for mercy for the wife:

> Even if Nin-dada daughter of Lu-Ninurta may have killed her husband, a woman, what can she do, that she should be killed?

The assembly then considered the wife's case and decided that she should be executed with the others. In this account, the facts had been proven; the only issue before the court was the possibility of clemency. It therefore seems to me appropriate that the culprits are referred to by the group arguing against mercy not as "dead" but as "not live," i.e., not worthy of mercy.

More than a thousand years later, a striking illustration of this elliptical usage is given in a report of a trial for high treason.[22] King Nebuchadnezzar II, having discovered a plot against him by a certain Babu-aḫḫa-iddina, "proved against him in the popular assembly the crimes that he had committed and looked upon him angrily and pronounced his not-living (*lā balassu iqbî*), and his throat was cut" (lines 17-20). The narrative omits mention of the death sentence, which is self-evident in a case of treason, and focuses on the king's prerogative of pardon, which presupposes a death sentence. The death penalty for treason resulted from a conviction by a court (the popular assembly, not the king); "not-living" resulted from the king's decision to deny mercy.

Finally, the same metonymy explains an enigmatic biblical law (Exod 22:17): "You shall not make a witch live." This law, in my interpretation, is addressed to the local authorities.[23] It is understood that witchcraft is a capital offense. The purpose of the law is to forbid the local authorities to exercise a prerogative of mercy with regard to witches.

Summary Justice

The effect of elliptical usage of one part of the dual phrase is to cast emphasis on that aspect. In certain contexts, when used as a speech formula, that emphasis is such as to give the phrase a slightly different nuance. In

22 *AfO* 17 2 (edition in Weidner 1954-56b: 1-3).

23 Westbrook 1986a: 62-66.

2 Kgs 10:19, king Jehu issues an order summoning the priests of Baal, without exception, and adds: "Anyone who is missing shall not live." We understand from this that the penalty for disobedience is death, but it adds little to emphasize that the king will not pardon the offender. The emphasis lies rather in its focus on the final stage of judgment to the exclusion of the preceding stages. Truncation of the legal phrase enables it to become part of the peremptory order and thus to be symbolic of the truncation of the judicial process. The offender will be put to death summarily, without trial, without being able to offer an explanation or excuse. Failure to appear is proof of his guilt; there is no need for legal niceties and no question of pardon. The same is true in Gen 31:32 when Jacob, accused by Laban of stealing his household gods, accepts a search, declaring: "He with whom your gods are found shall not live."

The use of the truncated phrase as a peremptory order is not confined to the Bible. In a letter from Mari dating to the 18th century, an official reports:

> I assembled the sheikhs of the cities of the Binu-Yamina, and I gave them the following strict order:[24] "Whoever you are, if a single individual leaves your city and you do not seize him and bring him to me, in truth you shall not live."[25]

Finally, returning to the Bible, in Exod 19:12-13, we find the full dual phrase but separated in a way that changes its emphasis. Moses, about to ascend Mount Sinai, is instructed to warn the people:

> Do not go up onto the mountain or touch its edge. Anyone who touches the mountain shall be killed. No hand shall touch him but he shall surely be stoned or shot. Whether beast or man, he shall not live.

24 *ašpuṭšunūti*. *CAD* translates *šapāṭu* "to issue orders" (Š/1 450) but for no apparent reason creates a second lemma (Š/1 451) with three examples—one uncertain, one in broken context, and this passage, which it translates, "I informed(?) them . . . ." In my opinion, the first meaning applies here also. Confirmation is provided by examples of the noun *šipṭu*, "ruling, strict order, reprimand," given in *CAD* Š/2 93.

25 ARM 2 92, line 122.

There is to be no trial, but instant death for trespassers, as postponement of the element "shall not live" until after the mode of execution indicates. It is not clear who was to carry out the stoning or shooting. The order seems to allude to the posting of guards, but a further possibility, which we shall discuss in the next section, is that it entitled ordinary Israelites to take law into their own hands.

Private Justice

In all the examples that we have examined from the ancient Near East, the power of life and death vests in the hands of the king or his delegates. There is, however, at least one example of the phrase being used in connection with private individuals. Zech 13:3 states:

> But if a man continues to prophesy, his father and mother who bore him shall say to him, "You shall not live, for you have spoken falsehood in the name of the LORD," and his father and mother who bore him shall pierce him through because of his prophesying.

False prophesy was a form of apostasy, a serious public offense for which the death penalty is prescribed in the laws of Deuteronomy (18:20; cf. 13:6, 9-11; 17:2-5). According to those laws, execution was to be by the community and only after a public trial, with procedural safeguards for the defendants, or after a formal inquiry by the public authorities (13:13-16; 17:2-7). Where the culprit has sought to suborn a close relative or friend in secret, however, the procedure is less elaborate. It is the duty of the relative or friend to denounce the culprit and personally to initiate the public execution by stoning (13:7-11). His sole testimony is sufficient because it is contrary to interest, namely, the natural ties of love and affection.[26]

26 Levinson (1996: 601-20) rightly points out that the procedural safeguard of two witnesses (Deut 17:6) should not be read into Deut 13:7-12. In the nature of the case, there can be no other witnesses. Levinson's conclusion that the addressee of the law must summarily execute the culprit should, however, be nuanced. The addressee of the

The prophetic passage goes a step further. The situation is considered so serious that the culprit's parents are given the right to execute summary justice themselves, without going through normal procedures. They assert that right by means of the speech formula "You shall not live," which, as we have just seen, is normally used by rulers when they order summary execution.[27] There is no preceding order, as there is in the case of rulers; instead, the parents arrogate to themselves legal authorization by naming the offense in their declaration. It is the grave, public nature of the offense that entitles them to act. For a brief moment, and in special circumstances, the parents are given the authority of a ruler or judge over a criminal: their own son.[28]

With this final example we have reached a meaning of the phrase that fits exactly our interpretation of the legal solution in the paragraphs of Codex Eshnunna. Those paragraphs, it will be recalled, ruled that an intruder caught breaking in at night "shall die; he shall not live." Our interpretation, following Yaron's original proposal, was that the householder was being given authority to kill the intruder on the spot. The case of the false prophet killed by his parents shows that the phrase could bear that meaning. It is a sub-category of the formula's use in reference to summary justice: the right of an individual to take the law into his own hands in special circumstances. It is true that in most cases of summary justice the formula is truncated, whereas here it is whole. The reason, we suggest, is

---

apostasy still has to bring the case to the public, who participate in the execution; he could not justify the slaying of a close friend or relative *ex post facto* by citing his apostasy, as would one who took the law into his own hands.

27 The difficulty of this phrase for commentators and the strained rationalizations that result are illustrated by a recent example: "the sentence here is expressed somewhat less directly, perhaps to ameliorate the harsh and extraordinary circumstances whereby parents are called upon to execute their own children" (Meyers and Meyers 1993: 374).

28 Another possible example of the phrase being used of an individual is a Mari letter, ARM 10 32. Unfortunately the text is incomplete and the context too obscure to be certain. A daughter writes to her father that unless he sends someone quickly to take her away, "I shall die; I shall not live" (line 32′). Since her request appears to arise from an incident related earlier in the letter (lines 13′–14′) in which a certain Ḫaya-Sumu threatened her—"since I will cause you to die, let your 'star' (= father) come and take you away!"—it may be that Ḫaya-Sumu was claiming (abusively?) the right to kill her summarily.

that in the Eshnunna paragraphs, the necessary context is lacking. The phrase does not follow upon a peremptory order, nor is it a speech formula. Nor does the context that is given in the protasis make the right self-evident. Theft and adultery are not public offenses that have to be stopped at all costs, in which action might be expected of a private person.[29] "Shall die" establishes that the culprit is liable to the death penalty—it plays the same role as the parents' naming of the offense in the case of false prophesy. The second part of the formula—"shall not live"—refers to the modalities of execution, as we have seen in Exod 19:12-13. By emphasizing seizure *in flagranti delicto*, the protasis indicates that summary justice is in issue, and in the circumstances described, the only possible executioner is the very person by whom the culprit is seized.

Conclusion

Seen through modern eyes, the second leg of the dual formula "he shall die; he shall not live" seems a redundant repetition, whose only effect is to heighten the dramatic impact of its first leg. We have attempted to show, however, that in its duality the formula functioned as a technical legal term. In this function, its second leg had an independent meaning of considerable importance. Depending on the context, it could refer to the power of pardon by a ruler, the exercise of summary justice by a ruler, or the right of a private person to execute summary justice. Accordingly, when the dual phrase occurs in the apodosis of three paragraphs of a law code, we are entitled to assume that its second leg is not redundant but indicates one of those three legal solutions. Legal logic and comparative evidence constitute a compelling argument in favor of the third solution: private summary justice.

29 Compare the case of Pinhas in Num 25:7-8, who brought to an end a plague by summarily killing apostates.

18

International Law in the Amarna Age

Abstract

This study explores the basic aspects of the system of international law in the ancient Near East, as it is revealed in the Amarna correspondence. It seeks to show that, despite apparent differences on the surface, the political powers of the era operated with similar conceptions of law and in adherence to entrenched traditions regarding international relations.

Where an international society exists, relations between its members will be governed not only by common political conventions but also by agreed rules of law. In the ancient Near East, international law had a venerable tradition, being attested virtually from the beginning of written records.[1] Formal treaties were a frequent instrument of foreign policy, and customary international law was appealed to in diplomatic protests and negotiations. Thus, although the Amarna Letters are not legal documents, international law is important to understanding them. This chapter provides a background to the worldview of the correspondents, by sketching in outline some of the fundamental legal conceptions upon which their diplomatic *dêmarches* were based.

* Originally published in *Amarna Diplomacy: The Beginnings of International Relations* (ed. R. Cohen and R. Westbrook; Baltimore: Johns Hopkins University Press, 2000), 28-41, 239-42. Used by permission.

1 The earliest account of a border dispute, between the Sumerian states of Lagash and Umma in the twenty-fifth century B.C.E., is a dramatic tale of treaties, breach, and consequences; see Cooper 1983b. Although individual legal systems varied greatly, there was a common legal tradition throughout the ancient Near East that continued into the first millennium B.C.E. As a result, it is possible to draw examples of a legal principle from different periods and countries.

The State

International law in modern theory is the system of law that governs relations between states (as opposed to domestic law, which is the ordinary law governing relations between individuals within a state or other political entity). It is therefore necessary first to establish whether, in the ancient Near East, states existed in a form to which we can meaningfully attribute a role in international law and, if so, what was meant by a state.

The modern concept of the state as a legal entity is based on the model of the corporation: an artificial person recognized by law, whose "acts" are the result of imputation to it of the acts of its officials. It is this existence separate from its members, albeit fictive, that gives the state capacity to be a subject of international law.[2]

Ancient law had not developed the concept of the corporation and could not therefore rely on it as a model. The usual form of government was monarchy, and all acts of the monarch were apparently personal; they were not attributed to his country acting as a separate person.[3] Ancient law could not conceive of the state as a legal entity.

The modern model, however, is not the only possible paradigm for a state. Ancient Near Eastern law achieved the same role for its political societies as states in modern international law but by a different route: the application of a model based on the particular structure of its own societies and their domestic law.[4] Other contributors to this volume have shown the

2 Kelsen 1961: 181-82, 191-93, 197-99.

3 Legal historians have, it is true, suggested that their role was no different from that of a modern ruler. Korošec called the Hittite emperor "der oberste Funktionär des Staates" (1931: 46). Similarly, Kestemont states that "en matière juridique publique, le chef d'État et la communauté nationale constituent deux pôles d'une seule et même personnalité morale: la communauté nationale est le siège réel des droits et obligations et le chef d'État en est le représentant" (1974: 48). All that these authors are doing, however, is unconsciously imposing the corporate model upon ancient polities, the result being jarring anachronism.

4 For the lay reader, it should be emphasized that the term "domestic" in this article has nothing to do with family or family law; it is simply used as defined above, in opposition to international law.

importance of the family metaphor in international politics.[5] For international law, the operative metaphor was that of the household.

Ancient Near Eastern society was strongly hierarchical. It was based not on the individual but on the household. The household, called the "house," was a socioeconomic unit headed by a "father," whose extended, multigenerational family lived under his authority. It was normally a geographical unit also, in the sense that "house" also meant land—a dwelling at least, if not agricultural land. Subordinate members of the household consisted not only of obvious family members such as wives, sons, daughters, daughters-in-law, and grandchildren, but also dependents in a client status and slaves.[6] A typical society consisted of a coalition of household units. The word "man" often referred not to any male individual, but to a head of household.

Within this structure, the king was regarded as no more than a householder on a larger scale, his household being the aggregation of households that made up a political society. The population of the state was his household and the territory within its borders the household land. In this regard he was often referred to simply as a "man," for example, "Aziru, the man of Amurru."[7] The constitutional relationship between king and citizens relied on a metaphor drawn from the hierarchy within a household: he was their master; they were his slaves. The metaphor of slavery would more accurately be regarded as a metonym, since it was only certain aspects of slavery, such as obedience and loyalty, that were regarded as applicable. In domestic law, there was a sharp distinction between free citizens and slaves.

The king was by no means the apex of the hierarchy. Above him stood the emperor, if he were a vassal king. He and his household, that is, the population of his country, were all slaves of the emperor. Again, the term was used metaphorically, to denote subordinate members of a household. Above the emperor was yet another stratum, that of the gods, to whom all

5 E.g., Cohen 1996: 11-26; Artzi 1980: 167.

6 See Stager 1985.

7 EA 162:1, rightly translated "ruler" by Moran. This was not an innovation of the Amarna Age; in the Old Babylonian period we find references such as "Hammurabi, the man of Babylon."

owed obedience, and even the pantheon itself could contain a hierarchy of households.

The state may be identified as a household at a median hierarchical level, at the point where the head of household, a king, came under the direct jurisdiction of the gods with regard to his own and his subordinates' actions.[8] It would be a distortion to speak of the king's actions being "imputed" to his household, as in the corporate model, but as we shall see below, other legal doctrines unknown to modern law provided channels through which the same result might be achieved.

The Amarna Letters provide evidence of the conscious use of this legal model. The greeting formulae of the Great Power correspondence follow a stereotyped pattern, a typical example of which is (EA 1:1-9):

> Say to Kadashman-Enlil, the king of Karadunishe, my brother: Thus Nibmuarea, Great King, the king of Egypt, your brother. For me all goes well. For you may all go well. For your household, for your wives, for your sons, for your magnates, your horses, your chariots, for your countries, may all go very well. For me all goes well. For my household, for my wives, for my sons, for my magnates, my horses, the numerous troops, all goes well, and in my countries all goes very well.

The apparently personal greeting is, in fact, an assertion of legal status. Paradoxically, its "personal touch" establishes that the correspondence between the writer and the addressee is not personal but is carried on in their official capacity. Not only are the official titles of both given but the salutation also moves from the personal household to those features identifying it as a median household in the hierarchy and, therefore, a state, namely officials, armed forces, and territory. Even as between suzerain and vassal, the legal model was alluded to: the Egyptian king was careful to address his vassals as "X, ruler (literally: 'man') of the city Y."[9]

8 The theoretical picture is complicated somewhat by the existence of vassal kings; see below.

9 EA 162, 367, 369, 370. See Moran 1992: xxvii, nn. 73, 74. The term "mayor" (*ḫazannu*), not used in the formal address, refers to their function in the Egyptian administration.

International Law

Jurisdiction

International law was a system of rules regulating relations between kings, as heads of median-level households. The system was under the jurisdiction of the gods, who constituted its court or courts. Enforcement was by the gods or by legitimate self-help, sanctioned by the gods. Three problems arise in this regard.

First, if jurisdiction is divine, then its rules might be considered as being in the realm of religion rather than of law. Kestemont regards them as extra-juridical norms, on a level with norms of honor, honesty, and conscience, which demonstrate the impotence of international law rather than its presence.[10] I would argue that there was no such separation in the ancient world. Everyone, without exception, believed in the gods: the gods were part of the real world as they saw it, just as they saw the earth as being flat. The divine legal system governed human behavior no less than human courts, and its sanctions, if less certain in their application (but not by much), were equally feared. Notwithstanding the occasional breach and the rationalization of misconduct, the behavior of states was conditioned by what they saw as an effective legal system. Natural calamities such as plague, drought, flood, and defeat in war were attributed to divine justice, and steps were taken to make legal reparation in light of them. In his Plague Prayers, the Hittite king Mursili identifies the cause of a plague afflicting Hatti as the breach of a treaty with Egypt by his father, Suppiluliuma. He seeks to assuage the gods by making reparations to Egypt and returning Egyptian prisoners.[11] A similar action was taken by David regarding a breach of treaty by his predecessor Saul, which was identified as the cause of a drought (2 Sam 21:1-11). From this perspective, one might even argue that ancient international law was more genuinely law than is its modern counterpart.

Second, the subjects of modern international law being essentially states, individuals have no standing before its tribunals. Not so the ancient divine courts. The gods judged everyone, whether king or commoner,

10 Kestemont 1974: 201-4.

11 Translated in Goetze 1969b: 394-96; see also Houwink ten Cate 1969: 97-98.

emperor or slave, and every individual within a state could seek direct recourse to divine justice through prayer. Ancient international law was distinguished from domestic law in the degree rather than in the total absence of accessibility. For the individual, the gods were a residual court, a tribunal that would punish those offenses that escaped human courts (for lack of evidence), and the ultimate court of appeal where human courts could not or would not provide justice.[12] In disputes between kings, in contrast, the divine tribunals were courts of first instance. There was no other authority to which they might have recourse.

Third, the system is further complicated by the existence of vassal kings. Such kings were subject to the jurisdiction of their emperor and thus one step removed from the jurisdiction of the gods. Two factors, however, need to be taken into consideration. One is that empires in the Amarna Age were not administrative units, but each contained a core state where the emperor would be a mere king, answerable to the gods and his peers, and ruling his subjects directly, in the manner of all other kings. The second factor is that domestic sovereignty could be distinguished from suzerainty by what I will call the "doctrine of impermeability." An ordinary head of household had a certain jurisdiction over the subordinate members of his house, subject to the rules of law and custom. His control, however, was not impermeable. The king's court regularly adjudicated inner-household disputes, between husband and wife, between two wives or wife and concubine, between father and son, and even between master and slave. For an emperor, however, the affairs of his vassals' subjects were beyond his reach. Litigants from within a vassal state could presumably petition the gods if unsatisfied with royal justice, but there is no evidence that they could ever go over the head of their own king by appealing his decision to the emperor. The suzerain did not interfere in the internal jurisdiction of his vassals; he only adjudicated disputes between vassal kings or between his own nationals and nationals of vassal states.

Vassal kings therefore had an independent domestic legal system, which is one of the essential characteristics of a modern state, and they occupied a place in the hierarchy above that of domestic households. As

12 There was no such thing as a spiritual sphere into which human courts would not enter: they saw it as within their jurisdiction to punish even "victimless" crimes against the gods, such as incest.

between themselves, they could conduct an active foreign policy, make alliances, and even acquire their own vassals, depending on the policy of the imperial power.[13] The Amarna Letters attest to alliances between vassals within the Egyptian empire against fellow vassals (EA 74, 149) and to the building of mini-empires such as those of Lab'ayu of Shechem and 'Abdi-Ashirta of Amurru (EA 244, 253, 254, 280; EA 83, 90). Only where they impinged directly on their interests would the Egyptians intervene. Accordingly, it is unwise to be too dogmatic: just as international law was not a hermetically sealed system but one characterized by degree, so the capacity of vassals to be the subjects of international law must be recognized as limited, but real. The juridical role of the gods, which became more direct as households rose in the hierarchical ladder, took on a qualitative difference at the level of kings, including vassal kings.

Doctrine

Certain doctrines of domestic law unfamiliar to modern systems enabled the household model to function effectively at the level of international law, endowing the actions of kings with the same effects as does the fiction of legal personality for the modern state. I would point to three in particular that are illustrated below.

1. The head of household had legal authority vis-à-vis outsiders: he could enter into legal obligations that bound his whole household or individual subordinates.

2. The head of household's own obligations could be enforced against his subordinates. Of particular importance for international law are the possibilities of vicarious or collective punishment. In the first instance, a subordinate member could be put to death for an offense that the head of household had committed, it being regarded as punishment of the head of

13 E.g., an Old Babylonian diplomatic dispatch reports that King Atamrum of Andarig, a vassal of King Zimri-Lim of Mari, has seven vassal kings of his own! (Joannès 1991: 172).

household himself.[14] In the second, the whole household could be destroyed, together with its head, where the latter had committed a serious offense against a hierarchical superior.[15]

3. The head of household in principle owned all family property; on his death the members of his household who constituted his primary heirs became his automatic, universal successors. In this way, a juridical continuity of the household was ensured.

Customary International Law

The two most important sources for international law are custom and treaty. Customary international law is difficult to identify in the ancient sources, since it does not derive from legal instruments. It is also difficult sometimes to distinguish a legal rule from a rule of etiquette, since the response to both, barring a serious legal infraction, was generally the same: a diplomatic protest.[16] In three areas, concerning envoys, foreign nationals, and extradition, there appear to have been customary rules.

Envoys

EA 30 is a passport or letter of credentials of a Mittanian envoy.[17] In EA 15, the envoy's credentials are included in the Assyrian king's message of

14 Code of Hammurabi 229-230: "If a builder builds a house for a man and does not make his work strong, and the house that he built collapses and causes the death of . . . the house-owner's son, the son of that builder shall be killed."

15 For the crime of treason and blasphemy, Naboth was executed along with his sons; see 1 Kings 21 and 2 Kgs 9:26.

16 The Amarna letters reveal a series of obligations that were taken very seriously but that were clearly no more than etiquette: e.g., inquiring after the health of a brother monarch, inviting a brother monarch to a special festival, sending greetings on accession to the throne, and declaring official mourning on the death of a brother monarch. See Korošec 1931: 47-48; Artzi 1980: 167.

17 On passports for envoys, see Meier 1988: 89-93.

introduction. Although it was an obvious diplomatic necessity, there is no evidence that such a letter was legally required in every case to establish an envoy's credentials. The envoy of a friendly state was regarded as a guest of the host monarch, who was responsible for his housing and maintenance. The length of stay was entirely at the discretion of the host, whose permission was necessary before the envoy could depart.[18] Inordinate retention of an envoy would lead to protests, but as it was, strictly speaking, legal, the reaction was muted. The Mittanian king retaliated in kind (retorsion) or sent a lower-level envoy (EA 29:155-61) but, at the same, time, appealed for Egyptian cooperation (EA 28).

The modern doctrine of diplomatic immunity, whereby a diplomat is not liable in the courts of the host country for his illegal acts, is not attested in ancient Near Eastern records. Indeed, the Amarna Letters suggest that at the very least, the host country could demand that the offending diplomat be tried and punished by his own country. In EA 29:173-81, Pharaoh demands that the Mittanian king impose the death penalty on two of his own diplomats (cf. EA 24 IV:35-39 = paragraph 28), whom Pharaoh claims committed (unspecified) crimes while in Egypt but who had since returned to Mittani. The Mittanian king points out that he has already conducted a judicial investigation in the presence of Mane, the Egyptian ambassador, apparently on the basis of an earlier demand, and has put them in chains and transported them to the border (in anticipation of extradition?). Nonetheless, he readily agrees to Pharaoh's new demand, on condition that proof be given of a capital offense: "Now, may my brother establish the nature of their crime, and I will treat them as my brother wants them treated."

There is evidence, however, of a doctrine of diplomatic inviolability, in that a serious attaint to the person or dignity of a diplomat by the host country would be regarded as an attack on the diplomat's country and, hence, *casus belli*.[19] In EA 16, the Assyrian king was in a delicate position. His envoys had complained to him about being made to stand for hours in the sun (along with the rest of the Egyptian court) at one of Akhenaten's

18 Meier 1988: 229-45.

19 As illustrated in the biblical account of the shameful treatment of King David's envoys. Half their beards were shaved off and their clothes cut off at the middle. David responded with an armed expedition; see 2 Sam 10:1-14.

interminable religious devotions.[20] He could not protest their treatment directly, for the envoys were treated no differently from the Egyptian courtiers and no diplomatic slight was intended. Instead, he argued: "If staying out in the sun means profit for the king, then let him (a messenger) stay out and let him die right there in the sun, (but) for the king himself there must be a profit" (lines 43-49).

The suggestion that the Egyptian king was entitled to kill envoys for his own profit must be taken as rhetorical; in practice, it would have been regarded as a serious breach of international law. At the same time, the appeal to self-interest is a telltale sign of the absence of firm legal grounds.

Foreign Nationals

There is substantial evidence of a rule of customary law imposing liability on the host government to compensate foreign nationals who had been the victim of serious crimes on their territory. The starting point is a doctrine of domestic law, recorded in the Code of Hammurabi 22-24:

> If a man commits robbery and is caught, that man shall be killed. If the robber is not caught, the person robbed shall declare his losses before the god, and the city and mayor in whose district the robbery was committed shall compensate him for his lost property. If it is life (i.e., murder), the city and mayor shall pay his family one mina of silver.

The local authority had a responsibility toward the victim akin to that of an insurer. It has been pointed out by Green that the same doctrine was applied to foreign victims, who were entitled to look to the local ruler for compensation, pending apprehension of the culprit.[21] In an Egyptian story set in the twelfth century, Wen-Amun, an Egyptian passing through the Phoenician port of Dor, had some valuables stolen from his ship by one of the members of his crew. He at once notified the prince of Dor, claiming that the losses were his responsibility. The prince admitted in principle an

20 Following the interpretation of Redford, cited by Moran 1992: 41 n. 16.

21 Green 1979: 116-17.

obligation to compensate Wen-Amun from his own treasury but found a legal loophole in the fact that the thief was from Wen-Amun's crew (a member of his own foreign household, so to speak). As Green points out, it is improbable that there was a treaty between Dor and Egypt at the time; so the basis of the prince's liability must have been customary law (1979: 117).

Several treaties from Ugarit almost contemporaneous with the Amarna correspondence stipulate compensation from the public purse for the robbery and murder of nationals of Ugarit in the territory of Karkemish, and vice versa. A curious feature of one of these treaties, in which the victims (significantly) are merchants, is that the public authority is liable to make a fixed payment of three minas of silver for murder victims, whether the murderers are caught or not, but are liable to pay simple compensation for goods stolen *only if the robbers are caught.*[22] I conclude that the purpose of the treaty was not to establish liability but to *limit* existing liability under customary law. The authorities were prepared to act as paymaster of first resort but were not prepared to accept open-ended liability for plundered caravans where there was no hope of recouping their expenditure from the actual culprits. In this light, the fixed payment for murder may also be seen as a limitation of liability. The normal system of retribution for murder in the ancient Near East was a dual right of the victim's relatives: to execute revenge or to accept ransom payment from the culprit in lieu of revenge.[23] Since the ransom demanded for the culprit's life could theoretically be considerably higher, the fixed sum of three minas represented a limit on the primary payment of compensation by the public authority, which it might not be able to recoup from the culprit, even if he was caught.

I have discussed these sources in detail because they are necessary to understanding the full legal significance of EA 313 and EA 8. In EA 313, the murder of Egyptian merchants by brigands on the territory of a vassal is dealt with by the vassal paying the local Egyptian commissioner "400 shekels of silver, plus 1000." Moran notes that it is a strange way to write 1,400 shekels. The point is that there are *two* payments for two separate matters: first, compensation in place of ransom and, second, compensation

22 RS 17.146; edited in Nougayrol 1956: 154-57.

23 See Westbrook 1988d: 39-83.

for goods stolen, in that order. The normal customary law is followed, unaffected by the vassal-suzerain relationship.

In EA 8, the Babylonian king informs the Egyptian king that some Babylonian merchants were robbed and murdered by Egyptian vassals in Canaan, and continues: "In your country I have been robbed. Bring them to account and make compensation for the money that they took away. Put to death the men who put my servants to death, and so avenge their blood" (lines 26-29).

The Babylonian king's identification with his merchants is the other side of the coin of vicarious punishment: an offense against a subordinate member of the household is an offense against the head of household. His demand for compensation directly from the Egyptian king fits in perfectly with the rule of customary law. But his demand that the Egyptian king execute vengeance on the killers, rather than pay compensation and exact ransom from them, was probably more than was required in strict law. For this reason, as we have seen in EA 16, the Babylonian king appeals to his counterpart's self-interest: "If you do not put these men to death, they are going to kill again, be it a caravan of mine or your own messengers, and so messengers between us will thereby be cut off" (lines 30-33).

We thus see the difference in this letter between a legal and a political argument: a legal claim needed no elaboration, since the relevant rule of customary international law was accepted by the parties as binding on them; a political demand needed support, by threat of sanction, offer of advantage, or appeal to self-interest.

Extradition

Kings had a traditional discretion to grant or refuse asylum to fugitives. As between kings of equal status, they were under no legal obligation to return fugitives upon demand, unless it was specifically provided for by treaty, which was frequently the case.[24] Of course, it might be considered an unfriendly act to harbor a fugitive, in which case a request for extradition would be granted as a favor.

24 See, for instance, the detailed provisions of the Egypt-Hatti peace treaty in Beckman and Hoffner 1996: 93-94 (no. 15, paragraphs 12-19).

As between suzerain and vassal, the former had no duty to extradite, but the latter certainly did.[25] The Egyptian king in EA 162 exercised his right with regard to various political refugees who had fled to Amurru, and the ruler of Amurru, so recalcitrant in other matters, showed no reluctance to comply.

Treaties

Legal Basis

In the domestic legal systems of the ancient Near East, a contract between heads of household would bind their respective households. It is no accident that *rikiltu*, the term for "contract" in Akkadian, the international lingua franca of the Amarna Age, was used without discrimination for international treaties. A treaty between kings was simply a contract that would bind their "households" in the same way.

In a domestic contract, it was often the practice to secure ancillary obligations by means of a promissory oath, for example, provisions against future revendication. The oath took the form of a curse that the speaker called down upon himself should he break his promise. In doing so, he invoked the name of the king or specific gods, who were expected to execute the curse. Where the obligations of the contract were entirely future or contingent, as in a contract of betrothal, it was possible for the contract to consist solely of an oath.[26] This was precisely the case with treaties, which only involved future or contingent obligations.

In some aspects, however, international treaties differed significantly from domestic contracts. Since kings were under the direct jurisdiction of the gods, treaty oaths were in the name of the gods alone. Domestic contracts were witnessed by the parties' peers, and disputes over breach could be brought before a variety of courts but ultimately before the king, as

25 The Hittites sometimes conceded limited extradition rights to their vassals in the vassal treaty. See, e.g., Treaty between Mursili II of Hatti and Kupanta-Kurunta of Mira in Beckman and Hoffner 1996: 75 (no. 11, paragraph 22).

26 E.g., Westbrook 1988b: 137 (YOS 8 51), and Falkenstein 1956-57: vol. 2, 27-28 (*NSG* 17).

fountainhead of justice. Domestic courts had the power to punish a party for breach of the divine oath.[27] In treaties, however, the role of witnesses was played by the gods, their names (and seals) being appended as witnesses to the treaty tablet. (The presence of human witnesses is rarely even mentioned.) In consequence, the gods had a dual role: as witnesses to the treaty and as "gods of the oath," in which capacity they were responsible for punishing any breach. As a treaty between Mursili II of Hatti and Tuppi-Teshup of Amurru pithily prescribes:[28] "If Tuppi-Teshup does not observe the terms of the treaty . . . then these oath gods will destroy Tuppi-Teshup, together with his person, his wife, his son, his grandsons, his house, his city, his land, and his possessions."

Although they were personal agreements between kings, treaties bound the populations of their respective countries by reason of the doctrine of householder responsibility. If there were a breach of the treaty, the gods could respond by destroying either the king himself (personal punishment), his subjects (vicarious punishment), or both (collective punishment). They bound the parties' successors under the doctrine of universal inheritance, although it was politically more prudent to gain a fresh, direct commitment from the new monarch.

In summary, treaties were contracts on the domestic model but gained their international character from two factors: the position of the contracting parties on the hierarchical scale, and their being purely within divine jurisdiction.[29]

27 E.g., *NSG* 17 (edited in Falkenstein 1956-57: vol. 2, 27-28.

28 Beckman and Hoffner 1996: 59 (no. 8, paragraph 22).

29 Two agreements that were identical in substance could be domestic or international, according to the status of the parties. The Assyrian emperor Esarhaddon designated as his successor a younger son and feared that disparate elements in the empire would revolt against the son after his death. He therefore concluded a series of treaties taking an oath of loyalty to his successor from members of the royal family, high officials, and vassal kings. The treaties are all identical in form, whether with internal subjects or with vassal kings (see SAA 2 6, discussed in Parpola and Watanabe 1988: xxviii-xxxi, 28-58). But where the Hittite kings dealt with primitive countries that had no monarchy, they contracted with the leading householders as representatives of their community, who were thus elevated to international status (Beckman and Hoffner 1996: 22-30 [no. 3]).

Formation

In contrast to modern law, treaties did not have to be in written form.[30] They were frequently committed to writing, especially when concluded through the agency of envoys, but the legal core of a treaty was an oral agreement, the written version being a record thereof and of evidentiary value only. The legally binding element was the promissory oath that the parties swore by the gods. The oath in fact achieved much the same purpose as writing in modern law: it was a ceremonial formality that emphasized the seriousness and durability of the undertakings. Hence, it is not surprising that references to treaties in the Amarna Letters sometimes simply use the word "oath." In EA 74, Rib-Hadda warns the Egyptian king that 'Abdi-Ashirta of Amurru has made an alliance against him with the revolutionary leaders of Ammiya. As Moran points out, the literal phrase is "placed an oath" (1992: 145 n. 13). In the same way, in EA 149, Abi-Milku of Tyre reports that Zimredda of Sidon exchanged oaths with the rulers of Arwada in preparation for a joint attack on Tyre.

In addition, there could be ceremonies attending the oath, which, if not legally necessary, further emphasized the formality of the agreement. For the oath-swearing reported in EA 74, 'Abdi-Ashirta assembled the parties in a temple, although the oath procedure did not strictly require it. Where the parties met face to face, there were various customary ceremonies, such as slaughtering an animal or sharing a meal or drink. Two Mesopotamian kings from the Old Babylonian period are reported to have sworn the oath, slaughtered an ass, sat down to drink together from the same cup, and finally exchanged presents.[31] In Gen 31:44-54, after Jacob and Laban had made a treaty in solemn form, the two sides ate bread together. In light of these sources, the Egyptian king's complaint to his vassal Aziru in EA 162 takes on new significance:

30 Article 2(1)(a) of the Vienna Convention on the Law of Treaties (1969, amended 1980) defines a treaty as "an international agreement between states in written form and governed by international law." Korošec considered the ancient treaty document dispositive (1931: 15-16), but so much evidence has since accrued of purely oral treaties that writing cannot have been a condition of legal validity. See, e.g., Charpin 1990: 109-16. The law was the same for domestic contracts: Renger 1977: 75-76.

31 ARM 26/2 404:60-63; see Joannès 1991: 175.

> Now the king (of Egypt) has heard as follows: "You are at peace with the ruler of Qadesh. The two of you take food and strong drink together. And it is true. Why do you act so? Why are you at peace with a ruler with whom the king is fighting? And even if you did act loyally, you considered your own judgment, and his judgment did not count."

The reference is not to mere conviviality; it is an unmistakable allusion to the celebration of a treaty.

Where the parties were separated, envoys had to be used to conclude the treaty. The envoy would present the king with a list of stipulations to which the latter had to swear. The procedure is well documented in Old Babylonian diplomatic records,[32] and it was still in use in the preparing of the Egypt-Hatti peace treaty.[33] It was evidently used by the Hittite king in the vassal treaty that he offered Addu-nirari of Nuhašše, reported in EA 51,[34] and by Aziru of Amurru in demanding a special oath of safe conduct from the Egyptian king and his high officials (EA 164:27-42).

Typology

Scholars normally divide ancient Near Eastern treaties into two separate categories: on the one hand, there are parity treaties and, on the other, vas-

32 See Charpin 1988: 144-45, 179-82; 1991: 144-45; and Eidem 1991. In a reciprocal treaty, there could initially be two tablets, each containing unilateral obligations. The practice of interleaving mutual obligations on a single tablet also existed, however, as can be seen already in the Ebla treaty from the twenty-fifth century; see Edzard 1992.

33 The two extant versions of the treaty reflect the procedure, although the tablets already contained the obligations of both parties. The version from the Hittite archives is an Akkadian original drafted by the Egyptian chancery, whereas the version on the temple at Karnak is an Egyptian translation of the Akkadian original drafted by the Hittite chancery (Spallinger 1981: 299). Although almost identical in substance, their difference in format reflects the insistence of each side on drafting the text to which the opposing monarch had to swear.

34 Moran's objections (1992: 122 n. 2) to Altman's surmise (1977: 30) are therefore unfounded, although there might have been a further tablet drafted as a record of the treaty, had it come to fruition.

sal treaties.[35] In the former, two independent rulers enter into an agreement on terms of reciprocity, usually with obligations that are substantially identical. Korošec wondered, though, how an independent ruler could have an obligation imposed upon him by another ruler without compromising his sovereignty.[36] The answer is that the ruler was not submitting to the other party but was submitting to the higher authority of the gods, recognized by both parties.

A vassal treaty in its purest form was unilateral: the vassal made a series of promises under oath to the suzerain. Promises under oath by the suzerain on specific issues were not excluded, however; even if not under oath, they were still binding insofar as their breach would release the vassal from his oath.[37] The balance of obligations depended on the relative bargaining power of the parties. Indeed, as Liverani has pointed out, a Hittite treaty with Kizzuwatna is presented as if it were a parity treaty, even with mutual oaths, but was in substance a vassal treaty.[38]

Serious doubts have been expressed as to the legal status of vassal treaties. Korošec regarded them as only partly creatures of international law: "halbvölkerrechtlich" (1931: 35-36). Other commentators have pointed to lack of consent or lack of sovereignty in the vassals as flaws in their status as instruments of international law.[39] We cannot go into these difficult questions at length here, but I will make two points that are of particular relevance to the Amarna correspondence.

First, in legal theory, if not in political reality, vassals entered voluntarily into a treaty with their overlords. Given a choice between death and vassalage, a threatened ruler would not unnaturally choose the latter. According to an Egyptian account, Canaanite rulers besieged in Megiddo begged mercy from Thutmose III, and in return for sparing their lives, he imposed upon them an oath.[40] Furthermore, the initiative might come from the greater power, if political circumstances made it expedient to court

35 E.g., Korošec 1931: 12-15.

36 Korošec 1931: 24, 25.

37 See Altman 1990: 180-82, 203-5.

38 Liverani 1973.

39 E.g., Schachermeyr 1928-29: 182.

40 Lorton 1974: 138, nos. 2 and 3, cf. 111, no. 4 (Tutankhamun). Cf. the ruse of the Gibeonites in Josh 9:3-27.

smaller states. In EA 51, Addu-nirari of Nuhašše proudly reported to his Egyptian suzerain his rejection of a Hittite offer of a vassal treaty.[41]

Second, a formal treaty was not a prerequisite for vassalage. Returning to the model of the hierarchical society, the political relationship between hierarchical superior and subordinate was characterized by membership of the former's household. This in itself gave rise to mutual obligations: loyalty and obedience by the subordinate on the one hand, and responsibility of the superior for actions by and wrongs to the subordinate on the other, using the metaphor "slave/master" or "father/son." Accordingly, the superior was entitled to punish the inferior for breach of the customarily expected duties.[42]

Nonetheless, a superior might regard his own authority as insufficient to ensure obedience and seek to strengthen his hold on the subordinate by adding a divine guarantor. For example, the Egyptian ruler Ramesses III used the oath to get one of his artisans to report misconduct among government workers.[43] The same rationale applied to vassals. The emperor could not maintain an army permanently on vassal territory. A treaty provided a supplementary mechanism for enforcing loyalty, through the oath and its divine sanctions.

For both these reasons, therefore, it is better to think of vassal treaties in terms of negotiated settlements (in a political market that could favor buyers or sellers) than of imposed edicts.[44] After all, all that a treaty added was the divine sanctions promised by the vassal's oath. If the overlord could impose his will by brute force, he would have no need of them.

The Egyptian and Hittite Systems

It has been argued that the Hittite and Egyptian conceptions of international treaties during the Amarna period were different in kind. The Hittite

41 Cf. the letter of the Hittite king Suppiluliuma to the king of Ugarit, offering him a treaty of vassalage as one of the rewards for giving military support; see Beckman and Hoffner 1996: 119-20 (no. 19).

42 See the Hittite Instructions for Temple Officials, Sturtevant and Bechtel 1935: 148-49.

43 Edgerton 1951: 141.

44 Cf. Parpola on Assyrian vassal treaties (Parpola and Watanabe 1988: xv-xvi).

system was formalized through treaties because it was based on agreement, whereas agreement with an inferior was excluded *a priori* for Pharaoh, who, in truth, regarded even equal powers as inferiors. Instead, the Egyptian model was the correct behavior expected of an official within the administration.[45]

I would qualify that view by arguing that any differences between the Egyptians and the Hittites were of political choice, not legal system. First, as we have seen, treaties are not necessary to a vassal relationship, so that the Egyptians' failure to use them would not necessarily be evidence of a different legal regime.

Second, the oath was by no means unthinkable to the Egyptians. We have seen its use in internal administration after the Amarna period. The Egyptians had indeed procured loyalty oaths from vassals at the logical time for such oaths, when they had been in an expansionist phase more than half a century earlier.[46] Although presented through the absolutist perspective of Egyptian propaganda, their very acceptance of oaths by the gods was an admission that they could not rely entirely on their own power in their relations with their vassals. Whether the practice of taking oaths continued with each successor to the vassal throne is not clear; there are certainly references in the Amarna Letters to oaths by the vassals (EA 148, 209).

Third, it was not unthinkable for the oath to be taken by the Egyptian king himself. The peace treaty with the Hittites required an oath, which Ramesses II did not hesitate to mention approvingly in a letter.[47] In EA 164, as we have seen, Aziru of Amurru, faced with an Egyptian demand that he present himself at the Egyptian court to explain his actions, insisted that the king and his senior officials first swear an oath guaranteeing him safe conduct. It is reasonable to suppose that Aziru's condition was met, since he subsequently traveled to Egypt and returned safely.

For all these reasons, I consider that in spite of Egypt's reticence on the subject, treaties—parity and vassal—formed as much a part of the Egyptian conception of international law as they did for the Asiatic states.

45 Cf. Liverani 1983: 49-51.

46 Thutmose III from the Canaanite rulers at Megiddo (*Urk.* IV 1234:17-1236:1); Amenhotep II from the ruler of Qadesh (*Urk.* IV 1304:2).

47 Beckman and Hoffner 1996: 124-25 (no. 22D).

In this light, the proposal of a treaty by Alashiya in EA 35:42-43 should be considered a serious offer to which a positive reply could be expected from Egypt. In EA 24 III:109-119, the Mittanian king quotes a standard military assistance clause from a treaty that is similar to the mutual clauses found in the Egypt-Hatti peace treaty.[48] Whether it refers to an existing treaty or a proposed one, it assumes that whatever political difficulties stood in its way, such a treaty with Egypt had no legal impediment.

Conclusions

In this brief sketch, I have only been able to touch upon some of the many aspects of international law revealed by sources from the ancient Near East. I hope, however, that enough has been covered to demonstrate the importance of law in the thinking of the correspondents to the Amarna Letters. In negotiations between both equal and unequal powers, all parties carried with them and deployed the common conceptions and long-standing traditions of a functioning system of international law.

48 Beckman and Hoffner 1996: 93 (no. 15, paragraphs 7, 9); cf. Beckman and Hoffner 1996: 73-74 (no. 11, paragraph 18). Artzi (2000) argues that Egypt's failure to intervene when the Mittanian king was murdered by a usurper (EA 17) is evidence that it had no treaty relations, since protection of the partner's dynasty was a standard treaty obligation. But the usurper did not ascend the throne himself; instead, he ruled as regent for the murdered king's son. To me, this suggests a concern to avoid triggering the terms of a treaty, by conserving the outward form of dynastic succession.

19

Babylonian Diplomacy in the Amarna Letters

Abstract

Modern commentators view the pattern of negotiations in the Amarna Letters as reflecting an imbalance between Egypt and the Asiatic great powers. The Asiatic kings try unsuccessfully to wrest gold and status from the Pharaoh and in doing so are often forced into humiliating concessions. The Babylonian dispatches are regarded as a prime example of this imbalance. Babylonian kings look, at best, self-abasing and, at worst, ridiculous, especially when describing their own actions and reactions in previous diplomatic incidents. A close analysis of Babylonian arguments, however, reveals a cunning and devious train of logic designed to gain the moral advantage over the Egyptian interlocutor. The Babylonian rulers used the cultural conventions of the day to send hidden messages, the meaning of which would nonetheless be unmistakable to the recipient.

In the fourteenth century B.C.E. the most powerful states of the Near East, Egypt, Hatti, Mittani, Babylonia, and Assyria, formed an international society, a "Great Powers' Club" with conventional forms of diplomacy and settled rules of protocol.[1] Their relations are detailed in some thirty-five items of correspondence in the Amarna Letters, with all but two

* Originally published in the *Journal of the American Oriental Society* 120 (2000): 377-82.

* The arguments in this article were first adumbrated at a conference on the Amarna Letters at the Rockefeller Center, Bellagio, in September, 1996. I am grateful to all the participants for the stimulating discussions that gave rise to my proposals. A summary version is presented in the publication of the conference proceedings (Cohen and Westbrook 2000), in the chapter of Christer Jönnsen. The present article is a revised version of a paper given to the Egyptology and Ancient Israel group of the AAR/SBL annual meeting, Orlando 1998.

1 See Tadmor 1979: 3-4; Liverani 2000: 15-27. On protocol, see Korošec 1931: 47-49; and Artzi 1980: 161-70.

being letters from the Asiatic kings to the Pharaoh.[2] In principle, they corresponded on a basis of equality, as "great kings" who referred to each other as "my brother." In practice, the Egyptian ruler enjoyed an advantage over his Asiatic counterparts. As the head of a mature hegemonic power, more self-sufficient in prestige goods than the other powers, and in particular enjoying a near monopoly on the production of gold, he was able to bargain from a position of strength. Modern commentators, therefore, view the pattern of negotiations as one in which the Asiatic kings try unsuccessfully to wrest gold and status from the Pharaoh and in doing so are often forced into humiliating concessions.[3]

The dispatches of the Babylonian kings appear to present an egregious example.[4] The Babylonian correspondent looks, at best, self-abasing and, at worst, ridiculous, especially when describing his own actions and reactions in previous diplomatic incidents.[5] But appearances can be deceptive. As Cohen has pointed out, the detailed negotiations in the letters were conducted on two levels: as subgames in which the nature of the relationship was assumed, and as metagames in which the issue was relative status.[6] At the metagame level, Babylonia did not need to assert its equal status, as did Assyria.[7] Nor did it seek a relationship of inter-dependence with Egypt like Mittani.[8] Rather, its aim was mutual advantage as between independent entities:

2 EA 1-30, 41-44. EA 1 and 5 are from the Pharaoh to the Babylonian king. EA 13, 14, 22, 25 are inventories. EA 18 may not belong to this correspondence. The numbers follow the edition of Knudtzon 1907-15 (rep. 1964). The most recent translation into English is Moran 1992. Unless otherwise stated, quotations from the letters use Moran's translation.

3 Zaccagnini 1973: 160-65; Schulman 1979: 188-91; Liverani 1990: 224-26.

4 The letters are from two kings, Kadashman-Enlil I and his successor Burnaburiash II. No attempt will be made in this article to distinguish between them, as in our view these letters, in spite of their personal tone, were at the very least the result of a consultative process between the king and his officials, if not the product of a chancery. As such, they represent a continuity of diplomatic tradition.

5 Cf. the analysis of Cohen 1996: 17-20.

6 Cohen 1996: 20-25.

7 EA 16:26-27: "I am the [equal] of the king of Hanigalbat."

8 EA 20:15-17: "I will now, this year, deliver my brother's wife, the mistress of Egypt, and they will bring her to my brother. On that day shall Hanigalbat and Egypt be [one]." See Artzi 2000: 205-11.

> as I am told, in my brother's country everything is available and my brother needs absolutely nothing. Furthermore, in my country everything too is available and I for my part need absolutely nothing. We have (however) inherited good relations of long standing from (earlier) kings, and so we should send greetings to each other. (EA 7:33-41)

Where the relationship was being negotiated, the Babylonian king was not averse to making peremptory demands, as where he insisted that Egypt not entertain a delegation from Assyria, whom he claimed as his vassal (EA 9:19-38).

In other instances, Babylonian tactics were capable of great subtlety. Aware of the disparity in their bargaining position with Egypt, the Babylonian kings might sometimes give the impression of negotiating at the metagame level, when in fact their goals were more modest. Making metagame demands enhanced their opening position, and allowed them ultimately to maximize the lesser gains for which they would settle. Furthermore, a close analysis of the Babylonian arguments reveals a cunning and devious train of logic, designed to gain the moral advantage over the Egyptian interlocutor, and a mordant sense of humor. The Babylonians used the cultural conventions of the day to send hidden messages, the meaning of which would nonetheless be unmistakable to the recipient. We will attempt to illustrate these points through three examples.

"As Plentiful as Dust"

The desire of Asiatic kings for Egyptian gold is often stressed, along with the fact that it put them in a weaker bargaining position.[9] Their approach to the question of gold, however, was not uniform. It is true that all saw gold, like other presents, as a measure of friendly relations: "If your purpose is graciously one of friendship, send me much gold" says the Assyrian king with characteristic directness (EA 16:32-33). For Mittani it was a sign of

9 Zaccagnini 1973: 165; Liverani 1990: 224. Edzard documents the change from silver to gold as a unit of account in Kassite Babylonia and its dependence on Egyptian gold (1960: 37-55).

"love," i.e., an affirmation of close alliance. But beyond this general symbolism, very different political functions were attributed to the receipt of generous shipments of gold. Mittani wished to use Egyptian gold as a means of acquiring (or maintaining) its status within the international community:

> May my brother send me much gold . . . may my brother show his love for me, that my brother greatly glorify me before my country and before my foreign guests. (EA 20:71-79)

Assyria reversed this reasoning:

> I am the [equal] of the king of Hanigalbat, but you sent me . . . of gold, and it is not enough for the pay of my messengers on the journey to and back. (EA 16:26-31)

Babylonia, however, stressed not status but the image of friendly relations that would be presented to the international community:

> That neighboring kings might hear it said: "The gold is much. Among the kings there are brotherhood, amity, peace, and good relations." (EA 11: reverse 19-23)

Theoretically, the image would redound to the benefit of both parties.

In negotiating for Egyptian gold, the Asiatic kings attempted to debase its value by stressing its abundance. The reasoning was that only large shipments are worthy of a Great King and, by implication, sufficient to reciprocate the gifts that the Pharaoh receives from his "brother."[10] In this connection, a standard phrase was used by the Assyrian and Mittanian kings: "(In your country,) gold is as plentiful as dust . . . ." The Assyrian king continues, with brutal directness: "Why are you so sparing of it?"[11]

The Babylonian king likewise complained about Egyptian parsimoniousness in its shipments of gold, but he adopted a more indirect approach.

10 Liverani 1990: 213-15.

11 EA 16:14-16 *ḫuraṣu ina mātika epiru šu . . . ammīni ina inēka isaḫḫur*. Cf. EA 19:61; 26:42; 27:106; 29:146, 164 (Mittani).

In EA 9, he first recalls the unbounded generosity of past generations, then states in a matter-of-fact way the amount of the current Egyptian shipment (two minas). He continues with a seemingly humble plea for whatever gold the Pharaoh can send (lines 12-13): ". . . if gold is plentiful, send me as much as your ancestors (sent), but if it is scarce, send me half of what your ancestors (sent)." Only then does he declare it inadequate to his present needs (a building project), still without criticizing the size of Egyptian shipments at large.

There is a conscious allusion in this disingenuous request to the formulaic assertion of Asiatic kings of abundance in Egypt. In conceding that the assertion may be untrue, the Babylonian king replaced direct complaint with biting sarcasm. The suggestion that the present Pharaoh might not be able to afford as much as his ancestors was deeply humiliating. At the very least, a king purported to equal the achievements of his ancestors and often boasted of exceeding them.[12] The Pharaoh might be willing to risk an accusation of stinginess, because a smaller than demanded shipment could be interpreted ambiguously: as a sign of diplomatic disfavor, or that the reciprocal gifts were inadequate. His prestige would be preserved by the common assumption that he could send more if he wished.[13] On the other hand, commiseration with his poverty, albeit insincere, was a trap. The Pharaoh could not then send a smaller shipment of gold without losing face. In choosing wit rather than bluster as his polemical weapon, the Babylonian king showed himself to be a subtle negotiator.

Distant Countries

In EA 7:14-32 the Babylonian king records an incident in an amount of detail which seems to be superfluous:

12 For example, Thutmoses III boasts in his annals of crossing the Euphrates and setting up a stela alongside that of his father, Thutmoses I (*Urk.* IV 697:4-5 = Breasted 1907: 478; cf. Spalinger 1978: 35-41).

13 Cf. Liverani's discussion of the Pharaoh's resolution of the contradiction between the boast of universal control and the boast of enlarging one's territory (1990:57): "The Pharaoh tries to solve the contradiction by stating that he extends his borders 'wherever he wants' . . . so implying that his will finds no external obstacles, but finds a limit in itself, in his own judgment."

> Furthermore, since I was not well and my brother showed me no concern, I for my part became angry with my brother, saying: "Has my brother not heard that I am ill? Why has he shown me no concern? Why has he sent no messenger here and visited me?" My brother's messenger addressed me, saying: "It is not a place close by so your brother can hear (about you) and send you greetings. The country is far away. Who is going to tell your brother so he can immediately send you greetings? Would your brother hear that you are ill and still not send you his messenger?" I for my part addressed him as follows, saying: "For my brother, a Great King, is there really a faraway country and a close-by one?" He for his part addressed me as follows, saying: "Ask your own messenger whether the country is far away and as a result your brother did not hear (about you) and did not send (anyone) to greet you." Now, since I asked my own messenger and he said to me that the country is far, I was not angry (any longer), I said no more.

The king was angry because the Pharaoh, in breach of diplomatic etiquette, had failed to send a "get well" message when the former was ill. An Egyptian diplomat managed to appease him by pointing out that the great distance between the two countries did not permit the Pharaoh to receive timely news of his sickness. The king, at first skeptical, finally accepted the envoy's excuse after his own staff confirmed its factual basis.

The incident described was therefore a non-incident, a minor misunderstanding at court which the Egyptian envoy managed to defuse before it grew into a real diplomatic incident. Why then bother to relate it to the Pharaoh, and in terms that only make the king look foolish and ignorant? The true reason emerges a little later in the letter.

By way of preliminary, it should be pointed out that the Babylonian king was almost certainly aware of the great distance between Egypt and Babylonia. It is true that there were no maps and little concept of geography, but long distances were measured in the time that it took to traverse them, not in miles, and envoys had been going back and forth between the two courts for many years. There was a more-or-less standard time for the journey and, barring diplomatic incidents, a standard time for the stay of an envoy at the host court.[14] It is difficult to imagine that the king would have been unaware of the pattern of arrivals and departures. The king's ignorance was merely a sham, and more important, he knew that the Pharaoh would know that it was a sham. That is the first of several such hidden signals in this letter.

The letter goes on to talk about the value of mutual gifts for their relationship, of (possibly) other matters in a section that is unfortunately broken, and of the retention of envoys. It then returns to the question of distance, but this time the shoe is on the other foot (7:53-60):

> Furthermore, as I am also told, the journey is difficult, water cut off, and the weather hot. I am not sending many beautiful greeting-gifts. I send to my brother four minas of beautiful lapis lazuli as a routine greeting-gift. In addition, I send my brother five teams of horses. As soon as the weather improves, my next messenger to come I will have bring many beautiful greeting-gifts to my brother.

The excuse for the smallness of the present is again a sham, and one that would have been obvious to the Pharaoh. The present did not consist of bulk goods; the same escort could presumably have brought eight minas of lapis or indeed twelve, instead of four. If teams of live horses could be sent, the lack of water could not have been desperate. The hidden message was therefore plain: the Babylonian king was discontented with the Egyptian and wished to register a diplomatic protest by sending a smaller than customary gift.

At this point, however, the king found himself on the horns of a dilemma. To avoid the accusation of stinginess or worse still, of poverty, the fiction of difficult conditions had to be preserved, but that fiction would cause him to lose face. It was in essence a plea of weakness in the face of natural difficulties, and how could a mighty emperor admit to weakness?

The key phrase is "as I am also told" (*u kî iqbûnimma*). The informant could have been none other than the Egyptian diplomat! There was no shame in the Babylonian king's inability to overcome physical space,

14 Caravans regularly plied the route between the two countries: EA 8; and see Meier 1988: 80-82, 245.

measured in time and difficulty of the journey, because the Egyptian side had already admitted to the same weakness. The earlier incident thus proved very useful. The Babylonian king took a minor exchange between himself and the Egyptian envoy, in which the envoy had merely been trying to be diplomatic, and, perhaps with some embellishment, adapted it to his own ends. Indeed, he neatly set up the whole argument (and revealed his true purpose) when he asked the rhetorical question: "For my brother, a Great King, is there really a faraway country and a close-by one?"

3. A False Daughter

In EA 4:4-14 the Babylonian king recounts the painful details of a double diplomatic snub:

> Moreover, you, my brother, when I wrote to you about marrying your daughter, in accordance with your practice of not giving a daughter, wrote to me, saying: "From time immemorial no daughter of the king of Egypt is given to anyone." Why not? You are a king; you do as you please. Were you to give a daughter, who would say anything? Since I was told of this message, I wrote as follows to my brother, saying: "Someone's grown daughters, beautiful women, must be available. Send me a beautiful woman as if she were your daughter. Who is going to say, 'She is no daughter of the king!'?" But holding to your decision, you have not sent me anyone.

Having failed in his bid for a daughter of the Pharaoh, he requested the daughter of a commoner whom he could pretend was of royal blood, and was again refused. How could the king debase himself so much, and why should he recall an incident that made him look weak and foolish? The answer lies in a devious stratagem to improve his bargaining position.

In the exchanges of Amarna diplomacy, there is no lack of undiplomatic, almost brutally frank, language. A gift is declared to be inadequate, "not enough for the pay of my messengers on the journey there and back" (16:29-31); envoys are referred to insultingly as nobodies ("an ass-herder") or liars (1:18-19, 73-76); an escort is declared too small (11:19-22). In one area, however, the bluntest of correspondents were reduced to embarrassed allusions, namely, when there was a danger of infringing their interlocutor's religious susceptibilities. Thus the Assyrian king wrote to the Pharaoh in uncharacteristically conciliatory and guarded language (16:43-55):

> Why should messengers be made to stay constantly out in the sun and so die in the sun? If staying out in the sun means profit for the king, then let him (a messenger) stay out and let him die right there in the sun, (but) for the king himself there must be a profit. Or otherwise, why should they die in the sun?

If Redford's interpretation of the background to these lines is correct, Assyrian envoys had complained to their own king about Akhenaten's practice of keeping the whole court, including foreign diplomats, standing in the blazing sun for hours on end as part of his new program of worshipping the sun disk.[15] Kings were not reluctant to relay their envoys' complaints about their treatment, but having to question a fellow ruler's religious practice in so doing would have put the Assyrian king in a delicate position.[16]

The sanctity of religious or traditional practice represented a diplomatic taboo, one of the few areas where cultural differences were acknowledged. Rulers were reluctant to ruffle the religious sensibilities of their fellow kings, but this reluctance had the effect of handing the other side a negotiating advantage, the ancient equivalent of "I'd love to make the concession that you demand, but unfortunately my hands are tied by domestic public opinion, which would never accept it."

15 Redford 1984: 235. The alternative explanation, that the theme is the difficulties of the route for messengers (given that the Pharaoh's gifts are so poor), seems to us less likely. (See, for this view, Artzi 1997: 320-36.) The Assyrian king had already made his views on that issue very plain earlier in the letter. The present lines follow his response to a complaint by the Pharaoh about the treatment of his envoys, where it would be natural to present a counter-complaint.

16 In EA 1:65-68 the Pharaoh is evidently responding to a complaint by the Babylonian king: "Now, we are brothers, you and I, but I have quarreled because of your messengers, since they report to you, saying, 'Nothing is given to us who go to Egypt.'"

The Pharaoh's first refusal was therefore not a snub but made with feigned reluctance.[17] Note that the marriage taboo is against "anyone," not just a foreigner. It has a remarkable parallel in the Bible. In Gen 29:16-26, Laban agrees to give his daughter Rachel in marriage to Jacob, in return for seven years' service. On the wedding night, however, Laban switches Rachel for Leah, her elder, and less attractive, sister. When Jacob discovers the trick the following morning, he angrily accuses Laban of fraud. Laban merely replies: "It is not deemed proper in our locality to give the younger daughter before the elder." He is able to play the taboo card, even against a charge of fraud.

The Babylonian king was faced with a similar taboo and was aware that it was equally deceitful. Reasons of state determined the Pharaoh's refusal, not religious sensibilities. The Babylonian king therefore adopted a strategy designed to call his bluff. The Pharaoh's argument was that his hands were tied; so the king offered him two means of escape.

Firstly, he argued that the Pharaoh, as a king, had the power to defy the tradition. He could go this far because it had been presented as a practice hallowed by time, not a rule laid down by divine command. In view of Egyptian monarchs' pretensions to divinity, this was a particularly effective argument, which would show that the Pharaoh was either weak-willed, and thus lower his prestige, or insincere. Secondly, he offered a ruse which the Pharaoh, if he were truly eager to give a daughter but only constrained by the taboo, could not refuse. Of course, the Pharaoh did refuse, and thereby exposed himself to a charge of hypocrisy. Diplomatic etiquette demanded strict reciprocity between Great Kings who acknowledged each other as equals—"brothers," as did the Egyptian Pharaoh and the Babylonian king.

The king then went on to press home his advantage, referring to the Pharaoh's own request for a daughter of the king in marriage (4:20-22):

17 We disagree with Schulman, who characterizes the Pharaoh's response as "rather insulting" and an "arrogant and curt refusal" (1979: 179, 191). Liverani correctly (in our view) saw that the Pharaoh was declaring himself bound by tradition, identifying the same tactic in EA 35:7-8 (1979: 29 n. 42, 31 n. 55). Liverani regards it, however, as an element of strength in negotiation. It is, but internal constraints can be a two-edged sword, since they paradoxically rely on the admission that one is weak.

> Should I, perhaps, since you did not send me a woman, refuse you a woman, just as you did to me, and not send her? But my daughters being available, I will not refuse one to you.

The Babylonian king had thus gained the moral upper hand, but the final purpose of this whole *dêmarche* was still to come. For again, it is highly unlikely that the king did not know in advance the answer to his request for a daughter, just as he knew the answer to his inquiry about geography to the Egyptian diplomat. The presentation of a request that he knew would be refused, and his insistence on a second attempt that, other than to call the Pharaoh's bluff, had no better chance of success than the first, were merely tactical maneuvers to improve his chances of gaining a lesser prize. That had been his main goal from the outset.

In the last section of the letter, a demand is made for gold, immediately, with the usual excuse that it is for a special building project. The demand, however, is then tied into the question of giving a daughter to the Pharaoh (4:41-50):

> If during this summer, in the months of Tammuz or Ab, you send the gold I wrote you about, I will give you my daughter . . . . But if in the months of Tammuz or Ab you do not send me the gold and (with it) I do not finish the work I am engaged on, what would be the point of your being pleased to send me gold? Once I have finished the work I am engaged on, what need will I have of gold? Then you could send me 3,000 talents of gold, and I would not accept it. I would send it back to you, and I would not give my daughter in marriage.

The very last phrase, "and I would not give my daughter in marriage," is the sting in the tail. Although in its strict sense based on an absurd contingency—late payment of a huge sum—the real contingency is clear. The king was demanding prompt payment of a large bride price as the condition for giving his daughter in marriage. The whole purpose of the letter was in fact to bargain for the highest possible bride price in negotiations for marriage between the Pharaoh and a daughter of the Babylonian king. The bid for a daughter of the Pharaoh, sure to be refused, was merely a tactic to put the Pharaoh further in the king's debt and thus increase the bride price by way of compensation for the Pharaoh's inexcusable failure to maintain the customary reciprocity between Great Kings.

Part Two

Biblical Sources

20

Biblical Law

Abstract

This is an introductory explanation of biblical law and reveals the law that was operative in ancient Israel and Judah. As an introduction, it summarizes a number of areas where scholarship has achieved a measure of consensus. Its particular value lies in its use of legal categories to explore what the Hebrew Bible says in regard to fundamental issues of law and society.

1. Political and Juridical Background

The biblical period of Jewish-Law dates from the mid-second millennium to the fourth century B.C.E. Traditionally, it covers five subperiods: patriarchal (sixteenth century?), exodus (thirteenth?), judges (twelfth and eleventh), monarchy (eleventh through sixth), and post-exilic (sixth through fourth).

In the narratives of the book of Genesis, the patriarchs are characterized as autonomous legal units, whose relationship to a wider legal system resembles that of states in international law. Indeed, each patriarch is head of an independent household which often appears as the equal of local rulers (Genesis 14). At other times, however, a patriarch may appear as an individual in an uneasy relationship of dependence upon the host society: Abraham and Isaac in Egypt and at Gerar (Gen 12:10-20; 20:1-18; 26:6-11), Abraham and the Hittites (Genesis 23). There is no mention of a court to whose jurisdiction they might be subject, but when Jacob is accused of

* Originally published in *An Introduction to the History and Sources of Jewish Law* (ed. N. S. Hecht et al.; Oxford: Oxford University Press, 1996), 1-17. Used by permission.

theft by Laban, he proposes submission to an *ad hoc* tribunal composed of members from both sides (Gen 31:36-37).

Nonetheless, the substantive law of the period does not differ significantly from that of later periods. The main difference would appear to lie in the fact that enforcement of legal rights is through self-help (see, for example, the rape of Dinah in Genesis 34). Where individuals are intended to represent later political units, political disputes are placed in the context of family law. Thus the later decline of the tribe of Reuben is depicted in terms of the partial disinheritance of Reuben by his father for the offense of sleeping with the latter's concubine (Gen 49:3-4). The head of household would appear to have had total jurisdiction over its subordinate members (Gen 42:37), but the latter could appeal to a divine tribunal (Gen 16:6).

According to the account in Exodus and Deuteronomy, the 40 years spent by the Israelites in the desert on their way from Egypt to the promised land are a seminal period, during which the laws and institutions of the later polity were established. Leadership, temporal and spiritual, is in the hands of Moses, to whom Aharon as high priest is subordinate. Moses judges the people, i.e., is head of the administration of justice, but there are several accounts of the delegation of his authority (see below). The substantive law is given by God to Moses at Mount Sinai, in the form of the Ten Commandments and of "judgments"—rules concerning everyday social and economic relations (Exodus 22-23). Further rules are established by God as precedents when consulted by Moses on cases that occur during the journey through the desert (e.g., Num 9:6-14).

The degree of historical reality present in the biblical account of this period is a matter of dispute among scholars. The legal system is idealized and has long been recognized as a projection back into Israel's past of institutions of later periods or even of ideological programs that may never have been put into practice. Much of the substantive law can be shown to be part of a wider ancient Near Eastern tradition, which stretches back at least to the third millennium B.C.E.

As in the previous period, political events are presented in terms of private law: the elaborate division of the promised land among the tribes by Joshua is structured upon the division of an estate by heirs, in accordance with general ancient Near Eastern practices.

After the settlement in Canaan, there existed a loose confederation of tribes which was occasionally united by charismatic war leaders known as judges. It was regarded by later generations as a period of anarchy, "when each man did what was right in his own eyes." Nonetheless, there was a universally accepted code of conduct, as epitomized by the incident of the Levite's concubine (Judges 19-20). When a traveler had sought hospitality in a city of the Benjaminites, the local inhabitants had seized and raped to death his concubine. The crime was regarded as so shocking that he was able to recruit all the other tribes for a war against the Benjaminites.

Government of cities was in the hands of local "lords" (Judg 9:6; 20:5). For the administration of justice, the focal point was the city gate, where the elders judged local cases and citizens transacted their affairs. The book of Ruth claims to describe events that took place "in the days when the judges judged" (Ruth 1:1). It paints a picture of an agricultural community with an established customary law that is well known to its members, who apply it before the elders at the city-gate (Ruth 4:1-12). Again, the substantive law, in its secular aspects at least, does not differ radically from that found in other periods. On the other hand, there is no consciousness of a code of Mosaic law that has to be followed by the local courts.

The period of the "judges" ends with the establishment of a monarchy (c. 1000 B.C.E.), first by Saul but then giving way to a dynasty founded by David and consolidated by his son Solomon (under whom the first temple was constructed). On Solomon's death, the kingdom divided into two (c. 922 B.C.E.): "Israel" in the north, "Judah" in the south, with its capital at Jerusalem.

During the monarchy, the king was the head of the legal system, but a dual system of courts appears to have existed beneath him, consisting of the local courts of the elders and courts presided over by royal officials. There was no legislature in the modern sense; the king issued decrees (1 Sam 28:9) and made judgments which might be regarded as precedents (cf. 1 Sam 30:23-25). There are occasional references to the *torah* of Moses (e.g., 2 Kgs 14:6 = 2 Chr 25:4), but these may be anachronistic insertions. Even if genuine, it is not clear that they refer to the body of pentateuchal commandments later identified in rabbinic jurisprudence. The "book of the law" (*sefer torah*) discovered in the temple during the reign of Josiah (2 Kgs 22:8) has generally been associated with the book of Deuteronomy or a part thereof.

The kingdom of Israel fell to the Assyrians in 722 B.C.E. and disappeared from history. The kingdom of Judah survived until 587 B.C.E., when it was conquered by the Babylonians under Nebuchadnezzar. Here begins the "exilic" period: many of the leaders of the community were taken to Babylon, where they appear to have thrived. The Babylonian Empire itself fell to the Persian conqueror Cyrus in 538 B.C.E., and the latter permitted the exiles to return to Jerusalem and to reestablish their political and legal institutions. The temple, destroyed when the city had fallen to the Babylonians, was rebuilt (the "Second Temple") and was later to be much enlarged under Herod.

Under the Persian empire, Judah was no longer a sovereign state but a province (called *Yehud*). Nonetheless, it retained a high degree of local autonomy under the rule of indigenous governors. The seminal figure of the period was Ezra, who came from Babylonia with an imperial commission to appoint judges to administer the community's own law (Ezra 7:25). Described as a priest and a "scribe skilled in the *torah* of Moses," he may be credited with laying the jurisprudential foundations of Jewish law as we understand it today. For he and his fellow priests read "from the book, from the *torah* of God, with interpretation" before the assembled people (Neh 8:18). Thus the legal system became based upon the idea of a written code of law interpreted and applied by religious authorities.

2. Sources

The term sources has two meanings: (1) authoritative texts applied by the courts in determining the law in a particular case and (2) primary data used by historians as evidence of the law in force at a particular period. In the post-biblical period the laws contained in the first five books of the Bible, the *Torah*, constituted a source of the first type, but as we have seen they did not achieve this status until almost the end of the biblical period. The main sources of law were tradition, precedent (Jer 26:17-19), and royal decree (1 Sam 14:24; Jer 34:8-10), with divine authorship frequently being attributed to the latter two forms (e.g., Num 27:1-11; Exod 20:22-26).

As regards historical sources, there is only one extant contemporary legal text: the *Meṣad Ḥashavyahu* inscription, a petition by a corvée worker to the local military commander dated to the reign of Josiah (seventh century B.C.E.). The principal source is of course the Bible itself, but its historical value is qualified by the fact that the version that has come down to us is the result of hundreds of years of compilation and redaction;

much of it cannot be dated with any certainty. Within the Pentateuch, scholars in the tradition of biblical criticism (deriving from Wellhausen and Graf) have identified several sources from different streams of tradition that have been interwoven in the final version. With very tentative dates, they have been labeled: J—eighth century B.C.E.; D(euteronomy)—seventh; E—seventh; P(riestly)—fifth. J, E, and P are interwoven in the first four books of the Pentateuch, while the Deuteronomic author is also regarded as responsible for the redaction of the historical narrative found in Joshua-Kings. Traditional scholars continue to maintain the claim to the unity of the Pentateuch. This chapter follows the critical approach.

The events of the monarchy are recorded in two parallel accounts: the books of Samuel-Kings, which are regarded as closer to the events that they portray, and 1-2 Chronicles, which are of post-exilic authorship. Moreover, much of the material used by biblical authors came from existing traditional sources such as songs, proverbs, rituals and laws. Scholars have attempted to isolate these sources on the basis of form, but the results are necessarily speculative and rarely datable.

The Pentateuch contains two discrete collections of non-sacral laws (i.e., laws governing relations between man and man). Exod 21:1-22:16 forms the core of a series of various cultic, ethical, and legal rules known as the Covenant Code (Exod 20:23-23:19), which is regarded by scholars as an independent source inserted into the account of the events at Sinai at some stage during the editing and combining of the J and E narratives. Its dating is uncertain, but it is generally considered to be of great antiquity, although not contemporary with Israel's sojourn in the desert. The agricultural content of many of the laws (e.g., Exod 22:4-5) places it after settlement in Canaan, while the absence of any mention of a king would seem to indicate the period of the judges (twelfth-eleventh century). Many scholars claim to see signs of development within the individual laws, either by way of reforms (e.g., in the law of *talion* in Exod 21:22-25) or scholastic exegesis (e.g., Exod 22:8). The strong affinity between the laws of 21:1-22:16 and the cuneiform law codes (see below) points to a separate origin for this unit within the Covenant Code.

The second collection of non-sacral laws is Deut 21:1-25:13. Since the cultic laws of Deuteronomy are associated with the reforms of King Josiah (7th century, Judah), the non-sacral laws too must have received their present form at the same time, although they contain earlier traditions. Several parallels to the Covenant Code suggest that the Deuteronomic author used the earlier code as a source or at least that there was a source common to both. It has also been suggested that the Deuteronomic author was responsible for redactional additions to the Covenant Code (e.g., Exod 21:8b). The style of the Deuteronomic laws is more heterogeneous than those of Exodus, with motive clauses, exhortation, and admonition. There are also scattered non-sacral laws found outside the main corpus, e.g., homicide (Deut 19:13), evidence (Deut 19:15-21), slave-release (Deut 15:12-18).

A further body of laws known as the Priestly Code, and dealing mostly but not exclusively with sacral matters, is to be found scattered through the narrative of Leviticus and Numbers (P-source). Within this source, a compact unit of mostly cultic rules in Leviticus 17-26 has been identified as a separate corpus, referred to as the Holiness Code. It is generally dated to the exilic period, due to close parallels with the writings of the prophet Ezekiel.

The Ten Commandments in themselves constitute an independent source which is found in two narratives: Exod 20:1-17 and Deut 5:6-21. Strictly speaking, however, they are not to be regarded as laws to be applied by the courts but as moral exhortation to the individual, since they contain no sanctions for disobedience.

An influential theory of A. Alt distinguished between two types of laws in the codes: casuistic laws, which are framed as a hypothetical case with the corresponding legal solution (e.g., "If an ox gores a man . . . , its owner shall be put to death . . ."), and apodictic laws, which are framed as concise commands (e.g., "Thou shalt not steal"; "He who curses his father and mother shall be put to death"). The former were said to derive (via a putative Canaanite law) from the Mesopotamian law codes (see below), which share the casuistic form, while the latter were regarded as a native Israelite creation. Subsequent evidence has not confirmed this theory, but the distinction between casuistic and apodictic laws is still routinely used by scholars in discussing their origins.

The law codes are by no means the only source for law in the Bible. The P narrative contains four reports of judicial decisions which supposedly represented the original precedents for later rules of law: a case of blasphemy (Lev 24:10-23), a second Passover for persons ritually impure (Num 9:1-14), the gatherer of wood on the Sabbath (Num 15:32-36), and the rights of daughters (here, those of Zelophehad) in intestate succession (Num 27:1-11; 36). Similar reports are found in juridical parables—a realistic account of a legal case presented to a king for judgment with the aim of leading him to draw a parallel with his own conduct: the poor man's lamb (2 Sam 12:1-14), the woman of Tekoah (2 Sam 14:1-20), and the negligent guard (1 Kgs 20:35-43).

Many of the narratives in Genesis, the historical books, and Ruth describe in a more incidental fashion legal institutions and procedures, such as a formal search for stolen goods (Gen 31:30-35), a herding contract (Gen 29:15-18; 30:31-34; 31:38-39), a treason trial (1 Kgs 21:8-14), and levirate marriage (Ruth 4:1-10). A further source of law is the use of metaphor by the prophets: the relationship between God and Israel is described in terms of human legal relationships such as guardianship and marriage, revealing modes of formation and penalties for breach, etc. (e.g., Hosea 2).

To reconstruct the legal system of ancient Israel, however, further sources are needed that can supplement the fragmentary information provided by the Bible and place it in context. One possibility is to look to the abundant material from the period immediately following: the Mishnah and early strata of the Talmud, the New Testament and the Dead Sea Scrolls, and commentaries on the biblical codes such the *Mek.* and that of Philo of Alexandria. While they undoubtedly preserve many earlier traditions, two difficulties arise in using these sources. First, the legal sources and commentaries do not represent academic historical inquiry but the needs of practical jurists to produce a system suited to the conditions of their own society, which were very different from those of biblical times. Second, the intellectual background of all authors of this period is Greek philosophy, which contains concepts far more sophisticated than those employed by the drafters of the biblical codes. It is very difficult therefore to distinguish in these later sources between genuine tradition on the one hand and legal development, interpretation, or rationalization on the other.

There is, however, a more closely related source that has come to light through the archaeological discoveries of the past 100 years: the legal systems of Israel's contemporary and earlier neighbors. Records from the ancient Near East, mostly in cuneiform script, begin at the end of the fourth millennium B.C.E. and continue until Hellenistic times. (Special note should be made of an archive of some sixty legal documents in Aramaic from a fifth century B.C.E. Jewish community at Elephantine in Egypt.) They include not only thousands of legal documents but records of all aspects of their societies' life and thought, providing their legal systems with a context that is mostly lacking in the biblical evidence.

These sources are of more than mere comparative value; there emerges from the cuneiform record evidence of a common legal tradition that stretched across the whole of the ancient Near East. That tradition is reflected especially in a form of jurisprudence that was developed in Mesopotamia as part of a wider intellectual system and transmitted beyond its boundaries through the medium of cuneiform scribal schools. An individual case is reformulated as a hypothetical problem (the casuistic form mentioned above) and discussed by considering variants on the facts, often according to a set pattern (e.g., varying the status of the victim). The system, however, lacks the ability to formulate abstract concepts or to define legal terms; it produces instead endless lists of examples. In the third and second millennia this technique finds expression in law codes that are remarkably similar in form and content. Six such codes have been recovered to date, in Sumerian, Babylonian, Assyrian, and Hittite, the best-known being the code of King Hammurabi of Babylon. The law codes of the Bible are heirs to this tradition, in varying measure. In the earliest of them, the Covenant Code, some three quarters of its content can be traced back to standard legal problems found in the cuneiform codes.

The later codes already show the first signs of the revolution in thought that was to replace the Mesopotamian science of lists by Greek philosophy, albeit the bulk of their material still derives from the old tradition. The shift from the Mesopotamian concept of a law code as a pedagogical tool to that of an authoritative source of law is, however, achieved only in the latest stratum of the Bible. For most of the biblical period the climate of thought and practice in which the law of Israel was created is that represented by the cuneiform sources.

3. Legal Practice

A. Courts

The *local court* sat in the open space behind the city gate. It consisted of leading citizens usually referred to as elders (Deut 21:18-21; 22:13-21; 25:5-10; 1 Kgs 21:8-11; Lam 5:14). In the P-source, the term "assembly" (*'edah*) seems to designate the same body (Num 35:12, 24-25; cf. Josh 20:19). The elders also have the power to extradite a fellow townsman from a city of refuge in order to stand trial for murder (Deut 19:12), and they are responsible for unsolved murders (Deut 21:2-3). They appear to have sat as a college.

The *king* is *ex officio* the supreme judge and sits alone (e.g., 1 Sam 8:5; Ps 72:1-4; Jer 22:15-16; cf. Judg 4:5). Solomon judged from a throne situated in the "courtyard of judgment" (1 Kgs 7:7). The king could judge cases at first instance (1 Kgs 3:16-28), possibly where a difficult question arose (cf. Exod 18:26). A party might petition him directly, by "shouting" to the king (2 Kgs 6:26-29), using the formula "Save, O king!" (2 Sam 14:4-11). There is no evidence of a formal system of appeals from the lower courts, but the petition may have been a method of overcoming failure to obtain justice at the local level (2 Sam 12:1-6; cf. 2 Kgs 8:3-6).

God in his capacity as divine king is also regarded as a judge (Jer 11:20). He may be petitioned directly, through prayer (e.g., Lam 3:59), or on behalf of others (Gen 18:25). God was the ultimate guarantor of justice when the human system had failed because of abuse by its officers (Isa 3:14). During the period of the monarchy a system of *royally appointed judges*, connected in some way with the military administration, was active in the capital and the provinces. Its relationship to the local courts of the elders is unclear. King Jehoshaphat (Judah, ninth century B.C.E.) is reported (2 Chr 19:5-11) to have appointed both (a) "judges in all the fortified cities of Judah" and (b) a special court in Jerusalem, consisting of levites, priests, and heads of households (i.e., elders). The scope of the latter's jurisdiction is not specified beyond the statement that it was presided over by a priest for "all matters of God" and by the governor (*nagid*) for "all matters of the king."

The three different accounts in the Pentateuch of Moses' appointment of subordinate judges have been interpreted by scholars as attempts to legitimize reforms of the court system by Jehoshaphat and other kings. In Exod 18:13-26 Jethro proposes the appointment of commanders (*śarim*) of thousands, hundreds, fifties, and tens to lighten the burden of judging for Moses, who is only to take the difficult cases. The model is that of the royal military organization. The appointees are to be able men from among all the people, but in Deut 1:9-17 Moses makes the same appointments from among all the "heads of the tribes," i.e., the elders, while in Num 11:16-25 seventy elders are appointed from the "elders and officials" (*šoṭrim*).

In the trial of Jeremiah (Jeremiah 26) the court consists of commanders and "all the people," but it may be an *ad hoc* court. It should be noted that in the *Meṣad Ḥashavyahu* document a petition is presented to the local military commander. In the post-exilic community the Persian emperor's mandate to Ezra authorized him to appoint judges (Ezra 7:25).

In Ezekiel's ideal constitution the levitical priests are to be judges (Ezek 44:24). Evidence for the role of priests as judges in practice is less clear. In Chronicles the levites are mentioned as officials and judges in Solomon's reign (1 Chr 23:4), but this may be an anachronism from a post-exilic source. The Chronicler also gives a priest jurisdiction over "all matters of God" in Jehoshaphat's reform, which could refer to sacral matters or simply to the priests' traditional forensic function of administering evidentiary procedures (cf. Deut 17:9 and 19:17-18 and see below). Possibly priests had jurisdiction within the precincts of the temple (cf. Jer 20:1-3).

B. Procedure

In private disputes, if the defendant is not present, the plaintiff must bring him to court to face charges, (Deut 21:18-21) or the court itself may summon him (Deut 25:8; 1 Sam 22:11). Some sources suggest a formal procedure of claim (Isa 5:1-7) and reply (Mic 6:2-4; 1 Sam 22:14-15) or counterclaim (Jer 2:29), but it is not always strictly observed (1 Kgs 3:17-22).

Evidence is usually given in the form of oral testimony; documentary evidence is not mentioned in a forensic context (although Job 31:35 appears to know of a written bill of indictment) but must have been admitted, since documents were sometimes used to attest to transactions. Reliance is also placed on evidentiary presumptions (Deut 22:24-27) and material evidence (Exod 22:12; Deut 22:16-17). An exculpatory oath procedure is applied for a bailee accused of fraud (Exod 22:10) and a wife accused of adultery (Num 5:21-23). It was administered by the priests (Num 5:21-23; cf. Deut 21:5), as were other supra-rational evidentiary procedures—the oracle (Exod 22:8; Josh 7:10-18; 1 Sam 14:38) and possibly the ordeal (Num 5:23-28). Perjury was punished by the talionic principle (Deut 19:19-21).

The verdict in actions *in personam* was a formula directed to the winning party: "You are in the right" (*ṣadik 'atah*; Prov 24:24). In actions *in rem* it was declaratory: "She is its mother" (1 Kgs 3:27).

For public offenses such as blasphemy, treason, and sacrilege the accused was brought to trial on the basis of a denunciation (Deut 17:4, 7; 1 Kgs 21:9-13) and held in custody until judgment was pronounced (Lev 24:12; Num 15:34). The denouncer, sometimes called a *śaṭan*, stands to the right of the accused (Zech 3:1). In the trial of Jeremiah the "priests and prophets" act as his accusers and demand the death penalty (Jer 26:11). A minimum of two witnesses is required for a conviction (Deut 17:6; 19:15; 1 Kgs 21:10), a principle apparently extended to all capital cases (Num 35:30).

Where the injured party is a hierarchical superior, he may act as both plaintiff and judge, bringing the defendant before his own court, e.g., Saul against Ahimelech (1 Sam 22:11-16), God against the elders and commanders of Israel (Isa 3:13-15).

Most contracts were oral (e.g., 1 Kgs 20:39-41), but some could be attested by documents: when Jeremiah buys land, it is recorded in a "double document" consisting of sealed and open parts (Jer 32:11). A document might accompany divorce (Deut 24:1, 3; Isa 50:1; Jer 3:8). Some transactions were witnessed at the city gate: Boaz convenes ten elders to witness an agreement over redemption of family land (Ruth 4:1-11).

4. Principal Legal Institutions

A. Marriage and Divorce

Marriage in biblical Israel was not so much a personal relationship as an alliance between two families for the purpose of producing legitimate heirs (Gen 34:8-10; 1 Sam 18:22; cf. Judg 11:1-2). Polygamy was permitted. On the question of prohibited degrees, the laws of Leviticus appear to be more restrictive than the practice attested in the narratives. The latter contemplate marriage between a half-sister and half-brother who do not share a common mother (Gen 20:12; 2 Sam 13:13), but even this degree is forbidden by Lev 18:9. Similarly, Jacob marries two sisters, but Lev 18:18 forbids such a union.

There are four stages in the formation of marriage:

(i) Agreement between members of the two families that the bride will be given in marriage to the groom. The parties are usually the father of the bride and the groom or his father. Jacob and David act for themselves, whereas Abraham sends his own agent to procure a bride for his son Isaac (Genesis 24). Even where the son chose his own bride, it was considered proper for his parents to open the negotiations (Gen 34:4; Judg 14:1-2, 5). Adult sons might participate with their father in the negotiations over their sister (Gen 34:13-18). The bride was thus the object of the agreement rather than a party thereto, but a widow or divorcee could contract on her own behalf (1 Sam 25:39-42; Hos 2:16-22; cf. Ezek 16:8, an orphan bride).

A subsidiary term of the agreement was the amount of betrothal payment (*mohar*) to be made by the groom to the bride's father. From ancient Near Eastern evidence this would normally have been in silver, as is provided in Exod 22:16. The two examples given in the biblical narratives are atypical: seven years' labor by Jacob (Gen 29:15-19) and a hundred Philistine foreskins from David (1 Sam 18:25).

(ii) Bringing of the *mohar* by the groom, who would customarily provide a banquet on the occasion (Judg 14:10). From this point in time the bride is betrothed (*'oraśah*). She is referred to as a wife (Deut 22:24; Judg 15:1), and as far as outsiders are concerned she is a fully married woman—rape or seduction by a third party will be treated with corresponding severity (Deut 22:22-25). In the cuneiform sources breach of the agreement by the father results in damages (see Codex Hammurabi 160). On the same principle, the Philistines recognize that Samson has a just claim when breach by his father-in-law leads him to take revenge, albeit incommensurate (Judg 15:1-2, 6). Nonetheless, it does not appear that a formal divorce was necessary to dissolve betrothal, as was the case in later law.

(iii) Claiming of the bride by the groom, on the strength of payment of the *mohar*. On completion of his seven years' service Jacob says to his father-in-law Laban: "Bring me my wife, for my days are completed" (Gen 29:21).

(iv) Completion of the marriage. It is the father-in-law's turn to give a banquet before delivering his daughter to the groom (Gen 29:22). Legal completion appears (in the absence of evidence as to special ceremonies or rites) to be constituted by consummation, which is referred to as the groom entering the bridal chamber, described variously as a tent (Gen 24:67), room (Judg 15:1), or *ḥuppah* (Joel 2:16; Ps 19:6), the term used in post-biblical periods for the bridal canopy under which the wedding ceremony takes place.

A man might be forced to marry under certain circumstances. According to Exod 22:15-16:

> If a man seduces an unbetrothed virgin and lies with her, he shall marry her with payment of *mohar*. If her father refuses to give her to him, he shall pay "the *mohar* of virgins" (i.e., the customary amount) in silver.

If the offense is rape, the conditions are harsher (Deut 22:28-29):

> If a man finds an unbetrothed virgin and seizes her and lies with her and they are caught, the man who lay with her shall pay the girl's father fifty shekels of silver and she shall be his wife. Because he degraded her, he shall not be able to divorce her all his days.

Under the law of the levirate, a man might be obliged to marry his deceased brother's widow. If he refused, he was subjected to a humiliating ceremony (Deut 25:5-10):

> If brothers dwell together and one of them dies and has no son, the wife of the deceased shall not be married outside to a stranger; her husband's brother shall go in to her and take her as his wife and perform the duty of a husband's brother to her. The first son whom she bears shall rise up upon the name of his deceased brother, that his name be not expunged from Israel. If the man does not wish to marry his brother's wife, then his brother's wife shall go up to the gate to the elders and say: "My husband's brother refuses to raise

> up a name to his brother in Israel; he will not perform the duty of a husband's brother to me." Then the city elders shall call him and speak to him, and if he persists, saying, "I do not wish to marry her," then his brother's wife shall go up to him in the presence of the elders, pull his sandal off his foot, spit in his face and declare: "So shall it be done to the man who does not build up his brother's house." And his name shall be called in Israel: "The house of the one whose sandal was pulled off."

The biblical levirate, unlike the later institution, applied not only to brothers. In their absence, the duty fell upon the closest relative. In Genesis 38, after Tamar is twice widowed and her father-in-law refuses to allow his third son to marry her, she tricks her father-in-law into performing the levirate himself. In Ruth 4:1-6, a more distant relative is potentially liable. On the other hand, the circumstances under which the law applies are narrower than in the later law (see section B on Inheritance below).

Although it receives scant mention in the Bible, the dowry (*šilluḥim*) must have played an important role in Israelite marriage. In Josh 15:18-19 (= Judg 1:13-15) and 1 Kgs 9:16, it consists of land. More typical items are personal slaves (Gen 29:24, 29; cf. 16:2-3; 24:59), jewellery, and clothing (Ezek 16:10-12). It is typically furnished to the bride by her father (being the functional equivalent of an inheritance share), but in Ezek 16:10-12, where the girl is an orphan, it is provided by the groom, and in Gen 24:53 it is supplemented by gifts from the groom's father. During marriage the dowry merged into the husband's property, but the wife might maintain control of certain personal items (Ezek 16:16-18), especially personal slaves (Gen 16:2-3; cf. *melug* in the Mishnah [*m. Yebam.* 7.1] = Akkadian *mulūgu*, Ugaritic *mlg*). From the usage of neighboring societies, it may be presumed that a primary purpose of the dowry was to support the wife in widowhood.

A special problem that is dealt with by several of the ancient Near Eastern law codes is that of the wife whose husband fails to return from a foreign country (e.g., Codex Hammurabi 133-137). Under certain circumstances the wife is allowed to remarry, but the second marriage is subject to annulment should the first husband return. There are no legal provisions of this nature in the Bible, but the story of David and Michal seems to reflect the same principles, in contrast to the harsher attitude of later Jewish law (*m. Yebam.* 10.1). After David has fled from Saul (1 Sam 19:11-17), the latter gives David's wife Michal to one Paltiel (1 Sam 25:44). After Saul's death David claims Michal back from his successor Ishbaal, who feels obliged to comply, in spite of the tearful objections of Paltiel and the fact that he is at war with David (2 Sam 3:14-16).

Divorce is a unilateral act by the husband, by means of a formal declaration such as: "She is not my wife and I am not her husband" (Hos 2:4), following the practice prevalent throughout the ancient Near East. The possibility of a wife divorcing her husband is not raised in the Bible, but the right existed at least in theory in the surrounding societies and is attested in practice among the Jewish community at Elephantine (see TAD B2.6, B3.3, and B3.8 in Porten and Yardeni 1989).

The husband is mentioned in sources from the period of the later monarchy as providing his wife with a "document of separation" (*sefer keritut* in Deut 24:1, 3; Isa 50:1; Jer 3:8) upon divorce. Possibly it served to furnish the wife with documentary evidence that she was free to remarry.

The main legal provision concerning divorce is Deut 24:1-4. While rabbinic jurisprudence regarded it as the basis of divorce law, the biblical text does not lay down any general principles. Rather, it deals with an exceptional case:

> If a man takes a woman and consummates the marriage, and it happens that she displeases him because he found in her some indecency and he writes her a document of separation and gives it to her and sends her from his house, and she leaves his house and becomes the wife of another and the latter hates her and writes her a document of separation and gives it to her and sends her from his house or the second man who married her dies, then her first husband who divorced her may not take her again as his wife, after she has been made unclean to him.

It presents a complicated scenario: (1) a husband finds "some indecency" (*'ervat dabar*) in his wife and divorces her; (2) she remarries, and her second husband either "hates" and divorces her or dies and leaves her a widow; (3) the first husband is then forbidden to remarry her.

The rationale for this provision becomes clear if it is placed against the background of the wider ancient Near Eastern legal tradition. If a husband divorces his wife without cause, the technical phrase being "hates and divorces," he must restore to her her dowry and pay compensation. If on the other hand she has done something to justify her being divorced (cf. *m. Ketub.* 7.6: immodest conduct), he may keep her dowry and need pay her nothing.

In the Deuteronomic law, then, the wife left the first marriage penniless, but not the second, whether as divorcee or widow. In prohibiting remarriage, the law imposes an estoppel on the husband to prevent him from profiting twice from his wife: first by claiming that she was not fit to be his wife, and subsequently by conceding that she *is*.

A husband is forbidden to divorce his wife altogether in two instances: in Deut 22:28-29, where he had raped a maiden and was forced to marry her, and in Deut 22:13-19, where he had falsely accused his wife of premarital infidelity:

> If a man takes a wife, has intercourse with her, hates her, makes a false statement about her, and gives her a bad reputation, saying, "I married this woman but when I slept with her I did not find in her the signs of virginity," but the girl's father and mother take the girl's signs of virginity and bring them out to the city elders at the gate, the girl's father saying to the elders, "I gave my daughter as a wife to this man and he hated her, so he made a false statement, namely, 'I did not find the signs of virginity in your daughter,' but here are the signs of my daughter's virginity," and spreading out the garment before the city elders, then the city elders shall take that man and beat him, fine him one hundred of silver, and give it to the girl's father, because he gave a virgin of Israel a bad reputation. She shall be his wife; he may not divorce her all his days.

B. Inheritance

The basic family unit was the "house of the father," a patriarchal household of three (or more) generations (Gen 7:7). On the death of the head of household, his sons (or grandsons inheriting *per stirpes*: Josh 17:1-6) divided the estate by lot (Num 26:55). The firstborn was entitled to an extra share. A father could transfer that share to another son but not to the son of a different mother, if his preference was based on favoritism towards the other wife (Deut 21:15-17). The firstborn could, however, lose his extra share by misconduct (Gen 49:3-4). He could also trade his future right to it: Esau (in Gen 25:27-34) sold his for a bowl of soup!

The brothers could choose to postpone division and remain as joint owners—technically known as "dwelling together" (Gen 13:1-6; Ps 133:1). If one died childless during this period, the other brothers could simply divide without him. To ensure the deceased his share, another brother was obliged to marry his widow, the product of this levirate marriage being deemed the deceased's heir who would divide on his behalf (Deut 25:5-6). The levirate duty also applied if the brother predeceased his father and the estate was therefore still undivided (Genesis 38) or if an undivided inheritance that had been sold was restored to the family by redemption (Ruth 4).

If there were no heirs in the house of the father, the estate passed to the nearest agnate in the clan (*mishpaḥah*), in the order of brother, uncle, etc. (Num 27:8-11). In the absence of sons, daughters counted as heirs (Num 27:8), but because their share was regarded as dowry, they were obliged to marry within their clan (Num 36:8).

5. For Further Reading

A. General

Daube 1947; Falk 1964; Greengus 1992; Jackson 1985; Jackson 1989; Patrick 1989; Welch 2005 [Editors' note: Westbrook had cited an earlier version of Welch's work, but its most easily accessible form is now the 2005 edition]; Westbrook 1988d; Yaron 1988a

B. Juridical Background

Dearman 1988; Noth 1967: 1-107

C. Sources

Alt 1934a: 81-132 (in the English edition); Fishbane 1985: 89-277; Jackson 1975: 75-107; Patrick 1985; Paul 1970; Porten and Yardeni 1989; Pritchard 1969 (contains translations of the cuneiform law codes and of selected private legal documents); Roth 1997; Westbrook 1985a; Yaron 1980

D. Legal Practice

Boecker 1980; Frymer-Kensky 1984; Jackson 1972: 203-250; McKenzie 1964; Reviv 1982

E. Marriage

Ben-Barak 1979; Levine 1968; Neufeld 1944; Westbrook 1986b; Yaron 1957

F. Inheritance

Daube 1950; Mendelsohn 1959; Westbrook 1991b

21

The Laws of Biblical Israel

Abstract

Biblical scholars continue to debate the origins and date of the laws of the Torah. This article focuses on the laws in Exodus and Deuteronomy (that is, in the Covenant Code and certain sections of the Deuteronomic Code) that govern legal matters between humans, as opposed to laws of a more religious nature. It argues that the laws in these codes originated in a manner similar to that of the provisions in other law codes from the ancient Near Eastern and Mediterranean world. The article thus argues against the evolutionary model, which detects in the biblical material a development from primitive law to more sophisticated law, and against the literary model, which sees direct textual dependence between the biblical codes and other ancient Near Eastern codes.

Laws and Law Codes

The most famous law code associated with the Bible is the Ten Commandments, but the Torah (Pentateuch) contains many more commandments—613 in all, according to Rabbinic tradition. Like the Ten Commandments, most of them regulate relations between humans and God, for example dietary rules, rules of personal purity, sacrifices and dedications by individuals, or priestly duties and cultic rules regarding the community as a whole. Other rules in the Torah prescribe purely ethical behavior, like helping one's neighbor, providing charity, or not oppressing the poor. Only about 60 provisions are what we would regard nowadays as law. They are rules that establish rights and duties as between individuals,

* Originally published in *The Hebrew Bible: New Insights and Scholarship* (edited by Frederick E. Greenspahn; New York: New York University Press, 2008), 99-119.

with regard to marriage, inheritance, property, contract, crime and tort, etc. They cover disputes that can be tried in a human court and give solutions that are enforceable by the normal machinery of justice.

These 60 laws are unevenly spread through the second to the fifth books of the Torah. They are embedded in three of the literary sources that scholars have identified in that segment of the Bible, which are thought to have been written at different times during the first millennium B.C.E. (although their exact dating is a matter of great dispute). Nearly half of the 60 laws are to be found in chapters 21 and 22 of Exodus, in a context usually associated with the Elohist (E) source. An equal number are found in the book of Deuteronomy, mostly concentrated in chapters 21 and 22, but with scattered examples from chapter 15 to chapter 25. Deuteronomy is considered to be an independent source. For the rest, a smattering of laws are found at various points in Leviticus, mostly incidental to regulations regarding purity or priestly functions, and three laws are expounded at length in Numbers. The latter two books contain what is called the Priestly (P) source.

The bulk of the laws in the Torah are thus concentrated in two main clusters. The first, in Exodus 21 and 22:1-16, is usually called the Mishpatim (Hebrew for "judgments") and is part of a larger unit referred to as the Covenant Code (Exod 20:22-23:33). It forms a solid block that is followed, after some transitional provisions (Exod 22:17-19), by a series of ethical rules, moral exhortations, and cultic regulations. The second cluster, in Deuteronomy 21 and 22, has a central block that is divided by a group of ethical rules (Deut 22:1-12) and other provisions scattered among mostly ethical and exhortatory material. The pervasive moral rhetoric of Deuteronomy is attached even to everyday laws: for example, legal sanctions are adorned with admonishments such as "you will purge the evil from among you, and all Israel will hear and be afraid" (Deut 21:20).

My concern to separate out laws from other normative or exhortatory material is not just the imposition of a modern category upon ancient sources. The laws already had a separate existence in antiquity. They represent a special type of literature that has remarkably close parallels among Israel's neighbors, both in style and in content. Indeed, the parallels to an external source are the closest of any literary genre in the Bible.

The external source in question is the so-called "law codes." The most famous example is Codex Hammurabi (CH) from Babylonia of the eighteenth century B.C.E., but the texts of no fewer than ten other codes, in whole or part, have been recovered, widely scattered in time and space. Seven are from the Near East and are written in cuneiform script. Of these, two are in Sumerian, from the cities of Ur (Codex Ur-namma—CU) and Isin (Codex Lipit-Ishtar—CL) in southern Mesopotamia dating to the twenty-first and nineteenth centuries respectively. Three are in Akkadian: one comes from Eshnunna (CE), a city to the north of Babylon, and is dated about thirty years earlier than CH; one is from Assyria dating between the fourteenth and eleventh centuries (Middle Assyrian Laws—MAL); and a small excerpt of a code comes from sixth-century Babylonia (Neo-Babylonian Laws—NBL). Finally, there is one in Hittite from the Hittite capital Hattusha in Anatolia (Hittite Laws—HL), covering a slightly earlier time span than the Middle Assyrian Laws.[1] Outside the Near East we have in Greek an excerpt from the laws of Drakon, ruler of Athens in the seventh century, and a large code from Gortyn (Crete), dated to the sixth century.[2] A Roman code called the Twelve Tables is traditionally dated to the fifth century.[3] The Greek and Roman codes are usually ignored by biblical scholars, but they share the same characteristics as the Near Eastern codes; they come from the Mediterranean region not very far from Israel, and they are a lot closer in time to the biblical sources than are most of the cuneiform codes.

All of these law codes are strikingly similar in form. Their salient characteristic is the *casuistic* sentence, namely, a conditional clause stating the circumstances of a hypothetical case, followed by a clause stating the legal consequences. For example: "If a man knocks out the eye of a man, his eye shall be knocked out" (CH 196).

The content of all of the codes is everyday law as would be practiced in the courts. The similarity in content, however, runs even deeper. Many of the same cases recur in different codes, not always with identical facts or with the same solution, but close enough to show that they drew upon the same situations and the same legal principles. For example, the case of an adulterer caught in the act is found in the Middle Assyrian Laws, the Hittite Laws, and the Gortyn Code, with variations in the punishment

1 All the cuneiform codes are translated in Roth 1997. For the Hittite Laws, see especially Hoffner 1997.

2 Drakon's law is translated by Stroud 1979, and the Gortyn Code by Willetts 1967.

3 Translated in Crawford 1996: vol. 2, 555-72.

inflicted, but all with some discretion in punishment allowed to the husband. The punishment of theft by payment to the owner of a multiple of the thing stolen is found in Codex Hammurabi, the Hittite Laws, and the Twelve Tables.

If we look at the biblical laws, we find that they fit perfectly into the same pattern. They are for the most part casuistic in form and contain many cases found in a number of law codes. In the Mishpatim we find multiple payments for theft, but also many other examples, such as the case of a man who suffers non-permanent injury in a fight and is entitled to damages for his loss of work and medical costs (Exod 21:18-19), which is also found in CH 206 and HL 10. From the Deuteronomic laws, the rape of a maiden who is betrothed but not married (Deut 22:23-27) is also found in CE 26 and CH 130, while the woman who seizes a man's genitals in a fight (Deut 25:11-12) is dealt with in MAL A 8. Even some of the instances in the Priestly source have parallels: the case of the daughter who inherits where there are no sons and must marry a male relative (Num 27:1-11; 36:5-9) has a parallel in the Gortyn Code (VII 15-IX 24). We are therefore justified in seeing in the clusters of everyday law in the Torah law codes of the same type as their Near Eastern and Mediterranean counterparts, notwithstanding their intermingling with sacral laws and ethical rules or the addition of moral exhortation.

The Nature of the Codes

When first discovered, Codex Hammurabi was assumed to have been royal legislation, a codification, or reform. It was subsequently noted, however, that neither it nor the other codes were ever cited in court or referred to as a source of law. A new theory was formulated, principally by Fritz Kraus[4] and Jean Bottéro,[5] that CH was an academic document, a product of the scribal school, not intended for citation in court. The cuneiform scribes of Mesopotamia tried to classify the world around them by means of lists—of flora, fauna, grammatical forms, gods, offices, precious stones. A more sophisticated form of list recorded conditions and consequences: medical

4 Kraus 1960.
5 Bottéro 1982.

symptoms and their diagnoses, omens and their meanings, actions and their legal redresses. The latter type of list was cast into the form of objective, hypothetical cases: "If a woman gives birth, and the left foot (of the child) is withered—that house will prosper."

The "laws" of CH present just such a list, albeit in another context. They are bracketed by a prologue and epilogue and inscribed on a monument. In the epilogue Hammurabi tells us himself what the foregoing list represents: "These are the just judgments that I decided . . . ." The judgments in question, however, if such they were, have been subjected to a process of editing. They have been stripped of all unnecessary details and turned into hypothetical cases that could serve as a rule for the future.

As Jacob Finkelstein demonstrates, the stone monument with its list of just judgments, set up in temples around his kingdom towards the end of his long reign, served as royal propaganda to show that Hammurabi had been a just king.[6] Some of the other law codes also had a monumental form, but still others were found in archives or scribal schools, so that we do not know for what purpose they had been created. In whatever context they are found, the codes' original composition relied on that same proto-scientific tradition, the Mesopotamian "science of lists."

In the biblical narrative, the laws of the Torah are presented as if they were legislation given by God and supposed to be applied in ancient Israel, although the kings of Israel and Judah were often neglectful of them. In post-biblical times, they were certainly applied in Jewish courts as normative law.

While modern scholarship questioned the historicity of the biblical account of law-giving, it did not at first doubt that in historical times, at least during the monarchy, the laws written in the Torah were the laws of the land. Scholars soon noted, however, as in the case of CH, that the laws were never mentioned in any historical context after the settlement. Citation only appears after the Babylonian exile, under Ezra the scribe. Here, then, is another characteristic shared by biblical and Mesopotamian law.

The biblical laws are located not in a law book or monument but in a religious historical narrative set in the distant past. The natural conclusion is that those everyday laws that occur at various places in the Torah were drawn from another source before being embedded in their present

6 Finkelstein 1961: 103.

context. That source was likely a law code or codes, or it at least arose independently through the same process that gave rise to the other law codes. The nature of the law codes is a vital element in determining the next question: the connection between them.

The Law Code Tradition

Assyriologists have not addressed the question of the relationship between the different law codes of Mesopotamia, except to assume that their transmission followed the path of the cuneiform script, which by the second millennium had spread from Mesopotamia, where it had been invented, across most of the Near East, with the exception of Egypt. Classicists have assumed a direct borrowing by the Romans of Greek law (as Roman legend relates) but have considered the relationship between the Greek or Roman codes and the Near Eastern codes only to the extent of expending significant energy on denying its existence. It has been left to biblicists to inquire into the connection between the law codes. On the one hand, they have focused on how the Mesopotamian format got into the biblical codes, and on the other they have examined the relationship, chronological and literary, between the biblical codes themselves. As biblical codes, they identify the Covenant Code (including the Mishpatim), the Deuteronomic Code, and the Priestly source (including a special section called the Holiness Code). In recent years, several different schools of thought have emerged. Most current scholars subscribe to one of two models: the evolutionary or the literary.

The Evolutionary Model

The main protagonists of this school today are Eckart Otto (in many publications from the 1980s to the present) and Bernard Jackson.[7] They rely heavily on a form-critical approach, which finds in the current form of a law evidence of its original setting. Their starting point is an influential theory developed by Albrecht Alt. Alt divided the biblical laws by form

7 E.g., Otto 1988b, 1988c, 1994, 2003. E.g., Jackson 2000.

into two types: casuistic, as we have just described, and apodictic, or direct commands (e.g., "Thou shalt not kill"). He took apodictic laws to be a native Israelite product, while casuistic laws were copied from Canaanite law codes, which in turn were copied from Mesopotamian law codes. The Covenant Code (and thus the Mishpatim), being mostly casuistic but with a smattering of apodictic commands, dated from the early Israelite settlement in Canaan.[8]

Otto has modified this theory, by proposing a different milieu for the two forms of law. Apodictic law evolved from within the family or clan, where the paterfamilias dictated rules and enforced them. Casuistic law evolved from precedents in disputes between families, which were settled by arbitration at the town gate. The two were fused together in the early monarchy to form the Covenant Code, which continued to undergo a complex process of editing as the society and its laws developed. Later in the monarchy, the Deuteronomic code was an adaptation and development of the earlier code. As for the connection with the cuneiform codes, Otto explains that the biblical material went through a parallel but separate developmental process as biblical casuistic law, derived from local precedents. The similarity of form derives from the fact that the Israelites adopted cuneiform drafting techniques they encountered in the Canaanite towns.

Jackson also attributes apodictic rules to a family setting, but his main distinction is between oral and written law. Following the theories of the anthropologist Jack Goody,[9] he considers that law changes entirely in character when written down. Early written texts, however, may retain features of primitive oral law—an "oral residue." The Mishpatim are early, primitive laws that retain many traces of their origins in pre-institutional dispute resolution. They are wisdom rather than binding law. The paradox of their close literary connection with the cuneiform law codes is to be explained by an oral tradition that preceded scribal formulation of these laws and had elements in common with the orally transmitted custom of the region. The Deuteronomic laws are more developed, but all biblical laws retain the character of wisdom literature until the time of Ezra, when they begin to be cited in court like modern law.

8 Alt 1934a.
9 E.g., Goody 1986.

The Literary Model

Most of the protagonists of the literary model rely on the work of Meir Malul. Malul casts doubt on any connection through common legal practice. Since the law codes are a literary product, their appearance in the Bible is a result of contact through scribal practice. Malul takes as his example the laws of the goring ox, where there is a remarkable affinity between the versions found in CE, CH, and the Mishpatim. Indeed, the law of an ox goring an ox in the Mishpatim (Exod 21:35) is almost identical to that in CE (§53). Malul therefore suggests that the biblical author or editor knew firsthand the Mesopotamian laws and that he may even have had a copy (or copies?) of them in front of him when he composed or edited his biblical version.[10]

Anne Fitzpatrick-McKinley adopts the same model of a scribal tradition, but in a more extreme form. She takes up a theory of Alan Watson that relates to the spread of Roman law in much later times. Watson argues that law is structurally autonomous. That is, it develops under its own momentum, to the point where there can be a marked divergence between the law and the needs of the society or its rulers.[11] Fitzpatrick-McKinley applies this theory to the much earlier law of the ancient Near East, including that of the Hebrew Bible, by means of Goody's distinction between the oral and the written. Like Jackson, she considers that with the introduction of writing in the ancient Near East the flexibility of the oral law, allowing gradual adjustments without apparent alteration, was lost. Writing has two effects. First, it severs rules from their original context, making the text of the law multipurpose. Some oral rules were incorporated into the text, but once incorporated, they would eventually cease to reflect social practice. Second, it creates a class of specialized scribes. The law codes are the work of such scribes: they were not legislation but wisdom-moral teachings propagated by scribes. The biblical laws were based on this literary tradition, shared with Israel's neighbors, that was developed by literary elites.[12]

10 Malul 1990b.

11 Watson 1985.

12 Fitzpatrick-McKinley 1999.

John Van Seters adopts the image projected by Malul of a scribe or scholar sitting in a library surrounded by texts. The writer plagiarizes those texts, or rather emulates them, writing material of his own creation that imitates or takes directly from the sources before him. The author of the Covenant Code thus borrowed material from other law codes at his disposal, which included the Deuteronomic and Priestly Codes but also the Babylonian codes, in the form of CH or its successor.[13] David Wright likewise considers that the author of the Mishpatim knew the Akkadian text of CH and drew directly from it, together with other cuneiform sources.[14]

Cutting across the question of which model applies to the biblical codes has been a furious debate over the dating of the codes. It has long been accepted that the book of Deuteronomy dates to the period of Assyrian hegemony over Israel in the seventh century. The Deuteronomic laws also have strong affinities to the Middle Assyrian Laws, both in style and in content. There is a broad consensus that the Priestly source dates to the Babylonian exile (after 587 B.C.E.) or the post-exilic period. The problem is the Covenant Code. Alt considered it to be a very old, premonarchic source, and although many would now place it in the monarchy, most scholars still agree that it predated Deuteronomy. This chronology has been challenged by Van Seters, who places the Covenant Code in the Babylonian Exile of the sixth century.

The issue at stake is the relationship between the Deuteronomic and Covenant Codes. Most scholars consider that the author of Deuteronomy knew the Covenant Code and introduced reforms to its long-standing provisions. Van Seters considers that it was the author of the Covenant Code who knew the Deuteronomic Code and adapted some of its laws. I have no wish to enter into this debate. There is no external evidence by which we could date the Covenant Code, and attempts to do so on the basis of its style or of the state of development of its laws are an exercise in futile speculation. My concern is rather with the mode of transmission of the laws that end up in the biblical codes.

13 Van Seters 2003.
14 Wright 2003.

Critique of the Current Models

Neither of the two current models furnishes an entirely satisfactory explanation of the origins of the biblical laws. The evolutionary model relies on a series of unwarranted assumptions.

1. It assumes that the present form reflects the circumstances in which the law was created: in a family setting, in inter-clan arbitration, from a foreign source, *et cetera*. There is not a shred of evidence to support this assumption. Legislation, such as there is in the ancient Near East, takes all sorts of forms.[15] It is true that the casuistic form is characteristic of Mesopotamian "scientific" style, but the law codes were not purely scientific documents like the omen or medical lists. They served other purposes, and some of them contain other forms when it suits them.

2. It imagines a world for which we have no evidence and which may never have existed. The model has its roots in nineteenth-century ethnology and the equation of ancient civilizations with contemporary primitive tribes. Already the earliest codes, however, come from long-standing urban civilizations, and the law-code tradition had existed for more than a millennium before the advent of the biblical codes.

3. The weakest point of this model is that it suits a self-contained society, isolated from its neighbors, and is embarrassed by the bib-

15 A decree of the Babylonian king Ammi-ṣaduqa (from the dynasty of Hammurabi), for example, contains a mix of different styles:

> §1 The arrears of feudal tenants, shepherds, knackers, seasonal herders and palace fee-payers—in order to give them support and deal equitably with them—are released. The debt-collector shall not dun the family of a fee-payer.
>
> §17 A taverness who has lent beer or barley shall not collect what she lent.
>
> §20 If a free man of Numhia, etc., has been bound by a debt and has sold or pledged himself, his wife, or his children, because the king has established equity for the land, he is released; his freedom is established.

> lical codes' close affinity with foreign law codes. Attempts to distinguish between local form and foreign content founder on the close correlation in content, while the projection of the connection back into a primitive pre-writing phase faces a chronological chasm of several thousand years between the Mesopotamian and Israelite experiences of such a phase.

At first sight, the literary model seems a simpler and more satisfying explanation. It is particularly suited to the reception of foreign sources. However, like all simple solutions, it would only work well if reality were as simple.

> 1. It assumes that each biblical code had a different document to copy from: MAL for Deuteronomy and CH for the Mishpatim. The MAL are not complete; so it is impossible to say whether or not they contain all the laws found in the Deuteronomic Code. CH, on the other hand, is virtually complete, so it is strange that the Mishpatim contain laws found in other cuneiform codes but not in CH.
>
> Wright's answer is to say that almost all the laws in the Mishpatim are in fact derived from or inspired by CH, even though the relationship may not be obvious at first sight. He can only achieve this result by special pleading, forcing the laws into categories that make them a match or seizing upon the most tangential resemblances as evidence of influence. Even then, there remain a hard core of laws that resist "Hammurabification," such as the case of the ox goring an ox (Exod 21:35), which is only found in CE (§53), or the burning of a neighbor's field (Exod 22:5), which is found only in HL (§106).
>
> Van Seters' answer is inconsistent. On the one hand, he wants to see CH as the Mesopotamian text the Covenant Code (the Mishpatim) used, and he tries to show that it was the model not only in content but also in structure and ideology, with Moses being portrayed as the Jewish Hammurabi. He speaks of a Babylonian legal tradition for the Covenant Code, whereas the

earlier Deuteronomic Code came from an Assyrian source.[16] On the other hand, he refers to other literary codes at the disposal of the Covenant Code's author and at times to the Mesopotamian legal tradition or the cuneiform legal tradition.[17] Yet again, he accounts for the existence of material in the Covenant Code that is not in CH by referring to a single text, namely CH's "literary descendant."[18]

2. For this model, it is important to know exactly when and how the biblical authors had the opportunity to read the Mesopotamian codes. Alt's idea of Canaanite law codes has been criticized, given the failure to discover any law code among the abundant legal material from Late Bronze Age sites in Syria and Canaan, such as Emar, Alalakh, and Ugarit. Malul assumes a cuneiform library that the Davidic monarchy inherited with the conquest of the Canaanite cities, but as has been pointed out, cuneiform died out in the region at the end of the Bronze Age. Wright therefore places both the Covenant and Deuteronomic Codes in the period of Assyrian hegemony, when there was access to Mesopotamian learning. Van Seters agrees as regards the Deuteronomic Code but puts the author of the Covenant Code in Babylonia during the exile, where he would have come in direct contact with the local culture.

Both of the latter scholars rely on a complete cultural discontinuity in the countries of the Eastern Mediterranean between the Late Bronze Age and the Iron Age, leading to total loss of knowledge of cuneiform law. Thus each biblical author came to the text that was his model in a pristine state. In a sense, it is the same technique of encapsulation that is employed by the evolutionary school to preserve the purity of their developmental model, and it is equally misleading, as we shall see.

3. The literary model divorces the text from any relationship with the law in force. This is of great advantage to biblical scholars,

16 Van Seters 2003: 43-45, 56-57.
17 Van Seters 2003: 123-24.
18 Van Seters 2003: 98.

who are trained in literary criticism and not in jurisprudence. Not all literature is alike, however, and legal literature is simply not the same as scientific literature or myth or historiography. Even if it is not legislation, or not binding in any way, legal literature cannot so easily escape consciousness of the living law of the society that produced it.[19] The codes themselves occasionally make conscious reference to the creation of rules they contain: CE 58 and HL 55 both explain that the rule in question had its origin in a royal decree. The Hittite Laws go further and consciously update the text in response to changes in the practice of law: "formerly the punishment was x; now it is y."

The biblical codes likewise were the product of the law in practice within the societies that produced them and not simply the product of other codes. A clear example is the case in Deut 21:1-9 of the corpse found murdered in a field. The law places responsibility upon the members of the local authority, who must undergo an exculpatory ceremony and take an exculpatory oath:

> If a corpse is found in the land which the LORD your God gives you to possess, lying in the open fields, and it is not known who killed him, your elders and magistrates shall go out and measure the distance of the towns around the corpse. The elders of the town nearest to the corpse shall take an unworked heifer not yet put to the yoke. The elders of that town shall bring the heifer down into a wadi with a constant stream, in which no plowing or sowing has been done, and they shall break the heifer's neck in that wadi . . . . And all the elders of that town near the corpse shall wash their hands over the heifer whose neck was broken in the wadi. And they shall say: "Our hands have not shed this blood and our eyes have not seen."

19 The fact that later legal systems sometimes develop rules in disregard of social reality (Fitzpatrick-McKinley 1999, following Watson) is irrelevant. In later systems such as Roman law those rules still had normative force; they impacted society even if they were anachronistic or unrealistic.

Exactly the same oath in the same situation is attested in practice in correspondence from the Canaanite city of Ugarit in the thirteenth century:[20]

> And concerning the case of the woman whose husband was killed in Arzigana along with the son of Hutiya, about which you wrote to me, now let the men of Arzigana swear in the town of Arruwa as follows: "We did not kill the woman's husband, brother of Abdi-Anatu in the town, nor do we know who killed him."

From the same city come international treaties regulating the liability of the local authorities for the unresolved homicide of foreign merchants.[21] Moreover, the principle of collective responsibility of the local community for unsolved homicides is found in HL IV and in CH 22-24.[22] There is thus an interplay between the codes and practice that continues over centuries.

The above example has equally important implications for the question of the biblical authors' access to sources. It completely destroys the argument that the demise of cuneiform script at the end of the Bronze Age consigned to oblivion all the law and learning that had been written in that medium. However influenced Deuteronomy may have been by Assyrian culture, it did not rely on the Assyrian law code as its sole source.

New Perspectives

The perspectives that the two models share may also be called into question. In this regard, it is necessary to reconsider two fundamental

20 The text is RS 20.22. It is edited in Nougayrol et al. 1968: 94-97.

21 RS 17.146 and 18.115; edited in Nougayrol 1956: 154-60

22 HL IV: "If a man is (found) killed in another's field, if he is a free man, he (the owner) shall give field, house, and 60 shekels of silver . . . . If it is not a field but uncultivated land, (they shall measure) 3 *danna* hither and 3 *danna* thither, and whichever town is reckoned within, he shall take those very persons."

CH 22-24: "If a man commits robbery and is caught, that man shall be killed. If the robber is not caught, the person robbed shall declare his losses before the god and the city and mayor in whose district the robbery was committed shall compensate him for his lost property. If it is life (i.e., murder), the city and mayor shall pay his family one mina of silver."

relationships. First, biblicists have concentrated on the relationship between the biblical and cuneiform codes and between the biblical codes themselves. Neither can be understood, it seems to me, without taking into account all the known codes, not only from the Near East but also from the Mediterranean basin.

The cuneiform codes are part of a long-standing scribal tradition, but their transmission is far from simple. Codex Hammurabi continued to be copied in Mesopotamia and perhaps elsewhere well into the Neo-Babylonian period (sixth century). The reason was not legal; it had become a classic work of literature in the scribal curriculum. The Hittite Laws and the Middle Assyrian Laws were not only copied but also developed for several centuries within those societies; MAL is also found in copies from Neo-Assyrian sources (seventh century), apparently as part of the Assyrian scribal tradition. The Sumerian codes were copied in Old Babylonian scribal schools (twentieth to sixteenth centuries), but not, apparently, in later times. CE and HL disappeared in the second millennium with the demise of their respective kingdoms, but provisions from them reappear in later times. Doubtless there were many more law codes than have survived, but such breaks in continuity make it more likely that an earlier law code was not the only medium through which laws could enter a later law code.

The Roman Twelve Tables is traditionally dated to around 450 B.C.E., in the early Republic, but only on the basis of later legends. It could be later or much earlier, from the time of the monarchy. The text exists only in fragmentary quotations from much later authors. With the discovery of CH, attempts were made to link the Twelve Tables with the Near Eastern Codes, but such efforts have met with resistance. The prevailing approach among Romanists is still to emphasize self-contained evolutionary development. This is in spite of close correlations in the law of injury, theft, and accidental homicide.

The Greek Gortyn Code is dated to the sixth century B.C.E., mostly on the basis of its language and writing, and is one of many legal inscriptions from Crete of that period. Surprisingly, Hellenists have been much more receptive to the idea of Near Eastern influence on early Greek law. The Code provides spectacular confirmation. It is headed, as are many similar Greek legal inscriptions, with a single word: Gods! Robert Pounder has traced the origins of this enigmatic heading through earlier Greek inscriptions back into the ancient Near East, into the curses and blessings that are common at the end of inscriptions such as CH.[23] Accordingly, our perspective needs to widen to account for the transmission of laws to these latter codes, beyond the bounds of imperial conquest.

Secondly, scholars from both schools have relied on the dichotomy between orality and writing as formulated by Goody. That dichotomy is not applicable to the transmission of law. According to Goody, oral tradition is a poor vehicle for transmitting legal texts, because of its inaccuracy over time. Biblical scholars have concluded from this that the written codes were the sole mode of transmitting theoretical statements of the law. Legal rules, however, do not need to be formulated in precisely the same language every time, unless they are the words of a statute, which, as we have seen, the law codes were not. In fact, there exists an immense body of evidence for the efficacy of oral legal tradition. It is called the Talmud. Committed to writing only in the fifth century C.E., it is a record of the "oral law"—cases and rulings transmitted orally by generations of rabbis over hundreds of years. Nor is the Talmud unique: the early Roman jurists had a similar source of law in "ancestral custom" (*mos maiorum*), despite reliance on written sources such as the Twelve Tables.

If anything, it would appear that in both these cases written sources and oral traditions reinforced each other as mnemonic devices. Rabbinic oral traditions had already been partially committed to writing before the Talmud, in the much smaller collection of the Mishnah from the second century C.E. The written Mishnah and the much larger oral traditions not included in it then continued side by side for several centuries until the latter were included in the Talmud. Moreover, although drawn from the post-biblical period, this model of intellectual coexistence between the written and the oral had deep roots in the ancient Near East. In a letter to king Esarhaddon from the seventh century B.C.E., his chief scribe and astrologer warns the king: "If Mars, retrograding, enters Scorpius, do not neglect your guard! The king should not go outdoors on an evil day. This omen is not from the Series [i.e., the written canonical series *Enuma Anu Enlil*]; it is from the oral tradition of the masters."[24]

Notwithstanding the strong scribal tradition in the ancient Near East, in legal matters writing remained secondary. Contracts were oral transac-

23 Pounder 1984: 243-50.

24 SAA 10 8, obverse line 24 through reverse line 2.

tions and although some types were usually recorded in writing, a document was not essential to their validity and could be rejected in favor of oral testimony. Even in the recording of judgments writing played a surprisingly minor role. The di-til-la documents of the Neo-Sumerian period (twenty-first century B.C.E.) are official records of court cases, presumably kept in a public archive. Nevertheless, when the court needed to hear evidence of a previous judgment, it relied not on the written record but on the testimony of a court officer (maškim), who had to be present at every case.

Affinities

The origin of the biblical law codes is thus only part of a wider question: why do the different legal systems of the ancient Near East and (to a lesser extent) of the ancient Mediterranean region show such close connections and continuity over a period of several thousand years? Seen in this light, there are elements in both models of biblical transmission that can contribute to the answer, which is complex and multi-layered. Three levels of affinity may be discerned.

First, there is some evidence for Jackson's idea of an orally transmitted custom of the region. There appears to be a deep structure of legal institutions. A prime example is inheritance, which displays the same underlying pattern in every legal system attested: universal inheritance by the legitimate heirs with a period of joint ownership until they divide by mutual consent. It is impossible to say when this pattern originated, but archaeological evidence suggests that it may date to prehistoric times, as far back as the eighth millennium B.C.E.[25] Any hypothesis as to its transmission would be highly speculative, facing the same barriers as attempts to trace the spread of prehistoric languages. But its widespread occurrence would not have been possible without long continuity as law in practice.

Second, there is the patent affinity of form and content between the law codes. Since the earliest known examples are from Mesopotamia and are closely associated with the protoscientific traditions of cuneiform literature, it is reasonable to posit a diffusion from that area into the rest of

25 Yoffee 1988: 119-30.

the Near East and even the Mediterranean basin. As Van Seters rightly observes, an obvious mode of transmission would have been copying and emulation, but it cannot provide the whole explanation. It would require the creation either of a "super-code" to cram in all the information scattered over the extant codes or of a law library for every budding author of a new code. Nor would it explain how a later code could be aware of the context of the words in an earlier text, especially one translated from a foreign language.

There is, I suggest, a third, intermediate level of affinity that derives from the intellectual activity through which law codes were created. The institution of inheritance provides a starting point. Its period of joint ownership gave rise to a myriad of problems that made the topic a favorite of the law codes, perhaps because of the intellectual challenge they presented. CE, MAL, Deuteronomy, Gortyn, and the Twelve Tables all tackle different problems arising from joint ownership by co-heirs, with little overlap between them.

Codex Eshnunna

(16) A loan of fungibles shall not be given to an undivided son or to a slave.

Middle Assyrian Laws

(B 2) If one of undivided brothers kills a person, they shall give him to the person's avenger. If he chooses, the avenger may kill him, or if he chooses he may accept composition and take his inheritance share.

(B 3) If one of undivided brothers utters treason or is a fugitive, the king may do as he pleases in respect to his inheritance share.

Deuteronomy

(25:5) If brothers dwell together and one of them dies and he has no son, the deceased's wife shall not marry outside to a stranger. Her brother-in-law shall come in unto her and take her as his wife and perform the levirate. The firstborn that she shall bear will rise up upon the name of his deceased brother, and his name will not be erased from Israel.

Gaius, *Institutes* (Roman)

(III 154a-b) But there is another kind of partnership special to Roman citizens. For at one time, when a father died, between his legitimate heirs there was a certain partnership at the same time of positive and natural law, which was called *ercto non cito*, meaning undivided ownership . . . . Now in this kind of partnership there was this peculiarity, that even one of its members by freeing a slave held in common made him free, . . . and also one member by selling a thing held in common made it the property of the person receiving it.

Justinian's *Digest* (Roman)

10.2 The Action for Dividing an Inheritance (*familia*)

(1) This action is derived from the Law of the Twelve Tables; for when co-heirs wished to dissolve their common ownership, it seemed necessary to establish some action by which the inherited property could be distributed among them (Gaius, *Prov. Ed.*, book 7).

Gortyn Code

(V 28-34) If some of the heirs wish to divide the inheritance while others do not, the judge shall order that all the property shall be in the possession of those who wish to divide until they divide.

Furthermore, these provisions were not simply an intellectual game: as testaments from Emar and Egypt attest, testators tried to create ingenious solutions to some of the difficulties that arose from joint ownership and management.

Arnaud *Textes syriens* 71 (Emar on the Euphrates, fourteenth century)

Dagan-bel, son of Itur-Dagan, spoke as follows: I have made my wife Ba'alat-ummi father and mother over my house. I have given my house and all my property to my wife Ba'alat-ummi. I have five sons: Harm, Baba, Amzahi, Himashi-Dagan, and Ibni-Dagan. My five sons shall honor [= support] Ba'alat-ummi, their mother and father. If they honor her, they may divide my house and all my property after her death. If any of my five sons, while

> Ba'alat-ummi their mother is still alive, says "(I claim) my share," he shall have no rights in my house and property. He shall place his garment on a stool and go where he pleases.
>
> Lawsuit of Mose (Egypt, thirteenth century)
>
> Testimony of Ramesses-Meiamun: I was the child of Huy, son of Urnero, daughter of Neshi. A share was allocated for Urnero together with her brothers and sisters in the great court in the time of king Haremhab . . . . Allocation was made for me together with my brothers and sisters. My mother, the citizeness Urnero, was made administrator (of the undivided estate) for her brothers and sisters.

Here then is a case where many law codes were focused on the same legal institution, were applying the same intellectual effort to analogous problems (in tandem with devices being applied in practice), but were not dependent on each other.

A second point of reference is the Talmud. Much of its discussion focuses on specific legal problems, derived either from a law in the Torah or from an actual case or possibly a fictitious case created for the sake of argument. The method is to ask, what if? What if we change the facts slightly—do we reach the same result, or should we change the legal consequence, on the basis of reasoning by analogy or because the new circumstances bring in to play another rule? It is a method of reasoning that is universally used in legal education to this very day. Looking backwards, it is also the method that lies behind the ancient law codes. For example, CH has the following sequence:

> 229 If a builder builds a house for a man and does not make his work strong and the house that he built collapses and causes the death of the householder, the builder shall be killed.
>
> 230 If it causes the death of the householder's son, they shall kill the builder's son.
>
> 231 If it causes the death of the householder's slave, he shall give slave for slave to the householder.

The sequence man, son, slave (or analogous degrees of status) frequently recurs in the law codes, giving the impression that it was a regular device used to expand the discussion of a case in a scholarly manner. I suggest that among the sources that made up a law code, alongside material taken directly from other law codes or directly from actual cases, were scholarly problems that were familiar objects of discussion. Since a law code cannot include all aspects of the discussion, different excerpts of the same problem would appear in different codes, with perhaps a different emphasis or with an extension of the discussion in a different direction. Consider the problem of the rape or seduction of a girl who is betrothed but not married, as discussed in the following law codes:

> Deuteronomy 22
>
> (23-24) If there is a maiden betrothed to a husband and a man finds her in town and lies with her, you shall take them both out to the gate of that town and stone them to death—the girl because she did not cry out in town and the man because he forced his neighbor's wife, and you shall purge the evil from your midst.
>
> (25-27) And if the man finds the betrothed girl in the country and seizes her and lies with her, the man who lay with her shall die and only he. To the girl you shall do nothing, she has no sin meriting death . . . for he found her in the country—the betrothed girl cried out but there was none to save her.
>
> (28-29) If a man finds a girl, a virgin who is not betrothed, and seizes her and lies with her and they are found, the man who lay with her shall give fifty of silver to the girl's father, and she shall be his wife. Because he forced her, he may not divorce her all his days.
>
> Codex Eshnunna
>
> (26) If a man brings the betrothal payment for a man's daughter but another seizes her and deflowers her without asking her father and mother, it is a case of life: he shall die.
>
> Codex Hammurabi
>
> (130) If a man binds and lies in the lap of the wife of a man who has not known a man and is (still) dwelling in her father's house and they seize him, that man shall be killed; that woman shall be freed.

Codex Ur-Namma

(6) If a man uses force with the virgin wife of a man and rapes her, he shall kill that man.

Exodus 22

(15-16) If a man seduces a virgin who is not betrothed and lies with her, he shall make her his wife with a betrothal payment. If her father refuses to give her to him, he shall pay silver like the betrothal payment of virgins.

Middle Assyrian Laws

(A 55) If a man seizes with force and rapes a virgin, a man's daughter who is living in her father's house . . . whose . . . has not been opened, who is not married and there is no claim against her father's house—whether in the city or in the country or at night or in the square or in a granary or at a town festival—the virgin's father shall take the wife of the man who had intercourse with his daughter and give her to be raped. He shall not return her to her husband; he shall take her. The father shall give his deflowered daughter in marriage to the man who slept with her. If he has no wife, the man who lay with her shall pay her father three times(?) the silver of the value of a virgin and he shall marry her. He shall not . . . her. If the father does not wish, he shall receive the silver, three-fold(?) that of a virgin, and give his daughter to whomever he wishes.

(A 56) If the virgin gave herself to the man, the man shall swear and his wife shall not be touched. He shall give three times(?) the silver of the value of a virgin. The father shall deal with his daughter as he chooses.

Hittite Laws

(197) If a man seizes a woman in the hills, it is the man's sin: he shall die. If he seizes her in a house, it is the woman's sin: she shall die. If the husband finds them and kills them, there is no liability upon him.

Deut 22:23-29 extends the discussion to include the rape of an unbetrothed girl. CE 26 and CH 130 discuss only the rape of a betrothed girl, while the

Mishpatim (Exod 22:15-16) consider only the seduction of an unbetrothed girl. MAL A 55 considers both rape and seduction, but only of an unbetrothed girl, and has a curious discussion of the site of the offense, the purpose of which is apparently to show that it is of no legal consequence. The rationale becomes clear from the Deuteronomic law, which contains an evidentiary test of the betrothed girl's complicity based on whether the offense took place in the town or in the country. That same test is found in HL 197, but in a very terse form with regard to the adultery of a married woman. Rather than assume that Deuteronomy had access to yet another law code that happened to spell out the distinction more explicitly, it is reasonable to suppose that Deuteronomy, MAL, and HL all were aware of the whole scholarly problem and were content to allude to it in their written versions.

Consequently, there existed behind the text of the law codes a penumbra of legal discussion to which the authors of the codes had access. This "oral law" (better regarded as a canon of traditional scholarly problems) informed the written text of codes but also existed as an independent source of law, or rather of wisdom about law.

Conclusions

The genre of text we call the law codes drew in varying measure upon three resources: an oral scholarly tradition, a written scribal tradition, and an inter-reaction with the law in practice. The first two stretched for thousands of years across the Near East and the Mediterranean, with no respect for borders or rulers.

The two clusters of everyday law in the Torah that we call law codes should be seen in this light. They are now embedded in a literary-historical account that is set during Israel's wanderings in the desert before the settlement of the promised land. They appear to have originated, however, in an intellectual tradition that biblical Israel shared with its neighbors to the east and west alike and that can be traced back more a thousand years earlier.

Scholars may continue to debate the date of the literary sources in which these biblical codes are embedded. But given the complex interaction of legal traditions behind law codes in general, it would be rash indeed to "date" the origins of the biblical codes, whether by suggesting that their contents could only have developed when certain social conditions prevailed within Israelite society or that they could only have been acquired when certain foreign texts became available.

22

Lex Talionis and Exodus 21:22-25

Abstract

The law in Exod 21:22-25 makes the local authorities responsible for maintaining peace and order in public places. If as the result of a brawl an innocent passerby is injured by persons unknown, the local authorities must pay him compensation. The pericope is not therefore concerned with the law of talio.

One of the most controversial topics in biblical law—in emotional as well as scholarly terms—is the talionic principle: "an eye for an eye." The debate over the nature of this principle has been complicated by the fact that the principal law in which it occurs itself bristles with contradictions and obscurities. Exod 21:22-25 reads (in the Authorized Version):

> If men strive, and hurt a woman with child, so that her fruit depart from her, and yet no mischief follows: he shall be surely punished, according as the woman's husband will lay upon him, and he shall pay as the judges determine. And if any mischief follow, then thou shalt give life for life, eye for eye, tooth for tooth, hand for hand, foot for foot, burning for burning, wound for wound, stripe for stripe.

Three problems emerge from the text. The first is one of syntax: the verbs of the opening protasis are in the third person plural (*ynṣw* "they fight," *ngfw* "they push"), but the first apodosis is in the singular (*y'nš* "he shall be punished"). In the second apodosis, moreover, the verb is in the

* Originally published in *Revue Biblique* 93 (1986): 52-69.

second person singular (*ntth* "you shall give"). In consequence, there seems to be no correlation between the perpetrator and the person to be punished. The second concerns the terminology. Two of the key terms in the law are of uncertain meaning. The term *'swn* is translated "mischief" in the Authorized Version, but this is little more than a guess based on the context. The context, however, itself depends upon the meaning of this term.[1] The second term, *pllym*, is traditionally translated "judges," which has served only to create problems of interpretation.[2] E. A. Speiser, who re-examined the meaning of the stem *pll* in Hebrew,[3] concluded that it meant "to estimate, assess, calculate," its use in our passage being explained by a parallel in the Hittite Laws. According to HL 17: "If anyone causes a woman to miscarry, if it is the 10th month, he shall give 10 shekels of silver; if it is the 5th month, he shall give 5 shekels of silver." The term *pllym* therefore means "calculation" of the damages according to the month of pregnancy.[4] This interpretation has been accepted by a number of modern translations,[5] but as we shall see presently, it serves only to exacerbate the problems of understanding the law.

The third problem is legal. The traditional interpretation is that the law deals with two alternatives: a miscarriage and the death of the mother (or injury to her). In the first instance the perpetrator must pay whatever the husband demands, subject to the discretion of the judges. In the second, he must suffer talionic punishment, unless monetary value is meant.[6]

The result is a law whose formulation is remarkably clumsy and whose substance is in contradiction with other rules in the same code. If the claim is assessed by judges, then the mention of the husband's discretion is oti-

1 The *Mek.* takes *'swn* to mean death (although it admits that there is no proof) on the assumption that the death of the pregnant woman is the occasion for the phrase "life for life" (Chapter VIII, *ad loc.*). Some modern translations extend it to injury as well, so as to cover all the eventualities listed in vv. 24-25, e.g., "other damage" (i.e., apart from miscarriage)—Jewish Publication Society (JPS), *The Torah*, 1962.

2 *Mek.*: *dayyanim*; Vulgata: *arbitri*. On the difficulties, see below.

3 Speiser 1963: 301-6.

4 Speiser 1963: 303.

5 E.g., Jewish Publication Society (see n. 1 above), New English Bible.

6 See the summary of ancient and modern opinions in Paul 1970: 72-74, and in Jackson 1975: 81-85.

ose. And if, as Speiser claimed,[7] it is not judges that are being referred to, but determination of the damages by an objective calculation, then the contradiction is even more apparent.[8] In the second instance, capital punishment is imposed where a pregnant woman is killed in the course of a brawl, whereas according to Exod 21:13, a killer who did not lie in wait for his victim has a right to asylum in a place of refuge. If the woman is only injured, the punishment is the same injury, whereas in Exod 21:18-19 only limited compensation, in the form of medical expenses and loss of time, is to be paid where a man suffers a non-fatal assault in the course of a quarrel. Even if the talionic formula is interpreted to mean monetary compensation, there would seem to be no reason for using a different basis of compensation, at least for non-permanent injuries.[9]

It is not surprising, therefore, that most modern scholars see the law as composite.[10] But what these commentators do not explain is why any ancient compiler would want to reduce two separate laws to one or turn a previously sensible rule into a less sensible one by additions or corrections. A notable exception is Jackson, who attempts to demonstrate that the original law went through a series of reforms achieved by deliberate interpolation.[11]

Jackson's basic thesis[12] is that the original law ended at the phrase "life for life" and considered two alternatives: premature birth (of a viable fetus) as the result of a blow to the mother; death of the fetus (*'swn*), i.e., miscarriage.[13] The addition of verse 24 ("eye for eye," etc.) changed the meaning of the original law, so that it now referred to the death of the fetus in the first alternative and to the death of (or injury to) the mother (*'swn*) in the second alternative, since a fetus cannot lose a tooth.

7 Speiser 1963: 303.

8 See the criticism in Jackson 1975: 80.

9 For an attempt at reconciling these sources, see Paul 1970: 74, and the criticism of Jackson 1975: 87-89.

10 See especially Budde 1891: 108-11, and Morgenstern 1930: 69-71, 83-84; but also Cazelles 1946: 56, and even Cassuto 1967: 276.

11 Jackson 1975: 81-85.

12 Jackson 1975: 95-96. We cannot do justice here to the whole of Jackson's extremely detailed analysis, which ascribes virtually every unexplained item in the law to interpolation and gives it a specific place in the historical development.

13 Adopting the interpretation of LXX and Philo (Jackson 1975: 96).

This theory has been severely criticized by S. E. Loewenstamm[14] on the grounds that the possibility of premature birth being an issue is unlikely and unattested by the ancient Near Eastern parallels, which all present the death of the fetus and of the mother as the two alternatives. Loewenstamm points out that the one, very late, piece of supporting evidence adduced by Jackson, a Greek papyrus from Egypt dated 89 B.C.E., does not in fact mention premature birth and was probably not concerned with that eventuality at all. Moreover, the technique of amendment suggested by Jackson is far too sophisticated for the biblical legislator, or any other in the history of law.[15] But in attempting to explain the law's inconsistencies other than in terms of legal-historical development, Loewenstamm can only suggest textual confusion: the text of a law dealing with a blow given to a pregnant woman has become mixed up with the text of another law providing for the consequences of blows which men dealt one another in a brawl.[16]

We shall not enter into a detailed discussion of the relative sophistication or clumsiness of the biblical draftsman since in our view all theories that assume changes in the text are on an unsound basis as long as two key words in that text remain unclear.[17] We propose an entirely different approach, starting from the assumption that the text is an organic whole and represents a single and perfectly sensible law.

Our method is to ask, on a simple reading of the text:

1. What is the legal problem raised by the protasis?
2. How would a reasonable law go about dealing with that problem?
3. What meaning could be attributed to our two key terms that would fit such a law?
4. Can the presumed meaning in each case be justified by reference to the other occurrences of the term in the Bible?

14 Loewenstamm 1977: 352-60.

15 Loewenstamm 1977: 353-55.

16 Loewenstamm 1977: 357.

17 Thus Loewenstamm (1977: 358) surmises that the terms *'swn* and *pllym* are unknown because they come from a dialect peculiar to the area where the law originated and where the standard of draftsmanship was low.

If by this means a law can be reconstructed that is objectively feasible and internally consistent, then further details can be elucidated by the usual methods of comparison with ancient Near Eastern laws and other parallels.

The protasis opens with the words "if men fight and they push a pregnant woman and her fetus comes out." The scene is one of a brawl, with an indeterminate number of participants. A pregnant woman who is passing is caught up in the melee and is jostled, perhaps knocked to the ground, and has a miscarriage. Who pushed her? The verb is in the third person plural, and since it is unlikely that they all pushed her at the same time, it must signify an indeterminate subject—one of them pushed her.

From these circumstances we may conclude that the legal problem involved was the question of responsibility for damage when the identity of the actual perpetrator cannot be ascertained. The legal discussion distinguishes between two alternatives: if it is a case of *'swn* or not. On our hypothesis, these alternatives will be concerned with the location of responsibility rather than the nature of the damage. We therefore suggest that the term *'swn* describes the problematic case, i.e., damage caused by an unknown perpetrator.

The next step is to see if this interpretation is valid in other contexts. The word *'swn* occurs only three times elsewhere in the Bible, all in the Joseph story, and indeed all in Jacob's statements of reluctance to send Benjamin to Egypt with his brothers.[18]

To understand why he is so reluctant, we must go back to the disappearance of Joseph and to the plan adopted by the brothers to conceal their responsibility. They dip Joseph's coat in blood and present it to Jacob.[19] The legal significance of this act has been elucidated by D. Daube.[20]

In biblical law, as set out in Exod 22:10-12, a shepherd is *prima facie* responsible for the safety of the herd entrusted to him and if an animal is lost or stolen he must pay for it, unless the cause was *force majeure*, in particular wild beasts. In the latter case he escapes liability altogether, the only condition being that he bring a remnant of the devoured animal by way of evidence.

18 Gen 42:4, 38; 44:29.
19 Gen 37:31-33.
20 Daube 1947: 3-15.

According to Daube, the brothers dyed Joseph's coat red and delivered it to Jacob as the only trace left of his child, in order to take advantage of the law. In other words, they claimed that not only were they innocent; they were not even negligent.[21]

The brothers submit formal evidence and ask Jacob to accept it: "They said: 'We found this: recognize it as your son's robe or not.'"[22] Jacob accepts their evidence, as he must, because they have fulfilled the conditions laid down by the law, and makes a formal declaration as to the cause of death: "He recognized it. He said: 'It is my son's robe. A wicked beast ate him. Joseph is surely torn to pieces.'"[23] Jacob's acceptance, however, is only formal. He did not really believe it, as we see from the reported statement of his in Gen 44:28: "The one went away from me—I said, 'He is surely torn to pieces,' and I have not seen him since." Jacob does not say that Joseph was killed by wild beasts but that he made a formal declaration to this effect, and his curious closing remark would not have been made were he convinced of Joseph's death. In other words, he still suspected Joseph's brothers.[24]

Now we can understand why Jacob will not let Benjamin accompany his brothers to Egypt, even though the family is starving. He fears that another *'swn* will happen to Benjamin as happened to Joseph, i.e., a disaster for which nobody can be blamed.[25] Jacob only changes his mind after two of the brothers agree to accept strict responsibility for Benjamin's safety.[26]

The texts in Genesis therefore confirm, if Daube's theory is accepted, that *'swn* refers to cases where responsibility cannot be located. Daube noted that his explanation of *'swn* as a technical legal term did not appear to apply to our passage in Exodus and found this curious, since the context

21 Daube 1947: 4-5.

22 Gen 37:32.

23 Gen 37:33. As Daube points out, the terminology is in fact identical to that of the law in Exod 22:12: *ṭrp ṭrp*.

24 Daube 1947: 9. We would add: not necessarily of murder. Kidnapping and sale into slavery (presumably abroad) was common enough practice (Exod 21:16; Deut 24:7).

25 Daube 1947: 10. According to Jackson, *'swn* stresses the effect of death or injury on some person other than the direct victim (1975: 78, 96). But Jacob fears that the *'swn* will befall "him," i.e., Benjamin, the direct victim. It doubtless would be a calamity for Jacob as well, but this is not what is stated.

26 Gen 42:37; 43:9. Daube 1947: 13.

is legal,[27] but on our interpretation of the law, it fits perfectly. The only difference is that in our passage, one man is certainly responsible, but since he cannot be identified, it is impossible to impose liability for punishment or compensation. Thus the first alternative envisaged by the law becomes clear: if it is *not* a case of *'swn* (v. 22), then the identity of the perpetrator must be known, and he alone must bear the penalty. Accordingly, the verb is expressed in the singular: "he shall surely be punished." The punishment is ransom, either of his own life or possibly of his son's life, since the death of a fetus was the damage caused.[28] This is made clear by the terminology used: "as the woman's husband shall impose (*yšyt*) upon him," which is the same as for the owner of a goring ox: "If ransom is imposed (*ywšt*) upon him, he shall pay as the redemption of his life all that is imposed (*ywšt*) upon him" (v. 30). It also explains the apparently unlimited discretion of the husband, because it is in the nature of a claim of ransom-money that there is no *legal* limit, but there is, on the other hand, a natural limit of how much a man is willing, or able, to pay for his own (or his son's) life.[29]

The exact measure of the ransom is not mentioned, because that is not the rule to be established by this law—it is already known. The point of the law is to establish the sole liability of the perpetrator. It is therefore reasonable to suppose that the final phrase of v. 22, "he shall give *bpllym*," refers not to the question of measure of damages—which is satisfactorily covered in the previous phrase—but to the idea of sole responsibility. We propose to translate: "he shall pay *alone*."

Again, we must see if this translation is valid elsewhere in the Bible. The form[30] is unique to our passage, but the stem *pll* appears as an adjective in two other contexts. In Deut 32:30-31 we read:

27 Daube 1947: 10.

28 Cf. CH 116, 210, 230; MAL A 55.

29 This limitation affects the plaintiff also. He may well regard the execution of the offender as empty satisfaction and therefore not claim more than the man can pay.

30 The grammatical form of *bpllym* is admittedly not clear. Possibly it is a noun, *plurale tantum*, with the adverbial prefix *b*-. On the other hand, the final *mem* may be the adverbial ending itself, but then one must assume that the *yod* is redundant and the prefix a hyper-correction like the post-biblical *bḥnm*. I am grateful to Dr. S. Kogut of the Hebrew University for drawing my attention to this point.

> How should one chase a thousand, and two put ten thousand to flight, except their Rock had sold them, and the LORD had shut them up? For their rock is not as our Rock, even our enemies themselves being judges.

The last clause, translating *w'ybynw plylym*, is clearly unsatisfactory. Speiser, who, as we have seen, took the stem *pll* to mean "reckon," proposed here: "even in our enemies' estimation."[31] But Israel's enemies surely did not regard their own deities as less efficacious than the God of Israel, and it seems to us doubtful that the biblical poet would make such an unlikely claim.[32] Far more appropriate to his theology is the rendering: "For their rock is not as our Rock; our enemies are *alone*." Other nations have no real god; only the God of Israel rules the destiny of all nations, and Israel cannot therefore be defeated except by a decision of its own God.

The term *'wn plyly(m)* occurs in Job 31:11 and 28. The Authorized Version translates: "an iniquity to be punished by the judge(s)," but in both cases it patently is not a justiciable offense.[33]

In vv. 9-10 a man conceives a secret lust for his neighbor's wife and lurks at her door, and in vv. 26-27 he is secretly tempted to worship the sun and the moon. Speiser translated "an assessable transgression,"[34] which gives no sense that we can discern. In our view the emphasis added by the term *plyly(m)* is on Job bearing sole responsibility for calamities that befall him, and not God, if they are the result of secret vices.[35] We

31 Speiser 1963: 303.

32 The JPS adopts Speiser's translation but then explains: "i.e., as everyone must admit"—which is not at all the same.

33 This is true of all the offenses listed in chapter 31. They are sins which must be punished by God, because they are not subject to human justice. Divine punishment will generally take the form of sickness. Such a list forms the subject matter of Tablet II of the Sumero-Akkadian incantation series, *Šurpu*, which beseeches the gods to forgive the sick, downcast patient who is suffering as a result of his moral or cultic offenses. Edited in Reiner 1958. Cf. Geller 1980.

34 Speiser 1963: 304.

35 The punishment in v. 10 for the man who secretly lusts after his neighbor's wife is: "Let my wife grind for another, and others bend over her." If the first verb is interpreted literally, i.e., that Job's wife will become another's slave and do menial tasks such as milling, then it would be an example of vicarious talio, where a member of the

shall see presently that the stem *pll* is employed in another case where the question is whether to locate responsibility with God or with man. Here it signifies "a sin for which I alone am responsible."

If the idea of sole responsibility underlines the stem *pll*, then the *piel* form of the verb should signify the shifting of responsibility unto either the subject or the object of the verb. Eli's admonition to his wicked sons in 1 Sam 2:25 has long been a crux of interpretation.[36] Following the conventional meanings attributed to *pll*, the literal translation is: "If a man does wrong against a man, God will judge him (*wpllw 'lhym*); but if a man does wrong against the LORD, who will pray for him (*ytpll lw*)?" This makes little sense, and even if, as is frequently proposed, the first or the second verb, or both, is rendered "intervene," "intercede" or the like, the result is no clearer.[37]

We translate: "If a man does wrong against a man, God may take the blame for him; but if a man does wrong against the LORD, who will bear responsibility for him?" *Prima facie*, it sounds absurd to contemplate God taking the blame for a human offense, but this is exactly what happens in Exod 21:13. A man who kills another is to be put to death, but not if "God caused it to happen to his hand" (*'nh lydw*). In modern terms, the perpetrator could claim that it was an accident, but the concept of causation in

---

offender's family suffers the same treatment as was suffered by the equivalent member of the victim family. (This can even include sexual abuse: MAL A 55.) It is nonetheless conceived of as punishment of the offender himself. Another possibility, which we tentatively propose, is that the verb *tṭḥn* ("she will grind") should be amended to read *tṭḥh* and translated "she will approach (sexually)," on the basis of the Akkadian cognate *ṭeḫû* (cf. *Šurpu* II 48). This would make perfect parallelism with the second verb but change the character of the wife's actions from punishment imposed on her to adultery of her own initiative. The sense would then be that if Job were to plan adultery for his part, it would be his own fault if his wife were to commit adultery for her part. This in fact is the traditional Jewish interpretation of the verse, assuming *ṭḥn* ("grind") to be a euphemism for sexual intercourse; see the *b. Soṭah* 10a.

36 See Houtman 1977: 412-17, who summarizes the various theories.

37 Speiser (1963) translates the first phrase "God can intervene." He does not explain how or why God would intervene, nor how this rendering is connected with the notion of calculating, which as we have seen is posited by him as the basic meaning of the stem. Houtman (1977) concludes that *'lhym* means a "good spirit," i.e., some exceptional person who ventures to intercede for the sinner. With respect, scholarly constructions such as these strike us as a *tabula in naufragio*.

biblical law does not allow for accident in the death of a man. It is the result of will, either divine or human. The accused, in pleading accident, would therefore do so by blaming God.

To return to Eli and his sons, the latter committed acts that were at the same time offenses against men (those bringing sacrifices) and God (the intended recipient). Eli's point is that his sons might find some legal excuse[38] for their conduct to avoid retribution at human hands; no such protection would be available against divine retribution.

Ps 106:30 provides a clearer example of the same idea: "Pinhas stood and *ypll*, and the plague was halted." What exactly Pinhas did is related in Num 25:7-8. He neither judged, prayed, nor interceded with God; instead: "he went after the man of Israel into the tent, and thrust both of them through, the man of Israel, and the woman through her belly. So the plague was halted." In the eyes of the Psalmist, Pinhas took upon himself the blood-guilt and relieved the community of liability.

In Ezek 16:51-52, the prophet compares Jerusalem unfavorably with her sister, Samaria:

> Neither hath Samaria committed half of thy sins; but thou hast multiplied thine abominations more than they, and hast justified thy sisters in all thine abominations which thou hast done. Thou also, which hast judged (*pllt*) thy sisters, bear thine own shame for thy sins that thou hast committed more abominable than they; they are more righteous than thou: yea, be thou confounded also, and bear thy shame, in that thou hast justified thy sisters (Authorized Version).

Speiser translates *pll* here "you have caused (re)assessment in favor of your sisters," but there is no need for such circuitous logic.[39] The prophet states expressly what has happened: by being so much worse than her sis-

38 Obviously not accident in this case, but there might have been some justification within the framework of the sacrificial rules. They might even have warded off complaints with the claim that their method reflected divine will.

39 Speiser 1963: 304. The logic of other recent translations is even more convoluted, e.g., "you must bear the humiliation which you thought your sisters deserved" (NEB); "you must bear the disgrace of serving as your sisters' advocate" (JPS).

ter Samaria, Jerusalem has taken over responsibility for the sins of the latter, who appears innocent in her light.

The final passage in which the *piel* form of the verb *pll* appears is Gen 48:11: "And Israel said to Joseph, 'I had not thought (*pllty*) to see your face.'" Here, at least, Speiser's hypothesis might seem acceptable. His rendering "counted on, figured"[40] reflects the obvious intent of the statement and is easily derived from the idea of assessment. Nonetheless, this passage stands apart from those discussed above in that the use of the verb is not legal, and some extended, figurative sense may therefore be allowed. We do not consider it stretching the basic meaning too far if the literal translation "I did not take upon myself the seeing of your face" were taken to convey the idea that Israel could not assume responsibility for holding out hope.

In summary, we submit that the above forms of the stem *pll* indicate, at least in a legal context, the basic notion of sole responsibility.[41]

We now turn to the second alternative: where it is a case of *'swn*—in our interpretation, a case of perpetrator unknown. From a theoretical legal point of view, two possibilities immediately present themselves: that there is no liability at all,[42] or that there is joint liability of all the participants in the brawl. The first is definitely excluded, since the apodosis does discuss

40 Speiser 1963: 304.

41 The stem *pll* also occurs twice in the form of a noun, in Isa 16:3 (*plylh*) and 28:7 (*plylyh*). In our view, they are not connected with the examples discussed above but with the Akkadian verb *palālu* ("to watch over, be watchful"), often describing the activity of a scout. (See Speiser 1968: 389-91; *AHw* 813). In the first verse God is asked to watch over (or act as scout or look-out for?) a group of refugees fleeing the enemy, and in the second, the participants in a drinking orgy are so drunk that they cannot see straight nor maintain watchfulness. We would likewise not attempt to connect the *hitpael* form, *htpll* "to pray," with our proposed meaning, except in the case of 1 Sam 2:25. It may be derived from a separate stem altogether; see *HAL*[3] 881-82. On the other hand, the cognate stems *pl'* and *plh* may show some semantic connection, as in phrases such as: "a man who takes upon himself an oath" (*ypl' ndr* in Lev 27:2) and "we have been set apart (*npl'nw*), I and your people, from all peoples" (Exod 33:16). I am grateful to Dr. S. Kogut for drawing my attention to this point.

42 This is the principle followed by Talmudic law in an analogous case: "When ten persons beat a man with ten sticks, whether simultaneously or successively, so that he died, none of them is guilty of murder" (*b. B. Qam.* 10b).

some sort of punishment, and the second finds no reflection in the laconic words "you shall give life for life, etc."

There is, however, a third possibility, suggested by comparative laws from the ancient Near East. Codex Hammurabi 22-24 provides:

> If a man commits robbery and is caught, that man shall be put to death. If the robber is not caught, the person robbed shall declare his lost property before the god, and the city and mayor in whose territory or district the robbery was committed shall replace his lost property. If it is a case of life (i.e., murder), the city and mayor shall pay his family one mina of silver.

The law is divided into two alternative cases, on the same pattern as our biblical text: if the perpetrator is found; if he is not found. In the former case, the robber must pay the penalty; in the latter, it is the local public authority, representing the community as a whole, that is held responsible.

The same solution is applied at Ugarit, in a series of treaties with neighboring states dealing with the problem of the murder and robbery of travelers from one state in the territory of the other. RS 17.230 reads:[43]

> 1-3 Ini-Teshub, king of Carchemish, has made this treaty with the "men of Ugarit."
> 4-6 If a man from Carchemish is killed in the land of Ugarit,
> 7-12 if they catch the one who killed him, he shall pay three times a man (lu$_2$ 3-*šu ú-ma-al-la*)[44] and three times the possessions that disappeared with him (the victim);
> 13-19 if they do not find the one who killed him, they shall pay three times a life (*napišta* [zi] 3-*šu ú-ma-al-lu-ú*) and the possessions that disappeared with him—*in simplum.*
> 20-23 And if a man from Ugarit is killed in the land of Carchemish, the same payment (*mu-ul-la-a*) applies.

43 Edited in Nougayrol 1956: 153-54.

44 Nougayrol (1956: 153-54) translates "ils paieront," but the verb is in the singular. Nor, as our discussion of the contents will show, need it be corrected to the plural, as does the *CAD*: "they (!) pay" (in M/1 182, s.v. *malû*, meaning 6e).

In addition to seeing the same pattern as in CH 22-24, and the same imposition of responsibility on the community for an unsolved murder, we obtain some interesting data on terminology. The phrase "pay a man" (line 9) is a synonym for "pay a life" (line 14), as the parallelism of the clauses shows,[45] and both are referred to as a *mullû* (line 23).

The term *mullû* occurs frequently at Ugarit to designate a penalty for murder or theft, in conjunction with verbs of payment: either *mullû*, *šullumu*, or *nadānu*.[46] A further treaty between Ugarit and Carchemish concerning the robbery and murder of expatriate merchants makes it clear that a money payment is involved.[47] Where merchants from Ugarit have been robbed and murdered in Carchemish, the "sons of Carchemish" must "pay as *mullû* for one man 3 mina of silver."[48] Where merchants from Carchemish have been robbed and murdered in Ugarit, the same penalty applies, expressed somewhat more explicitly as: "3 mina of silver as *mullû* for one man, for the blood."[49]

45 Cf. RS 17.251 (edited in Nougayrol 1956: 237), where a payment of "10 lives" is imposed for the illegal seizure of a person.

46 For references, see *CAD* M/2 189, s.v. *mullû* A.

47 RS 17.146 (Nougayrol 1956: 154-57). The verb *ml'* also exists in Biblical Hebrew with the meaning "to pay in full"; see 1 Sam 18:27.

48 Lines 12-14 *ù mu-ul-lu ša* 1-*en* 3 MA.NA KU$_3$.BABBAR DUMU.MEŠ KUR URU *kar-ka-meš ú-šal-la-mu-ni*

Lines 26-27 *ù* DUMU.MEŠ KUR URU *kar-kà-meš* 3 MA.NA KU$_3$.BABBAR.MEŠ *mu-ul-la-a ša* 1-*en* LU$_2$-*lim ú-šal-la-mu-ni*

While following the same basic pattern as the previous treaty, this treaty is considerably more complex, involving as it does royal merchants and mercantile guilds. Strangely enough, the guild is held liable not only when the murderers are not found, but even when they are, and in the latter case for reimbursement of goods as well. Logically, one would have expected the more severe penalty on the guild in the former case. The reason would seem to be that the guild is expected to guarantee a minimum compensation should the robbers be insolvent. It might also provide immunity from later proceedings should (as is likely) the stolen goods eventually find their way into some of their member's hands. On the strict liability of an innocent receiver of stolen goods, see Westbrook and Wilcke 1974-77.

49 Lines 34-35 *ù ša* 1-*en* LU$_2$-*lim* 3 MA.NA KU$_3$.BABBAR.MEŠ *mu-ul-la-a ša damê* (= UŠ$_2$.MEŠ) DUMU.MEŠ KUR URU *u-ga-ri-it ú-ma-al-lu-ni*

Cf. lines 43-44 *ú* DUMU.MEŠ KUR URU *u-ga-ri-it* 3 MA.NA KU$_3$.BABBAR.MEŠ *mu-ul-la-a ša* 1-*en* LU$_2$-*lim ú-ma-al-lu-nim-ma*.

Finally, in a lawsuit apparently based on a similar treaty, a merchant representing the king of Tarhudashi sues the "sons of Ugarit" over a merchant of Tarhudashi who was robbed and murdered in their territory.[50] The judgment (of the king of Carchemish) is that the "sons of Ugarit" must pay the *mullû* of that merchant. The text continues (lines 16-19): "the sons of Ugarit paid 180 shekels of silver (i.e., 3 mina) as *mullû* to Arshi-miga the servant of the king of Tarhudashi."[51]

It may therefore be concluded that the phrase "pay a life" refers to the payment of a fixed sum representing the value of a person. That value may be fixed by treaty or statute but often appears to be a matter of traditional law. The payment may be increased by multiplying the number of "persons/lives" (i.e., their fixed value) to be paid.

Furthermore, the phrase "to pay a life" is found not only in the context of murder but also of causing miscarriage. According to the Middle Assyrian Laws A 50, a person who strikes a pregnant woman and causes her to miscarry "shall pay a life" (*napšāte umalla*).[52] His penalty is therefore a sum representing the value of the life lost. Only if there are aggravated circumstances, such as the death of the mother herself, or the fact of the fetus being a firstborn son to her husband, is the penalty death.[53]

The solution proffered by the cuneiform sources to the problem of death by an unknown hand is therefore to place responsibility on the local public authority, which is obliged to pay the injured party[54] a money penalty. This principle obtained also in the Bible in the case of murder, as is evidenced by the ceremony of the heifer in Deut 21:1-9. Where there is an unsolved murder, the elders (*inter alia*) of the city in whose territory the corpse was found must take an exculpatory oath: "our hands did not shed this blood and our eyes did not see" (v. 7). In a letter from the king of Car-

50 RS 17.158 (see Nougayrol 1956: 169-71).

51 The term *mullû* also exists at Nuzi as the payment of a penalty for various offenses. The payment is in money, slaves, or animals, as fixed by the court. See the references in *CAD* M/2 189-90, s.v. *mullû* A.

52 Literally, "lives," but it is a *plurale tantum*, as its use in MAL B 2 shows. The same penalty for causing a miscarriage is found in paragraph 52 of Tablet A.

53 The connection of the paragraph with the texts from Ugarit and its meaning of money payment were pointed out by Paul 1970: 72 n. 6. For other views, see Driver and Miles 1935: 111-14; and Jackson 1975: 97-98.

54 The relatives of the deceased. See below.

chemish to the king of Ugarit[55] concerning a woman whose husband was murdered in the city of Arzigana, a virtually identical oath is imposed upon the "men of Arzigana": "we did not kill the husband of the woman, brother of X, in the city. We do not know who killed him."[56] If the "men of Arzigana" withdraw from the oath, they must pay a certain sum to the widow of the murdered man.[57]

Returning to our passage in the Bible, we submit that the phrase "you shall give a life" in v. 23 means that the community must pay the value of a life to the husband of the woman who miscarried in the case where the identity of the person whose blow caused the miscarriage cannot be ascertained, since:

i) this is the solution offered for death by an unknown hand in Codex Hammurabi and in the texts from Ugarit considered above, which all present the problem in the same terms that we have posited for our passage;

ii) the idea of community responsibility for death by an unknown hand is explicitly recognized in the Bible in Deut 21:1-9;

iii) the terminology of the Ugarit texts, "pay a life," is the same as that of v. 23;

iv) that same terminology is employed in the context of causing miscarriage in the Middle Assyrian Laws;

v) the phrase itself indicates a shift in the subject of the rule: "*you* (singular) shall give . . . ."

This final point needs some elaboration. The sudden and unexpected use of the second person singular here has long been a source of perplexity. For Cazelles, it indicated an attempt by the redactor to stitch

55 RS 20.22, edited in Nougayrol et al. 1968: 95, 97 (no. 27).

56 Lines 46-50.

57 Lines 52-55. It is not at all certain that the "men of Arzigana" entirely escaped liability by taking the oath. Line 51, which states the consequences, is unfortunately broken at beginning and end. Nougayrol (1968: 95-97 n. 2) suggests that the oath only relieved them of liability for compensation payable apart from the standard penalty. It might refer to the penalty for goods lost.

together two different laws.[58] For most other commentators, it is a clear case of interpolation.[59] Only A. Alt tried to give the form an original function, with the unlikely hypothesis that the verse originally referred to a cultic offering.[60]

We would point to another function of the second person singular, which is attested in the Book of the Covenant, namely to direct a law at the community as a whole (or its representatives), e.g., "from my altar you (singular) shall take him to die" (21:14); "you (singular) shall not suffer a witch to live" (22:17). The form "you shall give," therefore fits our reconstruction of the law perfectly, in terms of both the change in subject and the latter's identity.

Once the expression "give a life" is understood as the payment of a set sum at which a person's life is valued, then the continuation of the phrase in v. 23 "instead of a life" (*tḥt*[61] *nfš*) causes no difficulty. It merely identifies the loss for which the penalty is being paid. This can be done by naming the object lost (where the loss is total—actual or constructive)[62] or the nature of the damage where it is partial (e.g., burning). In the context of delict, a non-literal translation of the term "instead of" (*tḥt*) would, we suggest, be "as the penalty for."[63] The term does not assume that the penalty in question must necessarily be the mirror image of the loss caused. In the Book of the Covenant itself, a person who puts out his slave's eye must set the slave free "as the penalty for his eye" (*tḥt ʿynw*, 21:26), the owner

58 Cazelles 1946: 55-56.

59 E.g., Morgenstern 1930: 68-69, and 70 n. 72, discussing the older commentators; Jackson 1975: 100; and Phillips 1970: 89.

60 Alt 1934b: 303-5. Alt's only evidence is a votive stele to the god Saturn from Nicivibus (in North Africa), dated to around 200 B.C.E. He does not explain why no such offering is adumbrated in the other laws concerning homicide or unlawful wounding, or for that matter why, if an offering could be made for a wound, one should not be made for a lost fetus.

61 *HAL*[3] 1026: "an Stelle von, anstatt, für," from a basic meaning of "unterhalb von."

62 Thus in CH 245-246 payment is "an ox instead of (*kīma*) an ox," both where the plaintiff's ox is actually killed and where it suffers an injury so severe as to make it unfit for use as a farm animal.

63 There is certainly an element of compensation, as payment may be made to the injured party, but since the payment is by no means always an indemnity, we consider it more suitable—in this context—to emphasize the penal element.

of a goring ox that kills another's ox must pay[64] an ox "as the penalty for the ox" (*tḥt hšwr*, 21:36), and the thief of an ox must pay five cattle "as the penalty for the ox" (21:37). Payment of the penalty can thus take the form of the same type of item, a multiple of similar items, or an abstract legal act. Likewise in the Middle Assyrian Laws, in the case of a simple miscarriage, the person responsible must pay a life "as the penalty for her fetus" (*kimu ša libbiša*),[65] but where the circumstances are aggravated by the fact that the fetus was a firstborn son, he is put to death likewise "as the penalty for her fetus."[66]

The final problem that remains is the continuation of the formula in vv. 24-25, "an eye instead of an eye, a tooth instead of a tooth, etc." Although this list has been considered a later addition to the main text,[67] the very nature of the ancient Near Eastern law codes provides a ready explanation for its presence. The principle behind the imposition of liability on a city for cases of unsolved murder was the responsibility of the city for the safety of travelers on the roads of its territory. The principle behind the imposition of liability on the community in the law in Exodus was similarly the safety of passersby in the streets. But in neither case is the abstract principle given express formulation—this is not the method of the law codes. Instead the casuistic method typical of those codes is used. In the Exodus law, the principle of responsibility for safety in the streets is expressed firstly by a strong example, the pregnant woman who is jostled by brawlers, and this example "generalized" by adding a long list of further examples, to show that any injury to an innocent passerby will come under the same rule.[68]

To summarize: the law in Exod 21:22-25 provides that if an innocent passerby is injured as a result of a brawl and the person responsible is not caught, the community must pay a money penalty to the victim in lieu of the ransom-money that the victim could otherwise have claimed. The money penalty will be a fixed sum and is therefore likely to be lower than

64 Note that the variation between the verb *šlm* here and *ntn* in the law of the pregnant woman is paralleled by the interchangeable use in RS 17.146 of *šullumu* (lines 12, 27, 43) and *mullû* (line 34).

65 MAL A 50 (col. VII, lines 68-69, 72-73).

66 MAL A 50 (col. VII, lines 78-79).

67 Jackson 1975: 94, 106-7.

68 On this technique, see Bottéro 1982: esp. 434-35.

the ransom-money that could have been demanded from the perpetrator himself.[69]

Accordingly, we would translate the passage as follows:

> If men fight and a pregnant woman is pushed and has a miscarriage, if it is not a case of perpetrator unknown, he (the perpetrator) shall surely be punished as the woman's husband shall impose (ransom) upon him, and he shall pay alone. If it is a case of perpetrator unknown, you (the community) shall pay a life as the penalty for a life, an eye as the penalty for an eye, a tooth as the penalty for a tooth, an arm as the penalty for an arm, a leg as the penalty for a leg, a burn as the penalty for a burn, a wound as the penalty for a wound, a bruise as the penalty for a bruise.

The passage therefore provides no information as to the existence of a talionic principle for physical injuries in biblical law.

Excursus

Our investigation is now completed within the terms of reference that we set for it at the beginning of this article. It would be helpful, however, to try to explain the law in Lev 24:17-21 in the light of our findings. A modern idiomatic translation (JPS) reads:

> If a man kills any human being, he shall be put to death. One who kills a beast shall make restitution for it: life for life. If anyone maims his fellow, as he has done so shall it be done to him: fracture for fracture, eye for eye, tooth for tooth. The injury he inflicted on another shall be inflicted on him. He who kills a beast shall make restitution for it; but he who kills a human being shall be put to death.

69 In the treaties from Ugarit, the penalty on the community is always lower than that imposed on the perpetrator himself. Penalties such as death, ransom, or talio would in any case not be appropriate for a public body.

The law unambiguously demands literal retaliation, using the same terminology as in Exod 21:23-25. How can the two laws be reconciled, on our interpretation of the latter? We tentatively suggest that the Leviticus pericope is an exegesis of the law in Exodus (or one very similar in form) and a strained one at that. A more literal translation will make our point clear:

> A man who strikes dead any life of a human shall be killed. One who strikes dead a life of a beast shall pay it life instead of life. A man who gives a blemish in his fellow: as he did, so shall be done to him—fracture instead of fracture, eye instead of eye, tooth instead of tooth. As he put a blemish on his fellow so shall be put on him. One who strikes dead a beast shall pay it; one who strikes dead a human shall be killed.

What reasoning lies behind this extraordinarily prolix and repetitive language? This passage in Leviticus belongs to a source that is known for its bitter opposition to the common practice of accepting ransom-money in lieu of the murderer's execution.[70] Thus in Num 35:31-32 we read:

> You shall not take ransom-money for the life of a murderer who has done wrong deserving death, but he shall be put to death. Nor shall you take ransom-money in lieu of his fleeing to his city of refuge (or) returning to live on his land before the death of the priest. You shall not pollute the land in which you live, for blood pollutes the land, and the land can have no ransom for the blood which is shed on it except by the blood of him who shed it.

We surmise that the author of this passage had before him the text of the Exodus law, or one very similar to it, containing the well-known phrase "pay a life instead of a life"—which was known to mean money payment—and less well known phrases such as "an eye instead of an eye," which perhaps had been coined only for the particular law. This precedent needed to be distinguished if his view was to prevail, and he did so in the

70 The Priestly source. See Eissfeldt 1964: 235 (in the English edition); and McKeating 1975: 64-65.

passage in Leviticus by a method of reasoning that presages Talmudic interpretation: "life" in the text before us does not refer, as one would normally suppose, to *human* life, but to *animal* life, and the text is therefore not a precedent for accepting ransom-money for homicide.[71] The remaining members of the formula, now divorced from the familiar "pay a life," can therefore be interpreted as literal retaliation.[72] The final step is to summarize the results of this exegesis in the author's own words: "one who strikes dead a beast shall pay it; one who strikes dead a human shall be killed."

71 The interpretation is not entirely fantastic, since CH 245 rules that a man who, by neglect or by blows, kills another's ox, must replace "ox instead of ox." But the circumstances are the very specialized ones of a contract of hire; otherwise it is rare for people to kill oxen. Perhaps CH 245-248 provided the inspiration for the Levitical author's exegesis, since the sequence of injuries there (to the ox) are: life, fracture (of leg or neck), eye, horn (tooth?).

72 Note that the verb *šlm*, which can only refer to payment, is used in connection with the life of a beast, while the verb *ntn*, which as we have seen is synonymous with *šlm* in this context and is so used in the Exodus law (n. 64 above), but does have a broader range of meanings, is used in connection with the various injuries in the less usual sense of "put on" and thus can be interpreted as "inflict."

23

The Deposit Law of Exodus 22:6-12

Abstract

Exod 22:6-12 comprises two laws dealing with the responsibility of depositees. Both form coherent legal rules, consistent in their individual parts, that may be explained without recourse to theories of diachronic change or editing. The first concerns goods deposited for safekeeping in a house and tests the owner's claim of fraudulent breach of contract by the depositee by recourse to an oracular procedure. The second concerns a herding contract and provides for exculpatory oaths by the depositee, on the one hand, against a claim of misuse of an animal and by the owner, on the other, against a claim of fraudulent recaption.

The Covenant Code contains a number of rules relating to the responsibilities of the depositee. In a modern translation, Exod 22:6-12 reads:

> (6)When a man gives money or goods to another for safekeeping, and they are stolen from the man's house—if the thief is caught, he shall pay double; (7)if the thief is not caught, the owner of the house shall depose before God that he has not laid hands on his neighbor's property. (8)In all charges of misappropriation—pertaining to an ox, an ass, a sheep, a garment, or any other loss, whereof one party alleges, "This is it"—the case of both parties shall come before God: he whom God declares guilty shall pay double to the other. (9)When a man gives to another an ass, an ox, a sheep or any other animal to guard, and it dies or is injured or is carried off, with no witness about, (10)an oath before the Lord shall decide between the two of them that the one has not laid hands on

* Originally published in *Zeitschrift für die alttestamentliche Wissenchaft* 106 (1994): 390-403.

> the property of the other; the owner must acquiesce, and no restitution shall be made. [(11)]But if [the animal] was stolen from him, he shall make restitution to its owner. [(12)]If it was torn by wild beasts, he shall bring it as evidence; he need not replace what has been torn by beasts. (JPS)

Although the general purport of the law is clear, interpretation of many of its details is fraught with difficulty, due to apparent legal inconsistencies and to the ambiguity of its language. For v. 8 alone, Knierim lists some sixteen variant translations.[1] Accordingly, opinions differ greatly as to its meaning, and the tendency of modern scholars has been to see the text as composite, embodying several layers of different laws superimposed or at least the results of redactional changes to the original law. Special anomalies that frequently have been pointed out are the different divine names in vv. 7-8 and in v. 10, the absence of a penalty at the end of v. 7, the abrupt change in style and content in v. 8, and the third alternative in v. 9, "captured," which seems inconsistent with the first two.[2]

It is not our intention to enter into a discussion of the merits of individual proposals for dealing with these anomalies, since we propose an entirely different approach. We shall seek to show that the law is an organic whole, consistent in its individual parts, that may be explained without recourse to a diachronic deconstruction of its text. In doing so, we shall apply principally the method of legal logic, on the grounds that in a legal text, the sole criterion for resolving ambiguities of language is the most appropriate legal meaning. For that purpose it must be assumed that the law is coherent, and only if all attempts fail should recourse be had to explanations based upon error, inelegant editing, or unresolved difficulties arising from the historical development of legal conceptions.

The text contains two separate laws, in vv. 6-8 and 9-12, which we shall consider in turn. The first concerns the theft of goods deposited in a

1 Knierim 1965: 162.

2 Baentsch 1892: 42; Ehrlich 1908: 353; Jepsen 1927: 38-40, 66 69, 73; Noth 1962: 184; Horst 1961a: 169; Knierim 1965: 143; Paul 1970: 93 n. 1; Jackson 1972: 101-2; Otto 1988b: 14-19; Otto 1988c: 16-25; Schwienhorst-Schönberger 1990: 194-211. A recent interpretation apparently eschewing this approach is that of Schenker 1990: 27-34.

person's house for safekeeping. As Otto has pointed out,[3] the nub of the law lies in the situation where the thief is not caught and suspicion falls upon the depositee that he may have misappropriated the property for himself under cover of a claim that they were stolen by person or persons unknown. That is the question posed by the words "if he did not lay hands on his neighbor's property"—not whether the depositee was negligent, but whether he was in deliberate breach of contractual obligations.

The procedure for resolving this question is given in vv. 7-8. In our opinion, v. 8 is the direct continuation of v. 7. The apparent generality of its language is deceptive; in fact, it enters into details of the accusation against the depositee raised in v. 7. There is therefore nothing missing at the end of v. 7. Indeed, although it is not necessary to our argument, we would suggest that v. 7 is still part of the protasis, which should be read: "if the thief is not found and the householder has drawn near the *'ĕlōhîm* (to determine) if he did not lay hands on his neighbor's property." The circumstances of the case are thus set within the parameters of an accusation of bad faith which obliges the depositee to undergo an evidentiary procedure. The following verse then contains the resolution of that procedure.

Two main views have been expressed as to the nature of the procedure: that it is an oath, or that it is an oracular judgment.[4] We would reject the first possibility, for the following reasons:

1. The terminology is completely different to that of v. 10, where the oath procedure is described in explicit terms.
2. An oath by its nature is as to facts within the personal knowledge of the swearer. It is unlikely that the depositor in this case would have personal knowledge of the depositee's act of theft to which he could swear.
3. The description does not accord with the way the oath functions in litigation. Although evidence in the Bible is lacking, this aspect of the oath is well attested in the surrounding societies,

3 Otto 1988c: 17.

4 Bibliographical references in Jackson 1972: 237 n. 1. For the oath, see in particular Price 1929, and for the oracle Graf 1864. A further possibility (e.g., Cassuto 1967: 286, cf. 267) is that *'ĕlōhîm* means simply the court. But a statement that a dispute between two parties is to be tried by the court would be banal and superfluous in a law code.

> being among the oldest known and most widespread legal procedures in the ancient Near East.[5] It is a decisive form of evidence in litigation but is not automatically employed in every case.[6] In its simplest form, the court imposes on the defendant an exculpatory oath, whereby he may deny the allegations against him. If he swears the oath, he wins the case; if he refuses to swear, he loses. Such was the fear of the oath's consequences, i. e., divine punishment in the form of realization of the self-curses pronounced, that it was not infrequent for the defendant to refuse to swear,[7] or for the plaintiff to concede the case rather than let him swear,[8] or for the two parties to reach a compromise rather than proceed to the oath.[9]

On occasion, the court may impose the oath on the plaintiff instead of the defendant, and it will often impose the oath on the witnesses of one side or the other, sometimes together with the party in whose favor they are attesting.[10] In its judgment, a court at Ugarit allowed for two contingencies: if the plaintiff's witnesses confirmed his allegation, then they were to swear the oath thereto together with the plaintiff; if, however, they did not confirm his allegation (and thus became witnesses for the defendant), they were to swear to that effect together with the defendant.[11]

From the above analysis, the following characteristics of the litigation oath emerge:

5 The earliest known examples are from the Sargonic period: Edzard 1968: nos. 81, 96. In the declaratory version, which applies to evidence in litigation, the oath-taker invokes the name of a god (or king) and calls down upon himself various curses if the statement he is making should not be true. (The other version is the promissory oath which is used in contracts.) For the biblical oath, see Horst 1961b: 292-314.

6 The clearest analysis is provided by Driver and Miles 1940. For the neo-Sumerian period, see Falkenstein 1956: 66-68, and cf. Edzard 1976: 90-92.

7 Edzard 1976: 91; Driver and Miles 1940: 133, text no. 1; *ana ittišu* (MSL I 6 I 45-50; see Landsberger 1937: 177-78).

8 TCL 1 232 (= Schorr 1913: no. 265), Driver and Miles 1940: no. 7.

9 CT 4 13a, CT 4 47a, CT 6 33b.

10 See Loewenstamm 1980a.

11 RS 20.20 (edited in Nougayrol et al. 1968: 94-97) following Loewenstamm's interpretation of the identity of the second set of witnesses (1980a: 341-42).

1. It is imposed by the court in its discretion, after a preliminary hearing. This is expressed by such terms as "the judges gave/sent X to the oath."
2. It is imposed on one party only (and/or his witnesses).[12]
3. The act of swearing the oath (or failing to do so) in itself decides the case; there is no further judgment by the court or any other outside agency. The true judgment of the court has been in deciding which party is to take the oath.

These characteristics clearly do not fit the procedure as described in vv. 7-8, where both parties are involved and an outside agency renders judgment. On the other hand, the characteristics of an oracular proceeding are appropriate to that procedure. In the absence of other evidence, the oracle is perfectly apt to decide whether a person is lying or not, by answering yes or no. It functions by choosing between people (e.g., as between Saul and Jonathan in 1 Sam 14:42), and where the issue is the contradictory statements of two litigants, in choosing the one that lies it will automatically vindicate the other as telling the truth. Furthermore, the verb used in v. 7, *qrb*, is found in two accounts of oracular procedure, in Josh 7:14 and in 1 Sam 14:36.

Turning from procedure to substance, the key to understanding v. 8 is the word *pš'*, a common term for sin or wrongdoing. The long accepted view of Köhler that in this context it meant "Bestreitung," the contestation of a claim of ownership between two innocent parties,[13] has been refuted by Knierim, who points out that it can bear this meaning nowhere else in the Bible.[14] Knierim's own proposal, however, "Eigentumsdelikt" (property offense),[15] relies on a doubtful analogy. In 2 Kgs 8:20, 22, the verb clearly refers to the rebellion of Edom against

12 Price (1929: 27) in analyzing Exod 22:8 confuses oath with judgment: "Each party was obliged to face the taking of the oath and to swear by the severest of oaths. In case no guilt could be proved the judges freed the accused." It is possible to separate v. 7 from v. 8 and to take the former as the oath by the depositee alone and the latter as a different procedure (e.g., Noth 1962: 184), but only at the cost of presuming that v. 7 represents an incomplete law.

13 Köhler 1928.

14 Knierim 1965: 143-60.

15 Knierim 1965: 163.

Judean hegemony. According to Knierim, Edom is removing itself from sovereignty of Judah and thus robs Judah of part of its property.[16] While it is true that vassals in the ancient Near East (like subjects) were referred to as the "slaves" of their overlords, in no context is there any suggestion that the rules of property applied to them, e.g., that they could be bought and sold like domestic slaves. It is not possible, therefore, even with the help of legalistic subtlety, to reduce Edom's act to one of theft.[17]

Nevertheless, Knierim is correct in looking to its use in the context of rebellion to explain the meaning of the term in our text. The verb can simply mean "to rebel," as its use in tandem with *mrd* in Ezek 20:38 shows. As Cogan and Tadmor point out, however, it is not used in a neutral sense.[18] It occurs where the rebellion is a rebellion by a foreign vassal, such as Edom or Moab, against Israel or Judah,[19] while Judah's rebellions against Assyria or Babylonia employ the term *mrd*. It is thus a judgment on the vassal by the overlord that he has "sinned" in rebelling. It is paralled by the use of "to sin" in Akkadian texts condemning the rebellion of vassals.[20]

The reason why rebellion is a sin is that vassalage is based upon a treaty, entered into by solemn oaths (on the part of the vassal at least). Rebellion is a breach of that treaty and oath, which brings down upon the party in breach the sanctions (usually in the form of curses) provided for by that treaty. As a Neo-Assyrian treaty puts it:[21]

> If Mati-ilu sins against this treaty (*ina adê annûti*) with Aššur-nerari, king of Assyria, may Mati-ilu become a prostitute, his soldiers women . . .; may Ištar, the goddess of men, the lady of women, take away their bow, bring them to shame, and make

16 Knierim 1965: 150-51.

17 Knierim's reasoning as to the nature of the slave's offense is found in developed Roman law, in Justinian's Digest: "a runaway female slave is understood to commit theft of herself" (D.47.2.61).

18 Cogan and Tadmor 1988: 21-22.

19 2 Kgs 1:1; 3:5, 7; 8:20, 22; 2 Chr 21:8, 10. By analogy, Israel against the House of David (1 Kgs 12:19 = 2 Chr 10:19) and Israel and Judah against God (Isa 1:2ff.).

20 See *CAD* Ḫ 157b.

21 Parpola and Watanabe 1988: 8-13 (column V, lines 8-15).

them bitterly weep: "Woe, we have sinned against the treaty of Aššur-nerari, king of Assyria."

The annals of Aššurbanipal make the same connection in describing the regrets of defeated rebels:[22] "because we did not keep the great treaty[23] of Aššur, we sinned against the goodness of king Aššurbanipal." In the Bible, the same idea was given an additional dimension by the use of the treaty as a metaphor for the agreement between God and Israel whereby the latter were to accept God as their ruler,[24] generally translated "covenant" in English (the same Hebrew term, *bĕrît*, is used for covenant and treaty). Rebellion against God, using the term *pš'*, consists in breach of the covenant, as Ezek 20:37-38 makes clear when God states that he will purge Israel of rebels and sinners (*hammōrĕdîm wĕhappôšĕ'îm*) as part of the process of bringing Israel under "the obligation of the covenant" (*māsōret habbĕrît*).[25] The same association is expressed by Hos 8:1 through parallelism: "Because they broke my covenant (*'ābĕrû bĕrîtî*), and rebelled (*pāšā'û*) with regard to my commands."

In law, wrongs against another person can be committed *ex delictu* or *ex contractu*. There are many examples in the Bible of the use of *pš'* to express the former, as in Jacob's (alleged) theft of Laban's gods (Gen 31:36) or the son who robs[26] his parents (Prov 28:24). A treaty is not more than a contract in the sphere of international law. In domestic law, therefore, the term *pš'* would properly apply to a breach of contract, not perhaps to a minor or inadvertent breach, but to a fundamental willful breach, as is betokened by rebellion in the context of treaty. Since our text concerns a contract—of deposit—and since misappropriation of the property deposited amounts to just such a breach of that contract, it is reasonable to interpret the term *pš'* as the type of wrongdoing that is specifically *ex contractu*, i.e., a wrongful and willful breach of a fundamental term of the contract of deposit.

22 Streck 1916: 78-79 (column VII, lines 72-74).

23 On the term *adê* "treaty, covenant," see Parpola 1987: 180-83.

24 The fundamental study is that of Mendenhall 1955. For a survey of the considerable scholarship on this topic, see McCarthy 1978.

25 Translation from Greenberg 1983: 362.

26 Or oppresses (*gzl*). On the meaning of this term, see Westbrook 1988d: 23-30, esp. 26 n. 88.

The term by which *pš'* is qualified, *dbr*, has a multitude of possible meanings. We would select in this context the basic meaning "word," because the verse goes on to specify: it gives verbatim the words used in the allegation. Thus *dbr-pš'* is, in our interpretation, the statement of the owner as to breach of contract by the depositee,[27] which he then expresses with the phrase: *kî hû' zeh*. Of the two possible translations of this phrase,[28] the first, "it is that," must refer to an owner of lost property identifying his property, and is totally inappropriate to a dispute between owner and depositee where, as Knierim points out, the property cannot yet have been recovered.[29] We therefore adopt the second possibility: "he is it," meaning that he (the depositee) is the thief. The allegation of the owner is that the depositee himself is the thief, and not some person unknown as he has claimed.

We now come to the crucial part of v. 8, the list of animals or missing property, the formulation of which gives the impression of a rule of far more general import than the dispute hitherto described between owner and depositee. The most glaring discrepancy is that the property is not the same as that by which the contract of deposit was originally defined: silver or utensils. Why are asses and the like suddenly brought into the discussion? To understand their connection with the dispute, we must go back to the opening clause of the law: "if the thief is found, he shall pay double."

The fact appears to have been overlooked by commentators that if there is any clause that is out of place in this law, it is the express mention of the thief's penalty. If the issue is deposit, then the exact penalty imposed upon the thief is irrelevant to the dispute, and if the issue is one of theft, then it is of no consequence whatsoever from whom the thief steals, be it borrower, hirer, depositee or the owner himself; his penalty will always be the same. It becomes highly relevant, however, if the point is to locate the liability of the dishonest depositee on the scale of penalties that apply to theft.

27 Paul (1970: 89 n. 6) refers to the parallel Akkadian terms and *dabābu*, which mean both word and, in a legal context, case or allegation.

28 Knierim 1965: 162.

29 Knierim 1965: 153.

In both the cuneiform and biblical sources the same principles are applied in the treatment of theft and related offenses such as embezzlement,[30] receiving stolen goods,[31] dishonestly obtaining a pecuniary advantage,[32] etc. Punishment varies according to two criteria: the type of theft and the type of property stolen, and is usually expressed as a multiple of the latter's value. In CH, a penalty of ten-fold is imposed for the theft of animals, whether stolen (§8) or misappropriated by a dishonest shepherd (§265), but misappropriation by a dishonest overseer of feed-grain entrusted to him is punishable by a two-fold penalty (§8) and theft of a plough by a payment of five shekels (§259), or three shekels for a hoe (§260). In the Hittite Laws, the distinctions are sharper: the theft of a bull, stallion, or ram is punishable by a 15-fold payment (§§57-59), that of a draught ox or horse by ten-fold (§§60-61), that of a cow, mare, or ewe by six-fold (§§67-69), and that of a pig, bees, or grain by various smaller amounts (§81; §§91-92; §96). On the other hand, misappropriation of a bull, stallion, or ram by a dishonest finder of those animals when lost is punishable by a seven-fold payment only. The sole distinction is the absence of asportation which is a characteristic feature of ordinary theft. In the Covenant Code, the distinction is made in the case of ordinary theft between ox and sheep, for which five and four-fold penalties respectively are payable (Exod 21:37). In Exod 22:3, a two-fold payment is levied whatever the animal involved. We have argued elsewhere that the offense is the (innocent) purchase of stolen goods, i.e., the difference in penalty between the two cases is based on their being entirely different offenses and not on the legally irrelevant factor of what a thief does with his property after he has stolen it.[33] If we are correct, then one aspect of the distinction between the two offenses is the presence or absence of asportation.

To return to our text, the penalty for ordinary theft of an ox or a sheep is five- and four-fold, but for misappropriation by a dishonest

30 E.g., the dishonest shepherd who misappropriates animals entrusted to his care: CH 265.

31 E.g., MAL A 3-4.

32 E.g., Edict of Ammi-ṣaduqa 7. Cf. CH 8.

33 Westbrook 1988d: 111-19.

depositee it is only two-fold. The point of the verse, with its general list of items, is then that whatever the property involved, even if it normally carries a higher penalty, the offense is to be treated in the same way as theft of silver or utensils, with the same (relatively) low penalty as in that case.

Accordingly, we would translate the disputed part of the law: "if the thief is not found and the householder comes before the *'ĕlōhîm* (to determine) if he did not lay hands on his neighbor's property: on every allegation of wrongdoing, whether ox, ass, sheep, or garment or any missing property concerning which he (owner) says 'He (depositee) is it (the thief),' the word of both of them shall come to the *'ĕlōhîm*. The one whom *'ĕlōhîm* condemns shall pay two-fold to his neighbor."

The wrongdoing in question is willful breach of the contract of deposit by misappropriating the deposited property. This serious allegation obliges the depositee to submit to the oracular procedure, concerning which it is ruled that the penalty shall not exceed that for simple theft of silver or utensils in any case, that the accuser must also face the oracle (which presumably will point to one or the other as the liar), and that if his accusation is proved false, he must bear the potential penalty himself under the normal talionic principle.[34]

The second rule (vv. 9-12) takes us out of the house and into the realm of herding contracts. The same type of contract was concluded between Jacob and Laban, and there are now many examples from cuneiform records.[35]

In this type of contract the herdsman is automatically liable for losses from the herd due to theft (v. 11), so that the question of good

34 Schenker (1990: 29) attempts to explain the dishonesty of the depositee as a false claim that some valuable property of a neighbor in fact belongs to the claimant, who had only deposited it with the neighbor for safekeeping. It is difficult to reconcile this interpretation with the explicit statement in v. 8 that the property in question is lost. On Schenker's hypothesis, neither party would be claiming that the property had been lost: the "owner" would claim that it is with the depositee, and the depositee would claim that he had never received it.

35 Gen 29:15-18; 30:28-34. As befits their literary context, the terms are a trifle unusual, but 31:38-41 refers to standard liability clauses: see Finkelstein 1968: 30-36; and Morrison 1983: 155-64. For the cuneiform material, see Postgate 1975: 1-18.

faith does not arise.[36] On the other hand, he is exempt where loss is due to the depredations of wild beasts, provided he brings the remnant of the animal as proof (v. 12). Jacob notes that he did not do so and thus forfeited his exemption (Gen 31:39).

Complications arise with the herdsman's obligations in vv. 9-10. There are three difficulties. Firstly, the content of the oath is to the effect that the herdsman did not "lay hands" on the animal, as in the previous rule. As Schwienhorst-Schönberger points out, it is difficult to see why a herdsman would deliberately wound or kill an animal entrusted to him, and the language of the phrase excludes negligence, i.e., that the mishap was caused by an omission on the herdsman's part.[37] On that basis, it would apply only to the last of the three possible mishaps that are listed: the capture of the animal, where the herdsman is accused of misappropriating it himself.

This difficulty may readily be resolved if we remember the essential difference between a contract of deposit and a contract of hire. In the latter, the hirer pays the owner for the privilege of using his property; in deposit, the depositee, whether or not he is paid, holds the property for the owner's benefit and may not, unless special provision has been made, exploit it for his own benefit. Thus it is that the following law (v. 13) obliges the hirer of animals to compensate the owner for injury to or death of the animals during the period of hire, since these are risks that naturally arise from his use of them. The depositee, on the other hand, would not normally be held to such a standard, unless the suspicion arises that he did in fact use the animals, in breach of his contract. He therefore takes the oath to negate an allegation that he appropriated to his own use the animals in his charge, whether by exploiting their labor or their products or possibly even by consuming them. Jacob, in asserting his honesty to Laban, points out that during

36 The reason may lie in the fact that a herding contract includes compensation for the shepherd, whereas a contract of deposit with a householder would not automatically do so. The question of remuneration lay at the basis of the Rabbinic distinction: see the *Mek.*, *ad* v. 11. Schenker (1990: 30-31) considers that liability for theft falls on the shepherd because he had had the usufruct of animals, unlike the depositee of goods in vv. 6-7, and the owner had thus suffered an extra loss. But, as we shall see, the usufruct is exactly what the shepherd should not have had.

37 Schwienhorst-Schönberger 1990: 199.

his service as a herdsman "I did not eat the rams of your flock" (Gen 31:38). On the other hand, it must be admitted that the case of capture, which involves a dishonest claim that the animal was taken away by a third party, still seems to accord ill with the first two cases. We shall return to this question below.

The second difficulty also arises from the anomalous nature of the case of capture. In verse 10, following the oath, it is stated: *wĕlāqaḥ bĕʿālâw* "its owner shall take/has taken." If, as some commentators consider, it refers to the owner taking back the remains of the dead or wounded animal[38] (although, since the animal belongs to the owner anyway, this would seem to be a superfluous provision), then it cannot cover the case of capture, where the animal must have disappeared entirely. It would suggest that either this phrase or the case of capture is an ill-considered interpolation into the text. Accordingly, most commentators translate: "the owner shall accept (the oath)."[39]

Satisfactory as this solution may appear, and in spite of the fact that it preserves the integrity of the text, it is unacceptable, for legal reasons. As we have seen, in litigation, the exculpatory oath is imposed upon one of the parties by the court, in the exercise of its discretion. He will then win the case if he takes the oath and lose if (as not infrequently happens) he refuses to take the oath. The question of the other party "accepting" the oath as conclusive evidence simply does not arise. We must therefore reconsider the phrase in question.

The oath in verse 10 is qualified by a curious condition. This oath is said to be "between the two of them" (*bên šĕnêhem*). The very same expression occurs in 2 Sam 21:7, where David is said to take pity on Miphiboshet, the son of Jonathan, "because of the oath of YHWH between them (*bênōtām*), between David and Jonathan." The reference here is to the mutual oaths that the two friends swore to each other when David was forced to flee from Saul's court (1 Sam 20:42).[40] In our text, then, this

38 E.g., Cassuto 1967: 287, following the *Mek.*; Ehrlich 1908: 353; and Schenker 1990: 29.

39 Translation from the NRSV. Cf. the JPS: "the owner must acquiesce." See Schwienhorst-Schönberger 1990: 204 n. 42 for the earlier authorities.

40 "Between them" (*ina birīšunu*) is a standard phrase for expressing mutuality in Akkadian: *CAD* B 246-247. Its use to express mutual oaths is illustrated by the equal treaty between Ugarit and Amurru (RS 19.68; edition in Nougayrol 1956: 284-86):

means that *both* the owner and the herdsman were obliged to take an oath.[41]

The phrase "laid hands on his neighbor's property," however, can only refer to the herdsman's oath, since he is not the owner. The only possible reference to the owner's oath can be in the following phrase *wĕlāqaḥ bĕʿālâw*, which should then be translated with the past tense, as "his owner took." To identify the taking in question, we must look back to the wrongs listed in the previous verse. The first two, death and injury to the animal, have nothing to do with taking, but obviously relate to the herdsman's oath concerning exploitation of the animals, as we have seen. The third, "capture," furnishes a clear parallel.

The circumstances in which "capture" by the owner would be wrongful are when the owner surreptitiously takes back his own animal ("with none seeing") and then claims it from the herdsman. A similar act of dishonesty is described in CH 113, when a creditor surreptitiously takes grain from his debtor's granary. In neither case can it be called theft, since the owner (or creditor) is taking his own property, but any future claim for return of the property deposited or lent will clearly be fraudulent.

The two oaths in v. 10 are not cited directly but described through the perspective of their results, which are biased towards the innocent herdsman. Two situations are presented where the herdsman is cleared of liability through the oath procedure: (a) where he proves that he did not use the animal by taking the oath; (b) where it is proved that the owner did recapt his own animal by his refusing to take the oath. This is not to say that they are part of the same procedure. As we have seen,

---

"From this day, Niqmadu king of Ugarit and Aziru king of Amurru have made an oath between them" (lines 1-5: *ma-mi-tam i-na be-ri-šu-nu i-te-ep-šu-nim*).

41 Schenker (1990: 29-30) does indeed interpret the oath as mutual ("ob nicht einer [der beiden] seine Hand auf das Gut seines Nachbarn legen wollte"), seeing again here a false claim by the owner that he had lent an animal that was returned damaged or lost altogether. But his proposed scenario fits neither the term "captures" (the circumstances of the animal's disappearance are a matter of indifference to the owner) nor the terms of the oath as translated by him. Note Patrick's comment on v. 10 (1985: 82): "Although the initial clause 'an oath by Yahwe shall be between them' sounds as if both parties took an oath, it is clear from what follows ('to see whether he has not put his hand . . .') that the bailee alone is involved."

only one party to an action swears the oath, and here in any case there are two different accusations, deriving from different circumstances: the second is a counter to the claim that an animal is missing, not that it is dead or injured. At most, they could arise at the same time, when the animals are due to be returned, and might thus be consolidated in one suit. We therefore conclude that the two were conveniently lumped together by the framer of this text because they shared the oath procedure.[42]

The final difficulty is the discrepancy between the divine name that is used in the two rules, in vv. 7-8 and 10, which has indicated for many commentators the existence of different strata in the text.[43] We can only point out that the two entirely different procedures are involved. The oath is taken in the name of YHWH, the national god, which is in accordance with the normal pattern for oaths. The earlier procedure does not mention an oath at all. It is before *'ĕlōhîm*, which may refer to another god, to any god, or perhaps to no god at all, but to some institution or building, as seems to be the case in the other use of the term in the Covenant Code, in Exod 21:6.[44]

As we have no knowledge of the criteria applied by the ancient courts in deciding to employ the oracle, oath, or the other procedures available, it is impossible to say why the one was preferred over the other in this particular case. Some indication, however, of the conditions for allowing the depositee to take the oath is provided by CE 37, where the circumstances are analogous to those of vv. 6-8:

42 The consequences for the owner of having wrongfully recapted his animal are not stated. Possibly there were none—in the nature of the oath procedure, the owner would lose by refusing to take the oath and thus withdrawing his claim. From the parallel of CH 113, one might have expected some penalty on the owner, but this law seems to be concerned only with the question of the shepherd's liability.

43 E.g., Jepsen 1927: 73; Noth 1962; cf. Alt 1934a: vol. 1, 289 n. 3 (of the 1959 edition); and Schwienhorst-Schönberger 1990: 200-3.

44 Loretz (1960: 167-75) points to the fact that oaths were normally taken at the temple. Thus in CE 37, an oath concerning deposit is taken at the gate of the Tišpak temple. (Tišpak, it should be noted, was the national god of Eshnunna.) On the other hand, oaths are not the sole legal procedure that takes place at the temple, as Loretz himself admits, in arguing that the earpiercing ceremony of Exod 21:6 likewise was performed at the temple door. For further theories as to the meaning of *'ĕlōhîm* in this verse, see the literature cited by Schwienhorst-Schönberger 1990: 308 n. 191.

> If the man's house is ransacked(?)[45] and the house-holder's property is missing together with the deposited property (or, perhaps, property of the depositee),[46] the house-holder shall swear to him an oath at the Gate of Tišpak: "My property is indeed missing with your property; I have not committed fraud and deceit." He owes him no debt.

The meaning of the law is in part obscure due to textual difficulties, but that aspect which concerns us is fortunately clear. The theft includes property of the householder, who escapes liability by taking an exculpatory oath confirming this fact and denying wrongdoing.

In our view, the point of joint loss being mentioned here is that it enables the householder to cross the threshold of credibility that will make him eligible for the oath, by establishing a presumption of innocence in his favor.[47] The householder, to account for his inability to return the property, tells a story, introducing a possibly fictional third party. The exculpatory oath, which deals essentially in negatives, is not

45 Restoration of *luqqut* suggested by Landsberger 1968: 99.

46 Tablet A (IM 51059) iii 18 has *it-ti ma-ṣa-ar-tim*; Tablet B (IM 52614) iii 1 has *it-ti bu-še-e* ^{lú}*ma-ṣa-ar-tim*. Contrary to Landsberger's interpretation (1968: 99 n. 1), the term must be ^{lú}*maṣṣartum* (in the genitive) "watchman, guard." Cf. EA 52:38, 48.

47 The same consideration would appear to be behind mention of joint loss in CH 125: If a man gave his property for safekeeping and where he gave it his property was lost together with the householder's property through breaking in or climbing in, the householder who was negligent and caused the loss of the property given to him for safekeeping shall indemnify (literally: make complete and restore) the owner of the property. The householder may continue to search for his property and take it from its thief.

Koschaker (1917: 26-33) noted that the issue of joint loss is immaterial to that of liability for negligence, since the depositee could not have guarded the depositor's goods less well than his own. He concluded that the formulation of the law was confused due to its combination of older and later law. Under the older law, joint loss was automatically sufficient to relieve the depositee of liability, whether negligent or not. With the introduction of liability for negligence, the present text was drafted to show that it applied even to cases of joint loss, where it was previously exempt. There is no need, however, to assume confused editing or the existence of a mechanical and primitive rule. If our understanding of CE 37, discovered after Koschaker's commentary, is correct, then in CH 125 mention of joint loss is made only to exclude the question of fraud, since the paragraph wishes to concentrate entirely on liability for negligence.

the appropriate means for introducing such extraneous matters. *Prima facie* evidence of the alleged events must first be adduced in some other form. We tentatively suggest (since omission is not a reliable basis for argument in respect to ancient Near Eastern law codes) that in the absence of this factor in Exod 22:6-8, there was no evidentiary presumption that would make the oath appropriate in that particular case. In the second rule in vv. 9-10 the same objections do not arise. The oaths are purely negative—taken in reply to the accuser's allegations (of use on the one hand, and recaption on the other), not in support of any further allegations of the accused.

Summary and Conclusions

Exod 22:6-12 contains two laws on deposit, the first concerning property consigned to a person's house and the second livestock entrusted to a herdsman. As befits contractual obligations, liability is strict, but with some exceptions. In the first law, the depositee may be relieved of the duty to restore property lost if he can show that it was due to the wrongful act of a third party, namely the thief. If the depositee's claim is fraudulent, however, he becomes liable to a penal payment, a multiple of the goods lost, as for theft, but only at the low level as for theft of silver or utensils, whatever the type of property in fact lost. The procedure for testing the veracity of the depositee's claim, should the owner allege it to be fraudulent, is oracular, with the owner suffering the depositee's potential penalty should the oracle decide against him.

In the second case, the above exception does not apply, the herdsman being liable for animals lost due to theft. On the other hand, he is exempted from liability for animals killed by wild beasts, subject to production of their remains as proof, and for natural wastage. If, however, wastage was the result of the herdsman's exploiting the animals entrusted to him, contrary to the terms of a contract of deposit, he will be liable (in what amount is not stated). He may take the exculpatory oath to clear himself of such an accusation of breach of contract. By the same token, if the owner of the livestock surreptitiously recapts an animal for the purpose of a wrongful claim against the herdsman, he may take the oath to clear himself of this charge.

Both laws are concerned essentially with fraud and with the procedures necessary to rebut a charge of fraud. Neither of them deals directly with negligence, perhaps because it was not the subject of this traditional legal problem. Whether the exceptions to contractual liability could themselves be limited by an allegation of negligence remains an open question.[48]

48 It was claimed by Koschaker (1917) that the introduction of the concept of negligence by the depositee in CH 125 represented a major legal innovation. Most commentators regard CE 37 (and Exod 22:6-12) as representing an earlier stage of legal development. See, e.g., Yaron 1988b: 251; and Otto 1988c: esp. 25-27.

24

Who Led the Scapegoat in Leviticus 16:21?

Abstract

The longstanding conundrum of the phrase איש עִתִּי in Lev 16:21 is reexamined in the light of Hittite and Greek parallels. In addition, the etymology of עִתִּי is considered anew. Both the comparative and the philological evidence point to the idea that a criminal was the man who was to lead away the scapegoat as part of the Yom Kippur ritual.

A celebrated passage in the book of Leviticus prescribes the ritual of public atonement for the collective sins of the Israelites, to be performed by Aaron, the high priest, as part of the Yom Kippur purgation. It involves two goats, one to be sacrificed as a sin offering and the other to be led out into the wilderness. The procedure, according to Lev 16:21, is as follows:

> Then Aaron shall lay both his hands on the head of the live goat, and confess over it all the iniquities of the people of Israel, and all their transgressions, all their sins, putting them on the head of the goat, and sending it away into the wilderness by means of someone designated for the task (איש עתי). (NRSV)

The translation "someone designated for the task" reflects the later talmudic tradition that a priest was assigned the task of leading the goat out and ensuring that it did not return (*m. Yoma* 6.3). Other modern translations follow the LXX, which has ἀνθρώπου ἑτοίμου ("someone

* Co-authored with Theodore J. Lewis. Originally published in the *Journal of Biblical Literature* 127 (2008): 417-22.

at hand, ready, prepared") for איש עתי (cf. Vg.: *per hominem paratum*). Jacob Milgrom, for example, renders the phrase as a "man in waiting," and the Eberhard Bible as "(durch einen) bereitstehenden Mann."[1]

The descriptive phrase in all these translations is superfluous, telling us nothing of consequence about the man who is to lead the scapegoat. In this respect, the KJV's "a fit man" is no wit inferior. Like all the versions ancient and modern, it reflects the translator's difficulties with a *hapax legomenon* of uncertain meaning: עִתִּי. The apparent root is עֵת ("time, appointed time"), but translators have not succeeded in deriving a term from it that is appropriate to the context (cf. *Targum Onqelos*: *gĕbar dizĕmîn*).

We suggest that the description of the man involved was of great significance to the ritual and propose an entirely new interpretation based on parallel Hittite and Greek traditions[2] and on a different etymology of the word עִתִּי.

A number of Hittite rituals have been compared with the biblical scapegoat, but one is of particular interest because it involves both an animal and a human actor to accompany the animal. The Ritual of Ašhella prescribes the steps to be taken to rid the army camp of plague:[3]

4-7 At evening time, the army commanders, whoever they are, all prepare rams—whether white or dark does not matter at all.

11-14 At night they tie them in front of the tents and say as follows: ". . . Whatever god has made this plague (*henkan*), behold! I have bound up these rams for you: be appeased!"

15-17 At dawn I drive them out onto the steppe. And with each ram they bring a jug of beer, a loaf of thick bread, and a . . . jug, and they make an adorned (*unuwant*) woman sit down

1 See the comments of Milgrom 1991: 1045; and Levine 1989: 106.

2 By doing a comparative legal analysis of three neighboring societies, we are by no means embracing the myth-and-ritual approach of old nor implying any notion of a universal religious practice.

3 KUB IX 32:1-32 and duplicates: see *CTH* 394 (Laroche 1971). See the translation by Gurney 1977: 49.

before the king's tent and place with the woman a jug of beer and three loaves of thick bread.

18-24 Then the army commanders place their hands on the rams and say as follows: "Whatever god has made this plague, now behold! The rams are standing here and are very fat in entrails, heart, and loins. Let human flesh be hateful to him, and let him be appeased by these rams." And the army commanders bow to the rams and the king bows to the adorned woman.

25-32 Then they bring the rams and the woman and the bread through the camp and they drive them away onto the steppe. And they run away to the enemy's border without coming to any place of ours. And they say repeatedly as follows: "Behold! Whatever evil (*idalu*) there was in the camp among the men, oxen, sheep, horses, mules, and donkeys, now behold! These rams and this woman have taken it away from the camp. And the one that finds them, may that land take this evil plague (*idalu henkan*).

The ritual is explicitly designed to transfer the evil (*idalu*) that is the cause of the plague (*henkan*) from the soldiers to the rams. They are chased out of camp together with the woman, and both woman and sheep continue on until they reach enemy territory. There is thus a double dispatch: the king and his troops send away the woman and the rams, but it is she who has to herd the rams across the border. The woman acts as a buffer between the king and the rams, who are contaminated with the evil plague. In terms of a warriors' encampment, a woman, the symbol of weakness, held the lowliest possible status. Nonetheless, she is dressed in finery, apparently as a substitute for the king, just as the male rams are substitutes for the warriors. In another Hittite plague ritual, the king exchanges clothes with a prisoner of war, who is then described as "adorned" (*unuwant*).[4]

4 The ritual involves a prisoner of war and a captive woman. The former is expressly a substitute for the king. They are to be the focus of a plague-bringing *enemy* deity, male or female respectively, and are to carry the plague back into their own country. See *KBo* XV 1 I 6-22 in Kümmel 1967: 111-25.

In the Greek world of the first millennium B.C.E., more closely contemporary with the biblical source, the archetypal scapegoat is a person (φαρμακός), not an animal. Various sources attest to the chasing out (or killing) of a scapegoat in order to end a famine or plague, or else as part of an annual ritual.[5] In descriptions of actual rituals, as opposed to mythological accounts, the scapegoat was a marginal person, such as a criminal,[6] slave, or poor person. Indeed, the word φαρμακός became a term of abuse, as were other terms also used to describe the scapegoat, such as κάθαρμα ("offscourings") and περίψημα ("sweepings").

Notwithstanding his lowly status, the Greek scapegoat was sometimes dressed in finery, like the Hittite woman. J. Bremmer has explained the dichotomy by the fact that in theory aversion of the catastrophe demanded sacrifice of a valuable person, but in practice the upper ranks of society were unlikely to be forthcoming. Accordingly, an expendable subject was taken but was treated as an important person.[7] It may rather have been a question of substitution by appearance, as in the Hittite rituals.

In Strabo's description of a Leucadian custom, the qualification for the scapegoat in an annual ritual was not class or character in general, but actual criminal culpability (10.2.9):

> It was also the ancestral custom among the Leucadians every year during the sacrifice to Apollo for someone of those guilty (of crimes: τις τῶν ἐν αἰτίαις ὄντων) to be thrown from the cliff for

5 There is an extensive bibliography on the subject going back to 1913 (see Fraser 1966). The evidence is surveyed by Bremmer 1983: 299-320. See also Burkert 1979: 59-68, for a comparative analysis of the Greek, Hittite, and Hebrew sources. Some Greek sources suggest that the scapegoat was killed, but Hughes argues that the later lexicographers and scholiasts added the element of killing, whereas the earlier sources contemporary with the living custom speak only of expulsion (1991: 139-64; cf. Bremmer 1983: 315-17).

6 Douglas (2003: 121-22) writes against those such as R. Girard who make use of Greek scapegoat rituals that, she argues, "do not look remotely like the Bible" especially because "there is nothing obviously punitive about the levitical rite." Yet our understanding of the etymology of איש עתי (see below) would undercut Douglas's critique precisely on this point.

7 Bremmer 1983: 303-7.

> the sake of averting evil. To him were attached feathers of every sort and birds capable of reducing with their fluttering the force of the leap, and below many men would wait in a circle in small boats and take him up. And when he had been taken up they would do all they could to remove him safely beyond the borders.

Several points are to be noted. Although the victim is a criminal, the ritual is not punishment for his particular crime. Rather, it is apotropaic—to ward off a potential calamity to the community. The text gives the impression that the victim is selected more or less at random from a number of suitable candidates. Nor is the victim actually killed. Although he is required to make a hazardous leap into the sea, measures are taken to ensure his survival. He is then hastily expelled from the territory, perhaps without touching land again.

His banishment notwithstanding, in a sense it was the criminal's good fortune to be selected for this fate. The phrase ἔν αἰτίαις suggests that he has been found guilty but not yet punished.[8] Exile in this ritualistic way may well have been a means for him to escape a more severe punishment.

In the light of these scapegoat traditions from neighboring societies, we may reconsider the etymology of עִתִּי in Lev 16:21. The traditional understanding of עִתִּי is to see it as a form of עֵת, the Hebrew word for "time" from the root ענה, with the doubling of the ת being the result of the regular assimilation *nt* > *tt* (**ʿintī* > *ʿittī*). Owing to the contextual difficulties noted above, it seems more likely that עתי (again with the common *nt* > *tt* assimilation) is from the Semitic root ענת. Here our best evidence is from Syriac, Aramaic, and Arabic.

The noun *ʿett(ā')* is well attested in Syriac with the meaning "deceit, knavery, villainy, depravity."[9] R. Payne Smith notes that it often translates Hebrew אָוֶן, "trouble, wickedness."[10] C. Brockelmann points out that *ʿettā'* is used to translate חֲמָסִים, "lawlessness" (//רֶשַׁע, "wickedness") in Prov 4:17.[11]

8 The term αἰτία refers solely to guilt, blame (or the accusation thereof). See the references in LSJ 44, s.v. αἰτία I.

9 Payne Smith 1999: 3008; Payne Smith/Payne Smith 1988: 431; Brockelmann 1928: 535.

10 Payne Smith 1999: 3008.

11 Brockelmann 1928: 535.

The verbal root for *ʿettāʾ* would be *ʿnt*. It appears in its assimilated form (*nt* > *tt*) in Syriac *ʿt*(*t*) with the meaning "to defraud, be fraudulent, dishonest, wicked."[12] As pointed out by R. Payne Smith, the cognate form is well attested in Arabic as *ʿanita* (with lack of assimilation) meaning "to be in distress, to meet with hardship, to commit crimes, sins, or acts of disobedience deserving punishment."[13]

A cognate noun עַנְתָּא, "oppressor, wrongdoer," is used in the Targum of Prov 16:33 to translate the Hebrew *Vorlage* reflected by the LXX's ἀδίκοις, "ungodly, unrighteous, unjust" (not in the MT). Brockelman also lists the Arabic *ʿanatun* "crimen."[14]

Elsewhere one could reconsider the etymology of the Ugaritic warrior goddess ʿAnatu. Suffice it to say that numerous suggestions have been offered in the past with, in P. L. Day's opinion, "no conclusive results."[15] Though warriors can be painted in a positive light (cf. the Hebrew PN עַתַּי referring to one of David's mighty warriors in 1 Chr 12:12), their violent actions (such as ʿAnatu's decapitations and cutting off hands in *KTU* 1.3.2) can easily be cast in a negative light. Thus, the etymology underlying the Ugaritic DN ʿAnatu and the Hebrew PN עַתַּי may be cognate to the root *ʿnt* in Arabic, Syriac, and Aramaic mentioned above.[16]

Lastly the final *i* vowel on עִתִּי (אִישׁ) deserves comment. No satisfactory answer has been presented for this vowel, even among those who follow the traditional interpretation that the word designated a "timely" person. It is most likely not a remnant of the original case system or associated with the so-called *hireq compaginis*, which is mostly restricted to nouns in construct and participle forms in

12 Payne Smith 1999: 3008; Payne Smith/Payne Smith 1988: 431. See also Payne Smith Margoliouth 1981: 256; Brockelmann 1928: 535.

13 Payne Smith 1999: 3008; see Lane 1984: 2168-69.

14 Brockelmann 1928: 535.

15 Day 1999: 36.

16 There is a possibility that the root may also be found in the opening line of the larger of the two Arslan Tash inscriptions, which reads *lḥšt lʿtʾ* and could refer to an "incantation against evil" (see Garbini 1981: 277-94, who notes the Arslan Tash text, yet he takes the root to be *ʿwy* or *ʾwt*). Yet most scholars emend *lʿtʾ* to *lʿ<p>t*ʾ, "flyers," a word that is firmly attested later in the text.

poetry.[17] A better option would be the relational/adjectival suffix *î* (the so-called *nisbe* suffix), which is well known through its use on gentilics and ordinal numbers. According to B. K. Waltke and M. O'Connor, the *î* suffix can be used "to make adjectives from substantives" with examples such as רֶגֶל "foot" > רַגְלִי "foot-(soldier)," נֵכָר "strangeness" > נָכְרִי "strange," and תַּחַת "below" > תַּחְתִּי "lower."[18] Thus אִישׁ עִתִּי could designate a criminal man.

* * *

From the parallel rituals, the rationale for choosing such a person becomes perfectly clear. He is the ideal candidate for taking away the goat carrying the community's sins. As in the case of the Leucadian scapegoat, his crime is not specified, but it symbolizes impurity akin to that of the goat, except that the latter had to be made impure by a ritual of transference. Like the Hittite woman, he plays the role of a buffer between the high priest and the sin-ridden scapegoat, and there is a double dispatch: of the אִישׁ עִתִּי by the high priest and of the goat by the אִישׁ עִתִּי.

Unlike in the parallels, the biblical criminal could eventually return after dispatching the scapegoat and could presumably escape further punishment for his offense.[19] The difference is based on impeccable logic. Since the purpose of the biblical ritual is to remove not a plague (or similar divine punishment for sin) but the actual sins of every Israelite, the criminal must have had his sin removed as well.

17 Waltke and O'Connor 1990: §8.2; Joüon and Muraoka 2006: §93 l-q.

18 Waltke and O'Connor 1990: §5.7c.

19 He did, however, have to wash his clothes and bathe before he was allowed to reenter the camp (Lev 16:26). The one who burns the sacrificial bull and goat of the sin offering outside the camp must perform the same cleansing ritual (Lev 16:27-28).

25

The Prohibition on Restoration of Marriage in Deuteronomy 24:1-4

Abstract

The prohibition in Deut 24:1-4, that a woman's first husband may not remarry her after her second marriage has ended, becomes effective only in very particular circumstances. This article argues that those circumstances entail a first husband who divorced the woman with grounds (due to misconduct on her part) and a second husband who ended his marriage with the woman either by divorcing her without grounds or simply by passing away. A closer look at these circumstances helps to explain the rationale for the prohibition in this text.

The purpose of this article[1] is to re-examine the law in Deut 24:1-4 forbidding a man to remarry the wife whom he had divorced and whose subsequent marriage has now come to an end, and to propose a new solution to the problem that has troubled commentators both ancient and modern: what was the rationale behind this curious rule?

Although it later became the basis for the general principles of divorce in Jewish law, the text itself is concerned with a very narrow set of circumstances, which are set out in great detail:

> When a man takes a wife and marries her, if then she finds no favor in his eyes because he has found some indecency in her, and

* Originally published in *Studies in Bible* (ed. S. Japhet; Scripta Hierosolymitana 31; Jerusalem: Magnes Press, 1986), 387-405. Used by permission.

1 This article was first presented at a departmental seminar of the Hebrew University Law Faculty's Institute for Research in Jewish law in 1984. I wish to express my thanks to all the participants for their comments and criticisms, which greatly assisted in the drafting of the final version. Responsibility, of course, is entirely my own.

> he writes her a bill of divorce and puts it in her hand and sends her out of his house, and she departs out of his house, and if she goes and becomes another man's wife, and the latter husband dislikes her and writes her a bill of divorce and puts it in her hand and sends her out of his house, or if the latter husband dies, who took her to be his wife, then her former husband, who sent her away, may not take her again to be his wife, after she has been defiled; for that is an abomination before the LORD, and you shall not bring guilt upon the land which the LORD your God gives you for an inheritance (Revised Standard Version).

The lengthy protasis may be analyzed into eight steps which are necessary for the operation of the apodosis and which correspondingly narrow the circumstances to which the prohibition will apply:

1. The first husband (H1) marries the wife (W).
2. H1 finds "some indecency" (ערות דבר) in W.
3. H1 therefore divorces W.
4. W marries H2.
5. H2 "dislikes" (שנא) W.
6. H2 divorces W.
7. *Alternatively* (to steps 5 and 6) H2 dies.
8. H1 tries to marry W.

In order to understand the law's rationale, it is necessary to discover what is special about this particular combination of eight circumstances. The explanations offered to date, however, all fail to take into account at least one of the circumstances listed.

1. The earliest explanation is that proposed by Philo in *Spec. Laws*:[2]

> . . . she must not return to her first husband but ally herself with any other rather than him, because she has broken with the rules that bound her in the past and cast them into oblivion when she chose new love-ties in preference to the old. And if a man is will-

2 Philo *Spec. Laws* 3.30-31.

> ing to contract himself with such a woman, he . . . has lightly taken upon him the stamp of two heinous crimes, adultery and pandering. For such subsequent reconciliations are proofs of both.

In other words, the wife has committed adultery, and her former husband by remarrying her becomes a party thereto.

As Yaron points out,[3] this rationale ignores the legal character of the text. The wife's divorce and her subsequent marriage are both perfectly legal: she cannot have committed adultery.[4] If Philo is suggesting that adultery during her first marriage was the motive for her divorce and second marriage, then this is certainly not reflected in the text, where the first divorce is a unilateral act of the husband and clearly at his initiative.

2. S. R. Driver suggested,[5] that the prohibition acted as a deterrent to hasty divorce: the first husband could not lightly send away his wife with the assurance that he could always take her back again. But here also Yaron points out the unreality of such a rule: the divorcing husband is hardly likely to have in mind the possible circumstances following the dissolution of a subsequent marriage by his wife.[6] Once again the protasis is far too complex for the solution offered.

3. Yaron's own proposal takes up a further point made by Driver,[7] namely, that the woman who desired to return to her former home might

3 Yaron 1966: 6-7.

4 We suggest that the express mention of the bill of divorce in both cases was to emphasize the fact that both divorces were legitimate and that no question could arise of the woman not being free to remarry, i.e., her subsequent action could not be interpreted as adultery. Cf. the famous passage in Matt 5:31-32: "It has been said, 'Whoever shall put away his wife let him give her a bill of divorce.' But I say to you that whoever shall put away his wife, except for fornication, causes her to commit adultery." In our view, Jesus is here denying the efficacy of the bill of divorce to dissolve the old marriage (or rather, the husband's ability to dissolve and use the bill as evidence thereof), thus allowing the wife the freedom to remarry. Cf. an Old Babylonian bill of divorce (Meissner *BAP* 91): "H has divorced his wife W. She has . . . her . . .; she has received her divorce-money. If another marries her, H will not raise claims."

5 Driver 1896: 272.

6 Yaron 1966: 5.

7 Driver 1896: 272.

be tempted to intrigue against her second husband. The object of the prohibition, in Yaron's view, is to protect the second marriage from such an eventuality, or from the first husband attempting to get his wife back. The rule is therefore concerned with the stability and continuation of the second marriage, not the first .[8]

Yaron's theory, unlike its predecessors, accounts for the importance of an intervening marriage as a condition for the prohibition, but there remains one circumstance in the protasis that it fails to cover, namely the possibility of the second marriage ending with the death of the husband.[9] It is understandable that the law might wish to prevent the second marriage being terminated by divorce, but there is no reason for it to intervene where an external event has brought that marriage to a natural end. The express mention of this alternative shows, in our view, that marital discord was not the situation that the law had in mind.[10]

4. Another approach is to look at the motive clauses at the end of the apodosis. Wenham compares these to the motive clauses of the prohibition against incest in Leviticus 18 and 20 and concludes that the Deuteronomic text actually regards the restoration of marriage as a type of incest.[11] His reasoning is as follows: the incest prohibition applies to certain relations created by marriage and may even survive the end of the marriage that created the forbidden affinity. In the Bible, a wife was regarded as her husband's sister. Divorce did not terminate this relationship: she is counted as a very close relative. If a divorced couple remarry, it is an incestuous union, like a man marrying his sister.

We shall not enter here into a discussion of the validity of Wenham's analysis of the incest laws or of the nature of the marital relationship. It is sufficient to say that his analysis cannot possibly apply to the Deuteronomic law because it completely ignores the intervening marriage. The law does not, as Wenham assumes, prohibit remarriage as such, and there

8 Yaron 1966: 8-9.

9 As pointed out by Wenham 1979: 37.

10 The idea that the wife might consider murdering her second husband is too far-fetched and is not considered by Yaron, but Rashi suggests that she contributes to his death.

11 Wenham 1979.

is no way that we can see of the second marriage being a factor in the creation of incestuous affinity.

5. A final explanation is that there is a natural repulsion[12] against taking back a wife who had cohabited with another man. Yaron, however, points out that the Deuteronomic prohibition is unparalleled in any other legal system, which would suggest the opposite. Nonetheless C. Carmichael attempts to show that such an attitude did exist in ancient Israel and thus provided the rationale behind the law.[13] He finds evidence in a comparison of the two cases in Genesis where Abraham passes off Sarah his wife as his sister, first to the Pharaoh (chap. 12) who takes her as his wife, and then to Abimelech (chap. 20) who is prevented from doing so by a timely warning in a dream. According to Carmichael the author of the second passage is reacting against the situation in the first, where Sarah is actually taken as a wife, because he finds it offensive that Sarah could be taken by another man and then restored to Abraham. The Deuteronomic source shares this sensibility, which it transfers to the legal sphere.

Carmichael's analogy is inexact. The act which is found offensive by both sources is adultery. It is committed by the Pharaoh, and he is severely punished for it.[14] (Sarah, of course, is not punished, being under duress.) Abimelech is stopped on the verge and spared punishment. Carmichael attempts to overcome this objection by suggesting that Abraham had *de facto* divorced Sarah, thus re-establishing the analogy to the Deuteronomic law. But if Sarah was divorced, why punish the Pharaoh or threaten to punish Abimelech? As Wenham points out,[15] Carmichael's interpretation virtually reinstates Philo's view that the second marriage is adulterous, after that view had been discredited by Yaron.

We would suggest that, far from there being a natural repulsion, both biblical and ancient Near Eastern sources find nothing untoward in a man resuming relations with his wife after she has had relations with another,

12 See, e.g., Junker 1933: 100.

13 Carmichael 1974: 203-7.

14 The punishment is vicarious: the killing of members of Pharaoh's family is considered punishment of the head of the household.

15 Wenham 1979: 37.

even amounting to marriage, providing no other factor makes resumption of the marriage improper.

Our first piece of evidence is the very same source that Carmichael relies on, Genesis 12. The Pharaoh marries Sarah, the marriage is *prima facie* valid but in fact void due to a hidden defect. When the defect is discovered, Sarah is returned to her first husband, and the first marriage continues as if nothing had happened. The varying degrees of moral turpitude of the parties involved do not affect the validity of the marriage.

The second instance in the Bible is the marriage of David and Michal, which is likewise interrupted by the marriage of Michal to Paltiel.[16] The narrative appears to regard it as perfectly natural for Saul to give his daughter to another husband after David has fled for his life, and for Ishbaal later to accede to David's demand for her return. The reason has been elucidated by Z. Ben-Barak from a widespread practice in Mesopotamian law.[17] Codex Eshnunna (CE), Codex Hammurabi (CH) and the Middle Assyrian Laws (MAL) all contain provisions whereby a person who has been forcibly detained abroad and whose wife has remarried in the interim may on his return reclaim his wife.[18] The second marriage, if justified by the circumstances,[19] was perfectly valid, and children of that marriage followed their father—in other words, they were legitimate. Nonetheless, it was voidable at the first husband's instance, should he one day return. David's demand, according to Ben-Barak, is based upon a comparable law which explains both Ishbaal's acquiescence and the second husband's inability to resist the demand.[20]

The significance of the comparison from our point of view is that both in the biblical narrative and in the Mesopotamian laws a husband is found claiming the restoration of his wife after she has been married to another (and even had children by him), and nowhere is revulsion expressed at the idea. On the contrary, the law hastens to assist the original husband at the expense of the second marriage.

16 1 Sam 18:20-29; 25:44; 2 Sam 3:12-16; 6:16, 20-23; 21:8-9.

17 Ben-Barak 1979: 15-29.

18 CE 29, CH 133-135, MAL A 45.

19 CE requires only that the first husband have been absent "a long tine," whereas CH requires lack of subsistence. MAL sets a two-year period (and lack of subsistence).

20 Ben-Barak 1979: 25-29.

Ben-Barak saw a contradiction between the law behind David's claim to restoration of his marriage and the prohibition in Deuteronomy and concluded that the latter was not in force in David's time.[21] There is in fact no need to assume a contradiction, since the special circumstances of the husband's enforced absence[22] would constitute an obvious exception to any general prohibition. It will be our contention, however, that the prohibition in Deuteronomy was by no means so broad as to come into conflict with the practice in the case of the absent husband: it applied not to restoration of marriage as such, but to restoration in very particular circumstances.

Let us therefore return to the protasis of our Deuteronomic law and begin by examining the detail upon which so many of the theories stumble—the difference in the dissolution of the first and second marriages. In the former, the husband finds "some indecency" in his wife and divorces her. In the latter he "dislikes" her and divorces her or, in the alternative, dies. There must therefore exist some underlying factor which is on the one hand common to divorce for "dislike" and death, and on the other distinguishes these two types of dissolution from divorce for "indecency." That factor, we submit, lies in the property aspect of marriage—more exactly, in the financial consequences of its dissolution.

The Bible contains no direct evidence on this aspect of marriage, but there is sufficient evidence from both earlier cuneiform sources and from post-biblical Jewish sources to establish the existence of a continuous tradition.

To take the case of widowhood first, CH 171b-172 contains the basic principles:

> The wife shall be entitled to her dowry and to marital property that her (late) husband gave her in writing in a tablet. . . . If her husband has not given her marital property, they shall make good to her her dowry, and she shall take a share like one heir in the property of her husband's estate.

21 Ben-Barak 1979: 29.

22 The first marriage is deemed dissolved by death, but the facts may turn out to be otherwise.

More than a thousand years later, paragraph 12 of the Neo-Babylonian Laws (NB) applies the same principle, if in somewhat different measure:

> A wife whose husband has received her dowry, and she has no son or daughter of her own, and death has carried off her husband, then a dowry as much as the dowry shall be given her from her husband's property. If her husband has given her a marital gift,[23] she shall take her husband's gift together with her dowry and is quit. If she has no dowry, the judges shall assess her husband's property and something shall be given to her according to her husband's property.

Likewise in the Mishnah, the widow is entitled not only to her dowry[24] but also to her "ketubah," namely, the marriage settlement or the statutory minimum in the absence of a voluntary settlement.[25]

In the case of divorce, our earliest record of the financial consequences is Codex Ur-Namma (CU) 6-7:

> 6 If a man divorces his first wife, he must pay one mina of silver.
> 7 If it is a (former) widow whom he divorces, he must pay half a mina of silver.

That this was not the only payment is revealed by CH 138-140:

> 138 If a man divorces his first wife who has not borne children, he shall upon divorcing her give her money in the amount of her bride-money and make good to her the dowry that she brought from her father's house.
> 139 If there was no bride-money, he shall give her one mina of silver as divorce-money.

23 On the problems of the terminology, see Westbrook 1988b: chap. 1.

24 The rules are complicated by the division of the wife's property into categories called נכסי מלוג and נכסי צאן ברזל, but her basic entitlement is unquestioned. See, e.g., *m. Ketub.* 7.1.

25 These principles are regarded as so self-evident that it is difficult to find a direct statement of them. For clear indirect evidence, see e.g., *m. Ketub.* 10.1-2.

140 If he is poor, he shall give her one third of a mina of silver.

The sums set out in CU and CH are thus revealed as the minimum where there is no bride-price. The bride-price (*terḫatum*) is the equivalent of the biblical מהר and in divorce is used as the measure of compensation, parallel to the widow's marriage settlement.[26] It should be added that this measure of compensation was itself in lieu of contractually agreed divorce-money, which was the norm in marriage contracts throughout the ancient Near East.

The Middle Assyrian Laws, as we shall see below, contain the principle that at least the dowry is to be returned on divorce, if not always with additional compensation.[27] It is in the Mishnah, however, that the tenacity of the early Mesopotamian tradition is revealed. Apart from her dowry, the divorcée is entitled, like the widow, to the payment of compensation—her כתובה—which, in the absence of express agreement in the marriage contract, is a fixed minimum of 200 *zuz* for a virgin bride and one hundred for a former widow, i.e., the same distinction as in Codex Ur-Namma, and in exactly the same proportions.[28] Moreover, a *beraita* in the Babylonian Talmud[29] reveals that these fixed sums represent the transformation of the bride-money into divorce-money, the culmination of a development[30] which we have already seen at an earlier stage in Codex Hammurabi, where the bride-money was the measure of divorce-money.

26 Where the wife has had children, the financial consequences are more dramatic. The principle revealed by CE 59 and CH 147 is that the husband forfeits his whole property to the wife. See Westbrook 1988b: chap. 4.

27 MAL A 37 appears at first sight to allow the husband total discretion in whether to give his wife a divorce settlement, but as C. Cardascia (1969: 191-96) points out, it must be read in the light of paragraphs 20 and 38, which refer to the restoration of the dowry and forfeiture of the bride-price respectively. It should also be read in the light of the husband's contractual obligations, Assyrian marriage contracts being in no way special in this respect. Possibly paragraph 37 is denying a right to a statutory minimum as awarded by CH 6-7 and CH 138.

28 *m. Ketub.* 1.2.

29 *b. B. Qam.* 82b.

30 The interim stage is represented by a custom whereby the bride's father returns the bride-price to the groom via the bride, so that it becomes part of her dowry. The *beraita* reveals how this custom became law. See Geller 1978.

In summary, there is a tradition spanning the whole length of ancient Near Eastern law that, upon dissolution of the marriage, whether by divorce or by the death of the husband, the wife was entitled to a financial settlement consisting at least of the restoration of the dowry that she brought into the marriage, but generally also of a payment from the husband's resources. It is reasonable to suppose, therefore, that biblical law shared the same principle.

In the case of divorce, however, there is a complication. For if the wife had committed some wrong that justified the husband in divorcing her, then the financial consequences were entirely different. The principal marital offense that a wife could commit was adultery, but in Mesopotamia as in the Bible, the penalty was death, and not surprisingly, there is no word as to the financial consequences. On the other hand, CH also discusses cases where the wife has committed some wrong less serious than adultery.

CH 141 reads:

> If the wife of a man . . .[31] accumulates a private hoard, scatters her household, slanders her husband—on being found guilty, if her husband pronounces her divorce, he may divorce her without giving her anything, not her journey-money, not her divorce-money.

If the husband can prove, therefore, that his wife has been guilty of misconduct, here mostly of a financial nature, he can divorce her without paying the usual compensation. There is no mention of her dowry, but if she is to be expelled from the matrimonial home without even money for the way, it is reasonable to suppose that the husband was not obliged to restore it. Further evidence for this interpretation comes from the alternative to divorce given the husband in the same law: the wife will continue to live in his house "as a slave"—which implies that she is stripped of her property.

CH 142 deals, in our interpretation,[32] with the case of a woman who

31 The clause omitted contains complications that do not concern us here. See Westbrook 1988b: chap. 4.

32 The interpretation of the first part of the protasis is a matter of considerable scholarly dispute. See Westbrook 1988b: chap. 2.

refuses to marry her fiancé. If after investigation by the local court it is found that

> . . . she is chaste and has no sin and her husband (= fiancé) is going out and greatly slandering her, that woman has no penalty; she shall take her dowry and go to her father's house.
>
> If she is not chaste and is going out, scattering her house, slandering her husband, they shall cast that woman into the water.

The form of betrothal is known in modern scholarship as "inchoate marriage,"[33] being very close to full marriage, and the provisions of this paragraph may therefore be extended by analogy. Indeed, there is some evidence that misconduct by a fiancée in inchoate marriage was treated more harshly than misconduct by a wife.[34] At all events, the misconduct here is similar to that of the wife in CH 141 and in addition includes sexual misconduct. It is unlikely that the latter actually amounted to fornication (or at least this was not proved), since the usual explicit language is lacking,[35] and it is cumulated with other, less serious, offenses. What is important from our point of view is the fact that the woman, if proved innocent, is entitled to keep her dowry. The necessary inference is that her misconduct would lead to its forfeiture. By analogy, if she were a wife and divorced for such conduct, she would leave without her dowry.

The same principle as regards the wife's property is found in MAL A 29. The law first recites the rule that the wife's dowry and gifts from her father-in-law are reserved for her own children; her husband's family have no claim to them. It continues: "But if her husband *drives' her out*,[36] he may give it to his children at his choice." A rare Assyrian verb, *puāgu* "to drive out with force," is used instead of the standard verb for divorce, *ezābu*. According to Cardascia, the reason is that the wife is being expelled for misconduct, not merely divorced, and hence the rule that in these circumstances she forfeits her marital property.[37]

33 The term was coined by Driver and Miles 1952: 262-63.

34 Cf. Gen 38:24-25; Deut 22:20-21, 24.

35 Cf. CH 129, 131, 132, "lying with another man."

36 Following Cardascia's interpretation (1969: 161-63).

37 Cardascia 1969: 163.

Finally, the principle is stated explicitly in the Mishnah:[38]

> These are they that are put away without their Ketubah: a wife that transgresses the Law of Moses and Jewish custom. What (conduct is such that it transgresses) the Law of Moses? If she gives her husband untithed food, or has connexion with him in her uncleanness, or does not set apart dough-offering, or utters a vow and does not fulfill it. And what (conduct is such that it transgresses) Jewish custom? If she goes out with her hair unbound, or spins in the street,[39] or speaks with any man.

The first category of transgressions—against the Law of Moses—is entirely anchored in Scripture, but the second category has no obvious biblical basis and must derive, as the Mishnah claims, from ancient custom. And from the Mesopotamian sources it is clear that this custom was very ancient indeed.

Thus a second principle may be posited as common to ancient Near Eastern law (and thus presumed in biblical law as well): if the wife was guilty of misconduct, which could be in the sphere of her financial and household duties or, from the examples in CH and in the Mishnah, sexual misconduct not amounting to adultery but rather in the sphere of indecency or immodesty, her husband was justified in divorcing her without the usual financial consequences. She forfeited her right to divorce-money and apparently her dowry as well.

In our text in Deuteronomy, the first divorce comes about because the husband found "some indecency" (ערות דבר) in his wife. The term has been the subject of much debate, beginning with the famous dispute between the schools of Hillel and Shammai in *m. Giṭ.* 9.10. Of the modern scholars, only A. Toeg argued that the term means actual adultery, on the ground that in most occurrences in the Bible ערוה is employed as a euphemism for sexual relations (e.g., Lev 18:6).[40] But there can be no

38 *m. Ketub.* 7.6.

39 This involves exposing herself. Cf. *b. Giṭ.* 90a, which adds the example of bathing where men bathe.

40 Toeg 1970: vii. Toeg's argument is weakened by his claim that the clause is an interpolation, which relieves him of the need to find a role for it in the law.

question of sexual connotation in Deut 23:15, which is the only other biblical text to employ the identical phrase ערות דבר. In that passage, it is the physical cleanliness of an army camp that is the issue. Driver noted that the phrase must refer to something less than actual adultery,[41] since this is punished not by divorce but by death (Deut 22:22), and suggested "some improper or indecent behavior."[42] This seems to us the correct interpretation in light of the comparative material discussed above. In our view ערות דבר is the type of misconduct referred to in CH 141-142 and in *m. Ketub.* 7.6 and therefore justifies the husband in divorcing his wife without a financial settlement.

What of the second marriage? There, the husband does not claim misconduct but divorces his wife for "dislike." The verb, שנא, more usually rendered "hate," is found in the context of divorce not only elsewhere in the Bible but throughout the ancient Near East. J. J. Rabinowitz, on the basis of the Aramaic marriage contracts from Elephantine, claimed that "hate" in the Bible might sometimes be employed as a technical term for "divorce."[43] The Elephantine marriage contracts contain clauses setting out the financial consequences of divorce. The divorce itself was effected, as elsewhere in the ancient Near East, by the divorcing party pronouncing a formula, which in two of the documents is rendered "I hate PN my husband/wife."[44] Yaron accordingly translated: "I divorce . . . my husband/wife," noting also that divorce-money was called literally "silver of hatred."[45]

At first sight, this interpretation is supported by the evidence of cuneiform sources. The dissolution of adoption in cuneiform law uses the same verbal formula as marriage, *mutatis mutandis*, but in an adoption contract from Ugarit, the expected formula is replaced by the verb "hates" (*zêru*).[46] Moreover, in an Old Babylonian marriage contract, the clauses penalizing

41 Driver 1896: 271.

42 Driver 1896: 270.

43 Rabinowitz 1953: 91-97. The biblical example that he gave, however (Deut 21:15), is not convincing and has been rejected by Yaron (1957: 119).

44 TAD B2.6 (= Cowley 15); and TAD B3.3 (= Kraeling 2).

45 Yaron 1961: 54-55.

46 RS 15.92 (edited in Nougayrol 1955: 54-56): "If in the future A hates B, his son . . ." (lines 7-9). The normal repudiating formula is: "If in the future A says to B, his son, 'You are not my son.'"

divorce contain the following parallelism: "if H (husband) divorces W (wife) . . . / if W hates H . . . ."[47]

The impression given by these sources is, however, a false one. For further evidence reveals that they represent only an abbreviated version of a longer formula, "hate *and* divorce." Thus in a marriage contract from Alalakh, the clause penalizing divorce begins: "if W hates H and divorces him."[48] The same is found in a Neo-Assyrian marriage contract except that the conjunction is missing (a point whose significance we shall see below): "if W hates H (and) divorces."[49] In the scribal dictionary of legal formulae, *ana ittišu*, the full formula is given: "if a wife hates her husband and says 'You are not my husband'" (which is the standard divorce formula).[50] The point is made most clearly in the Elephantine documents themselves. While the two contracts cited above use the verb "hate" alone, a third has a fuller version: (a) "if H . . . says 'I hate my wife W, she shall not be my wife'";[51] and (b) "if W hates her husband and says to him 'I hate you, I will not be your wife.'"[52] It is the second clause which is the operative divorce formula and which was omitted, but implied, in the other two contracts.

The term "hate" is therefore an addition to the divorce formula which expresses not the divorce itself (for which there is another technical term) but some extra dimension thereof. This extra dimension must have been very common, since it was possible to abbreviate the formula already at a very early period. To understand what the dimension was, we must go beyond the realm of marriage and divorce. The verb "hate" is found in a variety of contexts in Codex Eshnunna and Codex Hammurabi as follows:

47 CT 6 26a.

48 *JCS* 8 7 no. 94, lines 17-19: *šum-ma* H W [*i-z*]*í-ir-šu ù i-zi-bu-šu.*

49 *Iraq* 16 37-39 (ND 2307), lines 49-50: *šum-ma* H *e-zi-ra e-zip-pi* SUM-*an*, "if H hates, divorces, he must pay." This lapidary formulation has led to various interpretations. Postgate (1976: 105-6) reads *e-sip-ši* SUM-*an*, "he shall pay (back the dowry) to her two-fold," but such a penalty is unknown and legally dubious. We would likewise reject interpretations based on emendations, such as that in *CAD* E 422 (s.v. *ezēbu*): *e-zib-ši*, "her dowry"; and that of Jakobson (1974: 116): *e-zib-tū*(!). As we shall see below, the parallel in Mal 2:16 proves the correctness of the unemended form.

50 MSL I 7 IV 1-5 (edited in Landsberger 1937: 103).

51 TAD B3.3 (= Kraeling 2), lines 21-22.

52 TAD B3.3 (= Kraeling 2), lines 24-25.

CE 30 If a man hates his city and his master and flees . . . .
CH 136 . . . because he hated his city and fled . . . .
CH 142 If a woman hates her husband (= fiancé)[53] and says, "You shall not marry me . . . ."
CH 193 If (he) . . . finds out the house of his father and hates his foster-father and foster-mother and goes to the house of his father . . . .

The verb invariably appears in combination with a verb of action, providing the motivation for that action. The motivation appears to turn what might otherwise be an innocent act into a guilty one, and we therefore feel justified in applying the terminology of modern criminal law: it is the *mens rea*, the "guilty mind," which is a necessary constituent of the offense.[54] The verb "hate" is used to show that the action arose from a subjective motive and without objective grounds to justify it—and for this reason is blameworthy.

In the context of marriage, the element of *mens rea* is explained by our earlier discussion. A husband could divorce his wife at will[55] but had to pay her a heavy financial settlement. Only if he could justify his action on the objective grounds of the wife's misconduct could he escape the usual financial consequences. The verb "hate" therefore expresses the fact that the divorce in this case is for purely subjective reasons, and the financial penalties, whether by contract or under the general law, will apply.

The combination "hate and divorce" is found in the Bible not only in the Deuteronomic law but also in Mal 2:16, and it is the latter that we wish to consider first, since our findings from the comparative material must be universally applicable to be valid.[56]

53 See n. 32 above.

54 The other being the *actus reus*, the guilty act. The terms are derived from the maxim *actus non est reus nisi mens sit rea.*

55 And in some systems, at least, a wife her husband. See Westbrook 1988b: chap. 4.

56 Yaron (1957: 117-18) suggests a third occurrence: "abandoned and hated" in Isa 60:15. It is true that the Hebrew verb "abandon" (עזב) is the same root as the Akkadian verb "divorce" (*ezēbu*), but divorce does not fit the context at all, and inversion of the formula is not to be expected. Accordingly, we prefer the traditional interpretation. Yaron further suggests that שנא alone means divorce in two passages, Judg 15:2 and Prov 30:23, but in both cases we consider the use of the verb to be non-technical,

The passage in Malachi is a famous crux,[57] most of the discussion turning around the two verbs שנא and שלח. The traditional Christian interpretation is that the verse expresses God's opposition to divorce, although this is difficult to reconcile with the form of the verbs. Thus the Authorized Version renders: "For the LORD saith that he hateth putting away: for one covereth violence with his garment," while the Revised Standard Version emends the text: "For I hate divorce . . . and covering one's garment with violence." A modern scholar, A. Tosato, has attempted to reconcile this interpretation with the syntax by taking the first verb as an imperative: "For 'Hate divorce!' the God of Israel has said. (Hate him who) covers his own garment with violence!'"[58]

The Jewish interpretation, on the other hand, is that the verse recommends a husband to divorce his wife if he hates her, although this is difficult to reconcile with the obvious words of disapproval in the second part of the verse.[59] One modern interpretation therefore combines recommendation of divorce with disapproval: "Wenn einer nicht mehr liebt, Ehe scheiden . . . aber derjenige besudelt mit Schande sein Gewand."[60]

We prefer simply to take the two verbs as finite,[61] and translate literally: "For he has hated, divorced . . . and covered his garment in injustice." The comparative material discussed above reveals to us the true significance of the first phrase: "For he has divorced *without justification*." The criticism is not of divorce as such but divorce for "hate," where the husband follows his own inclination and the wife has done nothing to deserve such a fate. The phrase "hated, divorced" without the conjunction has a striking parallel in the Neo-Assyrian marriage contract mentioned above[62] in the clause penalizing divorce, which suggests that it was taken from a standard legal idiom.

---

and the situation not to be marriage but inchoate marriage. The "hatred" will (or should, in the case of Proverbs) cause the marriage not to take place.

57 "This has been rightly called the most difficult section of the Book of Malachi" (Smith 1912: 47). For a summary of the research, see Locher 1981: 241-71.

58 Tosato 1978: 552.

59 Abravanel 1892 *ad loc.*

60 Schreiner 1979: 217-18.

61 Following Smith 1912: 55.

62 See n. 49 above.

Compared with the verse in Malachi, the use of hate and divorce in the Deuteronomic law is almost self-evident: it contrasts the second divorce, where the husband has no objective justification, with the first divorce, where the husband does have, or claims to have, such justification (ערוות דבר).

We therefore have before us the same distinction that exists throughout ancient Near Eastern law, and, it must be presumed, the same financial consequences. As we have seen from the comparative material, divorce with justification deprives her of that settlement. In the Deuteronomic law, divorce with justification is ranged against two alternatives: divorce without justification, and widowhood. The only feature that the latter have in common and which at the same time distinguishes them from the former is that they both result in a financial settlement for the wife. Consequently, as we submitted at the start of this discussion, it is the unspoken property aspect which runs like a thread through the whole protasis and accounts for its attention to detail and the distinctions that those details contain: it must therefore be the key to the law's rationale.

We are now in a position to reconstruct the scenario presented by the protasis. The first husband has divorced his wife on the grounds of her "indecency" and has therefore escaped the normal financial consequences—he paid her no divorce-money and most probably kept her dowry. The woman nonetheless managed to find another husband, and that marriage has ended in circumstances which leave her well provided for: her dowry (if she had received a second one from her family), possibly marital gifts from the second husband, plus divorce money or the widow's allowance. Now that she is a wealthy widow or divorcée, the first husband forgets his original objections and seeks to remarry her.

The effect would be that the first husband profits twice: firstly by rejecting his wife and then by accepting her. It is a flagrant case of unjust enrichment which the law intervenes to prevent. The prohibition on remarriage is based on what in modern law would be called estoppel. This is the rule whereby a person who has profited by asserting a particular set of facts cannot profit a second time by conceding that the facts were otherwise. He is bound by his original assertion, whether it is objectively the truth or not.

The estoppel is expressed by the phrase "after she has been defiled." A. Hurvitz has pointed out[63] that the form of the verb is curious and unattested elsewhere: הטמאה. The *hophal* form expresses causation, and the correct translation should be: "she has been caused to be unclean." The point is not whether the wife is in fact unclean, but that the first husband's earlier assertion that she was unclean makes her unclean now for the purposes of remarrying her. Having profited from the claim that she was unfit to be his wife, he cannot now act as if she were fit to marry him because circumstances have made her a more profitable match.

A final point is the Deuteronomic postscript to the law "for that is an abomination before the LORD, and you shall not bring guilt upon the land which the LORD your God gives you for an inheritance." The phraseology seems somewhat harsh for a case of unjust enrichment and has doubtless been a factor in scholars seeking the rationale for the law in some sexual taboo. But as Weinfeld notes, the word "abomination" (תועבה) is used in Deuteronomy (and in Proverbs) not in a sexual connection but essentially to emphasize the hypocritical attitude of the malefactor, the classic example being that of the falsifier of weights and measures.[64] The law in Deut 24:1-4, as we have explained it, is an excellent example of hypocrisy and may therefore have been used by the Deuteronomic author[65] not so much for its property-law implications as to illustrate an attitude that he wished to condemn.[66]

63 In an oral communication.

64 Weinfeld 1972: 267-69.

65 Most probably the law was taken verbatim from an existing code and only the postscript added.

66 Contrary to the views of most scholars (cf. Hobbs 1974: 23-29), we doubt whether the text of Jer 3:1 has any connection with the law in Deuteronomy. The dissolution of the second marriage is not mentioned, and it is the husband in the rhetorical example who is to return to the wife, whereas in marriage it would be the other way round. The reference may therefore be to an illicit liaison between the man and his former wife.

26

Riddles in Deuteronomic Law

Abstract

The structure and organizing principle of the Deuteronomic Code continues to puzzle scholars. This article proposes a new approach. Rather than applying legal logic as its primary criterion for analyzing the code's structure, this study uses the model of the riddle. Cuneiform literature confirms the aptness of this model for understanding organizational patterns within Near Eastern scribal traditions, from which the law codes derive.

The collection of special laws in Deuteronomy 12-26 presents at first sight a picturesque jumble of eclectic rules. For the modern scholar, it stands as an irresistible temptation to bring order out of chaos—small wonder then that in recent years much research has focused on their organizational structure.

In any random collection of laws, a close enough examination is bound to reveal some common factors—of language, form, or content. These in turn may be collected into patterns that enhance our appreciation of the text. The historian should nonetheless confine himself to those patterns that he considers to reflect ideas current at the time of the text's composition, if he is to avoid imposing upon the text modern categories or intellectual constructs.[1]

Before we consider how to search for ancient categories, however, certain preliminary questions need to be resolved, namely, whether the Deuteronomic laws were divided into categories at all, and if so, of what kind. A model is needed, from some other genre of literature in the Bible

* Originally published in *Bundesdokument und Gesetz: Studien zum Deuteronomium* (ed. G. Braulik; Freiburg: Herder, 1995), 159-74. Used by permission.

1 Kaufman 1979: 106-8.

where the same thought processes are employed but in a more accessible form. The one model which has been proposed, the Decalogue, does not meet these requirements.[2] It is not from a different genre, since it is *prima facie* no more than another set of specific rules. Whether those rules also had a secondary function as categories is a matter to be demonstrated, not assumed. Moreover, if they did have that function, then the thought processes behind the categorization are still no more accessible than for the special laws; on the contrary, the definition of what category each commandment represents remains a matter of scholarly controversy, being supplied from outside the text by interpretation.[3]

Without prejudice to the role of the Decalogue, we consider that on this preliminary level a more appropriate model exists, albeit in an unlikely source: the so-called numerical proverbs. To begin with the most famous example (Prov 30:18-19):

> Three things amaze me
> And four I cannot fathom:
> The way of an eagle in the sky,
> The way of a snake on a rock,
> The way of a ship on the high seas,
> And the way of a man with a woman.

It is a kind of riddle, in which we are given a heading (which tells us that it is a riddle), four parts and a clue. The clue here is the word דרך ("path," "way") which occurs in each part. As in all riddles, however, the parts appear to be entirely disparate phenomena, and the answer is that factor which unites them. In this case, the parts are not evenly balanced, for there is a sting in the tail. Using the clue, we can easily surmise the connection between the first three: they all use "paths" that are not paths—they are not marked out, there is no way of judging where the bird, snake, or ship will go next, and perhaps also they leave no trace behind them. The fourth path,

2 For a survey of current literature on this theory, see Braulik 1991: 15-17.

3 For example, the commandment "You shall not bear false witness against your neighbor" is reinterpreted by Kaufman as the category "fairness to one's fellow as regards both his substance and his dignity" (1979: 141), but by Braulik (1991: 102) as "Den Armen, sozial Schwachen and Schuldigen ihr Recht nicht verweigern."

then, is linked metaphorically. It is not a physical movement but a course of conduct that shares the same characteristics with the first three.

A more straightforward example, in which the parts are on an equal footing, is Prov 30:21-23:

> Under three things the earth trembles,
> And four it cannot bear:
> A slave who becomes king,
> A fool who eats his fill,
> A hated woman whose marriage is consummated,
> And a maidservant who succeeds her mistress.

In this case the unifying factor is clear—the undeserving who are nonetheless rewarded. By the same measure, the clue is less so, but perhaps lies in the fact that the riddle's parts arc presented not at random but in a logical sequence. The characters slave, fool, hated woman, and maidservant are chiastically arranged in terms of status (male slave, free male, free female, female slave), while the second limb, documenting the characters' achievements, reveals an independent, albeit similar, sequence: king, appetite for food fulfilled, appetite for sex fulfilled, mistress.

A model therefore exists within the Bible for the organization of the Deuteronomic laws into units of a small number of disparate laws with an unstated unifying factor. The next step for the historian is to find controls that will aid in the identification of unifying factors by ensuring that they are drawn from the text's historical context, in the sense of the intellectual tradition from which its contents are derived. In the case of the Deuteronomic laws, that means looking firstly to the genre to which they belong, namely, ancient law codes, as attested in other books of the Torah and in the cuneiform sources.[4]

Unlike their biblical counterparts, the cuneiform scribes provide us with explicit evidence that they consciously divided their law codes into categories by subject matter. Late Old Babylonian copies of Codex Hammurabi (CH) insert headings at certain points in the text, e.g., "rules concerning soldier and fisherman," ‘‘rules concerning field, garden, and

4 See Malul 1990b: 87-91, 153-59; Westbrook 1988a: 82-97.

house."[5] Not quite so explicit but equally clear is the native edition of the Middle Assyrian Laws (MAL), which are preserved on 14 tablets. Tablet A, the only complete tablet, is exclusively concerned with cases involving women. Tablet B, of which half is preserved, appears to concern cases involving land. It may therefore be presumed that the other tablets (insofar as they are not duplicates) were likewise dedicated each to a particular topic.[6]

The above divisions vary greatly in length: Tablet A of MAL contains approximately sixty paragraphs and Tablet B must originally have comprised about forty.[7] The heading "soldier and fisherman" covers ten paragraphs of CH, while "field, garden, and house" covers at least thirty (§§36-65, at which point there is a break in the text). Another late Old Babylonian copy has two headings preserved: "rules concerning *kiššātum*-service and debt" (= §§117-119) and "rules concerning [. . .] and safekeeping" (= §§120-126).[8] To discover more such divisions, especially the smaller units from which larger "chapters" were constructed, two means are available.

The first is suggested by the last two native headings mentioned above. Both classify the laws by legal categories; it should therefore be possible to apply legal logic to the codes in order to discern other legal categories. The pioneer in this approach is Petschow, who has shown in the case of CH and of Codex Eshnunna (CE) that the individual laws of those codes were organized in thematic units.[9] Some of those units are easy to discern: CH 1-5 have the theme "litigation," §§154-158 are all incest offenses, and §§185-193 all concern adoption. Even so, they rely on the subjective judgment of the modern scholar. It could be argued that the last-mentioned unit should really extend to §195, under the more general heading "children."[10] *A fortiori* where the proposed legal category is uncertain, unconventional, or possibly too abstract for ancient jurisprudence.

5 Finkelstein 1967: 42-43.
6 See Cardascia 1969: 19-22.
7 Cardascia 1969: 20 n. 1.
8 Finkelstein 1967: 48.
9 Petschow 1965: 146-72; 1968: 131-43. See further Eichler 1987: 81-84.
10 The difficulties of classification are discussed by Petschow 1965: 163, who uses a double heading for §§185-194: "Bestimmungen adoptions- and pflegschaftsrechtlicher Art."

As Petschow rightly stresses, the classification of ancient legal topics is not always identical with modern legal methodology.[11]

To return to our model of the riddle, the legal category is the answer to the riddle, and the individual laws its parts. The question therefore arises whether the other aspect of the riddle that we have seen, the possibility of an organized sequence that acts as a clue to the unifying factor, is present. Certainly, more confidence in the historical authenticity of a legal category can be gained if the laws within the proposed unit show some signs of logical arrangement. A clear example is chronological progression, which is frequently found in the law codes. Thus the lawsuit in CH 1-5 is followed through its chronological stages of accusation, trial, and judgment by giving examples that can occur at each, and in CE 25-35 the theme of marriage is illustrated by cases concerning betrothal, wedding, desertion, wet-nursing, and adoption, i.e., formation and dissolution of marriage, and children. A more complex pattern is found in the incest unit of CH 154-158:

> 154 If a man has intercourse with his daughter, they shall expel that man from the city.
> 155 If a man chooses a daughter-in-law for his son and his son has intercourse with her and afterwards he is caught lying in her lap, they shall bind him and throw him in the water.
> 156 If a man chooses a daughter-in-law for his son and his son has not had intercourse with her and he lies in her lap, he shall pay her half a mina of silver and restore to her whatever she brought from her father's house, and the husband of her choice shall marry her.
> 157 If a man after his father's death lies in the lap of his mother, they shall burn them both.
> 158 If a man after his mother's death is caught in the lap of his step-mother/nurse(?) who has borne children, that man shall be torn out from his father's house (i.e., disinherited).

Looking first at the protasis of these paragraphs, we note that the forbidden degrees follow a logical sequence: older man with younger woman, then

11 Petschow 1965: 170.

younger man with older woman, and within each of these variations the first case is that of a blood relative, followed by one of a relative by marriage. The penalties are not organized in the same way, but appear to follow a simple chiastic pattern: expulsion, death, compensation, death, expulsion. As in the riddle that we analyzed, there is a difference in the arrangement of the two members of the laws.

Organizational patterns of this kind are not merely for aesthetic reasons. The law codes belonged to a wider genre, which included medical, lexical, and divinatory texts. All were "scientific" texts, scholarly treatises on law, medicine, language, divination, etc.[12] For the Mesopotamian scribes, this type of literature belonged to the category of scribal wisdom, *emqutu*, the original setting for which was the scribal school.[13] The connection between law codes and numerical proverbs is therefore not so surprising; it is more intimate than merely structural. They both belong to the same way of looking at the world, the tradition of wisdom literature in the broad sense.[14]

The law codes share many features with the other types of scholarly literature, especially as regards form. The basic unit is the individual example, sometimes as in the law codes or omen texts expressed by the casuistic sentence, sometimes as in grammatical texts by paradigms, sometimes as in lexical texts by words or short phrases. The scientific purpose of the scribes was to classify all human knowledge, but in the absence of modern analytical tools such as vertical reasoning and definition of terms the result was endless lists of examples, in which analysis could at best be inferred but not expressed through the suggestive choice and grouping of examples.[15]

Thus the casuistic format used by the law codes is a poor tool of analysis, in which a few examples must serve to cover a whole area of the legal system. A tightly organized sequence of examples can help to alleviate some of the system's faults—the parameters of the topic, for example, can be indicated, if not delineated. Indeed, it can do more. In a true riddle,

12 Bottéro 1992: 156-79.

13 Kraus 1960: 290-92. On the pseudo-scientific disciplines of Mesopotamian wisdom, see Parpola 1993: xiii-xv, xxvii; on the scribal schools, see Sjöberg 1976: 159-79; and on the didactic aspects of the law codes, see Eichler 1987: 81-82.

14 The laws of the Covenant Code are identified with wisdom by Jackson 1992.

15 See Bottéro 1992: 134-36, 177-79.

the sport is in finding the most eclectic examples of the unifying factor; a law code, by contrast, would not consciously strive for obscurity, but the riddle technique gives a casuistic code the opportunity to be eclectic in the interests of science and stretch the topic to its farthest limits. To return to two earlier examples, in CH 1-5 the course of a lawsuit is illustrated not by commonplace examples but by attempts to pervert the course of justice by a party, a witness, and a judge; in CE 25-35 the examples that plot the course of a marriage are notable for their singularity, such the rape of a betrothed maiden, the disappearance of a husband abroad, and a slave woman who fraudulently gives a child away for adoption. Another function pertains to the scribal school, where the law codes were copied and taught. Examples are easier to learn if they conform to a familiar pattern. Thus chiasm is an excellent didactic device in a casuistic context for reviewing the full gamut of possible punishments for a discrete category of offenses.

In few cases, however, are organizational patterns as readily discernible in the law codes as legal themes. Since there are no explicit contemporary statements on which to rely, an even more cautious approach is needed than in finding substantive categories, if anachronism is to he avoided. The most reliable patterns are those like the chronological sequence, which are simple, found frequently, and act as a clue to the riddle, i.e., contribute to understanding the theme. Nonetheless, stylistic features in themselves are neither necessary nor sufficient to mark substantive categories. There is nothing to prevent the same text from containing several overlapping rhetorical patterns, fulfilling different purposes and by no means all designed to elucidate a particular thematic unit.

In the Deuteronomic law code, Wenham and McConville apply legal logic to ascertain the existence of a separate unit in 22:13-29.[16] The unity of theme is that "all the laws concern illicit sexual relations between men and women and prescribe appropriate penalties in each case."[17] The definition is perhaps too wide, since the next law following in 23:1 concerns incest and shows the difficulty of formulating ancient legal categories in modern terms. Nonetheless, it is understandable that the conventional sexual offenses of fornication, infidelity, and rape could be regarded as a

16 Wenham and McConville 1980: 248-52.

17 Wenham and McConville 1980: 249.

category apart from the more exotic sin of incest, which by being related but not included could act as a link to the next unit.[18] Wenham and McConville also claim support from the arrangement of the laws, dividing the text into six cases arranged in two parallel panels:

vv. 13-22	Offenses of married women	
	13-19	Offense in father's house
	20-21	Offense in father's house
	22	Adultery
vv. 23-28	Offenses by unmarried girls	
	23-24	Betrothed girl in city
	25-27	Betrothed girl in field
	28-29	Unbetrothed girl

The significance of the different scenes of the crime may be overstated, since it is difficult to see that the purported pattern serves any expository or mnemonic purpose. We would emphasize rather the three-fold sequence based on status: married woman, betrothed girl, unbetrothed girl. Our reason is that sequences based on status are a very common feature of the cuneiform codes, e.g., free man, son, slave (*passim* in CH and CE, although in different order); *awīlum, muškēnum*, slave (CH 196-223); married woman, betrothed woman (CH 129-130, 141-142). Status was of far greater significance in ancient than in modern systems and was used by the compilers of the law codes as a standard method of expanding the discussion of a single case.[19] We can thus be confident that in seeing such a sequence in Deuteronomy we are not making a subjective judgment.

The authors further note that the penalties are arranged chiastically: payment and divorce prohibited, woman executed, man and woman executed, man and woman executed, man executed, payment and divorce prohibited.[20] As we have seen in the numerical proverb and the incest laws in CH, the apodosis may follow a different sequence from the protasis.

18 On the use of paragraphs that could be included in either of two units as a link between them, see e.g., Petschow 1965: 163, on CH 195; and n. 42 below on *šumma ālu*.

19 See Westbrook 1988d: 58-61.

20 Wenham and McConville 1980: 250.

Mention should he made of a different methodology that is applied to the same text in order to identify a smaller unit within it, namely, vv. 22-29.[21] By tracing certain word patterns in these verses, Otto constructs a sequence consisting of a framework formed by 22 and 28-29 on the one hand and a central core with a concentric structure formed by 23-27 on the other.[22] In content, 22 and 28-29 form opposites: the death penalty for a married woman; a private remedy for the father of an unbetrothed girl. Verses 23-27 merely expand 22 by considering the question of consent, using a marginal case (betrothed girl) that falls between 22 (married woman) and 28-29 (unbetrothed girl). The basis of the unit is therefore 22 and 28-29 and the rationale for the unit lies not in a common theme but in its history: 22 and 28-29 stem from different sources—the former from laws based on the penal jurisdiction of the head of household (hence the death penalty), the latter from laws based on the inter-family conciliation tribunal that sat at the city gate (and which only had power to award simple compensation). Their combination represents the fusion of the two jurisdictions at some point in Israelite history.[23]

It is beyond the scope of this paper to enter into a discussion of the diachronic aspects of redaction, but it is germane to our inquiry to point out that the argument is an inverted pyramid, in which ever-widening assumptions are imposed one upon the other. From stylistic patterns found in the text substantive categories of law are presumed, and from those categories the existence of independent jurisdictions. A further diachronic dimension is added by presuming the existence of different collections based (originally) on jurisdiction and a process of editing that brings them together.[24] It seems to us that if accusations of unfounded speculation are

21 Otto 1993a: 274-81.

22 This summary slightly simplifies the verse count of the author, who excludes some parts of verses as extraneous redactional material.

23 The theory of two jurisdictions is argued in detail in an earlier work (Otto 1988c: esp. 61-68), on the basis of the difference in form between casuistic and apodictic laws.

24 As the penal law in Deut 22:22 is formulated casuistically and not apodictically as the theory demands, yet another diachronic layer of redaction has to be assumed to explain the discrepancy: "Dtn 22,22a gehört also in das ursprünglich in der Familie beheimatete todesrechtliche Sanktionsrecht und ist nur oberflächlich der kasuistischen Form angeglichen worden" (Otto 1993a: 278). Methodologically this could equally be seen as removing one of the steps upon which the pyramid itself is constructed.

to be avoided, the first step should be to establish the existence of different jurisdictions in the legal system by evidence independent of the text, then by the same method to demonstrate their fusion. Only then would the text be analyzed to see how that fusion was reflected in the structure of the current law code, and finally stylistic elements adduced to reinforce the structure posited by the previous steps. To extrapolate whole systems of courts from stylistic patterns in a text represents the triumph of form over substance.

A second instance in the Deuteronomic laws where a separate unit can be identified by legal logic is in our opinion 22:1-12.[25] Indeed, we would argue that the unifying factor is a jurisprudential distinction of the highest importance.

The passage contains nine laws: the obligation to care for a neighbor's animal by returning it when lost (vv. 1-3) or helping him lift it when fallen (v. 4), a prohibition on cross-dressing (v. 5), restrictions on taking from a nest (vv. 6-7), the obligation to add a parapet when building a house (v. 8), a prohibition on sowing seed in a vineyard (v. 9), on plowing with an ox and an ass (v. 10), on wearing mixed cloth (v. 11), and the obligation to wear tassels (v. 12).

These provisions are usually divided into two groups: (a) 1-4, 6-7, 8 and (b) 5, 9-12.[26] According to Braulik the intermingling of the two is deliberate: a "meshing" (German *Verzahnung*) of the humanitarian principle of the 5th Commandment—"preserve life"—and a sacral prohibition—"avoid mixtures"—which belongs to the sphere of the 6th Commandment.[27] There are thus not one but two unifying factors. Verse 12, however, fits neither of the two categories proposed. It is of course always possible to find some role for v. 12 within this context, but the discrepancy would remain. Thus Merendino explains the connection of v. 12 to the foregoing verses as a matter of "attraction":[28] "Sein Platz hier am Schluß der Perikope vv. 1-11 erklärt sich aus seiner inhaltlichen Entsprechung mit v. 11. Einem Gebot über die Art der Kleidung folgt ein Gebot über einen

25 These verses are regarded as a unit on formal grounds. See Barbiero 1991: 141-47.

26 Barbiero 1991: 159-60.

27 Braulik 1991: 73-74.

28 On the concept of attraction, see Petschow 1965: 171 and n. 152.

bestimmten Schmuck an der Kleidung."[29] This explanation, however, directly contradicts Merendino's previous assertion that "vv. 9-12 bilden inhaltlich eine Einheit. Sie enthält eine Bestimmung gegen das Zusammenbringen von ungleichartigen Dingen."[30] The presumed "meshing" cannot therefore be determinative of the content of the unit, whatever its stylistic contribution.

In our view there is but a single legal factor that unites this eclectic collection of rules, namely, that they are all about property: what one must or must not do with property. The property in question may be land (houses, fields, or vineyards) or movables (animals and garments). This is not, however, the primary distinction made by the text; rather, there is a neat division into three types of property.

The first section comprises the first three laws (vv. 1-5), which concern other people's property, namely, a neighbor's animal or the clothes of a member of the opposite sex. The second consists of but a single law, that of the hen and her eggs/chicks (vv. 6-7), which are ownerless property.[31] The third section, in the last four laws (vv. 8-12), concerns my property: my house, my land, my animals, and my clothing.

This division may not seem very important to us, but to a classical Roman jurist the categories of *res alien* and *res nullius* (as opposed to *res mea*) were fundamental.[32] *Res nullius*, ownerless property, which has little significance in modern legal systems, is discussed at length by the jurists, the principal example being, as it so happens, wild animals or birds, in which ownership was retained only as long as the creature remained in its captor's control.[33]

29 Merendino 1969: 257

30 Merendino 1969: 257.

31 It is difficult to see the purpose of vv. 6-7 as humanitarian. In the context of the law of warfare (cf. Gen 32:12 and Hos 10:14) the same principle would give one the right to slaughter children before their mothers' eyes. The purpose of the rule lies in the practicalities of property law: it is permissible to appropriate the fruits of ownerless property but not the capital, so that others may in their turn enjoy its fruits.

32 Justinian *Inst.* 2.1pr.: ". . . we turn to things. They either belong to us (*in nostro patrimonio*) or they do not belong to us. They can be: everybody's by the law of nature; the state's; a corporation's; or no-one's (*nullius*). But most things belong to individuals." (edition in Krueger 1912 [my translation]).

33 *Digesta* 41.1.1-5 (edition Krueger 1912 [my translation]).

The method of using Roman concepts from much later sources to explain an earlier Hebrew source is in this instance less singular than might be thought. A prime reason for the striking similarity between the provisions of the various law codes of the ancient Near East, in spite of the great distances of time and space that separated them, is their belonging to a scholastic tradition which from its place of origin, apparently Mesopotamia, spread throughout the region. In that tradition certain scholastic juridical problems, such as the goring ox, the betrothed maiden, and the thief caught breaking in at night, formed a canon of learning that was transmitted from generation to generation and from school to school. Thus they reappear again and again in different law codes, and with them the legal concepts and distinctions that they embodied. We have argued elsewhere that the Mediterranean basin including Rome was not isolated from this tradition.[34] Where then a discussion occurs among Roman jurists about wild animals as *res nullius*, the possibility arises that it stems from a scholastic juridical problem in the Near Eastern tradition, the only remnant of which to be preserved, unfortunately, is the law in Deut 22:6-7. It is significant that the Roman jurists cited in this connection are associated with academic law rather than practice, in particular Gaius, a jurist of the second century C.E., who is principally remembered as the author of a textbook for law students and whose work bears marks of the influence of ancient Near Eastern law.[35] It is therefore likely that the Roman classification of property goes back to Near Eastern sources, except that in the latter it is never stated expressly. Its existence in the minds of the ancient authors emerges from the structure in which they cast their casuistic rules.

To complete our discussion of the unit, it may be noted as regards its arrangement that the internal structure of the first and third sections follows a logical sequence based on another standard basis for categorizing property (cf. Exod 22:8): farm animals and clothes in the first section and land, farm animals, and clothes in the third.[36] Given that the unit applies

34 Westbrook 1988a: 97-118.

35 See de Zulueta 1946-53: 1-5; and Westbrook 1988a. The other jurist cited is Florentinus, who is known only as the author of a legal textbook.

36 It is tempting to see the references to land in the last law of the previous unit (21:23) as a "bridge" which introduces the new unit and completes the sequence land, animals, clothes in the first section. The temptation should be resisted as unwarranted speculation. Although a provision on land in the first section would indeed make an even neater pat-

the eclectic possibilities of the riddle to the full, ranging through birds' nests, parapets, and tassels, the familiar pattern of land, animals, and clothing provides the strongest of clues that the answer lies in the sphere of property.

Most of the laws in Deuteronomy do not yield to classification by legal logic. If their arrangement is not to be dismissed as random, then some other, non-legal, factors must he found that unify groupings of disparate laws. An attempt has been made by Carmichael with the five laws that make up Deuteronomy 21.[37] The first law lays down the ceremony to be performed to expiate a murder by persons unknown, the second regulates marriage of a captive slave girl, the third confirms the inheritance share of the firstborn son, the fourth punishes a rebellious son, and the fifth requires the body of a hanged criminal to be buried before nightfall. As Carmichael rightly points out, there is no link between them in terms of legal subject matter. Instead, he proposes a non-legal factor: these are all situations that have to do with death, each of them connected with wrongdoing. The corpse may cause defilement, the girl may be prevented from mourning her parents, a father settling his estate in contemplation of death may deny his firstborn's rights, a son has to die because of his conduct, a criminal's body may cause defilement.

There are grave methodological objections to Carmichael's hypothesis. The criteria by which the topic "death" was chosen are not clear. No evidence is produced to show that it was used elsewhere as a unifying factor, whether in legal or non-legal texts, in the Bible, or in other ancient literature. On the contrary, death is such a commonplace in the law codes, especially as a punishment, that it is hard to see how it could be used to distinguish one set of laws from any others. Nor does any thought appear to have been given to what purpose might be served, expository, didactic, or moralistic, by such a classification. If either of the first two, then it suffers from a fatal error. Four of the five laws might he claimed to be "situations that have to do with death," in that death forms part of the circumstances of the case, the protasis. The protasis of the rebellious son law, however, contains nothing about death; it is necessary to raid the apodosis

tern that accommodates modern sensibilities, its absence does not invalidate the logic of the sequence.

37 Carmichael 1979: 129-42.

to find a mention of death in the death penalty. Such an inelegance deprives the unit of any rhetorical structure that might aid the reader and reveals the artificiality of the purported common factor.[38] In methodological terms, it has been plucked out of the air, deriving not from the evidence of ancient sources but from the thought-processes of the modern mind.

How then may we find non-legal factors to classify these laws that represent the authors' or compilers' intentions? In seeking the appropriate controls, we turn once again to the cuneiform law codes, but this time to examine the non-legal context in which they arose.

We have mentioned that the law codes were part of the wider genre of scientific literature by which the scribes sought to classify knowledge and which included medical, lexical, and omen lists. It is reasonable therefore to draw upon such texts for reliable non-legal factors. The criteria for classification were seldom abstract: lexical texts were separated into lists of stones, plants, professions, etc; medical texts into lists of symptoms or body parts; divinatory texts were divided by vehicle of divination: fetuses, livers, or astronomical phenomena. A mechanical scribal device reveals that within these lists there were further divisions based on content. A ruled line on a clay tablet is used to mark matters of different content. In contracts, for example, it is often found between the terms and the list of witnesses or between the witnesses and the date. In the scientific literature it is employed with varying frequency. Its most frequent use is in first millennium lexical texts, where it marks off small groups of associated words. Such units appear to be designated by the technical term *sadīru in* Standard Babylonian.[39] In the early Mesopotamian law codes it is not found at all (or rather it is used simply to divide the individual lines of the text), while in copies of MAL and the Hittite Laws it is used to divide individual laws, which is most helpful, but not for our purposes.

Of course, ruled lines cannot tell us what factor united the text within them; only that one existed, and it is often difficult to discern what unites

38 Wenham and McConville (1980: 251) attempt to support Carmichael's analysis by claiming a chiastic structure for the unit. They succeed in showing that any chiasm can be constructed if one is sufficiently liberal in the elements used to constitute its members. The parallel of C, "unloved captive slave girl receiving her freedom," and C[1], "unloved first-horn son receiving inheritance," is a trifle forced. In addition, our earlier remarks on the limitations of purely stylistic structures apply.

39 *CAD* S 18, meaning 2b. See the discussion in Landsberger 1937: ix-x.

one unit and distinguishes it from the next.[40] A particularly clear and simple example from the omen series *šumma ālu* gives us some indication of scribal criteria. The protases of Tablet V set out the circumstances in which a house is built, with lines between the following sections:[41]

1-2	laying foundations on specific days
3-17	laying foundations in a specific month (in calendrical order)
18-21	events at the time of laying foundations
22-33	location, character, appearance of foundations
34-(x)	month in which house was built
(x)-45	animals (+ starlight in line 45) penetrate house
46-67	character (46-57), location (58-67) of gates
68-72	character, location of house (on street)
73-74	location of house in high or low place
75-90	location of house (in city: 75-76), features of parts of house: brickwork, front, roof, parapet, support, beam, wall
91-99	parts of house: threshold, bolt, courtyard
100-101	renovations (?)

These simple categories of time, space, part, and whole are typical of the non-legal divisions of cuneiform scientific texts.[42] In another omen series,

40 Such is unfortunately the case with a source that ought to be particularly appropriate, the lexical text *ana ittišu*. It is a sort of Sumero-Akkadian legal dictionary, a list of legal terms used in contracts and other legal documents. Its organization is complicated by the fact that two different principles are employed, thematic and acrographic, and the themes are further interspersed with small narratives, novellae, that illustrate the terms listed. The terms are divided into groups of anything from one to a dozen lines, and sometimes longer, as when a novella relates the history of a partnership (MSL I 6 I 9-II 5). The discernible themes are those of legal logic, such as hired labor, litigation, marriage, but they form chapters larger than the units designated by ruled lines. In his edition, Landsberger (1937: xii-xvii) discusses some of these problems and attempts a rough division of the contents.

41 Text: CT 38 10-13; edition in Nötscher 1928-30: 4-13.

42 Note also, in connection with our earlier discussion (n. 18 above) of the linking function of the incest law in Deut 23:1, the use of examples at the beginning or end of sections which could equally fit in the adjacent section but which are assigned by the ruled line to one section alone.

šumma izbu, concerning ominous fetuses, there is not the convenience of ruled lines, but the categories are still straightforward and relatively easy to isolate: sounds made by the fetus, fetus in shape of various animals, fetus in shape of various parts of the body, physical defects, twins, multiple births.[43] The material character of the categories chosen makes a useful control on the almost infinite possibilities of themes outside the bounds of legal logic. At the very least, they should mark the starting point for inquiry, rather than unattested abstract categories such as "death."

In the riddle, it will be recalled, the unifying factor was not at all legal. Theoretically then, the model of the riddle allows us to identify units in a law code where the unifying factor is not dependent upon legal logic. Nonetheless, we must bear in mind that the license afforded us by the riddle is to rule merely imaginary lines between groups of laws, and heed the limitations suggested by the evidence of cuneiform scientific literature.

As an example, we shall first take a case where the clue to the riddle is plainly stated at the outset. In Deuteronomy 20 and 21 eight laws are presented, the first and second set of four each beginning with the phrase "when you go out to war . . ." and incidentally ending with a corpse. Since the first four laws, 20:1-21:9, are in fact all set in the context of war, there is no reason to question the express evidence for their theme given in the opening line, which in its exhortational generalities is reminiscent of the heading with which numerical proverbs are introduced, but which also serves as a clue. The only difficulty arises with regard to the fourth law, 21:1-9, which is not usually associated by scholars with the previous three.[44] It concerns the ceremony of expiation to be performed by the local authorities where a murder victim is found in the open country, slain by an unknown hand. From the many cuneiform parallels, however, we know that this provision dealt with the problem of banditry, as it affected travelers through the countryside.[45] As Jackson has shown,[46] banditry was a recognized form of irregular warfare. In the conflict between Abimelech

43 Tablet I, lines 1-46. On the principal copy (CT 27 14-15, I, II) there are some ruled lines, but too few on a broken tablet to discern the smaller units. The final line marks off the library catch-line and the colophon. Edition in Leichty 1970: 32-35.

44 See Braulik 1991: 65-70; and Carmichael 1979: 129, for whom it is the first of a unit of five laws constituting Deuteronomy 21.

45 Dion 1982: 17; Westbrook 1986a: 62-65.

46 Jackson 1972: 6-7, cf. 35-40.

and the lords of Shechem, the latter waged war by setting ambushes on the hilltops and robbing passing travelers (Judg 9:25). Between friendly states, it led to international treaties which made the host state responsible for the losses of foreign merchants and to diplomatic protests, as when the rulers of Akko robbed and killed Babylonian merchants on their way to Egypt.[47] It is significant that the term used for the victim is חלל, which indicates elsewhere those slain in battle.

Seen in this light, 21:1-9 makes the fourth limb of a by now familiar arrangement: the chronological sequence. The first law (20:1-9) is situated prior to hostilities, laying down the procedure for reviewing the army and for mustering out ineligible or unsuitable recruits. The second law (20:10-18) brings us to a point in time just before an enemy city is attacked, regulating the terms of surrender that may be offered to the city for not offering resistance. With the third law (20:19-20) we finally find ourselves in the midst of war. It regulates one aspect of the conduct of a prolonged siege, namely, the destruction of trees. The fourth law is set at the end of a successful campaign, when the land is settled with Israelite towns and villages, but peaceful conditions are shattered by an act analogous to war.

The following law, 21:10-14, continues the chronological sequence but introduces a new thematic unit in that it takes place after the war is over and the troops have been sent home. It concerns purely domestic issues, as do the following three laws. Regrettably, elucidation of this unit cannot be pursued here, since it would require long digressions on questions of substantive interpretation that were best reserved for a separate study.

Our second example is a group of four laws in Deut 25:1-12: the prohibition of giving a man sentenced to beating more than forty blows, the prohibition on muzzling an ox while threshing, the levirate law, and the punishment of a woman who seizes a man's testicles in a fight.

Carmichael has attempted to link the muzzled ox law with the levirate by suggesting that it is not to be understood literally but as an allusion to the levir's duty.[48] The ox is a figurative term for an Israelite and "threshing" one for sexual intercourse. Thus the levir's refusal to give conception

47 RS 17.146 (Nougayrol 1956: 154-57), RS 17.158 (Nougayrol 1956: 169-71), RS 17.229 (Nougayrol 1956: 106); EA 8, lines 8-33 (edition in Moran 1992: no. 8).

48 Carmichael 1980: 250-52.

to his brother's widow constitutes muzzling the ox, because the dead man's threshing bears no fruit.

It is not clear to us what the purpose of an allegorical statement would be in the middle of a collection of laws otherwise drafted in plain language. It cannot have been a popular saying because the circumstances of its application, the levirate, are too narrow and complex. As an *ad hoc* phrase, on the other hand, it would not have been comprehensible even to the contemporary reader without the explicit terms of the levirate law that follows it. And as a pithy summary of those terms it is inexact. The levirate is a positive duty, whereas the muzzled ox law is formulated negatively, as a prohibition.

Another such interpretation, by Noonan, prefers to see in this law a prohibition on the sin of Onan (i.e., *coitus interruptus*).[49] "Do not muzzle" therefore means "do not deny the natural accompaniment of intercourse," namely, conception. The purpose of muzzling an ox, however, is to stop it from eating the grain, which, as Noonan admits, is an imperfect metaphor for *coitus perfectus*.

In our view, the unifying factor in these laws lies not in fanciful allegories or metaphors but in the traditions of ancient scientific literature. Let us begin at the most elementary level, in the curriculum of the scribal schools. An Old Babylonian list called *Ugu-mu* ("my skull") is a dictionary of Sumerian terms for parts of the body, proceeding systematically from head to toe. It evidently served as a means of oral instruction, wherein the (Akkadian-speaking) pupils had to recite aloud the Sumerian terms while pointing to the relevant part of the body.[50] The same system continued in use in later times, forming the basis of the first-millennium canonical lists Hh. XV and Nabnitu.[51]

Reference to parts of the body is found frequently in other types of cuneiform scientific literature, such as medical and divinatory texts. In the passage from *šumma izbu* referred to above, it is used as one means of classifying the ominous appearance of the fetus. It is also found in the law codes as the mode whereby unlawful wounding is analyzed, taking the

49 Noonan 1980: 172-75.

50 Cavigneaux 1983: 630 (18.3).

51 Hh. XV is edited in Landsberger and Civil 1967 (= MSL IX). The lexical series SIG$_7$ + ALAM = *nabnītu* is edited in Finkel 1982 (= MSL XVI).

form of a list of the affected parts of the body. Thus CE 42-46 lists injured parts according to the classification head (nose, eyes, tooth, ear, cheek), then limbs (finger, arm, leg), then body (collarbone).[52]

In Deut 25:1-12 the same system is applied in a more radical way to link four entirely different laws. The key lies not in their circumstances, which have no connection, but in the apodosis.[53] They all concern what is or is not to be done with parts of the body. The back is to be struck not more than forty times, the face is not to be covered, the face is to be spat in, the foot is to be uncovered, the hand is to be cut off.

The sequence would appear to be body, head, limbs—which is less symmetrical than the sequence in CE or systematic than that in *Ugu-mu*, but more so than *šumma izbu*, where the body parts appear to be listed in the order face, . . . finger, . . . membrane, . . . head, hand, wrist, foot, blood-vessel, "goat-horn," "gazelle-horn," . . . matted hair.[54] Another possibility arises from the suggestion of Eslinger that in the last law (vv. 11-12) the Hebrew term translated "hand" (כַּף) should be rendered "genitals."[55] The woman who seizes a man's genitals is thus punished talionically, by female circumcision. If this suggestion is correct, the sequence would then be symmetrical opposites: back, head, foot, front.

The factor unifying this group of laws is therefore not legal at all. If it seems disappointingly mechanical, a primitive categorization in our eyes, it had for its ancient audience the virtue of familiarity, being derived from the most elementary traditions of classification. It also makes an excellent riddle.[56]

52 Edition in Yaron 1969: 69-73; new readings by Roth 1997: 70-71 (in the 1995 edition).

53 For an example of a unit linked by the apodosis, see Exod 21:12-17.

54 Column I, lines 24-26. The complete sequence cannot be reconstructed due to breaks in the text and terms whose meaning is unclear.

55 Eslinger 1981: 269-81.

56 It is possible that the two following provisions, in vv. 13-19 (just weights and remember Amalek), form a unit that continues the same theme, but somewhat at a tangent. The common factor appears to be parts of the body, but in a different sense. The Hebrew term for weight is אבן "stone," which is also the standard euphemism for testicles. This verse is thus connected to the foregoing through a reference to the genitalia, albeit by way of an uncharacteristically vulgar pun. Amalek's crime was to have attacked the stragglers at the rear of the Israelite column, which is expressed in Hebrew by a verb deriving from the root זנב "tail." The two laws therefore follow the sequence front and back, but through punning.

27

The Trial of Jeremiah

Abstract

Jeremiah 26 provides one of the few records from the Near East in which a court debates points of law rather than facts. This article presents a legal analysis of the text that resolves a number of discrepancies and that shows how the text was composed to credit Jeremiah's defense speech as the decisive factor in his acquittal.

Chapter 26 of the book of Jeremiah belongs to an exceedingly rare category of trial report in the ancient Near East, in that it focuses on issues of law and not of fact. It is concerned not with the evidence but with the legal arguments that were presented to the court prior to its decision.[1] This small contribution in honor of Professor Wenham will review in brief scholarship on the forensic aspects of the report and attempt to provide a coherent account of the legal procedure involved in the prophet's trial.

The difficulties of the account in Jeremiah 26 have led to a long tradition among exegetes of excision, emendation, and source criticism.[2] Not a few have despaired altogether of making sense of the narrative. Thus one commentator remarks: "Too many discrete strands make up the story for a coherent account to be derived from it."[3]

* Originally published in *Reading the Law: Studies in Honour of Gordon J. Wenham* (ed. J. G. McConville and K. Möller; New York: T. & T. Clark, 2007), 95-107. Copyright © 2007. Reprinted by permission of Continuum International Publishing Group.

* A draft of this study was presented to the Department of Bible at Tel Aviv University on 2 January 2006. I am grateful to the members of the department for their comments and criticisms. Responsibility for the opinions expressed remains entirely my own.

1 There are many litigation records in cuneiform, but they report only the evidence and the bare verdict. The sole comparable report to Jeremiah 26 is the Nippur Homicide Trial, discussed below.

2 For a division into diachronic layers and a summary of scholarship, see Stipp 1992: 17-72.

3 Carroll 1986: 520. Likewise Hossfeld and Meyer, who take the view "dass wir einem Text mit erheblichen Unebenheiten gegenüberstehen" (1974: 32).

The biblical narrative should not, however, be dismissed as unrealistic or confused simply because it does not fit modern concepts of forensic jurisprudence or reporting. When seen in the context of ancient Near Eastern litigation, many of the seeming discrepancies fall away. The events described may be divided into a number of stages.

1. The Offense (vv. 1-6)

The facts in this case are not in dispute. Jeremiah has made in public the statements for which he is put on trial, and he does not deny them. The trial is about whether they constitute an offense under the law. The only relevant law in the Bible is Deut 18:20-22, which decrees the death penalty for a prophet who falsely purports to prophesy in the name of YHWH when he has no such mandate. To distinguish between a false and a real prophet, the law proposes a "wait and see" test: if the prophecy is fulfilled, it came from YHWH. We have no way of knowing whether the Deuteronomic law was in force or even in the minds of the participants in Jeremiah's trial.[4] What we are entitled to assume is that the Deuteronomic rules were not created *ex nihilo* and for the most part reflected traditional law. That said, the death penalty is a far more credible aspect of the law than its "wait and see" test.

2. Seizure and Accusation (vv. 7-9)

The seizure of Jeremiah by so many people at once may be dismissed as hyperbolic, but in a forensic context seizure can be a formality, a symbolic act to initiate pre-trial proceedings, especially when accompanied by formal words of accusation, as here in vv. 8-9.[5] In Deut 21:19, a father and mother are expected to "seize" their rebellious son and bring him before the elders—a daunting task for aged parents against a strapping young

4 The lack of citation is of no weight because the system of citation of statutes characteristic of Rabbinic law had not yet developed. It is attested with certainty only in post-exilic sources (Westbrook 2003d: 19-21).

5 Cf. Dombradi 1996: vol. 1, 295-302, for the Old Babylonian period, although she distinguishes between criminal and civil trials. In the former, the person may be physically detained until brought before the court.

man, if conceived in purely physical terms. In Jeremiah's case, the question of how he is brought before the court is moot, because the court comes to him.

The verbal accusation is: "You shall surely die! Why did you prophesy . . .?" (v. 9). As H. J. Boecker points out, it is common in the biblical idiom for the accusation to be formulated as a question to the accused.[6] The accuser may at the same time propose the punishment, which is the accuser's estimation of the seriousness of the offense.[7] Although presented as if it were a sentence, it is merely a proposal, conditional upon trial and conviction.[8]

Boecker notes that atypically the proposed punishment in this verse precedes the accusation, which he attributes to the heated emotions of the accusers.[9] It is noteworthy, however, that the accusation in question does not state what crime has been committed; it simply repeats the accused's words without any expression of wrongdoing. This is equally atypical for the interrogative form of accusation, where the offense is made explicit either before or after the question. Thus in 1 Sam 26:15-16, in a quasi-forensic context, David accuses Abner and his guard: "Why did you not guard your lord the king, for someone came to slaughter the king your lord. It is not good what you have done: by the life of YHWH, you are all deserving of death, because you did not guard your lord . . . ."

In Jeremiah 26, I suggest, the appropriate punishment precedes the accusation for two reasons. First, it serves to define the crime: Jeremiah can only face the death penalty if his prophecy in the name of YHWH is false. Second, the trial and the role of the accusers are atypical in that the facts are not at issue. There is no need to prove that the offense was committed.

3. The Court (vv. 9-10)

The three components of the accusers are the priests, the prophets, and "all the people" (כל העם). At the close of the accusation it is said that all the people gathered (v. 9, ויקהל) around Jeremiah in the Temple of YHWH.

6 Boecker 1964: 25-31, 67; see Bovati 1994: 75.

7 Boecker 1964: 72.

8 Bovati 1994: 85-88.

9 Boecker 1964: 59.

Some commentators translate the verb "thronged about," which raises difficulties in the sequence of events, since they must already have gathered around Jeremiah at the moment of seizure.[10] Far better is the view of those commentators who see in the use of the verb here the constitution of a court.[11] As Bovati puts it, "this phrase does not describe the threatening press of the crowd around Jeremiah so much as the formation of a juridically competent assembly which has a decisive role within the trial."[12] At this point, however, the nobles intervene. Furthermore, in v. 17 yet another group, the elders of the land, are mentioned as being present. The question is then: Which of these various groups formed the court and what role did they play?

Bovati hesitates to ascribe the role of a court to "all the people." That function belongs to the nobles, who will pass sentence. The public assembly acts "almost like the jury in a modern assizes" to endorse their decision.[13] Boecker likewise insists that the trial is conducted by the nobles, but with participation by the people, which may be a special feature of Jerusalem courts. He also invokes the idea of a jury, drawing on a parallel from German legal history.[14] H. C. Brichto refers to the king's officials and the עם as judge and jury respectively.[15]

A different approach is that of H. Schulz, who considers the only true court to be כל העם in v. 17. In his view, this is a special "cultic court" (*Kultgericht*) comprised of every other group mentioned—the priests, the prophets, the accused, the nobles, the elders, and the people—and at the same time separate from them. The scenario imagined by Schulz is that the various parties or groups address various other groups during the course of the proceedings, but only the elders address the whole court. Their opinion must therefore have been the one adopted by the court, although not actually recorded in the text.[16]

For V. H. Matthews and D. C. Benjamin, "all the people" is a technical legal term for a quorum, which means that enough people are present

10 Holladay 1989: 106; Lundbom 2004: 289-90. Cf. Brin 1983: 53, who regards the actions of the accusers as those of a lynch mob.

11 E.g., Rietzschel 1966: 97 n. 10; O'Connor 1989: 621.

12 Bovati 1994: 229.

13 Bovati 1994: 229.

14 The term he uses is "*Rechtssasse*" (Boecker 1964: 59 n. 1).

15 Brichto 1992: 228.

16 Schulz 1969: 120-22.

for the trial to be official. Wherever the term appears, it means "officially" rather than referring to a group of jurors or spectators. When "all the people" gather round Jeremiah, the state court was officially called into session.[17]

Whatever their individual merits, the difficulty with all these reconstructions is the models that they use. Bovati, Boecker, and Brichto rely on anachronistic parallels drawn from their own legal systems. Judges and juries in modern courts, whether in the Civil or Common Law systems, have different functions; such differentiation cannot be projected back into an ancient tribunal. Schulz and Matthews and Benjamin invent novel institutions that are otherwise unknown. Even if we accept the possibility of Schulz's special "cultic court," not elsewhere attested in the Bible, the idea of a forum in which some factions address other factions but not the plenum has no parallel in any recorded legal system. Nor is it surprising, since such a cacophonic arrangement between groups within earshot of each other would be unworkable.

Similarly, Matthews and Benjamin's idea of the totality being a quorum, if taken strictly, would mean that the court could never sit, since full attendance of every possible participant is unattainable in practice. If all the people means less than everyone, on the other hand, then the phrase begs the question of what is the minimum needed for a trial to be official. It also begs the question of what makes a group action official. The one biblical text that Matthews and Benjamin cite in support illustrates the problem. In Gen 19:4-5, all the men of Sodom gather outside the house in which Lot has two guests and demand that he produce them. It is difficult to see their demand as the authoritative act of a duly constituted assembly—as opposed to a threatening mob—given that the action that they are said to contemplate is hardly of a juridical nature. Nonetheless, both Schulz' and Matthews and Benjamin's analyses are helpful, as we shall see below, in their emphasis on the inclusive nature of the tribunal.

A better approach in my view is to examine the copious data from Israel's neighbors, from around the time of Jeremiah and previously. It is true that there is no evidence from the ancient Near East as to the actual formalities whereby a court was constituted. There is a great deal of evidence, on the other hand, about the composition of courts of law,

17 Matthews and Benjamin 1993: 236.

indicating cultural patterns that were long-standing and widespread. Three types of forum can be discerned:

a) A single official sitting as judge or a college referred to simply as "the judges."
b) A large assembly of lay persons (Sumerian: ukkin; Akkadian: *puḫrum*; Hittite: *pankuš*, *tuliya*). There is never any mention of a quorum, but the members are referred to as "citizens" (*mār banî*), "the men of GN," "the sons of GN," and the like (see below under c). The qualification for membership would thus seem to be the status of an adult male citizen.
c) A mixed tribunal of officials and citizens. This form of court was quite common. In the Neo-Babylonian and Persian periods, for example, an assembly (*puḫrum*) of free citizens (*mār banî*) or local elders (*šībūt āli*) in Babylonian cities is frequently found sitting as a court for both civil and criminal matters, sometimes alone and sometimes in conjunction with officials, both royal and temple.[18] In a case from the reign of Cambyses, employees of the Eanna Temple at Uruk who stole ducks from the temple are examined by an assembly consisting of temple administrators and free citizens (*mār banî*) and after they confess are sentenced by a plenary tribunal consisting of the chief administrator and the royal treasurer of the Eanna Temple, and the assembly of the men of Babylon and the men of Uruk.[19] In another case from the reign of Cyrus, the city scribe of Sippar, an official of the Shamash Temple, and the elders sit in a mixed tribunal to decide whether a slave is private or temple property (*Cyr.* 332), while in a property dispute from the reign of Neriglissar, the court is composed of the governor of Babylon, the judges, and the elders of the city (Dalley *Edinburgh* 69).[20]

The Hittite terms *tuliya* and *pankuš*, the subject of a philological study by G. M. Beckman, are particularly helpful in revealing the ancient conceptualization of large, mixed tribunals. The term *tuliya* is the equivalent

18 Dandamaev 1981: 45-49; Oelsner, Wells, and Wunsch 2003: 919.
19 *Iraq* 13 96 (edited in Figulla 1951: 95-102).
20 Edited by Joannès 2000: 234-37.

of Akkadian *puḫrum* and is used to describe an assembly, *inter alia*, acting as a court. The term *pankuš* as an adjective means "every." Beckman concludes that where the noun *pankuš* stands alone, it has the meaning "totality (of those present on a given occasion)"—it is inclusive, rather than exclusive. For example in a ritual text (KUB XII 8:3:1-4): "Then the men of GN enter. Three men wail and the congregation sings thus . . . ." When employed in the political and juridical sphere, it is synonymous with *tuliya*, or more precisely, the *pankuš* is assembled in a *tuliya*.[21]

In the light of this evidence, "all the people" (כל העם) should not be taken as an authoritative body in itself; it merely designates all those present in the Temple. It is through the action described by the verb that they constitute themselves as a court. Although mentioned separately, the priests and prophets are also a component of the court, since "all the people," like the *pankuš*, is an inclusive term. Thus in v. 8, Jeremiah can be said to have addressed "all the people" without mention of the priests and the prophets, even though the previous verse had informed us that the priests and the prophets heard it too. The court thus constituted is then joined by the nobles to form a mixed tribunal.

The whole process is referred to summarily in v. 17, where the elders address "all the קהל of the people," that is, those present constituted as a court. What formality was needed to give the court authority is not stated, but in this final form it included all those mentioned separately: the people, the priests and prophets, and the nobles. My conclusion thus supports the inclusive approach of Schulz and of Matthews and Benjamin but is based on real ancient models, not putative ones.

If there is a technical aspect to the phrase "all the people," it is that it cannot refer to every living soul even among those present. To qualify as a court, it must exclude persons who are not eligible, such as foreigners, women, and slaves, if any were present (cf. the merism in Gen 19:4: "young men and old, all the people"). On the other hand, it would have included not only Jerusalemites but the inhabitants of the towns of Judah, whom Jeremiah had been commissioned to address in the Temple. Some of them, the "elders of the land," publicly voice their opinion during the proceedings. The examples given above from Babylonian trials are sufficient to negate Matthews and Benjamin's judgment that "from a

21 Beckman 1982: 438.

sociological point of view these elders from a village assembly are out of place in a state court."[22]

To summarize: by the action described in v. 9 (ויקהל) the priests and prophets and the remaining male citizenry constitute themselves as a court in order to pursue Jeremiah in a formal trial. Their previous role as accusers, however, does not bode well for the fairness of the trial, for there was no rule in ancient law that precluded a man from being judge in his own cause.[23] The priests and prophets who are singled out as the motivating force behind the accusation have an obvious interest in protecting their monopoly over authorized prophecy. Fortunately, the nobles of Judah, evidently palace officials, intervene. In our understanding, they join the court that is about to sit in order to form a mixed tribunal of officials and citizens.

4. The Trial (vv. 11ff.)

Because the trial turns upon the law, not the facts, the proceedings have nothing of the character of a conventional hearing in which the prosecution and defense present conflicting narratives and adduce evidence in support, and the judges decide on the true version of events.

To place the biblical report in context, I would invoke the parallel of the only other known trial report of a purely legal issue from the ancient Near East. In a murder trial conducted before the assembly of Nippur, as reported in a literary account copied in Old Babylonian scribal schools, the established facts were that three men had conspired to kill a priest. After the murder, the conspirators had informed the victim's wife of what they had done, but she kept silent.[24] The central issue of the hearing being reported is the culpability of the victim's wife. The report presents it in the form of a debate among different factions within the Assembly. As in Jeremiah's trial, the guilt or innocence of all the accused is formulated in terms of their liability to the death penalty.

Nine men of various professions, such as bird-catcher and potter, who are clearly ordinary citizens, address the assembly, speaking in favor of the

22 Matthews and Benjamin 1993: 236.

23 Examples from the Bible are to be found in Wells 2004: 50-51.

24 Editions by Jacobsen 1970: 193-214; Roth 1998: 173-84.

death penalty for the conspirators and the wife. Two men, an army officer, and an orchard-keeper, then argue in the woman's defense. The Assembly then deliberates (line 43: en_3-tar-re-eš-am_3) and sides with the majority, adding its own arguments. It concludes: "her guilt exceeds (the guilt of) those who kill a man."

Here also we see the term assembly (*puḫrum*) is used in a non-exclusive manner. The report then states that the assembly, having resolved the case, delivered all four for execution.

On the basis of this parallel, I would argue that the report of Jeremiah's trial is in fact a series of orations by factions within the court. The only difference—and it is a significant difference for the structure of the narrative—is that the defendant gets to speak on his own behalf.

5. Oration of the Priests and Prophets (v. 11)

The priests and prophets reiterate the charges previously made against Jeremiah. They now refer to the defendant in the third person, addressing their remarks to the nobles and all the people. Boecker takes this change to indicate that a prosecutor is addressing a court officially in session.[25] The priests and prophets do not repeat the facts but take them as known ("as you have heard with your own ears"), even though a part of the court, namely, the nobles, had not in fact been eyewitnesses to Jeremiah's prophesying. The latter are deemed to be cognizant of the facts. The issue is thus one of pure law. When the priests and prophets put the case for the prosecution, they are not presenting to the court a version of events (nor, obviously, evidence to support it), but a legal argument. They function as a faction within the tribunal rather than as an external entity.

As we have seen, the offense is not made explicit in the accusation. It only emerges from Jeremiah's defense that he is accused of falsely purporting to prophesy in the name of YHWH. The argument of the priests and prophets appears to be that Jeremiah's lack of a mandate is self-evident from the content of his prophecy. They thereby infer that a "wait and see" test, such as prescribed in Deut 18:21-22 (if the prophecy is fulfilled, it came from YHWH), would not be applicable.

25 Boecker 1964: 71, 150 n. 4.

6. Jeremiah's Oration (vv. 12-15)

Jeremiah's speech to the court in his defense:

a) agrees upon the facts (v. 12, "all the words that you have heard");
b) asserts his divine mandate from YHWH;
c) points out that the prophecy is conditional, and may be averted by appropriate measures. This argument may also be an oblique reference to a "wait and see" test, effectively neutralizing its danger for Jeremiah. It places responsibility for his prophecy not being fulfilled with the government and people (cf. Jonah 3:4-10);
d) warns the court of the consequences of a guilty verdict. Bovati adduces this verse in support of his view that there is no such thing as a ''neutral'' defense; defense is to accuse the accuser.[26] His analysis, however, does not fit the account of the trial. Jeremiah addresses not those who have accused him ("the priests and prophets" or even "the priests and prophets and all the people") but emphatically the whole court ("all the nobles and all the people"). It is not a charge of false accusation that he is bringing, but a warning of perversion of justice through a wrongful verdict. If the trial had turned on an issue of fact, then the court, even if it had wrongly convicted the accused, could claim its innocence because it had been misled by the false evidence of the accusers. There is no such escape for the court here, where the issue is purely one of law: do Jeremiah's words amount to false prophecy (without allowing for "wait and see")? A guilty verdict would therefore be a conscious wrongdoing (according to Jeremiah), and execution of the death sentence would amount to murder. Furthermore, murder pollutes the immediate area where it is committed and the persons implicated. An official verdict of the Jerusalem court would pollute the members of the court, the city, and its inhabitants. Thus the wheel will come full circle: pollution in turn will

26 Bovati 1994: 331-32, especially n. 161.

bring down divine wrath, with similar consequences to the curse pronounced in the original prophecy.

7. Oration of the Nobles and All the People (v. 16)

The remainder of the court rejects the argument of the priests and prophets, addressing them as an isolated minority. Although the inference is that the overwhelming majority unreservedly embraces Jeremiah's argument, curiously, no reasoning is presented, only a conclusion of Jeremiah's innocence. It should logically mark the end of the report, even if not followed by an explicit notice of Jeremiah's acquittal. Instead, the narrative continues with notices of the fate of two other prophets.

It is these extra verses that have done most to persuade scholars that the chapter is a composite account that has lost any pristine coherence it might have had through editing.[27] It is true that they appear to disrupt the chronological (and logical) sequence followed hitherto and seem otiose after the climax of the court's pronouncement in v. 16. Brichto, however, has rightly discerned that a deliberate narrative technique is employed here: ". . . this chapter exploits the narrative technique of dividing the story into episodes, a synoptic episode relating the entire story in brief, followed by a resumptive episode in which additional details are provided."[28]

Brichto does not explain the advantage of this technique, which seems to result in a resounding anti-climax. That, in my view, is exactly the point. The narrative is not a dry court report but a propagandistic account of the trial. The purpose of the narrator (or editor) is to paint Jeremiah in the best light. The progress of the trial is sketched in the bold lines of a good courtroom drama: Jeremiah is accused, Jeremiah makes a magnificent speech in his own defense, the court acquits him. The impression is thereby given that it was Jeremiah's speech that won the day. There are, though, two inconvenient facts that would temper this impression, and for that reason they are relegated to postscripts. Paradoxically, the structure of

27 Typical is the judgment of O'Connor: "The inconsistencies and contradictions of these verses . . . indicate that vv 17-24 do not form part of the original narrative" (1989: 623).

28 Brichto 1992: 227.

the narrative, in seeking to play down uncomfortable facts, vouches for the basic credibility of the report.

8. Oration of Members of the Elders of the Land (vv. 17-19)

Those elders who address the court (apparently not all of them) are once again a faction within the forensic assembly. They are among the inhabitants of the cities of Judah who had come to Jerusalem to worship at the Temple and would thus have been among Jeremiah's audience who were subsequently constituted as a court, albeit (the text emphasizes) a small minority.

The elders present arguments that directly correspond to Jeremiah's (in a way that the statement of the court in v. 16 does not): a previous prophet had made a conditional prophecy of disaster; King Hezekiah's government had heeded him and taken the appropriate apotropaic measures; the disaster was thereby averted; to act otherwise in this case would be a wrongful act with dire consequences for the perpetrators. This argument from precedent may well have been decisive, as Schulz claims, or at least may have had more weight in the court's decision than Jeremiah's oration. Certainly, it was sufficiently important that it could not be omitted from a report of the trial. The narrative, however, relegates it to a postscript after the acclamation that Jeremiah's words receive, so as to give the impression that the latter's rhetoric brought about his acquittal.

9. The Case of Uriah (vv. 20-24)

A second example is given of a prophet who gave much the same message as Jeremiah, but who was pursued, extradited, and executed by King Jehoakim. The case is distinguished from the present one by the protection given Jeremiah by a royal official. Bovati argues that this and the previous notice are both part of the speech by the elders, who present two contradictory precedents. The latter is to be followed, since it was a decision of the reigning king. Accordingly, Jeremiah had by no means been acquitted by the nobles in v. 16, but the trial continues and would have ended in Jeremiah's execution were it not for the intervention of the official in an unstated manner.[29]

It is anachronistic to turn the elders into some form of legal experts who summarize the relevant precedents (like the official in some trials in modern Civil Law systems). From the pattern of the Nippur Homicide Trial, it is more likely that the elders argued for one point of view only. As elders, they would be the obvious repository of memories of a case that had occurred more than a hundred years earlier. Their expertise counter-balances any expertise that the priests and prophets could claim in the assessment of prophecy.

In my view, the second notice is not part of the forensic debate. A vague reference to the content of the prophecy cited as being "just like the words of Jeremiah" begs the very questions (the content of the prophecy and its conditionality) that are at issue. It uses the language of the outside narrator (the reliable narrator, as Brichto calls him), not the language of the participants in the debate, who refer to Jeremiah as "this man" (vv. 11 and 16).[30] On Bovati's hypothesis, it is difficult to explain how the intervention of the royal official Ahikam son of Shaphan could have taken place. For Ahikam neither presents arguments nor is he assigned any forensic role.

Above all other verses of the chapter, v. 24 is regarded by scholars as the ultimate misfit. Attributing the outcome of Jeremiah's trial to the intervention of a named official, in unexplained circumstances, seems to contradict the verdict, if not the whole of the proceedings just previously narrated. "Not only is Jeremiah's rescue mysterious in v 24; the reason he requires rescue is also obscure."[31] Nonetheless, it is my opinion that v. 24 is an integral part of the second postscript and vital to understanding the course of the trial and its result.

The second postscript, by the narrator, is a further acknowledgment that in reality it was not just Jeremiah's inspired rhetoric that won his trial.

29 Bovati 1994: 331-33 n. 161. Brichto attributes the second precedent to another set of elders, but no mention is made of them in the text (1992: 228-29).

30 Stipp suggests that the phrase "concerning this city and this land" in v. 20 indicates direct forensic speech (1992: 20-21). On the contrary, it is simply a quotation from the prophecy, to show its parallel with Jeremiah's prophecy "concerning this house" and "this city" (v. 6). The meaning of the verse is: there was another man who made an "about this house and city" prophecy just like Jeremiah. Cf. Hardmeier 1991: 177.

31 O'Connor 1989: 624.

The last-minute participation by the nobles ensured that the court was sufficiently stacked in Jeremiah's favor—enough to overcome the unfavorable reaction that his preaching had previously aroused in its audience. The nobles' intervention seems unmotivated until we realize that it was the work of Ahikam, who had persuaded his fellow courtiers to act.[32]

Thus it was the influence of Jeremiah's friends at court already at the outset of the trial, with help from a few local dignitaries who managed to dredge up an old precedent, that was really responsible for Jeremiah's acquittal.

32 For Ahikam's position, see Lundbom 2004: 298-99. On the role of the Shaphanides, see Seidel 1997: 28-53. The narrative implies in v. 10 that it was entirely an initiative of the nobles, without the king's knowledge. This time Jeremiah is being saved from the people, not from the king, but it would not be wise to let the king hear of it. In Jer 36:10-19, where the prophet's message has been committed to writing, courtiers sympathetic to him (including Ahikam's brother) feel themselves unable to hide it from the king; so they hide Jeremiah instead.

28

Legalistic "Glosses" in Biblical Narratives

Abstract

This article examines three narratives where logical discrepancies appear in relation to the legal issues at stake in each. It attributes the discrepancies to later scribes who attempted to justify or explain certain legal actions in the narratives by inserting citations from the laws of the Torah. But the citations and the actions that they are meant to support form a less than coherent match, because the narratives were not originally based on a literal reading of said laws.

The genealogy of Israel in the book of Chronicles contains the following notice: (1 Chr 2:34-35):

> Sheshan had no sons, only daughters; but Sheshan had an Egyptian slave named Jarha. Sheshan gave his daughter to his slave Jarha as a wife, and she bore him Attai.

Sheshan's purpose in marrying his daughter to his slave was to ensure that the offspring of the union would be regarded as his grandchildren. Moreover, as S. Japhet points out, the Chronicler has carefully crafted the details of the story, in particular the mention of a foreign slave, so that Sheshan's tactic will conform with the slave laws of the Torah.[1] According to Exod 21:2-6, the children would undoubtedly be the master's, since the master had given him his wife. Lev 25:41, however, suggests that an Israelite slave might be able to take his children with him on leaving.[2] The identity

* Originally published in *Israel Law Review* 33 (1999): 787-97. Used by permission.

1 Japhet 1992: 79-91.

2 Japhet 1992: 88-89.

of the father as a foreign slave avoids any difficulty on this point: he cannot leave his master at all, and any children sired by him are unquestionably his master's.

Such punctiliousness in conforming with the rules of the Torah is characteristic of the Chronicler and of contemporary sources, such as Nehemiah, and to a lesser extent the so-called Deuteronomistic Historian of the books of Samuel and Kings.[3] It is not the case with all biblical narratives, however. In 2 Sam 13:13, for example, Tamar proposes to her half-brother Amnon that he marry her rather than rape her, although such a union would theoretically fall foul of the incest prohibitions of the Torah (Lev 18:9, 11; 20:7; Deut 27:22). Scholars have wrestled with this passage, proposing various solutions, but in our view the most likely is that marriage to paternal half-siblings was still permissible, as it was elsewhere in the ancient Near East, the more stringent rules of the Levitical and Deuteronomic circles not yet being normative for the whole of Israelite society.[4]

It therefore remained a dilemma for later authors and editors, working at a time when the laws of the Torah were canonized and universally normative, that earlier accounts of Israelite history contained episodes which seemed not to be in conformity with the letter of the law. The extent of this concern is illustrated by a comment found in almost identical form in 2 Kgs 14:6 and 2 Chr 25:4. Young king Amaziah of Judah, after consolidating his power, ordered the execution of those royal officials who had assassinated his father, the previous king. Nonetheless:

> He did not have the sons of the assassins killed, as it is written in the Book of the Torah of Moses which God commanded, saying: "Fathers shall not be put to death for sons and sons shall not be put to death for fathers, but a man shall be put to death for his own offense."[5]

3 For the latter, see Noth 1981.

4 For a summary of the different theories, see McCarter 1984: 323-324. McCarter's own suggestion, that the marriage, although illegal, could be permitted by the king, seems to us less plausible. A king might pardon incest (cf. Hittite Laws 187-188), but he could not make an incestuous union, which was a sin against God rather than man, legitimate.

5 This is the version in Kings; Chronicles has "shall die."

The citation is of the law in Deut 24:16. It is highly improbable that king Amaziah's restraint was due to his concern for the law; rather, there would have been no particular reason of policy for him to extend his revenge to the family of officials. Not many years previously, on the other hand, Jehu had killed king Ahab's son, king Joram, by way of punishment for Ahab's murder of Naboth (2 Kgs 9:24-26). Jehu, however, was an insurgent, who had every interest in destroying the whole dynasty of Ahab and all the faction supporting him (cf. 2 Kgs 10:1-11). The contrast between the two cases gave the biblical historiographer an opportunity to embellish an annalistic account of royal deeds with a legalistic gloss on the protagonist's motives.

The same concern to reconcile an historical account with the codified law may be identified elsewhere in the Bible. In this study, we wish to draw attention to three narratives in which a reference to a law in the Torah is put into the mouth of a protagonist, reported in direct speech. In our view, the voice is the voice of a legal commentator.[6] Unlike the author of the late Jarha story, commentators on earlier episodes from the history of Israel could not fashion the details to match the law but had to work with an existing account. Where the match was less than perfect, the result is sometimes anomalies that modern interpreters of an individual passage have been at pains to explain away. When these three passages are considered together, however, a pattern of discrepancy emerges which enables us to identify the legal references as the handiwork of a legalistic glossator.

Inheritance and the Jubilee Law

In Num 27:1-11 the daughters of Zelophehad obtain a ruling granting them the right to inherit their father's estate in the absence of sons. In Num 36:3, their uncles, the deceased's brothers, object to the ruling:

6 Both the identity of such commentators and their exact role in the creation of the biblical text—author or editor—is open to discussion. M. Fishbane attributes the role of inner-biblical exegesis to the class of Jewish scribes that emerges in the Josianic period (1985: 25-37). Neither issue affects the validity of our findings. The legal method that we are describing would apply equally whether the commentator was an author glossing a known account, perhaps from royal annals, when incorporating it into the biblical canon, or a scribe glossing the biblical text that he copied.

> But if they are married to a member of another Israelite tribe, then their inheritance will be taken away from our ancestral inheritance and will be added to the inheritance of the tribe into which they marry and be taken away from our inheritance portion.

As a result, Moses adds a proviso to the ruling, whereby the daughters must marry into a clan within their father's tribe. In fact, they marry their cousins.

The proviso makes perfect sense. The deceased's brothers, his closest relatives in the clan, would normally have inherited his estate in the absence of sons. When the estate passes to a daughter, it takes on the character of dowry property which will pass to her children from her marriage, but the latter will of course belong to her husband's clan. Thus the property will ultimately pass out of the line of the deceased's clan, which means that it will no longer be available for inheritance by members of that clan should the direct line of heirs fail. By marrying their cousins, the daughters of Zelophehad ensure that the potential to inherit remains in their father's clan.

What does not make sense is a further possibility that is mentioned by Zelophehad's brothers in their objection to the ruling (36:4):

> And when the Jubilee of the Israelites comes, then their inheritance will be added to the inheritance of the tribe into which they marry; and their inheritance will be taken away from the inheritance of our ancestral tribe.

As has often been pointed out, the Jubilee law, as set out in Lev 25:13-16, is concerned with property that has been sold returning to the original seller or his heirs; it has nothing to do with the transfer of property through inheritance or marriage.[7] Some commentators have attempted to reconcile the brothers' statement with the law in Leviticus by suggesting that it means that the property will not return to the original family *even* in the

7 Noth 1967: 222; Snaith 1967: 345-46. Snaith is incorrect, however, in assuming that the ruling in Num 27:1-11 is bad law because it contradicts the levirate law (1967: 308-10). The two are not incompatible, although there might be some question as to the priority of the daughter's inheritance.

Jubilee year.[8] That is to distort the plain text of v. 4, which speaks of a transfer of the property at the Jubilee, not its retention in spite of the Jubilee. One could of course suppose that there existed a further rule of the Jubilee institution, not mentioned in Leviticus 25, to the effect that the wife's land passed to her husband on the Jubilee. It is difficult to see on what basis, however. Whereas the simultaneous return of all ancestral land previously sold to outsiders has a solid rationale within the context of social justice measures and is supported by parallels from elsewhere in the ancient Near East, no such support in logic or empirical evidence can be found for the simultaneous transfer of every woman's inherited property to her husband (or his family).[9]

It seems to us that v. 4 is a legalistic hyper-correction, based on the over-zealous desire of a glossator to find a basis for the brothers' objection in the laws of the Torah. On the one hand, it is assumed by the story that the wife's heirs will belong to her husband's family, as one would expect through the logic of the dowry and of an agnatic system of inheritance, but the devolution of female property is not explicitly treated in any of the laws of the Torah.[10] On the other hand, the Jubilee laws of Leviticus 25 assume that sale of land is the occasion for their operation but do not explicitly exclude other forms of transfer. They therefore provided a link of sorts to the written law, however weak. The glossator, being more concerned with legal authority than with legal logic, preferred to base the ultimate fate of the daughters' property on an express law rather than an implied one.

Royal Decrees and the Slave-Release Law

In Jer 34:8-16, king Zedekiah declares freedom for all Israelite slaves held by the nobles and free population of the kingdom, but the latter subsequently reenslave them. The prophet Jeremiah rebukes the slave owners, citing a slave-release law:

8 North 1954: 35. Compare Gray 1903: 478.

9 For Mesopotamian parallels, see Lewy 1958: 21-31. Royal decrees on the release of slaves (discussed below) also applied, *mutatis mutandis*, to release of land.

10 Compare Westbrook 1991b: 142-64.

> Every seventh year you shall release each man his Hebrew brother who is sold to you. He shall serve you for six years, and you shall set him free.

The text is closely modeled on Deut 15:12: "If your brother, a male or female Hebrew, is sold to you, he shall serve you for six years, and you shall set him free in the seventh year." The difficulty is that the law in question very clearly refers to an individual period of six years' service per slave, not to a general, simultaneous release as in the case of Zedekiah.

Commentators have sought to resolve the anomaly in various ways. Bright surmises that the general manumission by Zedikiah was a long overdue application of the law of individual release which, as v. 14 states, had been neglected for many years.[11] The biblical account makes clear, however, that Zedekiah's decree was more than merely the sum of individual manumissions. It applied to all slaves, regardless of their period of service to date, not only to those whose release was overdue. Moreover, the difference between the two laws was acknowledged by the biblical author. As Lemche points out, the anomalous opening phrase of the law that is cited, which does fit the rest of the text, has been grafted onto it from the debt-release law of Deut 15:1, which is universal and simultaneous in application.[12]

Most scholars accept that there is a discrepancy and seek an historical rationale. For David, it illustrates a development in the law, from individual manumission after six years of labor to a general one in a fixed year in which all slaves had to be set free simultaneously.[13] According to Sarna, it was more a question of the interpretation placed upon the earlier law at the time of Zedekiah: the six-year limit was regarded as a maximum that would be reduced by the incidence of the sabbatical year.[14]

Parallels from the ancient Near East provide the background to king Zedekiah's action and show that a legal development, whether by legislation or interpretation, is an unlikely explanation. It was a prerogative of kings to decree occasionally a universal cancellation of debts, often ac-

11 Bright 1965: 223-24.
12 Lemche 1976: 38-59.
13 David 1948: 74-75.
14 Sarna 1973: 148.

companied by the release of citizens enslaved by reason of debt.[15] Alongside this prerogative, there existed already at the time of the Hammurabi laws a provision for the release of individual debt-slaves after a fixed period of slavery, as shown by paragraph 117 of Codex Hammurabi, which orders the release of certain categories of slaves after three years' service.

Zedekiah's decree was the exercise of a royal prerogative inspired by the exceptional circumstances of a national crisis, the Babylonian siege of Jerusalem. It had no necessary connection with the periodic manumission of individual slaves, whether observed in practice at the time or not. The historiographer, however, wished to anchor the king's actions in a law from Deuteronomy, just as in the explicit case of king Amaziah discussed above.[16] That corpus of laws did not recognize a royal prerogative; it had been replaced by cyclical release, perhaps because of the very failure of Israelite kings to use it properly, which was the basis of Jeremiah's complaint.[17] The language of the cyclical release law that was the equivalent of a royal prerogative happened to refer only to debts, not to slaves. There was a cyclical slave-release law, but it was not directly relevant, being about individual release, not universal release. Accordingly, the historiographer adapted it by adding features from the debt-release law. In substantive legal terms this was perfectly logical, as laws and decrees concerning slave release were directed at debt slavery, and cancellation of debts would inevitably result in termination of slavery. Formally, however, we would argue that the law cited was factitious, the product of a legalistic glossator's concern to put the prophet's words on a scripturally authoritative basis.

Royal Misconduct and the Law of Theft

In 2 Sam 12:1-15 the prophet Nathan informs king David of the case of a rich man who, in order to entertain a visitor to their village, took a poor

15 They are best attested for the OB period but are found in other periods. See Kraus 1984; and Westbrook 1995f: 154-60. The biblical parallels, especially between Hebrew and Akkadian terminology, have frequently been commented upon. See, e.g., Lemche 1979.

16 See Noth 1981, for the identification of the Deuteronomistic historian.

17 See Westbrook 1995f: 160-61.

man's only lamb from him. David is outraged. He declares: "the man who does this deserves to die (literally, is a son of death)! And he shall repay the lamb four-fold."[18] Nathan then reveals that the case is only a parable of David's own misconduct as regards Uriah the Hittite and his wife Bathsheba, and that the king has in essence pronounced sentence on himself.

Commentators have been concerned with two main problems arising from the parable: the mismatch between the crime of the rich man (theft) and the crime of David (adultery and murder), and the appearance of the death penalty for theft. A third problem, the cumulation of the death penalty and multiple damages, has excited less comment. Those who seek to preserve the narrative's integrity adopt one of two approaches: eliminating the death penalty or finding some aggravating element in the theft.[19]

An example of the first approach is Phillips' reconstruction, according to which David is expressing regret that although morally the rich man deserves to die, the law allows only damages for theft. When Nathan reveals that the parable refers to David himself, the death penalty does apply, because David also committed murder and adultery.[20] Such an interpretation would seem to render Nathan's use of the parable altogether superfluous, since David has committed a capital offense anyway. Phillips further reduces the impact of the death sentence by suggesting that the Hebrew phrase "son of death" does not bear its commonly accepted connotation of "one who deserves to die" but should rather be translated "arch villain."[21]

Far from agreeing with this translation, either for "son of death" or for the comparable phrase "man of death," we suggest that in all cases where these phrases occur, they indicate that the person is subject to summary execution, as if he had already been condemned to death.[22] This is most evident in 1 Kgs 2:26, where king Solomon, having condemned his brother Adonijah to death, says to his co-conspirator Abiathar: "Go to Anathoth, to your estate. For you are a man of death, but today I will not put you to death." Abiathar is condemned to death by the king and then pardoned. His

18 Vv. 5-6 in the Masoretic text. The Septuagint has "seven-fold."

19 The difficulties for the unity of the narrative are summarized by Jones 1990: 96-100.

20 Phillips 1966: 242-44.

21 Followed by McCarter 1984: 299, who translates "a fiend of hell."

22 Compare the word "dead" to describe a condemned criminal; see Westbrook 1997.

offense was not that of being an arch villain or fiend of hell, but the very concrete one of high treason. Likewise, in 1 Sam 26:16, David's rebuke to Saul's retainers that they are sons of death derives its force from the assumption that the natural punishment for failing to guard one's king is summary execution (cf. 1 Kgs 20:39-42). In 1 Sam 20:31, Saul not unnaturally says of David, whom he has been trying to kill and who is at that moment an outlaw, that he is a son of death. The link between these very different cases and the parable of the ewe-lamb is not the moral opprobrium of the culprit for very diverse offenses, but their being subject to the death penalty. Only in 2 Sam 19:29 could Mephibosheth's statement that his family were all men of death to David be taken in either sense—that they were all villains as regards David or as if condemned to death by him.

The second approach is illustrated by Seebass, who emphasizes that the rich man's crime is a high-handed abuse of his powerful position in the local society. He can disregard a claim of theft by the poor man because the latter would not dare to sue him. The poor man therefore seeks the king's aid, and the king imposes the death penalty on the rich man for undermining the law, as well as the customary damages for theft. The king is guilty of the same abuse, in taking the wife of Uriah, who had no redress against him.[23]

We would take Seebass' insight a step further. The parable in our opinion has nothing to do with theft. The verb used is "take," not "steal," and it makes little sense for a rich man to steal a lamb like a common thief. It is more likely that the rich man was abusing a right to take the property of any villager for the purpose of feeding a guest of the village. Although his action was legal in a strict sense, it was illegal in its application and therefore an abuse of power punishable by death. By the same token, Nathan does not accuse David of theft (or adultery for that matter), but of having Uriah killed by the enemy and taking his wife in marriage (v. 9). Both actions were strictly speaking within the king's lawful powers: he could send soldiers to death in battle and could take their widows in marriage. In this case, however, the first was done in order to attain the second and was thus an illegal abuse, punishable by death (by a divine tribunal).[24]

23 Seebass 1974.

24 For a detailed discussion, see Westbrook 1988d: 30-35.

In the light of this interpretation, it is the penalty for theft in v. 6 that is intrusive. The point is that an editor of the narrative, failing to grasp the subtlety of the parallel, naturally assumed (as have most commentators) that the offense was theft. He therefore glossed the text with the appropriate penalty from the Torah, as laid down for theft of a sheep in Exod 21:37. It has long been noted that a scribe may have altered the text from seven-fold, as recorded in the Septuagint, in order to make it conform with the law.[25] Although more subtle and possibly earlier, the seven-fold penalty is in our view no less a gloss, for it is in itself a reference to the penalty for theft in Prov 6:31. There is a certain logic in using the precedent of a higher penalty, given that the standard penalty appears so inadequate for aggravated theft. Furthermore, since seven-fold in the proverb is taken to refer to an unpayable amount, it would make more sense to an editor who was assuming cumulation of penalties. The estate of the executed criminal would be transferred to the victim.

Conclusions

The three narratives discussed above have in common the fact that they all turn upon a point of law. There were potentially many possible sources for the law in question: a royal decree, customary law, or the provisions of a law code. For an author or editor from the time of Ezra and Nehemiah, if not earlier, the only possible source could be the canonical laws in the codes of the Torah. The connection was established with varying degrees of explicitness. In Jeremiah 34, a direct citation of a canonical law is put into the mouth of the prophet; in Numbers 36 the speakers refer expressly but obliquely to a canonical law; while in 2 Samuel 12 it is only the words of the sentence that reveals them to be a quotation from a canonical law. The commentators' method is exposed due to anomalies in the resultant text; doubtless there are other cases where a closer match between law in the narrative and codified law has left no trace of their handiwork, or at most, only debatable inferences.[26]

25 Driver 1913: 291.

26 E.g., the reference to two witnesses in the trial of Naboth (1 Kgs 21:10, 13)—either an integral part of the narrative or an added reference to the law in Deut 17:6 and 19:15.

The motivation of the commentators was certainly pious, but their method is evidence also of a new legal science. That science relied upon written texts as sources of law and derived rules and principles from the text through a special type of close reading. The legal consequences of actual cases depended upon the relationship of their facts to the exact words of the text. A characteristic feature was therefore a more legalistic approach to the sources of law. It is most familiar to us in later, more developed, forms, such as the works of the classical Roman or the Tannaitic jurists, but its hesitant beginnings were already manifest in biblical Israel of the post-exilic period.

Abbreviations

A	tablets in the collections of the Oriental Institute, University of Chicago
AAASH	*Acta Antiqua Academiae Scientiarum Hungaricae*
AASOR	*Annual of the American Schools of Oriental Research*
AB	Anchor Bible
ABAW	Abhandlungen der Bayerischen Akademie der Wissenschaften
AbB	Altbabylonische Briefe im Umschrift and Übersetzung
ABL	Harper, R., ed. 1892-1914. *Assyrian and Babylonian Letters Belonging to the Kouyunjik Collections of the British Museum*. 14 vols. Chicago: University of Chicago Press.
ADD	Johns, C. H. W. 1898-1924. *Assyrian Deeds and Documents*. 4 vols. Cambridge: Deighton, Bell.
AEM	Archives Epistolaires de Mari
ÄF	Ägyptologische Forschungen
AfK	*Archiv für Keilschriftforschung*
AfO	*Archiv für Orientforschung*
AfO Beiheft	Archiv für Orientforschung Beiheft
AHDO	Archives d'histoire du droit oriental
AHw	Soden, W. von. 1965-1981. *Akkadisches Handwörterbuch*. 3 vols. Wiesbaden: Harrassowitz.
AION	*Annali dell'Istituto Universitario Orientale di Napoli*
AJSL	*American Journal of Semitic Languages and Literature*
AnBib	Analecta biblica
ANET^3	Pritchard, J. B., ed. 1969. *Ancient Near Eastern Texts Relating to the Old Testament.* 3d ed. with supplement. Princeton: Princeton University Press.
AnOr	Analecta orientalia
AnSt	*Anatolian Studies*
AOAT	Alter Orient und Altes Testament
AoF	*Altorientalische Forschungen*
AOS	American Oriental Series

Aristotle *Ath. Pol.*	Aristotle, *Athenain politeia*
ARM	Archives Royales de Mari
Arnaud *Emar* 6	Arnaud, D. 1986. *Recherches au pays d'Aštata, Emar VI.* Vol. 3: *Textes sumériens et accadiens*. Paris: Éditions Recherches sur les civilisations.
Arnaud *Textes syriens*	Arnaud, D. 1991 *Textes syriens de l'âge du bronze récent.* AuOrSup 1. Barcelona: Editorial Ausa.
ArOr	*Archív Orientálini*
ARU	Kohler, J., and A. Ungnad. 1913. *Assyrische Rechtsurkunden, in Umschrift und Übersetzung nebst einem Index der Personen-Namen und Rechtserläuterungen.* Leipzig: Pfeiffer.
AS	Assyriological Studies
ASAW	Abhandlungen der Sächsischen Akademie der Wissenschaften
ASJ	*Acta Sumerologica*
ASOR	American Schools of Oriental Research
ASORSup	American Schools of Oriental Research Supplement Series
AT	Alalakh Tablets
AuOr	*Aula Orientalis*
AuOrSup	Aula Orientalis Supplement Series
Authorized Version	Authorized Version. See Hall, F., et al., eds. 1924. *The Holy Bible, Reprinted according to the Authorized Version, 1611*. London and New York: Nonesuch Press; Lincoln MacVeagh; Dial Press.
AV	Anniversary Volume
b. B. Qam.	Babylonian Talmud *Bava Qamma*
b. Giṭ.	Babylonian Talmud *Giṭṭin*
b. Soṭah	Babylonian Talmud *Soṭah*
BA	Babylonische Archive
BA	*Biblical Archaeologist*
BaghM	*Baghdader Mitteilungen*
BASOR	*Bulletin of the American Schools of Oriental Research*
BASP	*Bulletin of the American Society of Papyrologists*
BBB	Bonner Biblische Beiträge
BBSt.	King, L. W. 1912. *Babylonian Boundary Stones*, London: British Museum.
BE	Babylonian Expedition of the University of Pennsylvania, Series A: Cuneiform Texts
Beckman and Hoffner 1996	Beckman, G. M., and H. A. Hoffner, Jr. 1996. *Hittite Diplomatic Texts*. SBLWAW 7. Atlanta: Scholars Press.

Beckman *Emar*	Beckman, G. M. 1996. *Texts from the Vicinity of Emar in the Collection of Jonathan Rosen*. HANEM 2. Padua: Sargon.
Bib	*Biblica*
Bible de Jérusalem	École Biblique et Archéologique Française. 1974. *La Bible de Jérusalem: La Sainte Bible*. Paris: Éditions du Cerf.
BICSSup	Bulletin of the Institute of Classical Studies Supplement
BiMes	Bibliotheca Mesopotamica
BIN	Babylonian Inscriptions in the Collection of J. B. Nies
BISNELC	Bar-Ilan Studies in Near Eastern Languages and Culture
BM	tablets in the collections of the British Museum
BO	*Bibliotheca Orientalis*
Bo.	field numbers of tablets excavated at Boghazköi
Boyer *Contribution*	Boyer, G. 1928. *Contribution à l'histoire juridique de la 1ère dynastie babylonienne*. Paris: Geuthner.
BRM	Babylonian Records in the Library of J. Pierpoint Morgan
BT	Kutscher, R. 1989. *The Brockman Tablets of the University of Haifa*. Vol. 1. *Royal Inscriptions*. Haifa: Haifa University Press; Harrassowitz: Wiesbaden.
BWANT	Beiträge zur Wissenschaft von Alten und Neuen Testament
BZ	*Biblische Zeitschrift*
BzA	*Beiträge zur Assyriologie*
BZAR	Beihefte zur Zeitschrift für altorientalische und biblische Rechtgeschichte
BZAW	Beihefte zur Zeitschrift für die alttestamentliche Wissenschaft
c(a).	circa
CAD	Oppenheim, A. L., et al., eds.1956-. *The Assyrian Dictionary of the Oriental Institute of Chicago*. Chicago: Oriental Institute of the University of Chicago.
Caesar *Bell. gall.*	Caesar, *de bello gallico = Gallic War*
Camb.	Strassmaier, J. N. 1890. *Inschriften von Cambyses, König von Babylon (529-521 v. Chr.)*. Leipzig: Pfeiffer.
Cato *de agr.*	Cato, *de agri cultura origins*
CBS	tablets in the collections of the University Museum of the University of Pennsylvania, Philadelphia
CC	Covenant Code
CE	Code of Eshnunna
CH	Code of Hammurabi
CHANE	Culture and History of the Ancient Near East
chap(s).	chapter(s)

CHD	Güterbock, H. G., and H. A. Hoffner, Jr. 1980-. *The Hittite Dictionary of the Oriental Institute of the University of Chicago*. Chicago: The Oriental Institute.
Cicero *Att.*	Cicero, *Epistulae ad Atticum*
Cicero *de leg.*	Cicero, *de legibus*
Cicero *Dom.*	Cicero, *de domo sua*
Cicero *Fin.*	Cicero, *de finibus bonorum et malorum*
Cicero *pro Balbo*	Cicero, *pro L. Balbo*
Cicero *pro Tullio*	Cicero, *pro M. Tullio*
Cicero *Rep.*	Cicero, *de re publica*
Cicero *Verr.*	Cicero, *In Verrem*
CL	Code of Lipit-Ishtar
Claud. *Rap. Pros.*	Claudian, *de Raptu Proserpinae*
aCM	Cuneiform Monographs
Cod. Theod.	Theodosian Code; Codex Theodosianus
col(s).	column(s)
Coll.	*Mosaicarum et Romanarum legum collatio*
ConBOT	Coniectanea Biblica Old Testament Series
Cowley	Cowley, A. 1923. *The Aramaic Papyri of the Fifth Century B.C.* Oxford: Oxford University Press.
CQ	*Classical Quarterly*
CRRAI	Compte-rendu de la Rencontre Assyriologique International
CSA	Cahiers de la Société Asiatique
CT	Cuneiform Texts from Babylonian Tablets in the British Museum
CT Nebraska	Forde, N. W. 1967. *Nebraska Cuneiform Tests of the Sumerian Ur Dynasty*. Lawrence, Kansas: Coronado Press.
CTH	Laroche, E. 1971. *Catalogue des textes hittites*. Études et commentaires 75. Paris: Klincksieck.
CTN	Cuneiform Texts from Nimrud
CU	Code of Ur-Namma
Cyr.	Strassmaier, J. N. 1890. *Inschriften von Cyrus, König von Babylon (538-529 v. Chr.).* Leipzig: Pfeiffer.
D.	Corpus Juris Civilis, *Digesta* (author as applicable)
Dalley *Edinburgh*	Dalley, S. 1979. *A Catalogue of the Akkadian Cuneiform Tablets in the Collections of the Royal Scottish Museum, Edinburgh, with Copies of Texts*. Royal Scottish Museum Art and Archaeology 2. Edinburgh: Royal Scottish Museum.
Dar.	Strassmaier, J. N. 1890. *Inschriften von Darius, König von Babylon (521-485 v. Chr.).* Leipzig: Pfeiffer.

Demosthenes *Timocr.*	Demosthenes, *In Timocratem*
Dig.	Corpus Juris Civilis, *Digesta* (author as applicable)
Dio Cass.	Cassius Dio
Diodorus Siculus *Bib. Hist.*	Diodorus Siculus, *Biblioteca Historica*
Dion. Hal.	Dionysius (of) Halicarnassus
DN	divine name
EA	El-Amarna Letters, as edited in Knudtzon, J. A., ed. 1907-1915. *Die El-Amarna-Tafeln.* 2 vols. Vorderasiatische Bibliothek. Leipzig: Hinrichs.
Ea	lexical series ea A = *nâqu*; published in MSL XIV
ed(s).	editor(s)
EI	*Eretz-Israel*
Ent.	Entemena
Erimhuš	lexical series erimḫuš = *anantu*; published in MSL XVII
FAOS	Freiburger Altorientalische Studien
ff.	and following
FIOL	The Formation and Interpretation of Old Testament Literature
FIRA	Riccobono, S., and J. Baviera, eds. 1968. *Fontes iuris Romani anteiustiniani.* 3 vols. Florenz: Barbèra.
Florentinus *Dig.*	Corpus Juris Civilis, *Digesta* (Florentinus)
G.	Gaius, *Institutiones*
GAG	Soden, W. von. 1969. *Grundriss der Akkadischen Grammatik.* 2 vols. Analecta Orientalia 33 and 47. Rome: Pontifical Biblical Institute.
Gaius *Augustod.*	*Fragmenta interpretationis Gai institutionum Augustodunensia*
Gaius *Dig.*	Corpus Juris Civilis, *Digesta* (Gaius)
Gaius *Inst.*	Gaius, *Institutiones*
Gaius *Prov. Edict*	Gaius, *Ad Edictum Praetoris Provinciale = Commentary on the Provincial Edict*
Gell. *NA*	Gellius, *noctes Atticae*
GN	geographic name
GRBS	*Greek, Roman, and Byzantine Studies*
GRBM	Greek, Roman, and Byzantine Monographs
Gurney *MB Texts*	Gurney, O. R. 1983. *The Middle Babylonian Legal and Economic Texts from Ur.* London: British School of Archaeology in Iraq.

HAL[3]	Köhler, L., Baumgartner, W., and Stamm, J. J. 1967-96. *Hebräisches und Aramäisches Lexikon zum Alten Testament.* 3d ed. Edited by W. Baumgartner. Leiden: Brill.
HANEM	History of the Ancient Near East Monographs
HANES	History of the Ancient Near East Studies
HdO	Handbuch der Orientalistik
HG	Kohler J., A. Ungnad et al. 1904-23. *Hammurabis Gesetz.* 6 vols. Leipzig: Pfeiffer.
Hg.	lexical series ḪAR.gud = *imrú* = *ballu*; published in MSL V-XI
Hh.	lexical series ḪAR.ra = *ḫubullu*; published in MSL V-XI
HL	Hittite Laws
HSCP	*Harvard Studies in Classical Philology*
HSM	Harvard Semitic Monographs
HSS	Harvard Semitic Studies
HTR	*Harvard Theological Review*
HUCA	*Hebrew Union College Annual*
IBHS	Waltke, B. K., and M. O'Conner. 1990. *An Introduction to Biblical Syntax.* Winona Lake, Ind.: Eisenbrauns.
IBoT	Istanbul Arkeoloji Müzelerinde Bulunan Boğazköy Tabletleri
ICC	International Critical Commentary
ICK	Hrozný B. 1952-62. *Inscriptions cunéiformes du Kultépé.* Translated by M. David. 2 vols. Archív Orientální Monografie 14. Praha: Státni pedogogické nakl.
IEJ	*Israel Exploration Journal*
Il.	Homer, *The Iliad*
IM	tablets in the collections of the Iraq Museum, Baghdad
IOS	*Israel Oriental Society*
ITT	Constantinople Arkeoloji Müzeleri [Constantinople Archaeological Museum]. 1910-21. *Inventaire des tablettes de Tello conservées au Musée impérial ottoman.* 5 vols. Paris: Leroux.
J. Westenholz *Emar*	Westenholz, J. G. 2000. *Cuneiform Inscriptions in the Collection of the Bible Lands Museum Jerusalem: The Emar Tablets.* CM 13. Groningen: Styx.
JANES	*Journal of the Ancient Near East Society of Columbia University*
JAOS	*Journal of the American Oriental Society*
JBL	*Journal of Biblical Literature*
JCS	*Journal of Cuneiform Studies*

Jean *Tell Sifr*	Jean, Ch.-F. 1931. *Tell Sifr textes cunéiformes conservés au British Museum*. Paris: Geuthner.
JEN	Joint Expedition with the Iraq Museum at Nuzi
JEOL	*Jaarbericht van het Vooraziatisch-Egyptisch Genootschap "Ex Oriente Lux"*
JESHO	*Journal of the Economic and Social History of the Orient*
JHS	*Journal of Hebrew Scriptures*
JJP	*Journal of Juristic Papyrology*
JJS	*Journal of Jewish Studies*
JLA	*Jewish Law Annual*
JNES	*Journal of Near Eastern Studies*
JNSL	*Journal of Northwest Semitic Languages*
Jones and Snyder	Jones, T. B., and J. W. Snyder. 1991. *Sumerian Economic Texts from the Third Ur Dynasty*. Minneapolis: University of Minnesota Press.
JPS	Jewish Publication Society. 1985. *Tanakh*. New York: Jewish Publication Society.
JPS Torah Comm.	Jewish Publication Society Torah Commentary
JQR	*Jewish Quarterly Review*
JRS	*Journal of Roman Studies*
JSOT	*Journal for the Study of the Old Testament*
JSOTSup	Journal for the Study of the Old Testament Supplement Series
JSS	*Journal of Semitic Studies*
Justinian *Inst.*	Justinian, *Institutiones*
KadmosSup	Kadmos (Zeitschrift für vor- und frühgriechische Epigraphik) Supplement
KAH	Keilschrifttexte aus Assur historischen Inhalts
KAJ	Keilschrifttexte aus Assur juristischen Inhalts
KAR	Keilschrifttexte aus Assur religiösen Inhalts
KAV	Keilschrifttexte aus Assur verschiedenen Inhalts
KBo	Keilschrifturkunden von Boghazköi
KḪ	Kodex Ḫammurabi = Code of Hammurabi
Kienast *Altass. Kaufvertragsrecht*	Kienast, B. 1984. *Das altassyrische Kaufvertragsrecht*. FAOS 1. Altassyrische Texte und Untersuchungen 1. Stuttgart: Steiner.
Kraeling	Kraeling, E. 1953. *The Brooklyn Museum Aramaic Papyri: New Documents of the Fifth Century B.C. from the Jewish Colony at Elephantine*. Publications of the Department of Egyptian Art. New Haven: Yale University Press. Reprinted New York: Arno Press, 1969.

Kramer *AV* — Eichler, B. L., J. W. Heimerdinger, and Å. W. Sjöberg, eds. 1976. *Kramer Anniversary Volume: Cuneiform Studies in Honor of Samuel Noah Kramer*. AOAT 25. Kevelaer: Butzon & Bercker.

Kraus *AV* — Driel, G. van, et. al., eds. 1982. *Zikir Šumim: Assyriological Studies Presented to F. R. Kraus on the Occasion of His Seventieth Birthday*. Leiden: Brill.

KTS — Keilschrifttexte in den Antiken-Museen zu Stambul

KUB — Keilschrifturkunden aus Boghazköi

Lambert *BWL* — Lambert, W. G. 1960. *Babylonian Wisdom Literature*. Oxford: Clarendon.

LAPO — Littératures anciennes du Proche Orient

LCL — Loeb Classical Library

LHB/OTS — Library of Hebrew Bible / Old Testament Studies

LIH — King, L. W. 1898-1900. *The Letters and Inscriptions of Ḫammurabi, King of Babylon*. London: Luzac.

Livy — Titus Lilvius, *Ab urbe condita libri*

LQR — *Law Quarterly Review*

LSJ — Liddell, H. G., R. Scott, H. S. Jones et al., eds. 1996. *A Greek-English Lexicon*. Oxford and New York: Clarendon Press; University of Oxford Press.

LTBA — Soden, W. von, and Staatliche Museen zu Berlin, Vorderasiatische Abteilung. 1933-. *Die lexikalischen Tafelserien der Babylonier und Assyrer in den Berliner Museen*. 2 vols. Berlin: Vorderasiatische Abteilung der Staatliche Museen zu Berlin.

Lucilius — Gaius Lucilius, *The Twelve Tables*

LXX — Septuagint

m. Giṭ. — Mishnah *Giṭṭin*

m. Ketub. — Mishnah *Ketubbot*

m. Yebam. — Mishnah *Yebamot*

m. Yoma — Mishnah *Yoma* = Mishnah *Kippurim*

MA — Middle Assyrian

MAL — Middle Assyrian Laws

MAL A — Middle Assyrian Laws, Tablet A (and so forth through N)

MANE — Sources and Monographs. Monographs on the Ancient Near East

Manilius *Astr.* — Manilius, *astronomica*

MAOG — Mitteilungen der Altorientalischen Gesellschaft

Marcianus *Dig.* — Corpus Juris Civilis, *Digesta* (Marcianus)

MB — Middle Babylonian

MDP	Mémoires de la Délégation en Perse
MEFR	*Mélanges d'archéologie et d'histoire de l'école français de Rome*
Meissner *BAP*	Meissner, B. 1893. *Beiträge zum altbabylonischen Privatrecht*. Leipzig: Hinrichs.
Mek.	*Mekhilta*
MIO	*Mitteilungen des Instituts für Orientforschung*
MKNAW	Mededelingen der Koninklijke Nederlandse Akademie van Wetenschappen
MSL	Materialien zum sumerischen Lexikon I = Landsberger 1937 VI = Landsberger 1958 VIII/1 = Kilmer, Gordon, and Landsberger 1960 VIII/2 = Kilmer and Landsberger 1962 IX = Civil and Landsberger 1967 XII = Civil 1969 XIII = Civil 1971 XIV = Civil 1979 XVI = Finkel and Civil 1982 XVII = Cavigneaux et al. 1985
MT	Masoretic Text
MVAG	Mitteilungen der Vorderasiatisch-Ägyptischen Gesellschaft
MVN	Materiali per il vocabolario neo-sumerico
n(n).	note(s)
N.A.B.U.	Nouvelles Assyriologiques Brèves et Utilitaires
NA	Neo-Assyrian
Nabnitu	lexical series SIG$_7$ + ALAM = *nabnītu* published in MSL XVI
NB	Neo-Babylonian
NBL	Neo-Babylonian Laws
Nbn.	Strassmaier, J. N. 1889. *Inschriften von Nabonidus, König von Babylon (555-538 v. Chr.)*. Leipzig: Pfeiffer.
NCB	New Century Bible
NCBT	tablets in the Newell Collection of Babylonian Tablets, Yale University Library
ND	field numbers of tablets excavated at Nimrud (Kalhu)
New English Bible	Joint Committee on the New Translation of the Bible. 1970. *The New English Bible with the Apocrypha*. London and New York: Oxford University Press; Cambridge University Press.
NF / n.F.	Neue Folge
no(s).	number(s)

NRVN	Çiğ, M., and H. Kizilyay. 1965. *Neusumerische Rechts- und Verwaltungsurkunden aus Nippur I.* TTKY 6/7. Ankara: Türk tarih kurumu basimevi.
NS / ns	New Series
NSG	Falkenstein, A. 1956-1957. *Die neusumerischen Gerichtsurkunden.* 3 vols. ABAW philosophisch-historische Klasse n.F. 39, 40, 44. Munich: Bayerische Akademie der Wissenschaften.
NT	field numbers of tablets excavated at Nippur by the Oriental Institute and other institutions
OA	Old Assyrian
OB	Old Babylonian
OBC	Orientalia Biblica et Christiana
OBO	Orbis Biblicus et Orientalis
OBT Tell Rimah	Dalley, S., C. B. F. Walker, and J. D. Hawkins. 1976. *Old Babylonian Texts from Tell al Rimah.* London: British School of Archaeology in Iraq.
Od.	Homer, *The Odyssey*
OECT	Oxford Editions of Cuneiform Texts
OIP	Oriental Institute Publications
OLA	Orientalia Lovaniensia Analecta
OLZ	*Orientalische Literaturzeitung*
Or (NS)	*Orientalia (Nova Series)*
OrAnt	*Oriens antiquus*
Oros.	Orosius
OTL	Old Testament Library
OtSt	*Oudtestamentische Studiën*
Ovid *Fast.*	Ovid, *Fasti*
Ovid *Metam.*	Ovid, *Metamorphoses*
Oxford Bible	May, H. G., and B. M. Metzger, eds. 1962. *The Holy Bible: Revised Standard Version.* London and New York: Oxford University Press.
Papinian *Dig.*	Corpus Juris Civilis, *Digesta* (Papinian)
Paulus *Dig.*	Corpus Juris Civilis, *Digesta* (Paulus)
Paulus *Sent.*	Paulus, *Sententiae*
PBS	Publications of the Babylonian Section, University Museum, University of Pennsylvania
Petschow *MB Rechtsurkunden*	Petschow, H. 1974. *Mittelbabylonische Rechts- und Wirtschaftsurkunden der Hilprecht-Sammlung Jena.* ASAW philosophisch-historische Klasse 64/4. Berlin: Akademie-Verlag.

Philo *Spec. Laws*	Philo of Alexandria, *On Special Laws*
PIHANS	Uitgaven van het Nederlands Historisch-archeologische Instituut te Istanbul
pl.	plate
Plautus *Asin.*	Plautus, *Asinaria*
Plautus *Merc.*	Plautus, *Mercator*
Plautus *Pseud.*	Plautus, *Pseudolus*
Plautus *Rud.*	Plautus, *Rudens*
Pliny *Nat.*	Pliny (the Elder), *Naturalis historia*
PN	personal name
Pomponius *Dig.*	Corpus Juris Civilis, *Digesta* (Pomponius)
PRU	Le Palais Royal d'Ugarit
PY	Pylos (site where numerous Linear B texts were discovered; on additional sigla, see Bennett 1953).
Quintilian *Decl. mai.*	Quintilianus, *Declamationes maiores*
Quintilian *Decl. min.*	Quintilianus, *Declamationes minores*
Quintilian *Inst.*	Quintilian, *Institutio oratoria*
RA	*Revue d'Assyriologique et d'Archéologie orientale*
RAI	Rencontre Assyriologique Internationale
RB	*Revue Biblique*
RHA	*Revue hittite et asianique*
RHPR	*Revue d'Histoire et de Philosophie Religieuses*
RIDA	*Revue internationale du droit de l'antiquité*
Riftin	Riftin, A. P. 1937. *Staro-Vavilonskie iuridicheskie i administrativnye dokumenty v sobraniiakh SSSR*. Moscow: Izd-vo Akademii nauk SSSR.
RlA	*Reallexikon der Assyriologie*. Edited by E. Ebeling, et al. 16 vols. Berlin: de Gruyter, 1928–.
RN	royal name
RS	field numbers of tablets excavated at Ras Shamra
RSO	Rivista degli studi orientali
RSV	Revised Standard Version. See Burrows, M., et al., ed. 1952. *The Holy Bible: Revised Standard Version*. Toronto and New York: T. Nelson.
SAA	State Archives of Assyria
SAAS	State Archives of Assyria Studies
Sallust. *Bell. Cat.*	Sallustius, *Bellum catilinae*
Sallust. *Bell. Iug.*	Sallustius, *Bellum iugurthinum*

San Nicolò-Petschow *Bab. Rechtsurkunden*	San Nicolò, M., and H. Petschow. 1960. *Babylonische Rechtsurkunden aus dem 6. Jahrhundert v. Chr.* ABAW philosophisch-historische Klasse n.F. 51. Munich: Bayerische Akademie der Wissenschaften.
SANE	Sources from the Ancient Near East
SBH	Reisner, G. A. 1986. *Sumerisch-babylonische Hymnen nach Thontafeln griechischer Zeit.* Königliche Museen zu Berlin. Mitteilungen aus den orientalischen Sammlungen 10. Berlin: Spemann
SBLDS	Society of Biblical Literature Dissertation Series
SBLSymS	Society of Biblical Literature Symposium Series
SBLWAW	Society of Biblical Literature Writings from the Ancient World
SBS	Stuttgarter Bibelstudien
SCCNH	Studies on the Civilization and Culture of Nuzi and the Hurrians
Schol. ad Bas.	Scholiast on the *Basilica*
SDHI	*Studia et documenta historiae et iuris*
SDIOAP	Studia et documenta ad iura orientis antiqui pertinentia
Sen. *Clem.*	Seneca minor, *de clementia*
Sen. *Controv.*	Seneca maior, *controversiae*
Sen. *Ep. Mor.*	Seneca minor, *epistulae morales ad Lucilium*
SHA	*scriptores historiae Augustae*
Sigrist *Kutscher Mem. Vol.*	Rainey, A., et al., eds. 1993. Kinattūtu ša dārâti. *Raphael Kutscher Memorial Volume.* Tel Aviv Occasional Publications 1. Tel Aviv: Institute of Archaeology of Tel Aviv University.
Sigrist *Messenger Texts*	Sigrist, M. 1990. *Messenger Texts from the British Museum.* Potomac, Md.: Capital Decisions.
SJLA	Studies in Judaism in Late Antiquity
SLB	Studia ad tabulas cuneiformes collectas a F. M. Th. de Liagre Böhl pertinentia.
SMEA	*Studi Micenei e Egeo-Anatolici*
SMN	tablets excavated at Nuzi, in the Semitic Museum, Harvard University, Cambridge, Mass.
SNATBM	Ozaki (Gomi), T., and S. Sato. 1990. *Selected Neo-Sumerian Administrative Texts from the British Museum.* Soken kenkyu shiryo 7. Abiko: Research Institute, Chuo-Gakuin University.
Sollberger *Corpus*	Sollberger, E. 1956. *Corpus des inscriptions "royales" présargoniques de Lagaš.* Geneva: Dros.

SR	*Studies in Religion/Sciences religieuses*
SRU	Edzard, D. O. 1968. *Sumerische Rechtsurkunden des III. Jahrtausends aus der Zeit vor der III. Dynastie von Ur.* ABAW philosophisch-historische Klasse n.F. 67. Munich: Bayerische Akademie der Wissenschaften, with Beck.
Statius *Theb.*	Publius Papinius Statius, *Thebaid*
StBoT	Studien zu den Boğazöy-Texten
Strabo *Geo.*	Strabo, *Geographica*
StudBib	Studia Biblica
Studies Landsberger	Güterbock, H. G., and T. Jacobsen, eds. 1965. *Studies in Honour of Benno Landsberger on His Seventy-Fifth Birthday.* AS 16. Chicago: University of Chicago Press.
SubBi	Subsidia biblica
Szlechter *TJA*	Szlechter, E. 1963. *Tablettes juridiques et administratives de la IIIe dynastie d'Ur.* Publications de l'Institut de droit romain de l'Université de Paris 21. Paris: Recueil Sirey.
T.	(Twelve) Tables
Tac. *Hist.*	Tacitus, *Historiae*
TAD	Porten, B., and A. Yardeni, eds. 1989. *Textbook of Aramaic Documents from Ancient Egypt.* 2 vols. Texts and Studies for Students. Jerusalem: Hebrew University, Department of the History of the Jewish People; Winona Lake, Ind.: Eisenbrauns.
TAPA	Transactions of the American Philosophical Society
TCL	Textes cunéiformes du Louvre
TCM	Textes cunéiformes de Mari
TCS	Texts from Cuneiform Sources
Theophilus *Para.*	Theophilus, *Paraphrasis*
TIM	Texts in the Iraq Museum
TLB	Tabulae cuneiformes a F. M. Th. de Liagre Böhl collectae
trans.	translated by
transl.	translation
TTKY	Türk Tarih Kurumu Yayinlari(ndan)
TUAT	Texte aus der Umwelt des Alten Testaments
TuM	Texte und Materialien der Frau Professor Hilprecht Collection of Babylonian Antiquities im Eigentum der Universität Jena
TvR	*Tijdschrift voor Rechtsgeschiedenis*
UCP	University of California Publications in Semitic Philology
UET	Ur Excavations, Texts

UF	*Ugarit-Forschungen*
Ukg.	Urkagina = Uru-inimgina = Irikagina (the preferred reading of this name)
Ulpian *Dig.*	Corpus Juris Civilis, *Digesta* (Ulpian)
Urk. IV	Sethe, K., and Helck, W., eds. 1906-09; 1955-58. *Urkunden des ägyptischen Altertums IV: Urkunden der 18. Dynastie.* 22 vols. Leipzig: Heinrich (vols. 1-16, 1906-1909); Berlin: Akademie-Verlag (vols. 17-22, 1955-1958).
US	United States (Supreme Court) Reporter
v(v).	verse(s)
Val. Max.	Valerius Maximus, *Factorum et Dictorum Memorabilium Libri Novem*
Varro *L.*	Varro, *de lingua latina*
VAS	Vorderasiatische Schriftdenkmäler
Vienna Convention on the Law of Treaties	United Nations, International Law Commission. 1969. Vienna Convention on the Law of Treaties: drafted 1969, revised and adopted 1980.
Virgil *Aen.*	Virgil, *Aeneid*
VS	= VAS
VSAW	Verhandlungen der Sächsischen Akademie der Wissenschaften
VT	*Vetus Testamentum*
VTSup	Supplements to Vetus Testamentum
Waterman, *Bus. Doc.*	Waterman, L. 1916. *Business Documents of the Hammurapi* Period. Ancient Mesopotamian Tests and Studies. London: Ams Press (= *AJSL* 29-30 [1912-1914])
Westenholz *OSP*	Westenholz, A. 1975 & 1987. *Old Sumerian and Old Akkadian Texts in Philadelphia Chiefly from Nippur* (1 = BiMes 1, Malibu, Calif.: Undena Publications; 2 = Carsten Niebuhr Institute Publications 3, Copenhagen: Carsten Niebuhr Institute of Ancient Near Eastern Studies).
WMANT	Wissenschaftliche Monographien zum Alten und Neuen Testament
WO	*Die Welt des Orients*
WVDOH	Wissenschaftliche Veröffentlichungen der deutschen Orientgesellschaft
WZKM	*Wiener Zeitschrift für die Kunde des Morgenlands*
Xenophon *Cyn.*	Xenophon, *Cynegeticus*
YBC	tablets in the Babylonian Collection, Yale University Library

YNER	Yale Near Eastern Researches Series
YOS	Yale Oriental Series
YOSR	Yale Oriental Series, Researches
ZA	*Zeitschrift für Assyriologie*
ZAH	*Zeitschrift für Althebräistik*
ZÄS	*Zeitschrift für die Ägyptische Sprache und Altertumskunde*
ZAW	*Zeitschrift für die alttestamentliche Wissenschaft*
ZDMG	*Zeitschrift der Deutschen Morgenländischen Gesellschaft*
ZSSR (Rom. Abt.)	*Zeitschrift der Savigny-Stiftung für Rechtsgeschichte (Romanistische Abteilung)*
ZVR	*Zeitschrift für vergleichende Rechtswissenschaft*
ZVS	*Zeitschrift für vergleichende Sprachforschung*

Bibliography

Abarbanel, I. (dates: 1437-1508)

1892 *Perush 'al neviim aharonim* [*Commentary on the Latter Prophets*]. Jaffe. Republished Jerusalem: Sefarim Torah ve-Da'at, 1956.

Alster, B.

1974 *The Instructions of Šuruppak. A Sumerian Proverb Collection*. Mesopotamia 2. Copenhagen: Akademisk Forlag.

Alt, A.

1934a *Ursprünge des israelitischen Rechts*. VSAW philologisch-historische Klasse 86/1. Leipzig: Hirzel. Reprinted as pages 278-332 in vol. 1 of *Kleine Schriften zur Geschichte des Volkes Israel*. 3 vols. Munich: Beck, 1959. English edition: "The Origins of Israelite Law." Pages 81-132 in *Essays on Old Testament History and Religion*. Translated by R. A. Wilson. Oxford: Blackwell, 1966.

1934b "Zur Talionsformel." *ZAW* 52: 303-5. Reprinted at pages 341-44 in vol. 1 of *Kleine Schriften zur Geschichte des Volkes Israel*. 3 vols. Munich: Beck, 1959.

Altman, A.

1977 "The Justification Motif in the Historical Prologues to the Treaties of Shuppiluliuma I of Hatti." *Shnaton* 2: 27-49.

1990 "On the Legal Meaning of Some of the Assertions in the 'Historical Prologue' of the Kizzuwatna Treaty (KBo I,5)." Pages 172-206 in *Bar-Ilan Studies in Assyriology Dedicated to Pinhas Artzi*. Edited by J. Kline and A. Skaist. BISNELC. Ramat Gan, Israel: Bar-Ilan University Press.

Anbar, M.

1975 "Textes de l'époque babylonienne ancienne." *RA* 69: 109-36.

1978 "Textes de l'époque babylonienne ancienne II: Les archives de Šēp-Sîn." *RA* 72: 113-38.

Arnaud, D.

1973 "Un document juridique concernant les oblats." *RA* 67: 147-56.

1986 *Recherches au pays d'Aštata, Emar VI*. Vol. 3: *Textes sumériens et accadiens*. Paris: Éditions Recherches sur les civilisations.

1987 "La Syrie du moyen Euphrate sous le protectorat hittite. Contrats de droit privé." *AuOr* 5: 211-41.

1991 *Textes syriens de l'âge du bronze récent*. AuOrSup 1. Barcelona: Editorial Ausa.

1992 "Tablettes de genres divers du Moyen-Euphrate." *SMEA* 30: 195-245.

1996 "Mariage et remariage des femmes chez les Syriens du Moyen-Euphrate." *Semitica* 46: 7-16.

Artzi, P.

1980 "Mourning in International Relations." Pages 161-70 in *Death in Mesopotamia*. Edited by B. Alster. Mesopotamia 8. Copenhagen: Akademisk Forlag.

1997 "EA 16." *AoF* 24: 320-36.

2000 "The Diplomatic Service in Action: The Mittani File." Pages 205-11 in *Amarna Diplomacy: The Beginnings of International Relations*. Edited by R. Cohen and R. Westbrook. Baltimore: Johns Hopkins University Press.

Astour, M.

1996 "Who Was the King of the Hurrian Troops at the Siege of Emar?" Pages 25-56 in *Emar: The History, Religion, and Culture of a Syrian Town in the Late Bronze Age*. Edited by M. Chavalas. Bethesda, Md.: CDL.

Baentsch, B.

1892 *Das Bundesbuch*. Halle: Niemayer.

Baker, H., and C. Wunsch

2001 "Neo-Babylonian Notaries and Their Use of Seals." Pages 197-213 in *Seals and Seal Impressions, Pt. II*. Edited by W. W. Hallo and I. J. Winter. CRRAI 45. Bethesda, Md.: CDL.

Baldi, P.

1974 "Indo-European *sek^{w}-." *Journal of Indo-European Studies* 2: 77-86.

Barbiero, G.

1991 *L'asino del nemico: rinuncia alla vendetta e amore del nemico nella legislazione dell'Antico Testamento (Es 23,4-5; Dt 22, 1-4; Lv 19, 17-18)*. AnBib 128. Rome: Pontifical Biblical Institute.

Beal, R. H.

1988 "The ^{GIŠ}tukul-institution in Second Millennium Hatti." *AoF* 15: 269-305.

Beckman, G. M.

1982 "The Hittite Assembly." *JAOS* 102: 435-42.

1988 "Three Tablets from the Vicinity of Emar." *JCS* 40: 61-68.

1996a "Family Values on the Middle Euphrates." Pages 57-79 in *Emar: The History, Religion, and Culture of a Syrian Town in the Late Bronze Age*. Edited by M. Chavalas. Bethesda, Md.: CDL.

1996b *Texts from the Vicinity of Emar in the Collection of Jonathan Rosen*. HANEM 2. Padua: Sargon.

Beckman, G. M., and H. A. Hoffner, Jr.

1996 *Hittite Diplomatic Texts*. SBLWAW 7. Atlanta: Scholars Press.

Ben-Barak, Z.

1979 "The Legal Background to the Restoration of Michal to David." Pages 15-29 in *Studies in the Historical Books of the Old Testament*. Edited by J. A. Emerton. VTSup 30. Leiden: Brill. Reprinted at pages 74-90 in *Telling Queen Michal's Story: An Experiment in Comparative Interpretation*. Edited by D. J. A. Clines and T. C. Eskenazi. JSOTSup 119. Sheffield: JSOT Press, 1991.

1988 "The Legal Status of the Daughter as Heir in Nuzi and Emar." Pages 87-97 in *Society and Economy in the Eastern Mediterranean, c. 1500-1000 B.C.: Proceedings of the International Symposium Held at the University of Haifa from the 28th of April to the 2nd of May, 1985*. Edited M. Heltzer and E. Lipiński. OLA 23. Leuven: Peeters.

Bergmann, E.

1953 "Codex Hammurabi." Pages 255-69 in vol. 3 of *Reallexikon der Assyriologie*. Edited by E. Ebeling et al. 16 vols. Berlin: de Gruyter, 1928-.

Biggs, R. D.

1974 *Inscriptions from Tell Abū Ṣalābīkh*. OIP 99. Chicago: University of Chicago Press.

Birot, M.

1976 *Lettres de Yaqqim-Addu, gouverneur de Sagaratum*. TCM 1; ARM 14. Paris: Geuthner, 1976.

Black, H. C., J. R. Nolan, J. M. Nolan-Haley, M. J. Connolly, S. C. Hicks et al.

1990 *Black's Law Dictionary*. 6th ed. St. Paul: West Publishers.

Boecker, H. J.

1974 *Redeformen des Rechtslebens im Alten Testament*. WMANT 14. Neukirchen-Vluyn: Neukirchener Verlag.

1980 *Law and the Administration of Justice in the Old Testament and the Ancient East*. Translated by J. Moiser. London: SPCK; Minneapolis: Augsburg.

Borger, R.

1967-75 *Handbuch der Keilschriftliteratur*. 3 vols. Berlin: de Gruyter.

1973 "Die Weihe eines Enlil-Priesters." *BO* 30: 163-83.

1982a "Der Kodex Hammurapi." Pages 39-80 in *Rechtsbücher*. Edited by R. Borger et al. TUAT 1/1. Gütersloh: Gerd Mohn.

1982b "Die mittelassyrischen Gesetze." Pages 80-92 in *Rechtsbücher*. Edited by R. Borger et al. TUAT 1/1. Gütersloh: Gerd Mohn.

Borger, R., and O. Kaiser, eds.

1982 *Texte aus der Umwelt des Alten Testaments*. Vol. 1: *Rechts- und Wirtschaftsurkunden, historisch-chronologische Texte*. Lieferung 1: *Rechtsbücher*. Gütersloh: Gerd Mohn.

Bottéro, J.

1961 "Désordre économique et annulation des dettes en Mésopotamie à l'époque paléo-babylonienne." *JESHO* 4: 113-64.

1982 "Le 'Code' de Hammu-rabi." *Annali della Scola Normale Superiore di Pisa* 12: 409-44. English edition: "The 'Code' of Ḫammurabi." Pages 156-84 in *Mesopotamia: Writing, Reasoning, and the Gods*. Translated by Z. Bahrani and M. van de Mieroop. Chicago: University of Chicago Press, 1992.

1987 *Mésopotamie: L'écriture, la raison et les dieux*. Bibliothèque des Histoires. Paris: Gallimard.

1992 *Mesopotamia: Writing, Reasoning, and the Gods*. Translated by Z. Bahrani and M. van de Mieroop. Chicago: University of Chicago Press.

Bovati, P.

1994 *Re-Establishing Justice: Legal Terms, Concepts and Procedures in the Hebrew Bible*. Translated by M. J. Smith. JSOTSup 105. Sheffield: JSOT Press.

Boyer, G.

1928 *Contribution à l'histoire juridique de la 1ère dynastie babylonienne*. Paris: Geuthner.

1958 *Textes Juridiques*. TCL 29; ARM 8. Paris: Geuthner.

Braulik, G.

1991 *Die deuteronomischen Gesetze und der Dekalog: Studien zum Aufbau von Deuteronomium 12-26*. SBS. Stuttgart: Katholisches Bibelwerk.

Breasted, J. H.

1907 *Ancient Records of Egypt II*. Chicago: University of Chicago Press.

Bremmer, J. N.

1983 "Scapegoat Rituals in Ancient Greece." *HSCP* 87: 299-320.

Brichto, H. C.

1992 *Toward a Grammar of Biblical Poetics: Tales of the Prophets*. London and New York: Oxford University Press.

Bright, J.

1965 *Jeremiah*. AB 21. Garden City, N.Y.: Doubleday.

Brin, G.
1983 *Ha-Navi be-maavakav* [*The Prophet in His Struggles*]. Tel Aviv: Miph'alim University.

Brockelmann, C.
1928 *Lexicon Syriacum*. Halis: Niemeyer.

Burkert, W.
1979 *Structure and History in Greek Mythology and Ritual*. Sather Classical Lectures 47. Berkeley: University of California Press.

Burrows, M., et al., eds.
1952 *The Holy Bible: Revised Standard Version*. Toronto and New York: Nelson.

Cagni, L.
1980 *Briefe aus dem Irak Museum (TIM II)*. AbB 8. Leiden: Brill.

Cardascia, G.
1969 *Les Lois Assyriennes*. LAPO 2. Paris: Éditions du Cerf.
1980 "Kauf. C.II. Mittelassyrisch." Pages 514-20 in vol. 5 of *Reallexikon der Assyriologie*. Edited by E. Ebeling et al. 16 vols. Berlin: de Gruyter, 1928-.

Carmichael, C. M.
1974 *The Laws of Deuteronomy*. Ithaca, N.Y.: Cornell University Press.
1979 "A Common Element in Five Supposedly Disparate Laws." *VT* 29: 129-42.
1980 "'Treading' in the Book of Ruth." *ZAW* 92: 248-66.

Carroll, R. P.
1986 *Jeremiah*. OTL. Philadelphia: Westminster.

Cassin, E.
1958 "Quelques remarques à propos des archives administratives de Nuzi." *RA* 52: 16-28.

Cassuto, U.
1967 *Commentary on the Book of Exodus*. Translated by I. Abrahams. Publications of the Perry Foundation for Biblical Research in the Hebrew University of Jerusalem. Jerusalem: Magnes.

Cavigneaux, A.
1983 "Lexikalische Listen." Pages 609-41 in vol. 6 of *Reallexikon der Assyriologie*. Edited by E. Ebeling et al. 16 vols. Berlin: de Gruyter, 1928-.

Cavigneaux, A., et al.
1985 *The Series Erim-huš =* anantu *and An-ta-gál =* šaqû. MSL 17. Rome: Pontifical Biblical Institute.

Chantraine, P.
1968-80 *Dictionnaire étymologique de la langue grecque*. Paris: Klincksieck.

Charpin, D.

1980 *Archives familiales et propriété privée en Babylonie ancienne: étude des documents de "Tell Sifr."* Hautes études orientales 12. Geneva: Dros.

1986 *Le clergé d'Ur au siècle d'Hammurabi (XIXe-XVIIIe siècles av. J.C.).* Hautes études orientales 22. Geneva: Dros.

1987 "Les décrets royaux à l'Époque Paleo-Babylonienne." *AfO* 34: 36-44.

1988 *Archives épistolaires de Mari I/1-2.* 2 vols. ARM 26/1-2. Paris: Éditions Recherches sur les civilisations.

1990 "Une alliance contre l'Elam et le rituel du Lipit Napištim." Pages 109-18 in *Contribution à l'histoire de l'Iran. Mélanges offerts à Jean Perrot.* Edited by F. Vallat. Paris: Éditions Recherches sur les civilisations.

1991 "Un traité entre Ibâl-pî-El II d'Ešnunna et Zimri-Lim de Mari." Pages 139-66 in *Marchands, diplomates et empereurs. Études sur la civilisation mésopotamienne offertes à Paul Garelli.* Edited by D. Charpin and F. Joannès. Paris: Éditions Recherches sur les civilisations.

2002 "Esquisse d'une diplomatique des documents mésopotamiens." *Bibliothèque de l'école des chartes* 160: 487-511.

Chirichigno, G. C.

1993 *Debt-Slavery in Israel and the Ancient Near East.* JSOTSup 141. Sheffield: JSOT Press.

Çiğ, M., and H. Kizilyay

1965 *Yeni Sumer çagina ait Nippur hukukî ve idarî belgeleri* [*Neusumerische Rechts- und Verwaltungsurkunden aus Nippur*]. Türk tarih kurumu yayınlarından 6/7. Ankara: Türk tarih kurumu basimevi.

Civil, M.

1965 "New Sumerian Law Fragments." Pages 1-12 in *Studies in Honour of Benno Landsberger on His Seventy-Fifth Birthday.* Edited by H. G. Güterbock and T. Jacobsen. AS 16. Chicago: University of Chicago Press.

1969 *The Series Lú =* ša *and Related Texts.* MSL 12. Rome: Pontifical Biblical Institute.

1971 *Izi =* išātu, *Ká-gal =* abullu *and Níg-ga =* makkūru. MSL 13. Rome: Pontifical Biblical Institute.

1979 *Ea A =* nâqu, *Aa A =* nâqu, *with Their Forerunners and Related Texts.* MSL 14. Rome: Pontifical Biblical Institute.

Civil, M., and B. Landsberger

1967 *The Series ḪAR-ra =* ḫubullu. *Tablet XV and Related Texts. With Additions and Corrections to MSL II, III, V, and VII.* MSL 9. Rome: Pontifical Biblical Institute.

Cogan, M., and H. Tadmor
1988 *2 Kings*. AB 11. Garden City, N.Y.: Doubleday.

Cohen, R.
1996 "All in the Family: Ancient Near Eastern Diplomacy." *International Negotiation* 1: 11-28.

Cohen, R., and R. Westbrook, eds.
2000 *Amarna Diplomacy: The Beginnings of International Relations*. Baltimore: Johns Hopkins University Press.

Constantinople Arkeoloji Müzeleri
1910-21 *Inventaire des tablettes de Tello conservées au musée impérial ottoman*. 5 vols. Paris: Leroux.

Contenau, G.
1920 *Tablettes cappadociennes*. TCL 4. Paris: Geuthner.

Cooper, J. S.
1975 "Structure, Humor, and Satire in the Poor Man of Nippur." *JCS* 27: 163-74.
1983a *The Curse of Agade*. Baltimore and London: Johns Hopkins University Press.
1983b *Reconstructing History from Ancient Inscriptions: The Lagash-Umma Border Conflict*. SANE 2/1. Malibu: Undena.
1986 *Sumerian and Akkadian Royal Inscriptions*. Vol. 1: *Presargonic Inscriptions*. New Haven: American Oriental Society.

Cowley, A.
1923 *The Aramaic Papyri of the Fifth Century B.C.* Oxford: Oxford University Press.

Crawford, M. H., ed.
1996 *Roman Statutes*. 2 vols. BICSSup 64. London: Institute of Classical Studies, School of Advanced Studies, University of London.

Dalley, S.
1979 *A Catalogue of the Akkadian Cuneiform Tablets in the Collections of the Royal Scottish Museum, Edinburgh, with Copies of Texts*. Royal Scottish Museum Art and Archaeology 2. Edinburgh: Royal Scottish Museum.

Dalley, S., and B. Tessier
1992 "Tablets from the Vicinity of Emar and Elsewhere." *Iraq* 54: 83-111.

Dandamaev, M. A.
1981 "The Neo-Babylonian Citizens." *Klio* 63: 45-49.
1984 *Slavery in Babylonia: From Nabopolassar to Alexander the Great (626-331 B.C.)*. Edited by V. A. Powell and D. B. Weisberg. Translated by V. A. Powell. De Kalb, Ill.: Northern Illinois Press. Original 1974.

Daube, D.
1947 *Studies in Biblical Law*. Cambridge: Cambridge University Press. Reprinted New York: Arno, 1969.
1950 "*Consortium* in Roman and Hebrew Law." *Juridical Revue* 62: 71-91.
1986 "The Old Testament Prohibitions of Homosexuality." *ZSSR (Rom. Abt.)* 103: 447-48.

David, M.
1927 *Die Adoption im altbabylonischen Recht*. Leipziger rechtswissenschaftliche Studien, Leipziger Juristen-Fakultät 23. Leipzig: Weicher.
1948 "The Manumission of Slaves under Zedekiah: A Contribution to the Laws about Hebrew Slaves." *OtSt* 5: 63-79.

Day, P. L.
1995 "Anat." Pages 36-43 in *Dictionary of Deities and Demons in the Bible*. Edited by K. van der Toorn. 1st ed. Leiden and New York: Brill. 2d ed. Leiden and New York: Brill; Grand Rapids, Mich.: Eerdmans, 1999.

Dearman, J. A.
1988 *Property Rights in the Eighth-Century Prophets: The Conflict and Its Background*. SBLDS 106. Atlanta: Scholars Press.

Deller, K.
1987 Review of H. Freydank, *Mittelassyrische Rechtsurkunden und Verwaltungstexte II. VS 21 (NF 5, Berlin)*. *AfO* 34: 58-66.

Démare-Lafont, S.
1999 *Femmes, justice dans l'antiquité orientale: contribution à l'étude du droit pénal au Proche-Orient*. Fribourg, Switzerland: Suisse Éditions Universitaires; Göttingen: Vandenhoeck & Ruprecht.
2003 "Middle Assyrian Period." Pages 521-63 in vol. 1 of *A History of Ancient Near Eastern Law*. Edited by R. Westbrook. 2 vols. HdO 72. Leiden and New York: Brill.

Dijk, J. J. A. van
1959 "Textes divers du Musée de Bagdad III." *Sumer* 15: 5-14.
1962 "Neusumerische Gerichtsurkunden in Bagdad." *ZA* 55: 70-90.
1970 "Remarques sur l'histoire d'Elam et d'Ešnunna." *AfO* 23: 63-71.

Dion, P.-E.
1982 "Deutéronome 21,1-9: Miroir du développement légal et religieux d'Israël." *SR* 11: 13-22.

Dombradi, E.
1996 *Die Darstellung des Rechtsaustrags in den altbabylonischen Prozeßurkunden*. 2 vols. FAOS 20. Stuttgart: Steiner.
2000 "Studien zu *mitḫārum/mitḫāriš* und die Frage des Duplums: I. Zum semantischen Feld von *mitḫārum* in juristischem Kontext." *ZA* 90: 40-69.

Donner, H.
1969 "Adoption oder Legitimation? Erwägungen zur Adoption im Alten Testament auf dem Hintergrund der altorientalischen Rechte." *OrAnt* 8: 87-119.

Dossin, G.
1946-53 *Lettres*. 6 vols. TCL 22-27; ARM 1-6. Paris: Geuthner.
1967 *La Correspondance féminine*. TCL 31; ARM 10. Paris: Geuthner.
1972 "*adaššum* et *kirḫum* dans des textes de Mari." *RA* 66: 111-30.

Dougherty, R. P.
1923 *The Shirkûtu of Babylonian Deities*. YOSR 5/2. New Haven: Yale University Press.

Douglas, M.
2003 "The Go-Away Goat." Pages 121-41 in *The Book of Leviticus: Composition and Reception*. Edited by R. Rendtorff and R. A. Kugler. VTSup 93. Atlanta: Society of Biblical Literature.

Driel, G. van, et al., eds.
1982 *Zikir Šumim: Assyriological Studies Presented to F. R. Kraus on the Occasion of His Seventieth Birthday*. Leiden: Brill.

Driver, G. R., and J. C. Miles
1940 "Ordeal by Oath at Nuzi." *Iraq* 7: 132-38.

Driver, G. R., and J. C. Miles, eds.
1935 *The Assyrian Laws*. Oxford: Clarendon. Reprinted Aalen: Scientia, 1975.
1952 *The Babylonian Laws*. Vol. 1. Oxford: Clarendon.
1955 *The Babylonian Laws*. Vol. 2. Oxford: Clarendon.
1956 *The Babylonian Laws*. Reissued with revisions. Vol. 1. Oxford: Clarendon.
1960 *The Babylonian Laws*. Reissued with revisions. Vol. 2. Oxford: Clarendon.

Driver, S. R.
1896 *A Critical and Exegetical Commentary on Deuteronomy*. ICC. 2d ed. Edinburgh: T. & T. Clark.
1913 *Notes on the Hebrew Text and the Topography of the Books of Samuel*. 2d ed. Oxford: Clarendon.

Durand, J.-M.
1988 "L'ordalie." Pages 509-39 in *Archives Epistolaires de Mari 1/1*. ARM 26/1. Paris: Éditions Recherches sur les civilisations.

École Biblique et Archéologique Française
1974 *La Bible de Jérusalem: La Sainte Bible*. Paris: Éditions du Cerf.

Edgerton, W. F.
1951 "Strikes in Ramses III's Twenty-Ninth Year." *JNES* 10: 137-45.

Edzard, D. O.
1960 "Die Beziehungen Babyloniens und Ägyptens in der mittelbabylonischen Zeit und das Gold." *JESHO* 3: 37-55.
1963 "Sumerische Komposita mit dem Nominalpräfix nu-." *ZA* 55: 91-112.
1967 "Das sumerische Verbalmorphem /ed/ in den alt- und neusumerischen Texten." Pages 29-62 in *Heidelberger Studien zum Alten Orient*. Edited by D. O. Edzard. Wiesbaden: Harrassowitz.
1968 *Sumerische Rechtsurkunden des III. Jahrtausends aus der Zeit vor der III. Dynastie von Ur*. ABAW philosophisch-historische Klasse n.F. 67. Munich: Bayerische Akademie der Wissenschaften, with Beck.
1976 "Zum Sumerischen Eid." Pages 63-98 in *Sumerological Studies in Honor of Thorkild Jacobsen on His Seventieth Birthday, June 7, 1974*. Edited by S. J. Lieberman. AS 20. Chicago. University of Chicago Press.
1991 "Gilgameš und Huwawa A. II. Teil." *ZA* 81: 165-233.
1992 "Der Vertrag von Ebla mit A-bar-QA." Pages 187-217 in *Literature and Literary Language at Elba*. Edited by P. Fronzaroli. Florence: Dipartimento di linguistica, Università di Firenze.

Ehelolf, H.
1933 "Heth. *milit* = "Honig." *OLZ* 36:1-7.

Ehrlich, A. B.
1908-14 *Randglossen zur Hebräischen Bibel: Textkritisches, sprachliches und sachliches*. 7 vols. Leipzig: Hinrichs.

Eichler, B. L.
1973 *Indenture at Nuzi: The Personal* Tidennūtu *Contract and Its Mesopotamian Analogues*. YNER 5. New Haven: Yale University Press.
1987 "Literary Structure in the Laws of Eshnunna." Pages 71-84 in *Language, Literature and History: Philological and Historical Studies Presented to Erica Reiner*. Edited by F. Rochberg-Halton. AOS 67. New Haven: American Oriental Society.

Eichler, B. L., J. W. Heimerdinger, and Å. W. Sjöberg, eds.
1976 *Kramer Anniversary Volume: Cuneiform Studies in Honor of Samuel Noah Kramer*. AOAT 25. Kevelaer: Butzon & Bercker.

Eidem, J.
1991 "An Old Assyrian Treaty from Tell Leilan." Pages 185-207 in *Marchands, diplomates et empereurs. Études sur la civilisation mésopotamienne offertes à Paul Garelli*. Edited by D. Charpin and F. Joannès. Paris: Éditions Recherches sur les civilisations.

Eisser, G., and J. Lewy
1930 *Die Altassyrischen Rechtsurkunden vom Kültepe*. 2 vols. MVAG 33 and 35/3. Leipzig: Hinrichs, 1930-35.

Eissfeldt, O.

1964 *Einleitung in das Alte Testament*. 3d ed. Neue theologische Grundrisse. Tübingen: Mohr. Translated into English as *The Old Testament: An Introduction*. Translated by P. R. Ackroyd. New York: Harper & Row, 1965.

Eslinger, L. M.

1981 "The Case of an Immodest Lady Wrestler in Deuteronomy 25:11-12." *VT* 31: 269-81.

Fales, F. M.

1989 *Prima dell'alfabeto*. Venice: Erizzo.

Falk, Z.

1964 *Hebrew Law in Biblical Times: An Introduction*. Jerusalem: Wahrmann. 2d ed. Winona Lake, Ind.: Eisenbrauns, 2001.

Falkenstein, A.

1956-57 *Die neusumerischen Gerichtsurkunden*. 3 vols. ABAW philosophisch-historische Klasse n.F. 39, 40, 44. Munich: Bayerische Akademie der Wissenschaften.

1957-58 "Zur Grammatik der altsumerischen Sprache." *AfO* 18: 85-96.

1959 "Neue Rechts- und Gerichtsurkunden der Ur III-Zeit aus Lagaš." *ZA* 53: 51-92.

Faltz, L. M.

1985 *Reflexivization: A Study in Universal Syntax*. New York: Garland.

Figulla, H. H.

1951 "Lawsuit Concerning a Sacrilegious Theft at Erech." *Iraq* 13: 95-101.

Finet, A.

1973 *Le code de Hammurapi*. LAOP 6. Paris: Éditions du Cerf.

1978 "La 'gage' et la 'sujétion' (*nipūtum* et *kiššātum*) dans les textes de Mari et le Code de Ḫammurabi." *Akkadica* 8: 12-18.

Finkel, I. L., and M. Civil

1982 *The Series sig$_7$.alam = nabnītu*. MSL 16. Rome: Pontifical Biblical Institute.

Finkelstein, J. J.

1961 "Ammiṣaduqa's Edict and the Babylonian 'Law Codes.'" *JCS* 15: 91-104.

1965 "Some New *Mīšarum* Material and its Implications." Pages 233-51 in *Studies in Honour of Benno Landsberger on His Seventy-Fifth Birthday*. Edited by H. G. Güterbock and T. Jacobsen. AS 16. Chicago: University of Chicago Press.

1966 "Sex Offenses in Sumerian Laws." *JAOS* 86: 355-72.

1967 "A Late Old Babylonian Copy of the Laws of Hammurapi." *JCS* 21: 39-48.

1968 "An Old Babylonian Herding Contract and Genesis 31:38f." Pages 30-36 in *Essays in Memory of E. A. Speiser*. Edited by W. W. Hallo. AOS 53. New Haven: American Oriental Society.
1969a "The Hammurabi Law Tablet *BE* XXXI 22." *RA* 63: 11-27.
1969b "The Laws of Ur-Nammu." *JCS* 22: 66-82.
1970 "On Some Recent Studies in Cuneiform Law." *JAOS* 90: 243-56.
1981 *The Ox that Gored*. TAPA 71/2. Philadelphia: American Philosophical Society.

Fishbane, M. A.
1985 *Biblical Interpretation in Ancient Israel*. Oxford: Clarendon.

Fitzpatrick-McKinley, A.
1999 *The Transformation of Torah from Scribal Advice to Law*. JSOTSup 287. Sheffield: Sheffield Academic.

Fleishman, J.
1990 "The Authority of the Paterfamilias according to CH 117." Pages 249-53 in *Bar-Ilan Studies in Assyriology Dedicated to Pinhas Artzi*. Edited by J. Kline and A. Skaist. BISNELC. Ramat Gan, Israel: Bar-Ilan University Press.

Forde, N. W.
1967 *Nebraska Cuneiform Tests of the Sumerian Ur III Dynasty*. Lawrence, Kan.: Coronado Press.

Frankena, R.
1966 *Briefe aus dem British Museum (LIH und CT 2-33)*. AbB 2. Leiden: Brill.
1968 *Briefe aus der Leidener Sammlung (TLB IV)*. AbB 3. Leiden: Brill.
1974 *Briefe aus dem Berliner Museum*. AbB 6. Leiden: Brill.

Fraser, J. G.
1966 *The Golden Bough: A Study in Magic and Religion*. Vol. 6. *The Scapegoat*. 12 vols. 3d ed. (1906-1912). Reprinted London: Macmillan.

Freydank, D.
1994 "Nachlese zu den mittelassyrische Gesetzen." *AoF* 21: 203-11.

Friedrich, J.
1952 *Hethitisches Wörterbuch*. Indogermanische Bibliothek 2. Heidelberg: Winter.
1971 Die *hethitischen Gesetze*. Documenta et monumenta orientis antique 7. Leiden: Brill.
1974 *Hethitisches Elementarbuch, I. Teil*. Heidelberg: Winter.

Frymer-Kensky, T.
1984 "The Strange Case of the Suspected Soṭah (Numbers v 11-31)." *VT* 34: 11-26.

Gagarin, M.
1990 "The Function of Witnesses at Gortyn." Pages 29-54 in *Symposion 1985*. Akten der Gesellschaft für griechische und hellenistische Rechtsgeschichte 6. Köln: Weimar.

Garbini, G.
1981 "Gli incantesimi fenici di Arslan Taş." *OrAnt* 20: 277-94.

Gavison, R.
1987 *Issues in Contemporary Legal Philosophy: The Influence of H. L. A. Hart*. Oxford: Clarendon; New York: Oxford University Press.

Gelb, I. J.
1965 "The Philadelphia Onion Archive." Pages 57-62 in *Studies in Honour of Benno Landsberger on His Seventy-Fifth Birthday*. Edited by H. G. Güterbock and T. Jacobsen. AS 16. Chicago: University of Chicago Press.

Geller, M. J.
1978 "New Sources for the Origins of the Rabbinic Ketubah." *HUCA*: 227-45.

Goetze, A.
1930 *Neue Bruchstücke zum grossen Text des Hattusilis*. MVAG 34/2. Leipzig: Hinrichs.
1949 Review of H. G. Güterbock, *Kumarbi, Mythen vom churritischen Kronos aus den hethitischen Fragmenten zusammengestellt, übersetzt und erklärt*. *JAOS* 69: 178-83.
1956 *Laws of Eshnunna*. AASOR 31. New Haven: American Schools for Oriental Research.
1958 "Fifty Old Babylonian Letters from Harmal." *Sumer* 14: 3-78.
1967 *Die Annalen des Mursilis*. Darmstadt: Wissenschaftliche Buchgesellschaft. Reprint of MVAG 38. Leipzig: Hinrichs, 1933.
1969a "The Hittite Laws." Pages 188-97 in *Ancient Near Eastern Texts*. 3d ed. Edited by James B. Pritchard. Princeton: Princeton University Press.
1969b "Vow of Puduhepas." Pages 394-96 in *Ancient Near Eastern Texts*. 3d ed. Edited by J. B. Pritchard. Princeton: Princeton University Press.

Goody, J.
1986 *The Logic of Writing and the Organization of Society*. Studies in Literacy, Family, Culture, and the State. Cambridge and New York: Cambridge University Press.

Graf, K. H.
1864 "Was bedeutet der Ausdruck: Vor Gott erscheinen in den Gesetzen des Pentateuch Ex 21,6; 22,7.8." *ZDMG* 18: 309-14.

Gray, G. B.
1903 *A Critical and Exegetical Commentary on Numbers*. ICC. New York: Scribner.

Green, M.
1979 "Wenamun's Demand for Compensation." *ZÄS* 106: 116-20.

Greenberg, M.
1955 *The Ḫab/piru*. AOS 39. New Haven: American Oriental Society.
1983 *Ezekiel 1-20*. AB 22. Garden City, N.Y.: Doubleday.

Greenfield, J. C.
1982 "*Adi balṭu*: Care for the Elderly and its Rewards." Pages 309-16 in *Vorträge gehalten auf der 28. Rencontre Assyriologique Internationale in Wien*. Edited by H. Hirsch and H. Hunger. CRRAI 28; AfO Beiheft 19. Berger: Horn.

Greengus, S.
1966 "Old Babylonian Marriage Ceremonies and Rites." *JCS* 20: 55-72.
1969 "The Old Babylonian Marriage Contract." *JAOS* 89: 505-32.
1969-70 "A Textbook Case of Adultery in Ancient Mesopotamia." *HUCA* 40-41: 33-44.
1992 "Law." Pages 242-52 in vol. 4 of *The Anchor Bible Dictionary*. Edited by David Noel Freedman. 6 vols. New York: Doubleday.

Grimm, J., and W. Grimm
1878 *Deutsches Wörterbuch*. Leipzig: Hirzel.

Gross, K.
1987 "Daughters Adopted as Sons at Emar and Nuzi." Pages 81-90 in *La femme dans le Proche-Orient antique*. Edited by J.-M. Durand. CRRAI 23. Paris: Éditions Recherches sur les civilisations.

Gurney, O. R.
1977 *Some Aspects of Hittite Religion*. Schweich Lectures of the British Academy 1976. Oxford and New York: Oxford University Press.
1982 "A Case of Conjugal Desertion." Pages 91-94 in *Zikir Šumim: Assyriological Studies Presented to F. R. Kraus on the Occasion of His Seventieth Birthday*. Edited by G. van Driel. Leiden: Brill.
1983 *The Middle Babylonian Legal and Economic Texts from Ur*. London: British School of Archaeology in Iraq.

Güterbock, H. G.
1946 *Kumarbi, Mythen vom churritischen Kronos aus den hethitischen Fragmenten zusammengestellt, übersetzt und erklärt*. Istanbuler Schriften 16. Zurich and New York: Europaverlag.
1951 "The Song of Ullikummi: Revised Text of the Hittite Version of a Hurrian Myth." *JCS* 5:135-61.

1952 "The Song of Ullikummi: Revised Text of the Hittite Version of a Hurrian Myth (continued)." *JCS* 6:8-42.

1968 "Oil Plants in Hittite Anatolia." *JAOS* 88: 66-71.

Güterbock, H. G., and H. A. Hoffner, Jr.

1980- *The Hittite Dictionary of the Oriental Institute of the University of Chicago*. Chicago: The Oriental Institute.

Güterbock, H. G., and T. Jacobsen, eds.

1965 *Studies in Honour of Benno Landsberger on His Seventy-Fifth Birthday*. AS 16. Chicago: University of Chicago Press.

Haase, R.

1957 "Zur Bedeutung des Wortes *šakuwaššar*- in der hethitischen Gesetzestexten." *MIO* 5: 34-44.

Hall, F., et al., eds.

1924 *The Holy Bible, Reprinted according to the Authorized Version, 1611*. London and New York: Nonesuch Press; Lincoln MacVeagh; Dial Press.

Hallo, W. W.

1995 "Slave Release in the Biblical World in the Light of a New Text." Pages 79-93 in *Solving Riddles and Untying Knots: Biblical, Epigraphic, and Semitic Studies in Honor of Jonas C. Greenfield*. Edited by Z. Zevit, S. Gitin, and M. Sokoloff. Winona Lake, Ind.: Eisenbrauns.

Hardmeier, C.

1991 "Die Propheten Micha und Jesaja im Spiegel von Jeremia xxvi und 2 Regum xviii-xx: Zur Prophetie-Rezeption in der nach-joschijanischen Zeit." Pages 172-89 in *Congress Volume: Leuven, 1989*. Edited by J. A. Emerton. VTSup 43. Leiden: Brill.

Harper, R.

1892 *Assyrian and Babylonian Letters Belonging to the Kouyunjik Collections of the British Museum*. 14 vols. Chicago: University of Chicago Press.

Hart, H. L. A.

1961 *The Concept of Law*. Clarendon Law Series. Oxford: Clarendon. 2d ed. Oxford: Clarendon, 1994.

1983 *Essays in Jurisprudence and Philosophy*. Oxford: Clarendon; New York: Oxford University Press.

Harris, R.

1955 "The Archive of the Sin Temple in Khafajah." *JCS* 9: 91-120.

1975 *Ancient Sippar: A Demographic Study of an Old Babylonian City*. PIHANS 36. Istanbul: Nederlands Historisch-Archeologisch Instituut te Istanbul.

Hengstl, J.

1987 "Zum Kauf unter Rückkaufsvorbehalt in den altassyrischen Urkunden aus Kaniš." *ZA* 77: 98-116.

Hertel, T.

2006 Review of R. Westbrook, *A History of Ancient Near Eastern Law. Volume I and II*. *BO* 62: 299-315.

Hobbs, T. R.

1974 "Jeremiah 3:1-5 and Deuteronomy 24:1-4." *ZAW* 86: 23-29.

Hoffmann, I.

1984 *Der Erlass Telipinus*. Texte der Hethiter 11. Heidelberg: Winter.

Hoffner, H. A., Jr.

1974 *Alimenta Hethaeorum: Food Production in Hittite Asia Minor*. AOS 55. New Haven: American Oriental Society.

1997 *The Laws of the Hittites*. Documenta et monumenta orientis antique 23. Leiden: Brill.

Holladay, W. L.

1989 *Jeremiah 2, A Commentary on the Book of the Prophet Jeremiah, Chapters 26-52*. Hermeneia. Minneapolis: Fortress.

Holtz, S. E.

2009 *Neo-Babylonian Court Procedure*. CM 38. Leiden and Boston: Brill.

Horst, F.

1961a "Der Diebstahl im AT." Pages 167-75 in *Gottes Recht: Gesammelte Studien zum Recht im Alten Testament*. Edited by F. Horst and H. W. Wolff. Munich: Kaiser.

1961b "Der Eid im Alten Testament." Pages 292-314 in *Gottes Recht: Gesammelte Studien zum Recht im Alten Testament*. Edited by F. Horst and H. W. Wolff. Munich: Kaiser.

Horst, F., and H. W. Wolff, eds.

1961 *Gottes Recht: Gesammelte Studien zum Recht im Alten Testament*. Munich: Kaiser.

Hossfeld, F. L., and I. Meyer

1974 "Der Prophet vor dem Tribunal: Neuer Auslegungsversuch von Jer. 26." *ZAW* 86: 30-50.

Houwink ten Cate, P. H. J.

1968 "Hittite Royal Prayers." *Numen* 16: 81-98.

Hrozný, B.

1939 "Über eine unveröffentlichte Urkunde vom Kültepe." Pages 108-11 in *Symbolae ad iura orientis antiqui pertinentes Paulo Koschaker dedicatae*. Edited by T. Folkers et al. SDIOAP 2. Leiden: Brill.

1952 *Inscriptions cunéiformes du Kultépé*. Translated by M. David. Archív Orientální Monografie 14; ICK 1. Praha: Státni pedogogické nakl.

Hruška, B.
1973 "Die Innere Struktur der Reformtexte Urukaginas von Lagaš." *ArOr* 41: 4-13, 104-32.

Huehnergard, J.
1985 "Biblical Notes on Some New Akkadian Texts from Emar (Syria)." *CBQ* 47: 428-34.
1989 *The Akkadian of Ugarit*. HSS 34. Atlanta: Scholars Press.

Hughes, D. D.
1991 *Human Sacrifice in Ancient Greece*. London: Routledge, 1991.

Hunter, V.
1994 *Policing Athens*. Princeton: Princeton University Press.

Jackson, B. S.
1972 *Theft in Early Jewish Law*. Oxford: Clarendon.
1975 "The Problem of Exodus 21:22-25 (Ius Talionis)." Pages 75-107 in *Essays in Jewish and Comparative Legal History*. SJLA 10. Leiden: Brill. Reprint of *VT* 23 (1973): 273-304.
1985 "Law." Pages 548-51 in *Harper's Bible Dictionary*. Edited by P. J. Achtemeier. 1st ed. San Francisco: Harper & Row.
1989 "Ideas of Law and Legal Administration: A Semiotic Approach." Pages 185-202 in *The World of Ancient Israel: Sociological, Anthropological and Political Perspectives*. Edited by R. E. Clements. Cambridge: Cambridge University Press.
1992 "Practical Wisdom and Literary Artifice in the Covenant Code." Pages 65-92 in *The Jerusalem 1990 Conference Volume*. Edited by B. S. Jackson and S. M. Passamaneck. Jewish Law Association Studies 6. Atlanta: Scholars Press.
2000 *Studies in the Semiotics of Biblical Law*. JSOTSup 314. Sheffield: Sheffield Academic.

Jackson, B. S., and Watkins, T. F.
1984 "Distraint in the Laws of Eshnunna and Hammurabi." Pages 411-19 in vol. 5 of *Studi in onore di Cesare Sanfilippo*. 6 vols. Milan: Giuffrè.

Jacobsen, T.
1970 "An Ancient Mesopotamian Trial for Homicide." Pages 193-214 in *Toward the Image of Tammuz and Other Essays on Mesopotamian History and Culture*. Edited by W. L. Moran. HSS 21. Cambridge, Mass.: Harvard University Press.

Jacobsen, T., ed.
1970 *Toward the Image of Tammuz and Other Essays on Mesopotamian History and Culture*. Edited by W. L. Moran. HSS 21. Cambridge, Mass.: Harvard University Press.

Jakobson, V. A.
1974 "Studies in Neo-Assyrian Law. 1. Matrimonial Law." *AoF* 11: 115-19.
Janssen, C.
1991 "Samsu-iluna and the Hungry *nadītums*." *Northern Akkad Project Reports* 5: 3-40.
Japhet, S.
1992 "The Israelite Legal and Social Reality as Reflected in Chronicles: A Case Study." Pages 79-91 in *Sha'arei Talmon: Studies in the Bible, Qumran, and the Ancient Near East Presented to Shemaryahu Talmon*. Edited by M. Fishbane and E. Tov. Winona Lake, Ind.: Eisenbrauns.
Jas, R.
1996 *Neo-Assyrian Judicial Procedures*. SAAS 5. Helsinki: Helsinki University Press.
Jepsen, A.
1927 *Untersuchungen zum Bundesbuch*. BWANT 3/5. Stuttgart: Kohlhammer.
Jewish Publication Society
1985 *Tanakh*. New York: Jewish Publication Society.
Joannès, F.
1991 "Le traité de vassalité d'Atamrum d'Andarig envers Zimri-Lim de Mari." Pages 167-77 in *Marchands, diplomates et empereurs. Études sur la civilisation mésopotamienne offertes à Paul Garelli*. Edited by D. Charpin and F. Joannès. Paris: Éditions Recherches sur les civilisations.
2000 "Les textes judiciaires néo-babyloniens." Pages 234-37 in *Rendre la justice en Mésopotamie: Archives judiciaires du Proche-Orient ancien (IIIe-Ier millénaires avant J.-C.)* Edited by F. Joannès. Saint-Denis: Presses Universitaires de Vincennes.
Joannès, F., ed.
2000 *Rendre la justice en Mésopotamie: Archives judiciaires du Proche-Orient ancien (IIIe-Ier millénaires avant J.-C.)*. Saint-Denis: Presses Universitaires de Vincennes.
Johns, C. H. W.
1898-1924 *Assyrian Deeds and Documents*. 4 vols. Cambridge: Deighton, Bell.
Joint Committee on the New Translation of the Bible
1970 *The New English Bible with the Apocrypha*. London and New York: Oxford University Press; Cambridge University Press.
Jones, G. H.
1990 *The Nathan Narratives*. JSOTSup 80. Sheffield: JSOT Press.

Jones, T. B., and J. W. Snyder
1991 *Sumerian Economic Texts from the Third Ur Dynasty*. Minneapolis: University of Minnesota Press.

Jönsson, C.
2000 "Diplomatic Signaling in the Amarna Letters." Pages 191-204 in *Amarna Diplomacy: The Beginnings of International Relations*. Edited by R. Cohen and R. Westbrook. Baltimore: Johns Hopkins University Press.

Joüon, P., and T. Muraoka
1991 *A Grammar of Biblical Hebrew*. SubBi 14. Rome: Pontifical Biblical Institute.

Junker, H.
1933 *Das Buch Deuteronomium*. Bonn: Hanstein.

Jursa, M.
1996 "Akkad, das Eulmaš und Gubaru." *WZKM* 86: 197-211.

Kämmerer, T.
1994 "Zur sozialen Stellung der Frau in Emar." *UF* 26: 169-208.

Kaufman, S. A.
1978-79 "The Structure of the Deuteronomic Law." *Maarav* 1-2: 105-58.

Kelsen, H.
1961 *General Theory of Law and State*. Translated by A. Wedberg. 20th Century Legal Philosophy Series. New York: Russell & Russell. Original 1945.
1967 *Pure Theory of Law*. Translated by M. Knight. Berkeley: University of California Press. Reprinted California Library Reprint Series. Berkeley: University of California Press, 1978.
1991 *General Theory of Norms*. Translated by M. Hartney. Oxford: Clarendon; New York: Oxford University Press.

Kestemont, G.
1974 *Diplomatique et droit internationale en Asie occidentale (1600-1200 av. J.C.)*. Louvain-La-Neuve: Université Catholique de Louvain, Institut Orientaliste.

Kienast, B.
1960 *Die altassyrischen Texte des orientalischen Seminars der Universität Heidelberg und der Sammlung Erlenmeyer, Basel*. Untersuchungen zur Assyriologie und vorderasiatischen Archäologie 1. Berlin: de Gruyter.
1978 *Die altbabylonischen Briefe und Urkunden aus Kisurra*. 2 vols. Wiesbaden: Steiner.
1984 *Das altassyrische Kaufvertragsrecht*. FAOS 1. Altassyrische Texte und Untersuchungen 1. Stuttgart: Steiner.

Kilmer, A. D., and B. Landsberger
1962 *The Fauna of Ancient Mesopotamia. Second Part: ḪAR-ra* = ḫubullu. *Tablets XIV and XVIII.* MSL 8/2. Rome: Pontifical Biblical Institute.
Kilmer, A. D., E. I. Gordon, and B. Landsberger
1960 *The Fauna of Ancient Mesopotamia. First Part: Tablet XIII.* MSL 8/1. Rome: Pontifical Biblical Institute.
King, L. W.
1898-1900 *The Letters and Inscriptions of Ḫammurabi, King of Babylon.* London: Luzac.
1910 *Old Babylonian Letters in the British Museum.* CT 29. London: Trustees of the British Museum.
Klíma, J.
1940 *Untersuchungen zum altbabylonischen Erbrecht.* Monographien des Archív Orientální 8. Prague: Orientalisches Institut.
Klíma, J., H. P. H. Petschow, G. Cardascia, and V. Korošec
1971 "Gesetze." Pages 234-97 in vol. 3 of *Reallexikon der Assyriologie.* Edited by E. Ebeling et al. 16 vols. Berlin: de Gruyter, 1928-.
Knierim, R.
1965 *Die Hauptbegriffe für Sünde im Alten Testament.* Gütersloh: Gütersloher Verlagshaus.
Knudtzon, J. A., ed.
1907-15 *Die El-Amarna-Tafeln.* 2 vols. Vorderasiatische Bibliothek. Leipzig: Hinrichs. Reprinted Aalen: Zeller, 1964.
Kohler, J., and A. Ungnad
1913 *Assyrische Rechtsurkunden, in Umschrift und Übersetzung nebst einem Index der Personen-Namen und Rechtserläuterungen.* Leipzig: Pfeiffer.
Kohler, J., A. Ungnad et al.
1904-23 *Hammurabis Gesetz.* 6 vols. Leipzig: Pfeiffer.
Köhler, L.
1928 "Zu Ex. 22,8. Ein Beitrag zur Kenntnis des hebräischen Rechts." *ZAW* 46: 213-20.
Köhler, L., W. Baumgartner, and J. J. Stamm
1967-96 *Hebräisches und Aramäisches Lexikon zum Alten Testament.* 3d ed. Edited by W. Baumgartner. Brill: Leiden.
Korošec, V.
1931 *Hethitische Staatsverträge—ein Beitrag zu ihrer juristischen Wertung.* Leipziger rechtswissenschaftliche Studien 60. Leipzig: Weicher.
1964 "Keilschriftrecht." Pages 49-219 in *Orientalisches Recht.* Edited by E. Seidl, V. Korošec, and O. Spies. HdO 1/3. Leiden: Brill.

Koschaker, P.
1911 *Babylonisch-assyrisches Bürgschaftsrecht. Ein Beitrag zur Lehre von Schuld und Haftung*. Leipzig: Teubner.
1917 *Rechtsvergleichende Studien zur Gesetzgebung Hammurapis Königs von Babylon*. Leipzig: Hinrichs und Veit.
1924 [Title and pages not available]. In *Reallexikon der Vorgeschichte*. Edited by M. Ebert. Berlin: de Gruyter.
1928 *Neue keilschriftliche Rechtsurkunden aus der El-Amarna Zeit*. ASAW 39/5. Leipzig: Hirzel.
1931 *Über einige griechische Rechtsurkunden aus den östlichen Randgebieten des Hellenismus*. ASAW 42. Leipzig: Hirzel.
1936 "Randnotizen zu neueren keilschriftlichen Rechtsurkunden." *ZA* 43: 196-232.
Kouwenberg, N. J. C.
2002 "Ventive, Dative and Allative in Old Babylonian." *ZA* 92: 200-40.
Kraeling, E.
1953 *The Brooklyn Museum Aramaic Papyri: New Documents of the Fifth Century B.C. from the Jewish Colony at Elephantine*. Publications of the Department of Egyptian Art. New Haven: Yale University Press. Reprinted New York: Arno Press, 1969.
Kraus, F. R.
1955 "Neue Rechtsurkunden der altbabylonischen Zeit." *WO* 2: 120-36.
1958 *Ein Edikt des Königs Ammi-ṣaduqa von Babylon*. SDIOAP 5. Leiden: Brill.
1959 "Briefschreibübungen im altbabylonischen Schulunterricht." *JEOL* 16: 16-39.
1960 "Ein zentrales Problem des altmesopotamischen Rechtes: Was ist der Codex Hammu-rabi?" *Geneva NS* 8: 283-96.
1966 *Staatliche Viehhaltung im altbabylonischen Lande Larsa*. MKNAW 29. Amsterdam: North Holland.
1970 *Sumerer und Akkade, ein Problem der altmesopotamischen Geschichte*. MKNAW. Amsterdam: North Holland.
1973 *Vom mesopotamischen Menschen der altbabylonischen Zeit und seiner Welt. Eine Reihe Vorlesungen*. MKNAW 36/6. Amsterdam: North Holland.
1976 "Akkadische Wörter und Ausdrücke, X-XI." *RA* 70: 165-79.
1977 *Briefe aus dem British Museum (CT 52)*. AbB 7. Leiden: Brill.
1984 *Königliche Verfügungen in altbabylonischer Zeit*. SDIOAP 11. Leiden: Brill.
1987 *Sonderformen akkadischer Parataxe: Die Koppelungen*. MKNAW 50/1. Amsterdam and New York: North Holland.

Krecher, J.
1974 "Neue Sumerische Rechtsurkunden des 3. Jahrtausends." *ZA* 63: 145-271.
Kronasser, H.
1961 "Fünf hethitische Rituale." *Die Sprache* 7: 140-67.
1962a "Das hethitische Ritual KBo IV 2." *Die Sprache* 8: 89-107.
1962b "Nachträge und Berichtigungen zu 7/1961, 140-67." *Die Sprache* 8: 108-13.
Kruchten, J. M.
1981 *Le décret d'Horemheb: tradition, commentaire épigraphique, philologique et institutionnel*. Brussels: Éditions de l'Université de Bruxelles.
Krueger, P., et al.
1912 *Corpus iuris civilis*. 3 vols. Berlin: Weidmann.
Kühne, C.
1973 *Die Chronologie der internationalen Korrespondenz von El-Amarna*. AOAT 17. Neukirchen-Vluyn: Neukirchener Verlag.
Kümmel, H. M.
1967 *Ersatzrituale für den hethitischen König*. StBoT 3. Wiesbaden: Harrassowitz.
1974-77 "Ein Fall von Sklavenhehlerei." *AfO* 25: 72-83.
Kutscher, R.
1989 *The Brockman Tablets of the University of Haifa*. Vol. 1. *Royal Inscriptions*. Haifa: Haifa University Press; Wiesbaden: Harrassowitz.
Kwasman, T.
1988 *Neo-Assyrian Legal Documents in the Kouyunjik Collection of the British Museum*. Studia Pohl, Series Maior 14. Rome: Pontifical Biblical Institute.
Lacheman, E. R.
1940 "Nuzi Geographical Names I." *BASOR* 78: 18-23.
Lacheman, E. R., and D. I. Owen
1981 "Texts from Arrapḫa and from Nuzi in the Yale Babylonian Collection." Pages 377-432 in *Studies on the Civilization and Culture of Nuzi and the Hurrians*. Edited by M. Morrison and D. I. Owen. Winona Lake, Ind.: Eisenbrauns.
Lafont, S.
see: Démare-Lafont, S.
Lambert, W. G.
1960a *Babylonian Wisdom Literature*. Oxford: Clarendon.
1960b "Gilgameš in Religious, Historical and Omen Texts and the Historicity of Gilgameš." Pages 39-56 in *Gilgameš et sa légende: Études*

recueillies. Edited by P. Garelli. Cahiers du Groupe François Thureau-Dangin. Paris: Klincksieck.

Landsberger, B.

1924-25 "Schwierige akkadische Wörter." *AfK* 2: 64-70.

1924 "Solidarhaftung von Schuldnern in den babyl.-assyrischen Urkunden." *ZA* 35: 22-36.

1937 *Materialien zum sumerischen Lexikon: Vokabulare und Formularbücher, unter Mitwirkung von Fachgenossen*. Vol. I: *Die Serie* ana ittišu. Rome: Pontifical Biblical Institute.

1968 "Jungfräulichkeit: Ein Beitrag zum Thema 'Beilager und Eheschliessung.'" Pages 41-105 in vol. 2 of *Symbolae iuridicae et historicae Martino David dedicatae*. Edited by J. Ankum, R. Feenstra, and W. F. Leemans. 2 vols. SDIOAP 2. Leiden: Brill.

Lane, E. W.

1984 *Arabic-English Lexicon*. Rev. ed. Cambridge: Islamic Texts Society.

Laroche, E.

1965 "Mythologie anatolienne." *RHA* 23: 61-178.

1971 *Catalogue des textes hittites*. Études et commentaires 75. Paris: Klincksieck.

Larsen, M. T.

1976 *The Old Assyrian City-State and its Colonies*. Mesopotamia 4. Copenhagen: Akademisk Forlag.

Lautner, J.

1922 *Die richterliche Entscheidung und die Streitbeendigung im altbabylonischen Prozessrechte*. Leipziger rechtswissenschaftliche Studien 3. Leipzig: Weicher.

Leemans, W. F.

1957 "Some Aspects of Theft and Robbery in Old-Babylonian Documents." Pages 661-66 in *Scritti in Onore di Giuseppe Furlani*. Edited by Università di Roma, Istituto di Studi Orientali. RSO 32. Rome: Bardi.

1964 *Old Babylonian Legal and Administrative Documents*. TLB 1. Leiden: Nederlands Instituut voor het Nabije Oosten.

1968 "King Hammurapi as Judge." Pages 107-29 in vol. 2 of *Symbolae iuridicae et historicae Martino David dedicatae*. Edited by J. Ankum, R. Feenstra, and W. F. Leemans. 2 vols. SDIOAP 2. Leiden: Brill.

1988 "Aperçu sur les textes juridiques d'Emar." *JESHO* 31: 207-42.

1991 "Textes paléo-babyloniens commençant par une liste des personnes." Pages 307-31 in *Marchands, diplomates et empereurs. Études sur la civilisation mésopotamienne offertes à Paul Garelli*. Edited by D. Charpin and F. Joannès. Paris: Éditions Recherches sur les civilisations.

Leichty, E.

1970 *The Omen Series* šumma izbu. TCS 4. Locust Valley, N. Y.: Augustin.

Lemche, N. P.

1976 "The Manumission of Slaves—The Fallow Year—The Sabbatical Year—The Jubilee Year (Exodus 21:2f, 23:10-11; Deuteronomy 15:1-18; Leviticus 25; Jeremiah 34:8-10, Nehemiah)." *VT* 26: 38-59.

1979 "*Andurārum* and *Mīšarum*: Comments on the Problem of Social Edicts and Their Application in the Ancient Near East." *JNES* 38: 11-22.

Levine, B.

1968 "*mulūgu/melug*: The Origins of a Talmudic Legal Institution." *JAOS* 88: 271-85.

1989 *Leviticus = Va-Yikra: The Traditional Hebrew Text with the New JPS Translation*. JPS Torah Comm. Philadelphia: Jewish Publication Society.

Levinson, B. M.

1996 "Recovering the Lost Original Meaning of *wl' tksh 'lyw* (Deuteronomy 13:9)." *JBL* 115: 601-20.

Lewy, J.

1932 *Die Keilschrifttexte aus Kleinasien*. TuM 1; KTS 1. Leipzig: Hinrichs.

1956 "On Some Institutions of the Old Assyrian Empire." *HUCA* 27: 1-79.

1958 "The Biblical Institution of *deror* in the Light of Accadian Documents." *EI* 5: 21-31.

Liddell, H. G., R. Scott, H. S. Jones et al., eds.

1996 *A Greek-English Lexicon*. Oxford: Clarendon; New York: Oxford University Press.

Lipiński, E.

1994 "Kinship Terminology in 1 Sam 25.40-42." *ZAH* 7:12-16.

Liverani, M.

1973 "Storiografia politica hittita—I. Šunaššura, ovvero: della reciprocità." *OrAn* 12: 267-97.

1979 "'Irrational' Elements in the Amarna Trade." Pages 21-33 in *Three Amarna Essays*. Edited by M. Liverani. MANE 1/5. Malibu: Undena.

1983 "Political Lexicon and Political Ideologies in the Amarna Letters." *Berytus* 31: 41-56.

1990 *Prestige and Interest: International Relations in the Near East ca. 1600-1100 B.C.* HANES 1. Padova: Sargon.

2000 "The 'Great Powers' Club." Pages 15-27 in *Amarna Diplomacy: The Beginnings of International Relations*. Edited by R. Cohen and R. Westbrook. Baltimore: Johns Hopkins University Press.

Locher, C.
1981 "Altes und Neues zu Malachi 2,10-16." Pages 241-71 in *Mélanges Dominique Barthélemy: Études bibliques offertes à l'occasion de son 60e anniversaire*. Edited by P. Casetti, O. Keel, and A. Schenker. OBO 38. Fribourg, Switzerland: Suisse Éditions Universitaires.

Loewenstamm, S.
1977 "Exodus xxi 22-25." *VT* 27: 352-60.
1980a "The Cumulative Oath of Witnesses and Parties in Mesopotamian Law." Pages 341-45 in *Comparative Studies in Biblical and Ancient Oriental Literatures*. AOAT 204. Neukirchen-Vluyn: Neukirchener Verlag.
1980b "The Laws of Adultery and the Law of Murder in Biblical and Mesopotamian Law." Pages 146-53 in *Comparative Studies in Biblical and Ancient Oriental Literatures*. AOAT 204. Neukirchen-Vluyn: Neukirchener Verlag.

Lorton, D.
1974 *The Juridical Terminology of International Relations in Egyptian Texts through Dynasty XVIII*. Baltimore: John Hopkins University Press.

Luckenbill, D. D.
1930 *Inscriptions from Adab*. OIP 14. Chicago: The Oriental Institute of the University of Chicago.

Lundbom, J. R.
2004 *Jeremiah 21-36*. AB 21B. New York: Doubleday.

Lutz, H. L. F.
1931-46 *Legal and Economic Documents from Ashjâly*. UCP 10/1. Berkeley, Calif.: University of California Press.

Lyons, D., and R. Westbrook, eds.
2005 *Women and Property in Ancient Near Eastern and Mediterranean Societies*. Washington, D.C.: Center for Hellenic Studies. Electronic publication: <*http://www.chs.harvard.edu/publications.sec*>.

MacGinnis, J.
1993 "The Manumission of a Royal Slave." *ASJ* 15: 99-106.

Maekawa, K.
1973-74 "The Development of the É-MÍ in Lagash during Early Dynastic III." *Mesopotamia* 8-9: 77-144.

Magdalene, F. R.
2007 *On the Scales of Righteousness: Neo-Babylonian Trial Law and the Book of Job*. Brown Judaic Studies Series 348. Providence, R.I.: Program in Judaic Studies, Brown University.

Malul, M.

1989 "Susapinnu." *JESHO* 32: 241-78.

1990a "Adoption of Foundlings in the Bible and Mesopotamian Documents." *JSOT* 46: 97-126.

1990b *The Comparative Method in Ancient Near Eastern and Biblical Legal Studies*. AOAT 227. Kevelaer and Neukirchen-Vluyn: Butzon & Bercker and Neukirchener Verlag.

Matouš, L.

1950 "Contrats de vente d'immeubles provenant de Larsa." *ArOr* 18: 11-67.

1962 *Inscriptions cunéiformes du Kultépé.* ICK 2. Prague: Československá akademie věd.

1973 "Beiträge zum Eherecht der anatolischen Bevölkerung im 2. Jt. v.u.Z." *ArOr* 41: 309-18.

Matthews, V. H., and D. C. Benjamin

1993 *Social World of Ancient Israel 1250-587 BCE.* Peabody, Mass.: Hendrickson.

May, H. G., and B. M. Metzger, eds.

1962 *The Holy Bible: Revised Standard Version.* London and New York: Oxford University Press.

Mayrhofer, M.

1956-80 *Kurzgefaßtes etymologisches Wörterbuch des Altindischen: A Concise Etymological Sanskrit Dictionary.* 4 vols. Indogermanische Bibliothek 2. Heidelberg: Winter.

McCarter, P. K., Jr.

1984 *2 Samuel.* AB 9 Garden City, N.Y.: Doubleday.

McKenzie, D.

1964 "Judicial Procedure at the Town Gate." *VT* 14: 100-4.

Meek, T. J.

1913 "Cuneiform Bilingual Hymns, Prayers and Penitential Psalms." *BzA* 10: 1-127.

Meier, S.

1988 *The Messenger in the Ancient Semitic World.* HSM 45. Atlanta: Scholars Press.

Meissner, B.

1893 *Beiträge zum altbabylonischen Privatrecht.* Assyriologische Bibliothek. Leipzig: Hinrichs.

Mendelsohn, I.

1935 "The Conditional Sale into Slavery of Free-born Daughters in Nuzi and the Law of Ex. 21.7-11." *JAOS* 55: 190-95.

1959 "On the Preferential Status of the Eldest Son." *BASOR* 156: 38-40.

Mendenhall, G.
1955 *Law and Covenant in the Ancient Near East*. Pittsburgh: Biblical Colloquium.
Meyers, C. L., and E. M. Meyers
1993 *Zechariah 9-14*. AB 25C. New York: Doubleday.
Michalowski, P.
1989 *The Lamentation over the Destruction of Sumer and Ur*. Mesopotamian Civilizations 1. Winona Lake, Ind.: Eisenbrauns.
Mieroop, M. van de
1991 Review of R. Westbrook, *Old Babylonian Marriage Law*. *BO* 48: 567-74.
Milano, L.
1993 "Mehl." Pages 22-31 in vol. 8 of *Reallexikon der Assyriologie*. Edited by E. Ebeling et al. 16 vols. Berlin: de Gruyter, 1928-.
Milgrom, J.
1991 *Leviticus 1-16*. AB 3A. New York: Doubleday.
Moran, W. L.
1992 *The Amarna Letters*. Baltimore: The Johns Hopkins University Press.
Morrison, M.
1983 "The Jacob and Laban Narrative in Light of Near Eastern Sources." *BA* 46: 155-64.
Muffs, Y.
1969 *Studies in Aramaic Legal Papyri from Elephantine*. SDIOAP 8. Leiden: Brill. Reprinted as *Studies in the Aramaic Legal Papyri from Elephantine*. HdO 66. Leiden: Brill, 2003.
Müller, D. H.
1903 *Die Gesetze Hammurabis und ihr Verhältnis zur mosaischen Gesetzgebung sowie zu den 12 Tafeln*. Vienna: Hölder. Reprinted Amsterdam: Philo, 1975.
Mylonas, G. E.
1969 *Eleusis and the Eleusinian Mysteries*. Princeton: Princeton University Press.
Neufeld, E.
1944 *Ancient Hebrew Marriage Laws*. London: Longman; New York: Green.
Noonan, J. T., Jr.
1980 "The Muzzled Ox." *JQR* 70: 172-75.
North, R. G.
1954 *Sociology of the Biblical Jubilee*. AnBib 4. Rome: Pontifical Biblical Institute.

Noth, M.

1962 *Exodus*. Translated by J. S. Bowden. OTL. Philadelphia: Westminster.

1966 *Das vierte Buch Mose: Numeri*. Göttingen: Vandenhoek & Ruprecht.

1967 *The Laws in the Pentateuch, and Other Studies*. Translated by D. R. Ap-Thomas. Edinburgh: Oliver & Boyd; Philadelphia: Fortress.

1981 *The Deuteronomistic History*. Translated by J. Doull et al. JSOTSup 15. Sheffield: JSOT Press. German original 1943.

Nötscher, F.

1928-30 *Die Omen-Serie* šumma ālu ina mēlê šakin *(CT 38-40)*. Orientalia 51-54. Rome: Pontifical Biblical Institute.

Nougayrol, J.

1955 *Le Palais Royal d'Ugarit III: Textes accadiens et hourrites des archives est, ouest et centrales*. Mission Ras-Shamra 6. Paris: Imprimerie Nationale.

1956 *Le Palais Royal d'Ugarit IV*. Mission Ras-Shamra 9. Paris: Imprimerie Nationale.

Nougayrol, J., et al.

1968 *Nouveaux textes accadiens, hourrites et ugaritiques des archives et bibliothèques privées d'Ugarit*. Ugaritica 5. Mission de Ras Shamra 16. Paris: Geuthner.

O'Connor, K. M.

1989 "Do Not Trim a Word: The Contributions of Chapter 26 to the Book of Jeremiah." *CBQ* 51: 617-30.

Obermark, P.

1992 "Adoption in the Old Babylonian Period." Ph.D. diss. Hebrew Union College and Jewish Institute of Religion (Ohio).

Oelsner, J., B. Wells, and C. Wunsch

2003 "Neo-Babylonian Period." Pages 911-74 in vol. 2 of *A History of Ancient Near Eastern Law*. Edited by R. Westbrook. 2 vols. HdO 72. Leiden: Brill.

Oppenheim, A. L.

1955 "'Siege-Documents' from Nippur." *Iraq* 17: 69-89.

1956 *The Interpretation of Dreams in the Ancient Near East, with a Translation of an Assyrian Dream-Book*. TAPA 46/3. Philadelphia: American Philosophical Society.

Oppenheim, A. L., et al., eds.

1956- *The Assyrian Dictionary of the Oriental Institute of Chicago*. Chicago: Oriental Institute of the University of Chicago.

Otten, H.

1958 *Hethitische Totenrituale*. Akademie der Wissenschaften zu Berlin, Institut für Orientforschung 37. Berlin: Akademie-Verlag.

1961 “Eine Beschwörung der Unterirdischen aus Bogazköy.” *ZA* 54: 114-57.

Otto, E.

1988a “Interdependenzen zwischen Geschichte und Rechtsgeschichte des antiken Israels.” *Rechtshistorisches Journal* 7: 347-68. Reprinted at pages 75-93 in *Kontinuum und Proprium. Studien zur Sozial- und Rechtsgeschichte des Alten Orients und des Alten Testaments*. OBC 8. Wiesbaden: Harrassowitz, 1996.

1988b “Die rechtsgeschichtliche Entwicklung des Depositenrechts in altorientalischen und altisraelitischen Rechtskorpora.” *ZSSR (Rom. Abt.)* 105: 1-31. Reprinted at pages 139-63 in *Kontinuum und Proprium: Studien zur Sozial- und Rechtsgeschichte des Alten Orients und des Alten Testaments*. OBC 8. Wiesbaden: Harrassowitz, 1996.

1988c *Wandel der Rechtsbegründungen in der Gesellschaftsgeschichte des antiken Israel: Eine Rechtsgeschichte des ‘Bundesbuchs’ Ex XX 22-XXIII 13*. StudBib 3. Leiden: Brill.

1989 *Rechtsgeschichte der Redaktionen im Kodex Eshnunna and im Bundesbuch*. OBO 85. Freiburg: Universitätsverlag; Göttingen: Vandenhoeck & Ruprecht.

1992 “Der reduzierte Brautpreis. Ehe- und Zinsrecht in den Paragraphen 18 und 18a des Kodex Eshnunna.” *ZSSR (Rom. Abt.)* 109: 475-81.

1993a “Das Eherecht im Mittelassyrischen Kodex und im Deuteronomium: Tradition und Redaktion in den §§ 12-16 der Tafel A des Mittelassyrischen Kodex und in Dtn 22,22-29.” Pages 259-81 in *Mesopotamia – Ugaritica – Biblica: Festschrift für Kurt Bergerhof zur Vollendung seines 70. Lebensjahres am 7. Mai 1992*. Edited by M. Dietrich and O. Loretz. AOAT 232. Neukirchen-Vluyn: Neukirchener Verlag.

1993b “Die Einschränkung des Privatstrafrechts durch öffentliches Strafrecht in der Redaktion der Paragraphen 1-24; 50-59 des Mittelassyrischen Kodex der Tafel A (KAV 1).” Pages 131-66 in *Biblische Welten: Festschrift für Martin Metzger zu seinem 85. Geburtstag*. Edited by W. Zwickel. OBO 123. Freiburg: Universitätsverlag; Göttingen: Vandenhoeck & Ruprecht.

1994 “Aspects of Legal Reforms and Reformulations in Ancient Cuneiform and Israelite Law.” Pages 160-96 in *Theory and Method in Biblical and Cuneiform Law: Revision, Interpolation and Development*. Edited by B. M. Levinson. JSOTSup 181. Sheffield: Sheffield Academic.

2003 “Recht im antiken Israel.” Pages 151-90 in *Die Rechtskulturen der Antike. Vom Alten Orient bis zum Römischen Reich*. Edited by U. Manthe. Munich: Beck.

Owen, D. I.
1975 *The John Frederick Lewis Collection Texts from the Third Millennium in the Free Library of Philadelphia*. MVN 3. Rome: Multigrafica Editrice/Bonsignori Editore.

Owen, D. I., and R. Westbrook
1992 "Tie Her Up and Throw Her into the River! An Old Babylonian Inchoate Marriage on the Rocks." *ZA* 82: 202-7.

Ozaki (Gomi), T., and S. Sato
1990 *Selected Neo-Sumerian Administrative Texts from the British Museum*. Soken kenkyu shiryo 7. Abiko: Research Institute, Chuo-Gakuin University.

Paradise, J.
1980 "A Daughter and Her Father's Property at Nuzi." *JCS* 32: 189-207.

Parker, B.
1954 "The Nimrud Tablets, 1952: Business Documents." *Iraq* 16: 29-58.

Parpola, S.
1983 *Letters from Assyrian Scholars to the Kings Esarhaddon and Assurbanipal*. 2 vols. AOAT 5. Kevelaer: Butzon & Bercker.
1993 *Letters from Assyrian and Babylonian Scholars*. SAA 10. Helsinki: Helsinki University Press.

Parpola, S., and K. Watanabe
1988 *Neo-Assyrian Treaties and Loyalty Oaths*. SAA 2. Helsinki: Helsinki University Press.

Patrick, D.
1985 *Old Testament Law*. Atlanta: John Knox Press; London: SCM Press.

Patrick, D., ed.
1989 *Thinking Biblical Law*. Semeia 45. Atlanta: Scholars Press.

Paul, S.
1969 "Exod. 21.10: A Threefold Maintenance Clause." *JNES* 28: 48-53.
1970 *Studies in the Book of the Covenant in the Light of Cuneiform and Biblical Laws*. VTSup 18. Leiden: Brill.

Paulson, S. L., and B. L. Paulson, eds.
1998 *Normativity and Norms: Critical Perspectives on Kelsenian Themes*. Translated by B. L. Paulson, S. L. Paulson, and M. Sherberg. Oxford: Clarendon; New York: Oxford University Press.

Paulson, S. L., and M. Stolleis, eds.
2005 *Hans Kelson, Staatrechtslehrer und Rechtstheoretiker des 20. Jahrhunderts*. Grundlagen der Rechtswissenschaft 3. Tübingen: Mohr Siebeck.

Payne Smith, R.
1999 *Thesaurus Syriacus II*. 2 vols. Hildesheim: Georg Olms. Reprint of Oxford: Clarendon, 1879.

Payne Smith, R., and J. Payne Smith
1988 *A Compendious Syriac Dictionary*. Oxford: Clarendon; Winona Lake, Ind.: Eisenbrauns. Reprint of original edition, Oxford: Clarendon, 1903.

Payne Smith Margoliouth, J.
1981 *Supplement to the Thesaurus Syriacus of R. Payne Smith*. Hildesheim: Georg Olms. Reprint of original edition, Oxford: Clarendon, 1927.

Petschow, H. P. H.
1961 "Zur Unwirksamkeit verbotener Rechtsgeschäfte im altbabylonischen Recht." *ZA* 54: 197-200.
1965 "Zur Systematik und Gesetzestechnik im Codex Hammurabi." *ZA* 57: 146-72.
1968 "Zur 'Systematik' in den Gesetzen von Eshnunna." Pages 131-43 in vol. 2 of *Symbolae iuridicae et historicae Martino David dedicatae*. Edited by J. Ankum, R. Feenstra, and W. F. Leemans. 2 vols. SDIOAP 2. Leiden: Brill.
1975 "Hehlerei." Pages 247-51 in vol. 4 of *Reallexikon der Assyriologie*. Edited by E. Ebeling et al. 16 vols. Berlin: de Gruyter, 1928-.
1986 "Beiträge zum Codex Hammurapi." *ZA* 76:18-23.

Pfeiffer, R. H., ed.
1935 *State Letters of Assyria*. New Haven: American Oriental Society.

Pfeiffer R. H., and E. A. Speiser, eds.
1936 *One Hundred New Selected Nuzi Texts*. AASOR 16. New Haven: American Schools for Oriental Research.

Phillips, A.
1966 "The Interpretation of 2 Samuel xii 5-6." *VT* 16: 242-44.
1970 *Ancient Israel's Criminal Law: A New Approach to the Decalogue*. Oxford: Blackwell; New York: Schocken.

Porten, B., and H. Szubin
1995 "The Status of the Handmaid Tamet." *Israel Law Review* 29: 43-64.

Porten, B., and A. Yardeni, eds.
1989 *Textbook of Aramaic Documents from Ancient Egypt*. 2 vols. Texts and Studies for Students. Jerusalem: Hebrew University, Department of the History of the Jewish People; Winona Lake, Ind.: Eisenbrauns.

Postgate, J. N.
1973 "Assyrian Texts and Fragments." *Iraq* 35: 13-36.

1975 "Some Old Babylonian Shepherds and Their Flocks." *JSS* 20: 1-21.
1976 *Fifty Neo-Assyrian Legal Documents.* Warminster: Aris and Phillips.

Pounder, R.
1984 "The Origin of θεοί as Inscription-Heading." Pages 243-50 in *Studies Presented to Sterling Dow on His Eightieth Birthday.* Edited by A. L. Boegehold et al. GRBM 10. Durham, N.C.: Duke University Press.

Praag, A. van
1945 *Droit matrimonial assyro-babylonien.* Allard Pierson Stichting, Universiteit van Amsterdam, Archeologisch-historische bijdragen 12. Amsterdam: North Holland.

Pritchard, J. B., ed.
1969 *Ancient Near Eastern Texts Relating to the Old Testament.* 3d ed. with supplement. Princeton: Princeton University Press.

Puhvel, J.
1984- *Hittite Etymological Dictionary.* 7 vols. Trends in Linguistics Documentation 1, 5, 14, 22, 26. (vols. 1-6) Berlin and New York: Mouton; (vol. 7) Berlin and New York: de Gruyter.

Rabinowitz, J. J.
1953 "Marriage Contracts in Ancient Egypt in the Light of Jewish Sources." *HTR* 46: 91-98.

Radner, K.
1997 *Die neuassyrischen Privatrechtsurkunden als Quelle für Mensch und Umwelt.* SAAS 6. Helsinki: Neo-Assyrian Text Corpus Project.
2003 "The Neo-Assyrian Period." Pages 883-910 in vol. 2 of *A History of Ancient Near Eastern Law.* Edited by R. Westbrook. 2 vols. HdO 72. Leiden: Brill.

Rainey, A., et al., eds.
1993 Kinattūtu ša dārâti. *Raphael Kutscher Memorial Volume.* Tel Aviv Occasional Publications 1. Tel Aviv: Institute of Archaeology of Tel Aviv University.

Redford, D. B.
1984 *Akhenaten, the Heretic King.* Princeton: Princeton Univ. Press, 1984.

Reiner, E.
1958 *Šurpu: A Collection of Sumerian and Akkadian Incantations.* AfO Beiheft 11. Graz: Weidner.

Reisner, G. A.
1986 *Sumerisch-babylonische Hymnen nach Thontafeln griechischer Zeit.* Königliche Museen zu Berlin. Mitteilungen aus den orientalischen Sammlungen 10. Berlin: Spemann.

Renger, J.
1977 "Legal Aspects of Sealing in Ancient Mesopotamia." Pages 75-88 in *Seals and Sealing in the Ancient Near East*. Edited by M. Gibson and R. Biggs. BiMes 6. Malibu: Undena.
1984 "Patterns of Non-Institutional Trade and Non-Commercial Exchange in Ancient Mesopotamia at the Beginning of the Second Millennium B.C." Pages 31-123 in *Circulation of Goods in Non-Palatial Context in the Ancient Near East: Proceedings of the International Conference*. Edited by A. Archi. Incunabula Graeca 82. Rome: Edizioni dell'Ateneo.

Reviv, H.
1982 "The Traditions Concerning the Inception of the Legal System in Israel: Significance and Dating (Exodus 18:12-17; Numbers 11:16-25; Deuteronomy 1:9-17)." *ZAW* 94: 566-75.

Reynolds, F.
2003 *The Babylonian Correspondence of Esarhaddon and Letters to Assurbanipal and Sin-šarru-iškun from Northern and Central Babylonia*. SAA 18. Helsinki: Helsinki University Press.

Riccobono, S., and J. Baviera, eds.
1968 *Fontes iuris Romani anteiustiniani*. 3 vols. Florence: Barbèra.

Richardson, N. J.
1974 *The Homeric Hymn to Demeter*. Oxford: Clarendon; New York: Oxford University Press.

Ries, G.
1984 "Ein neubabylonischer Mitgiftprozess (559 v. Chr.): Gleichzeitig ein Beitrag zur Frage der Geltung keilschriftlicher Gesetze." Pages 345-63 in *Gedächtnisschrift für Wolfgang Kunkel*. Edited by D. Nörr and D. Simon. Frankfurt: Klostermann.

Rietzschel, C.
1966 *Das Problem der Urrolle: Ein Beitrag zur Redaktionsgeschichte des Jeremiahbuches*. Gütersloh: Gerd Mohn.

Riftin, A. P.
1937 *Staro-vavilonskie iuridicheskie i administrativnye dokumenty v sobraniiakh SSSR*. Moscow: Izd-vo Akademii nauk SSSR.

Rosen, B. L.
1977 "Some Notes on Eshnunna Laws 20 and 21 and a Legal Reform in the Laws of Hammurapi." *RA* 71: 35-38.

Roth, M.
1989a *Babylonian Marriage Agreements 7th–3rd Centuries B.C.* AOAT 222. Kevelaer: Butzon & Bercker; Neukirchen-Vluyn: Neukirchener Verlag.

1989b “A Case of Contested Status.” Pages 481-89 in *DUMU-E2-DUB-BA-A: Studies in Honor of Å. W. Sjöberg*. Edited by H. Behrens et al. Occasional Publications of the Samuel N. Kramer Fund 11. Philadelphia: Babylonian Section, University of Pennsylvania Museum, 1989.

1997 *Law Collections from Mesopotamia and Asia Minor*. 2d ed. SBLWAW 6. Atlanta: Scholars Press. 1st ed., 1995.

1998 “Gender and Law: A Case Study from Ancient Mesopotamia.” Pages 173-84 in *Gender and Law in the Hebrew Bible and the Ancient Near East*. Edited by V. H. Matthews, B. M. Levinson, and T. Frymer-Kensky. JSOTSup 262. Sheffield: Sheffield Academic.

Rowton, M. B.

1968 “The Use of the Permansive in Classic Babylonian.” *JNES* 21: 233-303.

Saarisalo, A.

1934 *New Kirkuk Documents Relating to Slaves*. Studia orientalia 5/3. Helsinki: Societas Orientalis Fennica.

Samuel, A. E.

1965 “The Role of Paramone Clauses in Ancient Documents.” *JJP* 15: 221-311.

San Nicolò, M.

1921 *Die Schlussklauseln der altbabylonischen Kauf- and Tauschverträge: Ein Beitrag zur Geschichte des Barkaufes*. Münchener Beiträge zur Papyrusforschung 4. Munich: Beck; 2d ed. by H. Petschow. Munich: Beck, 1974.

1930 “Über Adoption and die Gerichtsbarkeit der *mâr-bânî* im neubabylonischen Rechte.” *ZSSR (Rom. Abt.)* 50: 445-55.

1932 “Parerga Babylonica VII: Der §8 des Gesetzbuches Hammurapis in den neubabylonischen Urkunden.” *ArOr* 4: 327-44.

1938 “Diebstahl.” Pages 212-15 in vol. 2 of *Reallexikon der Assyriologie*. Edited by E. Ebeling et al. 16 vols. Berlin: de Gruyter, 1928-.

Sarna, N.

1973 “Zedekiah’s Emancipation of Slaves and the Sabbatical Year.” Pages 143-49 in *Essays Presented to Cyrus H. Gordon*. Edited by H. A. Hoffner, Jr. AOAT 22. Kevelaer: Butzon & Bercker.

Schachermeyr, F.

1928-29 “Zur staatsrechtlichen Wertung der hethitischen Verträge.” Pages 180-86 in *Altorientalische Studien. Bruno Meissner zum 60. Geburtstag am 25. April 1928 gewidmet von Freunden, Kollegen und Schülern*. MAOG 4: Leipzig: Harrassowitz.

Scheil, V. J.
1918 "Litige causé par la coïncidence du rachat et de la mort d'un esclave." *RA* 15: 139-41.
Schenker, A.
1988 "Affranchissement d'une esclave selon Ex. 21,7-11." *Bib* 69: 547-56.
1990 *Versöhnung und Widerstand: Bibeltheologische Untersuchung zum Strafen Gottes und der Menschen, besonders im Lichte von Exodus 21-22*. SBS 139. Stuttgart: Verlag Katholischen Bibelwerk.
Schindler, J.
1967 "Zu hethitisch *nekuz*." *ZVS* 81: 290-303.
Schorr, M.
1913 *Urkunden des altbabylonischen Zivil- und Prozessrechts*. VAB 5. Leipzig: Hinrich. Reprinted Leipzig: Zentral-Antiquariat, 1968.
Schreiner, S.
1979 "Mischehen – Ehebruch – Ehescheidung: Betrachtungen zu Mal 2,10-16." *ZAW* 91: 207-28.
Schuler, E. von
1957 *Hethitische Dienstanweisungen.* AfO Beiheft 10. Innsbruck: Biblio-Verlag. Reprinted 1967.
1959 "Hethitische Königserlässe als Quellen der Rechtsfindung und ihr Verhältnis zum kodifizierten Recht." Pages 435-72 in *Festschrift Johannes Friedrich zum 65. Geburtstag am 27. August 1958*. Edited by R. von Kienle. Heidelberg: Winter.
Schulman, A.
1979 "Diplomatic Marriage in the Egyptian New Kingdom." *JNES* 38: 177-93.
Schulz, H.
1969 *Das Todesrecht im Alten Testament.* BZAW 114. Berlin: Töpelman.
Schwienhorst-Schönberger, L.
1990 *Das Bundesbuch (Ex. 20,22-23,33): Studien zu seiner Entstehung und Theologie*. BZAW 188. Berlin: de Gruyter.
Seebass, H.
1974 "Nathan und David in 2 Sam 12." *ZAW* 86: 203-11.
Seidel, E.
1997 "Freunde und Feinde Jeremias unter den Beamten Judas der spätvorexilischen Zeit." *BZ* 41: 28-53.
Senn, A.
1957 *Handbuch der litauischen Sprache.* 2 vols. Indogermanische Bibliothek. Heidelberg: Winter.

Sethe, K., and Helck, W., eds.

1906-58 *Urkunden des ägyptischen Altertums IV: Urkunden der 18. Dynastie.* 22 vols. Leipzig: Heinrich (vols. 1-16, 1906-1909); Berlin: Akademie-Verlag (vols. 17-22, 1955-1958).

Siegel, B. J.

1947 "Slavery during the Third Dynasty of Ur." *American Anthropologist N.S.* 49 no. 1, part 2. Reprinted as *Slavery during the Third Dynasty of Ur*. Memoir Series of the American Anthropological Association 66. New York: Kraus Reprint Co., 1969.

Sigrist, M.

1990 *Messenger Texts from the British Museum.* Potomac, Md.: Capital Decisions.

1993 "Seven Emar Tablets." Pages 165-87 in Kinattūtu ša dārâti. *Raphael Kutscher Memorial Volume.* Edited by A. Rainey et al. Tel Aviv Occasional Publications 1. Tel Aviv: Institute of Archaeology of Tel Aviv University.

Simmons, S. D.

1959 "Early Old Babylonian Tablets from Harmal and Elsewhere, Pt. 1." *JCS* 13: 71-93, 105-19.

1960 "Early Old Babylonian Tablets from Harmal and Elsewhere, Pt. 2." *JCS* 14: 23-32.

Sjöberg, Å. W.

1973 "Nungal in the Ekur." *AfO* 24: 19-46.

1976 "The Old Babylonian Eduba." Pages 159-79 in *Sumerological Studies in Honor of Thorkild Jacobsen on His Seventieth Birthday, June 7, 1974.* Edited by S. J. Lieberman. AS 20. Chicago: University of Chicago Press.

Skaist, A. J.

1988 "The Chronology of the Legal Texts from Emar." *ZA* 88: 45-71.

1994 *The Old Babylonian Loan Contract: Its History and Geography.* BISNELC. Ramat Gan, Israel: Bar-Ilan University Press.

Skinner, J.

1930 *A Critical and Exegetical Commentary on Genesis.* ICC. 2d ed. Edinburgh: T. & T. Clark. Reprinted 1969.

Smith, J.

1912 *A Critical and Exegetical Commentary on Malachi.* ICC. Edinburgh: T. & T. Clark.

Snaith, N. H.

1967 *Leviticus and Numbers.* Century Bible. Nelson: London.

Soden, W. von
1949 "Kleine Beiträge zum Verständnis der Gesetze Hammurabis und Bilalamas." *ArOr* 17: 359-73.
1965-81 *Akkadisches Handwörterbuch*. 3 vols. Wiesbaden: Harrassowitz.
1969 *Grundriss der Akkadischen Grammatik*. 2 vols. AnOr 33 and 47. Rome: Pontifical Biblical Institute.
Soden, W. von, and Staatliche Museen zu Berlin, Vorderasiatische Abteilung
1933- *Die lexikalischen Tafelserien der Babylonier und Assyrer in den Berliner Museen*. 2 vols. Berlin: Vorderasiatische Abteilung der Staatliche Museen zu Berlin.
Soldt, W. H. van
1990-94 *Letters in the British Museum*. 2 vols. AbB 12-13. Leiden and New York: Brill.
Sollberger, E.
1956 *Corpus des inscriptions "royales" présargoniques de Lagaš*. Geneva: Dros.
1976 "Some Legal Documents from the Third Dynasty of Ur." Pages 435-50 in *Kramer Anniversary Volume: Cuneiform Studies in Honor of Samuel Noah Kramer*. Edited by B. L. Eichler, J. W. Heimerdinger, and Å. W. Sjöberg. AOAT 25. Kevelaer: Butzon & Bercker.
Spalinger, A.
1978 "A New Reference to an Egyptian Campaign of Thutmose III in Asia." *JNES* 37: 35-41.
1981 "Considerations on the Hittite Treaty between Egypt and Hatti." *Studien zur altägyptischen Kultur* 9: 299-358.
Speiser, E.
1956 "Nuzi Marginalia." *Or (NS)* 25: 1-23.
1964 "The Syllabic Transcription of Ugaritic [ḫ] and [ḥ]." *BASOR* 175: 42-47.
Stager, L.
1985 "Archaeology of the Family in Ancient Israel." *BASOR* 260: 1-35.
Starke, F.
1985 *Die keilschrift-luwischen Texte in Umschrift*. StBoT 30. Wiesbaden: Harrassowitz.
Steele, F. R.
1948 "Codex Lipit-Ištar." *JAOS* 52: 425-50.
Steible, H.
1982 *Die altsumerischen Bau- und Weihinschriften*. FAOS 5. Wiesbaden: Steiner.

Steinkeller, P.
1980 "(z)a-áš-da = *kiššātum*." *RA* 74: 178-79.
1982 "The Question of Marḫaši: A Contribution to the Historical Geography of Iran in the Third Millennium B.C." *ZA* 72: 237-65.
1989 *Sale Documents of the Ur III Period*. FAOS 17. Stuttgart and Wiesbaden: Steiner.
1993 "Early Political Development in Mesopotamia and the Origins of the Sargonic Empire." Pages 107-29 in *Akkad. The First World Empire: Structure, Ideology, Traditions*. Edited by M. Liverani. HANES 5. Padua: Sargon.

Stipp, H. J.
1992 *Jeremia im Parteienstreit*. BBB 82. Frankfurt am Main: Anton Hain.

Stol, M.
1986 *Letters from Collections in Philadelphia, Chicago, and Berkeley*. AbB 11. Leiden: Brill

Stolper, M.
1985 *Entrepreneurs and Empire: The Murašu Archive, the Murašu Firm, and Persian Rule in Babylonia*. PIHANS 54. Leiden: Nederlands Instituut voor het Nabije Oosten.
2000 "No Harm Done: On Late Achaemenid *pirku* Guarantees." Pages 467-77 in *Assyriologica et Semitica: Festschrift für Joachim Oelsner anlässlich seines 65. Geburtstages am 18. Februar 1997*. Edited by J. Marzahn and H. Neumann. AOAT 252. Münster: Ugarit-Verlag.

Strassmaier, J. N.
1889 *Inschriften von Nabonidus, König von Babylon (555-538 v. Chr.)*. Leipzig: Pfeiffer.
1890a *Inschriften von Cambyses, König von Babylon (529-521 v. Chr.)*. Leipzig: Pfeiffer.
1890b *Inschriften von Cyrus, König von Babylon (538-529 v. Chr.)*. Leipzig: Pfeiffer.
1890c *Inschriften von Darius, König von Babylon (521-485 v. Chr.)*. Leipzig: Pfeiffer.

Stroud, R. S.
1968 *Drakon's Law on Homicide*. University of California Publications, Classical Studies 3. Berkeley: University of California Press.

Sturtevant, E.
1942 *The Indo-Hittite Laryngeals*. Baltimore: Linguistic Society of America.

Sturtevant, E., and G. Bechtel
1935 *A Hittite Chrestomathy*. Special Publications of the Linguistic Society of America. Philadelphia: Linguistic Society of America, University of Pennsylvania.

Szlechter, E.
1954 *Les Lois d'Eshnunna*. Publications de l'institut de droit romain de l'Université de Paris 12. Paris: Recueil Sirey.
1963 *Tablettes juridiques et administratives de la IIIe dynastie d'Ur*. Publications de l'institut de droit romain de l'Université de Paris 21. Paris: Recueil Sirey.
1967 "Des droits successoraux dérivés de l'adoption en droit babylonien." *RIDA* 14: 79-106.

Tadmor, H.
1979 "The Decline of Empires in Western Asia ca. 1200 B.C.E." Pages 1-14 in *Symposia Celebrating the Seventy-fifth Anniversary of the Founding of the American Schools of Oriental Research (1900-1975)*. Edited by F. M. Cross. Cambridge, Mass.: American Schools of Oriental Research.

Thureau-Dangin, F.
1924 "La correspondance de Ḫammurapi avec Šamaš-ḫâṣir." *RA* 21: 1-58.

Thureau-Dangin, F., A. Barrois, G. Dossin, and M. Durand
1931 *Arslan-Tash*. Bibliothèque archéologique et histoire 116. Paris: Geuthner.

Toeg, A.
1970 "Does Deuteronomy 24,1-4 Incorporate a General Law on Divorce?" *Diné Israel* 2: 5-24.

Toorn, K. van der
1995 "The Domestic Cult at Emar." *JCS* 47: 35-49.

Tosato, A.
1978 "Il ripudio: delitto e pena (Mal. 2,10-16)." *Bib* 59: 548-53.

Tsukimoto, A.
1988 "Sieben spätbronzezeitliche Urkunden aus Syrien." *ASJ* 10: 153-89.
1990 "Akkadian Tablets in the Hirayama Collection (I)." *ASJ* 12: 177-259.
1991 "Akkadian Tablets in the Hirayama Collection (II)." *ASJ* 13: 275-333.

Uchitel, A.
1984 "Daily Work at Sagdana Millhouse." *ASJ* 6: 75-98.

Ulmann, C. C.
1872 *Lettisches Wörterbuch*. Vol. 1: *Lettisch-deutsches Wörterbuch*. Riga: Brutzer.

United Nations, International Law Commission
1969 Vienna Convention on the Law of Treaties: drafted 1969, revised and adopted 1980.

Van Seters, J.
2003 *A Law Book for the Diaspora: Revision in the Study of the Covenant Code*. Oxford: Oxford University Press.

Veenhof, K.

1978 "An Ancient Anatolian Money-Lender: His Loans, Securities, and Debt-Slaves." Pages 279-311 in vol. 2 of *Festschrift Lubor Matouš*. Edited by B. Hruška and G. Komóroczy. 2 vols. Budapest: Eötvös Loránd Tudományegyetem, Ókori Történeti tanszékeinek kiadványai.

1991 "Assyrian Commercial Activities in Old Babylonian Sippar: Some New Evidence." Pages 287-303 in *Marchands, diplomates et empereurs. Études sur la civilisation mésopotamienne offertes à Paul Garelli*. Edited by D. Charpin and F. Joannès. Paris: Éditions Recherches sur les civilisations.

1995 "'In Accordance with the Words of the Stele': Evidence for Old Assyrian Legislation." *Chicago-Kent Law Review* 70: 1717-44.

1997-2000 "The Relation between Royal Decrees and 'Law Codes' of the Old Babylonian Period." *JEOL* 35-36: 49-83.

1999 "Redemption of Houses in Assur and Sippar." Pages 599-616 in *Munuscula Mesopotamia. Festschrift Johannes Renger*. Edited by B. Bock, E. Cancik-Kirschbaum, and T. Richter. AOAT 267. Münster: Ugarit-Verlag.

2003 "The Old Assyrian Period." Pages 431-83 in vol. 1 of *A History of Ancient Near Eastern Law*. Edited by R. Westbrook. 2 vols. HdO 72. Leiden: Brill.

Veenker, R. A.

1967 "The Old Babylonian Judiciary and Legal Procedure." Ph.D. diss. Hebrew Union College-Jewish Institute of Religion (Ohio).

1974 "An Old Babylonian Legal Procedure for Appeal: Evidence from the *ṭuppi lā ragāmim*." *HUCA* 45: 1-15.

Wallace, R., and R. Westbrook

1989 Review of M. Gagarin, *Early Greek Law*. *American Journal of Philology* 110: 362-67.

Walters, S. D.

1970 *Water for Larsa: An Old Babylonian Archive Dealing with Irrigation*. YNER 4. New Haven: Yale University Press.

Waltke, B. K., and M. O'Conner

1990 *An Introduction to Biblical Syntax*. Winona Lake, Ind.: Eisenbrauns.

Waterman, L.

1916 *Business Documents of the Hammurapi Period*. Ancient Mesopotamian Texts and Studies. London: Ams Press (= *AJSL* 29-30 [1912-1914]).

1930-36 *Royal Correspondence of the Assyrian Empire*. University of Michigan Studies, Humanistic Series 17-20. Ann Arbor, Mich.: University of Michigan Press.

Watson, A.

1985 *The Evolution of Law*. Oxford: Blackwell; Baltimore: Johns Hopkins University Press.

Weidner, E. F.

1941-44 "Die astrologische Serie Enûma Anu Enlil." *AfO* 14: 172-95, 308-18.

1954-56a "Die astrologische Serie Enûma Anu Enlil (Fortsetzung)." *AfO* 17: 76-89.

1954-56b "Hochverrat gegen Nebukadnezar II." *AfO* 17: 1-9.

1954-56c "Hof- und Harems-Erlässe assyrischer Könige aus dem 2. Jahrtausend v. Chr." *AfO* 17: 257-93.

Weinfeld, M.

1970 "The Covenant of Grant in the Old Testament and in the Ancient Near East." *JAOS* 90: 184-203.

1972 *Deuteronomy and the Deuteronomic School*. Oxford: Clarendon.

Weisberg, D.

2001 "*Pirqūti* or *širkūti*? Was Ištar-ab-usur's Freedom Affirmed or Was He Re-Enslaved?" Pages 1163-77 in *Studi sul Vicino Oriente antico dedicati alla memoria di Luigi Cagni*. Edited by S. Graziani. 4 vols. Series Minor, Istituto universitario orientale, Dipartimento di studi asiatici 61. Naples and Rome: Istituto Universitario Universale and Herder.

2003 *Neo-Babylonian Texts in the Oriental Institute Collection*. OIP 122. Chicago: Oriental Institute.

Welch, J. W., ed.

2005 *Biblical Law Bibliography on CD-Rom*. Winona Lake: Eisenbrauns.

Wells, B.

2004 *The Law of Testimony in the Pentateuchal Codes*. BZAR 4. Wiesbaden: Harrassowitz.

Wenham, G. J.

1979 "The Restoration of Marriage Reconsidered." *JJS* 30: 36-40.

Wenham, G. J., and J. G. McConville

1980 "Drafting Techniques in Some Deuteronomic Laws." *VT* 30: 248-52.

Westbrook, R.

1971a "Jubilee Laws." *Israel Law Review* 6: 209-26. Reprinted at pages 36-57 in *Property and the Family in Biblical Law*. JSOTSup 113. Sheffield: Sheffield Academic.

1971b "Purchase of the Cave of Machpelah." *Israel Law Review* 6: 29-38. Reprinted at pages 24-35 in *Property and the Family in Biblical Law*. JSOTSup 113. Sheffield: Sheffield Academic.

1971c "Redemption of Land." *Israel Law Review* 6: 367-75. Reprinted at pages 58-68 in *Property and the Family in Biblical Law*. JSOTSup 113. Sheffield: Sheffield Academic.

1972 Review of S. Paul, *Studies in the Book of the Covenant in the Light of Cuneiform and Biblical Law. Israel Law Review* 7: 461-64.

1977 "The Law of the Biblical Levirate." *RIDA* 24: 65-87. Reprinted at pages 69-89 in *Property and the Family in Biblical Law*. JSOTSup 113. Sheffield: Sheffield Academic.

1982a "Old Babylonian Marriage Law." 2 vols. Ph.D. diss. Yale University.

1982b "Sabbatical Year" (in Hebrew). Columns 112-19 in vol. 8 of *Encyclopedia Biblica*. Edited by B. Mazar. 10 vols. Jerusalem: Bialik Institute, 1950-.

1984 "The Enforcement of Morals in Mesopotamian Law." *JAOS* 104: 753-56.

1985a "Biblical and Cuneiform Law Codes." *RB* 92: 247-65. Reprinted at pages 495-511 in vol. 1 of *Folk Law*. Edited by A. D. Renteln and A. Dundes. 2 vols. New York and London: Garland Publishing, 1994.

1985b "The Price Factor in the Redemption of Land." *RIDA* 32: 97-127. Reprinted at pages 90-117 in *Property and the Family in Biblical Law*. JSOTSup 113. Sheffield: Sheffield Academic.

1986a "Lex Talionis and Exodus 21, 22-25." *RB* 93: 52-69.

1986b "The Prohibition on Restoration of Marriage in Deuteronomy 24:1-4." Pages 387-405 in *Studies in Bible*. Edited by S. Japhet. Scripta Hierosolymitana 31. Jerusalem: Magnes.

1986c Review of M. Weinfeld, *Justice and Righteousness in Israel and Among the Nations*. *RB* 93: 602-05.

1988a "The Nature and Origins of the Twelve Tables." *ZSSR (Rom. Abt.)* 105: 74-121.

1988b *Old Babylonian Marriage Law*. AfO Beiheft 23. Horn: Berger.

1988c Review of D. Patrick, *Old Testament Law*. *Biblical Archaeologist* 51: 59-60.

1988d *Studies in Biblical and Cuneiform Law*. Cahiers de la Revue Biblique 26. Paris: Gabalda.

1989a "Cuneiform Law Codes and the Origins of Legislation." *ZA* 79: 201-22.

1989b "Restrictions on Alienation of Property in Early Roman Law." Pages 207-13 in *New Perspectives in the Roman Law of Property*. Edited by P. Birks. Oxford: Oxford University Press.

1990a "1 Samuel 1:8." *JBL* 109: 114-15.

1990b "Adultery in Ancient Near Eastern Law." *RB* 97: 542-80.

1991a "The Phrase 'His Heart is Satisfied' in Ancient Near Eastern Legal Sources." *JAOS* 111: 219-24.

1991b *Property and the Family in Biblical Law*. JSOTSup 113. Sheffield: Sheffield Academic.

1992a "Crimes and Punishments." Pages 546-56 in vol. 5 of *Anchor Bible Dictionary*. Edited by D. N. Freedman. 6 vols. New York: Doubleday.

1992b "The Trial Scene in the Iliad." *HSCP* 94: 53-76.

1993a "The Adoption Laws of Codex Hammurabi." Pages 195-204 in Kinattūtu ša dārâti. *Raphael Kutscher Memorial Volume*. Edited by A. Rainey et al. Tel Aviv Occasional Publications 1. Tel Aviv: Institute of Archaeology of Tel Aviv University.

1993b Review of C. Wright, *God's People in God's Land*. *Association for Jewish Studies Review* 18: 291-93.

1994a "The Deposit Law of Exodus 22,6-12." *ZAW* 106: 390-403.

1994b "Mitgift." Pages 273-83 in vol. 8 of *Reallexikon der Assyriologie*. Edited by E. Ebeling et al. 16 vols. Berlin: de Gruyter, 1928-.

1994c "The Old Babylonian Term *napṭaru*." *JCS* 46: 41-46.

1994d Review of C. Carmichael, ed., *Collected Works of David Daube*, Vol. 1: *Talmudic Law*. *ZSSR* (*Rom. Abt.*) 111: 702-3.

1994e "What Is the Covenant Code?" Pages 13-34 in *Theory and Method in Biblical and Cuneiform Law: Revision, Interpolation and Development*. Edited by B. M. Levinson. JSOTSup 181. Sheffield: Sheffield Academic. Reprinted 2006.

1995a "The Coherence of the Lex Aquilia." *RIDA* 42: 437-71.

1995b "A Death in the Family: Codex Eshnunna 17-18 Revisited." *Studies in Honour of Reuven Yaron*. Edited by M. Rabello. *Israel Law Review* 29: 32-42.

1995c "Muntehe." Pages 425-26 in vol. 8 of *Reallexikon der Assyriologie*. Edited by E. Ebeling et al. 16 vols. Berlin: de Gruyter, 1928-.

1995d "Riddles in Deuteronomic Law." Pages 159-74 in *Bundesdokument und Gesetz: Studien zum Deuteronomium*. Edited by G. Braulik. Herders Biblische Studien 4. Freiburg: Herder.

1995e "Slave and Master in Ancient Near Eastern Law." *Chicago-Kent Law Review* 70: 631- 76.

1995f "Social Justice in the Ancient Near East." Pages 149-63 in *Social Justice in the Ancient World*. Edited by K. Irani and M. Silver. Westport, Conn.: Greenwood Press.

1996a "Biblical Law." Pages 1-17 in *An Introduction to the History and Sources of Jewish Law*. Edited by N. S. Hecht et al. Oxford: Oxford University Press.

1996b "zíz.da/*kiššātum*." *WZKM* 86: 449-59.

1997 "A Matter of Life and Death." *JANES* 25: 61-70.

1998a "The Female Slave." Pages 214-38 in *Gender and Law in the Hebrew Bible and the Ancient Near East*. Edited by V. H. Matthews, B. M.

Levinson, and T. Frymer-Kensky. JSOTSup 262. Sheffield: Sheffield Academic.

1998b "Legal Aspects of Care of the Elderly in the Ancient Near East: Conclusion." Pages 241-50 in *The Care of the Elderly in the Ancient Near East*. Edited by M. Stol and S. Vleeming. Leiden: Brill.

1998c "Legal Aspects of Care of the Elderly in the Ancient Near East: Introduction." Pages 1-22 in *The Care of the Elderly in the Ancient Near East*. Edited by M. Stol and S. Vleeming. Leiden: Brill.

1999a "Codex Hammurabi and the Ends of the Earth." Pages 101-3 in vol. 3 of *Landscapes: Territories, Frontiers and Horizons in the Ancient Near East*. Edited by L. Milano et al. HANEM 3. Padova: Sargon.

1999b "International Law in the Amarna Age." Pages 28-41 in *Amarna Diplomacy: The Beginning of International Relations*. Edited by R. Cohen and R. Westbrook. Baltimore: Johns Hopkins University Press.

1999c "Legalistic 'Glosses' in Biblical Narratives." *Israel Law Review* 33: 787-97.

1999d "Lois Sumériennes." Columns 204-15 in *Supplément au Dictionnaire de la Bible*. Edited by J. Briend and M. Quesnel. Paris: Letouzey et Ané.

1999e Review of E. Dombradi, *Die Darstellung des Rechtsaustrags in den altbabylonischen Prozessurkunden*. *Or (NS)* 68: 122-27.

1999f "Vitae Necisque Potestas." *Historia* 48: 203-23.

2000a "Babylonian Diplomacy in the Amarna Letters." *JAOS* 120: 377-82.

2000b "Codification and Canonization." Pages 33-47 in *La codification des lois dans l'antiquité: Actes du Colloque de Strasbourg 27-29 Novembre 1997*. Edited by E. Lévy. Travaux du Centre de Recherche sur le Proche-Orient et la Grèce antiques 16. Paris: de Boccard.

2001a "I codici mesopotamici." Pages 377-83 in vol. 1 (*La scienza antica*) of *Storia della scienza*. Edited by S. Petruczioli. Rome: Istituto della Enciclopedia Italiana, 2001-.

2001b "Conclusions." Pages 327-39 in *Security for Debt in Ancient Near Eastern Law*. Edited by R. Westbrook and R. Jasnow. CHANE 9. Leiden: Brill.

2001c "Hard Times: CT 45 37." Pages 547-51 in *Veenhof Anniversary Volume: Studies Presented to Klaas R. Veenhof on the Occasion of his Sixty-fifth Birthday*. Edited by W. H. van Soldt and J. G. Dercksen. PIHANS 89. Leiden: Nederlands Instituut voor het Nabije Oosten.

2001d "Introduction." Pages 1-3 in *Security for Debt in Ancient Near Eastern Law*. Edited by R. Westbrook and R. Jasnow. CHANE 9. Leiden: Brill.

2001e "Noxalhaftung." Pages 605-6 in vol. 9 of *Reallexikon der Assyriologie*. Edited by E. Ebeling et al. 16 vols. Berlin: de Gruyter, 1928-.

2001f "The Old Babylonian Period." Pages 63-91 in *Security for Debt in Ancient Near Eastern Law*. Edited by R. Westbrook and R. Jasnow. CHANE 9. Leiden: Brill.

2001g "Social Justice and Creative Jurisprudence in Late Bronze Age Syria." *JESHO* 43: 22-43.

2002 Review of A. Fitzpatrick-McKinley, *The Transformation of Torah from Scribal Advice to Law*. *JNES* 61: 295-96.

2003a "The Case of the Elusive Debtors: CT 4 6a and CT 6 34b." *ZA* 93: 199-207.

2003b "Emar and Vicinity." Pages 657-91 in vol. 1 of *A History of Ancient Near Eastern Law*. Edited by R. Westbrook. 2 vols. HdO 72. Leiden and New York: Brill.

2003c "Evidentiary Procedure in the Middle Assyrian Laws." *JCS* 55: 75-85.

2003d "Introduction: The Character of Ancient Near Eastern Law." Pages 1-90 in vol. 1 of *A History of Ancient Near Eastern Law*. Edited by R. Westbrook. 2 vols. HdO 72. Leiden and New York: Brill.

2003e "Old Babylonian Period." Pages 360-430 in vol. 1 of *A History of Ancient Near Eastern Law*. Edited by R. Westbrook. 2 vols. HdO 72. Leiden and New York: Brill.

2003f "A Sumerian Freedman." Pages in 333-39 *Literatur, Politik und Recht in Mesopotamien. Festschrift für Claus Wilcke*. Edited by W. Sallaberger et al. OBC 14. Wiesbaden: Harrassowitz.

2004 "The Quality of Freedom in Neo-Babylonian Manumissions." *RA* 98: 101-8.

2005a "Elisha's True Prophecy in 2 Kings 3." *JBL* 124: 530-32.

2005b "Judges in the Cuneiform Sources." *Maarav* 12: 27-39.

2005c "Patronage in the Ancient Near East." *JESHO* 48: 210-33.

2005d "Penelope's Dowry and Odysseus' Kingship." Pages 3-23 in *Symposion 2001: Vorträge zur griechischen und hellenistischen Rechtsgeschichte*. Edited by R. W. Wallace and M. Gagarin. Akten der Gesellschaft für griechische und hellenistische Rechtsgeschichte 16. Vienna: Österreichische Akademie der Wissenschaften.

2005e "Polygamie." Pages 600-2 in vol. 10 of *Reallexikon der Assyriologie*. Edited by E. Ebeling et al. 16 vols. Berlin: de Gruyter, 1928-.

2005f "Reflections on Neo-Babylonian Law" (review article of C. Wunsch, *Urkunden zum Ehe-, Vermögens-, und Erbrecht aus verschiedenen neubabylonischen Archiven*). *NIN: Journal of Gender Studies in Antiquity* 4: 133-46.

2006a "Reflections on the Law of Homicide in the Ancient World" (review article of P. Barmash, *Homicide in the Biblical World*). *Maarav* 13: 143-70.

2006b "Response to Michael Gagarin." Pages 21-25 in *Symposion 2003: Vorträge zur griechischen und hellenistischen Rechtsgeschichte (Rauischholzhausen, 30. September-3. Oktober 2003)*. Edited by H.-A. Rupprecht. Akten der Gesellschaft für griechische und hellenistische Rechtsgeschichte 17. Vienna: Österreichische Akademie der Wissenschaften.

2006c "Witchcraft and the Law in the Ancient Near East." Pages 45-52 in *Recht gestern und heute: Festschrift zum 85. Geburtstag von Richard Haase*. Edited by J. Hengstl and U. Sick. Wiesbaden: Harrassowitz.

2007a "LH §§7 and 123: A Contradiction?" *N.A.B.U.* 2007: no. 27 (pp. 28-29).

2007b "Raub." Pages 269-70 in vol. 11 of *Reallexikon der Assyriologie*. Edited by E. Ebeling et al. 16 vols. Berlin: de Gruyter, 1928-.

2007c "The Trial of Jeremiah." Pages 97-107 in *Reading the Law: Studies in Honour of Gordon J. Wenham*. Edited by J. G. McConville and K. Möller. LHB/OTS 461. New York and London: T. & T. Clark.

2008a "The Laws of Biblical Israel." Pages 99-119 in *The Hebrew Bible: New Insights and Scholarship*. Edited by F. E. Greenspahn. New York: New York University Press.

2008b "The *napṭaru* at Ugarit." *JCS* 60: 53-56.

2009 "Drakon's Homicide Law." Pages 3-16 in *Symposion 2007: Vorträge zur griechischen und hellenistischen Rechtsgeschichte (Durham, 2.-6. September 2007)*. Edited by E. Harris and G. Thür. Akten der Gesellschaft für griechische und hellenistische Rechtsgeschichte 20. Vienna: Österreichische Akademie der Wissenschaften.

in press "Ancient Near Eastern Law." Forthcoming in *The Oxford International Encyclopedia of Legal History*. Edited by S. N. Katz. 6 vols. New York: Oxford University Press.

in press "Exile and Banishment in the Ancient Near East." *JAOS*: forthcoming.

in press "The Law and Politics of Rebellion in the Late Bronze Age." Forthcoming in *Rebellions and Peripheries*. Edited by S. Richardson.

in press "Law in Kings." Forthcoming in *The Books of Kings: Sources, Composition, Historiography and Reception*. FIOL. VTSup. Edited by B. Halpern and A. Lemaire. Leiden: Brill.

Westbrook, R., ed.

2003 *A History of Ancient Near Eastern Law*. 2 vols. HdO 72. Leiden: Brill.

Westbrook, R., and R. Cohen, eds.
2000 *Amarna Diplomacy: The Beginnings of International Relations*. Baltimore: Johns Hopkins University Press.
2008 *Isaiah's Vision of Peace in Biblical and Modern International Relations: Swords into Plowshares*. New York: Palgrave Macmillan.
Westbrook, R., J. S. Cooper, and G. Schwartz
2005 "A Mittani-Era Tablet from Umm el-Marra." Pages 3-18 in *General Studies and Excavations at Nuzi* 11/1. Edited by D. I. Owen and G. Wilhelm. SCCNH 15. Bethesda, Md.: CDL.
Westbrook, R., and R. Jasnow, eds.
2001 *Security for Debt in Ancient Near Eastern Law*. CHANE 9. Leiden: Brill.
Westbrook, R., and B. Lafont
2003 "Neo-Sumerian Period." Pages 183-226 in *A History of Ancient Near Eastern Law*. Edited by R. Westbrook. Leiden: Brill.
Westbrook, R., and T. J. Lewis
2008 "Who Led the Scapegoat in Leviticus 16:21?" *JBL* 127: 417-22.
Westbrook, R., and D. Lyons, eds.
2005 *Women and Property in Ancient Near Eastern and Mediterranean Societies*. Washington, D.C.: Center for Hellenic Studies. Electronic publication: <*http://www.chs.harvard.edu/publications.sec*>.
Westbrook, R., and D. I. Owen
1992 "Tie Her Up and Throw Her into the River! An Old Babylonian Inchoate Marriage on the Rocks." *ZA* 82: 202-7.
Westbrook, R., and R. Wallace
1989 Review of M. Gagarin, *Early Greek Law*. *American Journal of Philology* 110: 362-67.
Westbrook, R., and B. Wells
2009 *Everyday Law in Biblical Israel: An Introduction*. Louisville: Westminster John Knox.
Westbrook, R., and C. Wilcke
1974-77 "The Liability of an Innocent Purchaser of Stolen Goods in Early Mesopotamian Law." *AfO* 25: 111-15.
Westbrook, R., and R. Woodard
1990 "The Edict of Tudhaliya IV." *JAOS*: 110: 641-59.
Westenholz, A.
1975 *Old Sumerian and Old Akkadian Texts in Philadelphia, chiefly from Nippur: Part I*. BiMes 1. Malibu, Calif.: Undena Publications.
1987 *Old Sumerian and Old Akkadian Texts in Philadelphia, chiefly from Nippur: Part II*. Carsten Niebuhr Institute Publications 3. Copenhagen:

Carsten Niebuhr Institute of Ancient Near Eastern Studies, University of Copenhagen, Museum Tusculanum Press.

Westenholz, J. G.

2000 *Cuneiform Inscriptions in the Collection of the Bible Lands Museum Jerusalem: The Emar Tablets*. CM 13. Groningen: Styx.

Wilcke, C.

1968 "Einige Erwägungen zum § 29 des Codex Lipiteshtar." *WO* 4: 153-61

1969 "ku-li." *ZA* 59: 65-99.

1976 "Zu den spätaltbabylonischen Kaufverträgen aus Nordbabylonien." Festgabe für Herbert Petschow. *WO* 8: 254-85.

1979 "*abi ashlim*." *RA* 73: 95-96.

1980 "*šumṣulum* 'den Tag verbringen.'" *ZA* 70: 138-40.

1981 "Noch einmal: *šilip rēmim* und die Adoption *ina mê-šu*." *ZA* 71: 87-94.

1984 "CT 45,119: Ein Fall legaler Bigamie mit *nadītum* und *šugītum*." *ZA* 74: 170-80.

1985 "The Law of Sale and the History of Babylon's Neighbours." *Sumer* 41: 74-77.

1988 "Anmerkungen zu Konjugationspräfix /i/- und zur These vom silbischen Charakter der Sumerischen Morpheme anhand neusumerischer Verbalformen." *ZA* 78: 1-48.

1991 "Die Lesung von ÁŠ-da = *kiššātum*." *N.A.B.U.* 1991: no. 16 (pp. 13-14).

1992a "AḪ, die 'Brüder' von Emar. Untersuchungen zur Schreibertradition am Euphratknie." *AuOr* 10: 115-50.

1992b "Dieber, Räuber und Mörder." Pages 53-78 in *Außenseiter und Randgruppen: Beiträge zu einer Sozialgeschichte des Alten Orients*. Edited by V. Haas. Xenia 32. Konstanz: Universitätsverlag Konstanz.

Willetts, R. F., ed.

1967 *The Law Code of Gortyn*. KadmosSup 1. Berlin: de Gruyter.

Wiseman, D. J.

1953 *The Alalakh Tablets*. British School of Archaeology in Ankara, Occasional Publications 2. London: British School of Archaeology in Ankara.

1954 "Supplementary Copies of Alalakh Tablets." *JCS* 8: 1-30.

Wright, D. P.

2003 "The Laws of Hammurabi as a Source for the Covenant Collection (Exodus 20:23-23:19)." *Maarav* 10: 11-87.

Yamada, M.

1995 "The Hittite Social Concept of 'Free' in the Light of the Emar Texts." *AoF* 22: 301-16.

Yaron, R.
1957 "On Divorce in Old Testament Times." *RIDA* 4: 117-28.
1959 "Redemption of Persons in the Ancient Near East." *RIDA* 6: 155-76.
1961 *Introduction to The Law of the Aramaic Papyri.* Oxford: Clarendon.
1962a "Forms in the Laws of Eshnunna." *RIDA* 9: 137-53.
1962b "Vitae Necisque Potestas." *TvR* 30: 243-51.
1965 "Varia on Adoption." *JJP* 15: 171-83.
1966 "The Restoration of Marriage." *JJS* 17: 1-11.
1969 *The Laws of Eshnunna.* Jerusalem: Magnes.
1970 Review of Y. Muffs, *Studies in Aramaic Legal Papyri from Elephantine. RB* 77: 408-16.
1980 "Biblical Law: Prologomena." Pages 27-44 in *Jewish Law in Legal History and the Modern World,* Edited by B.S. Jackson. Jewish Law Annual Supplement 2. Leiden: Brill.
1985 "Quelques remarques sur les nouveaux fragments des Lois d'Ur-Nammu." *Revue historique de droit français et étranger* 63: 131-42.
1988a "The Evolution of Biblical Law." Pages 77-108 in *La Formazione del diritto nel vicino oriente antico.* Edited by A. Theodorides et al. Pubblicazioni dell'Istituto di diritto romano e del diritti dell'Oriente mediterraneo 65. Rome: Edizioni Scientifiche Italiane.
1988b *The Laws of Eshnunna.* 2d ed. Jerusalem: Magnes; Leiden: Brill.
1993a "*kurrum ṣibtam uṣṣab* 'das kor wird Zins hinzufügen': Weiteres zu §18A der Gesetze von Ešnunna." *ZA* 83: 206-18.
1993b "Stylistic Conceits: The Negated Antonym." *JANES* 22: 141-48.

Yildiz, F.
1981 "A Tablet of Codex Ur-Nammu from Sippar." *Or* 5: 87-97.

Yoffee, N.
1988 "Aspects of Mesopotamian Land Sales." *American Anthropologist* 90: 119-30.

Zaccagnini, C.
1973 *Lo Scambio dei Doni nel Vicino Oriente durante i Secoli XV-XIII.* Rome: Centro per l'Antichità e la Storia dell'Arte del Vicino Oriente.
1995 "War and Famine at Emar." *Or* 64: 96-100.
1996 "TÉŠ.BI = *mitḫaru/mitḫariš* at Emar and Elsewhere." *Or* 65: 89-110.

Zulueta, F. de
1946-53 *The Institutes of Gaius.* 2 vols. Oxford: Clarendon.

Index of Authors

Index of Subjects

Index of Ancient Sources

The sources listed below are arranged in the following order: Cuneiform, Biblical, Greek and Roman, Egyptian, Aramaic, and Rabbinic.

Cuneiform

Biblical